13. **CVS Corporation (NYSE / CVS)**
1 CVS Drive
Woonsocket, RI 02895
www.cvs.com
1999: $15,273,600,000
2000: $18,098,300,000

14. **Walgreen Company (NYSE / WAG)**
200 Wilmot Road
Deerfield, IL 60015
www.walgreens.com
1999: $15,306,600,000
2000: $17,838,800,000

15. **Lowe's Companies, Inc. (NYSE / LOW)**
1605 Curtis Bridge Road
Wilkesboro, NC 28697
www.lowes.com
1999: $13,330,540,000
2000: $15,908,595,000

16. **Winn-Dixie Stores, Inc. (NYSE / WIN)**
5050 Edgewood Court
Jacksonville, FL 32254
www.winndixie.com
1999: $13,617,485,000
2000: $14,136,503,000

17. **May Department Stores Company
(NYSE / MAY)**
611 Olive Street
St. Louis, MO 63101
www.mayco.com
1999: $13,048,000,000
2000: $13,869,000,000

18. **Rite Aid Corporation (NYSE / RAD)**
30 Hunter Lane
Camp Hill, PA 17011
www.riteaid.com
1999: $12,731,900,000
2000: $13,325,000,000

19. **Publix Supermarkets, Inc.
(OTC BB / PUSH)**
1936 George Jenkins Boulevard
Lakeland, FL 33815
www.publix.com
1999: $12,100,000,000
2000: $12,900,000,000

20. **Circuit City Stores (NYSE / CC)**
9950 Maryland Drive
Salisbury, NC 28145
www.circuitcity.com
1999: $10,810,468,000
2000: $12,614,390,000

21. **Best Buy Company, Inc. (NYSE / BBY)**
7075 Flying Cloud
Eden Prairie, MN 55344
www.bestbuy.com
1999: $10,064,646,000
2000: $12,494,023,000

22. **Toys R Us, Inc. (NYSE / TOY)**
461 From Road
Paramus, NJ 07645
www.toysrus.com
1999: $11,170,000,000
2000: $11,862,000,000

23. **The Gap, Inc. (NYSE / GPS)**
1 Harrison Street
San Francisco, CA 94105
www.gapinc.com
1999: $ 9,054,462,000
2000: $11,635,398,000

24. **Delhaize America, Inc. (NYSE / DZB)**
2110 Executive Drive
Salisbury, NC 28145
www.delhaize-americainc.com
1999: $10,219,474,000
2000: $10,878,684,000

25. **Office Depot, Inc. (NYSE / ODP)**
2200 Old Germantown Road
Delray Beach, FL 33445
www.officedepot.com
1999: $ 8,997,738,000
2000: $10,263,280,000

Retailing
Fourth Edition

Retailing
Fourth Edition

PATRICK M. DUNNE
Texas Tech University

ROBERT F. LUSCH
Texas Christian University

DAVID A. GRIFFITH
University of Hawaii

SOUTH-WESTERN

THOMSON LEARNING

Retailing, 4e

Patrick M. Dunne, Robert F. Lusch, David A. Griffith

Publisher:
Mike Roche

Acquisitions Editor:
Mark Orr

Developmental Editor:
Jana Pitts

Market Strategist:
Beverly Dunn

Project Editor:
Jim Patterson

Art Director:
Linda Beaupré

Production Manager:
Lois West

Compositor:
Progressive Information
Technologies

Printer:
R. R. Donnelly & Sons

Cover Image:
© IT International/Leo de Wys
Photo Agency

For permission to use material
from this text or product, contact
us by
Tel (800) 730-2214
Fax (800) 730-2215
http://www.thomsonrights.com

Library of Congress Catalog Card
Number: 00-111866

ISBN: 0-03-032696-6

To my professors, classmates, Coaches Don Ruberg and the late Joe Hawk, and teammates, especially Ben Cooper and Steve Thomas, from Xavier University. Thanks for the great education, encouragement, and life-long friendship.

—Patrick M. Dunne

To Mark and Stephen Lusch, who at age 14 were brave enough to take a journey in 2000 which allowed them to test their limits.

—Robert F. Lusch

To my wife, Monika, whose patience, support, and love provide me the courage to function as an idealist in a realist's world.

—David A. Griffith

Preface

This fourth edition of *Retailing*, like much of retailing itself, has undergone significant changes from prior editions. We have added many new and exciting features, but still kept the writing style conversational. In fact, given the influence of the Internet, the continuing growth of the service industry, and the many changes in the world's economic systems, there has never been a more exciting time to study retailing. As a result, every chapter of this edition features boxes covering these three topics in addition to the in-depth coverage within the text that you the reader have come to expect. Each chapter also has a fourth box that provides the reader with the Inside Story behind some recent retailing activity. As a result, we believe that students and instructors will like this edition even more than they did the highly-successful first three editions. A major contributor of the new ideas in this edition is our new co-author, Professor David Griffith. Dr. Griffith's interests and insights into e-tailing and the global retailing environment helped provide new focus for the text. We also believe that the students will appreciate his youthful insight into the world of retailing. And, if you happen to see a lot of Disney in this text, its attributable to David, a self-proclaimed Walt Disney junkie who has visited every Disney theme park throughout the world.

With retail providing one out of every five jobs in today's economy, then we, the authors, have a strong belief that retailing offers one of the best career opportunities for today's students. Thus, *Retailing* was written to convey that message, not by using boring descriptions of retailers and the various routine tasks they perform, but by making the subject matter come alive by focusing on the excitement that retailing offers its participants, in an easy-to-read conversational style filled with pictures and exhibits. This text demonstrates to the student that retailing as a career choice can be fun, exciting, and challenging. This excitement arises from selecting a merchandise assortment at market, determining how to present the merchandise in the store, developing a promotional program for the new assortment, or planning next season's sales in an ever-changing economic environment. While other texts may make retailing a series of independent processes, this edition like the first three editions of *Retailing*, highlights the excitement, richness, and importance of retailing as a career choice. *Retailing* provides the student with an understanding of the inter-relationship of the various activities that retailers face daily. To do this, we have attempted to show how retailers must use both creativity and analytical skills in order solve the problems of today's fast-paced environment.

In keeping with our goal of maintaining student interest, *Retailing* focuses on the material that someone entering the retailing field would need to know. We were more interested in telling the student what should happen, and what is happening, than in explaining the academic "whys" of these actions. Thus, when knowledge of a particular theory was needed, we generally ignored the reasoning behind the theory for a simple explanation and an example or two of the use of the theory. In presenting these examples we drew from a rich array of literature sources, as well as our combined 80 years of work in retailing.

Students and teachers have responded favorably to the "personality" of *Retailing* because of the numerous current examples, both in the text itself and in each chapter's various story boxes, which give realistic insights into retailing. One student wrote to say "thanks" for writing a book that was "so interesting and not too long." A faculty member noted she was "so pleased with the writing style because it was easier to understand, and the examples used were very appropriate and helped to present the material in a meaningful and easy-to-grasp manner for students." Still another liked *Retailing* because the writing style was "conversational," thus lending itself to very easy reading, so that she felt confident that her students would read the chapters. "The content coverage was excellent. Terms were explained in easy-to-understand language. And, although most of the topics of an advanced retailing text were presented, the extent and presentation of the material was very appropriate to an introductory course." Another reviewer was especially pleased that we were able to incorporate so many current examples.

Text Organization

Retailing, which features an attractive, full-color format throughout the entire text, is divided into five parts, which are in turn divided into 14 chapters that can easily be covered over the course of the term. Part I serves as an introduction to the study of retailing and provides an overview into what is involved in retail planning. Part II examines the environmental factors that influence retailing today, the behavior of customers, competitors, channels, as well as our legal and ethical behavior. Part III examines the role location plays in a retailer's success.

Part IV deals with the operations of a retail store. This section begins with a chapter on managing the retailer's finances. Special attention in this section is given to merchandise buying and handling, pricing, promotion and advertising, personal selling, store layout and design, and managing human resources. Part V deals with Retail Administration.

In addition, *Retailing* has an appendix on the role of fashion in merchandising, written by Dr. Mary Ann Eastlick, of the University of Arizona. This appendix follows the merchandise buying and handling chapter.

Chapter Organization

Each chapter begins with an **Overview** which highlights the key topic areas to be discussed. In addition, a set of **Learning Objectives** provides a description of what the student should know after reading the chapter. To further aid student learning, the text material is integrated with the learning objectives listed at the beginning of the chapters and the summaries at the end. A numbered icon like the one shown in the margin precedes each learning objective. The icons then appear in the margins and summaries to mark where each objective was fulfilled. In addition, the text features a prominent placement of key term definitions in the margin to make it easier for students to check their understanding of these key terms. If they need a fuller explanation of any term, the discussion is right there—next to the definition.

The body of the text will have **photos, exhibits, tables, and graphs** presenting the information and relationships in a visually appealing manner. Each chapter will have four **retailing boxes** featuring the inside story on a particular retailing event or

LO • 1
Define Retailing

decision (Retailing: The Inside Story), what is happening in the international retail market (Global Retailing), and how the on-line retailers (E-tailing) and retailers providing services (Service Retailing) have addressed the issues presented in that chapter. These boxes are typically lengthier real-world examples than can be incorporated in the regular flow of text material. Some of these box features are humorous, while others present a unique way to solve problems retailers face in their everyday operations. In addition, each chapter contains a **Managerial Question** within the body of the text asking the reader to relate how a retailer would use the chapter material in his or her business.

At the conclusion of each chapter is a **Student Study Guide.** The first feature of this addition to the text is a chapter **Summary** by Learning Objective followed by a list of **Terms to Remember**. These are followed by the traditional **Review and Discussion Questions**, which are also tied into the learning objectives for the chapter, and are meant to test recall and understanding of the chapter material, as well as provide students with an opportunity to integrate and apply the text material. Another feature is **Sample Test Questions,** a set of multiple-choice questions covering each of the chapter's learning objectives. The answers to these questions are in an Appendix at the end of the book.

The second half of the study guide is the **Application Section.** This section opens with a **Writing and Speaking Exercise** that is an attempt to aid the instructor in improving the students' oral/written communication skills, as well as their teamwork skills. Here the student, or group of students, is asked to make a one-page written report and/or oral presentation to the class incorporating the knowledge gained by reading the chapters. Some instructors may prefer to view these as "mini-cases."

A **Retail Project** is included that has the student visiting a library or a website and finding an answer to a current retail question.

The next feature of each chapter's Study Guide is a **Case**. Most of these are drawn from actual retail situations. The authors believe that the ability to understand the need for better management in retailing requires an explanation of retailing through the use of case studies. These cases will cover the entire spectrum of retail operations with cases involving department stores, specialty shops, direct retailing, hardware stores, grocery stores, apparel shops, discount stores, and convenience stores.

Since many of the students taking this class will one day open their own retail business, the next section is for them. **Planning Your Own Retail Business** presents a very specific problem based on the chapter's material that a small business manager/owner will face in his or her day-to-day operations.

Finally, **Key Terms and Concepts**, which will be presented in boldface type in the chapter, will have their definitions presented in the margins throughout the chapters.

Supplementary Material

Instructor's Resource Manual   This supplement includes an overview of each chapter, several detailed teaching tips for presenting the material, a detailed outline, the answers to questions for review and discussion, suggestions for handling the writing and speaking exercises, retail projects, cases, and planning your own business.

Test Bank   This printed ancillary contains more than 2,000 questions for professors to choose from. Varied levels of true-false and multiple-choice are organized by chapter and learning objectives. The test bank is available in both printed and electronic versions.

Computerized Test Bank   Available for Windows users, the computerized version of the printed test bank enables instructors to preview and edit test questions, as well as add their own. The test and answer keys can also be printed in "scrambled" formats.

Online PowerPoint Presentation   This is an innovative, easy-to-use presentation tool that will enable professors to custom design their own multimedia classroom presentations. Organized by chapter, this presentation will allow professors to use full-color slides of the figures, tables, and graphs from the text, as well as completely new material from outside sources in their classroom presentations. It is available on the publisher's web site at **http://www.harcourtcollege.com.**

Retail Spreadsheet Project   A computer spreadsheet called "The House," this project is set up for use with a computer, but it is possible to do all the required computations with a calculator or by hand. "The House" is about a small retail apparel shop and has two exercises for each chapter in the fourth edition of *Retailing*.

WebCT Study Guide   For professors interested in supplementing classroom presentations with online content, we and WebCT, can provide you with the industry's leading online courses.

Videos   The video package features companies such as Kmart, JCPenney, Pier 1 Imports and Fossil Watches. Each video segment supplements the ideas and concepts illustrated in the textbook.

Companion Web site   This site can be found at **http://www.harcourtcollege.com**. Go to Marketing to find the *Retailing* site. Besides the PowerPoint presentation, casebook, and retail spreadsheet project, there is a section on choosing retailing as a career, and advanced case for each of the five parts of the text, a detailed outline of each of the chapters, and 20 sample questions (10 true-false and 10 multiple-choice) for each chapter. Also, links to other important retail sites on the Web are provided.

Acknowledgments

Many people contributed to the development of this text. For their helpful suggestions as reviewers of the various editions of this text, we are especially grateful to the following:

Phyllis Ashinger, Wayne State University
Chad W. Autry, Bradley University
Steve Barnett, Stetson University
Barbara Bart, Savannah State College
Holly E. Bastow-Stoop, North Dakota State University
Jerry E. Boles, Western Kentucky University
David J. Burns, Youngstown State University
Louis D. Canale, Genesee Community College
Tim Christiansen, Purdue University
John Clark, California State University–Sacramento
Caroline Derozier, Texas Tech University
Roger Dickinson, University of Texas at Arlington
Janice Driggers, Orlando College
Joanne Eckstein, Macomb Community College
Jonathan Elimimian, Johnson C. Smith University
Sevo Eroglu, Georgia State University
Kenneth R. Evans, University of Missouri
Robert C. Ferrentino, Lansing Community College
Susan Fiorito, Florida State University
Sally L. Fortenbery, Texas Christian University
Jack Gifford, Miami University
Ellen Goldsberry, University of Arizona
D. Elizabeth Goins, University of Illinois at Springfield
Linda K. Good, Michigan State University
Donald H. Granbois, Indiana University
Blaine S. Greenfield, Bucks County Community College
Norman E. Hansen, Northeastern University
Shelley S. Harp, Texas Tech University
Joseph C. Hecht, Montclair State University
Stanley Hollander, Michigan State University
Patricia Huddleston, Michigan State University
Charles A. Ingene, University of Washington
Steve Inman, Texas Christian University
Marian H. Jernigan, Texas Woman's University
Julie Johnson-Hillery, Northern Illinois University
Laura Jolly, University of Kentucky
Mary Joyce, Bryant College
Jikyeong Kang, University of Wisconsin
William Keep, Quinnipiac College
J. Patrick Kelly, Wayne State University
Karen W. Ketch, University of Kentucky
Tammy Lamb Kinley, Western Illinois University
Jim Kress, Central Oregon Community College
Grace Kunz, Iowa State University

Frederick Langrehr, Valparaiso University
Marilyn Lavin, University of Wisconsin–Whitewater
Marilyn Lebahn, Northwest Technical College
Dong Lee, Fairmont State College
Melody L. Lehew, Kansas State University
Deborah Hawkins Lester, Kennesaw State University
Bruce Klemz, Winona State University
Michael W. Little, Virginia Commonwealth University
John W. Lloyd, Monroe Community College
Dolly D. Loyd, University of Southern Mississippi
Paul MacKay, East Central College
Michael McGinnis, University of Southern Alabama
Shawna L. Mahaffey, Delta College
Louise Majorey, Cazenovia College
Raymond Marquardt, University of Nebraska–Lincoln
Nancy McClure, Central Oklahoma University
Paul McGurr, Ashland College
Nancy J. Miller, Iowa State University
Diane Minger, Cedar Valley College
Linda Minikowske, North Dakota State University
Michelle A. Morganosky, University of Illinois–Urbana
Mark Mulder, Grand Rapids Junior College
David W. Murphy, Madisonville Community College
Lewis J. Neisner, University of Maryland
Elaine M. Notarantonio, Bryant College
Katherine A. Olson, Northern Virginia Community College
Jan P. Owens, University of Wisconsin–Parkside
Shiretta Ownbey, Oklahoma State University
Charles R. Patton, University of Texas at Brownsville
V. Ann Paulins, Ohio University
Kathryn Payne, Texas Tech University
Lynda Gamas Poloian, South New Hampshire University
John Porter, West Virginia University
Dawn Pysarchik, Michigan State University
Denise Reimer, Iowa Lakes Community College at Emmetsburg
R. Glenn Richey, University of Oklahoma
Lynne Ricker, University of Calgary
Jacquelene Robeck, University of Wisconsin–Stout
Thomas Rohrig, Texas Tech University
Marvin J. Rothenberg, Rutgers University
Rod Runyan, University of Wisconsin–Stevens Point
Ben Sackmary, State University College at Buffalo
Duane Schecter, Muskegon Community College

Jean Shaneyfelt, Edison Community College

Donna Smith, Ryerson Polytechnic University

Samuel A. Spralls III, Texas Tech University

Robert Stassen, University of Arkansas

Leslie D. Stoel, Ohio State University

Shirley Stretch-Stephenson, California State University–Los Angeles

Patrick Swarthout, Central Lakes College

Harriet P. Swedlund, South Dakota State University

William R. Swinyard, Brigham Young University

Paul Thistlewaite, Western Illinois University

Jane Boyd Thomas, Winthrop University

James A. Veregge, Cerritos Community College

Irena Vida, University of Tennessee

Mary Walker, Xavier University

Mary Margaret Weber, Emporia State Univeristy

Scarlett C. Wesley, University of Tennessee–Knoxville

Diane Wilemon, Texas Christian University

Mike Wittmann, University of Texas at San Antonio

Sarah B. Wise, University of South Carolina

Allen Young, Bessemer State Tech College

Deborah D. Young, Texas Woman's University

A special thanks must go to Mary Ann Eastlick, University of Arizona, for her excellent job writing Apparel Merchandising's Unique Role in Retailing, which is printed as Appendix 9A, following Chapter 9.

We would be remiss if we failed to thank all those in the retailing industry for their input in the text. We particularly want to thank David Overton and Tom Nicholson, Sears; Carol J. Greenhut, Schonfeld & Associates, Inc.; Bruce Van Kleeck, National Retailing Federation; Robert Grottke, Arthur Andersen; Paul Adams, Fleming Company; Steve Wilkinson, Kmart; Anne Alenskis, Albertson's; Suzanne Allford, HEB Grocery Company; Debbie Herd, JCPenney; Doral Chenoweth, USA Dinning Network; John Konarski, International Council of Shopping Centers; John Mount, Mount Marketing Services International; C. Beth Souther, Kurt Salmon Associates; Rick Segal and Martha Cass, Chapters Online Inc.; Marvin J. Rothenberg, Marvin J. Rothenberg Retail Marketing Consultants, Inc.; Molly Powers, Nielsen Marketing Research; William R. Davidson, Management Horizons; Whit and Sue Victory, Rix Funeral Home; and Fred Turner, York Group.

To the editorial team, we can only say we're glad you let us be a part of the team. These individuals include: Bill Schoof, acquisitions editor; Jana Pitts, developmental editor; Jim Patterson, senior project editor; Lois West, production manager; Linda Beaupre, creative director; Beverly Dunn, marketing manager; Linda Blundell, picture and rights editor; and Annette Coolidge, photo researcher.

Finally, we want to take this opportunity to thank our wives for their love and understanding, especially as seemingly endless deadlines approached. Thanks Judy, Virginia, and Monika.

Patrick Dunne
Lubbock, TX

Robert Lusch
Fort Worth, TX

David Griffith
Honolulu, HI

PATRICK M. DUNNE

Patrick Dunne, an associate professor at Texas Tech University, received his M.B.A. and Ph.D. in marketing from Michigan State University and his B.S. from Xavier University.

In over 30 years of university teaching, Dr. Dunne has taught a wide variety of marketing and distribution courses at both the undergraduate and graduate levels. His research has been published in many of the leading marketing and retailing journals. In addition, he has authored nine books. Dr. Dunne was the first academic to receive the Wayne A. Lemburg Award for "conspicuous individual accomplishments" from the American Marketing Association. Dr. Dunne has also been honored with several university teaching awards.

Previously Dr. Dunne served as Vice President of both the Publications and Association Developmental Divisions of the American Marketing Association. Professor Dunne is an active consultant to a variety of retailers, ranging from supermarkets to shopping malls.

ROBERT F. LUSCH

Robert F. Lusch, dean of the M. J. Neeley School of Business at Texas Christian University, received his Ph. D. in business administration from the University of Wisconsin and his M.B.A. and B.S. from the University of Arizona.

His expertise is in the area of marketing strategy and distribution systems. Professor Lusch has served as the editor of the Journal of Marketing. He is the author of over 150 academic and professional publications including 15 books. In 1997, The Academy of Marketing Science awarded him its Distinguished Marketing Educator Award and the American Marketing Association presented him the Harold Maynard Award.

Professor Lusch has served as President of the Southwestern Marketing Association, Vice President of Education and Vice President Finance of the American Marketing Association, chairperson of the American Marketing Association, and trustee of the American Marketing Association Foundation.

DAVID A. GRIFFITH

David A. Griffith, an associate professor at the University of Hawaii at Manoa, received his Ph.D. in business administration/marketing with a concentration on international business and his M.B.A. in general management from Kent State University. He received his B.S. in business administration/finance from the University of Akron.

His expertise is in the area of global marketing and electronic retailing. Professor Griffith has authored numerous academic and professional publications. Currently, Professor Griffith is on the Board of Directors of the American Marketing Association Global Marketing Special Interest Group. He has over ten years of consulting experience, has conducted numerous executive development seminars, is a contributing developmental professional to on-line executive development programs in the area of electronic commerce, and is involved in the strategy and planning of a number of on-line firms.

Brief Contents

Contents

Part II   The Retailing Environment   67

Chapter 3   Retail Customers   69

Chapter 6   Legal and Ethical Behavior   183

Chapter 13   Store Layout and Design   489

Part V   Retail Administration   533

Chapter 14   Managing Human Resources   535

Part I
Introduction to Retailing

Golf courses are primarily retailers of services. However, as they grow in popularity, the demand for golf clothing and equipment has similarly grown. This trend has benefited specialty golf stores, department stores, mail order catalogs, and Internet sites or e-tailers that cater to golfers.

Perspectives on Retailing

CHAPTER

1

Overview

In this chapter, we acquaint you with the nature and scope of retailing. We present retailing as a major economic force in the United States and as a significant area for career opportunities. Finally, we introduce the approach to be used throughout this text as you study and learn about the operation of retail firms.

Learning Objectives

After reading this chapter, you should be able to

1. explain what retailing is

2. explain why retailing is undergoing so much change today

3. describe five methods used to categorize retailers

4. understand what is involved in a retail career and list the prerequisites necessary for success in retailing

5. explain the different methods used for the study and practice of retailing

LO • 1
What is retailing?

What Is Retailing?

It is easy to overlook and take for granted the impact retailing has on a nation's economic growth and on how consumers obtain products. For example, consider the first major purchase that you will probably be making after graduation: the purchase of a new car. The retail automotive industry has undergone tremendous changes during the past 10 years and will continue to shape the manner in which consumers buy cars. Traditionally, making a car purchase was a time-consuming and frustrating process that began by reading magazines and the fine print in newspaper ads about various makes and models. Once this task was accomplished, you would spend a Saturday trudging from dealership to dealership to find just the right car. But the fun wasn't over yet. Once you found the car, you were usually treated to hours of haggling over the price.

Today, the buying process has been both transformed by, and is transforming, the retail automotive marketplace. The entrance of the auto superstore, where thousands of makes and models are available in a specific location, as well as on-line retailers and retail agents, such as Autobytel.com or AutoWeb.com, has dramatically changed how consumers shop and the manner in which retailers transact with their customers. Thus, when you begin that new car search you can expect a whole new buying process than the one your parents experienced. Today's auto consumer has the ability to get detailed information about prices, models, extras, and safety ratings on-line. Then, with just a click of a button the consumer can either initiate a car purchase or actually purchase the car. For example, when a customer initiates a car purchase at Autobytel.com, one of its over 3,000 accredited dealers leaps into action, contacting the customer within 24 hours. Merely 30 minutes after Ani Dominguez of Oklahoma City and her husband e-mailed their preferred model and target price to Autobytel.com, they received a response. By 5 p.m. the next day, the transaction was complete and they were the proud owners of a shiny new Ford Explorer XLT.[1] More recently, Autobytel.com has taken a step closer to click-and-purchase selling by offering new features such as real-time inventory, instant up-front pricing, trade-in options, competitive financing and insurance prices, and, most of all, home delivery. With a third of the company's 3,000-plus accredited dealers participating in its new Autobytel Direct Program, a customer can simply order a car and have it delivered. This is definitely a new era of retailing.

A recent study by J. D. Power & Associates indicated that 25 percent of all new car purchases were researched on-line, but fewer than 2 percent were sold using an on-line retail referral service such as Autobytel.com. However, the future looks bright as Forrester Research Inc., of Cambridge, Massachusetts, predicts that 470,000 cars will be sold on-line—with no dealer involvement—by the year 2003. This is probably not surprising to on-line retailers such as Amazon.com. It is no wonder Amazon.com's CEO Jeff Bezos, when asked what was the main advantage of the Internet as a shopping tool, answered that time was the consumer's most precious commodity.[2] This fact was highlighted by *Time* magazine when it chose Bezos as 1999's Person of the Year. According to *Time,* it was only fitting that the individual most credited with changing the way Americans would shop in the 21st century should be so honored. More details about Bezos are given in the E-tailing box presented in this chapter. Another Internet company, America Online, the preeminent provider of Internet access, was chosen *Advertising Age*'s Marketer of the Year for 2000.[3] Clearly, everybody seemed to agree that upon entering the 21st century our lives would forever be changed by the Internet.

In fact, retailing, which is responsible for matching the individual demands of the consumer with supplies of all the manufacturers, has made a significant contribution

E-tailing

Amazon.com: Retailing's New Wave

Winning on the Internet isn't necessarily about being first, or at least that is what some traditional retailers—such as Best Buy and Merrill Lynch, who were late to the game—hope. On-line success comes to those that execute best and those that know how to turn supposed liabilities into assets. Rewards today come not only from innovation, but also from great execution, and that execution is what's behind Amazon's Jeff Bezos as he seeks to become the earth's biggest seller of everything. All this despite the fact that Amazon.com is only expected to generate its first profitable quarter sometime in 2001.

Bezos first saw his vision of retailing's future in 1994, when as a 30-year old working for a New York investment banker, he was sitting at the computer exploring the still immature Internet. That afternoon he found a web site that measured Internet usage. Bezos couldn't believe it: the Internet was growing at a rate of 2,300 percent a year. "It was a wake-up call," he recalls. "I started thinking, O.K., what kind of business opportunity might there be here?" As a result he conceived an entirely new way of thinking about the ancient art of retailing, from creating a "flow experience" that keeps customers coming back to Amazon's web site to read product reviews or one another's "wish lists," to automating as much as possible a complex process that starts when you hit the e-tailer's "1-click" buy technology and ends when your purchase is delivered to your door. Even this delivery function is accomplished with a nationwide distribution network specially designed to handle e-tailing that was strategically placed in low- or no-sales-tax states around the United States. Each warehouse is 3 million square feet, built at a cost of $200 million, and designed to do what traditional warehouses can't do: deliver items directly and efficiently to customers rather than by pallet to retail stores. Such a process required new ways of thinking about employees and customers too, but Bezos had that creativity.

If all goes according to his daring—some might say outlandish—plan, his warehouses will be at capacity within the next few years and will store washing machines, cars, rubber gaskets, Prozac, exercise machines, model airplanes—everything but firearms and certain live animals. You name it, Amazon will sell it. Amazon will house nothing less than earth's biggest selection of goods, then Bezos will put them on his web site for people to find and buy; and Amazon won't just offer physical things that you can touch, but services too, such as banking, insurance, and travel. All of these advances will be based on Amazon's image for consistent, pleasant delivery and service, and perhaps its most valuable asset, its relationship with customers. "Small companies are good at taking risks; they have nothing to lose. Big companies lose their way when they stop taking big risks," Bezos says. "The only sure way to fail is to stop making bold innovations."

The sheer number of competitive web sites alone has put pressure on Amazon's growth and is the reason Bezos is adding categories as fast as he can. (After all, Wal-Mart, the world's largest retailer, only introduced a first-class web site in November 2000.) Thus, in addition to books, Amazon now e-tails video games and DVD movies, toys, electronics, software, home-improvement products, auctions, and zShops (on-line flea markets where anyone can sell anything). In addition, so as to not miss out on anything else dealing with e-tailing, Amazon also has minority stakes in other e-commerce companies such as Drugstore.com, Webvan, Gear.com, and Della.com, a wedding and gift registry.

Source: Based on "The Fast-Moving Internet Economy Has a Jungle of Competitors and Here's the King," "Cruising Inside Amazon," and "An Eye on the Future," all articles in *Time* magazine's Person of the Year feature, December 27, 1999: 50–87; "Note from the Editor," *Advertising Age*, March 6, 2000: s2; "E-Tail Gets Derailed," *Wall Street Journal*, April 5, 2000: A1 & A6; and the authors' observations.

to the economic prosperity that we enjoy so much. The nations that have enjoyed the greatest economic and social progress have been those with a strong retail sector. Retailers have become valued and necessary members of society. Although some may argue that we have too many retailers with too many stores operating today, we must not forget the social benefits that "overstoring" provides an economy. Some of the benefits

Global Retailing

Not Everybody Operates the Same Way

Although American retailers have made a significant contribution to this country's economic growth, the same cannot be said for retailers in all parts of the world. For example, Kmart found a totally different retailing philosophy when it expanded into Eastern Europe in the early 1990s after the fall of Communism.

When Kmart purchased a small department store chain in the former Czechoslovakia, the company found a retailing system totally different from the one in the United States. Like other retailers under the Communist system, the newly purchased chain failed to take markdowns or reductions in order to move older merchandise and use whatever money it got from the sale of this older merchandise to purchase newer and more "exciting" merchandise. Kmart also found that the chain's warehouses were full of decade-old state-manufactured sweaters, dresses, and underwear that offered very limited variations in assortment and price. Kmart was surprised to learn that under the Communist system, when an item didn't sell it was simply sent back to the warehouse and then returned to the shelves a few years later at its original full retail price for another try. This failure to take markdowns was terrifying to the retailer that was famous for unloading slow-moving items at giveaway prices by announcing a "blue-light" special.

If this wasn't enough to make shopping a "boring" event for the Eastern European consumer, Kmart also found another custom in Czechoslovakia that made shopping difficult. If they were unhappy with a product, Czech customers could bring it back to the store just like Americans could. However, whereas Americans are generally given either replacement merchandise, credit toward another purchase, or their money back, Czech customers were only given receipts and told to check back next month. Under the former Communist system, a refund committee, made up of store employees, would meet each month and decide on a case-by-case basis what to do with each returned item. Refund applicants could be denied or given refunds ranging from 10 to 100 percent of the purchase price. Any money left over would be split among the employees on the committee and the store. As a result, Kmart had to educate both the customers and their "new" employees as to what a "full refund policy" was all about. No wonder retailing didn't contribute to the economic growth of Eastern European countries as it did in the Western world and that Kmart left this market after only four years.

Wal-Mart waited until the latter part of the 1990s before entering Europe. When it entered Germany in 1997, the retailer immediately introduced "every day low pricing" (EDLP) and dropped existing prices by as much as 20 percent. The Bentonville, Arkansas, retailer was able to lower prices and not break German regulations prohibiting sales below cost by improving the efficiency of its distributions systems and working with suppliers.

However, when Wal-Mart purchased the British retailer ASDA in 1999, it found no such regulations but the toughest (overseas) market it ever encountered, with strong competition and a demanding consumer.

The lesson to be learned is that the retailer must also remember that customers and competitors are always different. For example, as Wal-Mart expands into more countries, it also faces the difficulty of catering to a wide variety of cultures. Using lessons learned from its stores in Mexico and South America, Wal-Mart tries to adapt some products to local customs. The image of Sam Walton's English setter on packages of its private-label dog food, Ol' Roy, was replaced with a terrier after Wal-Mart's German executives explained that terriers are popular in Germany, whereas Germans aren't familiar with setters. This fact of life about consumers being different is true not only when entering foreign markets but also, as we will point out in Chapter 3, when competing in different regions of the United States.

Source: Based on a presentation by several top Kmart executives to the American Collegiate Retailing Association, Troy, Michigan, April 23, 1993, and the authors' experiences with Wal-Mart.

that a vibrant retailing sector provides are easier access to products, not having to settle for a second or third choice when shopping for a particular product, greater customer satisfaction, and higher levels of customer service.[4]

However, perhaps the critical role of retailing in a society can best be illustrated when retailing doesn't perform as it should. Our Global Retailing box illustrates one of the reasons the Eastern European countries experienced a low rate of economic growth when they were under Communist control. Interestingly, when Toys "R" Us, Wal-Mart, Pizza Hut, and McDonald's opened for business in these countries, they became instant successes. The joy and excitement these new forms of retailing provided the citizens was amazing, which illustrates very well the value people of all cultures place on retailing that is responsive to their needs and wants.

> **Retailers that enter foreign markets and understand the local cultures and customs will be higher profit performers than those who don't understand the local cultures and customs.**

Dollars & Sense

Retailing, as we use the term in this text, consists of the final activity and steps needed to place a product in the hands of the consumer or to provide services to the consumer. In fact, retailing is actually the last step in a channel of distribution that may stretch from Europe or Asia to your hometown. Therefore, any firm that sells a product or provides services to the final consumer is performing the retailing function. Regardless of whether the firm sells to the consumer in a store, through the mail, over the telephone, through a television infomercial, over the Internet, door to door, or through a vending machine, it is involved in retailing.

Retailing
consists of the final activity and steps needed to place merchandise made elsewhere into the hands of the consumer or to provide services to the consumer.

The Nature of Change in Retailing

LO • 2
Why is retailing always undergoing so much change?

Many observers of the American business scene believe that retailing is the most "staid and stable" sector of business. Although this observation may have been true in the past, quite the contrary is occurring today. Retailing, which accounts for just less than 10 percent of the worldwide labor force and includes every living individual as a customer, is the largest single industry in most nations and is currently undergoing changes in many exciting ways.

Currently there are 1.9 million retail establishments in the United States with total sales of $2.9 trillion.[5] Based on U.S. Bureau of Census data, there are 23 retail establishments for every thousand households with average annual sales of more than $750,000. However, most retailers are smaller than the mean. Today more than 50 percent of retail establishments are small operations with annual sales of less than $400,000.

These figures also don't reflect the changes that have occurred behind these dollar amounts. The number of new retail enterprises that have been developed in the past two decades is truly amazing. Most of these new businesses have actually been new institutional forms, such as electronic retailing, warehouse retailing, supercenters (which are a combination of the discount department store and the supermarket), and home delivery fast-food businesses. Change is truly the driving force behind retailing today. We will now explore some of the trends that are affecting modern retailing.

E-tailing

The great unknown for today's retail managers is what will be the ultimate role of on-line shopping. Bill Gates, the legendary founder of Microsoft, believes that the Internet will soon become as indispensable to everyday life as the telephone.[6] Despite a slow start, some retailers are preparing for the soon-to-come day when, as people find the computer more user-friendly, e-tailing will account for more than 20 percent of total retail sales. (In 2000, e-tailing total sales were $20 billion or 1 percent of total retail sales.)[7] Still as we entered the 21st century, many undercapitalized e-tailers were being forced to seek new capital, merge with other e-tailers, or file for bankruptcy protection because almost as fast as Americans got used to buying goods on-line, they began to see the decline of many dot-com retailers. Although well-capitalized players such as Amazon.com will most likely make it, other once high-flying e-tailers appear doomed. For example, CDNow Inc., which Wall Street figured would dominate future sales of music to consumers, and Value America Inc., an on-line merchant that sold everything from barbecue sauce to personal computers, may not survive as their auditors have raised "substantial doubt" that these companies can make it as going concerns.[8]

Perhaps the very efficiency of e-tailing that contributed to the consumer's economic prosperity is turning out to be a principal cause of some e-tailer's demise. The Internet allows transactions without all the overhead of sales clerks and a store. But for many e-tailers, it has turned out to be too competitive. They have found that they have had to keep prices low, often via special promotions that never seem to end, to please customers who, with just the click of a mouse, can find competing e-tailers. Also, in the race to distinguish themselves from the crowd, e-tailers have been spending lavishly on advertising—ironically, in traditional media, especially during the Christmas season. They have also found themselves taking on more and more conventional retail practices, from building warehouses to adding service staff, thereby eliminating some of their alleged cost advantage. Others have disregarded these growth claims entirely and point out that the same claims were made about electronic shopping in the past. Still more threatening to e-tailers is the idea that many consumers use the Internet for research, then buy the product in regular stores.[9]

Finally, one of the most dramatic changes e-tailing is creating is a shift in power between retailers and consumers. Traditionally, the retailers' control over pricing information provided them the upper hand in most transactions. The information dissemination capabilities of the Internet are making more informed consumers and thus increasing their power when transacting and negotiating with retailers. Take, for example, the purchase of a new car that began this chapter. New e-tailers, such as Autobytel.com, have provided consumers pricing information thus enabling them to negotiate better deals. Other e-tailers, such as Priceline.com, are shifting power to consumers in new ways by allowing customers to set their own prices and let retailers fight for their business. Clearly, e-tailing is adding a new competitive dimension to retailing.

Price Competition

Some claim that America's fixation with low prices began after World War II when fair trade laws, which allowed the manufacturer to set a price that no retailer was allowed to sell below, paved the way for America's first discounter, E. J. Corvett. However, the current price revolution more likely began with the birth of Wal-Mart in Rogers, Arkansas, in 1962. At the time, there were 41 publicly held discount stores and another

Wal-Mart, the world's largest retailer, is also the world's leader in controlling selling, general, and administrative expenses. This is one of the keys to Wal-Mart's high profit performance.

two dozen privately owned chains already in business.[10] However, what Sam Walton did that forever changed the face of retailing was to realize before everybody else that most of any product's cost gets added after the item is produced and moves from the factory to the retailer's shelf and finally to the consumer. Therefore, Walton began enlisting suppliers to help him reduce these costs and increase the efficiency of the product's movement. Also, Walton, who never operated a computer in his life, made a major commitment in the 1980s to computerizing Wal-Mart as a means to reduce these expenses. As a result of the introduction of the computer to retail management, Wal-Mart's selling, general, and administrative costs as a percentage of sales fell to less than 16 percent while all of its competitors' operating expenses were still 2 to 4 percent higher. Simply put, Wal-Mart became the world's largest retailer by relentlessly cutting unnecessary costs and demanding that its suppliers do the same.

Retailers that control the costs incurred after the merchandise is acquired better than their competition will be higher profit performers.

Dollars & Sense

"Brick & mortar" retailers, such as Wal-Mart, aren't the only retailers to improve their efficiency by using the computer. As our Service Retailing box points out, service retailers are now using the computer to make better pricing decisions.

Service Retailing

Service Retailers Are Making Better Pricing Decisions

Although most "brick & mortar" retailers got savvy about using the computer to cut costs, few were as fast as their service counterparts in figuring how much money they were losing with old-fashioned pricing strategies. Lacking detailed information about market demand and their own available supplies, retailers routinely overpriced some merchandise and underpriced others.

This changed in the late 1980s when the airlines started using sophisticated computer programs to balance supply with demand. Hence, it is not uncommon for airline passengers, even those seated next to each other, to pay different prices for the same trip. Yet this sophistication didn't move beyond the airlines until their travel partners, hotels, began a similar system in the mid-1990s. Today, many service retailers have adopted such more enlighten pricing strategies.

Service products are vastly different than physical goods, because they come into existence at the same time they are bought and consumed. They are composed of intangible elements that are inseparable, they usually involve customer participation in some important way, they cannot be sold in the sense of ownership transfer, and they have no title. Thus, service retailing consists of the sale or rent of an intangible activity, which usually cannot be stored or transported but provides the user some degree of satisfaction even if it can't be owned. One of your favorite service retailers using a computer to set prices may be your local golf course.

Just as with airline passengers paying different prices for the same trip, golfers in the same foursome may pay different prices. Recently, one of our colleagues made plans to play one of the most famous public courses in Texas. She "booked" a twosome for 9 a.m. on a Saturday, 10 days in advance, and agreed to a $100-per-person greens fee. When she showed up, she found out that a third person was added to her group. After all, with a foursome in front and back of her, the golf course had some excess capacity. Therefore, the golf pro added this "other" person to her group and since he only made his reservation the night before over the Internet, his green fees was only $75.

Thus, just as airlines and hotels adjust prices from hour to hour to get a maximum yield from their fixed capacity (remember, there really wasn't much cost to adding that third golfer), some golf pros now preview demand for day, evening, and weekend tee times and adjust prices accordingly. Our colleague used such an Internet connection to play the course and the other major courses while on vacation in Phoenix a month later. These courses offered different prices for the next day's play depending on demand. In fact, two of the courses let you bid on tee times. It should not be surprising that future transactions with many service retailers, because of their perishable wares, may soon resemble electronic equities trading with bid prices and ask prices and frequent price changes.

Golf course green fees can vary depending on how reservations were made.

Demographic Shifts

Other significant changes in retailing over the past decade have resulted from changing demographic factors, such as the fluctuating birth rate, the growing importance of Generation-Y consumers, the Generation Xers starting to reach middle age, the baby boomers reaching retirement age, the redistribution of income levels, and the increasing number of women in the work force. Many people simply failed to realize how these factors, which had profound effects on our society, could also impact retailing. The successful retailers of the 21st century have become more service oriented (offering better "value" in price and quality), more promotion oriented, and better attuned to their customers' needs. For example, one of the reasons that Home Depot is now one of the nation's largest retailers is that it has listened to its customers. Today, 70 percent of the 50,000 items it carries have been suggested by customers.[11]

Also, with population growth slowing, retailers are no longer able to sustain their long-term profit projections by just gaining additional sales from new stores as they had been able to do in the past. Profit growth must come by either increasing same-store sales at the expense of the competition's market share or by reducing expenses without reducing services to the point of losing customers. (**Same-store sales** is a retailing term that compares an individual store's sales to its sales for the same month in the previous year. **Market share** refers to a retailer's sales as a percentage of total market sales for the product line or service category under consideration.) As a result, today's retail firms are run by professionals who can look at the changing environment and see opportunities, exert enormous buying power over manufacturers, and anticipate future changes before they impact the market, rather than just react to these changes after they occur. However, not even these experts are always in agreement about what the future will bring.

Same-store sales
compares an individual store's sales to its sales for the same month in the previous year.

Market share
is the retailer's total sales divided by total market sales.

Retailers who can spot upcoming demographic changes and adapt and not merely react after the changes occur will have higher profit performance.

Dollars & Sense

Store Size

Further insight about the changes occurring in retailing today can be obtained by looking at the average store size for various retail categories. The largest increase in store size in recent years has been in drugstores, a reflection of the rapid growth of chains such as Walgreens and Eckerd. In addition to drugs, these stores sell many different unrelated items, such as food products, convenience goods, greeting cards, seasonal items such as gardening supplies and Christmas decorations, and even clothing. This phenomenon is referred to as **scrambled merchandising.** For example, convenience stores are said to be using a scrambled merchandising approach when they sell gasoline, bread, milk, beer, cigarettes, magazines, and fast food. This scrambling of merchandise also applies to services, such as ATMs, phone cards, and car wash services at

Scrambled merchandising
exists when a retailer handles many different and unrelated items.

Retailers struggling to remain competitive and profitable have turned to scrambled merchandising where they stock their shelves with whatever sells even if the products offered are unrelated.

convenience stores. The effects of scrambled merchandising on retailing today can be most easily be seen in Exhibit 1.1, which shows the various locations where consumers can purchase different products.

There has also been an increase in the average store size for general merchandise stores, which in many cases are combining with supermarkets to form supercenters. In contrast, some other grocery stores have been shrinking in both size and the range of merchandise carried, reflecting their targeted customer's increased desire for convenience. In addition, stores have had to make better use of space because rents are rapidly increasing. Likewise, the average department store is now smaller because many of these retailers are closing their downtown stores, which often were their largest

Exhibit 1.1	The Effects of Scrambled Merchandising						
Store	**Loaf Bread**	**Hamburger**	**Dog Food**	**Candy**	**Paper Towels**	**Ice Cream**	**Motor Oil**
Fast Food Outlet		•		•		•	
Supermarket	•	•	•	•	•	•	•
Convenience Store	•	•	•	•	•	•	•
Supercenter	•	•	•	•	•	•	•
Club Store	•	•	•	•	•	•	•
Pet Food Store			•				
Drug Store	•	•	•	•	•	•	•
Home Improvement				•	•		•

Toys "R" Us pioneered the category killer format. Today, Toys "R" Us has taken this concept to over a dozen other countries.

stores, because the downtown areas of many cities have become "ghost towns." Thus, retailers today are seeing a trend emerge: retail stores are now either larger or smaller than their counterparts from the past. In fact, nowhere is this fact of retailing better described than with "category killers." The **category killer** got its name from its marketing strategy: carry such a large amount of merchandise in a single category at such low prices that it makes it impossible for customers to walk out without purchasing what they needed, thus "killing" the competition.

Toys "R" Us, which began operations in the 1950s, has the distinction of being the first category killer. Some well-known category killers today include Best Buy, Home Depot, Blockbuster Video, Circuit City, Office Depot, CompUSA, PetsMart, and Bed Bath & Beyond. Category killers have diverted business away from traditional wholesale supply houses. For example, Home Depot appeals to the professional contractor and Office Depot to the business owner who traditionally purchased supplies from hardware wholesalers and office supply and equipment wholesalers.

However, many other category killers from the past decade have suffered financial reverses. These specialty superstore chains failed because they had poor strategy, weak execution, and too much "me too" competition. The continued rapid growth of general merchandise discounters, such as Kmart, Target, and Wal-Mart, also contributed to their demise. Just For Feet Inc., which is now remembered more for its poorly executed ad during the 1999 Super Bowl (the ad showed a barefooted African runner being attacked by hunters and forced to wear shoes), was one of these hot retailers of the 1990s that failed to spot changes in the retailing landscape. It did not help the failed retailers that many time-strapped consumers started taking their business to the Internet or shopping at smaller more convenient outlets closer to home as we entered the 21st century.[12]

Therefore, success in retailing is dependent on a retail manager's ability to properly interpret what changes are occurring and what these changes mean to the store's customers, and building a strategy to respond to these changes. Therein lies the excitement and challenge of retailing as a career. After all, 30 years ago, the Wal-Mart strategy of building a major enterprise in small-town America and offering "everyday low prices"

Category killer
is a retailer that carries such a large amount of merchandise in a single category at such good prices that it makes it impossible for the customers to walk out without purchasing what they need, thus killing the competition.

was probably considered foolhardy. This was a time when retailers thought growth could be achieved only by competing in the big cities where large population bases were located. Yet someone who purchased 100 shares of Wal-Mart when it went public on October 1, 1970, for $16.50 a share would by 2000 be holding more that 204,800 shares worth nearly $13,000,000, not counting cash dividends, which could have been reinvested.[13]

Of course, the future cannot be predicted with certainty; after all, even today retail experts are still uncertain as to Amazon's future growth rate. This text, however, attempts to provide you with the tools to meet these upcoming challenges and be a success in retailing. Still the answer to what the future will bring lies in the disquieting fact that retailers do not operate in a closed environment; they operate in a continuously changing competitive environment. These changes are discussed in greater detail in Chapters 3 through 6. For now, we will concentrate on the following environmental elements: the behavior of consumers, the behavior of competition, the behavior of channel members (the manufacturers and wholesalers that the retailer buys from), the legal system, the state of technology, and the socioeconomic nature of society. Exhibit 1.2 depicts these elements.

A final comment about the changing face of retailing: Remember, business entrepreneurs, not obliged to conform to old legal and social standards, are free to forge new

Exhibit 1.2	External Environmental Forces Confronting Retail Firms

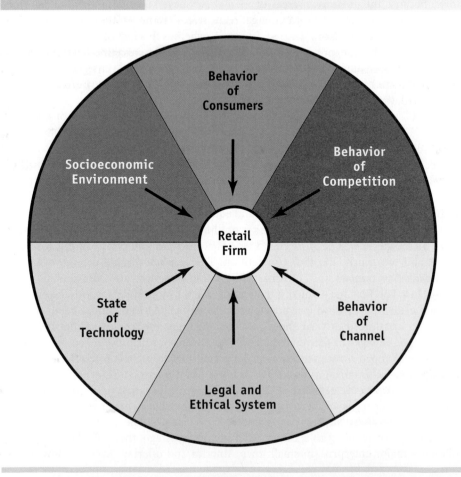

retail approaches that capitalize on emerging market opportunities. In retailing this is all the more evident when we consider fashion trends that in the past would have lasted for years, now may last only a few months.

Categorizing Retailers

LO • 3
What are the various methods used to categorize retailers?

Categorizing retailers can help the reader understand competition and the changes that occur in retailing. However, there is no single acceptable method of classifying retail competitors, although many classification schemes have been proposed. The five most popular schemes are described in Exhibit 1.3.

Census Bureau

The U.S. Bureau of the Census, for purposes of conducting the Census of Retail Trade, classifies all retailers using three-digit North American Industry Classification System (NAICS) codes. The web site for locating these codes is http://www.census.gov/epcd/www/naics.html. These NAICS codes include the following:

1. Motor vehicle and parts dealers (NAICS 441)—there are almost 123,000 of these retailers
2. Furniture and home furnishings stores (NAICS 442)—there are over 64,000 of these stores
3. Electronics and appliance stores (NAICS 443)—there are approximately 44,000 of these retailers
4. Building material and garden equipment and supplies dealers (NAICS 444)—there are roughly 93,000 of these dealers
5. Food and beverage stores (NAICS 445)—there are nearly 149,000 of these stores
6. Health and personal care stores (NAICS 446)—there are almost 83,000 of these retailers
7. Gasoline stations (NAICS 447)—there are approximately 127,000 gasoline stations
8. Clothing and clothing accessories stores (NAICS 448)—there are roughly 157,000 of these stores

Exhibit 1.3	Categorizing Retailers			
Census Bureau	**Number of Outlets**	**Margin/Turnover**	**Location**	**Size**
3-digit NAICS code	Single unit	Low margin/low turns	Traditional	By sales volume
4-digit NAICS code	2–10 units	Low margin/high turns	Central shopping districts	
5-digit NAICS code	11+ units	High margin/low turns	Shopping centers	By number of employees
		High margin/high turns	Free-standing nontraditional	

9. Sporting goods, hobby, book, and music stores (NAICS 451)—there are over 69,000 of these retailers

10. General merchandise stores (NAICS 452)—there are nearly 37,000 of these stores

11. Miscellaneous store retailers (NAICS 453)—there are almost 130,000 of these retailers

12. Nonstore retailers (NAICS 454)—there are roughly 45,000 of these retailers

Generally, these three-digit NAICS codes are too broad to be of much use to the retail analyst. The four-digit NAICS codes provide much more information on the structure of retail competition and are easier to work with. For example, NAICS 454 is nonstore retailing consisting of approximately 45,000 retailers. Within this are NAICS 4541, which consists of 10,000 electronic shopping and mail-order houses (Spiegel, Land's End, and L.L. Bean, for example), NAICS 4542, consisting of 7,000 vending machine operators, NAICS 4543, consisting of 27,000 direct-selling establishments, and so on.

In almost all instances, the NAICS code reflects the type of merchandise the retailer sells. The major portion of a retailer's competition comes from other retailers in its NAICS category. General merchandise stores (NAICS 452) are the exception to this rule. These stores, due to the merchandise carried, compete with retailers in most other NAICS categories. For example, general merchandise stores, such as department stores, compete with specialty apparel stores, such as The Gap and The Limited, mail-order retailers, such as Land's End and L.L. Bean, or off-priced stores, such as T.J. Maxx or Ross's Dress-for-Less, when someone is interested in buying clothing. In fact, most retailers must compete to a considerable extent with general merchandise stores, because these larger stores probably handle many of the same types of merchandise that smaller, more limited retailers sell. In a very broad sense, all retailers compete with each other since they are all vying for the same limited consumer dollars.

Most mail-order catalog retailers focus their efforts on a special market niche or segment.

A shortcoming of using NAICS codes is that they do not reflect all retailing activity. The Census Bureau definition equates retailing only with the sale of "tangible" goods or merchandise. However, by our definition, selling services to the final consumer is also retailing. This suggests that retailing can also be applied to businesses such as barber/beauty shops, health clubs, dry cleaners, banks, insurance agencies, funeral homes, movie theaters, amusement parks, maid services, medical and dental clinics, one-hour photo labs, and so on. For instance, NAICS 772, which is not classified under retail trade, consists of almost 490,000 eating and drinking establishments. Remember, any time the consumer spends money—either on tangibles (merchandise) or on intangibles (services)—retailing has occurred.

Number of Outlets

Another method of classifying retailers is by the number of outlets each firm operates. Generally, retailers with several units are a stronger competitive threat because they can spread many fixed costs, such as advertising and top management salaries, over a larger number of stores and can achieve economies in purchasing. However, single-unit retailers, such as your neighborhood IGA grocery store, do have several advantages. They are generally owner- and family-operated and tend to have harder-working, more motivated employees. Also, they can focus all their efforts on one trade area and tailor their merchandise to that area. In the past, such stores were usually able to spot emerging customer trends sooner and respond to them faster than the larger multiunit operations.

Any retail organization that operates more than one unit is technically a chain, but this is really not a very practical definition. The Census Bureau classifies chain stores into two size categories: 2 to 10 stores and 11 or more. We will use the 11 or more units when we use the term *chain stores.*

Exhibit 1.4 shows the importance of sales by **chain stores,** those retail operations having 11 or more units, as a percentage of total U.S. sales for some of the different merchandise lines. The statistics in Exhibit 1.4 reveal that chain stores account for 41

Chain stores
normally refers to operations having 11 or more units.

Exhibit 1.4	Importance of Chain Stores

Kind of Business	Percentage of Category
Durable Goods Stores	16
Eating Places	23
Auto and Home Supply Stores	37
Total U.S. Retail Sales	41
Nondurable Goods Stores	57
Women's Clothing Specialty Stores	62
Grocery Stores	63
Drug Stores	65
Shoe Stores	68
Family Clothing	80
General Merchandise Stores	96
Department Stores	99

percent of all retail sales (including 99 percent of all department store sales and 63 percent of all grocery store sales). Though large chain operations account for 57 percent of nondurable goods sales, they only account for 16 percent of durable goods sales, such as autos and furniture.

Not all chain operations enjoy the same advantages. Small chains are local in nature and may enjoy some economies in buying and in having the merchandise tailored to their market needs. Large chains are generally regional or national and can take full advantage of the economies of scale that centralized buying, accounting, training, and information systems and a **standard stock list** can achieve. A standard stock list requires that all stores in a retail chain stock the same merchandise. Other national chains such as Sears, recognizing the variations of regional tastes, use the **optional stock list approach,** which gives each store the flexibility to adjust its merchandise mix to local tastes and demands. After all, as one Sears executive told the authors, stores in the Rio Grande Valley in Texas sell a preponderance of smalls and mediums in men's shirts, whereas in Minnesota the chains sells a preponderance of larger sizes.

Both of these stock lists provide scale advantages in other retailing activities. For example, promotional savings occur when more than one store operates in an area and can utilize the same advertisements, even while tailoring specific merchandise to specific stores.

Finally, chain stores have long been aware of the benefits of taking a leadership role in the marketing channel. When a chain store retailer is able to achieve critical mass in purchases, it can get other channel members—wholesalers, brokers, and manufacturers—to engage in activities they might not otherwise engage in and is thus referred to as the **channel captain.** Some of the things the chain store retailer might get other channel members to do include direct-to-store deliveries, increased promotional allowances, extended payment terms, special package sizes, and so on that allow the retailer to operate in the most efficient manner.

Standard stock list
is a merchandising method in which all stores in a retail chain stock the same merchandise.

Optional stock list
is a merchandising method in which each store in a retail chain is given the flexibility to adjust its merchandise mix to local tastes and demands.

Channel captain
is the institution (manufacturer, wholesaler, broker, or retailer) in the marketing channel who is able to plan for and get other channel institutions to engage in activities they might not otherwise engage in. Large store retailers are often able to perform the role of channel captain.

Dollars & Sense

Retailers who can develop private branded merchandise better than their competition will experience higher profitability.

Private label branding
also often called store branding, occurs when a retailer develops its own brand name and contracts with a manufacturer to produce the merchandise with the retailer's brand on it instead of the manufacturer's name.

In recent years, chains, as will be discussed in greater detail in Chapter 4, have relied on their high level of consumer recognition to engage in **private label branding.** Private label branding, also sometimes called *store branding,* is when a retailer develops its own brand name and contracts with a manufacturer to produce the product with the retailer's brand on it instead of buying merchandise with the manufacturer's brand name on it. For example, Marks & Spencer, the English retailing giant, first applied the St. Michael private brand in 1928. The success of the St. Michael brand has enabled the firm to grow to more than 700 stores worldwide through a value orientation. Overall, private branding now accounts for almost 40 percent of department store sales and over 20 percent of total grocery units sold, and it is expected to surpass 30 percent of grocery sales by the year 2005.[14] Other retailers have borrowed from the success of the supermarkets and department stores with their private labels. Barnes & Noble now sells deluxe hardcover editions of many of the classics with its own publishing house imprint. Private labels usually have lower acquisition costs, which can be passed on to the consumer in the form of lower prices, thereby increas-

When a potential customer connects to Amazon.com they essentially help the retailer create a new location. A location with the ultimate in locational convenience; the home or office where the user's computer is located.

ing demand. Also, even though private brands have no national advertising costs, the retailer must spend more to develop local demand for the brand. As a result, retailers today are now competing with the national brand manufacturers as well as the store across the street.

A shortcoming of using the number of outlets scheme for classifying retailers is that it only addresses those retailers operating in a traditional brick & mortar space. As such, this scheme ignores many nontraditional retailers such as catalog-only and e-tailers. How many outlets does Amazon.com have? One could argue that each new on-line computer is a potential retail outlet for the e-tailing giant.

Margins versus Turnover

Retailers can be classified in regard to their gross margin percentage and rate of inventory turnover. The **gross margin percentage** shows how much **gross margin** (net sales minus the cost of goods sold) the retailer makes as a percentage of sales; this is also referred to as the gross margin return on sales. A 40 percent gross margin indicates that on each dollar of sales the retailer generates 40 cents in gross margin dollars. This gross margin will be used to pay the retailer's **operating expenses** (the expenses the retailer incurs in running the business other than the cost of the merchandise, e.g., rent, wages, utilities, depreciation, and insurance). **Inventory turnover** refers to the number of times per year, on average, that a retailer sells its inventory. Thus an inventory turnover of 12 times indicates that, on average, the retailer turns over or sells its average inventory once a month. Likewise, an average inventory of $40,000 (retail) and annual sales of $240,000 means the retailer has turned over its inventory 6 times in one year ($240,000 divided by $40,000) or every two months.

High-performance retailers, those who produce financial results substantially superior to the industry average, have long recognized the relationship between gross margin percent, inventory turnover, and profit. One can classify retailers into four basic types by using the concepts of margin and turnover.

Gross margin
is net sales minus the cost of goods sold.

Gross margin percentage
is the gross margin divided by net sales or what percent of each sales dollar is gross margin.

Operating expenses
are the expenses the retailer incurs in running the business other than the cost of the merchandise.

Inventory turnover
refers to the number of times per year, on average, that a retailer sells its inventory.

High-performance retailers
are those retailers that produce financial results substantially superior to the industry average.

Low-margin/low-turnover retailer
is one that operates on a low gross margin percentage and a low rate of inventory turnover.

Low-margin/high-turnover retailer
is one that operates on a low gross margin percentage and a high rate of inventory turnover.

High-margin/low-turnover retailer
is one that operates on a high gross margin percentage and a low rate of inventory turnover.

High-margin/high-turnover retailer
is one that operates on a high gross margin percentage and a high rate of inventory turnover.

Typically, the low-margin/low-turnover retailer will not be able to generate sufficient profits to remain competitive and survive. Thus there are no good examples of successful retailers using this approach. On the other hand, the low-margin/high-turnover retailer is common in the United States. Perhaps the best brick & mortar examples are the discount department stores, such as Target, the warehouse clubs, such as Sam's and Costco, and the category killers, such as Toys "R" Us. Amazon.com is probably the best known example of a low-margin/high-turnover e-tailer. High-margin/low-turnover brick & mortar retailers are also quite common in the United States. Furniture stores, TV and appliance stores, jewelry stores, gift shops, funeral homes, and most of the mom-and-pop stores located in small towns across the country are generally good examples of high-margin/low-turnover operations. Some click & mortar retailers using this approach include Coach and Sharper Image. Finally, some retailers find it possible to operate on both high-margin and high-turnover. As you might expect, this strategy can be very profitable. Probably the most popular examples are convenience food stores such as 7-Eleven, Circle K, Stop&Shop, or Quick Mart. However, because in the early stages of Internet retailing most retailers are using a low-margin to achieve a high-turnover rate, there are no examples of e-tailers using this strategy.

As indicated, the low-margin/low-turnover retailer is the least able of the four to withstand a competitive attack because this retailer is usually unprofitable or barely profitable, and when competitive intensity increases, profits are driven even lower. On the other hand, the high-margin/high-turnover retailer is in an excellent position to withstand and counter competitive threats because profit margins enable it to finance competitive price wars.

Although the margin/turnover scheme provides an encompassing classification, it fails to capture the complete array of retailers operating in today's marketplace. For example, service retailers, and even some e-tailers such as Priceline.com, have no inventory to turnover. As such, though this scheme provides a good way of analyzing retail competition, it neglects several important types of retailing.

Location

Retailers have long been classified according to their location within a metropolitan area, be it the central business district, a mall or strip shopping center, or as a freestanding unit. These traditional locations will be discussed in greater detail in Chapter 7. However, the past decade saw a major change in the locations that retailers selected. Retailers are now aware that the opportunities to improve financial performance could result not only by improving the sales per square foot of traditional sites but by operating in new nontraditional retail areas.

Dollars & Sense

Retailers that seek out nontraditional locations to reach customers will increase their chances of being highly profitable.

In the past, rather than expand into untested territories, many retailers simply renovated existing stores. Not today. Now retailers are reaching out for alternative retail sites. American retailers are testing all types of nontraditional locations to expand their businesses. For example, to get more people to eat pizza when they rent video tapes, Pizza Hut introduced kiosks in video rental stores with direct phone lines to the local Pizza Hut. McDonald's has tested locations in service stations along interstate highways. Loblaw, a Canadian grocer, has an in-store women's health club in its store near Toronto, and E*Trade, the on-line brokerage firm, is expanding its non-Internet presence with financial service centers in SuperTarget stores.

Also, given the high income levels of many airline travelers and the increasing amount of layover time between flights, many retailers have opened stores in airports, an idea that originated and has long been used by European and Asian retailers. Airport retailers have been able to succeed by offering fast service, convenience, a pleasant and clean appearance, product variety and quality, and entertainment.[15] However, as we enter the 21st century, probably the most significant of the new nontraditional shopping locations is one that combines culture with entertainment/shopping, something that would have been unheard of a decade ago. Today, locations such as the underground mall at the Louvre in Paris have proven that the edges are blurring between high-brow pleasures and entertainment for the masses.[16]

Dollar General, Jewel/Osco, Pathmark, Von's, and Sears have taken the lead in opening stores in inner-city neighborhoods. Also, KFC, Pizza Hut, and Taco Bell, which are all owned by Tricon Restaurants, are opening free-standing units near or on several large universities with all three fast-food chains under one roof where employees and facilities (parking lots, restrooms, etc.) can be shared in this nontraditional location. Other fast-food operators have combined two or more franchisees together. One popular example would be to combine a "meal" retailer (KFC) with a "dessert" operator (Haagen-Dazs).

Before ending our discussion of location, it is important to point out that this is one area of retailing that may undergo significant changes in the next decade. The Internet suggests that future locations may be as close as a consumer's computer. Some retailers are now able to operate out of their home office or car, communicating with the customer with the aid of a portable phone/fax.

Many fast-food retailers are opening two or more brand-name food franchises in the same location and under a single roof.

Size

Many retail trade associations classify retailers by sales volume or number of employees. The reason for classifying by size is that the operating performance of retailers tends to vary according to size, that is, larger firms generally have lower operating costs per sales dollar than smaller firms do. For example, the National Retail Federation, which categorizes U.S. department stores into three volume groups, found that operating expenses were 38 percent for firms having sales between $5 and $20 million, 38 percent for stores in the $20 to $100 million range, and only 34 percent for larger operations. Most retail trade associations provide similar breakdowns on gross margins, net profits, net markups, sales per square foot of selling space, and so forth. Retailers will find this information meaningful when comparing their results against others of a similar size. The inside covers of this text provide a description, along with the most recent sales figures, for the top 25 American retailers and the top 25 global retailers.

Although size has been useful in the past, it is unclear whether the changes brought about by technology will not make this factor obsolete. For example, imagine a fully automated retailer in which as a consumer places an order on-line, an automated warehouse packages the selected merchandise and forwards it to the shipping area to be sent by UPS to the customer. With this scenario in mind, is a brick & mortar retailer such as Wal-Mart comparable to Amazon.com in terms of the number of employees needed?

Managerial Question: Go to www.careersinretailing.com and pick any of the listed retailers. As a manager for your selected retailer, compare your retailer's web site to that of several other retailers. What changes would you make to your web site? Remember, you want to use your web site to make individuals interested in working for your retail enterprise.

<table>
<tr><td>**LO • 4**</td></tr>
<tr><td>What is involved in a retailing career?</td></tr>
</table>

A Retailing Career

Someone once said that managing a retail store is an easy job. All you have to do is get consumers to visit your store (traffic) and then get these consumers to buy something (convert the traffic into customers) while operating at a lower cost than your competition (financial management). Assuming this is correct, what type of person is needed to manage a retail store in the 21st century? A(n)

Economist	Yes ___	No ___
Fashion expert	Yes ___	No ___
Marketer	Yes ___	No ___
Financial analyst	Yes ___	No ___
Personnel manager	Yes ___	No ___
Logistics manager	Yes ___	No ___
Information system manager	Yes ___	No ___
Accountant	Yes ___	No ___

In reality, the answer is yes to all of these types, because a retail store manager needs to be knowledgeable in all these areas. As we have pointed out, few industries offer a more fast-paced, ever-changing environment where results are quickly seen on the bottom line than retailing. Few job opportunities will train you to become an expert not in just one field, but in all business disciplines. Retailing offers you the economist's job of forecasting sales up to six months in advance, the fashion expert's job of predicting consumer behavior and how it will affect future fashion trends, and the marketing manager's job of determining how to promote, price, and display your merchandise. Further, it offers the financial analyst's job of seeking to reduce the various expenses; the personnel manager's job of hiring the right people, training them to perform their duties in an efficient manner, and developing their work schedules; the logistics manager's job of arranging delivery of a hot item; the information system analyst's job of analyzing sales and other data to determine opportunities for improved management practices; and the accountant's job of arriving at a profitable bottom line.

In summary, a retailer is like a master chef. Anyone can buy the ingredients but only a master chef can make a masterpiece. Over the course of a career, you will have to deal with many issues. Among them are the following:

1. What product(s) or service(s) to offer
2. What group of customers to target
3. Where to locate the store
4. How to train and motivate your employees
5. What price level to use
6. What levels of customer service (store hours, credit, staffing, parking, etc.) to offer your customers
7. How to lay out the store
8. How to leverage the Internet to support your mission

If you consider that there are 10,000 possible combinations of products, and at least 10 possible combinations of the other seven issues, then there are more than 10 billion possible retailing formats. No wonder no other occupation offers the immediate opportunities and challenges that retailing does. Yet many students do not consider retailing when exploring career opportunities, or they do not consider all they can do in a retailing career. One of the greatest opportunities for people entering a retailing career is in on-line retailing, or e-tailing. One particular e-tailing field that is attracting many job seekers is the retailing of on-line information, which is providing unheralded opportunities to those seeking new challenges.

Common Questions about a Retailing Career

As a student considering your future career, you may have certain questions about what opportunities a career in retailing may offer. To help you understand both the positive and negative sides of retailing, we will examine a few of the most frequently asked questions.

Salary   Are salaries in retailing competitive? Generally, starting salaries in executive training programs will be around $30,000 to $40,000 per year. That, however, is only the short-run perspective. In the long run, the retail manager or buyer is directly rewarded on individual performance. Entry-level retail managers or buyers who do exceptionally well can double or triple their incomes in 3 to 5 years and often can have incomes twice those that classmates who chose other career fields will attain in 7 to 10 years. For example, it is not uncommon for a person in the supermarket industry who is within 5 to 7 years of their college graduation to be made a store director or manager and earn a six-figure income. However, although there is tremendous upside potential with a long-term retailing career, in general retailers offer starting salaries 5 to 10 percent lower than what many other business fields offer.

Career Progression   Can one advance their career rapidly in retailing? Yes. Obviously, this answer depends on both the retail organization and the individual. A person capable of handling more responsibility than he or she is given can move up quickly. There is no standard career progression chart, the www.careersinretailing.com web site shows career paths available with many of the country's leading retailers.

Geographic Mobility   Does a retailing career allow one to live in the area of the country where one desires? Yes and no. Retailing exists in all geographic areas of the United States where there is sufficient population density. In the largest 300 cities in the United States, there will be sufficient employment and advancement opportunities in retailing. In order to progress rapidly, a person must often be willing and able to make several moves, even if doing so may not be attractive in terms of an individual's lifestyle. Rapidly growing chain stores usually find it necessary to transfer individuals in order to open stores in new geographic areas. Fortunately, these transfers are generally coupled with promotions and salary adjustments. Finally, a person may stay in one geographic area if he or she desires. However, this may cost that person opportunities for advancement and salary increases.

Women in Retailing   Retailing has always been viewed as a good career for women. Today women constitute over 50 percent of all department store executives, making it the profession where women have attained the highest level of achievement. Although most female executives are at the lower levels of corporate management, women have recently made breakthroughs into the retail presidential ranks.

Societal Perspective   Professional merchants are considered respected and desirable members of their community, their state, and their nation. Leading retail executives are well-rounded individuals with a high social consciousness. Many of them serve on the boards of nonprofit organizations, as regents or trustees of universities, as active members of the local chambers of commerce, on school boards, and in other service-related activities. Retailers serve society not only outside their retailing career, but within it as well. For example, civic events such as holiday parades are often sponsored by local merchants. In addition, many retail firms support local groups and charities with cash, food, and other goods and services as a means to reinvest some of their profits in the communities they serve.

Unfortunately there are also unscrupulous, deceiving merchants that society can do without. This happens to be true in all professions. There are unscrupulous lawyers, doctors, and police officers who give their professions a negative image at times. On the other hand, there are professional and ethical lawyers, doctors, and police officers who are good for their professions and society as a whole. It is not the profession that dictates one's contribution to society but the soundness of one's ethical principles. Early in your career (preferably as a student), you need to develop a firm set of ethical principles to guide you throughout your managerial career.

Prerequisites for Success

What is required for success as a retail manager? Let's look at several factors that influence a retailer's success.

Hard Work   Most successful retailers, as will any successful individual, respond to the previous question with a simple "hard work." Beginning retailers have long known that they earn their salary 9 to 5, Monday through Friday, but earn their advancement on weekends and after 5 o'clock. Also, many entrepreneurs with little cash but a great idea and the willingness to work hard have found their fortunes in retailing.

Analytical Skills   The retail manager must be able to solve problems through numerical analysis of facts and data in order to plan, manage, and control. The retail manager is a problem solver on a day-to-day basis. An understanding of the past and present performance of the store, merchandise lines, and departments is necessary. It is the analysis of these performance data that forms the basis of future actions in the retailing environment. Today's retailer must be able to analyze all the financial data that are available before going to market. In addition, quantitative and qualitative analysis of customers, competitors, suppliers, and other constituencies often helps to identify emerging trends and innovations. Combined with current performance results and market knowledge, continual monitoring of these constituencies provides insight into past performance and alerts the retailer to new directions. Many retailers also get information from reading trade journals, such as *Women's Wear Daily, Progressive Grocer,* or *Chain Store Age,* discuss current happenings with their buying office, visit markets, and even talk to their competitors as a means to keep up.

Creativity   The ability to generate and recognize novel ideas and solutions is known as creativity. A retail manager cannot operate a store totally by a set of preprogrammed equations and formulas. Because the competitive environment is constantly changing, there is no standard recipe for retailing. Therefore, retail executives need to be idea people as well as analysts. Success in retailing is the result of sensitive, perceptive decisions that require imaginative and innovative techniques. For example, a buyer must be able to spot environmental changes and relate these changes to new needs or products in the marketplace.

Decisiveness   The ability to make rapid decisions and to render judgments, take action, and commit one's self to a course of action until completion is termed decisiveness. A retail manager must be an action person. Better decisions could probably be made if one had more time to make them. However, more time is frequently unavailable because variables such as fashion trends and consumer desires change quickly. Thus a manager must make decisions quickly, confidently, and correctly in order to be successful, even if perfect information is not always available. For example, buyers often make purchase decisions six months to a year before the merchandise arrives at the store.

Flexibility   The ability to adjust to the ever-changing needs of the situation calls for flexibility. The retail manager must have the willingness and enthusiasm to do whatever is necessary (although not planned) to complete the job. Because plans must be altered quickly to accommodate changes in trends, styles, and attitudes, successful retail managers must be flexible. For example, successful chains of prerecorded music were able to change from LP displays to CD and cassette displays almost overnight as a result of having interchangeable display bins. Today, changes in e-tailing occur continuously as retailers adjust prices and product offerings to changing consumer tastes and the competitive actions of other retailers.

Initiative   Retail managers are doers. They must have the ability to originate action rather than wait to be told what to do. This ability is called initiative. To be a success, the modern retail manager must monitor the numbers of the business (sales volumes, profits, inventory levels) and seize opportunities for action.

Leadership   The ability to inspire others to trust and respect your judgment and the ability to delegate, guide, and persuade others calls for leadership. Successfully conducting a retail operation means depending on others to get the work done; in any large-scale retailing enterprise, one person cannot do it all. A manager succeeds when his or her subordinates do their jobs.

Organization   Another important quality is the ability to establish priorities and courses of action for yourself and others and to plan and follow through to achieve results. This prerequisite is organization. Retail managers are often forced to deal with many issues, functions, and projects at the same time. To achieve goals, the successful retailer must be a good "time manager" and set priorities when organizing personnel and resources.

Risk Taking   Retail managers should be willing to take calculated risks based on thorough analysis and sound judgment; they should also be willing to accept responsibility for the results. Success in retailing often comes from taking calculated risks and having the confidence to try something new before someone else does. For example, no one can say that Jeff Bezos's decision to start Amazon wasn't without risk. All successful buyers have at one time or another purchased merchandise that could be labeled as "losers." After all, the buyer who never made errors was afraid to take risks and probably passed up many winners. However, successful buyers must have the ability to recognize when they make a mistake.

Stress Tolerance   As the other prerequisites to retailing success suggest, retailing is a fast-paced and demanding career in a changing environment. The retailing leaders of the 21st century must be able to perform consistently under pressure and to thrive on constant change and challenge.

Perseverance   Because of the difficult challenges that a retail career presents, it is important to have perseverance. All too often retailers may become frustrated due to the many factors that they cannot control. For example, a blizzard may occur just before Christmas and wipe out the most important shopping days of the year. Others may become frustrated with fellow employees; the long hours, especially the weekends; or the inability to satisfy some customers. The person with the ability to persevere and take all of this in stride will find an increasing number of career advancement opportunities.

Enthusiasm   Successful retailers must have a strong warmth of feeling for their job, otherwise they will convey the wrong image to their customers and associates in their department. Retailers today are training their salesforce to smile even when talking to customers on the telephone "because it shows through in your voice."[17] Without enthusiasm, success in any field will elude you.

Retail stores that have store managers who possess the 12 prerequisite characteristics of successful retail managers will be more profitable.

Dollars & Sense

The Study and Practice of Retailing

LO • 5

What are the different methods for the study and practice of retailing?

As we have seen, two of the prerequisites to success as a retail manager are analytical skills and creativity. These attributes also represent two methods for the study and practice of retailing.

Analytical Method

The analytical retail manager is a finder and investigator of facts. These facts are summarized and synthesized to make decisions systematically. In making these decisions, the manager uses models and theories of retail phenomena that enable him or her to structure all dimensions of retailing. An analytical perspective can result in a standardized set of procedures, success formulas, and guidelines.

Consider, for example, a manager operating a McDonald's restaurant, where everything is preprogrammed, including the menu, decor, location, hours of operation, cleanliness standards, customer service policies, and advertising. This store manager needs only to gather and analyze facts to determine if the preestablished guidelines are being met and to take appropriate corrective action if necessary.

Creative Method

Conversely, the creative retail manager is an idea person. This retail manager tends to be a conceptualizer and has a very imaginative and fertile mind capable of creating a highly successful retail chain. A good example of this is Leslie Wexner, founder and chairman of The Limited. When everyone else in the mid-1960s thought he was crazy (including his father) for selling only a "limited" line of women's apparel focusing on the 18- to 35-year old professional career women, Wexner had a gut feeling he was right. Such a retailer uses insight, intuition, and implicit knowledge rather than facts. The result is usually a novel way to look at or solve a retail problem that reflects a deeper understanding of the market. Is it possible to operate a retail establishment, in most part, with just creativity? Yes. However, in the long run, using only creativity will not be adequate. Witness the problem of a slowdown in sales at The Body Shop, a retailer with a very creative pro-environment focus, as other firms, including The Limited, were able to copy its creative focus.[18] Analytical decision making must also be used so that a manager can profitably respond to unforeseen events in the environment.

A Two-Pronged Approach

As shown through our McDonald's manager and Leslie Wexner examples, retailing can indeed be practiced from both perspectives. The retailer who employs both approaches is most successful in the long run. Aren't stores like McDonald's successful using only the analytical method? No. The McDonald's franchisee can operate analytically quite successfully. However, behind the franchisee is a franchisor who is creative as well as analytical. On the creative side was the development of McDonald's characters, such as Ronald McDonald, Grimace, and the Hamburglar, and selected menu items, such as Egg McMuffin, Arch Deluxe, and Big Mac. On the analytical side was the development of standardized layouts, fixtures, equipment, and employee training. It is the combination of the creative with the analytical that has made McDonald's what it is today.

Our Retailing: The Inside Story box provides an example of how one small-town retailer successfully combined analytical and creative methods to overcome the arrival of Wal-Mart in its market area.

The synthesis of creativity and analysis is necessary in all fields of retailing. Roger Dickinson, a former retail executive and now a retailing professor, has stated that "many successful merchandisers are fast duplicators rather than originators."[19] To decide who or what to duplicate requires not only creativity but also an analysis of the strategies that retailers are pursuing. This is an exercise in weighing potential returns against risks. Dickinson further states that "creativity in retailing is for the sake of increasing the sales and profits of the firm."[20] If creativity is tied to sales and profits, then one cannot avoid analysis; profit and sales statistics require analysis.

Retailers in the 21st century cannot do without either creativity or analytical skills. This text will develop your skills in both of these areas. At the outset, however, you should note that the analytical and creative methods for studying retailing are not that different. Whether you use creativity or analytical skills, they will be directed at solving problems.

Dollars & Sense

Retailers that practice both analytical and creative management will be consistently more profitable.

A Proposed Orientation

The approach to the study and practice of retailing that is reflected in this book is an outgrowth of the previous discussion. This approach has four major orientations: (1) environmental, (2) management planning, (3) profit, and (4) decision making.

Retailers should have an environmental orientation, which will allow them to anticipate and adapt continuously to external forces in the environment. Retailing is not static. With the social, legal, technological, economic, and other external forces always in flux, the modern retailer finds it necessary both to assess these changes in an analytical perspective and to respond with creative actions.

Retailers should have a planning orientation, which will help them to adapt systematically to a changing environment. Planning is deciding today what to do in the future.

Retailing: The Inside Story

Small-Town Retailers Can Compete with Wal-Mart

Many people mistakenly assume that the arrival of a Wal-Mart spells disaster for small-town retailers. This is not the case, if the retailer is able to differentiate itself from the competition. One such case occurred in southern Illinois. When Mrs. Bee, a hardware store owner, heard that a Wal-Mart was coming to her small town and locating a half-mile away, she was in shock. After all, the hardware store had been in her family for half a century. Her store, which offered a wide arrangement of housewares, sporting goods, appliances, hardware, gifts, and automotive parts, did have one thing going for it as it prepared to battle Wal-Mart. Five years earlier the store had moved from the downtown square to a small shopping center on the outskirts of the town of 6,000. This shopping center had a major supermarket chain for an anchor. With the supermarket, at least, Mrs. Bee knew that traffic would still be coming to the shopping center.

After thinking about the problem for a couple of days, Mrs. Bee decided to fight the competitive battle. She drove to Mt. Vernon, the nearest Wal-Mart, and spent a day combing the aisles, visiting with the manager (yes, Wal-Mart will try to help competitors survive when the chain enters a new mar-

ket), and filling a whole notebook with comments about Wal-Mart's merchandise, prices, and store layout.

For the next month, Mrs. Bee analyzed the data completely and concluded she could survive with Wal-Mart, but she would have to change her operations. First, she would have to drop her gifts, housewares, sporting goods, and automotive parts lines because she couldn't compete with Wal-Mart on either price or selection. She would now have to specialize in the appliance and hardware lines, offering a larger selection and better service—including advice on which products to purchase and how to use them—than Wal-Mart self-service merchandising could offer the customer.

Although she dropped what had been her strongest merchandise lines—they were also Wal-Mart's strongest—Mrs. Bee was soon operating at a higher profit level than before Wal-Mart arrived. However, Mrs. Bee also had to become much more creative with her business. The lack of competition had left her complacent in running the business before Wal-Mart. This has all changed.

Source: The above was based on information provided the authors by Marvin Lurie of the North American Retail Dealers Association.

A retailer who wants to have the competitive edge must plan for the future. We will place special emphasis on the development of creative retail strategies.

Retailers should have a profit orientation, since all retail decisions will have an effect on the firm's financial performance. The profit orientation will therefore focus on the fundamental management of assets, revenues, and expenses. Management tools that show how to evaluate the profit impact of retail decisions will be discussed.

Retailers should have a decision-making orientation, which will allow them to focus efforts on the need to collect and analyze data for making intelligent retail decisions. To aid in this process, a retail information system is needed to help retail executives program their operations for desired results.

The Book Outline

This book is composed of 14 chapters, each with its own study guide and application section. The materials are intended to reinforce each other. The end of chapter materials provide a way to bring the real world into your studies by launching you into the kind of situations you might face as a retail manager. Through careful analysis of this material and discussion with fellow students, you will discover retailing concepts that can be vividly retained because of the concrete context. Furthermore, this material will require you to think of yourself as a retail decision maker who must sometimes make decisions with less than perfect information.

Introduction to Retailing

This book is divided into five parts. The first part, Introduction to Retailing, has two chapters. In Chapter 2, Retail Strategic Planning and Operations Management, you are exposed to the basic concepts of strategic planning and operations results in retailing that will be used in the remaining chapters.

The Retailing Environment

The second part, The Retailing Environment, focuses on the external factors that the retailer faces in making everyday business decisions. The four chapters examine, in detail, the factors shown in Exhibit 1.2. Chapter 3, Retail Customers, looks at the behavior of the retail consumer and the socioeconomic environment. Chapter 4, Evaluating the Competition in Retailing, examines the behavior of competitors as well as the technological advances taking place in the market. Chapter 5, Channel Behavior, focuses on the behavior of the various members of the channel of distribution and their effect on the retailer. Chapter 6, Legal and Ethical Behavior, analyzes the effect of the legal and ethical constraints on today's retailer.

Market Selection and Location Analysis

It has often been said that the three keys to success in retailing are location, location, and location. In Chapter 7, Market Selection and Retail Location Analysis, we discuss the various elements considered in determining the feasibility of targeting a given market segment and entering a given retail market, and then we consider site selection.

Managing Retail Operations

In the fourth part, Managing Retail Operations, we discuss the merchandising operations of a retail firm. This part deals with the day-to-day decisions facing retailers. Chapter 8, Managing a Retailer's Finances, discusses various financial statements, the key methods of valuing inventory, and the development of merchandise planning budgets by retailers. Chapter 9, Merchandise Buying and Handling, looks at how a retailer determines what to buy for its market and how these purchases are made. The appendix following Chapter 9 discusses the merchandising of apparel goods. Chapter 10, Merchandise Pricing, discusses the importance to the retailer of setting the correct price. In addition to the various markup methods used by retailers, the chapter also looks at markdowns. Chapter 11, Advertising and Promotion, is devoted to a complete discussion of how a retailer can and should promote itself. The aspect of promotions that involves personal selling is covered in Chapter 12, Customer Services and Retail Selling, along with services offered by retailers. Chapter 13, Store Layout and Design, discusses the impact of proper layout and design on retail performance. Chapter 14, Managing Human Resources, examines the role of human resources in a retail firm.

The text concludes with a glossary of all major terms used in this text, as well as an index of the retailers mentioned. Also, the inside front cover of this text lists the top 25 U.S. retailing companies, including their financial performance for the most recent three years as well as the their addresses and web page listings. We have listed the top 25 global retailers on the inside back cover.

Student Study Guide

Summary

This chapter seeks to acquaint the reader with the nature and scope of retailing by discussing its impact on the economy, the types of retailers, and its prerequisites for success.

LO•1   What is retailing?

Retailing consists of the final activities and steps needed to place a product in the hands of the ultimate consumer or to provide services to the consumer.

LO•2   Why is retailing always undergoing so much change?

Retailing is not a staid and stable area of business; rather it is an exciting business sector that effectively combines an individual's skills to make a profit in an ever-changing market environment. That is why some retailers are successful and others, who are either unwilling or unable to adapt to this changing environment, fail.

LO•3   What are the various methods used to categorize retailers?

Retailers can be classified in a variety of ways. Five of the more popular schemes are by NAICS code, number of outlets, margins versus turnover, location, and size. None, however, sheds adequate light on competition in retailing.

LO•4   What is involved in a retailing career?

In the long run, a retailing career can offer an excellent salary, definite career advancement, and geographic mobility. In addition, a career in retailing incorporates the knowledge and use of all the business activities or disciplines (accounting, marketing, finance, personnel, economics, and even fashion). Besides, in retailing no two days are alike, each offers its own set of opportunities and problems. The prerequisites for success in retailing, besides hard work, include analytical skills, creativity, decisiveness, flexibility, initiative, leadership, organization, risk taking, stress tolerance, perseverance, and enthusiasm. These are all important, but it is especially important for the retail manager to work at developing an attitude of openness to new ideas and a willingness to learn. After all, the market is always changing.

LO•5   What are the different methods for the study and practice of retailing?

To be successful in retailing an individual must make use of the analytical and creative methods of operation. The four proposed orientations to the study and practice of retailing in this text are an environmental orientation, which allows the retailer to focus on the continuously changing external forces affecting retailing; a planning orientation, which helps the retailer to adapt systematically to this changing environment; a profit orientation, which enables the retailer to examine the profit implications of any decision; and a decision-making orientation, which allows the retailer to focus on the need to collect and analyze data for making intelligent, creative retail decisions.

Terms to Remember

retailing   category killer
same-store sales   chain stores
market share   standard stock list
scrambled merchandising   optional stock list

channel captain	high-performance retailer
private label branding	low-margin/low-turnover retailer
gross margin percentage	low-margin/high-turnover retailer
gross margin	high-margin/low-turnover retailer
operating expenses	high-margin/high-turnover retailer
inventory turnover	

Review and Discussion Questions

LO•1 What is retailing?

1. Which of the following transactions is considered to be a retailing transaction according to the text's definition? (a) a student buying an airline ticket from a travel agent, (b) a retired farmer setting up a trust account at a local bank, (c) a student buying a Mother's Day card, (d) a homemaker buying a magazine from a door-to-door salesperson, or (e) an appliance repair person coming to your home to fix a dishwasher.

LO•2 Why is retailing always undergoing so much change?

2. Retailing is often said to be a stable and never-changing sector of the economy because a Wal-Mart or McDonald's seldom change their layout or merchandise selection once they enter a market area. Agree or disagree and defend your answer.

3. Many environmental trends are taking place today that will have an effect on retailing operations over the next decade. Discuss three of these and their effects on retailing.

4. Currently there is a great deal of debate about the future impact of the Internet on retailing. What is your prediction concerning the Internet's impact on retailing in the year 2010? What support do you have for your prediction?

LO•3 Describe the five methods used to categorize retailers.

5. How can a retailer operate with a high-margin/high-turnover strategy? Won't customers avoid this type of store and shop at a low-margin store?

6. Isn't it better for a chain store operation to always use a standard stock list? After all, it would confuse the customer if a JCPenney's or Target in Portland, Oregon, is different than one in Portland, Maine.

LO•4 What is involved in a retailing career?

7. What concepts or techniques from economics or accounting do you believe would be most useful in retail decision making?

8. This chapter presented 12 prerequisites for success. Which one(s) do you think is (are) the most important? Why? Which ones do you think you already possess? Which ones do you think you need to improve?

LO•5 Be able to explain the different methods for the study and practice of retailing.

9. An individual who is both creative and analytical will definitely succeed in retailing. Do you agree or disagree with this statement? Defend your position.

10. Visit a local retailer who you would describe as creative and seek to determine which analytical skills that retailer also possesses.

Sample Test Questions

LO•1   Retailing

    a. may be defined as any cash purchase for merchandise
    b. is the same the world over
    c. is the final move in the flow of merchandise from producer to consumer
    d. is the sale of an item by the manufacturer to a wholesaler
    e. is not necessary to produce economic growth

LO•2   Which of the following words is descriptive of the retailing industry?

    a. changing
    b. stagnant
    c. unexciting
    d. staid
    e. boring

LO•3   Which of the following is not one of the ways by which retailers are categorized?

    a. number of outlets
    b. size
    c. margin versus turnover
    d. location
    e. gender of the manager

LO•4   Which of the following characteristics is it not desirable for a retail manager to possess?

    a. stress tolerance
    b. indecisiveness
    c. creativity
    d. leadership
    e. enthusiasm

LO•5   A convenience store manager is considering whether to offer home meal replacements (HMRs), which are "home-made" meals that customers can purchase on their way home from work. These meals only require heating in a microwave once the consumer gets home. The manager has gathered information on demographics, competitor sales in the trading area, and quality of HMR products that are available for her to sell. The manager was employing the _____ method of retail decision making.

    a. fact-based
    b. strategic
    c. creative problem-solving
    d. analytical
    e. tactical

Applications

Writing and Speaking Exercise

Halfway between your apartment and the campus is a small convenience store where you regularly purchase a cup of coffee to get you ready for those early morning classes. Over the past two years you have become friends with the owner. Late last night when you filled up your gas tank, you noticed that he was still there working on his books. While visiting with you, he stated that the store has been profitable, but he feels it could be more profitable if he could lower the high rate of employee turnover. He asks you for advice on this problem.

Prepare a short presentation for the owner listing what you think he should look for in hiring part-time employees. Also, list what employee traits he should seek to avoid.

Retail Project

At the beginning of this chapter we mentioned how you might be using the Internet to purchase your next car. Using the search engine on either your own computer or one at school, select two or three different auto web sites. List each web site address, such as Autobytel.com, and make a report describing what each company has on its web site. Which one did you like best? Why? Can you purchase on-line from each web site? What would be the buying process if you were to use these web sites? Can competitors gain anything from looking at these web sites? Finally, what is missing from these web sites that you feel should be on them?

Planning Your Own Retail Business

If you think you might want to be a retail entrepreneur, you can use the "Planning Your Own Retail Business" computer exercises at the end of each chapter to assist you in this process. Also, your teacher may have had you purchase *The House: Understanding A Retail Enterprise Using Spreadsheet Analysis* by Robert F. Lusch and Patrick Dunne, which can be used to help you understand the dollars and cents of retailing.

This first exercise is intended to acquaint you with how sensitive your retail business will be to changes in sales volume. Let's assume that you plan that your retail business will generate $500,000 per year in annual sales and that it will operate on a gross margin return on sales of 34 percent. If your fixed operating expenses are $90,000 annually and variable operating costs are 10 percent of sales, how much profit will you make? (*Hint:* Sales $\times$ Gross margin return on sales = Gross margin; Gross margin − Fixed operating expenses − Sales $\times$ Variable operating expenses as a percentage of sales = Net profit.) Use a spreadsheet program on your computer to compute your firm's net profits; next analyze what happens if sales drop 10 percent and if sales rise 10 percent. Why are bottom line results (net profits) so sensitive to changes in sales volume?

Endnotes

1. "Old Carmakers Learn New Tricks," *Business Week*, April 12, 2000: 116.
2. "Bricks-and-Mortar Blockheads," *Business Week*, December 13, 1999: EB 104.
3. "AOL's Marketing Builds Service into Powerhouse," *Advertising Age*, March 6, 2000: s2, s16.

4. David Reibstein and Paul Farris, "Do Marketing Expenditures to Gain Distribution Cost the Customer?" *European Management Journal*, March 1995: 31–38.

5. "Retailing," *Forbes*, January 10, 2000: 156–157.

6. "Why the Web Is Still a No-Shop Zone," *Fortune*, February 5, 1996: 127; and "Whose Internet Is It, Anyway?" *Fortune*, December 11, 1995: 120–142.

7. "Retailing," *Forbes*, January 10, 2000: 156–157.

8. Ibid.

9. "E-Christmas Failed to Faze Mall Sales," *Shopping Centers Today*, March 2000: 7.

10. From a list compiled by Robert Kahn.

11. "Profit in the Big Orange Box," *Forbes*, January 24, 2000: 122–127.

12. "Short Attention Span Retailing," PricewaterhouseCoopers's *E-Retail Intelligence Update*, October 1999.

13. Based on the authors' computations.

14. "Soap Opera at Wal-Mart," *Business Week*, August 16, 1999: 44.

15. "Airports Add More Concessions as Spending Takes Wing," *Shopping Center Today*, March 2000: 40.

16. "Shopping with Class," *Chain Store Age*, April 1999: 79–82.

17. "Americans Can't Get No Satisfaction," *Fortune*, December 11, 1995: 194.

18. "Can the Body Shop Shape Up?" *Fortune*, April 15, 1996: 118–120.

19. Roger Dickinson, "Creativity in Retailing," *Journal of Retailing* (winter 1969–1970): 4.

20. Ibid.

Successful retailers, such as Tower Records, excel at strategic planning and operations management.

Retail Strategic Planning and Operations Management

Overview

In this chapter, we will explain the importance of planning in successful retail organizations. To facilitate the discussion, we introduce a retail planning and operations management model, which will serve as a frame of reference for the remainder of the text. This simple model illustrates the importance of strategic planning and operations management. These two activities, if properly conducted, will result in the retail firm achieving results exceeding those of the competition.

Learning Objectives

After reading this chapter, you should be able to

1. explain why strategic planning is so important and be able to describe the components of strategic planning: statement of mission; goals and objectives; an analysis of strengths, weaknesses, opportunities, and threats; and strategy

2. describe the text's retail strategic planning and operation management model, which explains the two tasks that a retailer must perform and how they lead to high profit performance results

---

LO • 1

Explain why strategic planning is so important and describe its components.

Components of Strategic Planning

In most endeavors, a well-defined plan of action can mean the difference between success and failure. For example, a traveler does not go from Fargo to Kansas City without a well-defined plan of which highways to use. Political candidates and their advisors develop a campaign plan long before the election. Successful college students plan their assignments so that they are not forced to pull an all-nighter the night before an assignment is due. Similarly, a clearly defined plan of action is an essential ingredient of all forms of business management. This is especially true in the highly competitive field of retailing where in the past decade the number of stores has expanded faster than consumer demand.

Planning is the anticipation and organization of what needs to be done to reach an objective. This sounds simple enough, but as any retail buyer will tell you, it is difficult to know in advance of each upcoming season what styles, quantities, colors, and sizes the customers will want. Superior planning by retailers enables them to offset some of the advantages their competition may have, such as a good location. People not familiar with retailing often wonder how retailers can anticipate what consumers are going to want next season. In reality, success for all retailers, large and small, is generally a matter of good planning and then implementing that plan or plans. For example, today some of the nation's top retailers in terms of sales (Wal-Mart, Target, and Kmart) are rapidly replacing their older, 80,000- to 110,000-square-foot discount stores with new 160,000-square-foot supercenters. However, since their expertise is in dry goods and not perishable grocery items, they are relying on newly hired food merchants and their suppliers to aid them in developing the strategic plans for these supercenters. At the same time, these retailers didn't want to lose customers because the supercenter was too big, too busy, and not convenient. As a result, Wal-Mart is currently experimenting with 40,000-square-foot Neighborhood Market stores to compete with convenience stores and traditional supermarkets.

Failure to develop good plans can spell disaster for a retailer. Consider what appears to be a major planning error by Barnes & Noble and its www.barnesandnoble.com web site. The chain made the decision not to integrate the web site with its stores. Thus, at one of the company's typical brick-and-mortar stores, there is very little mention of the chain's on-line alternative. Compare this strategy to the decision by Canada's largest book retailer, Chapters. Each Chapter store has a large banner proclaiming its www.chapters.ca web site and tag line that it is "Always Open." In fact, many customers

Planning
is the anticipation and organization of what needs to be done to reach an objective.

Wal-Mart recognizes that its 160,000-square-foot Supercenters (see p. 9) cannot be located near all its potential customers. Therefore, to be more convenient to many customers, it is building Neighborhood Markets which will compete directly with convenience stores and traditional supermarkets.

actually think that the "Always Open" statement also refers to the physical store. Click & mortar integration (retailers using both on-line and physical stores) comes at a cost. Cannibalizing their established businesses is a risk for big-name retailers. Barnes & Noble may have 5 or 6 million customers on-line, but it has tens of millions walking through its stores. Why promote a web site that offers heavy discounts and no sales tax in most states to folks who might buy at full price? The answer is that if you don't, many of your customers will use Amazon's web site when the need arises. Chapters didn't want to lose any customers to its rivals and felt that although some of its store customers may shift a few purchases to its on-line location, those same customers would probably increase their total purchases. Thus, instead of just purchasing eight books in a store, the Chapters customer might now buy nine books, six in the store and three through its web site. Chapters, like many existing brick & mortar retailers, developed a plan that sought to translate its brand strength to its on-line venture by vigorously cross-promoting the two ventures, even if that meant cannibalizing its existing in-store sales. If Chapters did not pursue this strategy, it risked becoming just another dot-com upstart.[1]

Another example of good planning is the action taken by one the nation's largest food wholesalers, Fleming Companies, who has been working with its retailers to develop plans to withstand the onslaught of supercenters, and the possible entry of Wal-Mart's Neighborhood Market stores, into their trading area. Only by watching the changing environment and anticipating future changes was Fleming able to help the retailers make the necessary strategic plans to survive this new type of competition.[2]

Strategic planning is a type of planning that involves adapting the resources of the firm to the opportunities and threats of an ever-changing retail environment. Through the proper use of strategic planning, retailers achieve and maintain a balance between resources available and opportunities. Let's take a closer look at the components of the strategic planning process.

Strategic planning involves adapting the resources of the firm to the opportunities and threats of an ever-changing retail environment.

By promoting its on-line operations in their brick & mortar stores, Canadian bookseller, Chapters, has been able to capture a significant portion of the on-line marketplace.

Retailers who do a better job of planning than their competition can overcome some of the competition's natural advantages.

Strategic planning consists of four components:

1. Development of a mission (or purpose) statement for the firm
2. Definition of specific goals and objectives for the firm
3. Identification and analysis of the retailer's strengths, weaknesses, opportunities, and threats—referred to as SWOT analysis
4. Development of basic strategies that will enable the firm to reach its objectives and fulfill its mission

Mission Statement

The beginning of a retailer's strategic planning process is the formulation of a mission statement. The **mission statement is** a basic description of the fundamental nature, rationale, and direction of the firm. It provides the employees and customers with an understanding of where future growth for the firm is coming from. Not every retailer has a mission statement. In fact only about 50 percent of all businesses have written mission statements. Because so many businesses don't know where they want to go and how to get there, they end up as failures. The lack of a written statement, however, is not a cause by itself for failure if the firm has a clearly understood, even if unwritten, plan of action. For example, Wal-Mart doesn't have a written mission statement. Wal-Mart does, however, have a clearly defined sense of direction, which Sam Walton based on Marshall Field's directive to "give the lady what she wants."[3]

Although mission statements vary from retailer to retailer, good ones usually include three elements:

1. How the retailer uses or intends to use its resources
2. How it expects to relate to the ever-changing environment
3. The kinds of values it intends to provide in order to serve the needs and wants of the consumer

Consider the mission statement that was developed by Record World, a northeastern chain with more than 100 outlets:[4]

> Record World is in business to provide prerecorded entertainment in all modes desired by consumers. Our target market consists of all viable segments of the population shopping in locations, primarily malls, where our stores are situated in the northeast and mideast regions of the United States. In addition to a broad assortment of merchandise, we strive to provide our customers with both value and personal service. In the long-run, we will have the dominant market share in all the market segments we serve. We endeavor to double our sales in the next five years, primarily through improved market and merchandise development and secondarily through market penetration.

As this illustration points out, a mission statement really answers the question, What business should the retailer be in? Record World has used its mission statement not to be a record store leader but to be a value-oriented retailer of all prerecorded entertainment. The preceding mission statement illustrates how Record World overcame one of the major shortcomings of most retailers' mission statements—defining one's business too narrowly (i.e., being in the record business and not in the prerecorded entertainment business). A critical issue in defining a retail business is to do it at the most meaningful level of generalization. This is why most mission statements should be broad and general in nature, yet still provide direction as well as be motivational. Borders, for example, views its mission in a narrow sense as selling books through "a place where customers could always rely on a friendly, well-informed staff to find exactly what they were looking for, or browse solo for hours through shelves stocked with everything from African poetry to Zoroastrian theology."[5] As its mission statement implies Borders did not see itself selling books over the Internet. Therefore, rather than build a separate dot-com business that saps profits, Borders took a more modest approach. That's because Borders believed that on-line book sales were expected to capture less than 10 percent of book market worldwide by 2003.[6] Convinced that the

Mission statement
is a basic description of the fundamental nature, rationale, and direction of the firm.

opportunities are better in the brick & mortar world, Borders sought to develop its flagship chain by positioning its web site as a way to enhance the retail experience and build brand loyalty by offering access to borders.com within its superstores. Borders's own research showed that 80 percent of its customers are already buying on-line, so management figured it would be wasteful to spend money going after the already established separate web businesses.[7]

Dollars & Sense

> *Retailers that have missions that are broad and general in nature and motivate employees, yet still provide direction, will have higher profit performance.*

As a further example of what makes a good mission statement and what doesn't, consider how a poor mission statement can be improved. Avon Drive-in Theater, which was located in downstate Illinois, claimed it was "in the movie business and would only show PG13 movies at the lowest prices in its trading area." Maybe if Avon used a better statement, such as "We are in the entertainment business and we seek to show the movies that customers want at prices that reflect the market's price sensitivity," the theater might still be in business.

As our bookstore examples show, just having a mission statement is not enough. In today's business climate, the retailer must adhere to its mission and not change with every new fad.

Statement of Goals and Objectives

The second step in the strategic planning process is to define specific **goals and objectives.** These goals and objectives should be derived from, and give precision and direction to, the retailer's mission statement. Goals and objectives should identify the performance results that the retailer intends to bring about through the execution of its major strategies. Goals and objectives serve two purposes. First, they provide specific direction and guidance to the firm in the formulation of its strategy. Second, they provide a central mechanism by establishing a standard against which the firm can measure and evaluate its performance results. If the results are less than expected, then corrective actions need to be taken.

Although these goals and objectives can be expressed in many ways, usually retailers will divide them into two dimensions: **market performance,** which compares the firm's actions against those of its competitors, and **financial performance,** which analyzes its ability to provide an adequate profit level in order to continue in business. However, in addition to the market performance and financial performance objectives, some retailers may also establish **societal objectives,** which are phrased in terms of helping society fulfill some of its needs, and **personal objectives,** which relate to helping people employed in retailing fulfill some of their needs. Let us examine each of these goals and objectives in more detail.

Market Performance Objectives   Market performance objectives establish the amount of dominance the retailer has in the marketplace. The most popular measures

Goals and objectives
are the performance results intended to be brought about through the execution of a strategy.

Market performance objectives
represent how a retailer desires to be compared to its competitors.

Financial performance objectives
represent the profit and economic performance a retailer desires.

Societal objectives
are those that reflect the retailers' desire to help society fulfill some of its needs.

Personal objectives
are those that reflect the retailers' desire to help individuals employed in retailing fulfill some of their needs.

of market performance in retailing are sales volume and **market share.** Market share is the retailer's sales as a percentage of total market sales for the product line or service category under consideration.

Research has shown that profitability is clearly and positively related to market share.[8] Thus, market performance objectives are not pursued for their own sake but because they are a key profit path.

As retailers increase their market share, their financial performance will also increase in comparison to their competitors.

Dollars & Sense

Financial Objectives   Retailers can establish many financial objectives, but they can all be conveniently fitted into categories of profitability and productivity.

PROFITABILITY OBJECTIVES   Profit-based objectives deal directly with the monetary return a retailer desires from its business. When retailers speak of "making a profit," the definition of profit is often unclear. The most common way to define profit is the aggregate total of net profit after taxes—the bottom of the income statement. Another common retail method of expressing profit is as a percentage of net sales. However, most retail owners feel the best way to define profit is in terms of return on investments (ROI).[9]

This method of reporting profits as a percentage of investments is complicated by the fact that there are two different ways to define the term investment. Return on assets (ROA) reflects all the capital used in the business whether provided by the owners or by creditors. Return on investment (ROI), also referred to as return on net worth (RONW), reflects only the amount that the owners have invested in the business.

The most frequently encountered profit objectives for a retailer are shown in Exhibit 2.1, the Strategic Profit Model (SPM). The elements of the SPM start at the far left and move right. These five elements include the following:

1. **Net profit margin** is the ratio of net profit (after taxes) to net sales and shows how much profit a retailer makes on each dollar of sales after all expenses and taxes have been met. For example, if a retailer is operating on a net profit margin of 2 percent, it is making two cents on each dollar of sales. In general, retailers operate on lower profit margins than manufacturers. The net profit margin ratio is derived exclusively from income or operating statement data and does not include any measures from the retailer's balance sheet. Thus, it does not show how effectively a retailer is using the capital at its disposal.

2. **Asset turnover** is computed by taking the retailer's net sales and dividing by total assets. This ratio tells the retail analyst how productively the firm's assets are being utilized. Put another way, it shows how many dollars of sales a retailer can generate on an annual basis with each dollar invested in assets. Thus, if a retailer has a rate of asset turnover of 3.0 times, it is generating $3 in sales for each $1 in assets. The asset turnover ratio incorporates key measures from the income

Exhibit 2.1	**Strategic Profit Model**

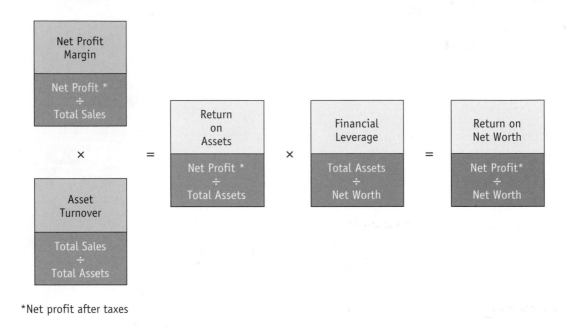

*Net profit after taxes

statement (sales) and the balance sheet (assets) and, as such, shows how well the retailer is utilizing its capital to generate sales. In general, retailers experience higher rates of asset turnover but lower profit margins than do manufacturers.

Return on assets (ROA)
is net profit (after taxes) divided by total assets.

3. **Return on assets (ROA),** which is net profit divided by total assets, depicts the profit return the retailer achieved on all assets invested regardless of whether the assets were financed by creditors or the firm's owners. As shown in Exhibit 2.1, ROA is the result of multiplying the net profit margin by asset turnover. For example, a retailer with a net profit margin of 2 percent and an asset turnover of 4.0 would have a ROA of 8 percent (2 percent times 4 equals 8 percent).

Financial leverage
is total assets divided by net worth or owners' equity and shows how aggressive the retailer is in its use of debt.

4. **Financial leverage,** which is total assets divided by net worth or owners' equity. This ratio shows the extent to which a retailer is utilizing debt in its total capital structure. The low end of this ratio is 1.0 and depicts a situation in which the retailer is using no debt in its capital structure. As the ratio moves beyond 1.0, the firm is using a heavier mix of debt versus equity. For example, when the ratio is 2.0 times, the firm has two dollars in assets for every dollar in net worth.

Return on net worth (RONW)
is net profit (after taxes) divided by owners' equity.

5. **Return on net worth (RONW),** which is net profit divided by net worth or owners' equity. Return on net worth is shown at the far right of the SPM and is usually used to measure an owner's performance. Note that, as shown in Exhibit 2.1, the ROA multiplied by financial leverage yields RONW. Thus if a retailer has a ROA of 8 percent and a financial leverage of 2.0, then its RONW would be 16 percent (8 percent times 2.0 equals 16 percent).

The important point to remember from this discussion of profitability is that department or specialty stores (which have higher gross margin and lower asset turnover rates) compete differently than discounters (which generally have lower gross margins but higher asset turnover rates, resulting in less inventory per dollar of sales and a lower need for capital assets outside of inventory). Discounters expect to gain a higher asset turnover by reducing their gross margins, and specialty stores expect a lower asset turnover rate with their higher gross margins.

Likewise, it must be remembered that attempts to increase asset turnover by merely reducing inventory levels can have serious consequences for a retailer. These lower inventory levels may produce higher turnover rates, but they could also lead to stockouts (where products are not available for customers), thus creating a dissatisfied customer who may never return.

Managers are usually evaluated on return on assets, because financial leverage is beyond their control. In addition to the five elements of the SPM, another measure of profitability is the gross margin percentage, which is gross margin (net sales minus cost of goods sold) divided by net sales.

All retailers establish some form of profit objective. The specific profit objectives developed will play an important role in evaluating potential strategic opportunities.

PRODUCTIVITY OBJECTIVES Productivity objectives state how much output the retailer desires for each unit of resource input. The major resources at the retailer's disposal are space, labor, and merchandise; productivity objectives for each may be established.

1. *Space productivity.* Space productivity is defined as net sales divided by the total square feet of retail floor space. (In this discussion, whenever we refer to net sales we are talking about annual net sales.) A space productivity objective states how many dollars in sales the retailer wants to generate for each square foot of store space.

2. *Labor productivity.* Labor productivity is defined as net sales divided by the number of full-time-equivalent employees. A full-time-equivalent employee is one who works 40 hours per week; typically two part-time workers equal one full-time employee. A labor productivity objective reflects how many dollars in sales the retailer desires to generate for each full-time-equivalent employee.

3. *Merchandise productivity.* Merchandise productivity is net sales divided by the average dollar investment in inventory. This measure is also known as the sales-to-stock ratio. Specifically, this objective states the dollar sales the retailer desires to generate for each dollar invested in inventory.

Productivity objectives are vehicles by which a retailer can program its business for high profit results. For instance, it would be impossible for a supermarket chain to achieve a respectable return on assets while experiencing dismal space (sales per square foot), labor (sales per full-time employee), and merchandise productivity (sales per inventory dollars). In short, productivity is a key determinant of profit in retailing.

Societal Objectives
Though generally not as specific or as quantitative as market and financial objectives, societal objectives highlight the retailer's concern with broader issues in our society. The five most frequently cited societal objectives are as follows:

1. *Employment objectives.* Employment objectives relate to the provision of employment opportunities for the members of the retailer's community. Many times they are more specific, relating to hiring the disabled, social minorities, or students.

Productivity objectives state the sales objectives that the retailer desires for each unit of resource input: floor space, labor, and inventory investment.

2. *Payment of taxes.* Paying taxes is the retailer's role in helping finance societal needs, from welfare programs to national parks, that the government deems appropriate.

3. *Consumer choice.* A retailer may have as an objective to compete in such a fashion that the consumer will be given a real alternative. A retailer with such an objective desires to be a leader and innovator in merchandising and thus provide the consumer with choices that previously were not available in the trade area.

4. *Equity.* An equity objective reflects the retailer's desire to treat the consumer fairly. The consumer will not be unnecessarily price-gouged in case of merchandise shortages. Consumer complaints will be handled quickly, fairly, and equitably. The retailer will inform the consumer, to the extent possible, of the strengths and weaknesses of its merchandise.

5. *Benefactor.* The retailer may desire to underwrite certain community activities. For example, many department store retailers make meeting rooms available for civic groups to use for meetings. Other retailers help underwrite various performing arts with either cash donations or by hosting social events that in turn help draw customers to their stores. Still others provide scholarships to help finance the education of the young. One of the best examples of a retailer with this objective is the late Milton Petrie, the founder and majority owner of Petrie Stores. Petrie had always been a generous individual, often sending checks to hard-luck cases he learned about in the morning paper. In his will, he not only remembered 383 individuals with gifts ranging from $5,000 to $15 million; but the majority of his $800 million in assets was placed in a trust not to fund charitable institutions but to continue his "passion for helping needy individuals."[10]

Retail stores in a community provide many employment opportunities for members of the retailer's community.

Personal Objectives   The final set of objectives that retailers may establish are personal. Personal objectives can relate to the personal goals of any of the employees of the retail establishment. Generally retailers tend to pursue three types of personal objectives:

1. *Self-gratification.* Self-gratification has as its focus the needs and desires of the owners, managers, or employees of the firm to pursue what they truly want out of life. For example, individuals may have opened up a sporting goods store because they enjoyed being around athletically oriented people. These individuals may also be avid amateur golfers, and by operating a sporting goods store they are able to combine work with pleasure. Basically, these individuals are experiencing and living the life they really wanted.

2. *Status and respect.* All humans strive for status and respect. In stating this type of objective, one recognizes that the owners, managers, or employees need status and respect in their community or within their circle of friends. Recognizing this need, the retailer may, for example, give annual awards to outstanding employees. Or when promotions occur, favorable coverage may be sought in local newspapers or trade journals such as *Stores* or *Chain Store Age.*

3. *Power and authority.* Objectives based on power and authority reflect the need of managers and other employees to be in positions of influence. Retailers may establish objectives that give buyers and department managers maximal flexibility to determine their own destiny. They are given the power and authority to allocate scarce resources such as space, dollars, and labor to achieve a profit objective. Having the power and authority to allocate resources makes many of these managers feel important and gives them a sense of pride when they excel because they know they controlled their own destiny.

Exhibit 2.2 is a synopsis of the market performance, financial performance, societal, and personal objectives that retailers can establish in the strategic planning process. Clearly revealed in this exhibit is the fact that all retail objectives, of whatever type, must be consistent with the overall mission of the retailer. The retailer's objectives must reinforce its mission.

Returning to our earlier discussion, let's now look at Record World's goals and objectives.

1. Open or acquire five to ten new stores over the next year.
2. Remodel six to eight stores over the next year.
3. Increase the net profit margin in each store by 1 percent for each six-month period.
4. Increase video sales in existing stores by 20 percent over the previous year.
5. Improve sales in classical music by increasing merchandise productivity by 1 percent over the preceding year.
6. Improve the quality of promotion activities, including in-store appearances, publicity, contests, cross-promotions, school promotions, and in-store circulars.
7. Increase awareness/recognition levels of consumers in newer market areas (e.g., Florida) equal to that in the New Jersey/Long Island area.
8. Improve teamwork among top-level executives, especially those at similar management levels.

| Exhibit 2.2 | **Retail Objectives** |

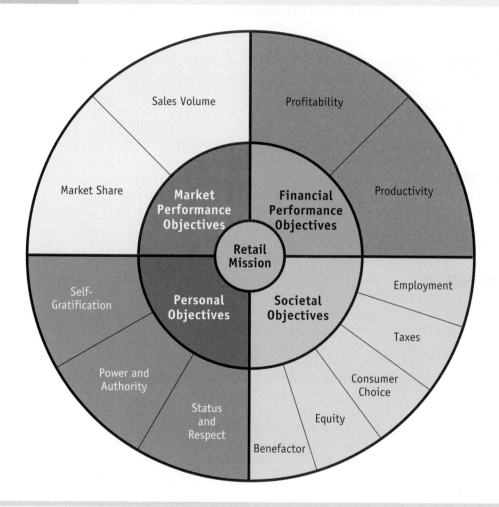

9. Restructure the buying operation to better interact with other corporate activities.

10. Target 2 percent of each store's profits to the favorite local charity of the store manager.

11. Have disabled applicants account for 10 percent of all new company-wide hires.

12. Maintain labor costs between 7.5 and 9 percent of sales.

Notice how goal 3 did not just say that Record World wanted to increase net profits, but stated an amount that it wanted to increase net profits by (1 percent over each six-month period). To be effective, goals should identify what the company wants to accomplish, the level that it wants to achieve, and the time period involved. In other words, goals should be measurable and schedulable.

A little noticed but high-performance retailer is Dollar General, which has succeeded by selling a limited assortment of groceries and general merchandise in small no-frill stores at prices 2 percent to 4 percent below those of the major discount chains. Dollar General, by maintaining strong control of operating costs and focusing on low-income customers, is able to locate 6,000-square-foot stores in small towns or in larger cities in neighborhoods near larger Wal-Marts. Dollar General, which sells a mix of basics such as jeans, motor oil, and snack foods, has fewer objectives and goals, but no less direction:

1. To achieve increases in same store sales and, consistent with that primary objective, to open as many productive new stores as possible. There are many opportunities to do so in our 23-state market.

2. To reduce our overhead as a percentage of sales, enabling us to further sharpen our low everyday prices.

3. To increase the return on our largest financial asset—inventory.

4. To develop our "number one" resource, human assets, to its fullest potential and to provide future management primarily by promotion from within.[11]

As shown here, goals and objectives should be established for each department or performance area in the business. In our example from Record World, goals and objectives 1, 2, 6, 7, 8, and 9 are market performance oriented; numbers 3, 4, 5, and 12 are financial performance oriented; numbers 10 and 11 are societal objectives; and number 10 could be a personal objective (self-gratification) for the store managers. Dollar General's first and fourth goals and objectives are market performance oriented and the second and third are financial performance oriented.

Managerial Question: How should a retailer determine the proportion and the number of market performance, financial performance, societal, and personal objectives?

Retailers that develop strategies to build traffic, convert traffic to customers, and lower the costs of serving these customers while maintaining their service level will achieve a high profit performance.

Strategies

After developing a mission statement and establishing some goals and objectives, a retailer must develop a strategy. A **strategy** is a carefully designed plan for achieving the retailer's goals and objectives. It is a course of action that when executed will produce the desired levels of performance. Retailers can operate with as few as three strategies:

1. Get shoppers into your store. Many retailers think this is one of the most difficult tasks in retailing—getting people to visit your web site or to come into your store. Our Service Retailing box shows a technique that Wal-Mart uses. This

Strategy
is a carefully designed plan for achieving the retailer's goals and objectives.

Service Retailing

Is Wal-Mart a Service Retailer?

During a recent family vacation to the Rockies, one of the authors was amazed to notice along the way that the largest, most crowded campgrounds for RVs weren't KOA Kampgrounds but Wal-Mart parking lots. In fact, most of Wal-Mart's 2,985 parking lots (including the parking lots for Sam's Clubs) across the United States, even those with precious little greenery, have become campgrounds for the trailer and recreation-vehicle set.

These locations are more appealing than those other "spaces for rent" campgrounds outside town because the stores are open all night and they sell gear, groceries, auto supplies, and souvenirs. Besides, Wal-Mart does not require reservations. Trying not to offend either competitors or townspeople, Wal-Mart doesn't advertise its open invitation to campers nor does its free parking spaces provide hookups for water, power, or sewage disposal. It also asks campers not to stay more than three nights. Thus, visitors sooner or later are going to have to go to a real "for rent" campsite.

Still, Wal-Mart caters to RVers in not-so-subtle ways. After all, the chain does not want to offend the regular camp-ground operators, who are probably big customers. Still, the retailer from northwest Arkansas understands the value of getting customers into its stores. Sam's and its main competitor, Costco, recently improved their fresh fruit and grocery selections for that reason. By stocking more fresh items, the average customer now visits a wholesale club store every 2 to 4 weeks, compared to the average 4 to 8 weeks in the past when customers would only shop to purchase nonperishable supplies in bulk. Using the same idea, the customized Rand McNally road atlas sold at all Wal-Marts includes the address of each store and its map coordinates. Campers, after all, are profitable customers as stores in heavily traveled areas stock extensive recreation-vehicle and camping supplies, which have high gross margins.

Trade association data show that there are more than 32 million RV enthusiasts in the United States, and many expect the number to grow as baby boomers retire. These people like to travel, like the comforts of their own home, and best of all have money to spend. Thus, it seems that Wal-Mart will continue as a service retailer.

general merchandise discounter becomes sort of a retailer of services to generate additional store traffic.

2. Convert these shoppers into customers by having them purchase merchandise. This means having the right merchandise, using the right layout and display, and having the right salesforce.

3. Do this at the lowest operating cost possible that is consistent with the level of service that your customers expect. Remember, as we pointed out in Chapter 1, most of a product's cost gets added after the item is produced and moves from the factory to a retailer's shelf and finally to the consumer. Thus, good strategies to reduce operating costs while providing the appropriate level of service present significant opportunities for retailers.

Although these three strategies may seem too simple to be operational, they actually do summarize the tasks that every retailer must perform. Many retailers go further and use strategies that enable them to differentiate themselves from the competition in order to accomplish these three tasks.

However, one of the greatest failings in retailing today is that too many retailers have concentrated on just one means of differentiation—price. Price promotions usually attract, but rarely hold, customers. The customers you gain with these promotions are just as apt to switch to another retailer when it cuts its price below your price. As a result, retailers have taught consumers that if they wait—and in many cases this wait is only a matter of days—the desired merchandise will go on sale. Unless a retailer has substantially lower operating costs, such as Wal-Mart does in comparison to its competitors, this is a very dangerous strategy to use because it can easily be copied by the competition and will result in reducing profits or causing losses. Some better forms of differentiation for a retailer are the following:

1. *Physical differentiation of the product,* such as the strategy Target uses for its brilliant and innovative "upscale" merchandise that really catches trends before the other mass merchandisers. Another company using this differentiation strategy is Lane Bryant, the plus-sized women's clothier, which recently dropped its dowdy, baggy styles and refocused on body-hugging fashions that previously were aimed only at smaller sized women.

2. *The selling process,* such as the way Nordstrom's or Neiman-Marcus uses its excellent customer service to connect with its target customers.

3. *After-purchase satisfaction,* which some of the major retailers, such as L.L. Bean Inc., achieve with their "satisfaction guaranteed" programs that enable customers to return an item of clothing for a new one after years of wear.

4. *Locational,* which Family Dollar excels at with more than 3,000 small stores that are usually located in strip centers en route to a nearby supercenter on the outskirts of a city. The chain hopes to intercept shoppers who would rather pick up that toothpaste and motor oil in a convenient manner instead of facing a cavernous building offering tires and tomatoes, shirts and soup, and bananas and car batteries. In addition, the small size of their stores also gives the retailer advantages in negotiating leases, thus reducing the retailer's operating costs in comparison to those of other chains.

5. *Never being out-of-stock,* which means being in stock with regard to the sizes, colors, and styles that the target market expects the retailer to carry. For example, Nordstrom offers a free shirt if it is out of stock on basic sizes.

These means of differentiation will not only get more consumers into your store, but will result in their buying more merchandise once they are in the store. Note also

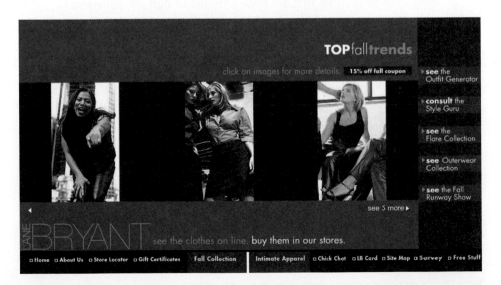

Lane Bryant, the plus-size women's clothier, promotes its sleek and sexy fashions on-line in an effort to position itself in the marketplace as a hip apparel retailer.

that in all these examples, the retailers are able to develop their own unique niches in the minds of the consumer and avoid price wars.

So how does a retailer develop a strategy to differentiate itself? This starts with an analysis of the retailer's strengths and weaknesses as well as the threats and opportunities that exist in the environment. This process, which is often referred to as **SWOT** (i.e., strengths, weaknesses, opportunities, and threats) **analysis,** involves the following elements:

SWOT analysis
is the assessment of a retailer's strengths, weaknesses, opportunities, and threats.

Strengths

What major competitive advantage(s) do we have? (This could be lower prices, better locations, better store personnel, etc.)

What are we good at? (This might be the ability to anticipate customer demands better than the competition so that the merchandise is there when the customer wants it, etc.)

What do customers perceive as our strong points? (Customers might perceive that we offer the best value for the dollar.)

Weaknesses

What major competitive advantage(s) do competitors have over us? (Do they have lower prices, better locations, more salespeople, etc.?)

What are competitors better at than we are? (Do they do a better job at merchandise selection or demand anticipation?)

What are our major internal weaknesses? (Do we do a poor job of employee training, are our stores in need of remodeling, etc.?)

Opportunities

What favorable environmental trends exist that may benefit our firm? (Is our market size growing, are family income levels rising in our market, is merchandise priced correctly for the target market, etc.?)

What is the competition doing in our market? (Are new firms entering or are existing firms leaving and what is the impact on us?)

What areas of business that are closely related to ours are undeveloped? (Is it possible for us to expand into a related field serving the same customers and take advantage of our good name in the marketplace?)

Threats

What unfortunate environmental trends exist that may hurt our future performance? (Has inflation caused consumers to become more price sensitive, or has it prevented us from raising our prices in order to pass increasing costs on to consumers, etc.?)

How could our competitor's actions [price, new products, services, etc.], the entrance of new competitors, or the possible loss of suppliers hurt us?

What technology is on the horizon that may soon have an impact on our firm? (Will some new electronic equipment soon replace our manual way of performing activities?)

In our Retailing: The Inside Story box we look at what could be the SWOT analysis for a family owned hardware store in your neighborhood.

Now the retailer is ready to develop some strategies to accomplish its objectives. Again, notice the close relationship between a retailer's goals and objectives and its strategies. Objectives indicate what the retailer wants to accomplish and strategies indicate how the retailer will attempt to accomplish those goals with the resources available.

A retail marketing strategy with strong financial elements must be developed . The retailer should have a fully developed marketing strategy, which should include the following:

1. The specific target market. A **target market** is the group or groups of customers that the retailer is seeking to serve.

2. A **location(s)**—which could either be a traditional store in a geographic space, a person's home in relation to print catalog or television shopping, or a virtual store in cyberspace—that is consistent with the needs and wants of the desired target market.

3. The specific retail mix that the retailer intends to use to appeal to its target market and to thereby meet its financial objectives. The **retail mix** is the combination of merchandise, price, advertising and promotion, customer services and selling, and store layout and design that the retailer uses to satisfy the target market.

Target market
is the group or groups of customers that the retailer is seeking to serve.

Location
is the geographic space or cyberspace where the retailer conducts business.

Retail mix
is the combination of merchandise, assortment, price, promotion, customer service, and store layout that best serves the segments targeted by the retailer.

The Retail Strategic Planning and Operations Management Model

LO • 2

Describe the text's retail strategic planning and operations management model.

Exhibit 2.3, our strategic planning and operations management model, suggests that a retailer must engage in two types of planning and management tasks: strategic planning and operations management. Each of these tasks is undertaken in order to achieve high profit performance results. At this point, take a few moments to reflect on this model.

As explained in Chapter 1, this book has an environmental orientation, a management planning orientation, a profit orientation, and a decision-making orientation. You will note that the environmental orientation is represented by the top and bottom parts of Exhibit 2.3, the management planning orientation by the center section (strategic planning and operations management) of the model that goes left to right, the profit orientation by demand for high profit performance shown at the far right of the model, and the decision-making orientation by all the decisions that the retailer must make throughout this model.

Retailers who develop strategic plans are better able to withstand competitive onslaughts and have better long-term profitability.

Retailing: The Inside Story

SWOT Analysis Shows How Many True Value Hardware Stores Continue to Succeed

The family operated and locally owned hardware store dates back more than one hundred years. Although many of these small hardware stores have fallen prey to strong national chain competition from the big box giants such as Home Depot and Lowe's, many continue to survive and prosper in their local communities. This has often been attributed to these independents joining a wholesale cooperative or buying group that helps them achieve efficiencies rivaling those of the national chains. During the 1930s John Cotter founded Cotter & Company as a retailer-owned wholesale buying cooperative. Cotter & Company was able to pool the purchasing power of many independent retailers to obtain significant buying and distribution economies, which allowed the small hardware retailer to compete with the rapidly growing chain stores. In 1997 Cotter & Company merged with ServiStar Coast to Coast, another large retailer-owned wholesale buying cooperative. The combined cooperative was renamed TRU*SERV and had annual sales of more than $6 billion. Today TRU*SERV supplies more than 6,500 members, which operate nearly 10,000 stores. Below is what a SWOT analysis might look like for a successful family operated True Value Hardware Store.

Strengths

What are the major competitive advantages a True Value Hardware store has over the competition?

A catchy name that combines a key brand (True Value) with the name of a local owner—for example, Jim Ruhl's True Value Hardware Store. Thus the store has the integrity of a respected national brand combined with the name of a well known and respected local operator.

The commitment that comes from management owning the business. The stores are almost all operated by the people that own the stores. This aligns the interest of the day-to-day managers with the customers. Customer service is generally high because if customers are not served well and do not return, then the owner/manager immediately feels the financial impact.

Because the stores are locally owned and managed, the managers have a very good sense of their trade area and the needs of people in that trade area. Because buying is not centralized like it is in a big retail chain, the buying for the store is more in tune with local demand patterns. Many owner/managers know what specific households in the trade area might need and thus order merchandise in anticipation of selling to these households on an individual level. Also, these managers know the names of virtually all of their regular customers and personally greet them when they enter the store. In short, they practice micromarketing.

Most True Value stores are in lower rent facilities that are owned and free of a mortgage or debt payments. This allows these retailers to have lower break-even points and better withstand competitive assaults.

Weaknesses

What major competitive advantages do big box retailers have over a True Value Hardware Store?

Home Depot and Lowe's have a strong promotional orientation. Often these retailers have local and national television advertising coupled with a heavy use of newspaper inserts. Many times they will run 24 to 36 newspaper inserts per year. Thus these large national chains do a better job of creating customer awareness.

Home Depot and Lowe's offer more than 60,000 items or SKUs (stock-keeping-unit, which is the lowest level of identification of merchandise) compared to a True Value Store, which may have less than 15,000 items. A big box store will be more 100,000 square feet versus a True Value store, which will generally be less than 12,000 square feet.

Home Depot and Lowe's are much more aggressive in terms of pricing frequently purchased and highly visible items. On

Strategic Planning

Strategic planning, as pointed out at the beginning of the chapter, is concerned with how the retailer responds to the environment in an effort to establish a course of action to follow. In principle, the retailer's strategic planning should best reflect the line(s) of high-turnover items such as garden hoses, popular lumber sizes, small tools, and gardening items, they are low price point competitors.

What are some of the major internal weaknesses of a typical True Value Hardware Store?

A typical store is not operated by computer-savvy managers. Although some True Value operators are capitalizing on information technology, many other owners do not recognize or purse the potential of a fully computerized inventory management and purchasing system.

Most stores lack depth of management. If the owner is absent from the store for an extended time due to illness, becomes disabled, or dies, there is often no other person in line to take over operations and ownership. Also, because some stores are independently owned, True Value stores sometimes present an inconsistent image across the country. Some stores are immaculate and clean and well organized, while other stores may be dusty and cluttered. But there is little that True Value can do about this problem. After all, it is difficult to enforce standards of operations to an independent store owner.

Many stores do not have seven day a week, morning to night operating hours because they are operated by the owners. A big box store is open seven days and more than 75 hours a week, whereas a True Value store is often open six days and fewer than 60 hours per week.

Opportunities

What favorable environmental trends exist that may benefit a True Value Hardware Store?

Due to the scarcity of time available to dual-income families, people want to shop closer to home. Trips to large malls and shopping areas are declining and trips to neighborhood shopping centers are on the rise. Also, people are finding that 100,000-square-foot stores are often too big when one only needs a few items. Most True Value stores are small in size and located in small community or strip malls. (It is noteworthy that Home Depot has recognized this opportunity and is building a new chain of small stores called Villager Hardware.) The number of homeowners planning do-it-yourself home improvement projects has been increasing yearly for two decades. Although many homeowners enjoy doing these projects, they often need advice during the project. True Value retailers, with their focus on customer service and knowledgeable staff, can provide excellent service to this highly profitable customer segment.

As a result of the phenomenal growth of the Internet, many more households are hopping on-line for hardware and home improvement items. This is an opportunity for True Value Hardware Stores because the co-op has built an e-tailing site that allows local customers to purchase an expanded assortment of products from their local True Value retailer. Rather than being restricted in items (SKUs) due to space constraints, True Value Retailers can now offer their customers more than 100,000 SKUs.

Threats

What unfortunate environmental trends exist that may hurt our future performance?

Many owners are finding that their children do not want to take over the family hardware business. These children are moving to other geographical areas and pursuing other careers.

The government reporting requirements on small single-unit businesses are often as numerous as for a multiunit chain store. Having the time to comply with local, county, state, and federal regulations and paperwork is becoming more burdensome.

Source: The authors want to acknowledge the assistance of Professor Leslie D. Stoel, The Ohio State University, with this SWOT analysis.

trade in which the retailer will operate, the market(s) it will pursue, and the retail mix it will use. Remember, strategic planning requires a long-term commitment of resources by the retailer. After all, as pointed out in our Global Retailing box (on page 57) about Toys "R" Us, a long-term commitment is necessary to overcome some of the adversities of operating globally. Specifically, effective strategic planning can help protect the retailer against competitive onslaughts.

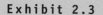

| **Exhibit 2.3** | **Retail Strategic Planning and Operations Management Model** |

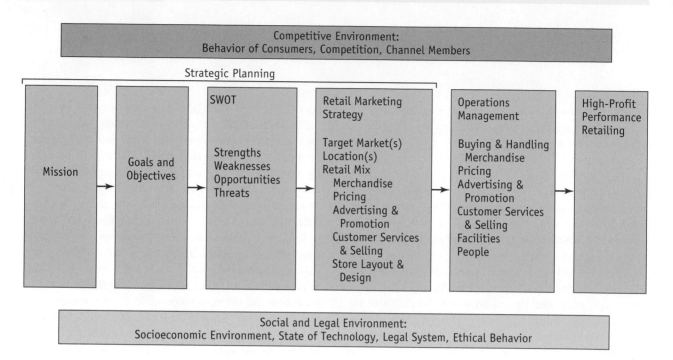

The initial steps in strategic planning are to define the firm's mission, establish goals and objectives, and perform a SWOT analysis. The next step is target market selection followed by the selection of an appropriate location(s). Of particular note is the fact that most retail managers or executives have little control over location decisions. A newly appointed manager for a chain department store could change promotional strategy, personnel, service levels, credit policies, and even prices but would in all likelihood be constrained by a long-term lease agreement. In fact, only the senior management of most chains is ever involved in decisions about location. For the small retailer just starting out, however, or retailers considering expansion, location is an important decision. A full discussion of location and site selection is presented in Chapter 7.

Following the target market selection and location decision is the development of the firm's retail mix. Retailers can best perform this strategic planning only after assessing the external environment. They should be looking for an opportunity to fulfill the needs of a defined group of consumers (i.e., their target market) in a method different from competition. In other words, retailers should strive to seek a differential advantage over the competition. Retailers will rarely discover a means of gaining a differential advantage over their competitors by merely reviewing their own internal operations or by focusing exclusively on the conventional industry structure. Strategic planning opportunities are to be found in the realities of a constantly changing environment. An effective retail strategy can only result from matching environmental forces with a retail marketing program that satisfies the customer better than any other retailer can. For example, Foot Locker has found success by concentrating on a narrow segment of the shoe market but offering a large selection.

Exhibit 2.3 also profiles the major environmental forces that should be assessed. Briefly these are as follows:

Global Retailing

Toys "R" Us—Commitment to the Japanese Marketplace

For centuries the Japanese marketplace has enticed U.S. retailers. However, government regulations had created barriers to the marketplace. Toys "R" Us, the U.S. category killer in the toy segment, had dominated U.S. retailing and was looking toward international expansion. While already establishing itself in Canada, Western Europe, Hong Kong, and Singapore, the tremendous growth in the Japanese economy in the 1980s and early 1990s set all the signals in place for Japan to be the next international location for Toys "R" Us. However, entrance and success in the Japanese marketplace would take careful planning and long-term commitment by the retailer if it were to attempt to overcome the large-store law aimed at protecting the country's politically powerful small shopkeepers from powerful large retailers who could offer lower prices. This is important as the typical Japanese toy store stocks between 1,000 and 2,000 different items, compared to Toys "R" Us, which typically carries over 15,000.

Robert C. Makasone, vice-chairman of Toys "R" Us in 1988, knew that in order to successfully overcome the large-store law and to adjust to local Japanese consumer behavior, he would need a local partner. As such, Makasone solicited the services of Den Fujita, president of McDonald's Co. (Japan). Fujita's local governmental contacts and understanding of technical characteristics of the larger-store law was valuable. Under the law, local communities are allowed to block new large retailers for up to 10 years. Fujita was able to help Makasone accelerate the process to a mere 18 months. With Toys "R" Us owning 80 percent of Toys "R" Us Japan and McDonald's Co. (Japan) owning 20 percent, the retailer opened to great fanfare, and 1,500 shoppers swarmed the 3,300-square-foot store in Ami, just north of Tokyo, on December 20, 1991. But opening the first store was just the beginning of the plan set in place. Upon entering the Japanese market, Toys "R" Us set forth a goal to open 10 new stores ever year.

As Toys "R" Us continued its commitment to expansion throughout the 1990s, the Japanese economy was undergoing dramatic changes. The tremendous growth Japan had experienced during the 1980s and early 1990s was turning into inflation and economic recession. As the economy continued to slow, Toys "R" Us continued expansion and by early 2000 had established 93 stores across Japan, accounting for 10 percent of Toys "R" Us's annual worldwide sales as well as approximately 10 percent of the Japanese toy market. The impact on the small shopkeeper has been dramatic. Kanoko Oishi of McKinsey & Co.'s Asian retail practice indicates that while 5 years ago 70 percent of toy stores charged full retail prices, only 30 percent do today. As such, Toys "R" Us has not only brought Japanese consumers greater selection by offering more items than traditional Japanese toy retailers, but they have also lowered the overall prices.

Trouble on the domestic front for U.S. parent company Toys "R" Us necessitated the spin-off of Toys "R" Us Japan in an effort to raise capital. Toys "R" Us Japan went public in 2000 to help its parent company gain necessary cash inflows and debt reductions to enhance the firm's balance sheet and increase a declining stock price. Retail experts felt this allowed Toys "R" Us to sell off an interest in an earnings stream at a very high valuation and repurchase shares of the parent company at a much lower valuation. However, Toys "R" Us will still be a significant shareholder in Toys "R" Us Japan and will continue its commitment to the Japanese market.

Source: Based on a March 20, 2000, Standard & Poor's press release, the initial public offering, and the authors' observations.

1. *Consumer behavior.* The behavior of consumers will obviously have a significant impact on the retailer's future. Specifically, the retailer will need to understand the determinants of shopping behavior so that likely changes in that behavior can be identified and appropriate strategies developed.

2. *Competitor behavior.* How competing retailers behave will have a major impact on the most appropriate strategy that the retailer should develop. Retailers must develop a competitive strategy that is not easily imitated.

Foot Locker has witnessed increased competitive activity from athletic shoe category killers such as Just For Feet. Also, some department and discount department stores have increased their athletic shoe assortments.

3. *Channel behavior.* The behavior of members of the retailer's distribution channel can have a significant impact on the retailer's future. For example, are certain channel members, such as manufacturers and wholesalers, establishing their own Internet sites in order to bypass retailers? Our E-tailing box describes such a situation. Or are wholesalers requiring larger minimum orders and offering less attractive credit terms? Behaviors such as these could have implications for the retailer's strategy.

4. *Socioeconomic environment.* The retailer must understand how economic and demographic trends will influence revenues and costs in the future and adapt its strategy according to these changes.

5. *Technological environment.* The technical frontiers of the retail system encompass new and better ways of performing standard retail functions. The retailer must always be aware of opportunities for lowering operating costs.

6. *Legal and ethical environment.* The retailer should be familiar with local, state, and federal regulations of the retail system. It must also understand evolving legal patterns in order to be able to design future retail strategies that are legally defensible. At the same time, the retailer must operate at the highest level of ethical behavior.

Detailed discussions of these forces are provided in Chapters 3 through 6. For now, realize that these forces are uncontrollable by a single retailer; but that threats emanating from these forces are often translated into opportunities by successful retailers. For example, Macy's once was an independent operation that catered to the working classes of New York, but now has become a trendy boutique store owned by Federated Department Stores catering to the top 25 percent of families.

After reviewing its mission, objectives, environment, and developing its retail marketing strategy, the retailer should be able to develop alternative uses of resources in or-

E-tailing

Is Detroit Trying to Bypass the Car Dealers?

Eager to cash in on the on-line boom, Detroit's car manufacturers want to use the Internet to sell built-to-order cars directly to consumers and bypass the traditional dealers that currently control access to customers in the $350 billion new-vehicle business. Such an overhaul requires that General Motors Corp. and Ford Motor Co., which have in the past flirted with the idea of buying and operating existing large auto-mall dealerships, change existing state laws.

Today, the legislatures in more than 40 states have laws favoring the car dealers, whose sheer numbers ensure that they are among the most influential political lobbyists. State franchise laws prevent Detroit from selling directly to consumers, either with their own physical auto malls or over the Internet. These state laws, which mandate that only franchised dealers can sell a new vehicle, ensure that independent on-line sites such as Autobytel.com, DriveOff.com, and CarOrder.com are just fronts for existing franchised car dealers. Some states have also legislated that only franchised dealers can get the cars at true wholesale cost and bar the manufacturers from giving price-breaks to high-volume dealers but not to others. Thus your local car dealers have a lot more protection from Internet invaders than your local book stores did from Amazon.com.

Although most consumers may not care who controls auto retailing over the Internet, they should be aware that the current system is notoriously inefficient. Despite the introduction of a dozen or so publicly held retail selling groups, such as

AutoNation and CarMax, that were supposed to improve the current channel, estimates are that inefficiencies still add about 10 percent to the cost of a car. It may be even more in cities with too many dealers selling the same vehicles. In addition, on-line vending, coupled with made-to-order manufacturing, could drastically reduce the expense of financing dealer inventories.

Meanwhile the fight is moving its way to Washington, where dealers are asking Congress to amend federal arbitration law. Their concern is that some auto makers have added clauses to their dealer contracts requiring dealers to resolve disputes with manufacturers through binding arbitration. Dealers want to be able to take disagreements, particularly over the issue of manufacturer-owned dealerships, directly to court, and to amend the law to exempt the auto industry from federal binding-arbitration requirements.

Regardless of who wins this battle, one thing is clear: Americans in the future will buy more cars, in a more efficient manner, through the Internet, but it is not clear as to who will be the seller. Indeed, the current car battle offers a warning to every manufacturer who dreams of cutting out the intermediary and selling directly to customers on-line.

Source: Based on "Is the Showroom Dead," *Forbes*, November 1, 1999: 128; "To Sell Cars in Texas, Online Firms Are Forced to Enter the Real World," *Wall Street Journal, Texas Edition*, January 26, 2000: T1; "Car Sales Evolving on Net," *Dallas Morning News*, April 29, 2000: 1F–2F; and "Auto Dealers, Fearing That Detroit Will Hog the Web, Fight Back," *Wall Street Journal*, May 10, 2000: A1, A12.

der to obtain the highest performance level. After determining which strategy will yield the best results, the retailer is now able to concentrate on operations management.

Operations Management

Operations management is concerned with maximizing the efficiency of the retailer's use of resources. Operations management converts resources into sales and profits. In other words, its aim is to maximize the performance of current operations.

Most of the retailer's time and energy is devoted to the day-to-day activity of operations management. Our Retail Strategic Planning and Operations Management Model (Exhibit 2.3) shows that operations management involves managing the buying and

Operations management deals with activities directed at maximizing the efficiency of the retailer's use of resources. It is frequently referred to as day-to-day management.

handling of merchandise, pricing, advertising and promotion, customer services and selling, and facilities. All of these activities require day-to-day attention. For example, the selling floor must be maintained, customers served, merchandise bought and handled, advertisements run, and pricing decisions made each and every day. In other words, operations management is running the store.

Part 4 of this text will focus on operations management, the real guts of retailing. In the first several years of a retailing career, your primary concern will be almost exclusively with the operations management side of retailing. The strategic planning duties will be handled by senior executives. However, if you enter retailing via a small or medium-sized firm, you may be making decisions, even strategic ones, immediately. Nonetheless, when a retailer is able to do a good job at operations management, that is—efficiently using the resources available—then the retailer is said to be operations effective.

Dollars & Sense

To be a high profit performance retailer, the retailer needs good strategic planning coupled with good operations management.

High-Performance Results

The far-right portion of the retail strategic planning and operations management model suggests that the cumulative effect of well-designed and executed strategic and operations plans will be the achievement of high profit performance. Mistakes in either of these two areas will severely hamper the retailer's performance and prevent it from being among the leaders in its industry. For instance, in the early 1990s The GAP was hailed as the most successful innovator in the retail apparel industry. However, by 2000, early baby boomers had already reached age 50 and had all the clothes they needed. As a result, total home furnishing sales exceeded total apparel sales for the third year in a row, something that didn't happen in the previous decade.[12] In addition, younger adults, those in their 20s and 30s, found the merchandise at the chain's Old Navy stores less exciting and geared too much toward teenagers. After all, adults didn't want multi-pocketed cargo pants. Analysts also attributed GAP's recent failure to a decision made in early 2000 to stock new items less frequently in order sell clothes at full price longer. Although margins improved, customers often left empty-handed in search for fresh ideas. Compounding GAP's problems, the head of GAP's successful on-line operations left for Wal-Mart.

The need to strive for high profit performance is tied to the extremely competitive nature of retailing. It is still relatively easy to start a retail business in comparison to starting a business in other industries. Thus new retail entrepreneurs are continually entering the marketplace. As a consequence of this increased competition, profit levels naturally deteriorate with more chains using the same format. A retailer is therefore well advised to set high profit objectives so that if its planned profits are not achieved, at least the retailer has a chance of achieving average profitability. The retailer that aims only for an average profit will often find itself having to confront a rather sobering financial performance. Exhibit 2.4 shows how the SPM results of high performance retailers compare to the median performance for similar retailers. As a general rule,

Exhibit 2.4	The SPM for Some of the Country's Top Retailers								

	Net Profit / Net Sales	×	Net Sales / Total Assets	=	Net Profit / Total Assets	×	Total Assets / Net Worth	=	Net Profit / Net Worth
Abercrombie	14.5%		2.7%		40.1%		1.6%		65.1%
Gap	9.6		2.4		23.2		2.4		56.1
WalMart	3.4		2.7		9.1		2.7		24.4
Sears*	3.9		1.1		4.4		5.4		24.0
Tiffany	10.4		1.2		12.9		1.8		23.4
The Limited	4.9		2.4		11.9		1.9		23.1
Target	3.6		2.0		7.3		3.0		21.9
Home Depot	6.1		2.4		14.5		1.5		21.8
Walgreens	3.5		3.3		11.5		1.7		19.7
Pier 1	6.1		1.9		11.3		1.6		17.9
Kohls	5.6		1.8		9.9		1.7		16.9
Talbots	5.3		2.0		10.5		1.6		16.8
Nordstrom	3.9		1.7		6.5		2.6		16.7
Lowe's	4.4		1.9		8.4		2.0		16.6
Costco	1.9		4.0		7.6		2.1		16.1

* Includes credit operations

retailers should strive for the following goals when planning their SPM: net profit margin of 2.5 to 3.5 percent; asset turnover of 2.5 to 3.0 times; and financial leverage of 2.0 to 3.0 times. Achieving such goals would produce a return on assets of 8 to 10 percent and a 18 to 25 percent return on net worth.

Student Study Guide

Summary

This chapter explains the importance, as well as the use of, planning in retail management. Toward that end, the chapter introduces a model of retail planning.

LO•1 Explain why strategic planning is so important and describe its components.

Planning and the financial performance of the retailer are intertwined. High profit performance does not just happen; it is engineered through careful planning. Not all retailers can be leaders, but the ones that do well will be those that did the best job of planning and managing. The components of strategic planning include development of a statement of purpose or mission for the firm; definition of specific goals and objectives for the firm; an identification of the retailer's strengths, weaknesses, opportunities, and threats; and development of basic strategies that will enable the firm to reach its objectives and fulfill its mission.

LO•2 Describe the text's retail strategic planning and operations management model.

Retailers must engage in two types of planning and management tasks: strategic planning and operations management. Strategic planning consists of matching the retailer's mission and goals with available opportunities. The retail marketing strategy that results from this consists of a target market, location(s), and retail mix. Operations management consists of planning the efficient use of available resources in order to manage the day-to-day operations of the firm successfully. When retailers succeed at these two levels, they will achieve high profit results.

Terms to Remember

planning	return on assets (ROA)
strategic planning	financial leverage
mission statement	return on net worth (RONW)
goals and objectives	productivity objectives
market performance objectives	strategy
financial performance objectives	SWOT analysis
societal objectives	target market
personal objectives	location
market share	retail mix
net profit margin	operations management
asset turnover	

Review and Discussion Questions

LO•1 Explain why strategic planning is so important and describe its components.

1. Why should a retailer always define its line or type of business in the most general terms? Doesn't this make planning more difficult?

2. How do the retail firm's mission statement and goals and objectives statement relate to the retailer's development of competitive strategy?

3. Most college students have unfavorable opinions of their bookstore. Suppose you were asked to advise your bookstore. What items would you consider in your SWOT analysis?

4. Is strategic planning more important for a small retailer than for a large retailer? Explain your answer.

5. Can a mission statement be too narrow in scope? Too broad in scope? Explain your answer.

6. Sewell Motors, a automobile dealer based in Dallas, has the following mission statement: "We will provide the best vehicle sales and service experience for our customers. We will do this in a way that will foster the continuous improvement of our people and our company. We will be a top-performing, thoroughly professional, and genuinely caring organization in all that we do." Would you change this mission statement? If so, why?

LO•2 Describe the text's retail strategic planning and operations management model.

7. What major environmental forces must a retailer face? Is any one more important than the others?

8. Does strategic planning become more or less important as the uncertainty the retailer faces increases?

9. When doing the strategic planning and operations management tasks described in the model, does the retailer use creative thinking or analytical problem solving?

10. A wise person once said that "a good plan will always overcome poor operations management." Agree or disagree with this statement and explain your reasoning. Use current examples, if possible, in your answer.

11. Why is it so important for a retailer to seek high profit performance? Isn't it enough to seek to be above average?

Sample Test Questions

LO•1 When a retailer sets goals based on a comparison of its actions against its competitors, it is establishing _____ goals.

  a. competitive analysis
  b. market performance
  c. geo-market performance
  d. societal performance
  e. financial performance

LO•2 The best way for a retailer to differentiate itself in the eyes of the consumer from the competition is to

  a. increase advertising of sale items
  b offer the lowest prices in town
  c. always be well stocked with the basic items that customers would expect to find in your store
  d. not sell any of the brand names the competition is selling
  e. increase its strategic planning effort

Applications

Writing and Speaking Exercise

William Lewis owns several copy shops near college campuses, known as Quick Copies. In the past, he has run his shops very informally—he likes to claim that he is successful because he doesn't think too much and that he makes most of his decisions by the "seat of his pants." Over the past five years profits at each shop have increased between 5 and 7 percent each year. Lewis hasn't given much thought to changing his original plans for his copy shops. However, competitors are beginning to appear near some of his shops. As a result, Lewis feels that it is time to develop a more structured approach for his business and asks you as part of your summer internship to research the strategic planning process. You are to prepare a memo on the basic steps and tasks that are involved in developing a strategic plan. Be sure to include in your memo a mission statement and a list of objectives that Quick Copies should seek to achieve.

Retail Project

Go to the library and either look at the most recent annual reports for four or five of the top 25 U.S. retailers or the top 25 global retailers listed on the inside covers of this text or locate the 10-Ks of those firms on the Internet. (*Note:* All publicly held firms need to file their SEC 10-Ks, a more complete financial analysis of the firms performance, electronically. The address for looking up this information is www.sec.gov) Using the SPM described in Exhibits 2.1 and 2.4, calculate your own SPM numbers for these retailers. Finally, after calculating these numbers, which retailer do you believe is the best at achieving financial superiority?

Case

The Dancer's Studio

Mary Jo Watkowski has been involved with the performing arts in some manner since childhood. At a young age, she began taking ballet lessons and, as a teenager, began performing with a local dance troupe. Watkowski eventually auditioned for and was hired by a ballet company that performed throughout the United States. At the age of 24, Watkowski resigned from the company so that she could pursue a degree in arts administration on a full-time basis.

Watkowski has recently completed her degree and has begun working for The Dancer's Studio, a company which operates seven dance instruction studios throughout Dallas. Before Watkowski's arrival, the owner of the company, Emmitt Helm, had conducted business based purely on intuition. Helm hired Watkowski in hopes that she could assist him in instituting a more formalized strategic planning process.

In the past, customers seeking dance lessons from The Dancer's Studio had ranged from two years old to sixty-two years old. Helm encouraged the managing instructors at each of his studios not to turn anyone away—he felt that "a customer is a customer" and that the managers should be grateful for any business they could get. Most of the instructors that taught for The Dancer's Studio were trained in ballet, jazz, and, to a limited extent, tap dancing. Yet they often found themselves in situations where meeting all the needs of the customers forced them to give lessons on types of dancing (for example, Texas two-step, ballroom, contemporary, and folk) in which they were not skilled.

Over the past several years, approximately 55 percent of the studio's customers have ranged from 5 to 13 years of age and have resided in the somewhat affluent suburbs that surround Dallas. Sales increased last year by $20,000 to a total of $200,000. Patrons seemed to have become aware of the studios primarily through word of mouth or from Dancer Studio's advertisement in the classified section of the area telephone books.

Although Helm has concentrated on his real estate development interests in the past, he now plans to devote his energies to developing the business and reputation of The Dancer's Studio. There are virtually no limitations on the financial resources that Helm will make available for this purpose.

Develop the following for Mary Jo Watkowski to present to Helm and the other members of the management team:

1. A mission statement for The Dancer's Studio.

2. Two possible market performance objectives and two feasible financial performance objectives.

3. A statement describing the market or members of the market that The Dancer's Studio will be targeting.

Planning Your Own Retail Business

In the "planning your own retail business" exercise in Chapter 1, you learned how to estimate the net profits that your business might earn. You saw what would happen if your sales estimate was off by 10 percent. Now it is time to analyze the dollar investment you would need in assets to support your business and how you might finance these assets.

Your investment in assets would need to cover inventory, fixtures, equipment, cash, customer credit (i.e., accounts receivable), and perhaps other assets. These assets could be financed with debt or by investments you make in the business or perhaps other investors.

Compute the strategic profit model ratios under the assumption that your first year sales are $500,000, net profit is $15,000, total investment in assets is $200,000, and the total debt to finance these assets is $100,000. (*Hint:* Net worth is equal to total assets less debt.) What would happen to these ratios if net profit rose to $20,000?

Endnotes

1. The above discussion was based on a presentation by Rick Segal, president of Chapter's On-Line Inc., at the ACRA Spring Conference, May 4, 2000. Used with his written permission.

2. Based on a "Competing against Alternative Formats" presentation by Paul M. Adams in Phoenix, Arizona, on May 16, 2000.

3. This was provided to the authors by Robert Kahn.

4. Reprinted with permission of Record World.

5. The Borders Story at www.borderstores.com.

6. "What New Economy?" *Forbes*, April 17, 2000: 478.

7. "Can Borders Turn the Page," *Business Week*, April 3, 2000: 75–78.

8. Sidney Schoeffler, "Nine Basic Findings on Business Strategy," *PIMS Letter, No. 1*, The Strategic Planning Institute, 1977.

9. For a detailed discussion of this material with examples, see "The Profit Wedge: How Five Measure Up," *Chain Store Age*, May 1998: 60–68.

10. "He Sure Didn't Take It with Him," *New York Times*, November 20, 1994: F6.

11. *Dollar General*, Annual Report to Shareholders, 1996.

12. "The Changing Marketplace," Barnard Retail Consulting Group, May 2000.

Part II
The Retailing Environment

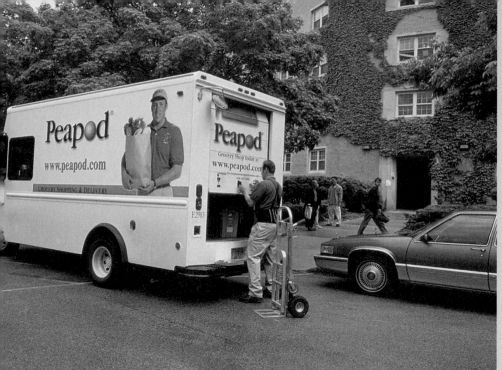

With households experiencing an increasing poverty of time, but rising incomes, more households are shopping for groceries on-line and having them delivered to their homes.

Retail Customers

Overview

In this chapter, we examine the effects of the external environment on retailing. We discuss the effects of recent changes in population, social, and economic trends on the way the consumer behaves and the implications of these changes for retailers. We conclude with the development of a consumer shopping/purchasing model incorporating all of these factors to describe overall shopping and buying practices.

Learning Objectives

After reading this chapter, you should be able to

1. explain the importance of population trends to the retail manager

2. list the social trends that retail managers should regularly monitor and describe their impact on retailing

3. describe the changing economic trends and their effects on retailing

4. discuss the consumer shopping/purchasing model, including the key stages in the shopping/purchasing process

Introduction

In Chapter 1 we said that retailing consisted of the final activities and steps needed to place a product or service in the hands of the consumer. In Chapter 2 we pointed out that to be a high performer, a retailer must be able to differentiate itself from the competition. In doing this retail managers must realize that, with the possible exception of a supermarket, a retailer can't serve all possible customer types. Some consumers will never shop at Wal-Mart and others will never shop at a Nordstrom or Neiman-Marcus. Therefore, before developing any plans, the successful retailer must first target a specific segment(s) of the overall market to serve and study the environmental factors (competition, the behavior of the other channel members, and legal and ethical factors) affecting that segment(s). Only then can retailers develop the rest of their retail mix—that is, the combination of merchandise assortment, price, promotion, customer service, and store layout that best serves the segment(s) targeted by the retailer.

The easiest way for retailers to differentiate themselves is to satisfy the customer's needs and wants better than the competition. This customer satisfaction, as we will use the term, is different than customer service. **Customer satisfaction** is determined by whether the total shopping experience has met or exceeded the customer's expectation. If it has, the customer is said to have had a rewarding shopping experience. This is important because it costs the average retailer four times as much money to get a new customer into its store as it does to retain a current customer.

However, studies have shown that for most customers, not only in this country but worldwide, shopping experiences haven't always met their expectations resulting in an unsatisfying experience. (The recent customer satisfaction data for the nation's leading retailers can be found at the University of Michigan's American Customer Satisfaction Index at www.bus.umich.edu/research/nqrc. This index is updated quarterly. Also, a primer on how to conduct a customer satisfaction survey can be found at http://customersat.com.) A part of the shopping experience, in addition to the physical product or service offered for sale, is the services included as part of the offering. These **customer services** are the activities performed by the retailer that influence (1) the ease with which a potential customer can shop or learn about the store's offering, (2) the ease with which a transaction can be completed once the customer attempts to make a purchase, and (3) the customer's satisfaction with the product after the purchase. These three elements are the pretransaction, transaction, and posttransaction components of customer service. Some common services provided by retailers, in addition to having the product on hand that satisfies the customer's needs and wants, include alterations,

Customer satisfaction occurs when the total shopping experience of the customer has been met or exceeded.

Customer services include the activities the retailer performs that influence (1) the ease with which a potential customer can shop or learn about the store's offering, (2) the ease with which a transaction can be completed once the customer attempts to make a purchase, and (3) the customer's satisfaction with the purchase.

fitting rooms, delivery, gift registries, check cashing, credit, extended shopping hours, short checkout lines, gift wrapping, parking, layaway, and merchandise return privileges, as well as the availability of in-home shopping facilities such as television, print catalogs, or Internet shopping. It must be remembered that none of these services are actually the merchandise or service offered for sale; they merely enhance the shopping experience for the customers the retailer is targeting.

Managerial Question: Given the wide variety of population, social, and economic trends, and the importance to retailers of targeting specific consumer groups, what segments provide the greatest opportunities for new retailers today?

If the customer is dissatisfied with either the product offered or the services provided; then that customer is less likely to choose that retailer in the future, thus decreasing future sales.(In the rest of this chapter we will use the term *product* to designate either the physical product or service offered for sale and the term *service* to refer to the services the retailer uses to facilitate that sale. However, in the case of a service retailer, the product is in fact the service.) Knowing what products to carry, as well as determining which customer services to offer, is a most challenging problem for retailers as they seek ways to improve the shopping experience. Imagine listening to a radio with no tuning or volume knob. The receiver picks up so many different signals—some in harmony, some in conflict—that the result coming through the speaker is noise. You're getting something, but you can't understand it. To make sense of the confusing array of information, retailers use market segmentation techniques to tune in segments of the population, hoping to hear a series of clear messages that can then be constructed into some overall meaning.

It should be noted that some retailers claim that this declining level of satisfaction may not actually be a bad sign. They view the decline as a function of rising expectations from the customer. They claim that their merchandise/service is much better today than it was a decade ago, but that customer expectations have increased at a faster rate. Today's consumers are fussier than ever and demand perfection. Their nearby home improvement store might have great merchandise and low prices, but the checkout line was too long. Understanding different customer segments and their need for convenience might stimulate the retailer to offer products through its web site, providing a critical service component to enhance the customer's experience. Therefore, as Exhibit 3.1 points out, it is important that the retailer know and understand its customer.

Exhibit 3.1 illustrates the three important trends—population, social, and economic—that all retailers must monitor because they will affect the way customers undertake the shopping process. As pointed out in Chapter 2, retailers must perform three strategies:

1. Get as many consumers as possible into their store.
2. Convert these consumers into customers by having them purchase products.
3. Do this at the lowest operating cost possible that is consistent with the level of service that their customers expect.

If the retailer doesn't understand its customer, it won't be able to accomplish the first two strategies.

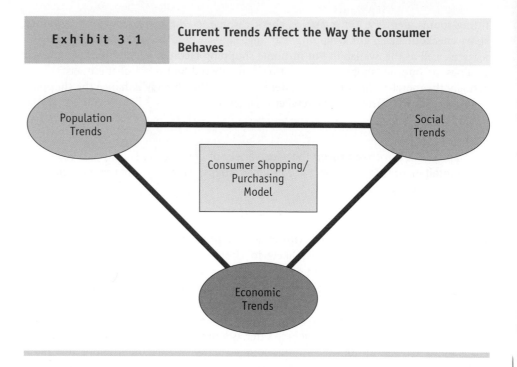

| Exhibit 3.1 | Current Trends Affect the Way the Consumer Behaves |

Market segmentation
is the dividing of a
heterogeneous consumer
population into smaller, more
homogeneous groups based
on their characteristics.

Market segmentation is a method retailers use to examine ways to segment, or break down, heterogeneous consumer populations into smaller, more homogeneous groups based on their characteristics. Market segmentation helps retailers understand who their customers are, how they think, and what they do, thus enabling retailers to build a meaningful picture of consumer needs, desires, perceptions, shopping behaviors, and the image these consumers have of the retailer in comparison to its competitors. Only by completing these market segmentation activities can a retailer hope to satisfy the consumers' needs better than the competition. Failure to spot changes in the marketplace before the competition means that the retailer will only be able to react and adapt to what more sensitive retailers have already spotted. Thus, whereas the high-performance retailer will have spotted an emerging trend and made the necessary changes in its retail mix, the average retailer can only be a follower or look-alike retailer. Being a "me-too" retailer has led many retail businesses into financial difficulties because little or no differential advantage is offered to the customer.

Retailers who focus on understanding a well-defined customer niche, in order to serve the customer in this niche with a differentiated offer, will be higher profit performers than their competitors.

One retailer who does a great job of understanding the customer is France's Marches Usines Auchan, one of the world's largest retail chains, by designing its store so that employees must interact with the customers. Its main store is approximately 400,000 square feet, with all of its divisions and offices—buying, research and development, workshops, staff restaurant, meeting rooms, travel agency, and so on—arrayed around the store. There is only one entrance through which everyone—customers, the store staff, and the headquarters personnel (who cannot avoid being informed as to what is happening in the store's departments)—must enter. As a result of this setup, the buyers must spend some time on the floor with customers; and if they identify themselves to the customers, they most likely receive an earful about what the customers liked and what could be improved.

This behavior is especially significant when it is compared to what so many other large retailers have done. Some large retailers have built their corporate offices to look like palaces, full of sculpture, brass, and marble, and far removed from their nearest retail outlet. When top management does visit one of the chain's retail outlets, store management is warned ahead of the visit, thus preventing senior management from really understanding how the store appeals to the customer every day.

Now, let's begin our study of the changing consumer to see how an understanding of population, social, and economic trends can help a retailer select a market segment to target.

Population Trends

> **LO • 1**
>
> **Explain the importance of population trends on retail planning.**

Retailers often find it useful to group consumers according to **population variables,** such as population growth trends, age distributions, and geographic trends. This is useful for two reasons: First, such data are often linked to marketplace needs; second, the data are readily available and can easily be applied in analyzing markets.

Population variables include population growth trends, age distributions, and geographic trends.

Population Growth

Retailers have long viewed an expanding population base as synonymous with growth in retail markets.[1] Unfortunately, this growth rate in market size has been declining during the past three decades as families have fewer children. From a historical viewpoint, the fertility rate in the United States—the average number of births per woman—has never been as low as its current level. The fertility rate was 2.2 children per woman in the 1930s, rose to 3.6 in the 1950s—the peak of the "baby boom era"—and dropped to 1.9 in 1995. By 1999, this figure had risen slightly to 2.1 and it is expected to remain stable around 2.0 for the next 15 years. Despite this decreased fertility rate, the total number of births, as shown in Exhibit 3.2, is still higher than it was during the 1970s and most of the 1980s. This increase in births has been dubbed the "baby boomlet" or "echo." However, as the last stage of baby boomers, those born between 1946 and 1964, move beyond childbearing years, total childbirths are not expected to rise.

Two other important influences on population growth are life-expectancy rates and net immigration totals. As Americans live longer the population base becomes larger. In 1970, the average life expectancies for a male and female at birth were 67 and 75 years, respectively; by 1997, these figures had increased to 74 and 79 years. Because immigration laws are under the control of Congress and difficult to predict, we will not project their impact on future population other than to report that the current estimate on future net immigration, both legal and illegal, is 820,000 a year, up from 542,000 in 1990. Of course, the economic conditions existing in this and other countries could greatly influence this figure. Nonetheless, the general consensus among forecasters is that most immigrants to the United States over the next two decades will come from Asia and Latin America.

Exhibit 3.2 Number of Births by Year

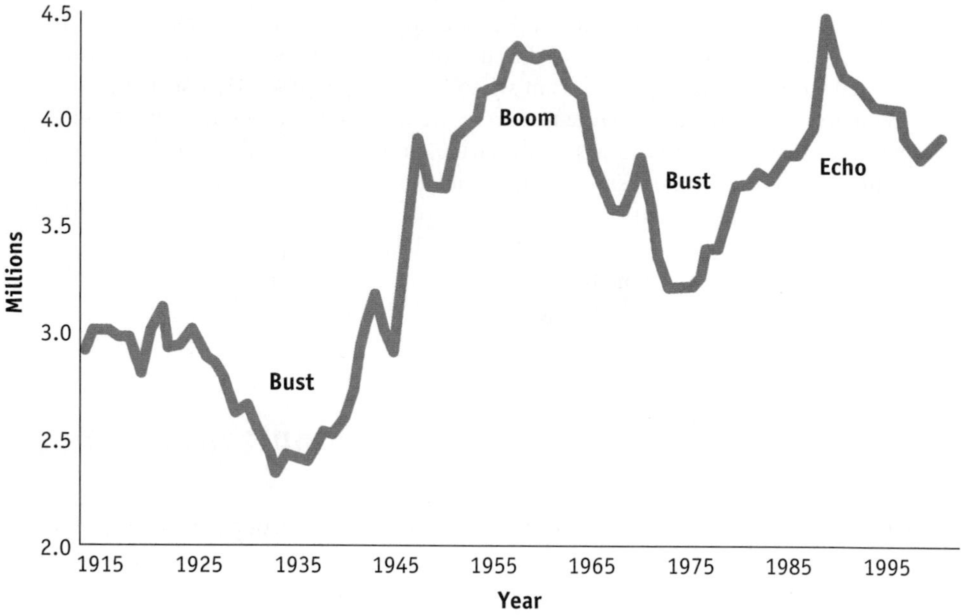

IMPLICATIONS FOR RETAILERS Overall, population is expected to grow, but at a slower rate. If current average projections for the fertility, immigration, and death rates are correct, the U.S. population will increase 10 percent (from 271 million in 1998 to 298 million) in 2010 and by 24 percent (to 335 million) by 2025. An increase in population growth will mean an increased demand for goods and services domestically, but nowhere near the 80 percent increase experienced over the past half century. Consequently retailers will focus on taking market share from competitors, managing gross margin through selling price and cost control, and, as shown in our Service Retailing box, increasing the productivity of existing stores. Another key will be international expansion. The global population is greater than six billion and will probably reach 12 billion before it stabilizes due to declining birthrates.[2] As a result, many retailers will look to global expansion as an avenue for future growth.

Age Distribution

The age distribution of the U.S. population is changing significantly. In 1980 the median age was 30 but by 1998 it had risen to 35. The most significant change today is the bulge of baby boomers moving into their late forties and fifties. In the 1980s, the baby boomers with incomes and energy to "shop till they drop" fueled the rapidly expanding retail sector, especially with regard to apparel sales. But today, as the first wave of boomers reach age 60 and older—a demographic group known as the "gray market"—they are not spending as they did in the past. Many are aggressively saving for retirement because of increasing concern over the long-term viability of social security and uncertainty about corporate downsizing, which has left many mature adults unemployed or underemployed. In the future, it is assumed that this first wave of

Service Retailing

Movie Theaters Find a Way to Improve Productivity

Monday nights have always been a slow night for theaters. Whether it's a night of rest after a long weekend, a continuation of the malaise of going back to work or school, or the attraction of Monday Night Football in the fall, most folks don't want to go out on Monday night.

A small four-screen theater in Pennsylvania has developed a rather novel way of improving its productivity with a "Monday Night Is Baby's Night" promotion. Here parents with infants can come in with their baby and watch a movie with the knowledge that they are welcome and that their baby will not disturb others in the theater. After all, because many others in the theater will also have babies in tow, they will likely be understanding. The only catch is that children over the age of one are not invited, as they may want to walk around and tend to be more restless. Others may come to watch a movie, but they are warned ahead of time of the presence of the babies.

The theater has bottle warmers ready in the outer lobby and spare diapers if needed. The movies don't start until 7:30 p.m. so that most of the babies actually sleep during the show.

Although Monday's are still slow, the theater attendance has doubled on Mondays with this creative promotion. Besides, it may prove to have a positive long-term effect as these new parents may get used to the idea of relaxing with a night out at the movies.

boomers will spend less on apparel and clothing and more on medicine and recreation and focus more on financial security, good health, comfort, their homes, and safety.[3] Today's younger boomers, those between 45 and 55, are paying off mortgages and car loans and saving for their children's education. This is a significant trend when one recognizes that over 27 percent of the population is over 50.

Seniors should, however, not be perceived as homogeneous. In the past, seniors were viewed as anyone over 60. Because people are living longer there are new, more useful categories. Octogenarians are people aged 80 to 89, nonagenarians are 90 to 99, and centenarians are 100 and older. In the United States there are more than 65,000 centenarians. By 2050 the number of centenarians is expected to increase by more than

Today's seniors, or the gray market, are more active and recreationally oriented than prior generations of seniors.

1,200 percent.[4] Another useful way to categorize seniors is in terms of their health (good/poor) and wealth (inadequate/adequate). Thus there are four types of seniors: good health/adequate wealth, good health/inadequate wealth, poor health/adequate wealth, and poor health/inadequate wealth. Because seniors in general have more wealth than seniors did several generations ago due to improved social security benefits, Medicare, and retirement savings, and because these seniors are relatively more healthy, the largest market growth has been with "active" seniors who have both the health and wealth to enjoy themselves.

"Baby busters," or "Generation Xers"—those born between 1965 and 1977—are an often overlooked age group. Unlike the baby boomers, this age group is a declining percentage of the population. Today there are 46 million of these consumers. While a relatively small group when compared to boomers or Gen Yers, Gen Xers represent a diverse consumer group. Often considered skeptical of product claims, retailers targeting this group must make concrete efforts to both understand the needs of this group and provide easily confirmed claims in a creative manner.

"Generation Y", "echo boomers," or the "millennium generation" are those born between 1978 and 1994 and number more than 75 million strong. They are emerging as a major buying and consuming force in the economy.[5] This generation is racially diverse; more than one in three is not Caucasian. Three out of four have a working mother and one out of four is in a single parent household. There is emerging evidence that the Gen Yers values are more traditional and they have a conservative lifestyle, such as not living together before marriage. Gen Yers want a professional career but place a higher priority on family and home. Many Generation Yers have never wound a watch, purchased a record, used a typewriter, or dialed a phone; however they think nothing of formatting a computer disk or downloading music off the Internet. In many ways, they are the most optimistic generation in this country's history. They tend to have higher disposable incomes than their age group in prior generations, are interested in good health, and tend not to rely on others for their success.

This group is not only different in age, but has a unique buying behavior that will be difficult for retailers to respond to unless they make a well-considered effort. The teens in this group are not buying the apparel brands their boomer parents bought. Rather than purchasing Levi's, Converse, and Nike; they are purchasing Mudd, Paris Blues, In Vitro, and Cement. Many Gen Yers are purchasing from catalogs and web sites. For example, teen girls are heavy purchasers from Delia, an apparel catalog catering to Generation-Y teen girls. Instead of typical mass-market advertising, Delia uses local campaigns including catalog drops at schools. The catalog not only features fashionable apparel but also offers advice on how to wear the apparel. No wonder, as Exhibit 3.3 illustrates, many retailing executives, themselves baby boomers, claim not to be able to understand this age group and its behavior. Because Gen Y is highly diverse, it is not easy to reach members of this group, and this effort has been heavily influenced by the fragmentation of media due to the explosion in magazines, cable channels, and Internet sites.

Retailers who understand the implications of the country's age distribution will be more apt to identify opportunities that will improve their profit performance.

Exhibit 3.3	Boomers, Xers and Yers

	Boomers, Busters and Echo Boomers		
	Baby Boomers	**Baby Busters**	**Echo Boomers**
Names	Boomers	Gen X	Gen Y Millennium Generation Digital Generation
Dates of Birth	1946–1964	1965–1977	1978–1994
Number in U.S.	76 million	46 million	75 million
Annual Spending	Over 900 billion	Over 125 billion	35–100 billion
Experienced	Birth of Rock and Roll	Growing Divorce Rate	Age of Technology
	Space Exploration	Gang Violence	Multi-layered Information
	Racial Divides	Pop Culture	Growth in Branding
	Sexual Revolution	Information Explosion	Recycling
Respond to	Authority	Creativity	Learning
Perspective on Technology	Fearful	Proficient	Indoctrinated
Attitude	Realistic	Pessimistic	Optimistic

IMPLICATIONS FOR RETAILERS   The most significant effect of an aging population is negative for retailers because, especially with regards to boomers, their big spending years are behind them. Retailers must remember what motivates consumers to spend money. Younger adults are by their very nature acquisition oriented. These first-time renters and home buyers need to acquire material objects and usually judge their progress by such possessions. Older adults tend to conserve what they have already acquired. Thus, as the population ages, a significant driving force for total economic growth dries up.

In view of the fact that as consumers age they change their spending habits, the high profit performance retailers of the next decade will be those that best adapt to these changes.

Dollars & Sense

Also, because different retailers tend to serve different age groups, the changing distribution of the U.S. population poses many challenges and opportunities. Retailers should be aware of what was pointed out earlier—consumers over 50, the first wave of baby boomers, tend to focus more on their families and finances than those in other age groups. They also spend more on medical services and travel. Thus, the products and services that appealed to these older consumers as free-spending younger consumers will not necessarily be the ones that appeal to them now as grandparents and home owners. In addition, this older market is expected to utilize the services of others

Echo boomers have been indoctrinated with computer technology and thus fearlessly embrace it.

more than they did when they were younger. This has begun to cause the softening of the do-it-yourself (DYI) market, as there are now more people over 35 than under 35. As the population ages, there are more people becoming "do-it-for-me's." This do-it-for-me trend is also expanding in the services arena. For instance, two emerging do-it-for-me services are home cleaning and yard care. These services have become especially popular among dual income households over 35, where there is little discretionary time but ample discretionary income for do-it-for-me services.

The "graying of America" will have enormous consequences for business in general, not just retailing, as most older consumers are skeptical and uninterested in shopping. Retailers must be able to speak the older consumer's language and not talk down to or patronize them, avoid tendencies of "phony friendliness," and in a tactful manner recognize that as they age, people have a declining ability to deal with spatial relationships, thus necessitating easy to navigate store layouts and clearly labeled merchandise.[6] However, it is doubtful that the baby boomers will behave as their parents did a generation before them. Retailers who assume that baby boomers will behave as their parents will be mistaken. A 50-year-old in 2005 will not act like a 50-year-old in 1985. In fact, they may act like a 30-year-old in 1985 (which is what they were), just older and wiser. Many of these "Pepsi Generation" types will probably enter the "gray market" kicking and screaming. They will demand that retailers embrace their values, such as youthfulness and invincibility, no matter what the product or service: food, insurance, entertainment, or medicine. Therefore, besides the increase in health care services and travel, restaurants (where the over-60 category accounts for more than 30 percent of the breakfast and dinner trade) will have to consider such items as the design of their tables and seats; financial service firms will have to reconsider their product offerings to this fixed-income category of consumers; malls will offer valet parking and lounges with concierge services that not only make shopping easier but make the shopper feel pampered,[7] and retailers in general will have to use bigger print, brighter parking lots, and fewer displays blocking store aisles, as well as rethink the way they portray and target senior citizens in their advertising.

Retailers shouldn't forget about the Gen Xers and Gen Yers. As noted earlier, these groups are not only different in age but they have what many boomers consider to be a significantly different buying behavior, which will be difficult for retailers to reach unless they make a well-considered effort.[8] Young consumers today don't want **conspicuous consumption**, which is consumption that is highly visible and attracts special attention. In fact, they are more sophisticated than previous generations when it comes to shopping and seem to be turned off by promotions that don't take them seriously. They want entertainment or events when they shop.[9] That means different promotions that are relevant to them, funny, and say "we understand." Retailers dealing with this market can't fake it.

Geographic Trends

The location of consumers in relation to the retailer often affects how they buy. In this third section covering population trends, we will take a closer look at how geographic trends affect retail operations.

Shifting Geographic Centers   Retailers should be concerned not only with the number of people and their ages, but also with where they reside. Consumers, especially as they get older, will not travel great distances to make retail purchases. Consumers want convenience and will therefore patronize local retail outlets. Because the U.S. population for the past 200 years has been moving toward the West and the South, growth opportunities in retailing should be greatest in these areas. Consider that between 1990 and 2000 the 10 fastest growing states were all in the West (Washington, Oregon, Idaho, Nevada, Utah, Arizona, Colorado) and South (Georgia, Florida, and Texas).

Over the past half century the South, now with 35 percent of the country's population versus 31 percent in 1960, and the West, now with 22 percent versus 16 percent, grew as the other two regions, Midwest (24 versus 29 percent) and Northeast (20 versus 25 percent), declined in population share. Demographers expect that this trend will continue.

IMPLICATIONS FOR RETAILERS   This changing geographic shift means Northeastern and Midwestern retailers are experiencing slower growth, and national retailers are adding stores and distribution centers (warehouses) in the South and West. Furthermore, one of the biggest mistakes that retailers make is to assume that all the consumers in a certain geographic area have the same purchasing habits. For instance, as a percent of consumer expenditures, households in the Northeast spend more on education, food, housing, and apparel; whereas those in the Midwest spend more on entertainment and tobacco and smoking supplies; those in the South spend relatively more on transportation, health care, and make more cash contributions; and those in the West spend more on personal insurance and pensions, housing, and entertainment. Exhibit 3.4 shows that not even consumers living in the same state, Texas, have similar shopping habits. In fact, the same differences have been found to occur in different parts of the same city. As a result, many of the leading retailers, such as Sears, have developed "micromarketing" merchandising strategies. **Micromarketing merchandising** involves tailoring merchandise in each store by using the optional stock list approach, discussed in Chapter 1, to match the preferences of its neighborhood. This is made possible by the use of computer software programs that match neighborhood demographics with product demand. Two of the biggest Sears stores in the Chicago area are nearly the same size and do about the same annual sales volume. However, the merchandise makeup of the two stores is different. The urban store, which is in close proximity to many fine bakeries, doesn't carry breadmakers; yet breadmakers are popular items in the more upscale suburban store 15 miles away.

Conspicuous consumption
is consumption that is highly visible and attracts special attention.

Micromarketing merchandising
is the tailoring of merchandise in each store to the preferences of its neighborhood.

| | **Exhibit 3.4** | | **Texas Consumers Percentage of National Average Usage** | |

Product	Dallas Fort Worth	Houston	San Antonio Corpus Christi	West Texas New Mexico
Biscuits/Dough	148%*	122%	103%	85%
Butter	51%	57%	39%	57%
Fresh Eggs	94%	112%	141%	110%
Juice/RFG	74%	104%	76%	66%
Lard	26%	121%	**	419%
Canned Ham	39%	21%	22%	28%
Sausage	134%	179%	219%	73%
Baked Beans	82%	76%	51%	60%
Cocktail Mixes	118%	79%	82%	112%
Pasta	71%	80%	72%	76%
Rice/Popcorn Cakes	84%	69%	58%	73%
Cosmetics	237%	133%	329%	221%
Cold/Sinus Tab/Cough Drops	157%	113%	125%	105%
Deodorant	119%	118%	125%	86%
Hair Coloring	137%	122%	238%	130%
Laxatives	152%	116%	164%	117%
Cat Food	88%	73%	81%	67%
Diapers	115%	135%	160%	74%
Facial Tissue	82%	66%	64%	78%
Paper Napkins	71%	74%	78%	68%
Motor Oil	112%	92%	279%	114%
Shoe Polish & Accessories	147%	145%	171%	147%
Tape	163%	105%	175%	149%
Hosiery	164%	126%	156%	110%

*National average = 100%.

**Not measured in this market.

Used with the permission of Information Resources, Inc.

Dollars & Sense

Retailers who develop micromarketing merchandising strategies will have higher profit performance.

Retailing: The Inside Story

Small Regional Discount Chains Can Be Successful If They Choose Their Locations Carefully

As the national chains expand by entering markets usually held by regional chains, many of these smaller chains have been forced to close their doors. One retailer who hasn't is Omaha-based Pamida, which was acquired by Shopko in 1999. Pamida, with annual sales of $800 million, has come to grips with its expenses and prepared itself for the stiffer competition of the national chains. In doing so, the chain has proved that there is still a place for regional discounters in the marketplace, if they choose their locations carefully.

With its new prototype 42,500-square-foot stores, which is only a quarter of the size of a national chain's supercenter, Pamida has found success by locating in towns of 10,000 to 15,000 in the rural Midwest, North Central, and Rocky Mountain states. By choosing such locations, Pamida doesn't have to face the Wal-Marts, Targets, and Kmarts storefront to storefront. For example, in 1992 Pamida competed with Wal-Mart in 28 percent of its markets versus only 18 percent today. By locating in these smaller markets first, Pamida has developed a base of customer loyalty and made it difficult for a larger chain to enter and fight over market share. With the majority of its sales coming from convenience goods (underwear, hard goods, toothpaste, socks, snacks, etc.), Pamida, with low prices and national brands, has given its customers a good reason not to drive 20 to 30 miles to a much larger national chain operation.

However, what has made Pamida successful is that it knows how to compete with its limited floor space in small towns. A couple of key illustrations are the following:

1. Because many people are willing to drive great distances to save money on prescription drugs, the chain has in-store pharmacies in 40 stores. These competitive-priced pharmacies give customers a reason to come back consistently, day after day.

2. More than 75 percent of the chain's 157 stores have an expanded in-store pantry that features a refrigerator case and frequently replenished consumables.

3. Without disregarding its more traditional hard-goods lines, Pamida has increased the percentage of floor space devoted to ready-to-wear in its prototypes to 45 percent from the 25 percent in its older stores. This additional space enabled the firm to stress its selection of daily wear and avoid the more competitive dress wear where the national chains had an advantage.

4. Home furnishings, with its higher margins, have been moved into the center of the store with stationery, domestics, and ready-to-assemble (RTA) furniture.

5. Pamida has invested millions of dollars in updating its information systems technology, which allows store managers to use information to help them make better decisions. In the past, Pamida had the problem of most regional chains: Its buyers and store managers knew how to buy the right merchandise, and how to display it and reorder it if it was selling; however, they were lost when it came to reacting to merchandise that wasn't moving. Now, with the new information system, managers can spot trends and react immediately without calling the home office in Omaha.

Urban Centers   Most of the U.S. population resides in metropolitan areas with populations greater than 50,000, which the U.S. Census Bureau calls **metropolitan statistical areas** (MSAs). The proportion of the population residing in these cities has increased dramatically, from 64 percent in 1950 to over 78 percent today. However, the urban or metropolitan population varies considerably by state. For instance, California, Massachusetts, and New Jersey are over 95 percent urban/metro; whereas Idaho, Maine, Mississippi, Montana, South Dakota, Vermont, and Wyoming are less than 40 percent urban/metro. This migration to MSAs is directed more to suburban than central city areas.

Metropolitan statistical areas are freestanding urban areas with populations in excess of 50,000.

IMPLICATIONS FOR RETAILERS   Every shift in population patterns of consumers has major implications for retailers, especially regarding where expenditures are made for household products. Although these recent shifts have resulted in a decline in downtown retail sales, sales increases in malls and free-standing suburban locations have more than made up for any decline.

However, there are opportunities for retailers in the smaller markets. During the past decade, retailers have witnessed a rapid growth in retail activity in secondary markets, areas with populations of less than 50,000. Historically, most chain retailers have ignored these markets. Secondary markets are also attractive because of the low level of retail competition, lower building costs, cheaper labor, and fewer building and zoning regulations. But as MSAs began to stabilize, secondary markets became more attractive. Some retailers have been successful in moving into small town America, as our Retailing: The Inside Story box indicates.

Mobility   In many countries, people are born, raised, married, widowed, and die in the same city or immediate geographic area. Although this was once true in the United States, it certainly is not true of contemporary America, due, in some degree, to this country's increasing divorce rate and trend toward higher levels of education. Typically, Americans change residence about a dozen times in a lifetime. This is twice the rate as for the British and French and four times as often as the Irish. Of those that move each year about 62 percent remain in the same county, about 19 percent move to a new county but stay in the same state, and approximately 19 percent move to a new state. The farther one moves from his or her prior residence—and this is especially true in moving to another state—the more one needs to establish new retail shopping patterns.

IMPLICATIONS FOR RETAILERS   A recent study regarding mobility has found that in almost half of large families where the children don't go to college, one child will live within five miles of the parent(s) when the parent(s) reaches age 60; and in more than three-quarters of the cases the offspring will live within 50 miles of the parent(s).[10] Thus, in view of the recent trends toward higher education, which is discussed in the next learning objective and results in more job variations, retailers can only expect that mobility will increase. This presents a problem because retailers tend to serve local markets and tend to cater to well-defined demographic groups. If the population moves, the retailer may find that its target market no longer resides in its immediate area. Likewise, retailers in areas undergoing population growth will want to be prepared to serve these new consumers as many retail-oriented decisions will have to be made quickly. After a move, consumers must locate new sources for food, clothing, household goods, and recreation. This presents an advantage for chain operations, in that a consumer moving from Des Moines, Iowa, to New Orleans, Louisiana, knows what to expect at a Sears, Target, JCPenney's, Burger King, or Pizza Hut. However, consumer mobility influences e-tailers less as these retailers are not bound by consumer movements. For instance, when a consumer moves from Bangor, Maine to San Francisco, California, they can still go on-line to shop at Amazon.com.

LO • 2

What social trends should be monitored and what are their impacts on retailing?

Social Trends

In this section, we continue our examination of demographic factors affecting the modern retailer by looking at several social trends: the increasing level of educational attainment, the state of marriage and divorce, the makeup of the American household, and the changing nature of work.

Education

The education level of the average American is increasing. Exhibit 3.5 shows that in 1998, 83 percent of individuals over age 25 had a high school diploma and 24 percent had a college degree, this latter statistic is nearly equal the 22 percent of those over 25 in 1920 who had a high school diploma. The Baby Boomers, those between the ages 38 and 56 in 2002, are the most educated generation ever. More than one in four has completed four years of college. This statistic is slightly higher for men and slightly lower for women. However, this trend is rapidly changing since already at many colleges and universities the women outnumber the men. It is forecast that by 2007 women will earn 58 percent, up from the 55 percent in 2000, of the bachelor's and master's degrees in U.S. colleges.[11] And women are increasingly pursuing high-paying career fields such as business, psychology, biology/life sciences, and engineering.[12]

IMPLICATIONS FOR RETAILERS Educational attainment is the single most reliable indicator of a person's income potential, attitudes, and spending habits. Thus college-educated consumers differ in their buying behavior from other workers of the same age and income levels. They are more alert to price, quality, and advertised claims. However, often overlooked when using education to segment the marketplace are the 30 million Americans over the age of 25 who have some college experience but not a degree. In many ways, people with some college best describe the term "average" American.[13] They have more money than high school graduates, but less than college graduates. They also fall between the groups in their propensity to shop in department stores, spend on apparel, buy new cars, travel, read books, watch TV, and invest in stocks and bonds.

Exhibit 3.5	**U.S. Education Levels**

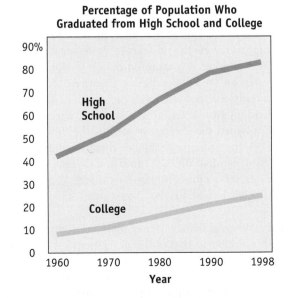

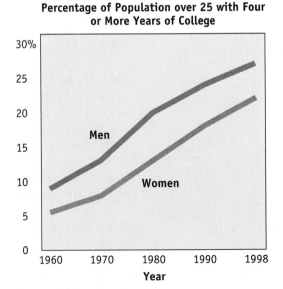

Source: U.S.Bureau of the Census, Statistical Abstract of the United States: 1999 (119th edition), Washington, D.C. 1999. Tables 263, 264.

Because education levels for the population, in aggregate, are expected to continue to rise, retailers can expect consumers to become increasingly sophisticated, discriminating, and independent in their search for consumer products. They will also demand a staff capable of intelligently dealing with their needs and wants.

Education is a key determinant of the use of the Internet for shopping. Today's middle-aged consumers grew up with the computer and feel comfortable with it. With their higher level of education they are more prone to shop electronically because they don't need the assurances or hand-holding that some retailers provide. This may present problems for many traditional sellers of services. For example, travel agencies may be left out of the loop as cyber shoppers "surf the net" to purchase airline tickets, hotel rooms, rental cars, and cruises.

Marriage and Divorce

State of Marriage   A relatively new social phenomenon has occurred during the past quarter century. In 1970, less than 10 percent of the U.S. male population between the ages of 30 and 34 had never married and just over 6 percent of the same aged female population had never married. In 1998 these percentages increased to 29 and 22 percent, respectively. Married couples are one of the slowest-growing household types not only in this country but worldwide. In 1970 males married at a median age of 23 and females at 21; today the median age for males is over 26 and for females it is 25. Not only are some people postponing marriage, some are choosing not to marry at all.

IMPLICATIONS FOR RETAILERS   For the retailer this trend toward single individual households presents many opportunities because the need for a larger number of smaller-sized houses complete with home furnishings will occur. This is especially true for the young adult market. The retailer's store hours may also require an adjustment to accommodate the needs of this market. Also, with more men living alone, supermarkets will have to direct promotions toward their needs and habits, because men tend to focus on getting specific items and then getting out of the store.

Divorce   Since 1960, the divorce rate in the United States has increased by 250 percent. It may be interesting at this point to review the findings of Professor Gary Becker of the University of Chicago. Professor Becker was awarded the 1992 Nobel Prize in economics for his 1981 book *A Treatise on the Family*. Becker theorized that families, just like businesses, rationally make decisions that maximize benefits. The theory suggests that in the traditional family, working husbands and stay-at-home wives each performed labor that when combined provided the greatest payoff for the time involved. However, as women's wages rose, it became more profitable for them to enter the labor force. As a result, spouses became less dependent on each other and divorces increased. An interesting statistic is that when divorce occurs it is at approximately 7.2 years after marriage; confirming the conventional wisdom about the "7-year itch."

IMPLICATIONS FOR RETAILERS   When a divorce occurs, many retail purchases are stimulated. A second household, quite similar to that of the never-married individual, is formed almost immediately. These new households need certain items such as furniture and kitchen appliances, televisions and stereos, and even linens. Once settled into their new homes, divorce may impact the way people shop. Retailers must make specific adjustments for a divorced, working parent with children by adjusting store hours, providing more consumer information, and changing the product assortment.[14]

Makeup of the American Household

Because households are the basic consumer unit for most products, household growth and consumer demand go together. Yet, because of the differing sizes and habits of various generations, the change in the makeup of households is notoriously hard to predict. The number of households without children increased 27 percent in the 1970s, 14 percent in the 1980s, and only 7 percent between 1990 and 1998.

Some interesting trends have occurred over the past two decades. For example, between 1980 and 1998 the number of people living alone ("home-aloners") increased by 44 percent. This trend, which represented nearly one-fourth of all households, is the result of an increased desire for privacy, an increase in young adults delaying marriage, an increasing number of divorces, an increase in never-marrieds, and a large increase in the number of people who live alone after the death of a spouse. Also, the number of unmarried couples ("mingles") increased by 167 percent since 1980. This trend, although it represents only 7 percent of all couple-households, is significant to the retailer because it represents a purchasing unit that is hard to understand by conventional household or family norms. The retailer, as well as the social scientist, has little knowledge of how joint decision making occurs or does not occur in such households.

Finally, there is one more interesting facet about the changing American household formation: the **boomerang effect**—so called because the parents think the children have left for good, but they just keep coming back. Between now and the year 2010, it is estimated that 40 percent of children will return to live with their parents after they have previously left home. Although this projection is extremely sensitive to future economic conditions, several factors will account for the projected 7 million boomerang households in 2010: people who marry in their twenties are just as likely to divorce as those who marry as teens, high school dropouts will not be able to find permanent work, and so on.

Boomerang effect occurs when grown children return home to live with their parents.

IMPLICATIONS FOR RETAILERS   Today, the combination of home-aloners, mingles, singles, and "dinks" (dual income, no kids) accounts for nearly 75 percent of all U.S. households. This market is not concerned about "back-to-school" sales and other family-oriented retail activities. This segment of the market is more interested in CD and DVD players, high social image, and gourmet foods. However, it is important that retailers recognize the differences in this market. Younger women will normally spend more on clothing and men will spend more on alcohol, cars, and dining out. As they age, women will begin to spend more than men on cars and entertainment while men will remain the best customers for dining out. The older segment of the single household market will require special attention from today's retailers. After all, between now and 2005, the "wild and crazy single guys" of the 1980s and early 1990s will turn into "tired and pudgy older guys" who no longer live as college students.

As you can see in our Global Retailing box, this changing structure in the makeup of households is not just an American trend, but a worldwide trend.

Changing Nature of Work

In the United States and other industrialized economies, work has become less central to life. In the past, work was often the way people identified themselves and obtained a meaningful life. Perhaps because of deterioration in institutional confidence or perhaps because of the overall prosperity of our economy and way of life, we are identifying less with our work. At the same time people are doing more work as a hobby.

Global Retailing

Worldwide Changes in Household Structure

The United States isn't the only country in which nontraditional households are becoming mainstream. Retailers in other developed countries are facing similar trends.

For example, the rise in the number of single parents, unmarried couples, and people living alone is common to most countries in the developed world. The difference is in the pace at which these trends are progressing.

Four main factors have changed the makeup of households and families in the past two decades: Women are having fewer children, more children are being born out of wedlock, populations are aging, and marriage is down while divorce is up.

Japan remains the most traditional of the developed nations, with low rates of divorce and low rates of out-of-wedlock births. It also has the largest share of married couples. Sweden and Germany have the largest shares of single-person households, in part because they have older populations.

Scandinavia has been setting the pace for out-of-wedlock births and cohabitation. Sweden and Denmark have the largest shares of births to unmarried couples, yet they don't have the highest shares of single parents, because many unmarried mothers in these countries live with partners.

It's not clear which country has the highest shares of mingles, or cohabitating couples, because some countries now include them with married couples in official household statistics. One estimate shows that virtually all young Swedes cohabitate before they marry.

The United States tops the list for single parents, partly because of high divorce rates, but also because single parents in the United States are more likely to be young, never-married women on their own, rather than cohabitaters.

People are gardening, investing time and money in learning to cook, and doing projects around the house. Also there is a rise of self-employed and home-based workers. In 1997 there were nearly 11 million self-employed individuals. By the late 1990s there were an estimated 5.5 million home-based businesses in the United States.[15] Most of these individuals enjoy the solitude of working at home. These individuals clearly have a distinctive lifestyle. For instance, they are very active in hiking, camping, bird-watching, antique shopping, and visiting art museums. They are heavy subscribers to Internet services and read magazines such as *Architectural Digest, Forbes,* and *House Beautiful.*

In increasing numbers, people are obtaining meaning from consumption. Some are literally durable goods junkies with RVs, boats, workshops, big screen televisions, swimming pools, and so forth. Often to pay for these extras, people hold multiple jobs. By the late 1990s, nearly 9 million individuals had multiple jobs. Many of these individuals were starting a small business, while holding their main job, while others were earning money to purchase something special or save for future consumption or to retire early so they would not have to work.

IMPLICATIONS FOR RETAILERS   Because people are finding less meaning in their work, they are less loyal to their employers. Nearly 30 percent of workers have held their job for less than 12 months, and the median length of service in a job is 3.6 years. In retailing, for entry-level personnel, turnover approaches 75 percent or more per year. Consequently, retailers need to find ways to enrich job experiences and lower turnover. One recent study found that turnover in the supermarket industry costs $5.8 billion annually. A cashier that departs costs $4,212, a department manager $9,354, and a store manager $56,844. Costs of employee turnover include paperwork errors, inventory shrinkage, and improper use of equipment. All of these errors occur due to the lack of experience of new employees. These errors lead to lower levels of customer service, which further leads to lost sales and profits.[16] One major opportunity for retailers is to employ home-based and disabled workers. Home-based workers can handle telephone inquiries and do clerical work or bookkeeping, and disabled workers can represent a previously untapped pool of talent for the retailer.

Finally, because many individuals are holding multiple jobs, retailers can tap into this pool of individuals for part-time workers. They have done this in the past but mostly at the retail clerk level. Today there are opportunities for retailers to employ these part timers in a variety of positions including accounting, inventory control, merchandising, buying, and store management.

Economic Trends

> **LO • 3**
> How do the changing American economic trends affect retailing?

In this section, we look at the effect on the modern retailer of income growth, the declining rate of personal savings, the increase in the number of working women, and the widespread use of credit in our economy.

Income Growth

In the late-1990s, the median household income was slightly over $37,000, which after adjusting for inflation was up less than 4 percent since 1980. As incomes rise, families tend to have higher disposable incomes. But all groups have not shared this income increase equally. During this time frame, African American family households experienced a rise in annual income of 16 percent to $29,000; Hispanic family households had a $28,000 annual income in 1997, however they experienced virtually no income growth from 1980 to 1997; and Caucasian family households experienced a 9 percent growth in income to a level of $47,000 in 1997. Notably, Asian-Pacific Islander family households, which were not tracked in 1980, had the highest household family income, which stood at $52,000 in 1997.

There has also been, as shown in Exhibit 3.6, a shifting of incomes among the various classes of Americans. Today, the upper classes of Americans have a higher share of

Exhibit 3.6	Share of Aggregate Income Received by Each Fifth and the Top 5 Percent of U.S. Households, 1970–1997					
Year	Lowest Fifth	Second Fifth	Third Fifth	Fourth Fifth	Highest Fifth	Top 5%
1997	4.2%	9.9%	15.7%	23.0%	47.2%	20.7%
1990	4.6	10.8	16.6	23.8	44.3	17.4
1980	5.3	11.6	17.5	24.4	41.1	14.6
1970	5.4	12.2	17.6	23.8	40.9	15.6

the nation's aggregate income in comparison to 1970. Today, the top fifth of all households by income level accounts for 47 percent, up from 41 percent in 1970, of the nation's income while the bottom two-fifths, or lowest 40 percent of the population, are earning only a seventh (14.1 percent) of the nation's income, down from 17.6 percent in 1970. The distribution of wealth is even more pronounced where 1 percent of the population holds 40 percent of the wealth. Thus, it appears that the rich are getting richer and the poor are getting poorer. However, this is in part misleading because income mobility in the United States is high. A significant proportion of the lowest income households move up the income scale over a 10-year period and similarly a significant proportion of the richest households move down the income scale over a 10-year period.

IMPLICATIONS FOR RETAILERS   The imbalance in income growth across households has created increased demand for value-oriented retailers such as discounters and manufacturers' outlets, and it explains why many of the upscale retailers (such as Macy's, Nordstrom, and Neiman Marcus) have not suffered the economic pressures facing many of their lower-scale counterparts. Also, retailers of luxury automobiles, luxury foreign vacations, and executive-style houses in gated communities have done well due to the explosion in millionaires. During the last half of the 1990s, 1 million new millionaires were created in the United States.[17] At the same time the low income level and low income growth among some segments of the population explain the growth of chains such as Dollar General.

Economists tend to view income from two perspectives: disposable and discretionary. **Disposable income** is simply all personal income less personal taxes. For most consumers, disposable income is their take-home pay. **Discretionary income** is disposable income minus the money needed for necessities to sustain life, (minimal housing, minimal food, minimal clothing, etc). Retailers selling necessities, such as supermarkets, like to see incomes rise and taxes decrease; knowing that although consumers won't spend all their increased disposable income on the retailer's merchandise, they will nevertheless increase spending. Retailers selling luxury goods want to see either disposable income increase and have the costs of necessities either decline or at least increase at a slower rate than income increases.

Disposable income
is personal income less
personal taxes.

Discretionary income
is disposable income minus
the money needed for
necessities to sustain life.

Personal Savings

A major criticism of the U.S. economic system is that it does not reward personal savings. Savings, which is expressed as a percentage of disposable income, have dwindled from a post–World War II high of 8.8 percent in 1981, to 5.4 percent in 1992, and to a dismal minus 0.2 percent in 2000. Though this may seem odd, it is important to note that during the past decade, the economy and stock market have been experiencing exceptionally strong growth. As a result people have quit saving and begun to invest in the stock market, which some consider a form of savings despite its additional elements of risk. (It should be pointed out that when using the government's numbers regarding the savings rate, the government fails to address the treatment of capital gains. When the government measures disposable income, it counts wages, interest earned, and dividends—but not realized or unrealized capital gains.) The government's rate tends to undermeasure savings because it fails to consider the wealth effect. The *wealth effect* claims that for every hundred dollars of additional wealth generated in an individual's stock market holdings, the individual will spend $4 (4 percent). Such spending will lower the nation's savings rate because when the stock market goes up, spending will increase without wages and salaries increasing. Saving will also be decreased in this example because the government will subtract the taxes on the stock market gains from disposable income.

Nevertheless, the savings rate in the United States is far below that of Japan, Germany, and France which all are over 10 percent. However, given national differences in the measurements of income and savings, comparisons between countries are unclear.

IMPLICATIONS FOR RETAILERS Retailers have enjoyed continued sales growth over the past decade because even though median household income in fixed dollars has increased only slightly, spending and not saving was the focus of the consumer. However, retailers must be prepared for the next millennium with baby boomers and Gen Xers planning for retirement by reducing their spending and increasing savings. Such savings would also mean less consumer spending. Other economists fear that in another decade, when more boomers retire, they will start to take money out of the stock market, which could cascade into a declining market, which could cause a reverse wealth effect because as consumers lose money in the stock market, they tend to save more. However, if the stock market continues to rise, consumers will spend more.

Women in the Labor Force

Over the past five decades women have become a dominant factor in the labor force. Three decades ago, 43 percent of all women over the age of 16 were in the labor force; this participation is expected to reach 61 percent in 2006. This trend is true of all age groups, even women age 25 to 34, who some might expect to be raising families. Seventy-six percent of all women age 25 to 34 are currently in the labor force. The percentage of all married women in the labor force who have preschoolers increased from 30 percent in 1970 to 64 percent in 1998. As we discussed earlier, more women are obtaining college degrees and over 82 percent of women with college degrees are in the work force.

This significant rise in the number of working women has protected many households from inflation and recession. In fact, many economists suggest that the working woman has been the nation's secret weapon against economic hardships. For example, annual household income for married households where both spouses were in the work force rose by over 27 percent (after adjusting for inflation) between 1980 and 1997 to more than $60,000. In addition to the working wife, another reason for the huge increase in household income for dual wage-earner families is that where once a professional man would marry a secretary or schoolteacher (admirable occupations, but not the highest paid), today many professional men are marrying professional women. As a result, the household incomes for these couples is increasing above the norm. This is also another cause of the polarization of income shown in Exhibit 3.6.

High profit performance retailers will be those that realize that the increase of women in the labor force is a two-edged sword. It will increase disposable income for the family, but it will reduce the time available for shopping; making it imperative that retailers make shopping a pleasant, convenient experience.

Exhibit 3.7	Dual Wage Earners and Their Effect on Hours Spent Shopping

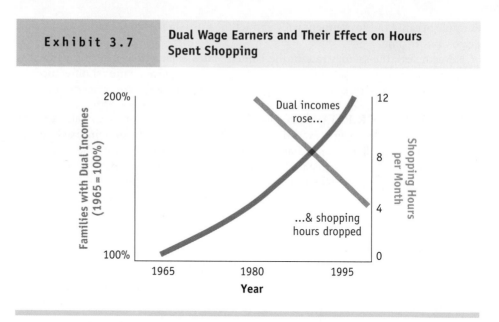

Source: *Vision for the New Millennium . . .* (Atlanta: Kurt Salmon Associates, 1997). Used with permission.

IMPLICATIONS FOR RETAILERS   The rise in the number of working women has many retail implications. As shown in Exhibit 3.7, the increase in dual wage earner families means that many families have less time for shopping and are more prone to look for convenience and services from retailers. Working men and women are often unable to shop "8 a.m. to 6 p.m. Monday through Saturday," thus preferring that retailers hold sales and special events in the evening or on weekends. Time-pressed shoppers find that price is sometimes less important than convenience, availability, and service. One study found that part-time working mothers of preschoolers tend to do more in-home shopping.[18] Retailers must develop strategies, such as extending store hours (early mornings, evenings, and weekends) and adding additional services such as baby-sitting. Brick & mortar retailers should also provide alternatives to in-store shopping such as catalogs or on-line shopping if they want to compete, such as described in our E-tailing box, for the time-pressed shopper's store loyalty.

Widespread Use of Credit

Retailers, especially department stores and those selling big-ticket items, have long offered their own credit to customers. However, today the trend is away from the retailer's store-brand credit cards that can be used only in that store and toward third-party cards (Visa, MasterCard, Discover, American Express, etc.). Spurred on in recent years by an active promotional campaign, these third-party firms are getting consumers to rack up credit card debt faster than the growth in their paychecks. Credit card debt is now over a half trillion dollars in the United States and more than two-thirds of households have a credit card. Among households with more than $50,000 in annual income, over 90 percent have at least two credit cards. Credit card firms offer promotional incentives such as free airline miles, rebates on new auto purchases, or rebates on other future purchases. For the retailer, credit card use has increased sales and profits. As a result, retailers from supermarkets to the family veterinarian are now

E-tailing

<u>Does the Most Dreaded of Shopping Chores Have a Place On-line?</u>

Next to a trip to the dentist, most consumers rank grocery shopping as their least favorite activity. There is no doubt that grocery shopping is not most people's idea of a good time. Consumers can think of more productive things they could do as opposed to the relatively repetitive task of moving up and down grocery store aisles putting the same products in their cart week after week. It is this frustration, and the added convenience for time-starved consumers, that companies such as Peapod, Webvan, and a number of other on-line grocers are counting on.

In the $450 billion U.S. grocery marketplace, on-line grocers are counting on shopping avoiders (those short on time or those who are limited in their ability to go to the store) as well as new technologists to drive the success of the on-line grocery industry. With just a click of the button, consumers can now have fresh vegetables, prime cuts of meat, and any other grocery product they would normally buy, delivered to their door. The driving force behind the on-line grocery industry has been Peapod. Peapod Inc., which was founded in 1989 by brothers Andrew and Thomas Parkinson and was recently acquired by the Netherlands' Ahold Corporation, has grown to be America's leading on-line grocer. With a mission of being a multichannel purveyor of food in the United States, Ahold will provide Peapod with goods, services, and fulfillment centers. Although Peapod already works with several of Ahold's U.S. chains, the deal will provide Peapod with entry into other markets in which Ahold operates and aids the e-tailer in being the leading and preferred provider of interactive grocery shopping services. Peapod has already penetrated eight markets from Chicago to Dallas. Its continued commitment to high-quality products and convenient delivery has enabled it to continually increase its customer base to more than 90,000. With the use of a centralized distribution system, Peapod has been able to reduce its overall costs and thus is moving closer to profitability.

Although the outlook for the on-line grocery business looks good, the question is whether on-line grocers can last until the number of on-line grocery shoppers reach a level for profitability. Peapod.com lost $28.5 million in 1999. Although this may seem like a lot, Webvan.com lost $76.3 million. Clearly, many consumers desire a way to reduce the amount of time they spend grocery shopping. However, the question is whether these e-tailers can penetrate their markets to reach profitability before running out of cash.

---

forced to accept these third-party cards and other retailers, such as Kroger Co., Wal-Mart, Nordstrom Inc., and Toys "R" Us, are now co-branding their names with these third-party issuers.

IMPLICATIONS FOR RETAILERS   Although the use of third-party credit cards has contributed to the increase in retail sales over the past decade, it may lead to problems in the future, especially during any economic slowdown or significant downturn in the stock market.[19] This becomes clear when one examines Exhibit 3.8, where the growth in consumer credit versus personal income is shown during the mid to late 1990s. Because the growth in credit has been outstripping the growth in personal income it becomes evident that as income growth slows or becomes negative, households will face a liquidity crisis.

In the late-1990s, total consumer debt including mortgages, home equity lines of credit, car loans, and credit card charges exceeded $6 trillion. Seven in 10 American families with credit cards carry balances over from month to month, with the outstanding balance averaging $3,900. Nearly 20 percent of household disposable income each month is now dedicated to paying off credit card debt. In addition, more

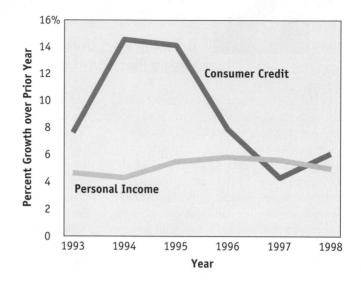

Exhibit 3.8	Growth in Consumer Credit vs. Personal Income

Source: U.S. Bureau of the Census, *Statistical Abstract of the United States, 1999* (119th edition), Washington, D.C. 1999, Tables 727, 824.

* Not including home mortgage and home equity debt.

consumers are taking out home equity loans to help finance purchases or to pay off high-interest rate credit card debt. It is estimated that home mortgage debt is at least 40 percent of middle-income assets, up from 29 percent in 1989.[20]

Consumer Behavior Model

LO • 4

What is involved in the shopping/purchasing model, including the key stages in the buying process?

Now that we have examined the population, social, and economic trends, we can develop a model that describes, and to some degree predicts, how these factors come together to affect consumer buying patterns. We call this the consumer shopping/purchasing model. Consumers are typically confronted with fundamental decisions when it comes to filling their needs: What products or brands can potentially fill their need and where should they purchase these products or brands? Our model is sufficiently general to deal with both of these decisions.

Retailers can use their understanding of their target consumer's buying behavior to improve their profit performance.

Consumer Shopping/Purchasing Model

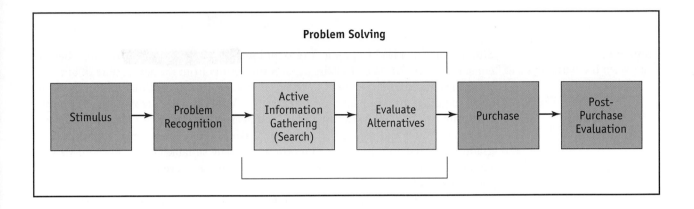

Examine the consumer shopping/purchase model in Exhibit 3.9. This model suggests that consumer behavior is a process, with a series of stages or steps. The six stages in the model include stimulus, problem recognition, search, evaluation of alternatives, purchase, and post-purchase evaluation.

Stimulus

A **stimulus** involves a cue (external to the individual) or drives (internal to the individual). A **cue** is any object or phenomenon in the environment that is capable of eliciting a response. Common examples of retail marketing stimuli are advertisements, point-of-purchase displays, coupons, salespeople, and free samples. However, all of these examples are cues controlled by the seller or retailer. In addition, there are cues that the retailer does not control. For example, word-of-mouth advertising is common in retailing. Many visits to e-tailing sites are the result of a visitor having a good experience and telling others about the site.

A second type of stimulus is internal to the individual and is referred to as a drive. A **drive** is a motivating force that directs behavior. Drives can be physiologically based (hunger and the need to stay warm in the cold) or learned (the desire to spend spring break in Cancun). When drives are strong they are more likely to prompt purchase behavior. The old adage "never go grocery shopping when you are hungry" illustrates this point.

Individuals can be exposed to both of these stimuli. For instance, a person may see an advertisement (cue) for a restaurant at the same time that he is hungry (drive), or a person living in Minnesota may be coping with a long, cold winter and browsing the Internet when she sees an advertisement for a vacation on the sunny beaches of Hawaii.

In an information economy as consumers move through their daily routine they are constantly exposed to hundreds of messages regarding products and services and where to purchase them. As a result, one of the scarcest resources is human attention. All retailers are competing with virtually all other organizations and individuals for the attention of the consumer. Consequently, the individual is always involved in **passive information gathering,** which consists of receiving and processing information regarding the existence and quality of merchandise, services, stores, shopping

Stimulus
refers to a cue that is external to the individual or a drive that is internal to the individual.

Cue
refers to any object or phenomenon in the environment that is capable of eliciting a response.

Drive
refers to a motivating force that directs behavior.

Passive information gathering
is the receiving and processing of information regarding the existence and quality of merchandise, services, stores, shopping, convenience, pricing, advertising, and any other factors that a consumer might consider in making a purchase.

convenience, parking, advertising, and any other factors that a consumer might consider in making a decision of where to shop and what to purchase.

Problem Recognition

Stimuli can often lead to problem recognition. **Problem recognition** occurs when the consumer's desired state of affairs departs sufficiently from the actual state of affairs to place the consumer in a state of unrest so that he or she begins thinking of ways to resolve the difference. Consider a few examples. While driving across town you notice that your car's gas tank is almost empty; you hear an advertisement for a new Sony CD player and tuner and realize that your 10-year-old stereo needs replacing; you will be graduating from college shortly and do not own any suitable clothes for your new career; or you receive your tax refund and realize you now have money to go to Cancun for spring break.

Not all problems will stimulate the same level of problem-solving activity. The level of one's desire to resolve a particular problem depends on two factors: the magnitude of the gap between the desired and actual states and the importance of the problem. Consider the example about the gas tank. If a quarter of a tank remained, the problem would be less urgent than if the gas gauge were on empty. Next, compare your recognition of the problem about replacing your old CD player and tuner with your recognition of the problem of acquiring a career wardrobe. In all probability, one of these problems would be more important to you, and thus you would be more motivated to solve it first.

Problem Solving

The next two stages in the consumer shopping/purchasing model—active information gathering (or search) and evaluation of alternatives—will determine the degree of problem solving that occurs. Individuals solve problems by searching for information and by evaluating their options or alternatives. The search for information and careful evaluation of alternatives occurs to reduce risk. If consumers do not select the best product, they can incur financial loss (financial risk), personal harm (safety risk), or decline of respect from family and friends (social risk). The amount of problem-solving activity consumers engage in varies considerably depending on their prior experience and the need to reduce financial, personal, and social risk. Consumers learn quickly, and once they find the product brands and retailers that are good at satisfying their needs at a low or acceptable risk level, the degree of problem solving decreases. Exhibit 3.10 illustrates three levels of problem solving. Note that these levels are determined by whether or not the consumer has a strong preference for a specific brand and retail store.

Habitual Problem Solving   With **habitual problem solving,** the consumer relies on past experience and learning to convert the problem into a situation in which less thought is required. The consumer has a strong preference for the brand to buy and the retailer from which to purchase it. Some consumers are not only habitual users of products but also heavy users. For instance, in fast food restaurants the heavy user is only one in five persons; however, heavy users account for 60 percent of fast food restaurant visits.[21] Using past experience, the consumer has arrived at an adequate solution for many consumer problems. Frequently purchased products of relatively low cost and low risk tend to belong in this category (e.g., toothpaste, milk, bread, soda pop); however, products of higher value may also be in this category. For example, when confronted with the need for a new automobile, some people can be loyal to both

Exhibit 3.10	Degrees of Consumer Problem Solving in Shopping/Purchasing

Brand Preference / Retailer Preference	Strong	None or Weak
Strong	Habitual Problem Solving	Limited Problem Solving
None or Weak	Limited Problem Solving	Extended Problem Solving

a particular brand and a specific retailer. Such an individual may be loyal to Ford, as well as having a favorite Ford dealer in their geographic area they patronize.

Limited Problem Solving

Limited problem solving occurs when the consumer has a strong preference for either the brand or the store, but not both. The consumer may not have a store choice in mind but may have a strong preference or may even have decided on the brand to purchase. Because the brand has been determined, the consumer has, in a sense, restricted the problem-solving process to deciding which retailers to patronize among those that carry the brand. Because the consumer may not know all the retailers that carry the item, some searching may be required. To illustrate, assume your TV fails and you decide to get a new one. You know that you want a Sony portable set, but because you are new in town, you do not know where to get the best buy. Also you recognize that your search does not need to be limited to retailers in your community and the Internet can help you locate the retailer with the lowest price. You prefer a local retailer who can service your set; however, you have decided that this additional convenience is not worthwhile if the local retailer has a price more than 10 percent above what an out-of-town retailer would charge for the set. Although we refer to this category as limited problem solving, there may be extensive decision making in regard to deciding which brand or store to select. Problem solving should be viewed as a continuum.

> **Limited problem solving** occurs when the consumer has a strong preference for either the brand or the store, but not both.

Extended Problem Solving

Extended problem solving occurs when the consumer recognizes a problem but has decided on neither the brand nor the store. For example, a woman in her early twenties has recently received a promotion and a 25 percent raise from the bank that employs her. Over the past year, she has postponed purchasing several major durable goods that she wants—a car, living room furniture, and a DVD player. With the 25 percent raise, she can afford some, but not all, of those items. She has little prior information and experience regarding alternative brands and retailers that sell these products, therefore she must engage in extensive problem solving to select the products she should buy, to determine which are the appropriate brands, and to learn which retail outlets carry what she wants. Extensive problem solving typically involves infrequently purchased expensive products of high risk. Here,

> **Extended problem solving** occurs when the consumer recognizes a problem but has decided on neither the brand nor the store.

the consumer desires a lot of new information, which implies a need for extensive problem solving.

Problem Solving Stages

Once consumers recognize that a problem exists and believe a potential solution involves going to the marketplace to purchase a product or service, then they will engage in problem solving. The first step is **active information gathering,** which is when consumers proactively gather information. Consumers are then confronted with a second stage in problem solving, which is the evaluation of alternatives. The evaluation of alternatives typically involves three stages:

Active information gathering
occurs when consumers proactively gather information.

Attributes
refers to the characteristics of the store and its products and services.

1. Development of a set of attributes on which the purchase decision will be based. The set of **attributes** refers to the characteristics of the store and its products and services. In fact, a store and its products and services can be thought of as a bundle or set of attributes, which can include such things as price, product quality, store hours, knowledgeable sales help, convenient parking, after-sale service, and so on. These attributes are often based on general information sources such as preexisting knowledge, advertising, discussions with friends and relatives, and reading magazines such as *Consumer Reports*, as well as the many information sources on-line.

2. In the second stage, consumers narrow the consideration set to a more manageable number of attributes. Although, consumers want to think that they have considered a wide range of options so as not to miss a golden opportunity, they do not want to be confused by a myriad of options. In the second stage, consumers might visit stores or browse on-line to gather more specific information, including price ranges, to narrow their list.

3. In the final stage, consumers directly compare the key attributes of the alternatives remaining on their short list. Here, consumers are very active in their search for specific information and often begin ascertaining actual prices through either store visits, browsing the web, or preliminary negotiating when appropriate.

One of the most important variables of problem solving is the information resources used by consumers. It is important for retailers to understand what information resources their target market prefers to use, then match their communication programs to these variables.

Purchase

Based on information gathered and evaluated in the problem-solving stage, the consumer decides which product and retailer to choose. Of course, a possible outcome of the problem-solving stage is a decision not to buy or to delay the purchase. A consumer might conclude that an adequate product or service isn't available or that the cost (financial or otherwise) is greater than previously thought. Although the consumer has not made a purchase, the information he or she has gathered is often mentally recorded and influences future shopping processes.

The purchase stage may include final negotiation, application for credit if necessary, and determination of the terms of purchase (cash, credit card, etc.). Sometimes last-minute unexpected factors can intervene during the transaction phase to preempt the purchase. For instance, the consumer can become aware of unanticipated costs such as taxes, delivery charges, or other items and decide not to buy.

Retailers often use the purchase stage as an opportunity to use suggestion selling to sell add-on or related products such as extended service warranties, batteries for toys, or impulse items. Both on-line and brick & mortar retailers use this technique. For instance, once you select books to purchase at Amazon.com, the company suggests other titles you might be interested in purchasing. If handled properly, consumers view this selling practice as a customer service, as if the retailer were looking out for the customer's long-term satisfaction. On the other hand, if handled poorly, the customer can view this as an attempt to gouge them. In extreme cases, the customer may even decide to cancel the initial transaction.

Post-Purchase Evaluation

The consumer shopping and purchase process does not end with the purchase. Ultimately, consumers are buying solutions to their perceived needs, and successful retailers take an active interest in ensuring that customers feel satisfied over the long term that their need has been resolved. The consumer's use and evaluation is therefore a critical, although sometimes overlooked, stage in the consumer behavior process.

The first important moment in the use and evaluation stage is immediately after the transaction, in the first hours and days during which the consumer uses the product or service. During this critical time, consumers form lasting impressions regarding the soundness of their purchase decision that in turn influences all future purchase decisions. If the consumer is dissatisfied, a condition can emerge known as **post-purchase resentment,** in which the consumer's dissatisfaction results in resentment toward the retailer.

If post-purchase resentment is not identified and rectified by the retailer, it can have a long-term negative influence on the retailer's ability to recapture the consumer as a satisfied customer because a satisfied customer tells a few friends, whereas a dissatisfied customer tells a dozen, or in an on-line chat room or Internet complaint site the unhappy customer can spread his or her story to millions. Consequently, it is less expensive to take care of a dissatisfied customer than it is to convert a noncustomer into a customer. Fortunately, if the retailer is proactive in its customer satisfaction program and responds quickly to budding resentment, it can be overcome. The problem is that many unhappy consumers do not report their dissatisfaction, so retailers must be vigilant in their monitoring of customer satisfaction. This process begins with the establishment of proactive policies such as full-satisfaction guarantees, which should be boldly communicated to the shopper. This tells consumers that if they do have a problem, the retailer wants to hear about and rectify it. Beyond this, many retailers have started customer follow-up programs, such as customer satisfaction reply cards, given out at the time of purchase or mailed to the customer several days later. Electronic cash registers have aided in this process by efficiently gathering the names, addresses, and telephone numbers of customers, recording the merchandise purchased, and automatically mailing the customer satisfaction surveys. It is important that retailers seek to find out why some past customers no longer shop at their stores.

Many large retailers—especially chains in which individual stores are not under central control, such as franchises and dealerships—have taken this customer satisfaction process one step further. They have instituted programs that measure customer satisfaction on an ongoing basis and compare customer service ratings of individual retail locations against preestablished benchmarks or a chainwide average.

Post-purchase resentment
arises when after the purchase the consumer becomes dissatisfied with the product, service, or retailer and thus begins to regret that the purchase was made.

Student Study Guide

Summary

This chapter concentrated on how, in order to satisfy the consumer, the retailer must continuously monitor the changes in the environment that affect consumer demand. It should be clear that the rapid changes occurring in the environment demand both sensitive management and good retail information systems in the retail industry. Retailers need managers who can provide leadership in meeting the challenges of, and likewise profiting from, the opportunities these changes present.

LO•1   Explain the importance of population trends on retail planning.

We began Chapter 3 with a discussion of the major population trends occurring in the United States today and their implications for the future of retailing. These trends include a slowing down of the population growth rate, a changing age distribution as America ages, the geographic shifting of the population to the South and West, the growth of large urban centers, and ever-increasing consumer mobility.

LO•2   What social trends should be monitored and what are their impacts on retailing?

Five major social trends and their implications for how retail managers must deal with these changes were discussed. These five trends were the increasing educational levels of consumers, the changing state of marriage (including the expanding never-married population), the effect of higher divorce rates, the changing makeup of the American household, and changes in the nature and importance of an individual's work.

LO•3   How do the changing American economic trends affect retailing?

The chapter next considered the effects of income growth, level of personal savings, women in the labor force, the widespread use of credit, and their impact on retailing in the 21st century.

LO•4   What is involved in the shopping/purchasing model, including the key stages in the buying process?

Shopping and purchasing can be viewed as a six-stage process. A stimulus (stage 1) triggers problem recognition (stage 2), which leads to problem solving. Problem solving consists of two stages: active information gathering or search (stage 3) and evaluation of alternatives (stage 4). The degree of problem solving can vary from habitual, which occurs when the consumer already has a strong preference for the brand and the retailer from which to purchase it, to extended problem solving, which occurs when the consumer has not decided on the brand or the store. Evaluation of alternatives can lead to purchase (stage 5) and finally purchase is followed by post-purchase evaluation (stage 6).

Terms to Remember

customer satisfaction
customer services
market segmentation
population variables

conspicuous consumption
micromarketing merchandising
metropolitan statistical areas
boomerang effect

disposable income
discretionary income
stimulus
drive
passive information gathering
problem recognition

habitual problem solving
limited problem solving
extended problem solving
active information gathering
set of attributes
post-purchase resentment

Review and Discussion Questions

LO•1 **Explain the importance of population trends on retail planning.**

1. Is it important for a retailer to understand that baby boomers are different from both Gen Xers and Gen Yers in their shopping behavior? Is there one example from current events that you can use to emphasize your argument?

2. What type of retailers would be most affected by changes in the age distribution of the population?

3. Compare your lifestyle with that of your parents. What opportunities do any differences present for different types of retailers?

4. What actions should retailers take in the face of slower population growth?

LO•2 **What social trends should be monitored and what are their impact on retailing?**

5. What are the short- and long-term retailing implications of people delaying marriage to a later age?

6. Should a retailer care about a changing trend such as the delay or even postponement of marriage by modern Americans? After all, how does an increase in the average age of a first marriage affect women's apparel retailing? Restaurant retailing? E-tailing?

7. A recent survey found that employees are less loyal to their employers than in the past. What actions can retailers take to reduce turnover among retail employees?

LO•3 **How do the changing American economic trends affect retailing?**

8. Should retailers be concerned about the recent decline in the personal savings rate? Does the behavior of the stock market affect purchase decisions?

9. How does a trend, such as the increasing number of working women, affect women's apparel retailing? Recreational retailing? Grocery retailing?

10. How are global lifestyles different than U.S. lifestyles?

LO•4 **What is involved in the consumer behavior model, including the key stages in the buying process?**

11. Why is the shopping/purchase behavior model presented in the text called a process model? Explain how this would affect a retailer's actions.

12. Does a consumer begin the shopping/purchase process at the need recognition stage?

13. Why should a retailer care about a customer after a sale has already been made?

Sample Test Questions

LO•1 Which of the following statements regarding current U.S. population trends is correct?

a. The baby boomers are now moving into their thirties and forties.

b. Americans change their residences about a dozen times in their lifetimes.

c. Markets with fewer than 50,000 people do not present many opportunities for retailers.

d. The fertility rate today in the United States is at an all-time high.

e. The country's total population is expected to grow at a record rate during the first half of the 21st century.

LO•2 The boomerang effect is a relatively new phenomenon that describes

a. the recent trend for firms to seek bankruptcy protection

b. the way styles from years ago come back as today's most popular styles

c. the recent trend of children returning to live with their parents after having already moved out

d. the use of price as the main means to attract new customers

e. the recent trend of having most companies report losses for the current quarter

LO•3 Discretionary income is

a. all personal income after taxes and retirement savings

b. all personal income after savings

c. all personal income minus the money needed for necessities food, clothing, housing, and so on

d. all personal income after taxes minus the money needed for necessities

e. all personal income after taxes

LO•4 The final stage of the consumer shopping/purchase model around which all other stages revolves is the

a. buy decision stage

b. active information gathering stage

c. purchase stage

d. post-purchase evaluation stage

e. payment stage

Applications

Writing and Speaking Exercise   You have recently been hired as the assistant manager for a large regional mall in Sacramento, California. One of the first things you notice on an early inspection tour of the mall is a lack of benches in the common areas for seniors and parents with children to sit on so that they can rest while shopping. It is said that benches reduce the selling area that the mall can rent to various temporary vendors, such as arts-and-crafts shows. You also find a memo from your predecessor banning the early opening of the mall commons so that elderly exercise groups cannot use the mall for walking and exercise classes. Prepare a one-page memo agreeing or disagreeing with the current mall policy and explaining your reasoning.

Retail Project   By the time you read this chapter, much of the demographic data mentioned in it will be outdated. You can get up-to-date data one of two ways. You can go to the government document section of your local library and use the most current issue of the *Statistical Abstract of the United States*, or you can use your computer to connect with the Census Bureau's web site (www.census.gov). A series of easy directions will guide you to the most current available data for any geographic area—from the entire nation to any county or town in any state. You can easily specify what kind of information you want. Also since the census does more than just count people, you can obtain breakdowns by different variables than the ones used in this chapter; including occupation, home value, and even households with indoor plumbing.

Case   Med-Center Drugstore

There are three Med-Center Drugstores operating in Rio Bravo, Texas. Until the past five years, Rio Bravo had basically been a retirement town, with adults over the age of 60 accounting for the largest segment of the population. This situation made it fairly simple for Med-Center Drugstores to target and serve the senior citizen market. Recently, though, the area has experienced a migration of young families and middle-aged couples who wanted to escape the city life. Whereas 50 percent of the population had once been in the 60-years-and-over category, the 35 to 45 years age group and the senior citizens group now each share 35 percent.

Older consumers originally had been attracted to Med-Center Drugstores because they did not have to worry about dealing with many children when shopping, they knew that they would not have to wait in long checkout lines, and they would not have difficulty maneuvering themselves or their carts in the extra-wide aisles. Many of these attractions no longer exist. Families with young children have become regular customers of the stores, store traffic has been increasing, and aisle widths have shrunk so that additional shelves could be installed as a means of displaying more merchandise and, ultimately, generating more sales.

Albert Clemens, president of the company that owns the drugstores, realizes that if the stores continue to operate as they are presently, there is a distinct possibility that older customers will begin shopping elsewhere. Although he wishes to continue to cater to the loyal senior citizen customers who helped Med-Center Drugstores achieve its current success, he does not want to ignore the potentially lucrative baby boomer market that is beginning to form in Rio Bravo. As Clemens's assistant, you are to consider and answer the following questions:

1. Should Med-Center Drugstores concentrate on only the baby boomer or on the senior citizen market? Both? Neither? Explain your position.

2. What types of marketing strategies could Med-Center Drugstores implement that would meet the needs of both age groups?

3. How might the changing marketplace affect Med-Center Drugstores merchandise assortment? What types of merchandise might management want to add, delete, or expand?

4. Should Med-Center Drugstores open an on-line store to target this market?

Planning Your Own Retail Business   In this chapter you learned that how broadly or how selectively you define your market is a major determinant of performance in retailing. In planning your retail business it will be important that you develop your retail marketing strategy to appeal to a particular market—either broadly or narrowly defined. For example, a women's apparel store could cater to all age groups, professional working women, or teens; it could also target various income groups such as low, moderate, or high income. Further, it could target women of different sizes from petite to full figured.

Assume for the store you are planning that there are 20,000 households in your community and these are within a reasonable driving distance of your store. You have determined that if you broadly define your store's market, that 75 percent of households in the community would be shoppers at the store and shop there an average of 2.7 times per year. On the other hand, if you define your market much more selectively by focusing on a well-defined niche, you estimate only 28 percent of households would shop at the store but they would shop an average of 9.2 times annually.

In this situation would a broadly or more narrowly defined market create more customer visits to the store? (*Hint:* Total store visitors, also referred to as traffic, is equal to the total number of households in the market multiplied by the proportion that would shop at the store multiplied by their average shopping frequency.) What other factors should you consider in deciding how narrowly or broadly to define your market?

Endnotes

1. The material in this section is taken from the most recent data and estimates available from various government publications.
2. "Six Billion Served" *American Demographics*, June 1999: 14–15.
3. *Vision for the New Millennium* (Atlanta: Kurt Salmon Associates, 1996).
4. Cynthia G. Wagner, "The Centenarians Are Coming," *The Futurist*, May 1999: 16–21.
5. "Targeting Tomorrow's Consumers," *Progressive Grocer*, July 1998: 55–58, and "Generation Y," *Business Week*, February 15, 1999: 81–88.
6. "Older Consumers Don't Believe You," *Advertising Age*, August 14, 1995: 14.
7. "Tapping the Graying Market," *Shopping Centers Today*, February 1996: 1, 22.
8. "Generation Y," *Business Week*, February 15, 1999: 80–88.
9. "Xtreme Retailing," *Business Week*, December 20, 1999: 120–128.
10. "A Bigger Family Stays Closer to the Nest," *Wall Street Journal*, April 1, 1994: B1.
11. "My Daughter, the PhD," *Business Week*, March 27, 2000: 30.
12. "Where the Boys Aren't," *U.S. News & World Report*, February 8, 1999: 47–55.
13. "Going the Distance," *American Demographics*, September 1999: 59–64.
14. For a complete discussion of the consumer's behavior, especially differences between male and female shoppers, see Paco Underhill, *Why We Buy* (New York: Simon & Schuster, 1999).
15. Carol Leonetti Dannhauser," Who's in the Home Office?" *American Demographics*, June 1999: 50–56.
16. "Turnover Costs Sack Retailers," *Chain Store Age*, March 2000: 100–102.
17. "The Rich Get Richer," *U.S. News & World Report*, February 21, 2000: 39–46.

18. Jean C. Darian, "In-Home Shopping: Are There Consumer Segments?" *Journal of Retailing*, Summer 1987: 163–186.
19. "Riding High on the Market," *American Demographics*, April 2000: 45–54
20. "A Penny Earned Is a Penny Spent Nowadays," *U.S. News & World Report*, March 22, 1999: 49.
21. "Hamburger Joints Call Them 'Heavy Users'—But Not to Their Face," *Wall Street Journal*, January 12, 2000: A1, A10.

With the birth and rapid growth of e-tailing, the competitive playing field in retailing has intensified.

Evaluating the Competition in Retailing

Overview

The behavior of competitors is an important component of the retail planning and management model. Effective planning and execution in any retail setting cannot be accomplished without the proper analysis of competitors. In this chapter, we begin by reviewing the various models of retail competition. The types of competition in retailing are described next. We then discuss the evolution of retail competition. Finally, we examine the upcoming retail revolution in nonstore retailing, developing retail formats, global and technological changes, and the use of private labels as a strategic weapon.

Learning Objectives

After reading this chapter you should be able to

1. explain the various models of retail competition
2. distinguish between various types of retail competition
3. describe the three theories used to explain the evolution of retail competition
4. describe the changes that could affect retail competition

<table>
<tr><td>LO • 1

What are the various models of retail competition?</td><td></td></tr>
</table>

Models of Retail Competition

In this chapter we look at the effects of competition on a retailer's performance. As noted in Chapter 1, retailing was once a growth industry that was able to increase profits solely on the basis of an increasing population base. Today's slower population growth rates have turned retailing into a business where successful regional and national retailers can only grow by taking sales away from competitors. The opposite is true, however, when discussing retail competition at the local level. Here, as a result of the makeup of the area's economy, the area's population and disposable income could be growing even while the country's is slowing. Consider, for example, what is occurring in California's Silicon Valley area. The computer has made this America's top growth market. Here a retailer could grow without having to take sales away from a competitor. Just the opposite would occur in those areas, such as Mansfield and Youngstown, Ohio, which are experiencing an economic slowdown.

Nevertheless, a high-profit retailer must always be on the offensive by studying the changing competitive environment, especially its local competition, and differentiating itself from that competition. Only by establishing a differential advantage that is extremely difficult in terms of time and money for others to follow, will a retailer reap all the rewards the industry offers. Prime examples of such differentiation are category killers, such as Home Depot and Lowes, with their large selection, Wal-Mart with a technologically advanced distribution system that enables it to operate with significantly lower operating costs than its competitors, Amazon with its significant presence on the Internet, and the Walt Disney Company (highlighted in this chapter's Service Retailing box) with its excellent customer service. A retailer's performance will be substandard if it is always forced to copy the actions of others and isn't able to differentiate itself. This, however, does not mean that a retailer should not pay close attention to what the competition is doing. Only by visiting the neighboring Wal-Mart, Target, or Kmart, will the small local retailer know what items the discounters are carrying and what they are not. These large discounters usually carry only a limited selection within

High-profit retailers develop strategic plans that provide them a differential advantage that competitors can only overcome with a substantial investment of time and money.

Service Retailing

Disney: Retailing's Benchmark for Service

Throughout the world, when one speaks of theme parks, one name comes to mind: Disney. Disney's service is not only the best in the theme park industry, but is also considered to be the best overall by many retail experts. It is for this reason that many service retailers throughout the world use the service at Disney theme parks as a benchmark of excellence. Further, it is this quality of service that has supported Disney's global expansion efforts by spreading the "pixie dust," or the "Disney magic," from California to Tokyo.

At the heart of Disney's success is its commitment to pioneering service concepts in the theme park industry. Disney research indicated that one area of service improvement in the parks was related to the length of lines. Although Disney is renowned for pioneering the concept of line management (through the use of themed areas to entertain guests during their wait for an attraction), Disney insiders knew it could be done better. One outcome of Disney's commitment to service is the Fastpass system, which was recently introduced on Disney's most popular attractions throughout Walt Disney World in Florida.

The Fastpass system was designed to increase customer satisfaction and smooth ride demand during peak seasons. Here's how it works: In front of Disney's most popular attractions, a clock shows the estimated wait time as well as a specified time period that a customer can return to visit the attraction if they decide to use the Fastpass system. Let's say that you enter the Animal Kingdom at 11 a.m. and find a long line at Kilimanjaro Safaris (with a wait of over an hour), and the Fastpass return time is between 1 p.m. and 2 p.m. If you decide to use the Fastpass system, you simply insert your theme park ticket into the Fastpass dispenser. Out pops your theme park ticket as well as your Fastpass ticket for Kilimanjaro Safaris. Then you are free to visit other theme park attractions instead of waiting in line. When you return to Kilimanjaro Safaris during your designated time (between 1 p.m. and 2 p.m.), you'll enter through a Fastpass entrance and proceed to the boarding area with little or no wait. To maximize overall customer satisfaction, Disney limits each customer to one Fastpass ticket at a time. When one of the authors recently tested the Fastpass system at Space Mountain at the Magic Kingdom, waiting in line would have taken just over one hour. However, with the Fastpass the author and his family were able to visit three other attractions before returning at the specified time. Less than 10 minutes later they were on board Space Mountain. Has this increased the industry service standard once again? You bet it has.

a product category. Rather than saying he or she would never be caught dead in a Wal-Mart, it is to the small appliance store owner's benefit to know which televisions the discounter is carrying. This way, as was pointed out in the Retailing: The Inside Story box in Chapter 1, the retailer can match the price on similar units and offer better services and a more complete range of units.

Yet no retailer, however clever, can design a strategy that will totally insulate it from the competitive actions of others. This is true despite the fact that the retailer may have done an excellent job in developing and following its mission statement, setting its goals and objectives, and conducting its SWOT analysis. After all, some merchandising innovations can be easily copied and cannot be patented. Furthermore, the relatively low cost of entry into a retail business, in comparison to other businesses, means that retailers can count on being copied by others when they unveil a profitable strategy. The rapid growth of discount department stores, convenience stores, and e-tailer web sites attest to this fact.

If you plan to become a retailer, you must develop the talent for designing and implementing innovative competitive strategies. Furthermore, you need to recognize that in retailing, competition is a fact of life.

The Disney Fastpass Distribution System has shortened wait times for popular rides giving Disney theme parks a differential competitive advantage.

Competition in retailing, as in any other industry, involves the interplay of supply and demand. One cannot appreciate the nature and scope of competition in retailing by studying only the supply factors—that is, the type and number of competing retailers that exist. One must also examine the consumer demand factors highlighted in Chapter 3. Let's explore a formal framework for describing and explaining the competitive environment of retailing.

The Competitive Marketplace

Retailers generally compete for customers on a local level, unless they are catalog or electronic retailers. Household members will typically not travel beyond local markets to purchase the goods they desire. When they do travel beyond local markets, however, it is usually because their city or town is too small to support retailers with the selection of merchandise that the consumer desires. Although some customers will always want to shop out of town, most cities with a population over 50,000 can provide the consumer with sufficient selection in almost all lines of merchandise. In cities with fewer than 50,000 citizens, household members may need to travel to another town or city only for large purchases, such as a new automobile, television, furniture, or for a special item of clothing, such as a wedding dress.

> *Retailers that attempt to study and respond to the local retail competition will be more profitable than retailers who don't understand that national competitive trends don't always affect every market.*

Market Structure

Economists use four different economic terms to describe the competitive environment in the retailing industry: pure competition, pure monopoly, monopolistic competition, and oligopolistic competition.

Pure competition occurs when a market has the following:

1. Homogeneous (similar) products.
2. Many buyers and sellers, all having perfect knowledge of the market.
3. Ease of entry for both buyers and sellers—that is, new retailers can start up with little difficulty and new consumers can easily come into the market.

In pure competition, each retailer faces a horizontal demand curve and must sell its products at the going "market" or equilibrium price. To sell at a lower price would be foolish, because you could always get the market price. Of course, you could not sell your product at a higher price.

The second type of economic environment does not occur too often in real life. In **pure monopoly,** the seller is the only one selling the product under question and will set its selling price accordingly. Nonetheless, as the retailer seeks to sell more units, the retailer must lower the selling price. This is because consumers who already have one unit will tend to place a lower value on an additional unit. This is called "the law of diminishing returns" or "declining marginal utility." After all, a hot fudge sundae would taste great right now, but would the second, third, or tenth one, purchased and consumed today, be as satisfying as the first?

Monopolistic competition is a market situation that develops when a market has the following:

1. Different (heterogeneous) products in the eyes of consumers that are still substitutable for each other. Here two or more retailers may be selling the same product, but one retailer is able to differentiate itself by providing better service. Thus, consumers perceive the retailers to be selling different products.
2. Sellers who feel that even though they may be the only ones selling a particular brand, they do face competition from other retailers selling similar goods.

The word *monopolistic* means that each seller is trying to control its own segment of the market. However the word *competition* means that there are substitutes for the product available, for example a Pepsi-Cola is a substitute for a Coca-Cola. The degree of the seller's control is dependent on the similarity of the competitor's product. This is

Pure competition
occurs when a market has homogenous products and many buyers and sellers, all having perfect knowledge of the market, and ease of entry for both buyers and sellers.

Commodities

Pure monopoly
occurs when there is only one seller for a product or service.

Monopolistic competition
occurs when the products offered are different, yet viewed as substitutable for each other and the sellers recognize that they compete with sellers of these different products.

why with monopolistic competition the retailer attempts to differentiate itself by the products or services it offers. Some of the common means of achieving differentiation are by offering better customer service, credit, more convenient parking, larger merchandise selection, cleanliness, free setup and delivery, and so on, as well as with the brand or store image created and developed through advertising.

Oligopolistic competition occurs when a market has the following:

1. Essentially homogeneous products, such as air travel.
2. Relatively few sellers or many small firms who always follow the lead of the few large firms.
3. The expectation that any action by one party will be noticed and reacted to by the other parties in the market.

As in pure competition, oligopolists face a long-run trend toward selling at a similar price, because everybody knows what the others are doing. Nonprice competition, relying on product or service differences other than price, is extremely difficult because consumers view the products and services as essentially similar. This is why when sell-

---

Oligopolistic competition
occurs when relatively few sellers, or many small firms who follow the lead of a few larger firms, offer essentially homogeneous products and any action by one seller is expected to be noticed and reacted to by the other sellers.

At a local level, most gasoline stations face oligopolistic competition since gasoline is essentially homogeneous, there are few sellers in each neighborhood, and price changes by one retailer will be quickly matched by the other retailers.

ing retail airline tickets, the major airlines such as American Airline and Delta almost always match each other's prices on identical travel routes.

Retailing can be characterized as monopolistic or, in rare cases, oligopolistic competition. The distinction between monopolistic competition and oligopolistic competition lies in the number of sellers. An oligopoly means there are few sellers, so any action by one is noticed and reacted to by the others. Conventional economic thought suggests that for an oligopoly to occur, the top four firms have to account for over 60 to 80 percent of the market. Although some national retailers do have large market shares (for example, in 1998, the top ten on-line retailers accounted for 43 percent of total on-line retail sales),[1] oligopolistic competition does not actually occur on a national level. However, it is common at a local level, especially in smaller communities, for food stores and department or discount department stores to operate as oligopolists. However, if prices become too high, merchandise selection too limited, or services too poor, residents of these communities will travel to larger communities to shop. This is known as **outshopping**. However, even when retailing becomes concentrated at the local level, there are several checks on the retailers' power:

> The country is full of automobiles, so most customers have large numbers of alternatives. Moreover, many modern retailers are becoming less specialized. The supermarket that sells nylons and the drugstore where you cannot find the drug counter are famous. Any seller who tries to maintain high prices is apt to find the grocers or the gas stations or someone equally far removed trying to take over his profitable lines. At any rate, there seems to be a continuous supply of new shopkeepers, ready to appear whenever prospects are good, and often even when they are not. It takes a good deal more to break into such fields as food retailing than it once did, but the cost of entry is still much lower than in most concentrated segments of manufacturing.[2]

In addition, one of the checks on a retailer at a local level is mail-order shopping or shopping over the Internet. If prices at department and specialty stores were to become too excessive, then local shoppers may increase their use of nonstore shopping alternatives.

The Demand Side of Retailing

Most retailers face monopolistic competition, and we assume such a market structure in the remainder of the text. In a monopolistically competitive market, the retailer will be confronted with a negatively sloping demand curve. That is, consumers will demand a higher quantity as price is lowered. The typical retailer thus faces a demand function as shown in Exhibit 4.1.[3]

Higher prices, in most cases, result in less demand, because households have limited incomes and many alternatives for allocating those dollars. If a retailer raises prices, and all else remains unchanged, then households will try to shift some of their purchasing power to other retailers with lower prices. This should suggest to you that retailers cannot be profitable by setting prices at the highest possible levels. Retailers will find it necessary to set prices somewhere below the maximum possible price but above zero. As prices approach zero, the retailer will sell large quantities but not generate sufficient revenue to cover costs. This implies that the retailer will not sell the maximum quantity. But where should retailers set prices? It seems reasonable that retailers would want to set prices to maximize profits over the long run. To do so, however, they need knowledge of their costs, and this involves an examination of supply factors.

outshopping
occurs when individuals in one community travel usually to a larger community to shop.

Exhibit 4.1	Demand as a Function of Price

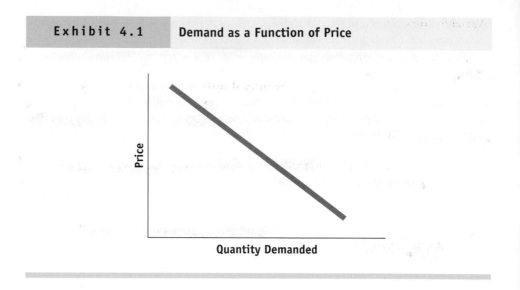

The Supply Side of Retailing

Fixed costs
are those that the retailer incurs regardless of the quantity of goods or services sold.

Retailers cannot operate without incurring costs, which can be classified as fixed or variable. These costs are portrayed graphically in Exhibit 4.2. **Fixed costs** are those that the retailer incurs regardless of the quantity of goods or services sold. These costs are in most part related to the size of the store and the costs of maintenance and finance, regardless of whether the store is open or closed. Examples of fixed costs in retailing include insurance, taxes, rent or lease payments, technology systems, and security guards.

Exhibit 4.2	Cost Functions in Retailing

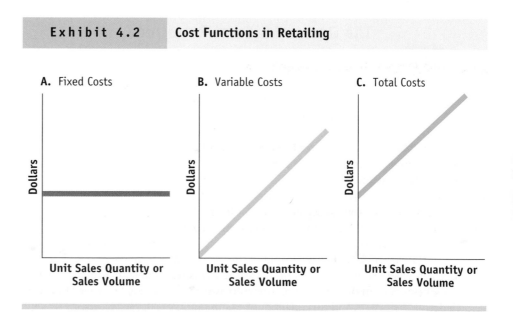

Variable costs are those that increase proportionately with sales volume. The two largest variable costs in retailing are the cost of the goods or services sold and some wages, such as commissions.

Without a doubt, not all of the costs of operating a retail store can be categorized strictly into fixed and variable costs. **Semifixed costs** are constant over a range of sales volume, but past a crucial point they increase to a higher plateau and then again remain constant at another higher sales volume range. For example, labor may be viewed as semifixed. Before the doors of the store can be opened each day, a staff of employees must be on hand, but as store traffic volume rises past a crucial point, more employees would need to be added because the existing staff would be inadequate.

Regardless of the exact form of the retailer's cost function, these costs must be examined in order to set a profit maximizing price.

Variable costs
are those that increase proportionately with sales volume.

Semifixed costs
are constant over a range of sale volume, but past a crucial point they increase to a higher plateau and then again remain constant at another higher sales volume range.

The Profit-Maximizing Price

A profit-maximizing price seeks to get as much profit as possible from the sale of each unit sold. In this situation the retailer seeks to charge a price in which the marginal revenue (the change in total revenue that results from the sale of one more unit) is equal to the marginal costs (the change in total costs that results from the sale of one more unit). If the marginal revenue (MR) is greater than the marginal cost (MC) for a grocery store selling milk, then the store will increase total profits by selling one more unit, or gallon, of milk. Likewise, if MC is greater than MR for that extra gallon of milk, then the store will reduce total profits by selling it. This doesn't mean the store will lose money by selling that extra gallon, only that profits will be lowered. Part of the reason for this phenomenon is that the store can't sell milk at different prices to different customers. If the store wants to sell extra milk it has to lower the price not just for a single customer but for all customers, or at least for a segment (for example, giving senior citizens or students a discount with special coupons).

Nonprice Decisions

All too often retailers believe that they must always compete on price—that is, they must always match or be lower than the competitor's price. In fact, that is not always the case. Many customers place a value on attributes other than price when selecting a place to shop. After all, why do some consumers choose to pick up a loaf of bread at a convenience store when it is cheaper at a supercenter or supermarket? The answer is that these customers want convenience because they have placed a value on their time. Therefore, the retailer has to make decisions about the other elements of the retail mix (merchandise mix, advertising and promotion, customer services and selling, and store layout and design) in order to influence the quantity of merchandise it sells and the profit level it achieves. If store location is fixed (the retailer has a long-term lease) in a poor location, some of the nonprice variables available are advertising, special promotions, personal selling, and store atmosphere. These nonprice variables are directed at enlarging the retailer's demand by drawing in more customers. One recent study by *Progressive Grocer* found that the most important criterion for selecting a supermarket was cleanliness. Other essential criteria in addition to low prices, were accurate scanners, having prices clearly labeled, friendly checkout clerks, and fresh products.[4]

Another advantage of using nonprice variables as a means of competing is that price is the easiest variable for the competition to copy. All the competitor has to do is change the price scanner and the shelf marker if it is a brick & mortar retailer or adjust the prices on its web site if it is an e-tailer. Therefore, retailers who rely primarily on price to gain an advantage may be creating a no-win situation. In 1999, for example, *Advertising Age* reported that the six major on-line drugstores mounted such a price battle to gain new customers that they wound up spending $2 on ads for every $1 in revenue on products with very little profit margins.[5] What retailers really should be trying to do is to develop a differential advantage that will take the competition a great deal of time and money to match or overcome. Besides, using price as a weapon to gain loyal customers does not always work. In February 2000, CDNow offered a $10 coupon on its web site that could be used on any $15 purchase. The promotion was expensive because not only did the e-tailer lose $2.8 million for the quarter, but customer orders dropped substantially once the $10 offer was dropped.[6]

Dollars & Sense

Retailers that are able to remove themselves from price competition by using some other means of differentiating themselves will be higher profit retailers than those that aren't able to do this.

Consider some of the ways a retailer could make use of nonprice competition to achieve a protected niche:

1. The retailer could position itself as different from the competition by altering its merchandise mix in the direction of higher quality goods, great personal service, or specializing in a specific size range. (In **store positioning,** one identifies a well-defined market segment using demographic or lifestyle variables and appeals to this segment with a clearly differentiated approach.) This would increase the maximum price that consumers will pay and also increase the distance consumers would travel to shop for these goods, thereby enlarging the retailer's trade area. Marshall Field's, Neiman-Marcus, Nordstrom's and Lane Bryant have done an excellent job of positioning themselves using this strategy.

2. The retailer can offer private label merchandise that customers consider to be different in terms of value from its competition. Exhibit 4.3 lists the private labels for some of the major retailers. The strategy of using private label branding to secure a protected niche is discussed in detail at the end of this chapter.

3. The retailer could provide customers with free parking or gas, which would effectively lower transportation costs for customers; for example, one West Texas car dealer promotes the fact that he will fill any out-of-town shopper's gas tank, up to 20 gallons. The lower transportation costs would increase the distance the customer would be willing to travel to shop, thereby increasing the retailer's trade area.

4. The retailer could strive to always have its basic merchandise in stock. Consider a retailer, such as Nordstrom, who strives to always have men's dress shirts in stock and will give the consumer a free shirt if it is ever out of stock on the basic sizes. Now compare this policy with a competitor who only has key items in stock 95 percent of the time. If you go into this store to pick up just five items, the chances

Store positioning
is when a retailer identifies a well-defined market segment using demographic or lifestyle variables and appeals to this segment with a clearly differentiated approach.

| Exhibit 4.3 | Private Labels of Major Retailers | | | |

Wal-Mart	JCPenney	Target	Kmart	Sears
Sam's Choice	The Original Arizona Jean Co	Cherokee	Martha Stewart	Kenmore
Faded Glory	Worthington	Xhileration	Route 66	Craftsman
Equate	Jaquelin Ferrar	Honors	Thom McAn	Fieldmaster
Great Value	St. John's Bay	Merona	Benchtop	Apostrophe
Ol' Roy	Hunt Club	Trend Basics	Penske	Canyon River Blues
Riders	Stafford	Furio	Bass	Crossroads
Catalina	Towncraft	Greatland	Blues Clues	DieHard
Vasarette	USA Olympic	Michael Graves	Sesame Street	Kenmore Elite
GE (small appliances)	City Streets	Pro Spirit	Premiere	TKS Basics
McKids	Michael James	Utility		WeatherBeater
Spring Valley	New Moves			
Ever Active	Okie Dokie			
Ever Start				
White Cloud	**Nordstrom**	**Saks Fifth Avenue**		
Sam's American Choice	Norsport	The Works		
	Faconnable	SFA Collections		
	Baby N	Real Clothes		

are one in four that the store will be out of stock on at least one item (.95 × .95 × .95 × .95 × .95 = .773; therefore, the store will have all five of your desired items just 77.3 percent of the time).

Remember, most retail decision variables, whether price or nonprice, are directed at influencing demand. Of course, the profitability of the decisions depends on the marginal cost of the action versus the marginal revenue it generates.

Competitive Actions

We just saw that most retailers attract customers from a limited geographic area and that as prices are lowered this area expands. But even at a zero price, households can only afford to travel a certain distance to get the goods and services retailers offer. Therefore, in most cities there are several, if not many, retailers in each line of retail trade.

When too many retail establishments are competing in a particular city, the profitability of all the retailers will suffer. Eventually, some retailers may leave the market. If there are too few retailers, profits may be high enough to attract new retail competitors, or existing retailers may be enticed to expand. A market is in equilibrium in terms of number of retail establishments if the return on investment is high enough to justify keeping capital invested in retailing, but not so high as to invite more competition.

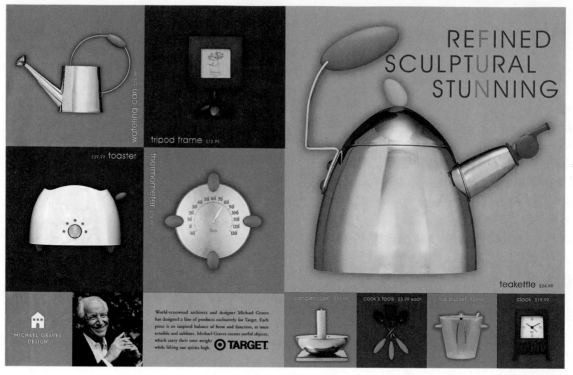

Target often uses private label merchandise so it will not have to compete directly with other discount department stores.

Overstored
is a condition in a community where the number of stores in relation to households is so large that to engage in retailing is usually unprofitable or marginally profitable.

Understored
is a condition in a community where the number of stores in relation to households is relatively low so that engaging in retailing is an attractive economic endeavor.

A good measure of competitive activity in a market is the number of retail establishments of a given type per thousand households. If the stores are of the same approximate size, then as the number of stores per thousand households increases, the degree of competition intensifies. This intensified competition will tend to decrease the retailer's profit. When the number of stores per household gets too large, the market can be characterized as **overstored**. However, if there is only a small number of stores per thousand households, in comparison to other markets, the market will be characterized as **understored**. Importantly, in overstored markets the average return on investment that retailers earn in that market is below what is needed to keep all of them doing business in that market and some will thus eventually exit the market. On the other hand, in understored markets the average return on investment that retailers earn in that market is above what is needed to keep all of them doing business in that market. This will in fact be an invitation for some retailers in the market to expand by opening more stores or for other retailers to enter this market.

Competition is most intense in overstored markets, because many retailers are achieving an inadequate return on investment. These retailers face a major performance imperative and will implement both price and nonprice actions in an all-out attempt to increase sales and profit levels. Because retailers operate in a relatively closed geographic market, with a fixed number of households and a limited number of dollars to compete for, any action by one retailer to increase its sales or profit level will warrant an action from competitors. (Although e-tailers are not exactly in a close geographic proximity to each other, they are close in the sense that they are accessible via an individual's computer. Thus, the early exit of many e-tailers in specific segments was the result of the Internet being overstored.)

Types of Competition

It is possible to merge the preceding discussion of competition in retailing with the classification schemes used by the Department of Commerce in conducting the Census of Retail Trade.

Intratype and Intertype Competition

Intratype competition occurs when two or more retailers of the same type, as defined by NAICS (North American Industrial Classification System) in the Census of Retail Trade, compete directly with each other for the same households. This is the most common type of retail competition: Circuit City competes with Best Buy; Avon competes with Mary Kay; Mail Boxes Etc. competes with Pack & Mail; Family Dollar competes with Dollar General; MCI WorldCom competes with AT&T for your phone service; and Amazon competes with Borders in the United States, and in Canada both compete with Chapters. Due to the changing nature of the retailing environment, retailers are often forced to change their strategy as their competition changes. For example, Sears, in the early 1990s wanted to compete head-on with low-priced discounters such as Wal-Mart and Kmart. Today, after doing its own SWOT analysis and concluding that consumers do not like to push shopping carts through malls, where most of its stores are located, it repositioned itself against the middle-of-the-road merchants JCPenney and May Department Stores by appealing to women and emphasizing apparel.

Recently, Kohl's moved into what had been Wal-Mart's territory (Denver and Dallas markets), the same way Wal-Mart moved into Kmart's trading areas a decade before. Also, many retailers have been competing by using a scrambled merchandising strategy. As discussed in Chapter 1, scrambled merchandising is when a retailer carries many different unrelated product lines as a means of enhancing the one-stop shopping convenience for its customers. Some examples include the following:

- Discount department stores (such as Kmart, Target, and Wal-Mart) are handling more cosmetics and fragrances, which were traditionally the province of the department stores. These discounters, as well as smaller operations like Pamida, are now handling refrigerated food items.
- Supermarkets (such as Albertsons, Kroger, and Food Giant) have taken market share away from fast-food restaurants with their Home Meal Replacements (HMRs). In addition, their banks and pharmacies have also changed the competitive landscape.
- Convenience food stores (such as 7-Eleven) are not only selling motor oil and related auto care products, but are adding fast-food, lottery tickets, and ATMs.

Every time different types of retail outlets sell the same lines of merchandise and compete for the same limited consumer dollars, **intertype competition** occurs. In each of the following examples, as intertype competition expanded, gross margins on the respective merchandise lines declined. For example, combination mail-order/on-line pharmacies have gained a growing share of prescription drugs. Their market share is now close to 20 percent, and the impact on the locally operated or chain-operated retail drugstore has been dramatic. Consequently, the average gross margin return on sales of drugs has declined due to this increased competition. This increased competition has caused both types of drug retailers to seek the lowest priced drugs available, as

Intratype competition occurs when two or more retailers of the same type, as defined by NAICS codes in the Census of Retail Trade, compete directly with each other for the same households.

Intertype competition occurs when two or more retailers of a different type, as defined by NAICS codes in the Census of Retail Trade, compete directly by attempting to sell the same merchandise lines to the same households.

Supermarkets are confronted by intense intertype competition from restaurants, fast food restaurants, and other places people can grab a bite to eat during their busy day.

different drug manufacturers produce virtually identical medicines for arthritis, ulcers, and other common ailments. As a result, the inflation rate for prescription drugs is the lowest of any medical category.

Furthermore, new retailers are always entering the marketplace creating greater intratype and intertype competition. As our E-tailing box describes, the Internet and eBay have made it possible for anyone to be an e-tailer.

Divertive Competition

Divertive competition occurs when retailers intercept or divert customers from competing retailers.

Another concept that helps to explain the nature of competition in retailing is **divertive competition.** This occurs when retailers intercept or divert customers from competing retailers. For example, an individual may recognize that she needs to get a birthday card for a relative and will probably do this the next time she visits the local shopping mall, which has a very well stocked Hallmark Card Store. However, one day while picking up a prescription at the drugstore she walks by the card stand and decides to purchase the greeting card at the drugstore. The drugstore retailer has intercepted this customer from the Hallmark store.

Another divertive ploy in use today is when a retailer adds a gas station on its property to catch those customers who have already stopped at the store and do not want to make another stop to get gas once they get on the highway to return home. Privately held Meijer's now sells gas at 103 of its 127 supercenters in the Midwest, and Wal-Mart sells gas at nearly 300 of its supercenters and discount stores.

Break-even point is where total revenues equal total expenses and the retailer is making neither a profit nor a loss.

To comprehend the significance of divertive competition, which can be either intertype or intratype competition, one needs to recognize that most retailers operate very close to the **break-even point** (the point where total revenues equal total expenses), but aren't really aware of this fact. For instance, supermarkets, with their extremely low gross margin return on sales, tend to have high break-even points, ranging from 94 to

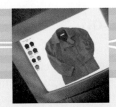

E-tailing

eBay Provides a New Arena for Microretailers

eBay, the on-line auction giant who has close to 6 million registered members/users and records more than 2.5 million auctions on any one given day, has become the new arena for "microretailers" to reach a global marketplace. Microretailers are small, one-or-two-person retail organizations.

Microretailers are not new. For example, microretailers specializing in hotdogs, pretzels, and other consumables can easily be observed operating in the downtown area of almost any major city. In the past, their relatively small trade area (restricted to a few city blocks) and merchandise assortment limited their competitive threat to more traditional retailers. However, the world is changing, and eBay is providing the arena for this dynamic competitive threat.

Imagine for a moment competing against the world's best-known retailers out of your living room. Omar Nuno, a Medicare specialist by day and owner of Grandwatches by night, is no longer imagining. After a long day of work he comes home to put listings for new brand-name watches, such as Seiko, Omega and others, for sale at eBay. His low overhead compared to other jewelry retailers allows him to offer deep discounts, thus providing him a competitive advantage in the high-margin world of high-quality watches.

Trading area you ask? Unlike microretailers in the brick & mortar world, on-line microretailers operate globally, as exemplified by the fact that Nuno has sold watches to customers around the world. Ebay provides a global reach and the global brand name to drive customers to a microretailer's doorstep, thus minimizing initial cash investments in virtual storefronts and advertising.

If you thought that eBay was just a glorified swap meet, consider the case of a California real estate broker who sold antiques in his spare time. After three years of selling antiques as a hobby, he wasn't extremely successful financially. However, within months of posting his antiques on eBay, his sales went through the roof. An antique peanut roaster that he bought for $250, and could not sell at the local antique mall, went for $2,950 on eBay. In just three short months his sales exceeded $70,000 of which about $30,000 was profit.

eBay is clearly revolutionizing the opportunities for microretailers. In as much, eBay can be credited with reinvigorating retailing in the world economy. The tremendous potential for not only financial freedom, but work flexibility, has everyone asking themselves not only "How much would someone pay for this stuff I don't want?" but "With the limited investment needed to sell items on-line, why haven't I become a microretailer already?"

Source: Based on "Can You Survive the eBay Economy?" *Inc.*, March 2000: 88–95, and the authors' own experiences with eBay.

96 percent of current sales. General merchandise retailers with a higher gross margin return on sales face lower break-even points of 85 to 92 percent of their current sales. In either case, a modest drop in sales volume could make these retailers unprofitable and fuel the growth of scrambled merchandising.

Retailers should attempt to operate at a sales volume of 20 percent above their break-even point because this will allow them to weather major competitive assaults and thus be able to achieve a higher profit over the long term.

Evolution of Retail Competition

LO • 3

What three theories are used to explain the evolution of retail competition?

Have you ever thought about how the various types of retailers you use have evolved to where they are today? Using the concepts of the evolution of retailing we can not only better understand the history of these retail formats, but we also may be able to make predictions about where they are going. Several theories have developed to explain and describe the evolution of competition in retailing. We review three of them briefly.

The Wheel of Retailing

Wheel of retailing theory describes how new types of retailers enter the market as low-status, low-margin, low-price operators; however, as they meet with success, these new retailers gradually acquire more sophisticated and elaborate facilities, and thus become vulnerable to new types of low-margin retail competitors who progress through the same pattern.

The **wheel of retailing theory,** illustrated in Exhibit 4.4, is one of the oldest descriptions of the patterns of competitive development in retailing.[7] This theory states that new types of retailers enter the market as low-status, low-margin, low-price operators. This is the entry phase and allows these retailers to compete effectively and take market share away from the more traditional retailers. However, as they meet with success, these new retailers gradually acquire more sophisticated and elaborate facilities, thereby becoming less efficient, in a trading-up phase. This creates both a higher investment and a subsequent rise in operating costs. Predictably, these retailers will enter the vulnerability phase and must raise prices and margins, becoming vulnerable to new types of low-margin retail competitors who progress through the same pattern. This appears to be the case today with outlet malls. Once bare-bones warehouses for manufacturers' imperfect or excess merchandise, outlet malls have quickly evolved into fancy, almost up-scale malls where retailers try to outdo each other's accent lighting, private dressing rooms, and generous return policies. As a result, with the cost of operating at such locations increasing and with the regular department stores becoming more competitive, there is now little difference in the outlet's prices and the department store's sale prices. Holiday Hospitality Corporations, which is owned by Bass, recognizing that it can become vulnerable by constantly upgrading its lodging units, has developed four distinct hotel/motel formats. Holiday Inn Express is targeted at the in-and-out business person or traveler who is willing to forgo some amenities for a lower price. Holiday Inn Select is similar to the Express but is aimed at the business traveler staying for a longer

Exhibit 4.4	**Wheel of Retailing**

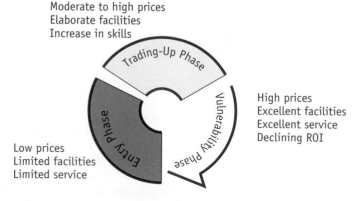

Moderate to high prices
Elaborate facilities
Increase in skills

Trading-Up Phase

High prices
Excellent facilities
Excellent service
Declining ROI

Vulnerability Phase

Entry Phase

Low prices
Limited facilities
Limited service

Holiday Inn is constantly developing and refining new retail formats so it can survive through the evolution of retail competition.

period of time who desires a few more amenities, such as dataport connections and conference rooms. The traditional Holiday Inn is targeted at the middle-class market and provides higher cost features such as a restaurant, a lounge, conference rooms, and a swimming pool. The Holiday Inn Crowne Plaza is targeted at the more upscale or serious business traveler and features luxurious furnishings and restaurants, health spas, business services, conference rooms, and other amenities. Realizing that consumers may have different lodging needs depending on the circumstances, Holiday Hospitality has tied these four formats together with the same loyalty program—the Priority Club.

The Retail Accordion

Several observers of the history of retailing have noted that retail institutions evolve from outlets that offer wide assortments to specialized stores that offer narrow assortments to their customers, and then return to the wide assortment stores to continue through the pattern again and again. This contraction and expansion of merchandise assortment suggests the term **retail accordion**.[8]

Retail accordion describes how retail institutions evolve from outlets that offer wide assortments to specialized stores and continue repeatedly through the pattern.

Retail historians have observed that, in the United States, retail trade was dominated by the general store until 1860. The general store carried a broad assortment of merchandise ranging from farm implements to textiles to food. After 1860, due to the growth of cities and roads, retail trade became more specialized and was concentrated in the central business districts of cities. By 1880 to 1890, department and specialty stores were the dominant competitive force. Both carried more specialized assortments than the general store. In the 1950s retailing began to move again to wider merchandise lines. Typical was the supermarket, which added produce and dairy products, nonfood items such as kitchen utensils, health and beauty aids, and small household appliances. Today specialization in merchandise categories once again became a dominant competitive strategy. Witness, for example, the recent success of Venator's (formally Woolworth's) Foot Locker stores, Barnes & Noble Bookstores, the spin-offs from The Limited of Intimate Brands (the Victoria's Secret division) and Abercrombie & Fitch Co. Even Wal-Mart is testing the idea of reducing store size and assortments with its new freestanding 40,000-square-foot Neighborhood Markets grocery stores.

The Retail Life Cycle

Retail life cycle
describes four distinct stages that a retail institution progresses through: introduction, growth, maturity, and decline.

The final framework we will examine in the evolution of retail competition is the **retail life cycle.** Some experts argue that retailing institutions pass through an identifiable cycle. This cycle includes four distinct stages that starts with (1) *introduction*, (2) proceeds to *growth*, (3) then *maturity*, and ends with (4) *decline.* Each stage is discussed briefly.

Introduction   This stage begins with an aggressive, bold entrepreneur who is willing and able to develop a different approach to retailing certain products. Most often the approach is oriented to a simpler method of distribution and passing the savings on to the customer. Other times it could be centered on a distinctive product assortment, shopping ease, locational convenience, advertising, or promotion. For example, Jiffy Lube and other quick oil change service retailers offered faster "while you wait" service at more convenient locations with lower prices than conventional service stations and automobile dealers and changed the way consumers serviced their cars. During this stage profits are low, despite the increasing sales level, due to amortizing developmental costs.

Growth   During the growth stage, sales, and usually profits, explode. New retailers enter the market and begin to copy the idea. Toward the end of this period cost pressures that arise from the need for a larger staff, more complex internal systems, increased management controls, and other requirements of operating large, multiunit organizations overtake some of the favorable results. Consequently, late in this stage both market share and profitability tend to approach their maximum level.

Maturity   In the maturity stage, market share stabilizes and severe profit declines are experienced for several reasons. First, managers have become accustomed to managing a high-growth firm that was simple and small, but now they must manage a large, complex firm in a nongrowing market. Second, the industry has typically overexpanded. Third, competitive assaults will be made on these firms by new retailing formats (a bold entrepreneur starting a new retail life cycle).

Decline   Although decline is inevitable, retail managers try to postpone it by changing the retail mix. These attempts can postpone the decline stage, but a return to

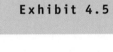

| Exhibit 4.5 | Retail Institutions in Their Various Stages of the Retail Life Cycle |

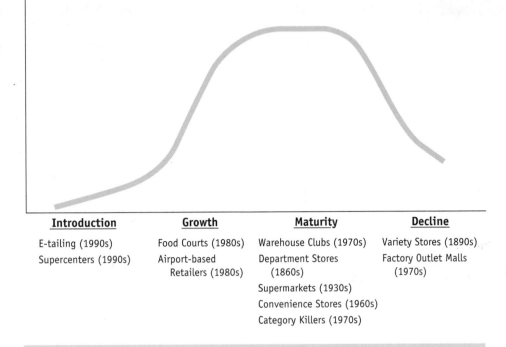

Introduction	Growth	Maturity	Decline
E-tailing (1990s)	Food Courts (1980s)	Warehouse Clubs (1970s)	Variety Stores (1890s)
Supercenters (1990s)	Airport-based Retailers (1980s)	Department Stores (1860s)	Factory Outlet Malls (1970s)
		Supermarkets (1930s)	
		Convenience Stores (1960s)	
		Category Killers (1970s)	

earlier, attractive levels of operating performance is not likely. Sooner or later a major loss of market share will occur, profits fall, and the once promising idea is no longer needed in the marketplace.

The retail life cycle is accelerating today. New concepts now move quickly from introduction to maturity as the leading operators have aggressive growth goals and their investors demand a quick return on equity. In addition, larger retailers with the capital and expertise in concept roll-out acquire many entrepreneurs in the early stages of the retail life cycle. Exhibit 4.5 lists the various stages of the retail life cycle for many of our current retail institutions.

The Inside Story box describes the history of theme parks. After reading it, you can determine for yourself if theme parks fit into one of the theories of the evolution of retail competition.

Future Changes in Retail Competition

LO • 4

What future changes could affect retail competition?

Retailers in today's ever-changing marketplace can expect dynamic changes in retail competition. A few of the trends shaping the retail landscape include an increase in competition from nonstore retailers, the advent of new retailing formats, heightened global competition, the integration of technology into operations, and the increasing use of private labels.

Retailing: The Inside Story

The Evolution of the Retail Format of the Theme Park

Many trace the beginnings of the whole amusement/theme park industry to medieval fairs in Europe. These fairs featured live entertainment, dancing, games, and even crude amusement rides. These entertainment retailers remained extremely popular until the early 1700s when political unrest caused many to close.

It wasn't until the late 1800s when the medieval fairs of the past were revived by American trolley companies that typically built amusement facilities at the end of their line to stimulate weekend ridership. The typical trolley developed entertainment retail format consisted of little more than picnic facilities, complemented with dance halls, restaurants, and a few amusement rides.

Near the end of the century, the amusement parks most of us are familiar with began to take form. In 1895 Paul Boynton opened an amusement park at Coney Island in New York. Two key innovations were brought forth by Coney Island. First, Coney Island was the first amusement park to use rides as the main attraction. Second, it was the first amusement retailer to charge an entrance fee.

The turn of the century saw tremendous growth in the amusement park industry. By the early 1920s there were well over 1,500 amusement parks as consumers became enthralled with the retail format. However, the Depression reduced the number to just over 400 by the mid-1930s and pushed the industry to the verge of collapse.

Enter Walt Disney. After finding relatively low service standards and poorly maintained facilities at amusement parks in the 1940s and 1950s, Disney believed that if a firm could provide service excellence in a family-themed environment, success would follow. So he went on to design a completely new concept of retail entertainment and called it the theme park.

Many were skeptical of the Disneyland project Walt Disney wanted to build in California. Without the traditional attractions, many wondered why people would attend. In fact, Disney had trouble gaining financing for the venture given the fact that people just didn't think it would work. However, Disney believed that children of all ages would become enthralled with the high quality of customer service that his venture could provide. Disney was right, and a new era of theme parks was born in 1955 with the opening of Disneyland.

Over the rest of the 20th century many others throughout the world have tried to copy the theme park concept that Disney developed. Some were successful, some were not. At the beginning of the 21st century, the retail entertainment industry is booming. Universal Studios and Six Flags in America, Asterix in France, and Huis ten Bosch and Sega parks in Japan, are just a few of the theme parks that have established themselves as successful competitors in the industry. Currently, Disney continues to maintain its premier standing; however, the retail environment continues to evolve. Given the theories of retail evolution that you have read about, what do you predict? Will Disney continue to maintain its position, or will it fall victim to retail evolution?

Source: National Amusement Park Historical Association and personal experience.

Nonstore Retailing

Several retail analysts predict that, as a result of several key forces at work today, nonstore sales (especially those that utilize the Internet) will experience significant growth during the next decade. With accelerated communication technology and changing consumer lifestyles, the growth potential for nonstore retailing, such as direct sellers, catalog sales, and e-tailing, is explosive. Kurt Salmon Associates expects that by the year 2005, nonstore retailing will account for 55 percent of total general merchandise, apparel, and furniture (GAF) sales, up from 15 percent a decade earlier.[9] Some of the forces contributing to this growth are as follows:

Consumers' need to save time

The erosion of fun in the shopping experience

The lack of qualified sales help in stores to provide information

The explosive development of the telephone, the computer, and telecommunications

The consumers' desire to eliminate the middleman's profit as a means of reducing prices

Therefore, traditional retailers need to continuously monitor developments in non-store retailing.

Direct Selling   Direct selling establishments are primarily engaged in the retail sale of products on an in-person basis, through party plans (Tupperware Home Parties) or one-on-one in the home or workplace (Avon Products), away from a fixed place of business. In the United States sales from direct selling total about $15 billion annually and are made by more than 4 million individuals who are not employed by the organization they represent but are independent contractors. Worldwide, direct selling sales total $50 billion, with Japan being the largest direct selling country. Major products sold include personal care items (Mary Kay Cosmetics), decorative home products (Princess House, Home Interiors and Gifts), cookware (West Bend, CUTCO), and encyclopedias (World Book, Encyclopedia Britannica). Today, with women increasingly out of the home, little "cold canvassing" is done, with many companies telephoning customers only when they need to make appointments to show the merchandise. In addition, traditional direct selling techniques are being merged with newer marketing channels, such as mail order and catalogs, and merchandise is being shown and sold anywhere people gather, such as at state fairs, in shopping malls, and at airports. The major attributes of direct selling remain the same: support for the independent contractor, knowledge and demonstration of the product by the salesperson, excellent warranties and guarantees, and the person-to-person component.

Catalog Sales   Mail-order retailers sell products by catalog and mail order. Catalog sales continue to be a $60 billion industry. Included are book and music clubs, jewelry firms, novelty merchandise firms, specialty merchandisers such as sporting goods (L.L. Bean), children's apparel retailers (Right Start), and kitchenware (Williams-Sonoma). While most mail-order retailers continue to offer their products through print catalogs, almost all have also begun to offer their catalog products on-line.

E-tailing   As pointed out in earlier chapters, the general belief among retail experts is that electronic, interactive, at-home shopping is definitely the place to be. Every major player in the retail industry, computer industry, telecommunications industry, and the transaction-processing industry is committed to this growth. The only prerequisite needed for the Internet's success is having enough homes with personal computers. Already half of the American households are connected either at home or at work.

Retailers can improve their long-term profit potential if they begin today to experiment with selling in the virtual world.

Dollars & Sense

Still, what is happening today is only the beginning of the explosion that is about to occur. As the Internet grows to allow real time, fully immersive three-dimensional video, Americans will spend more of their time in cyberspace. This in turn will create a whole new shopping experience. The shoppers of the next millennium will opt for the convenience and heightened experience of virtual shopping. Browsing will be even easier and the choices more extensive. Consumers will still want social activity outside the home; however, this won't constitute shopping but real entertainment, such as attending a sporting event or concert where, incidentally, a lot of merchandise and food will be for sale. The Net will allow consumers to shop with family and friends, even if they live half the world away. However, before conceding that e-tailing will replace the traditional store, it may be advisable to consider several key facts.

1. The Internet will not increase overall consumer demand. In terms of overall consumer spending, on-line sales will definitely cannibalize store and catalog sales. PricewaterhouseCoopers estimates that this cannibalization will vary across product categories. The consulting firm believes that on-line shopping will be big for books, music, video, and tickets. However, on-line shopping will remain only a minor player, at least until technology dramatically improves, for all other categories.[10]

2. Click & mortar strategies that integrate a single message will be more powerful than a pure e-tailing strategy. This will be especially true once click & mortar retailers learn the importance of reinforcing their Internet presence with in-store kiosks.[11]

3. E-tailers must pay better attention to customer service. Most e-tailers tend to do a good job during busy seasons, such as Christmas. However, in an effort to curtail operating costs, they reduce their service standards at other times. Customers are demanding such basic services as e-mail confirmation of orders, availability of real-time inventory, and free shipping. Because, as pointed out in the previous chapter, customer service is an area where traditional retailers are especially vulnerable, e-tailers should seek their niche here. Just listing an e-tailer's toll-free phone number and utilizing skilled call-center employees would be a plus for most e-tailers.[12]

New Retailing Formats

The practice of retailing is continually evolving. New formats are born and old ones die. Innovation in retailing is the result of constant pressure to improve efficiency and effectiveness in a continual effort to better serve the consumer. The pressure to improve service has also resulted in a shortened life cycle for retail formats. However, just as retailers find it extremely difficult to predict what will be the "hot new item" for an upcoming season, especially Christmas, they have the same trouble predicting the success of new retail formats.

For example, in the late 1980s, most retail experts agreed that hypermarkets (which are one and a half times the size of a supercenter) would be retailing's success story of the 1990s. However, despite their overwhelming success in Europe and their limited success in the United States with Meijer's in Michigan and Fred Meyer's in the Northwest, these super-large stores, which looked like airplane hangars, were instead retailing's biggest failure for the 1990s. What happened?

Probably, customers felt that any store that had rest areas and stockers wearing roller skates was just too big to shop in. Also, shoppers were unnerved by ceilings and shelves that rose several stories high. In addition, category killers, such as Toys "R" Us and

Sports Authority, offered greater selection, wholesale clubs offered better prices, and supermarkets and discounters offered more convenient locations.

Another retail format that didn't achieve the success predicted was the off-price retailer. **Off-price retailers** are similar to discounters with one important difference. Whereas discounters offer continuity of brands—that is, they carry the same brands day-in and day-out—off-pricers, which were more opportunistic, carried only brands that they were able to get on special deals from the manufacturer. Thus, the off-price retailers failed because the regular merchants, including discounters, became more price competitive on the brands the off-pricer was currently selling.

Although these retailing formats have not lived up to expectations, three formats brought about in part by the poor economic conditions of the early 1990s are expected to continue their success: supercenters, stores focusing on the recycling of usable merchandise that is in good condition, and liquidators. These three formats have one thing in common—they offer the consumer value by developing a partnership with suppliers.

Supercenters   The **supercenter**, which is a cavernous, one-stop combination supermarket and discount department store that carries from 80,000 to more than 100,000 products (ranging from televisions to peanut butter to fax machines), should continue to be the key growth format for the mass merchants. These stores offer the customer one-stop shopping (and as a result are capable of drawing customers from a 60- to 80-mile radius in some rural areas) and lower the customer's total cost of purchasing in terms of time and miles traveled without sacrificing service and variety. This is exactly what today's time-pressed consumer needs. Because, as Exhibit 4.6 shows, Wal-Mart, Meijer, Kroger, Kmart, and Target are banking their future on this new format, it is difficult to predict failure for the supercenter.

Off-price retailers
sell products at a discount but do not carry certain brands on a continuous basis. They carry those brands they can buy from manufacturers at closeout or deep one-time discount prices.

Supercenters
combine a discount store and grocery store and carry 80,000 to 100,000 products in order to offer one-stop shopping.

Exhibit 4.6	Number of Supercenters by Retailer		

	1998	1999	2000
WAL★MART	564	721	894
MEIJER	117	127	144
Kroger *	105	126	135
BIG K mart **	102	105	115
TARGET ***	14	16	31

Source: Company records
*Through Kroger's Fred Meyer Store subsidiary
**Kmart plans on adding 200 new supercenters by 2005
***Target will add another 200 supercenters over the next decade

Nevertheless, it is doubtful that the supermarket operators will surrender peacefully to the supercenters. For example, Kroger has joined the discounters by lowering prices. The other supermarkets, which have always operated with paper-thin net profit margins of 1 to 2 percent, will be forced to match the supercenters' prices by gaining better control over their inventory to achieve cost savings. In the past, unlike the discounters, supermarkets mostly allowed their buying plans to be dictated by the food manufacturers' promotional programs. Now they are joining the discounters in letting the customers' purchasing habits determine their purchasing and inventory decisions. By using "just-in-time" (JIT) methods, grocers are now reordering only when and what their computer, which is connected to their in-store bar-code scanners, deems necessary. This way grocers will be able to reduce costs and meet the discounters' prices head on.

The supercenter concept has even branched out into the automobile market. Glitzy, computerized auto superstore chains, such as AutoNation, Driver's Mart Worldwide, and CarMax Auto Superstores, are giving nightmares to the nation's 22,000 traditional car dealers. Since their introduction in the mid-1990s, this new breed of retailer has streamlined an industry in which over 20 percent of a car's price had covered the retailer's expenses and has made shopping easier for the customer. These massive publicly traded chains sell new and used cars using "cheap" Wall Street money to finance, sell, rent, lease, and repair cars. Just like the supercenters in the grocery industry, these auto superstores are making competition tougher for other retailers.

Recycled Merchandise Retailers

Recycled merchandise retailers are establishments that sell used and reconditioned products.

Recycled Merchandise Retailers Due to their very small numbers just a decade ago, recycled merchandisers have experienced the fastest growth of any retail format over the past five years. Originally a product of the great depression, **recycled merchandise retailers**—which sell castoff clothes, furniture, sporting goods, and computers—include pawn shops, thrift shops, consignment shops, and even flea markets. Even as a record number of retailers were seeking bankruptcy protection in mid-1990s, these recycled merchandise retailers were growing by 10 percent a year. No longer is conspicuous consumption chic. With the advent of the Gen Yers, this is a period of time when consumers would rather gloat about a good buy than an expensive product. Besides, selling clothes one no longer needs increases an individual's income.

Now that many preowned clothes shops are using the same media as traditional retailers to advertise their products, shoppers today find it difficult to distinguish between today's recyclers and small specialty shops. Because so many of the products are new or nearly new, looking like a Salvation Army Thrift Store is no longer appropriate. Recyclers have been developed to serve specific markets, such as pregnant women, large sizes, or children, or even specific merchandise, such as toys, sporting goods (including camping and backpacking equipment), outerwear, CDs, tools, or jewelry. The apparel group accounting for the fewest resale and thrift store sales is men's clothing. It seems that men hang onto their clothes longer than women and children do, leaving much less available for resale.

Recycling is not just an American phenomenon, it is also big in Europe and Latin America. However, nowhere is it growing faster than in Japan where this retail format is expanding at nearly a 20 percent annual rate. Japanese companies from kimono stores to catalog retailers have jumped on the secondhand bandwagon. One of the most popular stores in Japan is called "Per Gramme Market," which sells items at eight cents a gram. Thus a secondhand T-shirt would cost around $8.50, but a silk scarf would sell for $2.80.[13]

Liquidators With more than 15,000 retailers seeking the protection of the bankruptcy courts annually, a new growth industry (albeit from a very small starting point) has developed: liquidators. Often called retailing's undertakers or vultures, this small and all-but-invisible retail format comes in and liquidates leftover merchandise when an established retailer shuts down or downsizes. Firms like Schottenstein Professional Asset Management, which is part of the Value City family, purchase the entire inventory of the existing retailer and run the "going-out-of-business" (GOB) sale. They make their money by seldom paying more than 30 cents on the wholesale dollar for the closeout merchandise. This handful of firms does almost $5 billion in sales annually.

Some might question why don't retailers do this job themselves, such as some manufacturers do with outlet malls. Well, for starters, these retailers usually have problems—or else they wouldn't need the liquidator's service in the first place. Second, most liquidators pay cash for the merchandise—a plus for the strapped retailer—and then they take all the risks and gain the rewards. Other liquidators will only conduct the sale, but guarantee a minimum payout to the retailer. Finally, by having outsiders run the closeouts, management can focus on operating the continuing stores.

Running closeouts requires some special retailing skills. Liquidators have a talent for pricing merchandise and estimating the expense of everything from ad budgets and payrolls to utility bills. And because most of the employees know they will be out of a job as soon as the liquidation is complete, liquidators have to develop special incentive plans to make it more profitable for store personnel to stay and work rather than quit or walk off with merchandise.[14]

Heightened Global Competition

The rate of change in retailing around the world appears to be directly related to the stage and speed of economic development in the countries concerned, but even the least-developed countries are experiencing dramatic changes. Retailing in other countries, however, exhibits greater diversity in its structure than it does in the United States. In some countries, such as Italy, retailing is composed largely of specialty houses carrying narrow lines. Finnish retailers generally carry a more general line of merchandise. The size of the average retailer is also diverse, from the massive Harrod's in London and Mitsukoshi Ltd. in Japan, both of which serve more than 10 thousand customers a day, to the small one- or two-person stalls in developing African and Latin American nations.

The United States is not alone, however, in developing new retail formats. New types of retailing have emerged from all countries. These changing formats can be attributed to a variety of economic and social factors that are the same worldwide: a widespread concern for health, a steady increase in the number of working women and two-income families, the consequent upsurge in price levels, consumerism, and so forth. These factors, and their effects on consumer lifestyles, encouraged high-profit retailers around the world to seek new market segments, make adjustments in the retail mix, alter location patterns, and adopt new multisegment strategies. In the process, many new retail concepts and formats have emerged and spread.

Still, it is amazing that retailers from larger countries often do not have the success when entering a new country that retailers from smaller countries do. Consider, for example, the fact that while Wal-Mart was operating successfully on foreign shores, with 572 discount stores, 383 supercenters, and 49 Sam's Clubs at fiscal 2000 year end, other major American retailers experienced problems with their international expansion plans.

Retail experts attribute this failure by large country retailers to two factors. Some think it is a lack of understanding of the new country's culture. Wal-Mart made several

Global Retailing

IKEA

One word, "IKEA," says it all. IKEA is the world's largest retailer that specializes in furniture and home furnishings. Out of the woods of southern Sweden, IKEA has taken the relatively sedate (which some also call boring) product category of furniture and completely revolutionized it. Many credit IKEA with creating a mass market for a category where none previously existed.

Founded by Ingar Kamprad in Sweden in 1943, IKEA (formed from the founder's initials, I. K., plus the first letters of Elmtaryd and Agunnaryd, the farm and village where he grew up) has identified a global consumer segment for furniture and home furnishings. IKEA's success is built on its commitment to focusing on a combination of good design, good function, and good quality with prices so low that as many people as possible can afford the products. By emphasizing this singular focus, IKEA has been able to connect with consumers the world over. Currently operating in well over 25 countries as diverse as Australia, Kuwait, Slovakia, Taiwan, and Saudia Arabia, IKEA's underlying mission has rewarded it with global success.

So what makes IKEA so different? A consumer visiting an IKEA can expect more than 12,000 items to choose from in a typical full-line store. Much like other furniture stores, IKEA offers customers a chance to view product displays of furniture and home furnishings. But that is where the similarity ends. Unlike traditional furniture retailers where a salesperson assists customers with their purchase decision as well as scheduling delivery, IKEA is completely self-serve. Each product on the display floor has an identification tag that specfies the item's location in the IKEA inventory area. Once a customer has decided on an item, he or she simply proceeds to the inventory area, pulls the flat carton from the shelf (which contains the disassembled product), and heads to the checkout counter.

There is no doubt that the combination of quality products, convenience, and low prices has allowed IKEA to become one of the world's leading retailers. However, as global competition increases, new and innovative retailers will continually challenge IKEA. How IKEA responds to these competitive threats will determine its long-run success.

major mistakes when it entered international markets. When it entered Canada, Wal-Mart made one of the classic cultural mistakes when it distributed English-language circulars in French-speaking Quebec. When entering Mexico, the chain built large parking lots at some stores only to realize that most of their customers rode the bus to the store and then had to cross these large, empty parking lots carrying bags full of merchandise. Wal-Mart responded by creating a shuttle bus service.[15] This was especially embarrassing for Wal-Mart because one of the key factors for its overall success was the fact that the retailer started and stayed in small rural markets until it completely understood its customers and the channel partners.

Michael O'Connor, the former president of Super Market Institute and now a consultant, has another explanation. He feels that the failure of many retailers to succeed in international markets is because these retailers come from larger countries which have had successful economies. Retailers in smaller countries are not used to this and thus tend to take more time and be more careful with key decisions. According to O'Connor, by being a little less sure of themselves, smaller country executives will seek more counsel and listen to more opinions before developing strategic plans.[16] Along the same lines, these smaller country retailers have always had to deal with international issues if they were to expand. One smaller country retailer who has made an impact on international retailing is Ingar Kamprad, president of IKEA, who was the first to successfully develop a warehouse retailing format that could be followed around the world. IKEA is spotlighted in this chapter's Global Retailing box. The firm's warehouse format—which is based on economies of scale in the areas of marketing, purchasing, and distribution and which utilizes customer participation in the assembly and transportation of the merchandise—generates almost 90 percent of its revenues from global operations, more than any other major worldwide retailer.[17]

Integration of Technology

One of the most significant trends occurring in retailing involves technological innovations. Technology is having and will continue to have a dramatic influence on retailing. Technological innovations can be viewed under three main areas: supply chain management, customer management, and customer satisfaction. The plethora of supply-chain management techniques such as quick response (QR), just-in-time (JIT), and Efficient Consumer Response (ECR) are already being enhanced by new initiatives such as direct store delivery (DSD) and as collaborative, planning, forecasting, and replenishment (CPFR) systems. DSD systems have the potential to fully automate all retail inventory operations from tracking vendor and item authorization to pricing and order taking. DSD systems provide greater accuracy and increased administrative efficiency allowing retailers employing such systems to achieve cost advantages. Advancements in DSD systems will create more efficient operations and stronger partnerships and retailers as global competition increases. For example, United States–based Giant Food Inc. eliminated a tremendous amount of paperwork, dramatically increasing administrative efficiency with the implementation of a DSD system. Many industry experts believe that DSD is the engine that will drive industry profits. However, gross profit numbers alone don't tell the story and, in fact, can be somewhat misleading when it comes down to calculating the direct and incremental costs of warehouse-delivered products. Rather, it is activity-based costing analyses that demonstrated that in categories with mixed distribution, DSD products consistently outperform those going through the warehouse. Other supply chain systems—such as collaborative planning, forecasting, and replenishment—though still in its infancy, have the potential to take retailers and manufacturers far beyond continuous replenishment models in terms of reducing excess inventory levels, cutting out-of-stocks at retail, and efficiently meeting consumer demand. The bottom line is eliminating costly variations and distortions throughout the supply chain. However, technological systems, such as DSD and CPFR are but the beginning of the technological revolution occurring within the supply chain. Retailers who continue to use technology in innovative ways within the supply chain will achieve greater efficiency in their operations.

One of the keys to success in retailing is developing the ability to monitor the environmental changes taking place, especially those pertaining to technology, and adopting the technology to improve the retailer's profitability.

Dollars & Sense

Retailers on the forefront of technology who understand their consumers will achieve higher levels of effectiveness in their efforts. For example, retailers can use technology to better target their customers, thus allowing the retailers to provide better service. For example, Talbots provides enhanced value by locating its stores in the most appropriate areas. Talbot's uses its catalog information to open retail outlets. Talbots determines new store locations by examining clusters of ZIP codes, which have accounted for $150,000 or more of classic women's and children's apparel. Believe it or not, some of the most sophisticated users of database technology are casinos. In the past, one had to be a high roller to gain any "comps" (free products or services given to customers, e.g., free tickets to shows or a free night's stay). Today, when customers use the casino's gaming facilities (such as gambling at a slot machine), they can insert a card which has been assigned to them that tracks their gaming behavior. The customers then present these cards to the casino to receive individual rewards based on their use of the gaming facilities. Through the use of these cards a casino not only gains a much better understanding of its customers, allowing the casino to develop more effective retail strategies, but it can also reward customers at all levels, thus increasing customer satisfaction.

As technology continues to penetrate the retail marketplace, advancements in customer service and convenience will continue to be made. For example, what replacements are in store for the bar-code scanners? One cause of long lines at the supermarket checkouts is that each item has to be taken out of a shopper's cart, individually scanned, and then bagged. How might technology change this? Recent testing of radio frequency identifiers (RFID) on products might eliminate this process completely. In operation, the RFID reader generates a low-level radio frequency magnetic field that resonates with the tag's metal coil and capacitor, creating an electrical signal that powers the computer chip, which then transmits its stored data back to the reader—and this can all be done directly in the customer's shopping cart. The process works well, but the tags are expensive—as much as $200 each. However, recently that cost has fallen to less than $1 per tag. Although still too costly to use on anything but high-priced items, advancements in technology will soon be available to make this system affordable to implement. Imagine bagging your groceries while you shop. Once you have finished you simply push your cart to the checkout and within a few seconds the cashier scans your entire cart, you pay, and off you go.

These technological advances are but a few of the thousands that will change the nature of retailing. What technological innovations do you see on the horizon for retailers?

Increasing Use of Private Labels

As retailing continues to change, the improved use of private labels has again come to the forefront as a key business asset in developing a differential advantage for retailers. Private labels can set the retailer apart from the competition, and they can get customers into the store (or web site) and bring them back.

Today retailers are shifting their emphasis on the development of private label brands into high gear by using a variety of strategies to build the image of their brands, expand their brand recognition, and raise their brand images in the marketplace.

In the past retailers believed that national brands drew customers into the store, set the standard, and lent credibility to the retailer. At the same time, retailers felt private-label brands could help retailers differentiate their offerings, reach customers seeking lower prices, and boost margins due to the lower costs of private-label merchandise.

Today the thinking has changed. Leading retailers, as shown in Exhibit 4.3, are focused on developing strong proprietary private-label brands as leading brands and

JCPenney is a retailer which has built a major part of its image around private labels including its very popular Arizona Jeans Co.

supporting these brands with major advertising and promotional programs. Today brands such as JCPenney's "The Original Arizona Jean Company" are effectively serving as destination draws in their own right while still providing many of the same benefits of traditional private label programs.

Managerial Question: Should retailers advertise the fact that they are the owners of private label brand(s) they sell? Explain your reasoning.

Some of the private label branding strategies currently being used by retailers include the following:[18]

1. *Developing a partnership with well-known celebrities, noted experts, and institutional authorities.* Celebrity partnerships — or the use of people as private-label brands — allow retailers to align with an individual whose personal reputation creates immediate brand recognition, image, or credibility. Target uses noted architect Michael Graves and Kmart uses Martha Stewart.

2. *Developing a partnership with traditionally higher-end suppliers to bring an exclusive variation on their highly regarded brand name to market.* Wal-Mart recently signed an exclusive trademark licensing agreement to use the General Electric name on small appliances. (General Electric had sold the use of its name for small appliances to Black & Decker in the mid-1980s. B&D sold its small appliance division in 1999. Starting in 2001, Wal-Mart began using the GE label on products manufactured by Hamilton Beach/Procter-Silex.) These

partnerships offer both parties a win-win situation. The retailer gets an exclusive private label with a great image and the opportunity to expand customer appeal, ratchet up price points, and raise margins. The manufacturer builds volume and gains access to a broad new market spectrum.

3. *Reintroducing products with strong name recognition that have fallen from the retail scene.* Old brand names do not die. They get recycled. Retailers can add cachet to their store image by resuscitating former upmarket brands that have been discontinued but have not lost their image. Recycled brands can help a retailer achieve differentiation through exclusivity and attract consumers unwilling to risk buying an unknown brand name. By reviving a well-known brand with a pedigree, the retailer is able to leverage the brand's equity while still having a proprietary line. Today Kmart has reintroduced the Thom McAn shoe label that was popular for more than 50 years, and Wal-Mart has purchased the rights from Procter & Gamble to its discontinued White Cloud label on diapers and toilet tissues. Wal-Mart did the same with Faded Glory. In early 2000, Procter & Gamble decided to sell two more of its famous brand names, Prell shampoo and Coast soap, and it is expected that a retailer will soon acquire one or both of these brand names and build a product line around that name.

4. *Branding an entire department or a business; not just a product line.* In an approach designed to differentiate its supercenter food offer from the others, Target has taken its private label branding strategy one step further by branding its entire supermarket section with the Archer Farms name. Not only does the Archer Farms name readily draw an association with the Target brand (the archer's target or bullseye), but it also enables Target to separate the two sections of the store. In fact, many consumers believe it to be a different company entirely. This may be a plus for Target with consumers who might not otherwise shop for groceries in a discount store. The Archer Farms market positioning strategy leads the consumer to believe that it is an upscale grocer by placing more emphasis on quality and freshness than price. Such a strategy reinforces Target's protected niche image as the "discounter for consumers who don't want to be seen in a discount store." A "fresh from the farm" tag line underscores the market positioning message. Store design features—such as green neon perimeter lighting, graphics depicting farm scenes, colorful illustrations of major food categories, and product descriptions and use suggestions—all help create a differentiated grocery shopping environment. The Archer Farms name was also carried into a private-label program featuring approximately 100 stock-keeping units (SKUs).[19]

Target uses its Archer Farms brand to create a more up-scale image in the grocery section of its supercenters.

Student Study Guide

Summary

The behavior of competitors is an important component of the retail strategic planning and operations management model. Effective planning and operations management in any retail setting cannot be accomplished without the proper analysis of competitors.

LO•1 What are the various models of retail competition?

Competition in retailing, as in any other industry, involves the interplay of supply and demand. Various models of retail competition were described to aid in illustrating certain principles of retail competition. These models suggested that retail competition is typically local; the retail industry is monopolistically competitive and not a pure monopoly, pure competition, or oligopoly. Retailers today are in a struggle to develop strategies that allow them to protect themselves from competitive threats on the basis of having achieved some type of differential advantage over their competition. As a result of this goal, retailers are developing price and nonprice strategies that look at the supply as well as the demand side of retailing. This opening learning objective concluded by looking at how competitive activity can make a market attractive or unattractive.

LO•2 What are the various types of retail competition?

Competition is most intense in retailing, and various classification schemes were used to describe this intensity. Intratype and intertype competition descriptions were employed to determine if the retailers competing against each other were in the same line of retail trade or if they were in different lines of retail trade but still competing for the same customer with similar merchandise lines. Divertive competition was used to describe retailers who sought to intercept customers planning to visit another retailer.

LO•3 What are the three theories used to explain the evolution of retail competition?

Retail competition is both revolutionary and evolutionary. Three theories of viewing changing competitive patterns in retailing were reviewed. The wheel of retailing proposes that new types of retailers enter the market as low-margin, low-price, less efficient operators. As they succeed, they become more complex, increasing their margins and prices and making them vulnerable to new types of low-margin competitors, who, in turn, follow the same pattern. The retail accordion theory suggests that retail institutions evolve from outlets offering wide assortments to specialized narrow assortment stores and then return to the practice of offering wide assortments to repeat the pattern. Finally, the retail life cycle theory views retail institutions, like the products they distribute, as passing through an identifiable cycle during which the basics of strategy and competition change.

LO•4 What future changes could affect retail competition?

We followed with a discussion of changes that could affect retail competition. Industry analysts contend that nonstore retailing (direct selling, catalog sales, and e-tailing) will be a major competitive force in the future. These various types of nonstore retailing were discussed. We also looked at three examples of possible new retailing formats that evolved as an outgrowth of the economic slowdown in the early 1990s: supercenters, recycled merchandise retailers, and liquidators.

Just as the introduction of new retailing formats in one part of the United States will impact retailers in other parts of the country, so it is for international retailing. Retailing in other countries exhibits even greater diversity in its structure than retailing in the United States. The rate of change in retailing appears to be directly related to the stage and speed of economic development in the countries concerned, but today even the least-developed countries are experiencing dramatic changes in retailing; thereby heightening global retail competition. The global analysis section ended with a discussion as to why retailers from smaller countries tend to do better in international competition.

Other changes in retail formats will result from the significant development of technological advances for use in retailing. The chapter concluded with an in-depth discussion of private-label branding and the various strategies for its use today.

Terms to Remember

pure competition	intratype competition
pure monopoly	intertype competition
monopolistic competition	divertive competition
oligopolistic competition	break-even point
outshopping	wheel of retailing theory
fixed costs	retail accordion
variable costs	retail life cycle
semifixed costs	off-price retailers
store positioning	supercenter
overstored	recycled merchandise retailers
understored	

Review and Discussion Questions

LO•1   What are the various models of retail competition?

1. Can a retailer ever operate in a pure monopoly situation? If you agree that this is possible, provide an example and explain what dangers this retailer faces? If you disagree, explain why not.

2. Develop a list of expenses or costs for a department store and categorize them as fixed, variable, and semifixed.

3. Why is it so important for a retailer to develop a protected niche?

LO•2   What are the various types of retail competition?

4. Provide an example of intratype competition that was not mentioned in the text. Provide an example of intertype competition that was not mentioned in the text. Can a retailer face both intratype and intertype competition at the same time? Explain your response.

5. Can divertive competition only occur in intertype competition—that is, where two different types of retailers with a similar product compete with each other?

LO•3   What three theories are used to explain the evolution of retail competition?

6. Describe the wheel of retailing theory of retail competition. What is the theory's major strength and weakness? Does this theory do a good job of explaining what has happened to retailers in your hometown?

7. Describe the retail accordion theory of competition. What is this theory's major strength and weakness?

8. Would strategies for retailers differ in the four stages of the retail life cycle? What strategies should be emphasized at each of the four stages?

9. A friend told you this afternoon that it was almost impossible to find just an ordinary cheeseburger on the menu anymore, that the elegant simplicity of the original McDonald's has given way to a smorgasbord of menu items that are too complicated to comprehend. What evolution theory of retailing does this suggest?

LO•4 What future changes could affect retail competition?

10. Will nonstore retailing continue to grow? Provide a rationale for your response.

11. Many experts disagree over the future of shopping via the Internet. What is your opinion on the subject?

12. If a new retail format is a hit in one country, it generally will be successful in all countries. Do you agree or disagree?

13. In the chapter, several possible explanations were given as to why retailers, such as IKEA, from smaller countries tend to do better when entering foreign markets. Do you agree or disagree with these explanations? Explain your reasoning.

14. Some people claim that the increasing use of technology by retailers is making the stores less customer friendly. Do you agree or disagree with this statement? Explain your reasoning.

15. Is it better for a retailer to develop a new private-label brand or to try to revive a once prestigious brand that has been discontinued? Explain your reasoning.

Sample Test Questions

LO•1 What type of competitive structure are most retail firms involved in?

a. horizontal competition

b. monopolistic competition

c. vertical competition

d. pure competition

e. oligopolistic competition

LO•2 When Wal-Mart competes with Kroger, Albertsons, and Safeway by adding groceries to its general merchandise products in its new supercenters, what type of competition is this?

a. extended niche

b. intratype

c. scrambled

d. intertype

e. category killer

LO•3 Walking back to the dorm after class, your roommate complains that she wished there were an old-fashion hamburger joint she could go to for a simple hamburger, not a fancy triple-decker burger with 17 secret sauces, and not a fast food restaurant

with a playground for 50 kids. Her dilemma describes which theory of retail evolution?

a. retail violin

b. retail life cycle

c. bigger-n-better

d. wheel of retailing

e. compound growth

LO•4 **With regard to international trends in retailing, which of the following statements is true?**

a. Because of its sheer size, retailing in the United States is more diverse in its structure than it is in any other country.

b. Success with a retailing format in one country usually guarantees success in all countries.

c. The size of the individual stores do not tend to vary.

d. U.S. retailers haven't been as successful in international expansion as some of their competitors from smaller countries.

e. No new successful retailing format has been developed outside of the United States in the past half century.

Applications

Writing and Speaking Exercise As a summer intern at a locally owned Ford dealership in a city with 120,000 people, you have been asked to develop an outline of what the firm should do as it faces a new type of competition. Within the last 18 months, AutoZone has opened two new stores, a new Kmart Supercenter has a complete automotive service department, and Pep Boys has opened a 23,000-square-foot automotive parts supermarket that appeals to both the do-it-yourself auto enthusiast and the person who wants auto service done by others. This latter person can purchase parts and accessories at a Pep Boys at discount prices and have them installed by Pep Boys technicians. During this time period, service sales at your dealership has declined by 20 percent. Previously, sales had been growing 10 percent annually. Don Ruberg, the owner of the dealership, has asked you what strategies can be implemented to combat this increased competition and put the dealership back on a sales growth curve in service sales. He wants your report by Friday morning so he can have the weekend to think it over.

Retail Project You are thinking about buying a Ford Explorer after you graduate this semester. Use the Internet to see if you can get a better deal than you could get from a traditional auto retailer. All you will have to do is make three on-line connections, all free.

Start at DealerNet (www.dealernet.com), created by Reynolds & Reynolds, which provides computer services to dealers. You can see a picture of the Explorer and find out how it compares with competitors like the Jeep Grand Cherokee in such key areas as trunk space, fuel economy, and price.

Suppose you settle on a four-door, four-wheel-drive XLT model. Key over to the prices posted by Edmund Publications (www.edmunds.com), a longtime compiler of such information. There you discover what the current sticker price is for the XLT as well as what the dealer pays. You also learn a little-known fact: the XLT carries a 3 percent holdback—essentially a rebate for each Explorer that Ford pays to the dealer at the end of the year. This may help you in evaluating the price your dealer quotes.

When you're ready to order, type in http://www.autobytel.com. There are several buying services on the web, but Autobytel is free. From here you can buy the car using Autobytel direct or place your order, and you'll get a call from a nearby dealer. The dealer will charge you a fixed amount over the invoice and deliver the car. Now, you have saved enough to buy a copy of this text for all your friends.

Case — Tough Times for Grocers

In search of new ways to woo shoppers, the nation's 30,000 supermarkets have become a marketing test ground. The industry is still struggling to fight new competition and demographic changes that have been building for years. Baby boomers, one of the largest and most affluent groups of shoppers, have aged and now eat out frequently and shop on the run. The evidence of their lifestyle is ubiquitous: convenience stores and pharmacies now carry an array of groceries, and purveyors of prepared foods are flourishing.

The liberal spending by baby boomers has helped cause food sales to soar. But supermarket shopping sprees have not weighed heavily in the increase. Since 1965, food spending in America has climbed 46 percent, in real terms, to $534.5 billion in 2000, according to the Agriculture Department. But over that period, spending on food to be consumed at home—purchased mainly from supermarkets—grew by only 20 percent, to $291.2 billion. Spending on food eaten away from home—at fast food restaurants, delis, and other retailers that prepare food—shot up by 89 percent, to $243.3 billion according to the agency.

In addition, the increased competition from the discounters' supercenters has forced at least a thousand weaker supermarkets a year to shut down. And in an attempt to be as attentive to customers' needs as the corner grocers of the past, supermarkets are stocking twice as many products as they did a decade ago, further increasing their costs. Many have added conveniences like in-store restaurants, banks, pharmacies, and delis with hot prepared foods. They are using computer scanners to track individual purchases and to improve their marketing. Some are holding events like sampling extravaganzas to make shopping more exciting.

Service, value, convenience, and quality, rather than price, are the carrots that lure time-pressed shoppers today. "Retailers are moving away from featured sales," said the president of an advertising agency that specializes in the food industry. "No longer do you pile it high and sell it cheap."

Questions

1. What strategies can supermarkets adopt to fight off competition from fast food restaurants and minimarts?

2. Do you believe the trend in spending for food that is eaten away from home will continue in the future? Explain your response.

3. Can supermarkets compete with supercenters?

4. Should supermarkets worry about on-line grocers trying to take away their customers?

Starting Your Own Business   As a knowledgeable retail entrepreneur, you recognize how harmful new retail competitors entering the market can be to your business. You opened your bookstore only 18 months ago and already you have experienced healthy sales. In the year just ended sales reached almost $782,000. You have estimated of the 41,000 households in your market, 38 percent visit your store an average of 4.1 times a year. Due to your excellent merchandising and retail displays, 90 percent of visitors to your store make a purchase (referred to as closure) for an average transaction size of $13.59. Unfortunately, last week you learned that Borders (a category killer bookstore that also sells music tapes and CDs and serves coffee, pastries, and other refreshments) has signed a lease to be part of a new shopping mall in a city of 405,000 located 20 miles north of your store. This mall will also feature a Home Depot and an Office Max.

Predictably, you are quite concerned about how Borders will take customers from your store. It is hard for you to predict the impact of this new competition, and you remind yourself that at least they are 20 miles away. Nonetheless you believe that the percentage of households in your market that will shop your store will decline from 38 percent to 34 percent and average shopping frequency will decline from 4.1 times per year to 3.9 times per year. You believe you can maintain your excellent closure rate and average transaction size. What is the estimated sales impact of Borders becoming your competitor? (*Hint:* Annual sales can be obtained by multiplying the number of households in the market by the percent that patronize your store multiplied by their average shopping frequency or number of visits per year; this can then be multiplied by the closure rate and this result multiplied by the average transaction size.)

Endnotes

1. *Ten Trends for the Turn of the Millennium* (Columbus, OH: PricewaterhouseCoopers, 2000): 3.

2. Leonard W. Weiss, *Case Studies in American Industry* (New York: John Wiley and Sons, 1971): 222–223.

3. However, in real life retailers are not confronted by such a curve because they face a three-dimensional demand function. The three dimensions are (1) quantity demanded per household, (2) price at the retail store, and (3) distance from the individual's residence or place of work to the store. The quantity demanded by a household is inversely related to the price charged and distance to the store. This discussion is, however, beyond the scope of this text.

4. "What Shoppers Want," *Progressive Grocer*, April 2000: 37.

5. "Drugstores Wage a Pricey Online Battle," *Advertising Age*, August 30, 1999: 26.

6. "Buy AOL, Get Time Warner for Free," *The Motley Fool*, June 8, 2000.

7. Malcolm P. McNair, "Significant Trends and Developments in the Postwar Period," in A. B. Smith (ed.), *Competitive Distribution in a Free High-Level Economy and Its Implications for the University* (Pittsburgh, PA: University of Pittsburgh Press, 1958).

8. Stanley C. Hollander, "Notes on the Retail Accordion," *Journal of Retailing*, Summer 1966: 29–40, 54.

9. *Vision for the New Millennium* . . . , (Atlanta: Kurt Salmon Associates, 1997).

10. "Ten Trends for the Turn of the Millennium."

11. Ibid.

12. "Laughing All The Way to the (Phone) Bank," *U.S. News & World Report*, May 29, 2000: 46–47.

13. "Used Products Are Hot as Japanese Discover the Joy of Buying Second-Hand," *Wall Street Journal*, June 22, 2000: A1.

14. "Everything Must Go—To The Liquidators," *Business Week*, January 15, 1996: 52.

15. Wal-Mart's 2000 Annual Report.

16. Michael J. O'Connor, "Global Marketing: A Retail Perspective," *International Trends in Retailing*, December 1998: 19–35.

17. For an interesting discussion of IKEA and its founder, see "Folk Fortune," *Forbes*, September 4, 2000: 66–69.

18. The following is based on the May 2000 issue of "Key Trends and Issues" by PricewaterhouseCoopers. Used with permission.

19. This information was derived from an information kit supplied by Target.

Channel Behavior

CHAPTER

5

Overview

At the outset of this text, we pointed out that retailing is the final movement in the progression of a product from producer to consumer. Many other movements occur through time and geographical space, and all of them need to be executed properly for the retailer to achieve optimum performance. Therefore, in this chapter, we examine the retailer's need to analyze and understand the marketing channel in which it operates. The chapter discusses all the activities in the marketing system that either the retailer or another channel member must perform. It then looks at the various institutions involved in a marketing channel. This is followed with a review of the various types of marketing channels and the benefits each one offers the retailer. The chapter concludes with some practical suggestions to improve channel relationships.

Learning Objectives

After reading this chapter, you should be able to

1. discuss the retailer's role in the larger marketing system

2. describe the institutions involved and the functions that must be performed in every marketing system

3. describe the types of marketing channels by length, width, and control

4. define the terms *dependency, channel power,* and *channel conflict,* and explain why cooperation is so important in channel management

---

LO • 1

What is the retailer's role in the larger marketing system?

The Marketing System

Consider the following example. The final movement of a retail item occurred on November 17 at 10:47 a.m. when a UPS truck delivered a sport coat to a customer in suburban Chicago. The customer purchased the sport coat on-line from JCPenney just three days earlier. At some prior time (probably six months to a year earlier) that sport coat was manufactured in Mexico. Later it was warehoused, and then it was placed on display in the manufacturer's showroom. Next, JCPenney purchased a large quantity of these coats to be sold at its stores throughout the country, as well as on its web site. This particular coat was shipped to the retailer's Alliance, Texas, warehouse, later shipped to another JCPenney fulfillment center in Columbus, Ohio, and finally shipped to the customer on November 15th.

In this sport coat example, manufacturing occurred in Mexico, a Mexican motor carrier was used to transport the coats by truck to the United States, and after going through customs the coat was warehoused by the manufacturer in a duty-free warehouse in El Paso prior to being shipped to JCPenney. Thus, before the final retail transaction could take place, many physical movements were needed; involving many firms other than the retailer. Retailers cannot properly perform their roles without these other firms; they are part of a complex marketing system—an important component, but not the only one.

To understand the retailer's role in this larger marketing system, the retailer should be viewed as a member of one, or even several, marketing channels. A **marketing channel is** a set of institutions that moves goods from the point of production to the point of consumption. For example, the marketing channel might include manufacturers, wholesalers, and retailers. The manufacturer could sell directly to an individual for household usage; sell to a retailer for sale to the individual; or sell to a wholesaler(s) for sale to the retailer, who then sells to the individual. As such, marketing channels consist of all the institutions and all the marketing activities (for example, storage, financing, purchasing, transporting, and so on) that are spread over time and geographical space in the marketing process. If the retailer is a member of the marketing channel that collectively does the best job, it will be better able to compete with other retailers.

Why should the retailer view itself as part of a larger marketing system? Why cannot it simply seek out the best assortment of goods for its customers, sell the goods, make a profit, go to the bank, and forget about the system? In reality, the world of retailing is not that easy. Profits sufficient for survival and growth will be difficult if not impossible

Marketing channel is a set of institutions that moves goods from the point of production to the point of consumption.

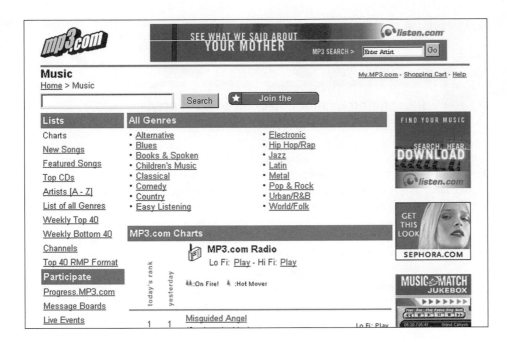

MP3.com is one of several innovative organizations that have revolutionized the marketing channel for prerecorded music.

to achieve if the retailer ignores the channel. This does not mean that the system can never be changed. Sometimes an innovative channel member, like a retailer, might break out of the existing system and replace it with a new system. For example, discounters established a new relationship with vendors by buying in large quantities, warehousing the merchandise in efficiently run distribution centers, and shipping to their stores as a means of obtaining lower prices. Another revolution is occurring in the channel for prerecorded music. MP3.com, for example, which sells music in digital format on-line, enables music lovers to get their music anywhere by downloading it from the company's servers. In addition, MP3.com allows the users to purchase music on-line or through a catalog and then listen to the music immediately, without having to go to a store. The Service Retailing box describes how the traditional channel for purchasing travel tickets is changing.

The **marketing system** consists of institutions performing marketing functions (activities), the relationships between these institutions, and the functions that are necessary to create exchange transactions with target populations or consumers. We will view the marketing system as largely synonymous with the marketing channel.

Exhibit 5.1 illustrates the marketing system. Study it closely. This exhibit portrays many of the links between institutions and functions that are necessary to bring about final exchange with target populations. Note that the marketing system is affected by five external forces: (1) consumer behavior, (2) competitor behavior, (3) the socioeconomic environment, (4) the technological environment, and (5) the legal and ethical environment. These external forces cannot be completely controlled by the retailer or any other institution in the marketing system, but they need to be taken into account when retailers make decisions. For example, a change in the minimum-wage law will usually increase the retailer's cost of doing business. A retailer cannot ignore these external forces. The retail strategic planning and operations management model (Exhibit 2.3) also dramatizes the importance of these external forces in retail decision making.

Marketing system
is the set of institutions performing marketing functions (activities), the relationships between these institutions, and the functions that are necessary to create exchange transactions with target populations or consumers.

Service Retailing

A Changing Channel Structure Has Placed Some Travel Agents Out in the Cold

The nature of the channel structure in the travel industry is undergoing a dynamic evolution. What was once a relatively tight-knit group of closely aligned agencies and travel service providers (such as airlines, hotels, and resorts) has developed into a highly competitive retail marketplace consisting of the traditional travel agents, new on-line travel service providers, and even the travel service suppliers themselves.

The travel industry is approximately a trillion-dollar-a-year industry. On-line travel bookings, though they represented only a billion dollars at the turn of the century, will represent more than $15 billion by 2005 (even by conservative estimates). This news, though good for most on-line travel services, is numbing to traditional travel agencies who are struggling as they realize that many of the marketing functions they performed in the channel are being replaced by more efficient on-line travel services.

The function of the travel agent has always been to find out what the customer wanted and then match the customer to the best available source of supply. As such, travel agents have performed the information-gathering and selling functions. Take for example the traditional travel agent transaction. A customer would either call to set up an appointment or stop by to visit a travel agent at the agency. A travel agent would then help the customer to narrow down his or her options based on the agent's resources (companies aligned with the travel agency) and then book the necessary reservations, such as hotels and airlines. However, for many travelers, the only role travel agents played was making the reservations. For these consumers, the Internet has facilitated the development of a whole new type of service retailer.

Today, on-line travel services, such as Travelocity.com or Expedia.com, provide travelers the opportunity to not only search their databases for destination information but also search hundreds of airlines and thousands of hotels for the lowest prices available. For example, let's say that you are planning to spend next summer backpacking through Europe. Rather than asking a travel agent or buying any books on traveling through Europe, you might visit on-line information retailers, such as Ricksteves.com or Lonelyplanet.com. After gathering some basic information you might head over to Expedia.com or Travelocity.com to find the lowest airline rates and to book your tickets. Given the information-gathering functions of the web and the ability to search multiple airlines for the lowest possible fare, many on-line travel services have become more efficient channel members than traditional travel agents.

However, the future is uncertain for Travelocity.com and Expedia.com as travel suppliers themselves enter the retail marketplace. Why book at Travelocity.com when you can book directly with the provider? For example, if you would like to stay at one of the Sheraton hotels in Buenos Aires, Argentina, you can simply go on-line and within minutes you can not only view the hotel and read about its amenities, but you can also book a reservation. Want a vacation at Walt Disney World? Simply go to Disney.com and make your reservations. However, sometimes a customer may wish to have a selection of service providers. In response, some service providers have strengthened their retail mix by banning together. For example, within the airline industry a consortium of six airlines — including America West, Continental, American, Northwest, and United — has developed its own on-line travel service, called Hotwire.com, to compete directly with Travelocity.com, Expedia.com, traditional travel agents, and Priceline.com. Hotwire will let customers select an actual discount fare based on their chosen route, but it will mask the identity of the airline, the routing (nonstop, one stop, or a connection), and the precise time of day of the flights until the consumer makes a purchase. Hotwire gives the airlines more control over the pricing of these discounted, nonpublished fares. However, there is a risk: Will Hotwire make fares so transparent to competitors that it will undermine regular retail prices?

Clearly, the channel structure of the travel industry is changing. As the channel structure changes, the marketing functions that each member performs changes. Many of the functions once performed by travel agents are being performed by the service providers themselves. Although the member of the channel who performs the functions may change, notice that the underlying functions do not. Someone is still needed to gather information and sell.

Exhibit 5.1	The Marketing System

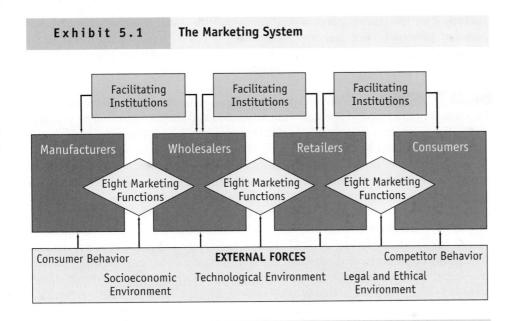

The Marketing Functions

What marketing functions need to be performed in the marketing system? Eight functions are necessary: buying, selling, storing, transporting, sorting, financing, information gathering, and risk taking. Each will be discussed briefly, but the retailer need not perform all these functions. They can be performed by any member of the channel, but they must be done by someone in the channel.

Buying   Before a retailer can sell merchandise to the final consumer, the retailer must purchase the merchandise from a supplier, either the manufacturer or a wholesaler who gets it from the manufacturer. Buying the merchandise is as important to the retailer's overall success as is selling merchandise. Sometimes the buying function is not as easy to perform as it seems. For example, it is difficult for high-end apparel retailers in smaller cities, such as Racine, Wisconsin, and Cheyenne, Wyoming, to constantly travel to New York or Los Angeles to visit the top designers. Today such retailers can cut back on these trips by using the Internet to keep up with current trends.

Because the cost of merchandise is a major expense area for most retailers, retailers that do a superior job at managing the buying function will be more profitable.

Selling   Selling is the function that most consumers associate with retailing, and it obviously is important. It involves all activities that are necessary and incidental to contacting customers and persuading them to purchase. Selling activities include advertising, personal selling, and sales promotions. Just as with the buying function, the Internet can ease the selling function. The retailer can use a web site to reach out to a larger number of customers in a wider geographic area.

Storing   Storage is necessary for many retailers because there is usually a difference between the time when products are manufactured and the time consumers purchase them. For example, an apparel manufacturer may produce a thousand blue dresses within two days, but because the demand for those dresses is not immediate, storage becomes necessary. The storage function involves many expenses, such as rent for the warehouse, insurance, fixtures, wages, ticketing the floor-ready merchandise with retailer-specific price tags, and so on. However, for service providers and some e-tailers, such as information-based retailers, storage of inventory takes on new issues. For example, storage for service retailers is impossible due to the fact that services cannot be stored. For instance, consider our golf example in Chapter 1. A golf course has the ability to provide its services throughout the day. If a threesome is scheduled, the golf course can take a loss unless it can introduce another player to make the match a foursome. As such, forecasting and pricing become paramount. Further, storage for e-tailers of information—such as the Great Outdoor Recreation Pages (www.gorp.com), which provides travel and recreation information—consists of the technical hardware storage devices and reliable web servers so that the e-tailer can provide consumers access to their information at a moment's notice.

Because for many retailers it costs money (i.e., finance charges and warehousing costs) to carry inventory, today's channels are starting to substitute information for inventory. Many suppliers have little information about when and how consumers use their products and therefore must build inventory to cover all scenarios. Retailers are now supplying that information. For example, through the use of systems such as electronic data interchange (EDI) retailers are able to provide suppliers with critical information to develop more effective working partnerships in the marketing channel. Or consider for a moment why most grocery stores offer shopping club cards that allow members to receive special discounts on products. Each time a consumer uses a shopping club card, the consumer's purchase information is tracked. As such, information gathered on individuals over time, coupled with hundreds of thousands of members worldwide, provide retailers with specific information that can be analyzed to reduce inventories and operate more efficiently. The Internet also helps retailers who cannot quickly find alternative merchandise sources when markets change. As a result, channels are developing Internet-based systems that have the ability to share information quickly and adjust to market conditions.

Transporting   Transportation is necessary when production occurs in geographical locations different from where consumers need the product and as a result the merchandise needs to be transported. Transporting merchandise from the store to the customer is also considered to be a part of the transportation function.

Transportation does not only mean physically moving an item to the consumers by way of a truck or a train and then storing the merchandise. MP3.com, as pointed out earlier, uses the Internet as its transportation vehicle and thus relies on networks, hubs, and routers to provide its products to customers.

Sorting   Sorting occurs because both demand for and supply of products are heterogeneous or different from each other. Matching these dissimilar demands and supplies involves four sorting processes: sorting out, accumulation, allocation, and assortment. Exhibit 5.2 uses the glass of orange juice you drink in the morning as an example of the sorting process.

The first step in the sorting process is sorting out, which involves separating large, heterogeneous supplies into smaller, more homogeneous groups. For example, if you go to an orange grove, you will quickly realize that not all oranges are suitable for processing into orange juice. Some will be too ripe, some will be diseased, and others may not be ripe enough or may be better suited to be sold as eating oranges. Sorting out occurs with eggs, wheat, and many other crops and raw materials. Many manufacturers, especially those working with apparel goods, complete a similar process to sort out imperfects or seconds.

The second step in the sorting process is accumulation. Accumulation consists of assembling groups of homogeneous supplies from many different sources in sufficient quantity for mass production or mass marketing. Sunkist, for example, must accumulate large quantities of high-quality oranges for its orange juice. There is a class of wholesalers who will buy in small quantities in order to accumulate the large quantities that food processors like Sunkist desire.

The third step in the sorting process is allocation, which consists of separating large amounts of processed goods into smaller quantities suitable for resale to retailers and wholesalers. Once again, the wholesaler enters the picture. A food wholesaler will buy Sunkist orange juice by the truckload (approximately 2,000 cases) and then sell it in smaller quantities to various supermarkets.

Assortment is the final step in the sorting process. Assortment occurs when someone, usually the retailer, assembles diverse supplies in a single place to meet customer demand. Surely you do not want to go to separate stores for the bacon, eggs, bread, and butter you eat with your juice! All retailers are in the business of building assortments that match the demands of the consumers who shop at their stores.

Every once in while someone thinks that he or she can skip the sorting function, only to find out one cannot. As the Retailing: The Inside Story box illustrates, such was the case for Value America, once one of Wall Street's darlings.

Financing

If we recognize that there are discrepancies between the time demand occurs and the time supplies are created, and also between geographic points of production (supply) and geographic points of consumption (demand), then it becomes clear that someone needs to finance these discrepancies. Ideally, the final consumer pays the retailer for the merchandise before the retailer must pay its supplier, but this generally does not happen. For example, most retailers have to pay for their Christmas merchandise before the Christmas selling season is over. Retailers would find it difficult to operate without credit from manufacturers. Many manufacturers, especially the smaller ones that sell to retailers, cannot afford or do not care to finance the inventory, and in these cases they sell their receivables (what the retailers owe the manufacturer) to what are referred to as "factors." **Factors** buy receivables from channel members (manufacturers, wholesalers, or retailers) at a discount and then assume the risk of collecting these accounts. Sometimes manufacturers are urged by credit rating agencies to show caution in shipping new merchandise on credit to certain retailers.

Information Gathering

Retailers must find out not only what their customers want and need, but also the best available source of supply. In some cases this may be on-line, but in other cases, especially when the consumer needs to try the product on to determine the correct size, it may require going to a brick & mortar retailer. In addition, without an exchange of information, the retailer cannot tell the consumers that it has the merchandise that will satisfy their needs. Information from the Internet

Factors
are institutions in the marketing system that buy receivables from channel members (manufacturers, wholesalers, or retailers) at a discount and then assume the risk of collecting these accounts.

Exhibit 5.2   Sorting Process

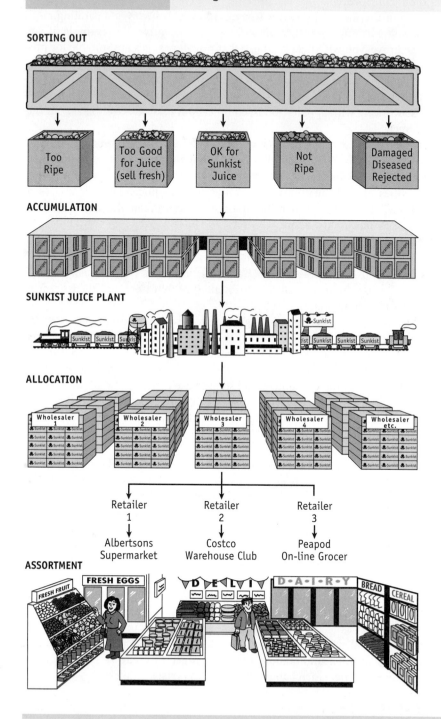

Source: Virginia Newell Lusch, used with permission.

Retailing: The Inside Story

Value America's Attempt to Eliminate the Sorting Function

Probably no company represents the failure of e-tailers to live up to their high expectations than Value America with its ultimate stock plunge. The stock went public at an initial public offering price of $23 a share in early 1999 and tripled to nearly $75 a share. After all, this stock represented the mind-set of the new economy. It was going to forever change the face of retailing. Instead Value America became the story of a business model flawed by the mistaken belief that a firm could eliminate one of the channel functions, the sorting function.

Value America's on-line operation was supposed to harness every efficiency promised by the web to create a new paradigm in retailing. What was the retailer's breakthrough idea? The store would carry no inventory and ship no products; thus it would have no need to complete the sorting process. Instead it would pick up orders from consumers and immediately transmit them to manufacturers who would ship IBM computers and Knorr soups, Panasonic televisions and Vicks VapoRub, directly to customers. Value America's business model was to sell a thousand brand names without having to carry any inventory.

Although the story was mesmerizing, the execution was a failure. Insiders say the on-line retailer never understood why other retailers used a marketing channel. Value America tried to do too much, too soon, by itself. Customers waited and waited to get orders filled. Discounting and advertising drained cash and wiped out any chance of profitability. Returned merchandise piled up in the halls of the company's offices. Some say Value America just tried to grow too fast. In retrospect, the chain forgot that someone had to perform the basic marketing functions.

Splashy expenditures on promotion worked for awhile in hiding some fundamental problems with the firm's business model. In signing up as many vendors as possible, there was little regard to whether their products were suited for sale via the web. However, the real problem was that many manufacturers simply were not capable of shipping a single box of Tide or a bottle of Advil. Manufacturers such as Procter & Gamble had always used wholesalers or sold directly to the retailers and therefore had no experience in shipping directly to consumers. One of the authors tried ordering some basic household items and was promised a three-day delivery. It took three weeks for the merchandise to arrive, and when it did the order was missing several items. Indeed, Value America's basic premise of eliminating the middleman never happened. Most orders had to be handled by the ultimate middleman: the old-fashioned wholesaler. This in turn raised the e-tailer's costs and increased its loses. In fact, Value America's stock was selling for less than $0.75 per share when it filed for bankruptcy on August 11, 2000.

---

can greatly reduce the spatial gap between production and consumption, which is essential to match suppliers properly with the demands of the retailer's market. It is not useful for suppliers to produce videotape recorders when the marketplace wants DVD players.

Risk Taking   It is obvious that demand cannot be forecast precisely. Products may be produced or purchased for resale, but the demand for those products might not materialize. In that case, the retailer can incur a loss. Consider the case of toy retailers. If they incorrectly forecast the demand for certain toys at the Christmas toy show in June and July, they may under- or overstock certain toys. Either way, a loss will occur. Another example of risk taking is a doctor's office. If the doctor's staff schedules too many appointments at one time, there is the risk of patients waiting and becoming dissatisfied. However, if the staff adjusts the amount of patients that the doctor can normally see in a given time period and some patients do not show, the doctor will miss out on

All retailers, including this medical care office, perform the risk taking function when they attempt to adjust the supply of a product or service to an uncertain demand.

some revenue. A final example of risk taking was highlighted in Chapter 1 in the discussion of Jeffery Bezos and the risks he took when starting Amazon. No wonder retailers say "risk taking's reward is profit."

Nonelimination of the Functions

Whether the economic system is capitalistic, socialistic, or somewhere in between, these eight marketing functions will exist. As pointed in the Retailing: The Inside Story box, they cannot be eliminated. They can, however, be shifted or divided among the different institutions and the consumer in the marketing system.

All forms of retailing were created by rearranging the marketing functions among institutions and consumers. For example, department stores were created specifically to build a larger and better assortment of goods. They capitalized on the opportunity to perform more of the sorting process. No longer was it necessary to travel to one store for a shirt, another for slacks, and yet another for shoes; the necessary assortment was available in a single store. Supermarkets increased consumer participation by shifting more of the information gathering, buying, and transporting functions to them. Before supermarkets, consumers could have the corner grocer select items and deliver them. But with the supermarket came self-service. Consumers had to locate the goods within the store, select them from an array of products, and transport them home. For performing more of these marketing functions, the consumer was compensated with lower prices.

A marketing function does not have to be shifted in its entirety to another institution or to the consumer but can be divided among several entities. For example, the manufacturer who does not want to perform the entire selling function could have the retailer perform part of the job through in-store promotions, local advertising, or promoting the product on its web site. At the same time, the manufacturer could assume some of the task through national advertising and developing its own web site to answer questions concerning the product itself (e.g., its installation, cleaning directions, and the manufacturer's warranty).

Retailers who understand the importance of the eight marketing functions and utilize the abilities of other channel members to most efficiently operate the channel will tend to be higher profit performers than those who do not understand their dependency on other channel members.

No member of the marketing channel would want, or be able, to perform completely all eight marketing functions. For this reason, the retailer must view itself as being dependent on others in the marketing system.

Marketing Institutions

LO • 2

What are the institutions involved and functions that must be performed in every marketing system?

What institutions are involved in performing the eight marketing functions? There are many more than you might initially think. These institutions can be meaningfully broken into two categories: primary and facilitating. **Primary marketing institutions** are those channel members that take title to the goods. **Facilitating marketing institutions** are those that do not actually take title but assist in the marketing process by specializing in the performance of certain functions. Exhibit 5.3 classifies the major institutions participating in the marketing system.

Exhibit 5.3   **Institutions Participating in the Marketing System**

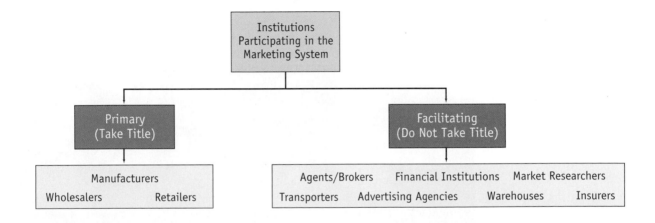

Primary marketing institutions are those channel members that take title to the goods as they move through the marketing channel. They include manufacturers, wholesalers, and retailers.

Facilitating marketing institutions are those that do not actually take title but assist in the marketing process by specializing in the performance of certain marketing functions.

Primary Marketing Institutions

There are three types of primary marketing institutions: manufacturers, wholesalers, and retailers.

Often, we do not think of manufacturers as marketing institutions because they produce goods. But manufacturers cannot exist by only producing goods; they must also sell the goods produced. Also, to produce those goods, the nation's 400,000 manufacturers must purchase many raw materials, semifinished goods, and components. In addition, manufacturers often need the assistance of other institutions in performing the eight marketing functions.

A second type of primary marketing institution is the wholesaler. Wholesalers generally buy merchandise from manufacturers and resell to retailers, other merchants, industrial institutions, and commercial users. There are nearly 500,000 wholesalers in the United States, each performing some of the eight marketing functions.

The third type of primary institution is the retailer. There are 2.4 million retail stores or establishments/institutions and over 1.8 million service establishments in the United States. Retailers can perform portions of all eight marketing functions.

It is possible that some firms, such as the membership warehouse clubs (Sam's or Costco), can act as both a wholesaler, selling to small businesses, and as a retailer, selling to households. However, for statistical purposes, the Census Bureau considers all membership warehouse clubs to be wholesalers, because the majority of their business involves wholesale transactions.

Facilitating Marketing Institutions

A variety of institutions facilitate the performance of the marketing functions. Most of these institutions specialize in one or two functions; although none of these institutions

Costco is a primary marketing institution that acts as both a wholesaler (selling to small businesses) and a retailer (selling to households).

takes title to the goods. Institutions that facilitate buying and selling in the marketing system include the following:

1. The **freelance broker** who has no permanent ties with any manufacturer and may negotiate sales for a large number of manufacturers. There is no limit on the territory in which sales may occur, but the broker is strictly bound by the manufacturer specifications on prices, terms, and conditions of sale.

2. The **manufacturer's agent** acts as the sales force for several manufacturers at the same time within a prescribed market area. The manufacturer's agent has a rather loose arrangement with the manufacturer that is seldom permanent beyond a year. This arrangement is usually renewed but can also be terminated on notice. The manufacturer's agent, like the freelance broker, is strictly bound by the manufacturer regarding prices, terms, and conditions of sale but is additionally bound by territory. Manufacturer's agents usually have jurisdiction over only a part of the manufacturer's total output. Manufacturer's agents are extremely important in product lines like furniture, dry goods, clothing, and accessories.

3. The **sales agent** has long-term arrangements with one or very few manufacturers. The sales agent sells the entire output for the manufacturer and has no limitation on territory, prices, terms, or conditions of sale. The sales agent also frequently finances the manufacturer. The sales agent is generally used for such product lines as home furnishings, textiles, and canned goods.

4. **Purchasing agents** specialize in seeking out sources of supply for some members of the channel. They operate on a contractual basis for a limited number of customers and receive a commission just as sales agents do. Purchasing agents, who are sometimes known as **resident buyers** and who once were a way of life for retail buyers, especially in the apparel industry, usually operate in New York City. They were the buying arm and intelligence service for out-of-town retailers and provide information on the availability of products; what showrooms to shop and not shop; the reliability of suppliers; present and future market trends; and special deals, prices, shipping, and other considerations involving the purchase of merchandise. Today, however, because of advances in communication and the advent of mega-retailers, only a few major resident buying offices remain.[1]

These facilitating agents and brokers are independent businesspeople who receive a commission or fee when they are able to bring buyer and seller together to negotiate a transaction. In addition to not taking title to the merchandise, agents and/or brokers seldom take physical possession of the merchandise. The purchasing agents assist in buying and the others assist in selling for manufacturers. One of the new breed of e-tailing brokers is Priceline.com, which has pioneered a unique e-commerce pricing system known as a "demand collection system," which allows it to act without holding any inventory. Priceline's system enables consumers to use the Internet to make bids on a wide range of products and services while enabling sellers to generate incremental revenue. Using its "name your own price" proposition, Priceline collects consumer demand, in the form of individual customer offers guaranteed by a credit card, for a particular product or service at a price set by the customer. Priceline then either communicates that demand directly to participating sellers or accesses participating sellers' private databases to determine whether Priceline can fulfill the customer's offer and earn its brokerage commission. Priceline's unique business model can be applied to a broad range of products and services and is already being copied.

Freelance broker
is a broker who has no permanent ties with any manufacturer and may negotiate sales over any territory for a large number of manufacturers.

Manufacturer's agent
is an agent who acts as the sales force for several manufacturers at the same time within a prescribed market area.

Sales agent
is an agent who has long-term arrangements with one or very few manufacturers to sell their entire output and has no limitation on territory, prices, terms, or conditions.

Purchasing agent
is an agent who operates on a contractual and commission basis for a limited number of customers and specializes in seeking out sources of supply for some members of the channel.

Resident buyers
are purchasing agents that reside in the central market for a particular line of merchandise and represent several retailers in that market.

The New York Stock Exchange is a facilitating institution that provides public-held retailers access to equity capital that can be used to finance marketing functions.

Advertising agencies also facilitate the selling process by designing effective advertisements and advising management on where and when to place these advertisements.

Institutions that facilitate the transportation function are motor, rail, and air carriers, and pipeline and shipping companies. Transporters can have a significant effect on how efficiently goods move through the marketing system. These firms offer differing advantages in terms of delivery, service, and cost. Generally, the quicker the delivery, the more costly it is. However, there is usually a trade-off in that the higher transportation costs will enable the channel to have lower warehousing costs. As a result, Federal Express and UPS are often viewed by Wall Street as e-tailing stocks, because e-tailers need these two transportation companies to deliver their merchandise.

The major facilitating institution involved in storage is the public warehouse. A **public warehouse** stores goods for safekeeping for any owner in return for a fee. Fees are usually based on cubic feet used per time period (month or day). Frequently, retailers take advantage of special promotional buys that manufacturers offer but often have no space for the goods in their stores or warehouses. As a result, they find it necessary to use public warehouses.

Public warehouse is a facility that stores goods for safekeeping for any owner in return for a fee, usually based on space occupied.

A variety of facilitating institutions also assist in providing information in the marketing system. For example, the role of the computer specialists, referred to as "system integrators," in setting up computer systems for transmitting information is evident throughout the business world. Retailers can now order many types of merchandise using an on-line computer. In fact, many retail analysts believe that Wal-Mart's leap into the number 1 spot in retail sales stems directly from the deployment of sophisticated electronics to run a huge supply and distribution network in which more than 7,000 of its suppliers access Wal-Mart's system about 120,000 times a week.[2] Today most of the major retailers require that all their vendors be linked electronically to the retailer's computer, permitting the vendors to automatically ship replacements without purchase orders and receive payment by electronic funds transfers. As a result of this saving in

Insurance agents are a vital facilitating institution that help firms manage the risk taking function by offering insurance services on such things as inventories, warehouses, and transportation vehicles.

distribution costs, the majority of retailers have been able to hold their selling prices constant despite a slight increase in merchandise costs.

There are also facilitating institutions that aid in financing, such as commercial banks, merchant banks, savings and loan associations, stock exchanges, and venture capital firms. These institutions can provide, or help the retailer obtain, funds to finance marketing functions. Retailers frequently need short-term loans for working capital requirements (to handle increased inventory and accounts receivables) and long-term loans for continued growth and expansion (adding new stores or remodeling).

Finally, insurance firms facilitate by assuming some of the risks in the marketing system. Insurance firms can insure inventories, buildings, trucks, equipment and fixtures, and other assets for the retailer and other primary marketing institutions. They can also insure against employee and customer injuries.

Having reviewed the various functions and institutions in the marketing system, we are now ready to examine how the primary marketing institutions are arranged into a marketing channel.

Types of Marketing Channels

LO • 3
What are the different types of retail channels?

A large part of the marketing system consists of the marketing functions and the primary marketing institutions that perform them. But how are these functions and institutions arranged into a marketing channel? Exhibit 5.4 shows that there are actually three strategy decisions to be made when designing an efficient marketing channel that can compete with other channels: channel length, channel width, and control of the channel.

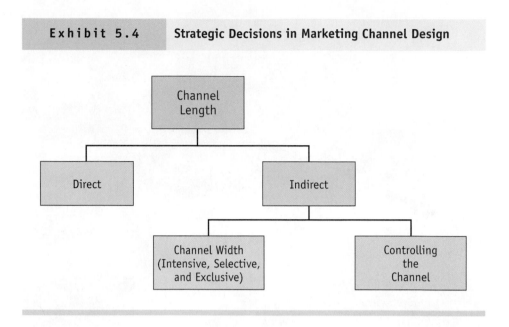

Exhibit 5.4   **Strategic Decisions in Marketing Channel Design**

Channel Length

Direct channel
is the channel that results when a manufacturer sells its goods directly to the final consumer or end user.

Indirect channel
is the channel that results once independent channel members are added between the manufacturer and the consumer.

As shown in Exhibit 5.5, channels can be direct or indirect. A **direct channel** occurs when a manufacturer sells its goods directly to the final consumer or end user. Here the manufacturer performs all the functions, although the consumer does make the final purchase. An example of such a channel is when Firestone sells some of its tires through company-owned retail outlets to the consumer. The channel becomes an **indirect channel** once independent channel members (wholesalers and retailers) are added between the manufacturer and the consumer. Indirect channels, as shown in Exhibit 5.5, may just have a retailer added or may have both a retailer and a wholesaler. For example, when Whirlpool produces a washer that meets Sears' specifications to be sold under the retailer's Kenmore private label and then Sears sells it to the consumer, the channel is described as an indirect manufacturer-to-retailer-to-consumer channel. When Kmart purchases Hunt's catsup from Fleming, a large food wholesaler, who had already purchased the catsup from its manufacturer, ConAgra, the channel is said to be an indirect manufacturer-to-wholesaler-to-retailer-to-consumer channel.

Sometimes the length of a channel is hard to determine. For example, when a consumer purchases cosmetics from Avon's web site, the channel is said to be a direct manufacturer-to-consumer channel. However, if the consumer made the identical purchase from an Avon sales representative, the channel would actually be an indirect one; manufacturer-to-retailer (the Avon lady is an independent businessperson)-to-consumer.

The desired channel length is determined by many customer-based factors, such as the size of the customer base, the customers' geographical dispersion, and their particular behavior patterns. The nature of the product, such as its bulk and weight, perishability, value, and technical complexity, can also be very important in determining channel length. For example, expensive, highly technological items such as music systems for your home will generally use short channels because of the high degree of technical support needed by customers, which may only be available directly from the manufacturer. Moreover, length can also be affected by the size of the manufacturer, its

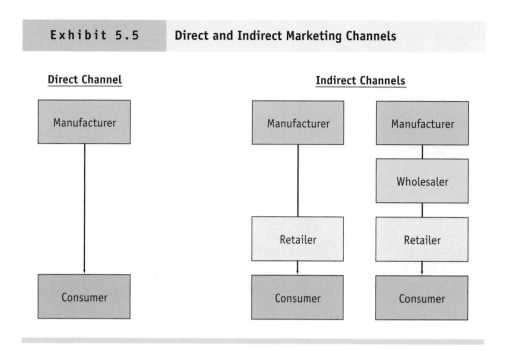

Exhibit 5.5 — Direct and Indirect Marketing Channels

financial capacity, and its desire for control. In general, larger and more well-financed manufacturers have a greater capability to bypass intermediaries and use shorter channel structures. Manufacturers desiring to exercise a high degree of control over the distribution of their products are also more likely to use shorter channel structures because the shorter the channel, the higher the degree of control. The product being sold will affect the channel's width. However, retailers do not always have a lot of control over their channel length. For example, retailers entering Japan will find that their channel's long length is to a great extent predetermined. Japan's channel structure (often referred to as a multitiered distribution system) was formed back in feudal times and has always been accepted the way it is. Therefore, sometime the retailer must learn to operate efficiently within marketing systems that may seem inefficient.

Channel Width

Channel width, shown in Exhibit 5.6, is usually described in terms of intensive distribution, selective distribution, or exclusive distribution. Channel width pertains to the number of retailers used to serve a given trading area. **Intensive distribution** means that all possible retailers in a trading area are used. **Selective distribution** means that a moderate number of retailers in a trading area are used. **Exclusive distribution** means only one retailer is used to cover a trading area. Although there are many exceptions, as a rule intensive distribution is associated with the distribution of convenience goods, which are products that the consumer is not willing to spend a great deal of effort in purchasing; selective distribution is associated with shopping goods, which are goods for which the consumer will make a price/value comparison before purchasing; and exclusive distribution is associated with specialty goods, which are products that the consumer expressly seeks out. Thus, soft drinks, milk, and greeting cards (convenience goods) tend to be carried by very large number of retailers, whereas home appliances and apparel (shopping goods) are handled by relatively

Intensive distribution
means that all possible
retailers are used in a trade
area.

Selective distribution
means that a moderate
number of retailers are used
in a trade area.

Exclusive distribution
means only one retailer is
used to cover a trading area.

Exhibit 5.6	**Width of Marketing Channel**

Exclusive Distribution

```
Manufacturer
     |
  Retailer
```

Only one retailer
in trading area
with manufacturer's
product(s)

Selective Distribution

```
      Manufacturer
       /      \
  Retailer   Retailer
```

Moderate number of retailers
used in each trading area

Intensive Distribution

```
            Manufacturer
         /    |    |    \
  Retailer Retailer Retailer Retailer
```

Product(s) is/are offered for sale by all
possible retailers in the trading area

---

fewer retailers, and specialty goods such as Rolex watches or Rolls Royce automobiles are featured by only one dealer in a trading area.

Channel Control

The previous discussion was concerned with the length and width of a marketing channel. However, a more pressing issue is who should control the channel. After all, most channels are made up of independent business firms who without the proper leadership may/will tend to look out for themselves to the detriment of the other channel members. For this reason, no channel will ever operate at a 100 percent efficiency level. All channel members must have as their goal "to minimize the suboptimization" of the channel.

In seeking to control or manage a channel, there are two basic channel patterns: the conventional marketing channel and the vertical marketing system. Exhibit 5.7 provides an illustration of these major channel patterns.

Conventional marketing channel
is one in which each channel member is loosely aligned with the others and takes a short-term orientation.

Conventional Marketing Channel   A **conventional marketing channel** is one in which each member of the channel is loosely aligned with the others and takes a short-term orientation. Predictably, each member's orientation is toward the next institution in the channel and "what is happening today" as opposed to "what will happen in the future." Thus the manufacturer interacts with and focuses efforts on the wholesaler, the wholesaler focuses efforts on the retailer, and the retailer focuses efforts on the final consumer. In short, all of the members focus on their immediate desire to close the sale or create a transaction. Thus the conventional marketing channel consists of a series of pairs in which the members of each pair recognize each other but not necessarily the other members of the system.

The conventional marketing channel, although historically predominant in the United States, is a sloppy and inefficient method of conducting business. It fosters intense negotiations within each pair of institutions in the channel. In addition, channel

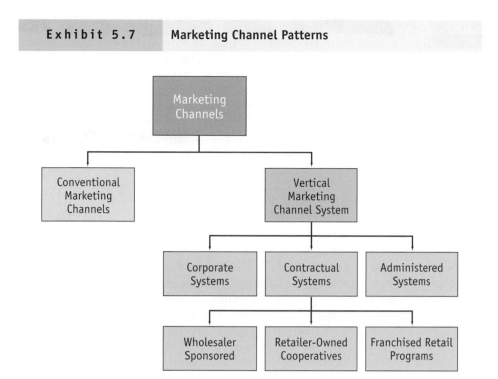

Exhibit 5.7   Marketing Channel Patterns

members do not see the possibility of shifting or dividing the marketing functions among all channel participants. Therefore, it is an unproductive method for marketing goods and has been on the decline in the United States since the early 1950s.

Vertical Marketing Systems   Vertical marketing systems are capital-intensive networks of several levels that are professionally managed and centrally programmed to realize the technological, managerial, and promotional economies of a long-term relationship orientation. The basic premise behind the idea of vertically managing a channel is to operate as close to that elusive 100 percent efficiency level as possible. This is done by eliminating the suboptimization that exists in conventional channels and improving the channel's performance by working together.

Vertical marketing systems
are capital-intensive networks of several levels that are professionally managed and centrally programmed to realize the technological, managerial, and promotional economies of a long-term relationship orientation.

Virtually every high profit performance retailer in the U.S. economy is part of a vertical marketing system.

Formerly adversarial relationships between retailers and their suppliers are now giving way to new vertical channel programs of channel partnership to minimize such inefficiencies.[3] Because vertical channel members now realize that it is impossible to offer consumers value without being the low-cost, high-efficiency channel, they have

Quick response (QR) systems,
also known as **efficient consumer response (ECR) systems,** are integrated information, production, and logistical systems that obtain real-time information on consumer actions by capturing sale data at point-of-purchase terminals and then transmitting this information back through the entire channel to enable efficient production and distribution scheduling.

Category management (CM)
is a process of managing all SKUs within a product category and involves the simultaneous management of price, shelf space, merchandising strategy, promotional efforts, and other elements of the retail mix within the category based on the firm's goals, the changing environment, and consumer behavior.

Corporate vertical marketing systems
exist where one channel institution owns multiple levels of distribution and typically consists of either a manufacturer that has integrated vertically forward to reach the consumer or a retailer that has integrated vertically backward to create a self-supply network.

Contractual vertical marketing systems
use a contract to govern the working relationship between channel members and include wholesaler-sponsored voluntary groups, retailer-owned cooperatives, and franchised retail programs.

developed either **quick response (QR) systems** or **efficient consumer response (ECR) systems.** These systems, which are the same despite the different names adopted by various retail industries, are designed to obtain real-time information on consumers' actions by capturing SKU (stock-keeping-units are the lowest level of identification of merchandise) data at point of purchase terminals and then transmitting this information back through the entire channel. This information is used to develop new or modified products, manage channel-wide inventory levels, and lower total channel costs. Category management is an important part of ECR. **Category management (CM)** is a process of managing all SKUs within a product category, not a single SKU or alternatively the entire store's merchandise. Category management involves the simultaneous management of price, shelf space merchandising strategy, promotional efforts, and other elements of the retail mix within the category based on the firm's goals, the changing environment, and consumer behavior. CM is accomplished in a channel establishing a team—made up of channel members who in a conventional channel would have acted independently—to apply the ECR concept to an entire category of merchandise.

The goal for most CM-oriented retailers is to optimize the operations of each part of the store by allocating space that maximizes gross margin dollars produced per unit of space. For a supplier working with a CM retailer, the goal is to become the lead supplier for that category. The names of the channel members who are active in CM read like a who's who list: at the retail level the names include Wal-Mart, H-E-B Grocery, Dominick's, and Schnuck's; at the wholesale level are Fleming and SuperValue, among others; at the manufacturing level the list includes General Electric, Procter & Gamble, Kraft/General Foods, M&M/Mars, Quaker Oats, VF Corp. (manufacturer of Lee Jeans), and Hallmark.

There are three types of vertical marketing systems: corporate, contractual, and administered. Each has grown significantly in the past 50 years.

CORPORATE SYSTEMS   **Corporate vertical marketing systems** typically consist of either a manufacturer that has integrated vertically forward to reach the consumer or a retailer that has integrated vertically backward to create a self-supply network. The first type includes manufacturers such as Sherwin Williams (paint), Hart, Schaffner and Marx (men's apparel), and Famolare (shoes), which have created their own warehousing and retail outlets. The second type includes retailers such as Holiday Inns. For example, Holiday Inns has vertically integrated to control a carpet mill, furniture manufacturer, and numerous other suppliers needed to build and operate its hotels.

In corporate systems it is much easier to program the channel for productivity and profit goals, because a well-established authority structure already exists. Independent retailers that have aligned themselves in a conventional marketing channel are at a significant disadvantage when competing against a corporate vertical marketing system.

CONTRACTUAL SYSTEMS   **Contractual vertical marketing systems,** which include wholesaler-sponsored voluntary groups, retailer-owned cooperatives, and franchised retail programs, are channel systems that use a contract to govern the working relationship between the members. Each of these channel types allows for a more coordinated and system-wide perspective than conventional marketing channels. However, they are more difficult to manage than corporate vertical marketing systems because the authority and power structures are not as well defined. Channel members must give up some autonomy to gain system economies of scale and greater market impact.

Wholesaler-sponsored Voluntary Groups   **Wholesaler-sponsored voluntary groups** are created when a wholesaler brings together a group of independently owned retailers (independent retailers is a term embracing anything from a single mom-and-pop store to a small local chain), grocers for example, and offers them a coordinated merchandising and buying program that will provide them with economies like those their chain store rivals are able to obtain. In return, the independent retailers agree to concentrate their purchases with that wholesaler. It is a voluntary relationship; that is, there are no membership or franchise fees. The independent retailer may terminate the relationship whenever it desires, so it is to the wholesaler's advantage to build competitive merchandise assortments and offer other services that will keep the voluntary group satisfied. Nonetheless, some retailers will reach a level of sophistication and sales volume at which they believe they can handle their own distribution. Fleming Companies (one the nation's largest food wholesalers and an early pioneer in voluntary group wholesaling with annual sales in excess of $16 billion) has lost customers such as West Texas's United Supermarkets when United, upon reaching 50 stores, decided to build its own warehouse and transportation systems.

The voluntary group wholesaler commonly offers the retailer the following services: store design and layout, store site and location analysis, inventory management systems, accounting and bookkeeping systems, insurance services, pension plans, trade area studies, advertising and promotion assistance, and employee training programs. The better the services and merchandising programs offered by the wholesaler, the more loyal the retailer and the more the wholesaler can direct and organize the channel's activities. Associated Wholesale Grocers, for example, has developed a special program for its retailers facing competition from supercenters entering their trading area. A year in advance of the supercenter's arrival, Associated helps its retailers adjust prices, remodel or relocate stores, add bakeries and delis, and develop other strategies to successfully combat the supercenters.

In the past, local food wholesalers got practically all of their business from independent grocers. Recently, however, as transportation costs have risen, major chains operating over a wide geographic area have also started using local or national wholesalers. While welcoming this new business, wholesalers have tried to keep their independents happy (as they still account for over 40 percent of their business) by offering them even more services.

Wholesaler-sponsored voluntary groups have been a major force in marketing channels since the mid-1960s. They are now prevalent in many lines of trade. Independent Grocers' Alliance (IGA)and National Auto Parts Association (NAPA) are both examples of wholesaler-sponsored voluntary groups.

Retailer-owned Cooperatives   Another common type of contractual vertical marketing system is **retailer-owned cooperatives,** which are organized and owned by retailers and are most common in hardware retailing. They include such wholesalers as TRU*SERV (which was highlighted in the Inside Story box in Chapter 2), Ace, and Handy Hardware. They offer scale economies and services to member retailers, allowing their members to compete with larger chain-buying organizations.

Finally, it should be pointed out that in theory, wholesale-sponsored groups should be easier to manage because they have only one owner, the wholesaler, versus the many owners of the retailer-owned group. In retailer-owned wholesale cooperatives, individual members tend to want to keep their autonomy and be less dependent on their supplier-partner for support and direction. In reality, however, just the opposite has been true. A possible explanation for this is that retailers belonging to a wholesale co-op may make greater transaction-specific investments in the form of stock ownership, vested supplier-based store identity, and end-of-year rebates on purchases that combine to erect significant exit barriers.[4]

Wholesaler-sponsored voluntary groups involve a wholesaler that brings together a group of independently owned retailers and offers them a coordinated merchandising and buying program that will provide them with economies like those their chain store rivals are able to obtain.

Retailer-owned cooperatives are wholesale institutions, organized and owned by member retailers, that offer scale economies and services to member retailers, which allows them to compete with larger chain-buying organizations.

Genuine Auto Parts Company has organized a highly successful wholesale sponsored voluntary group which operates under the NAPA banner.

Franchise

is a form of licensing by which the owner of a product, service, or business method (the franchisor) obtains distribution through affiliated dealers (franchisees).

Franchises   The third type of contractual vertical marketing system is the franchise. A franchise is a form of licensing by which the owner of a product, service, or method (the franchisor) obtains distribution through affiliated dealers (franchisees). In many cases the franchise operation resembles a large chain with trademarks, uniform symbols, equipment, storefronts, and standardized services, products, and practices as outlined in the franchise agreement.

Franchising is a convenient and economic means of fulfilling the desire for independence that many individuals have with a minimum amount of risk and investment and maximum opportunities for success. This is possible through the utilization of a proven product or service and marketing method. However, the owner of a franchise gives up some freedom in business decisions that the owner of a nonfranchised business would have. To maintain uniformity of service and to ensure that the operations of each outlet will reflect favorably on the organization as a whole, the franchisor usually exercises some degree of control over the operations of franchisees, requiring them to meet stipulated standards of product and service quality and operating procedures.

Franchisors can be found at any position in the marketing channel. The franchisor could be a manufacturer, such as Chevrolet and Midas Mufflers; a service specialist, such as Kelly Girl, Mail Boxes Etc, AAMCO Transmissions, H&R Block, Jenny Craig Weight Loss Centers, Supercuts, and Century 21 Real Estate; a retailer that rents formalwear, such as Gingiss Formalwear, or a fast-food retailer, such as McDonald's, Dunkin' Donuts, Subway, Domino's Pizza, and KFC. Exhibit 5.8 lists some of the major advantages and disadvantages of owning a franchise.

Franchisors that focus their expansion efforts internationally will experience a higher profit potential.

Exhibit 5.8	Advantages and Disadvantages of Franchise Ownership

Advantages to Franchisee

1. Franchisor provides managerial skills that are taught to franchisee.
2. Franchisee can begin a business with a relatively small capital investment.
3. Franchisee can acquire a relatively well known or established line of business.
4. Franchisee can acquire rights to a well-defined geographical area.
5. The standardized marketing programs and operating procedures enable the franchisee to be competitive immediately.
6. Because they own a piece of the action, franchisees tend to be more motivated and bottom-line oriented than managers.

Disadvantages to Franchisee

1. Too many franchises can be located in a geographical area.
2. Too many franchisors make promises they cannot keep (e.g, overstating the income potential of a franchise).
3. Franchisors can include a buyback agreement whereby the franchisee must sell back the franchise at a given point in time or the franchise agreement is for a short duration.
4. Under most franchise agreements, payments to the franchisor are a percentage of sales regardless of a franchisee's profitability.
5. Franchise systems may be too inflexible in terms of operating procedures (hours, product selection, etc.) for the franchisee. In short, the franchisee must surrender its freedom to make many decisions.

Although only a third of U.S. franchisors are currently operating in foreign countries, another third are looking to expand internationally within the next five years. After all, as the Global Retailing box indicates, why compete in overstored U.S. markets when many foreign markets are available? Although franchising is seen as an economic-development tool for poor countries, the most widely considered foreign markets are Canada, Japan, Mexico, Germany, the United Kingdom, and more recently Southeast Asia (Philippines, Thailand, Taiwan, Singapore, and Indonesia).

ADMINISTERED SYSTEMS   The final type of vertical marketing system is the administered system. **Administered vertical marketing systems** are similar to conventional marketing channels, but one of the channel members takes the initiative to lead the channel by applying the principles of effective interorganizational management, which is the management of relationships between the various organizations in the channel. Administered systems, although not new in concept, have grown substantially in recent years. Frequently, administered systems are initiated by manufacturers because they have historically relied on their administrative expertise to coordinate the retailers' marketing efforts. Suppliers with dominant brands have predictably experienced the least difficulty in securing strong support from retailers and wholesalers. But many manufacturers with "fringe" items have been able to elicit such cooperation only through the use of liberal distribution policies that take the form of attractive discounts (or discount substitutes), financial assistance, and various types of concessions that protect resellers from one or more of the risks of doing business.[5]

Administered vertical marketing systems exist when one of the channel members takes the initiative to lead the channel by applying the principles of effective interorganizational management.

Global Retailing

The Master Franchisor: The Middleman in Global Franchising

Global franchising is a driving force in retailing and global economic development. Franchising has spread its success to every corner of the globe, penetrating streets, plazas, shopping centers, malls, metro stations, and even the Internet with products and services that are replicates of their originals. By taking a successful retail format (whether it be product or service based) and transferring it with slight modifications to a world market, retailers such as McDonald's (United States), The Body Shop (United Kingdom), and Benetton Group (Italy) have become globally successful. With each new successful foreign expansion, entrepreneurial individuals, as well as firms, are increasingly becoming interested in becoming franchisees.

One aspect of franchising which is unique to the global arena is known as "master franchising." A **master franchisor** is positioned between the franchisor and its franchisees in a foreign market, providing both a cultural link and the critical managerial experience and funding necessary for the franchisees' success. Here's how a master franchisor arrangement works. Let's say that a German master franchisor believes that there is an incredible opportunity to have a Brazilian fast-food retailer in Germany due to a recent trend in Germany for exotic foods. The German master franchisor would acquire the franchise development rights for the country (or a particular region) from the franchisor (the Brazilian fast-food retailer). The master franchisor would then be responsible for selecting local franchisees, providing them with managerial assistance, collecting the franchise fees, and the like.

As one might expect, the use of a master franchisor has a significant number of advantages. Master franchisors are well versed in business operations, have capital available, and are intimately knowledgeable about local culture. In addition, they typically also have many political connections that can facilitate the quick entry into sometimes difficult to enter markets.

However, as you might guess, the master franchisor also creates a number of potential problems for successful franchising. The use of a master franchisor eliminates the direct link between the franchisor and the franchisee, thus limiting to some degree the effectiveness of the communication and control of the franchisor with its franchisees. Consider, for example, the franchisee in Germany of the Brazilian fast-food retailer. The franchisee has obtained their franchise from the master franchisor. However, the franchisee is a franchisee of the Brazilian fast-food retailer. When the master franchisor and the franchisor are telling them to do two contradictory things, whom should they listen to?

Although master franchisor systems have the potential to create inefficiencies in operations, most franchisors entering the global marketplace believe that the benefits far outweigh the costs. However, each individual franchisor must weigh the costs and benefits to determine what is in their firm's best interest.

Master franchisor
is a business positioned between the franchisor and franchisee in a foreign market, providing a cultural link and critical managerial experience and funding necessary for the franchisee's success.

Some of the concessions manufacturers offer retailers are liberal return policies, display materials for in-store use, advertising allowances, extra time in paying for the merchandise, employee-training programs, assistance with store layout and design, inventory maintenance, computer systems support, and even free merchandise.

Manufacturers that use their administrative powers to lead channels include Sealy (on its Posturepedic line of mattresses), Villager (on its dresses and sportswear lines), Scott (on its lawn-care products), Norwalk (on its upholstered furniture), Keepsake (on diamonds), and Stanley (on hand tools). Retailers can also dominate the channel relationship. For example, Wal-Mart, one of the earliest adopters of ECR and CM systems, administers its relationships with almost all of its suppliers by asking that all advertising allowances, slotting fees, end display fees, and so on be taken off the price of goods.

Many retailers, including McDonald's, have used the franchise system of distribution to expand globally.

Managing Retailer-Supplier Relations

LO • 4

How does dependency, power, cooperation, and conflict influence channel relations?

Retailers who are not part of a contractual system or corporate channel will probably participate in several marketing channels, because they will need to acquire merchandise from many suppliers. Predictably, these marketing channels will either be conventional or administered. If retailers want to improve their performance in these channels, they must understand the principal concepts of interorganizational management. In this case, it involves a retailer managing its relations with wholesalers and manufacturers.

What are the basic concepts of interorganizational management that a retailer needs to understand? They are dependency, power, conflict, and managing cooperative relations.

Dependency

As we mentioned earlier, all marketing systems need to perform eight marketing functions. These functions are performed by a multitude of institutions in the marketing channel. None of the respective institutions can isolate itself; each depends on the others to do an effective job.

Retailer A is dependent on suppliers X, Y, and Z to make sure that goods are delivered on time and in the right quantities. Conversely, suppliers X, Y, and Z depend on retailer A to put a strong selling effort behind the goods, displaying the merchandise and helping to finance consumer purchases. If retailer A does a poor job, each supplier can be adversely affected; if even one supplier does a poor job, retailer A can be adversely affected. In all channel alignments, each party depends on the others to do a good job.

When each party is dependent on the others, we say that they are interdependent. Interdependency is at the root of cooperation and conflict in marketing channels. To better understand cooperation and conflict between retailers and suppliers, an understanding of power is necessary.

Power

We can use the concept of dependency to explain power; but first we must define power. **Power** is the ability of one channel member to influence the decisions of the other channel members. The more dependent the supplier is on the retailer, the more power the retailer has over the supplier. For example, a small manufacturer of grocery products would be very dependent on a large supermarket chain if it wanted to reach the most consumers. Or many suppliers to Wal-Mart are very dependent on it because Wal-Mart is their biggest customer. For example, Wal-Mart accounts for 36 percent of the annual sales for National Picture & Frames, a manufacturer of frames and mirrors, making National Picture & Frames highly dependent on Wal-Mart.[6]

There are six sources of power:

Power
is the ability of one channel member to influence the decisions of the other channel members.

1. **Reward power** is based on B's perception that A has the ability to provide rewards for B. For instance, a retailer offers a manufacturer a prominent display area in exchange for additional advertising monies and promotion support.

Reward power
is based on B's perception that A has the ability to provide rewards for B.

2. **Expertise power** is based on B's perception that A has some special knowledge. For example, Midas Muffler (a franchisor) has developed an excellent training program for store managers. Thus franchisees view the franchisor as an expert.

Expertise power
is based on B's perception that A has some special knowledge.

3. **Referent power** is based on the identification of B with A. B wants to be associated or identified with A. Examples of this would be the auto dealers that want to handle BMWs or Mercedes because of the cars' status or a manufacturer that wants to have its product sold in Neiman Marcus because of the image that retailer projects.

Referent power
is based on the identification of B with A.

4. **Coercive power** is based on B's belief that A has the capacity to punish or harm B if B does not do what A wants. A franchisor, Burger King, for example, has the right to cancel a franchisee's contract if it fails to maintain standards concerning restaurant cleanliness, food, hours of operation, and employees.

Coercive power
is based on B's belief that A has the capability to punish or harm B if B doesn't do what A wants.

5. **Legitimate power** is based on A's right to influence B, or B's belief that B should accept A's influence. The appearance of legitimate power is most obvious in contractual marketing systems. A manufacturer may, for example, threaten to cut off a retailer's supply if the retailer does not properly display the manufacturer's products. Also, if the retailer accepts co-op advertising dollars, the manufacturer may control the minimum retail price, as this subject is usually covered in the agreement. Otherwise the retailer is free to set the selling price. To do otherwise without an agreement specifically covering retail price would be a violation of certain federal antitrust laws, which we will discuss in the next chapter.

Legitimate power
is based on A's right to influence B, or B's belief that B should accept A's influence.

6. **Informational power** is based on A's ability to provide B with factual data. Though not to be confused with expertise power, informational power is when the factual data is provided independently of the relationship between A and B. An example of this power would be a small retail store sharing scanner data with a vendor.

Informational power
is based on A's ability to provide B with factual data.

Retailers and suppliers that use reward, expertise, referent, and informational power can foster cooperation. On the other hand, the use of coercive and legitimate power tends to elicit conflict and destroy cooperation.

Conflict

Conflict between retailers and suppliers is inevitable because retailers and suppliers are interdependent. After all, every channel member is dependent on every other member. As such, interdependency has been identified as the root cause of all conflict in marketing channels. There are three major sources of conflict between retailers and their suppliers: perceptual incongruity, goal incompatibility, and domain disagreement.

Perceptual incongruity occurs when the retailer and supplier have different perceptions of reality. A retailer may perceive that the economy is entering a recession and therefore may want to cut inventory investments, whereas the supplier may perceive that the economy will remain strong and therefore may feel that inventory investments should be maintained or possibly increased. Perceptual incongruity is a major source of conflict in the marketing channel. For example, consider the following areas, which the retailer and supplier might perceive differently: the quality of the supplier's merchandise, the potential demand for the supplier's merchandise, the consumer appeal of the supplier's advertising, and the best shelf position for the supplier's merchandise.

A second source of conflict is **goal incompatibility,** a situation in which achieving the goals of either the supplier or the retailer would hamper the performance of the other. An example of the retailer's goals being incompatible with the supplier's goals is a situation known as dual distribution. Dual distribution occurs when a manufacturer that sells to independent retailers decides to also sell directly to the final consumer through its own retail outlets or through an Internet site. Thus the manufacturer manages a corporately owned vertical marketing system that competes with independent retailers, which it also supplies through a conventional, administered, or contractual marketing channel. Retailers tend to become upset about dual distribution when the two channels compete at the retail level in the same geographic area. For example, some manufacturers, such as Liz Claiborne, London Fog, Guess, Bass, and Esprit, have factory outlet stores that sell directly to the public at 50 to 70 percent off regular retail prices. These outlets traditionally were only located near a manufacturer's factory, but now the trend is to open these stores in factory outlet malls. This practice has angered traditional retailers that buy from these manufacturers and can have an adverse effect on manufacturer-retailer relationships. Two independent retailers who used the courts successfully to stop what they considered to be an unfair dual distribution system by Levi Strauss were Macy's and JCPenney.[7] In this case, Levi not only wanted to sell through the retailers' stores, but via its own Internet site, as well. The following E-tailing box illustrates how one major retailer handled possible dual distribution problems.

The problem of goal incompatibility is not necessarily one of profit versus image goals. Even if the retailer and supplier both have a return on investment (ROI) goal, they can still be incompatible, because what is good for the retailer's ROI may not be good for the supplier's ROI. Consider the price element in the transaction between the supplier and the retailer. If the supplier obtains a higher price, its ROI will be higher, but the ROI of the retailer will be lower. Similarly, other key elements in the transaction between the retailer and supplier such as advertising allowances, cash discounts, order quantity, and freight charges can result in conflict.

Perceptual incongruity occurs when the retailer and supplier have different perceptions of reality.

Goal incompatibility occurs when achieving the goals of either the supplier or the retailer would hamper the performance of the other.

E-tailing

The E-tailing Opportunities for Traditional Manufacturers May Create Channel Conflicts

The role of retailers in facilitating the transfer of a manufacturer's product to their customers is critical to a manufacturer's success. Manufacturers realize the value that retailers provide and recognize that strong channel relationships can create a competitive advantage in the marketplace. As such, over the past few decades manufacturers have invested heavily in developing strong relationships with their retailers.

However, the world of retailing is undergoing tremendous changes with the introduction of the Internet. The Internet provides new opportunities for manufacturers to not only develop closer relationships with their customers by interfacing with them directly but to offer their products directly to consumers. What is the cost to a manufacturer of becoming an e-tailer? What does a manufacturer's move to become an e-tailer do to its existing channel relationships? And how would a manufacturer's retail partners react?

One of the first, but most certainly not the last, conflicts to emerge between manufacturers and retailers resulting from the opportunities created by the Internet involved one of the nation's most well-regarded retailers, Home Depot, and one of its major suppliers. In the spring of 1999 Home Depot was in the final stages of planning its e-tailing strategy. The company had decided that in order to be competitive, it would employ a strategy of partnering with its manufacturers. In doing so, Home Depot would become the only on-line retailer of its manufacturers' products. However, some of Home Depot's suppliers had already ventured into the on-line retail marketplace.

Home Depot, being the primary retailer in the industry, considered their options. Then, in early 1999, Home Depot sent a letter to its most valued suppliers that stated "We recognize that a vendor has the right to sell through whatever distribution channels it desires. However, we too, have the right to be selective in regard to vendors we select, and we trust that you can understand that a company may be hesitant to do business with its competitors."[8]

Was this a threat? Maybe it was. Whether it was or wasn't is not as important as the fact that when a manufacturer becomes an e-tailer it not only becomes a competitor of its retail partners, but it also threatens the very relationships it has invested so much to build. It may come down to a simple question: If the retailer refused to sell the manufacturer's products, could the manufacturer survive by selling solely online? For example, given Home Depot's dominance in the industry, could any manufacturer afford to lose it as a retail partner?

Home Depot performs some of the selling functions for Kohler, a manufacturer of plumbing fixtures, by its use of in-store displays and sales promotion.

Esprit and other apparel manufacturers create conflict between themselves and traditional retailers when they open factory outlet stores that sell directly to the public at deep discounts from regular retail prices.

Managerial Question: How can a manufacturer employ an e-tailing strategy while maintaining a strong partnership with its retailers?

A third source of conflict is **domain disagreements**. "Domain" refers to the decision variables that each member of the marketing channel feels it should be able to control. When the members of the marketing channel agree on who should make which decisions, domain agreement exists. When there is disagreement about who should make decisions, domain disagreements exist.

Consider the case of an automobile manufacturer and an automobile dealer. The dealer believes it should be able to make decisions regarding employees, local advertising, retail pricing, hours of operation, and remodeling and expansion. However, the manufacturer believes that it should be consulted on hours of operation and remodeling and expansion. As a consequence, there exists some domain disagreement in the auto manufacturer–auto dealer relationship.

Another controversial domain disagreement practice that occurs in today's retail marketing channels is when retailers sell merchandise they purchased from the vendor not to the final consumer but to discounters who the manufacturer does not want selling its products. A diverter is an unauthorized member of a channel who buys and sells excess merchandise to and from authorized channel members. For instance, suppose a retailer could buy a name-brand appliance intended to retail for $389 at $185 if it purchases 100 units. However, if the retailer orders 200 units, it can purchase each item at $158. What does the retailer do? Some retailers will purchase 200 units even though they only need 100. They in turn sell the 100 extra units at a slight loss, for example at $155, to a discount store which may retail the item for $219. The net result is that the retailer loses $3 a unit on 100 units or $300; however, it has the remaining 100 units at $27 a unit less, for a savings of $2,700. The retailer is $2,400 ahead on the transaction;

Domain disagreements occur when there is disagreement about which member of the marketing channel should make decisions.

Gray marketing
is when branded merchandise flows through unauthorized channels.

however, the manufacturer is upset because the appliance has been diverted into a retail channel it did not intend. This practice is known as gray marketing. **Gray marketing** is when branded merchandise flows through unauthorized channels. Gray market channels develop when environmental conditions are conducive to profits.

Although gray markets exist domestically, environmental conditions in the global market are much more conducive to their development. For example, imagine a German camera equipment manufacturer who sells products to North America. Because of local market price competition, the company's premier camera sells for $850 in the United States, but sells for only $600 (in U.S. dollars) in Canada. It does not take long for distributors to realize the profit potential of diverting the cameras headed for Canada to the United States.[9] Another example can be seen in the retailing of cigarettes. With a 50 percent increase in domestic cigarette prices in recent years, the foreign gray market has increased substantially.[10] In effect, gray marketing activities cannot be stopped unless the channel member who sells to the diverter has expressly violated terms of its contract with the manufacturer. After all, the seller owned the goods that were sold to the diverter. However, recent laws enacted in the European Union have placed a ban on gray market activity resulting in legal action being taken against retailers and wholesalers dealing in unauthorized distribution.

Free riding
is when a consumer seeks product information, usage instructions, and sometimes even warranty work from a full-service store but then, armed with the brand's model number, purchases the product from a limited-service discounter or over the Internet.

Diverting can lead to another problem for the channel-free riding. **Free riding** is when a consumer seeks product information, usage instructions, and sometimes even warranty work from a full-service store but then, armed with the brand's model number, purchases the product from a limited-service discounter or over the Internet.

Not all conflict, however, in a channel is bad. Low levels of conflict will probably not affect any channel member's behavior and may not even be noticed. A moderate level of conflict may even cause the members to improve their efficiency, much the same as happens with some of your classmates when you are working on a team project. However, high levels of conflict will probably be dysfunctional to the channel and lead to inefficiencies and channel restructuring.

Managing Cooperative Relations

Although all channels experience some degree of conflict, the dominant behavior in most retail channels is cooperative. Cooperation is necessary and beneficial because of the interdependency of retailers and suppliers and because most retailers and suppliers must develop a partnership if they want to deal with each other on a long-term and continuing basis. As a result, many channel members have begun to follow a new set of channel management best practices listed in Exhibit 5.9. This supplier partnership is often a critical factor for the retailer who does not want to confuse the final consumer with constant adjustments in product offerings that result from always changing suppliers.

Those retailers who treat their fellow channel members as partners and not as the enemy will tend to have a better profit performance over the long term than those who do not.

Exhibit 5.9	Channel Management Best Practices

1. All channel members must remember that satisfying the retail consumer is the only way anyone can be successful.
2. Successful partners work together in good times and bad.
3. Never abandon a channel partner at the first sign of trouble.
4. Work together with your partners to offer products at appropriate prices. No one will win if either partner is not honest and fair with the other or with the retail customer.
5. Never abuse power in negotiations. Rather, understand your partner's needs prior to negotiations and work to satisfy those needs.
6. Share profits fairly among partners.
7. Limit the number of partners for each merchandise line. By doing so you can signal greater commitment and trust to your partners, thus building stronger relationships.
8. Set high ethical standards in your business transactions.
9. Successful partners plan together to help the channel operate efficiently and effectively.
10. Treat your partner as you would wish to be treated.

The management of cooperative relations is facilitated by three important types of behaviors and attitudes. These are mutual trust, two-way communication, and solidarity.

Mutual Trust   **Mutual trust** occurs when the retailer trusts the supplier and the supplier trusts the retailer. In continuing relations between retailer and suppliers, mutual trust, which is built on past and present performance between the channel members, is critical. This trust allows for short-term inequities to exist. If mutual trust is present, then each party will tolerate these inequities because each knows that in the long term it will be fairly treated. For example, a vendor suggests that the retailer purchases a certain product. The retailer does not believe that the product will be successful in its market. However, the vendor insists that many buyers in other markets are purchasing that particular item and even agrees to "make good" if the product does not sell. The buyer will probably buy the merchandise knowing that the supplier can be trusted to make an appropriate adjustment on the invoice amount, provide markdown money, or make up this inequity some other way in the future if the product does not sell.

Without mutual trust, retail supply channels would disintegrate. On the other hand, if trust exists it will be contagious and allow the channel to grow and prosper. This occurs because of reciprocity. If a retailer trusts a supplier to do the right thing and the supplier treats the retailer fairly, then the retailer develops more trust and the process of mutual trust continues to build. Trust in retail channels grows over time.

Two-Way Communication   As noted earlier, conflict is inevitable in retail channels. Consequently two-way communication becomes the pathway for resolving disputes, which allows the channel relation to continue. **Two-way communication** occurs when both parties communicate openly their ideas, concerns, and plans. Because of the interdependency of the retailer and supplier, two-way communication becomes necessary to coordinate actions. For example, when Jockey decides to have a national promotion on its underwear, it needs to coordinate this promotion with its retail channels so that when customers enter stores to shop for the items nationally advertised they

Mutual trust
occurs when both the retailer and its supplier have faith that each will be truthful and fair in their dealings with the other.

Two-way communication
occurs when both retailer and supplier communicate openly their ideas, concerns, and plans.

E x h i b i t 5 . 1 0	**Keys to Developing a Channel Partnership**

- A close relationship based on mutual trust, admiration, and respect.
- The development of an interdependency in establishing and maintaining the same high standards to achieve common goals and objectives.
- Creating and maintaining a business climate based on cooperation, fairness, and mutual success.
- Open, honest, and constant communication of ideas, concerns, needs, and plans.
- A total focus on quality and outstanding customer service and satisfaction must be a part of every decision and action taken.
- Performance plays a major role in maintaining a long-term relationship, but it is equally important to utilize innovative, visionary leadership in identifying opportunities and ways to assist one another. Collectively plan your strategies for the future and always stay at least one step ahead of the competition.

will find them displayed and in stock. This requires coordination, and two-way communication is critical to accomplishing this coordination.

Communication is not independent of trust. Disputes can be resolved by good two-way communication and this improves trust. Furthermore, trust facilitates open two-way communication. The process is circular and builds over time.

Solidarity

exists when a high value is placed on the relationship between a supplier and retailer.

Solidarity

Solidarity exists when a high value is placed on the relationship between a supplier and retailer.[11] Solidarity is an attitude and thus is hard to explicitly create. Essentially, as trust and two-way communication increase, a higher degree of solidarity develops. Solidarity results in flexible dealings where adaptations are made as circumstances change. When solidarity exists, each party will come to the rescue of the other in time of trouble. For example, in the early-1990s when the economy was weak, many retailers, already operating under intense competitive pressure and operating on thin margins, sought and obtained assistance, such as, advertising or building in-store displays, from suppliers with whom they had developed strong relationships in the past. Usually these activities are the responsibility of the retailer, but given the business climate, the vendor was able to assist. On the other hand, when solidarity does not exist, each party will abandon the other in time of trouble. This often occurs when retailers have developed poor relationships and conflict with their suppliers. If the retailer then experiences a liquidity crisis, suppliers are likely to refuse shipment of needed merchandise. This is already happening with many cash-starved e-tailers in the early part of the 21st century.

Exhibit 5.10 lists some of the factors that should be used in establishing a relationship with your channel partners.[12]

Student Study Guide

Summary

LO•1 What is the retailer's role in the larger marketing system?

The marketing system must be viewed as the solution. If the retailer ignores the marketing system in order to maximize short-run profits, then in the long run the system will work against the retailer. And if the system overlooks the retailer, profits sufficient for survival and growth will vanish. In learning to work within the marketing system, the retailer needs to recognize the eight marketing functions necessary in all marketing systems: buying, selling, storing, transporting, sorting, financing, information gathering, and risk taking.

LO•2 What are the institutions involved and functions that must be performed in every marketing system?

The retailer can seldom perform all eight functions: buying, selling, storing, transporting, sorting, financing, information gathering, and risk taking, and therefore must rely on other primary and facilitating institutions in the marketing system. Although the marketing functions occur throughout the marketing system, they can be shifted or divided among the institutions in the marketing system.

LO•3 What are the different types of retail channels?

Marketing channels can be arranged by length, width, and control. Length is concerned with the number of primary marketing institutions in the channel. A channel is said to be direct if it goes from manufacturer to consumer. An indirect channel has either a retailer or wholesaler included in the channel. The channel's width measures the number of retailers handling the product in a given trading area.

Control looks at the two primary marketing channel patterns, conventional and vertical. A conventional marketing channel is one in which each member of the channel is loosely aligned with the others, each member recognizing only those it directly interacts with and ignoring all others. Conventional marketing channels are on the decline in the United States and vertical marketing systems are becoming dominant. In the vertical marketing system, all parties to the channel recognize each other and one party programs the channel to achieve technological, managerial, and promotional economies. Three types of vertical marketing systems are corporate, contractual, and administered.

LO•4 How does dependency, power, cooperation, and conflict influence channel relations?

To operate efficiently and effectively in any marketing channel, the retailer must depend on other channel members for assistance. When a retailer becomes highly dependent on other channel members, the other channel members gain power over the retailer. However, other channel members (manufacturers and wholesalers) are also dependent on the retailer, resulting in interdependency and a sharing of power. Although power and interdependency can lead to conflict, it actually is more likely to create a high desire for cooperative relationships. Cooperation is critical to performing marketing functions effectively and efficiently and to managing the marketing channel for the benefit of the consumer.

Terms to Remember

marketing channel
marketing system
factors
primary marketing institutions
facilitating marketing institutions
freelance broker
manufacturer's agent
sales agent
purchasing agent
resident buyers
public warehouse
direct channel
indirect channel
intensive distribution
selective distribution
exclusive distribution
conventional marketing channel
vertical marketing systems
quick response (QR) systems
efficient consumer response (ECR) systems
stock-keeping units (SKUs)

contractual vertical marketing systems
wholesaler-sponsored voluntary groups
retailer-owned cooperatives
franchise
master franchisor
administered vertical marketing systems
power
reward power
expertise power
referent power
coercive power
legitimate power
informational power
perceptual incongruity
goal incompatibility
domain disagreements
gray marketing
free riding
mutual trust
two-way communication
solidarity

Review and Discussion Questions

LO•1 **What is the retailer's role in the larger marketing system?**

1. Why must a retailer to be successful in the 21st century view itself as a member of a larger marketing system?

2. Define the sorting process and its four steps. Give an example of each step in your answer that was not used in the chapter.

3. Must a retailer be involved in performing all the marketing functions? If it can rely on other members of the channel, what are the functions they can perform and who else can perform them?

LO•2 **What are the institutions involved and functions that must be performed in every marketing system?**

4. Facilitating marketing institutions are powerless in the marketing channel. Agree or disagree with this statement and explain your reasoning.

5. Some say that it is easy to see how a facilitating institution, such as a manufacturer's agent, helps manage a channel without taking title to the goods. However, they question the contribution of other institutions, such as advertising agencies and computer specialists. How would you resolve this dilemma?

LO•3 **What are the different types of retailing channels?**

6. Why should a retailer be concerned about a channel's length and width? After all, should not the retailer just care about making a profit, or does a channel's makeup affect a member's performance?

7. What is a vertical marketing system? What is the primary difference between a conventional marketing channel and a vertical marketing system?

8. Can a retailer lead the marketing channel? Why or why not? Give an example of a retailer who might lead a channel.

LO•4 **How does dependency, power, cooperation, and conflict influence channel relations?**

9. Why are retailers so dependent on other channel members? Couldn't they simply perform all eight marketing functions themselves?

10. Define and give an example of the six sources of power that can be used by a retailer in the marketing channel.

11. What are the major sources of conflict in a channel? Are all these conflicts the fault of retailers?

12. Looking over the list of channel management best practices in Exhibit 5.9, which of these best practice suggestions is the most important for all the channel members to follow if they want to improve channel cooperation? Why?

Sample Test Questions

LO•1 **Which of the following marketing functions is one the retailer could not perform?**

a. selling

b. sorting

c. location analysis

d. buying

e. financing

LO•2 **Facilitating institutions may best be described as specialists that**

a. take title but not possession of the merchandise

b. take title to the merchandise in order to facilitate the transaction

c. manage the channel so as to increase over-all efficiency above 100 percent

d. facilitate the transaction by performing all eight marketing functions

e. perform certain marketing functions, in which they have an expertise, for other channel members

LO•3 **A marketing channel in which each member is loosely aligned with the others is a**

a. highly efficient system

b. contractual system

c. marketing channel capable of achieving 100 percent efficiency

d. marketing channel based on the ideals of cooperation and partnership

e. conventional marketing channel

LO•4 **The basic root of all conflict in a marketing channel is**

a. that each member wants all the power

b. that each member is dependent on the other members of the channel

c. that each member is fully capable of performing all eight marketing functions

d. that partnership agreements tend to expire after a year

e. the fact that everybody wants to work independent of the other members

Applications

Writing and Speaking Exercise   Your sister opened a backpacking store in Durango, Colorado 10 years ago. Since then, she has added four more brick & mortar stores (two in the suburbs of Denver, one in Santa Fe, and one in Albuquerque) and one on-line store (thus increasing her trading area). Up to now, your sister has handled almost all of the marketing functions internally. However, because of the tremendous success of her click & mortar strategy, it seems unfeasible for this practice to continue. Your sister does not believe that she has adequate personnel to perform all of the related duties, nor does she think that she is carrying out the functions at the highest level of efficiency and effectiveness. During a discussion with her on a recent visit, you promise to send her a one-page memo making some suggestions concerning what to do and what marketing functions she could have other marketing institutions perform.

Retail Project   In Chapter 4 we discussed divertive competition and introduced the topic of the break-even point, or the point where total revenues equal total expenses. Let's see how this topic will aid us in determining whether to join a franchise system or to stay independent.

Assume that you own a sandwich shop. In looking over last year's income statement you see that the annual sales were $250,000 with a gross margin of 50 percent, or $125,000. The fixed operating expenses were $50,000; the variable operating expenses were 20 percent of sales, or $50,000; and your profit was $25,000, or 10 percent of sales.

In discussions with your spouse, you wonder if joining a franchise operation, such as Subway or Blimpie, will improve your results. Your research has determined that Subway requires a $10,000 licensing fee in addition to an 8 percent royalty on sales and a 2.5 percent advertising fee on sales. Blimpie, though it requires an $18,000 licensing fee, only charges a 6 percent royalty and a 3 percent advertising fee.

Assuming that you wanted to break even, what amount of sales would you have to generate with each system during the first year, as both your fixed and variable expenses would increase? Remember, the beak-even point (BEP) is where gross margin equals total operating expenses, or in equation form:

$$\text{Gross margin} = \text{Fixed operating expenses} + \text{Variable operating expenses}$$

Thus with Subway, your fixed expenses would increase from $50,000 to $60,000 and your variable expanses would increase from 20 percent of sales to 30.5 percent (20% + 8% + 2.5%). Blimpie's would increase fixed expenses by $18,000 and variable expenses by 9 percent. Using the equation we can calculate the BEP for both.

Subway's BEP:

$$50\% \text{ (Net sales)} = \$60,000 + 30.5\% \text{ (Net sales)}$$
$$\text{Net sales} = \$307,692$$

Blimpie's BEP:

$$50\% \text{ (Net sales)} = \$68,000 + 29\% \text{ (Net sales)}$$

$$\text{Net sales} = \$323,809$$

As a result of the increased expenses, by joining a franchise just to break even, you would have to increase sales over 20 percent. To make the same profit you already are making, you would have to add that profit figure to the equation.

Gross Margin = Fixed operating expenses + Variable operating expenses + Profit

Subway's BEP with a $25,000 profit:

$$50\% \text{ (Net sales)} = \$60,000 + 30.5\% \text{ (Net sales)} + \$25,000$$

$$\text{Net sales} = \$435,897$$

Blimpie's BEP with a $25,000 profit:

$$50\% \text{ (Net sales)} = \$68,000 + 29\% \text{ (Net sales)} + \$25,000$$

$$\text{Net sales} = \$442,857$$

Thus, to keep the same profit as you currently have, a franchise would have to help you increase sales by over 75 percent. There is no doubt the image of the franchise will draw additional customers and its management may even help cut some of your other expenses. However, as these numbers point out, joining a franchise system is not always a sure-fire guarantee of success.

Now, either by using a franchise directory in the library (i.e., the Worldwide or International Franchise Directory) or by using a franchisor's web site home page on the Internet; look up two competing franchise systems in the same line of retail trade. After locating the information about these franchises, do the same cost analysis we just did and determine, if based on these figures, joining a franchise is a good investment.

Case   LockerRoom

Matt Mettler owns and operates five LockerRoom sporting goods stores in the St. Louis market. The layout and atmosphere of Mettler's stores is more upscale than that of other area sporting goods stores, which seems to be a key feature for attracting new customers and maintaining customer loyalty.

While Mettler is pleased with his sales volume, he is unhappy with the fact that his cost of goods sold and operating expenses are reducing profits below what he has determined to be a satisfactory level. Mettler is responsible for ordering all the merchandise for the stores. However, he is frustrated because he has been unable to negotiate significant price breaks and promotional packages, similar to what Woolworth's gets with its Foot Locker stores, from many of the manufacturers and wholesalers he uses.

Recently, Mettler was approached by the vice-president of a wholesaler-sponsored voluntary group of sporting goods stores based in Chicago about the possibility of LockerRooms becoming part of the chain. The vice-president strongly reassured Mettler that he could operate LockerRooms as he has in the past. However, in addition to savings on merchandise, the group would provide him information on services, bookkeeping, and layout that could improve sales and reduce operating expenses. However, he would not be required to make use of any of these benefits.

Mettler has many hesitations about letting others tell him how to run his business. He is also worried that joining the group would cause him to relinquish control of the stores he worked so hard to develop, especially when the stores are experiencing such success. Yet he feels that he must somehow lower his operating cost if he is to maximize profits.

1. What negative consequences might Mettler experience if he joins the group? How might Mettler's current situation improve if he were to join?

2. Would it be better for Mettler to just join a franchising chain instead, even if it meant having to drop his name for theirs?

Planning Your Own Business   Upon graduation you decide that you wish to get in on the ground floor of the e-tailing revolution and develop your own on-line business. You decide that a large opportunity exists in providing private label apparel to a niche segment of Generation-Y consumers. In the process of planning your business, your preliminary sales forecasts lead you to believe that your first year's sales will be $220,000. You have identified two major manufacturers who can make the merchandise that you can purchase to sell on-line. One manufacturer is in a distant city and is able to promise seven-day delivery on orders of more than $5,000. The second manufacturer is located in a city 80 miles south and provides next-day delivery on orders of more than $500 placed by 1 p.m. Unfortunately, the nearby manufacturer has slightly higher prices. Consequently, you estimate that by purchasing through this source your gross margin percent would be 42 percent versus 44 percent by purchasing from the more distant manufacturer. However, because the nearby manufacturer is able to provide more frequent and smaller deliveries, you estimate that your average inventory would be $21,000 versus $25,500 if you used the more distant manufacturer as a supply source. Each manufacturer sells on terms of 2 percent/10 net 30. This means that if the invoice is paid within 10 days a 2 percent discount can be taken, and if not the net invoice is due within 30 days. Which supply source should you select? (*Hint:* Compute the gross margin return on inventory investment, which is defined as the gross margin dollars divided by average inventory investment.)

Endnotes

1. "Buying Offices: Once a Staple, Now Few Exist," *Shopping Center Today*, May 1997: 76, 86.

2. "Who's Afraid of Wal-Mart?" *Fortune*, June 26, 2000: 186–196; "Wal-Mart Expands Access to Product Sales History," *Wall Street Journal*, July 18, 1999: B8.

3. For a more complete discussion on this subject, the reader should consult Robert Buzzell and Gwen Ortmeyer, "Channel Partnerships Streamline Distribution," *Sloan Management Review*, Spring 1995: 85–96.

4. F. Robert Dwyer and Sejo Oh, "A Transaction Cost Perspective on Vertical Contractual Structure and Interchannel Competitive Strategies," *Journal of Marketing*, April 1988: 21–34.

5. Bert C. McCammon Jr., "Perspectives for Distribution Programming," in Louis P. Bucklin, ed., *Vertical Marketing Systems* (Glenview, IL.: Scott, Foresman, 1970): 45. Reprinted with permission of the author.

6. "The Big Squeeze," *Forbes*, March 11, 1996: 45–46.

7. "Levi Strauss & Co. Site Doesn't Pan Out," *InfoWorld Publications*, November 22, 1999.

8. Katrina Brooker, "First: Awfully Nervous," *Fortune*, August 16, 1999: 28–29.

9. Matthew B. Myers and David A. Griffith, "Strategies for Combatting Gray Market Activity," *Business Horizons*, 42(6) 1999: 2–8.

10. "As Cigarette Prices Soar, A Gray Market Booms," *Wall Street Journal*, January 28, 1999: B1.

11. Jan B. Heide and George John, "Do Norms Matter in MarketingRelationships?" *Journal of Marketing*, April 1992: 32–44; James C. Anderson and James A. Narus, "A Model of Distributor Firm and Manufacturer Firm Working Partnerships," *Journal of Marketing*, January 1990: 42–58.

12. The authors acknowledge the assistance of Drayton McLane in developing this list.

Given the restrictions on retail hours in different countries, products are often made available via automated merchandising systems to enhance convenience.

Legal and Ethical Behavior

Overview

In this chapter, we will discuss how the legal and ethical environment impacts the retailer in making decisions. The discussion revolves around the legal aspects of decisions made on pricing, promotion (including the use of credit), products or merchandise, marketing channels, and concludes with a discussion of the major ethical decisions facing a retailer today.

Learning Objectives

After reading this chapter, you should be able to

1. explain how legislation constrains a retailer's pricing policies
2. differentiate between legal and illegal promotional activities
3. explain the retailer's responsibilities with regard to the products sold

4. discuss the impact of governmental regulation on a retailer's behavior with other channel members

5. describe how various state and local laws, in addition to other federal regulations, must also be considered in developing retail policies

6. explain how a retailer's code of ethics will influence its behavior

In addition to studying the changing consumer (Chapter 3), competition (Chapter 4), and channel environments (Chapter 5), the dynamic nature of retailing requires that the legal environment also be monitored. Most large retailers, especially those operating in foreign countries where the laws and regulations are different, maintain legal departments and lobbyists to keep abreast of, interpret, and even influence government regulations. Such activities are usually beyond the resources of small businesses. However, governments and the business press do a reasonably good job of keeping retailers informed of pending and new legislation. (For example, the reader might want to visit the Federal Trade Commission's web site, www.ftc.gov, and review some of the basic primers on the various activities related to the United States to be discussed in this chapter.) In addition, there are retailer associations in most of the major countries, as well as every state in the United States, that help to keep retailers abreast of proposed changes in state laws and attempt to protect the retailers' interests.

We will now explore the final set of external constraints that influence retail decisions: legal and ethical decision making. These forces are shown in Exhibit 6.1. Consider the impact on convenience stores when the U.S. Food and Drug Administration (FDA) required a photo ID from any person appearing to be under 18 years of age that wanted to buy cigarettes or smokeless tobacco. Think about the impact of various state laws that only allow retailers to conduct one yearly promotional game of chance. What about the cities that regulate garage sales? What about those cities that have "sign ordinances" regulating the retailer's use of billboards and even the sign on the retailer's building? What about state regulations restricting the retailer's use of product samples? All these laws control the ability of retailers to serve the needs of their target market. In addition, ethical issues will impact retailers when making decisions.

Retailers who are familiar with the various laws regulating business will be less apt to make costly mistakes and thus more likely to be higher profit performers.

To avoid costly blunders, the retailer needs to understand its legal and ethical constraints of each of the countries it is doing business in. Some of the philosophical concepts used in developing laws and regulations in other countries are described in the chapter's Global Retailing box. In fact, as the box indicates, the differences in the laws of each nation can drive global retailers crazy. However, these laws do present some interesting opportunities for the retailer who is alert enough to take advantage of the

Exhibit 6.1   **Ethical and Legal Constraints Influencing Retailers**

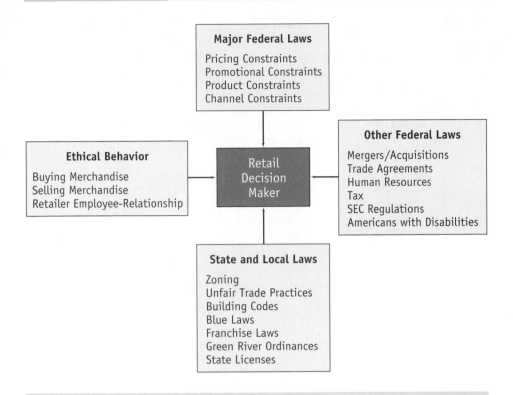

Major Federal Laws

Pricing Constraints
Promotional Constraints
Product Constraints
Channel Constraints

Ethical Behavior

Buying Merchandise
Selling Merchandise
Retailer Employee-Relationship

Retail Decision Maker

Other Federal Laws

Mergers/Acquisitions
Trade Agreements
Human Resources
Tax
SEC Regulations
Americans with Disabilities

State and Local Laws

Zoning
Unfair Trade Practices
Building Codes
Blue Laws
Franchise Laws
Green River Ordinances
State Licenses

In Quebec, Canada, the law mandates that if a retailer wants to have a sign in another language, that the sign must be in French first and then in the other language.

Global Retailing

All Laws Governing Retailing Are Not the Same

Each nation's regulations reflect and reinforce its brand of capitalism — predatory in the United States, paternal in Germany, and protected in Japan — and its social values. As a result, sometimes government regulations in foreign nations can drive retailers crazy.

As a result of these different philosophies, here are some of the "unusual" laws regulating retailers around the world:

In Germany, comparative advertising is banned; also local authorities can — and do — bar new stores if they believe existing stores will be hurt. Germany's paternal approach to protect existing firms impacted Lands' End in 1999 when the retailer tried to use its trademarked "Money Back Guarantee, No Matter What." It seems that the Center for the Fight Against Unfair Competition felt this guarantee would be unfair to traditional German retailers. The German courts ruled the American retailer could honor the guarantee, just not advertise the fact. Lands' End got around this when its German web site did not mention the guarantee, but had a link to a separate web site that did.

Retailers in Germany are also restricted in the number of hours they may be open. The law allows a retail store to stay open until 8 p.m. on weekdays, until 4 p.m. on Saturday, and, with the exception of bakeries (which can be opened for three hours), retailers cannot be open on Sunday. Also, certain transportation terminals are permitted to be open longer hours during the week and on Sunday for the convenience of travelers.

In addition, the sale of any item in Germany costing more than 300 Euros ($300 U.S.) requires the registration of the customer's name and address. One German law that many American consumers might appreciate is that mail carriers have to obey "no advertising" (i.e., junk mail) stickers that many Germans attach to their mailboxes. However, such a law may be disheartening for retailers.

In Japan, local merchants can legally demand concessions when a new store opens nearby. This can often delay construction for years. Japan also has a law, designed to protect small retailers, stating that giant retailers can stay open to 8 p.m. but are required to close their stores at least 20 days a year for "holidays." In addition, self-service gas stations, and any discounter who might want to introduce them, are banned in Japan on the ground that they are a fire hazard.

Still, while it is more difficult to open and operate retail outlets in these two countries than in the United States, it is easier to open a bank branch in those countries than it is to open one in all but a few states in the United States. However, this is rapidly changing as more and more banks are merging, thus creating the need for branch banking.

Other unique regulations can be found throughout the world. Consider these examples:

situation. Always remember that retailers cannot freely make decisions without regard for the laws society has established to regulate all business trade. For example, the legal environment in the United States consists of those federal, state, and local laws that limit the retailer's flexibility and freedom in making business-related decisions.

Due to the country-specific laws described in the Global Retailing box, this chapter will deal mainly with the various federal constraints that can affect the retailer's decision-making process with regard to pricing, promotion, products, and channel relationships in the United States.

Due to their complexity, we will not be able to discuss all of the other federal laws that impact retailers in this chapter. In addition, because state and local laws are quite varied, we will only make general comments on some state and local laws. We will, in most part, leave it up to you and your class discussions to investigate the impact of state and local laws on retail activities in your state and community.

- Quebec, a Canadian province that is 80 percent French-speaking, allows English on commercial signs only if French words dominate.
- In Italy, retailers may operate 44 hours per week provided that they close on Sunday.
- In Mexico, the clock on cash discounts (discounts given to retailers by vendors for early payment) does not start ticking until the retailer receives the bill and determines it is acceptable.
- In Australia, store hours are regulated separately by each state, resulting in confusion across the country. Also, supermarkets in Australia that have conveyor belts on their checkouts must pay an annual $25 "weights and scaffolding" fee for each one.
- The Netherlands sets minimum selling prices for goods produced within the country, but none for imported items.
- The size of a store in France is limited to 1,000 square meters if it is located in a city with a population of less than 40,000. If the city is larger, the size may increase to 1,500 square meters. Also, in France, the funeral business until recently was treated as a utility. Retailers had to bid for the right to operate in a certain city at fixed prices.
- Retailers in the United Kingdom, the country from which our "blue laws" were copied, have to cope with laws that make it legal to buy food for a mule on Sunday, but not for your baby. Also, pornographic material may be sold on Sunday, but not a Bible to take to church. British retailers do get around these laws. One British furniture dealer, for example, sells a box of matches for 1,000 British pounds ($1,650 U.S.), then gives the customer a "free" suite of furniture.
- Norway, also, bans all Sunday retailing, except for filling stations that are smaller than 150 square meters (1,600 square feet), grocery stores that are smaller than 100 square meters, and certain transportation terminals.
- China has backtracked away from a blanket ban on all direct door-to-door selling to allow direct sales companies that invest at least $10 million in China (e.g., Amway) to sell door to door.

However, an international retailer seeking to open a store in the United States must be prepared for some of our unusual local laws. For example, a law in Kansas City prohibits the sale of capguns to children, but not shotguns.

As Exhibit 6.2 shows, most federal laws affecting retailing seek to "promote competition." These fall into several categories. First, the Sherman Anti-Trust Act, the Clayton Act, the Federal Trade Commission Act, the Celler-Kefauver Antimerger Act, and the Hart-Scott-Rodino Act were passed to ensure a "competitive" business climate. Second, the Robinson-Patman Act was designed to regulate pricing practices. Third, the Wheeler-Lea Act was created to control false advertising. Although some may question if all these regulations are bleeding the economy, many do believe that they sometimes boost competitiveness. Other laws have been passed to protect consumers and innocent third parties. A sampling of these consumer protection laws is shown in Exhibit 6.3.

Note that all aspects of retailing—price, promotion, product, and channel membership—are regulated. We will begin our discussion of how federal laws impact a retailer's decision-making ability by looking at pricing regulations.

Exhibit 6.2	Primary U.S. Laws That Affect Retailing

Legislation	Impact on Retailing
Sherman Act, 1890	Bans (1) "monopolies or attempts to monopolize" and (2) "contracts, combinations, or conspiracies in restraint of trade" in interstate and foreign commerce
Clayton Act, 1914	Adds to the Sherman Act by prohibiting specific practices (e.g., certain types of price discrimination, tying clauses) "whereas the effect . . . may be to substantially lessen competition or tend to create a monopoly in any line of commerce"
Federal Trade Commission Act, 1914	Establishes the Federal Trade Commission, a body of specialists with broad powers to investigate and to issue cease-and-desist orders to enforce Section 5, which declares that "unfair methods of competition in commerce are unlawful"
Robinson-Patman Act, 1936	Amends the Clayton Act, adds the phrase "to injure, destroy, or prevent competition." Defines price discrimination as unlawful (subject to certain defenses) and provides the FTC with the right to establish limits on quantity discounts, to forbid brokerage allowances except to independent brokers, and to ban promotional allowances or the furnishing of services or facilities except when made available to all "on proportionately equal terms"
Wheeler-Lea Amendment to the FTC Act, 1938	Prohibits unfair and deceptive acts and practices regardless of whether competition is injured
Lanham Act, 1946	Establishes protection for trademarks
Celler-Kefauver Antimerger Act, 1950	Amends Section 7 of the Clayton Act by broadening the power to prevent corporate acquisitions where the acquisition may have a substantially adverse effect on competition
Hart-Scott-Rodino Act, 1976	Requires large companies to notify the government of their intent to merge

LO • 1

Does legislation constrain a retailer's pricing policies?

Pricing Constraints

Retailers continuously establish prices for the many items they offer to consumers. Pricing laws also influence retailers in determining what price they should pay for a product. In making these decisions they have considerable, but not total, flexibility. The major constraining factors are summarized in Exhibit 6.4.

Horizontal Price Fixing

Horizontal price fixing occurs when a group of competing retailers (or other channel members operating at a given level of distribution) establishes a fixed price at which to sell certain brands of products.

Horizontal price fixing occurs when a group of competing retailers establishes a fixed price at which to sell certain brands of products. For example, all retail grocers in a particular trade area may agree to sell eggnog at $2.19 a quart during the Christmas season. Regardless of its actual or potential impact on competition or the consumer, this price fixing by the retailers would violate Section 1 of the Sherman Antitrust Act, which states, "every contract, combination in the form of trust or otherwise, or conspiracy, in restraint of trade or commerce among the several states, or with foreign nations is

Exhibit 6.3	**Examples of Laws Designed to Protect Consumers**
Legislative Action	**Impact or Change in Consumer Environment**
Mail Fraud Act, 1872	Makes it a federal crime to defraud consumers through use of the mail
Pure Food & Drug Act, 1906	Regulates interstate commerce in misbranded and adulterated foods, drinks, and drugs
Flammable Fabrics Act, 1953	Prohibits interstate shipments of flammable apparel or material
Automobile Information Disclosure Act, 1958	Requires auto manufacturers to post suggested retail prices on new cars
Fair Packaging and Labeling Act, 1966	Regulates packaging and labeling; establishes uniform sizes
Child Safety Act, 1966	Prevents the marketing and selling of harmful toys and dangerous products
Truth in Lending Act, 1968	Requires lenders to state the true costs of a credit transaction; established a National Commission on Consumer Finance
Fair Credit Report Act, 1970	Regulates the reporting and use of credit information; limits consumer liability for stolen credit cards to $50
Consumer Product Safety Act, 1972	Creates the Consumer Product Safety Commission
Magnuson-Moss Warranty/ FTC Improvement Act, 1975	Empowers the FTC to determine rules concerning consumer warranties and provides for consumer access to means of redress, such as the "class action" suit; expands FTC regulatory powers over unfair or deceptive acts or practices
Equal Credit Opportunity Act, 1975	Prohibits discrimination in credit transactions because of gender, marital status, race, national origin, religion, age, or receipt of public assistance

Exhibit 6.4	**Pricing Constraints**

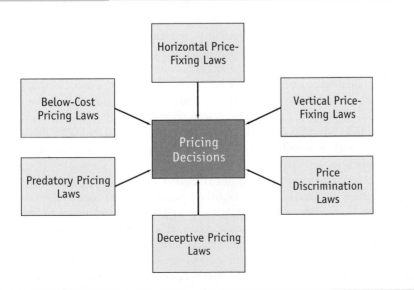

declared to be illegal."[1] It is also illegal for retailers to reach agreements with one another regarding the use of double (or triple) coupons, rebates, or other means of reducing price competition in the marketplace.

Occasionally, retailers have argued that the Sherman Act does not apply to them because they operate locally, not "among the several states," the definition of interstate commerce. However, because the merchandise retailers purchase typically originates in another state, the courts view retailers as involved in interstate commerce even if all their customers are local. Also, most states have laws similar to the Sherman Act, prohibiting such restraints of trade as horizontal price fixing on a strictly local level.

Vertical Price Fixing

Vertical price fixing
occurs when a retailer collaborates with the manufacturer to resell an item at an agreed-on price.

Vertical price fixing occurs when a retailer collaborates with the manufacturer or wholesaler to resell an item at an agreed-upon price. This is also often referred to as resale price maintenance or "fair trade." These agreements are illegal and have been viewed as a violation of Section 1 of the Sherman Act. This does not mean that manufacturers cannot recommend to retailers a price at which they would like to see an item sold, but they cannot establish a price at which the retailer must sell the product, unless, as discussed in the last chapter, the retailer has signed a "co-op" advertising agreement requiring a specific price. Nor can manufacturers legally threaten retailers with supply cutoffs if they do not sell at the recommended price. Resale price maintenance agreements, which made an illegal act (the fixing of a price) legal, were allowed between 1937 and 1975. These agreements were established as a means for small retailers to combat the price advantages of the chain stores during the depression of the 1930s. They were banned finally in 1976.

Although their use is being urged by some manufacturers and retailers as a means to combat the inroads of discounters such as Wal-Mart, Target, Kohl's, and Kmart as well as the warehouse clubs, the Federal Trade Commission (FTC) has vowed to "treat vertical price fixing as per se illegal." In May 2000, for example, the FTC announced that it wanted to reconsider this issue, so even if the retailer accepts co-op advertising dollars, the manufacturer may not always control the minimum retail price. The FTC was concerned about a policy called "minimum advertised price" (MAP) that kept the prices of CDs artificially high and stifled competition. With MAPs, a record company might fund a retailer's entire ad budget for a top CD. In return, the retailer agreed not to advertise or sell the CD for a price below that stated on the label. Such action was an attempt to make sure that CDs were never discounted. Although the intent may have been good—the small retailer wanted to prevent discounters from slashing the prices on CDs as an attempt to lure customers into its store and then sell them other higher gross margin items—it nevertheless limited competition.

Although manufacturers or franchisors cannot require that their retailers or franchisees sell their products at an established price, the U.S. Supreme Court recently ruled that they are allowed to cap retail prices. This is not identical to strict vertical price fixing because retailers or franchisees can sell at lower than the capped retail price that manufacturers or franchisors establish. Also the U.S. Supreme Court decided that alleged violations will be decided by a "rule of reason" analysis, which means that each price cap should be evaluated on its own merits to determine if it unreasonably restrains competition.

Price Discrimination

Laws can also influence the price that the retailer has to pay for the merchandise it wants to sell. **Price discrimination** occurs when two retailers buy identical amounts of "like grade and quality" merchandise from the same supplier but pay different prices. However, these laws do not mean that the retailer cannot sell identical products, for example, a new car, to two different customers at different prices. These laws are meant to protect competition by making sure that the retailers are treated fairly by suppliers.

Not all forms of price discrimination are illegal, however. Federal legislation addressed the legality of price discrimination in the Clayton Act, which made certain forms of price discrimination illegal. The Clayton Act was amended and strengthened by the passage of the Robinson-Patman Act. This act had two primary objectives: (1) to prevent suppliers from attempting to gain an unfair advantage over their competitors by discrimination among buyers either in price or in providing allowances or services and (2) to prevent buyers from using their economic power to gain discriminatory prices from suppliers so as to gain an advantage over their own competitors.

For price discrimination to be considered illegal, it must meet three conditions. First, the transaction must occur during interstate commerce. Trade between states, which is the definition of interstate commerce, covers all retailers, because the items they produce or market typically originate in another state. Second, the actual competition does not have to be lessened, only the potential of a substantial lessening of competition must exist. Third, the buyer who knowingly receives the benefit of discrimination is just as guilty as the supplier granting the discrimination.

Considerable attention has been given to the phrase "commodities of like grade and quality." What does this phrase mean? To begin with, commodities are goods and not services. This implies that discriminatory pricing practices in the sale of advertising space or the leasing of real estate are not prohibited by the act. For example, shopping

Price discrimination occurs when two retailers buy an identical amount of "like grade and quality" merchandise from the same supplier but pay different prices.

If two different households negotiate a different price for the same brand or model of a new car, this is not illegal price discrimination.

center developers frequently charge varying rates for equal square footage depending on the tenant and the type of merchandise to be sold.

"Like grade and quality" has been interpreted by the courts to mean identical physical and chemical properties. This implies that different prices cannot be justified merely because the labels on the product are different. Therefore, private labeling of merchandise does not make it different from identical goods carrying the seller's brand. However, if the seller can establish that an actual physical difference in grade and quality exists, then a differential in price can be justified.

The preceding discussion may have led you to believe that the illegality of price discrimination is clear cut and that retailers no longer have to fear being discriminated against. This is not always the situation. A variety of defenses are available to buyers and sellers that enable some types of price discrimination to occur. These defenses include cost justification, changing market conditions, and meeting competition in good faith.

Retailers effectively using legal price discrimination to purchase merchandise will be more profitable.

Cost Justification Defense   Such a defense would attempt to show that a price differential could be accounted for on the basis of differences in cost to the seller in the manufacture, sale, or delivery arising from differences in the method or quantities involved. The burden of such a defense is with the seller.

Changing Market Conditions Defense   This defense would attempt to justify the price differential on the danger of imminent deterioration of perishable goods or on the obsolescence of seasonal goods.

Meeting Competition in Good Faith Defense   The seller can attempt to show that its lower price to a purchaser was made in good faith in order to meet an equally low price of a competitor provided that this "matched price" did actually exist and was lawful in itself.

Therefore, it is legally possible that one retailer, a large warehouse club purchasing 10,000 cases, for example, might have a lower cost per case than a smaller retailer purchasing only 15 cases. However, the retailer that knowingly receives a discriminatory price from a seller (assuming the goods are of like grade and quality) should be relatively certain that the seller is granting a defensible discrimination based on any of the three preceding criteria. Fleming Company retained its Megafoods account by agreeing to match, not beat, the lower prices that Safeway had offered Megafoods. Although the Robinson-Patman Act is mainly concerned with illegal activities of the sellers, if a buyer knowingly misrepresents to the seller a price that another seller is willing to offer and the seller meets that "factious" offer, the buyer and not the seller is liable.

Sellers are not only prohibited from discrimination in price; they are also banned from providing different services and payments to different retailers. These services and payments frequently include advertising allowances, displays and banners to promote the goods, in-store demonstrations, and distribution of samples or premiums. The Robinson-Patman Act deals specifically with these practices and states that such services and payments or consideration must be made available on proportionately equal terms to all competing customers. Finally, it is important to point out that most of the United States' trading partners do not have laws, such as the Robinson-Patman Act—that ban price discrimination, as well as many of the other regulations discussed in this chapter. As a result, many U.S. retailers have been shocked by what they perceived as an "unfair" playing field when they entered foreign markets. For example, price and quality of product are not always the most important issue when setting up a channel in some foreign countries.

Deceptive Pricing

Retailers should avoid using a misleading price to lure customers into the store. Advertising an item at an artificially low price and then adding hidden charges is a **deceptive pricing** practice, which is an unfair method of competition. The Wheeler-Lea Amendment of the Federal Trade Commission Act made illegal all "unfair or deceptive acts in commerce." Not only is the retailer's customer being unfairly treated when the retailer uses deceptive pricing, but the retailer's competitors are being potentially harmed because some of their customers may deceitfully be diverted to that retailer. In addition, FTC Guide 233.1 prohibits the advertisement of an inflated former price to emphasize a price reduction (a clearance or sale). Also regulated by the FTC is the comparison of a price lower than a competitor's price for the same product and use of additional "free" merchandise to be given to a customer when purchasing a particular product at the price usually offered by the retailer.

Deceptive pricing occurs when a misleading price is used to lure customers into the store; usually there are hidden charges or the item advertised may be unavailable.

Predatory Pricing

Predatory pricing exists when a retail chain charges different prices in different geographical areas in order to eliminate competition in selected geographic areas. This is in violation of the Robinson-Patman Act, which also forbids the sale of goods at lower prices in one area for the purpose of destroying competition or eliminating a competitor, or the sale of goods at unreasonably low prices for such purpose. Generally, predatory pricing charges are difficult to prove in federal court.

Predatory pricing exists when a retail chain charges different prices in different geographic areas to eliminate competition in selected geographic areas.

Promotion Constraints

LO • 2
Is there a difference between legal and illegal promotional activities for a retailer?

The ability of the retailer to make any promotion decision is constrained by two major pieces of federal legislation, the Federal Trade Commission Act and the Wheeler-Lea Amendment of the FTC Act. The retailer should be familiar with three promotional areas that are potentially under the domain of the FTC Act and the Wheeler-Lea Amendment. These areas are deceitful diversion of patronage, deceptive advertising, and deceptive sales practices. Exhibit 6.5 depicts these three areas of constraint.

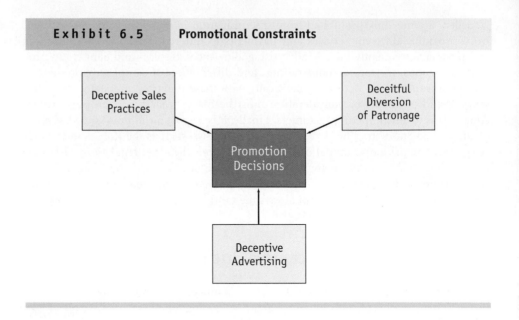

Exhibit 6.5   **Promotional Constraints**

Deceptive Sales Practices

Deceitful Diversion of Patronage

Promotion Decisions

Deceptive Advertising

Deceitful Diversion of Patronage

If a retailer publishes or verbalizes falsehoods about a competitor in an attempt to divert patrons from that competitor, the retailer is engaging in an unfair trade practice. The competitor would be afforded protection under the FTC Act but also could receive protection by showing that the defamatory statements amounted to libel or slander. In either case, the competitor would have to demonstrate that actual damage had occurred.

Another form of deceitful diversion of patronage that occurs in retailing is palming off. **Palming off** occurs when a retailer represents that merchandise is made by a firm other than the true manufacturer. For example, an exclusive women's apparel retailer purchases a group of stylish dresses at a bargain price and replaces their labels with those of a top designer. This is deception as to source of origin, and litigation can be brought under the FTC Act and the Wheeler-Lea Amendment. If the designer's dress label is a registered trademark, protection would also be afforded under the major piece of federal trademark legislation, the Lanham Act (1946).

According to a 1999 study by the International AntiCounterfeiting Coalition, U.S. firms lose $200 billion a year as a result of the counterfeiting of trademarked U.S. products.[2] Hundreds of different products, all fakes, have been copied overseas and shipped to the United States for retail sale. The top categories for fake products are video games and other electronic software, apparel, watches, and golf clubs. Not all the blame for such actions should be placed on retailers. After all, a great deal of the merchandise sold in the United States is made in many foreign countries. For many of these foreign countries, trademark law is relatively new and the concept of such protection is not always clear to the workers. In fact, most of the $200 billion in sales was probably unwittingly sold by U.S. retailers who will cease to do so when informed. Columbia Sportswear Co. noted a suspect item in a recent Sears catalog. When Sears was contacted, it canceled the order while the ship bringing the merchandise from a Taiwanese factory was still at sea. Wal-Mart has agreed to pay $6.4 million to Tommy Hilfiger after the retailer was found to have sold fake Tommy Hilfiger apparel and ignored a court order to stop. Wal-Mart claimed that it thought the apparel was authentic.

Palming off
occurs when a retailer represents that merchandise is made by a firm other than the true manufacturer.

The Pokémon product (Pikachu) on the left is counterfeit. Note that the product on the right has a softer covering and a tag written in English.

In early 2000, Wal-Mart won an unanimous Supreme Court decision that made it harder for companies to prove their products are distinctive enough to deserve trademark protection. Wal-Mart had contracted with a supplier to manufacture a line of children's clothing based on photos of products sold by Samara Brothers. The court ruled that trademark law did not protect Samara's line of clothing because "design, like color, is not inherently distinctive."[3] This ruling would not affect "highly" distinctive styles, such as Coach handbags; a Coca-Cola bottle; or labels, such as those on Levi jeans.

Today with Internet auctions, such as eBay, becoming so popular with consumers, federal authorities are investigating whether trademark laws are being violated when the sale of fake products is exposed.

Deceptive Advertising

Deceptive advertising occurs when a retailer makes false or misleading advertising claims about the physical makeup of a product, the benefits to be gained by its use, or the appropriate uses for the product. Deceptive advertising is illegal. However, it is often difficult to distinguish between what is false or misleading and what is simply "puffery" or "laudatory language," which retailers can legally use. Puffery occurs when a retailer or its spokesperson states what is considered to be an opinion or a judgment about a product, not a statement of fact—for example, saying "this is an excellent buy, and you cannot afford to pass it up." Probably most important for the retailer to

Deceptive advertising occurs when a retailer makes false or misleading advertising claims about the physical makeup of a product, the benefits to be gained by its use, or the appropriate uses for the product.

recognize is that the FTC's concern is not with the intent of the advertiser but with whether the consumer was misled by the advertising. When the FTC challenges any claim contained in advertising or promotional material, several requirements must be met before the commission can find actionable deception: (1) the FTC must prove that the challenged claim is contained in the advertisement; (2) the claim must be deceptive; and (3) the deceptive claim must be material.[4] Although there is disagreement over whether this was a change in, rather than a summary of, FTC policy toward deception, it appears that an example of a case that would not be judged deceptive would be an ad for "Danish pastry." This advertisement would not be considered deceptive because "a few misguided souls believe . . . that all 'Danish pastry' is made in Denmark." In 1999, the courts made an important distinction between puffery and trademark. The Boston Beer Company applied for a trademark registration for a phase used in its ads, "The Best Beer in America." The court ruled that the phase was "highly laudatory and descriptive" and as such it cannot be made into a trademark.[5]

Sometimes retailers may claim that another retailer is using deceptive advertising. One case involving a product most are familiar with, pizza, is discussed in the Service Retailing box.

Retailers who engage in any type of deceptive promotional activities will damage their reputations and be unable to achieve long-term high profit results.

Bait-and-switch advertising is promoting a product at an unrealistically low price to serve as "bait" and then trying to "switch" the customer to a higher-priced product.

Bait-and-switch promotions present another type of deceptive advertising. Bait-and-switch advertising is promoting a product at an unrealistically low price to serve as "bait" and then trying to "switch" the customer to a higher-priced product. However, the scope of the FTC's ban on bait-and-switch practices is much broader than the typical bait-and-switch scenario, and this strictness could, at least theoretically, pose problems for many retailers. For example, federal regulations outlaw all acts or practices of an advertiser that would discourage the purchase of the advertised merchandise as part of a bait scheme to sell other merchandise. Among those forbidden acts or practices are the following:

1. Refusing "to show, demonstrate, or sell the product offered."
2. Disparaging, by word or deed, the advertised product or the "guarantee, credit terms, availability of service, repairs or parts, or in any other respect, in connection with it."
3. Failing to have sufficient quantities of the advertised product to meet "reasonable anticipated demands" at all outlets listed in the advertisement, unless the ad clearly discloses that supply is limited or available only at certain locations.
4. "The refusal to take orders for the advertised merchandise to be delivered within a reasonable period of time."
5. The "use of a sales plan or method of compensation for salesmen . . . designed to prevent or discourage them from selling the advertised product."[6]

Service Retailing

So Who Does Make the Best Pizza?

Two of the premier pizza retailers, Papa John's and Pizza Hut, both found out that you can sometimes go a little too far in your puffery and competitive advertising. Well, at least that is what the courts were trying to tell them.

The case, which began in 1998, was initiated with a charge by leading pizza retailer Pizza Hut, which claimed that Papa John's was running misleading advertisements denigrating its products. What was Pizza Hut referring to? The company was concerned about Papa John's use of the advertising slogan "Better Ingredients, Better Pizza." Papa John's began using the slogan in 1995 to emphasize its belief in using only the best ingredients to provide customers with the highest quality pizza (which was backed by two taste tests that compared Papa John's ingredients to those used by other pizza retailers). Usually, such vague subjective claims are viewed as puffery. But the Papa John's case was different. Not only did Papa John's use the slogan "Better Ingredients, Better Pizza," in its advertising, but in 1997 Papa John's also mentioned Pizza Hut in the ad, thus suggesting that Pizza Hut was not using the highest quality ingredients to make its pizza. This created a new twist to the traditional puffery that usually goes on in advertising, because it made a direct claim against a competitor.

In response, Pizza Hut filed a lawsuit claiming that Papa John's dough and sauce are not as fresh as some of its ads suggest. Further, in an attempt to sway public opinion, Pizza Hut aired ads that questioned the quality of Papa John's dough. Hence, a counter-suit was filed and the legal system was forced to examine who really had the best pizza made with the best ingredients.

After hearing all of the evidence, and tasting all of the pizza, a judge found both pizza retailers guilty. Papa John's was ordered to cease and desist using their slogan "Better Ingredients, Better Pizza," and was forced to pay more than $450,000 in damages.

It wasn't until September of 2000 in a 3-0 ruling by the 5th U.S. Circuit Court of Appeals that the slogan amounted to puffery given that it so exaggerated the company's product that it could not by itself be misleading. Critics are unclear as to what effects this controversy will have on advertising. For the 5th Circuit Court of Appeals indicated that if Pizza Hut could have proven that consumers were swayed by the ad then it would have viewed the slogan as misleading and ruled against Papa John's. The interpretation by the lower and upper courts has some suggesting that retailers put warning labels on their menus stating "This food item may not be as good as a competitor's product." Others, however, contend that it will most likely have little effect at all. But, as always, the court of public opinion will not be swayed by a court ruling determining who has the best pizza. In the end, consumers, and their taste buds, will determine who has the best pizza.

In our Retailing: The Inside Story box you can decide whether or not a retailer was involved in bait-and-switch advertising.

Deceptive Sales Practices

There are basically two deceptive sales practices that are illegal. These practices are (1) failure to be honest or to omit key facts in either an ad or the sales presentation and (2) using deceptive credit contracts.

With regard to deceptive credit, federal laws attempt to "assure a meaningful disclosure of credit terms so that the consumer will be able to compare more readily the various credit terms available to him and avoid the un-informed use of credit."[7] These laws

Retailing: The Inside Story

You Be the Judge

After reading all the facts, you decide whether this retailer was guilty of using bait-and-switch advertising.

American TV & Appliance of Madison, Wisconsin, ran the following radio advertisement:

> There are lots of good-quality washers and dryers on the market. But when you ask which ones are the best automatic washers and dryers, well, it's simple. There's Speed Queen, Maytag, and all the rest . . . at American TV & Appliance we have both of them and they're on sale for our January white sale. A clearance sale on the finest washers and dryers you can buy. This week a Speed Queen washer and dryer set is reduced to $499 . . . You can buy the finest for less than $500 . . . Why pay more at Sears?

However, the court determined that the dealer:

1. Lost money on each sale of the advertised set.
2. Ordered only 20 of the sale sets, but 133 additional more expensive Speed Queen sets.
3. Did not pay a sales commission on the advertised sets.
4. Accepted credit cards for the purchase of the more expensive sets, but not on the advertised sets.
5. Only sold four of the advertised sets.

Whether the retailer actually did intend to engage in bait-and-switch advertising was never proven. However, the retailer was found guilty. Do you agree with the court?

Source: Based on State of Wisconsin vs. American TV & Appliance of Madison, Inc., 140 Wis. 2d 353, 410 N.W. 2d 596 (Wisc. Ct. App. 1987).

were the result of unscrupulous practices on the part of retailers attempting to hide the true cost of merchandise in unrealistically (and sometimes illegal) high credit terms. For example, the retailer might sell a car at a very low price but then tack on a high (and often hidden) finance charge. Many states have laws limiting these hidden charges.

To ensure that the consumer can make informed purchases when using credit, federal law requires that the customer receive information on the following details:

1. The total amount financed
2. The finance charge as an annual percentage rate (APR)
3. The finance charge in dollars
4. Information on payments (number, amount, due dates, early repayment, etc.)
5. Disclosure of any other fees or charges (late payment, insurance, etc.)

If the credit agreement involves merchandise bought on time, creditors are also required to provide the following:

1. A description of the merchandise
2. The cash price
3. The "deferred payment" price (price plus total interest)
4. The amount of any down payment or trade-in

These credit disclosure rules apply not only to in-store selling but also to all promotional activities of the retailer.

Product Constraints

A retailer's major goal is to sell merchandise. To accomplish this goal, the retailer must assure customers that the products they purchase will not be harmful to their well-being and will meet expected performance criteria. Three areas of the law have a major effect on the products a retailer handles: product safety, product liability, and warranties. They are highlighted in Exhibit 6.6.

Product Safety

Retailers are in a difficult position when it comes to product safety. Most retailers do not produce the goods they offer for sale but purchase them from wholesalers or manufacturers. Retailers have little to say about product quality or safety. Their only weapon is deciding to use reputable suppliers so as not to carry merchandise they consider to be unsafe. You might therefore believe that retailers are not responsible for the safety of products they sell; this is definitely not the case.

A retailer who does not recognize that it is responsible for the safety of products it sells will have lower long-term profits than a retailer that ensures it sells safe products to its customers.

Exhibit 6.6   **Product Constraints**

```
  ┌──────────────┐                    ┌──────────────┐
  │   Product    │                    │   Product    │
  │  Warranties  │                    │    Safety    │
  └──────────────┘                    └──────────────┘
            \                          /
             \     ┌──────────────┐   /
              \    │   Product    │  /
                   │   Decisions  │
                   └──────────────┘
                          │
                   ┌──────────────┐
                   │   Product    │
                   │  Liability   │
                   └──────────────┘
```

During the Firestone Tire recall of tires on Ford SUVs, in 2000, the manufacturer also enlisted the assistance of BF Goodrich retailers, who helped to replace the unsafe Firestone tires.

According to the Consumer Product Safety Act (1972), the retailer has specific responsibilities to monitor the safety of consumer products.[8] Specifically, retailers (as well as manufacturers, other intermediaries, and importers) are required by law to report to the Consumer Product Safety Commission any possible "substantial product hazard." Furthermore, included in the description of substantial hazards is any failure to comply with an existing safety standard. Thus a retailer may unknowingly violate the law by reselling products that do not conform to existing safety standards; such recently happened to Burger King when it had to stop a Pokemon giveaway because a small Pokemon toy could be swallowed by a child. In addition, a retailer may violate the law by not cooking its meals to a required temperature. Retailers may further violate the law by failing to repurchase from customers nonconforming products sold after the effective or expiration date of a health standard or for a number of other reasons. For example, a supermarket might sell a product after the expiration date marked on the product. Examples abound. For instance, although an appeals court substantially reduced a lower court award of $2.9 million against McDonald's, the retailer was still guilty of serving a "too hot" cup of coffee. Finally, for years the famous "30-minute delivery guarantee" was part of the Domino's product. The company, however, was forced to discard this guarantee in fear for being sued as a result of any traffic accidents involving a delivery person.

Product liability laws deal with the seller's responsibility to market safe products. These laws invoke the "foreseeability" doctrine, which states that a seller of a product must attempt to foresee how a product may be misused and warn the consumer against the hazards of misuse.

Product Liability

Product liability laws invoke the "foreseeability" doctrine, which states that a seller of a product must attempt to foresee how a product may be misused and warn the consumer against the hazards of misuse. The courts have interpreted this doctrine to suggest that retailers must be careful in how they sell their products. This is of particular importance to restaurant, nightclub, and bar owners who fail to consider the consequences of serving a consumer who appears intoxicated. In addition to the federal laws covering product liability, all states have their own regulations.

Product Warranties

Retailers are also responsible for product safety and performance under conventional warranty doctrines. Under the current warranty law, the fact that the ultimate consumer may bring suit against the manufacturer in no way relieves the retailer from its responsibility for the fitness and merchantability of the goods. The disheartening fact that confronts the retailer is that in many states the buyer has been permitted to sue both the retailer and the manufacturer in the same legal suit.

Retailers can offer expressed or implied warranties. **Expressed warranties** are the result of negotiation between the retailer and the customer. They may be either written into the contract or verbalized. They can cover all characteristics or attributes of the merchandise or only one attribute. An important point for the retailer (and its salespeople) to recognize is that an expressed warranty can be created without the use of the words "warranty" or "guarantee." For example, a car salesperson might tell a buyer, "Everybody we've sold this type of car to has gone at least 60,000 miles with no problems whatsoever, and I see no reason why you cannot expect the same. I would not be surprised if you are able to go 100,000 miles without any mechanical problems." This statement could create an expressed warranty. The court would, however, be concerned with whether this was just sales talk (puffery) or a statement of fact or opinion by the salesperson.

Implied warranties are not expressly made by the retailer but are based on custom, norms, or reasonable expectations. There are two types of implied warranties (which overlap a bit): an implied warranty of merchantability and an implied warranty of fitness for a particular purpose.

Every retailer selling goods makes an **implied warranty of merchantability.** By offering the goods for sale, the retailer implies that they are fit for the ordinary purpose for which such goods are typically used. The notion of implied warranty applies to both new and used merchandise. For example, imagine that a sporting goods retailer located close to the ocean sells inflatable rafts and a consumer purchases one. The raft bursts while the person is floating on it, and the person subsequently drowns. This retailer may be held liable. Because of the potential legal liability that accompanies an implied warranty, many retailers will expressly disclaim at the time of sale any or all implied warranties. This is not always legally possible; some retailers will not be able to avoid implied warranties of merchantability.

The **implied warranty of fitness** for a particular purpose arises when the customer relies on the retailer to assist or make the selection of goods to serve a particular purpose. Consider a customer who is about to make a cross-country moving trip and plans to tow a 4-foot-by-4-foot two-wheel trailer behind her automobile. She needs a pair of tires for the rear of the automobile and thus goes to a local tire retailer and asks the salesperson for a pair of tires that will allow her to tow the loaded trailer safely. The customer in this regard is relying on the expertise of the retailer. If the retailer sells the customer a pair of tires not suited for the job, then the retailer is liable for breach of an implied warranty of fitness for a particular purpose. This is true even if the retailer did not have in stock a pair of tires to safely perform the job but instead sold the customer the best tire in stock.

Expressed warranties are either written or verbalized agreements about the performance of a product and can cover all attributes of the merchandise or only one attribute.

Implied warranty of merchantability is made by every retailer when the retailer sells goods and implies that the merchandise sold is fit for the ordinary purpose for which such goods are typically used.

Implied warranty of fitness is a warranty that implies that the merchandise is fit for a particular purpose and arises when the customer relies on the retailer to assist or make the selection of goods to serve a particular purpose.

Consumer product warranties frequently have been confusing, misleading, and frustrating to consumers. As a consequence, the Magnuson-Moss Warranty Act was passed. Although nothing in federal law requires a retailer to warrant a product under this act, anyone who sells a product costing the consumer more than $15 and gives a written warranty (though only written warranties are covered by federal laws, many types of warranties are subject to state laws) to the consumer is required to provide the consumer with the following information:[9]

1. The identity of the persons to whom the warranty is extended.

2. A clear description of the products, parts, characteristics, components, and properties covered by the warranty; if necessary for clarity, those items excluded from the warranty must be described.

3. A statement of what the warrantor will do in the event of a defect, malfunction, or failure to conform to the written warranty, including those items or services the warrantor will pay for, and, if needed for clarity, those items or services he or she will not pay for.

4. The point in time when the warranty begins (if it begins on a date other than the purchase date) and its duration.

5. A step-by-step explanation of the procedure the consumer should follow to obtain performance of the warranty obligation and information regarding any informal dispute-settling mechanisms that are available.

6. Any limitations on the duration of implied warranties or any exclusions or limitations on relief (such as incidental or consequential damages) together with a statement that under some state laws the exclusions or limitations may not be allowed.

7. A statement that the warranty gives the consumer certain legal rights, in addition to his or her other rights under state law, which may vary from state to state.

It is the retailer's responsibility to provide the prospective buyer with the written terms of the warranty for review prior to the actual sale. In this regard, the retailer has two options: clearly and conspicuously displaying the text of the written warranty near the product or making warranties available for examination by consumers upon request and posting signs advising consumers of the presale availability of warranties.

Managerial Question: How should a retailer balance express and implied warranties in offering products to customers?

LO • 4

How does governmental regulation influence a retailer's behavior with other channel members?

Channel Constraints

Retailers are restricted in relationships and agreements they may develop with channel partners. These restrictions can be conveniently categorized into four areas as shown in Exhibit 6.7.

| Exhibit 6.7 | **Channel Constraints** |

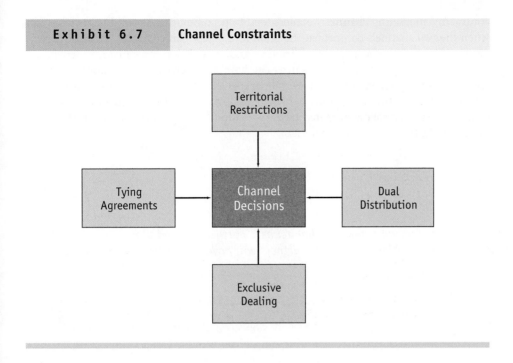

Territorial Restrictions

As related to retail trade, **territorial restrictions** can be defined as attempts by a supplier, usually a manufacturer, to limit the geographical area in which a retailer may resell its merchandise. The courts have viewed territorial restrictions as potential contracts in restraint of trade and in violation of the Sherman Antitrust Act. Thus, even though the retailer and manufacturer may both favor territorial restrictions, because of the lessening of competition between retailers selling the brand in question, the courts will often frown on such arrangements. The law does not, however, prevent manufacturers and retailers from establishing territorial responsibilities as long as they do not exclude all other retailers and restrict the sale of the manufacturer's products. Franchise agreements have long had territorial restrictions that provide a protected zone for the franchisee. Because of these zones, the franchisee is to develop a primary demand for the product without fear of cannibalization by another entry in the protected zone. In cases where the franchisor has permitted another franchisee to invade the "exclusive territory" of another franchisee as outlined in a contract, the original franchisee could sue the parent chain under a breach of contract claim. However, a 1999 federal appeals court ruling found that when a franchise contract expressly spells out that a franchisee does not have an exclusive territory, the franchisor has the power to place other outlets nearby.[10]

Territorial restrictions are attempts by the supplier, usually a manufacturer, to limit the geographic area in which a retailer may resell its merchandise.

Dual Distribution

As discussed in the previous chapter, a manufacturer that sells to independent retailers and also through its own retail outlets is engaged in dual distribution. Thus the manufacturer manages a corporately owned vertical marketing system that competes with independent retailers, which it also supplies through a conventional, administered, or contractual marketing channel. Retailers tend to become upset about dual distribution when the two channels compete at the retail level in the same geographic area. For example, Nike has wholly owned retail outlets and, in addition, uses major independent retailers as outlets. Such channel strategy can have an adverse effect on supplier-retailer relationships. Independent retailers will argue that dual distribution is an unfair method of competition and thus is in violation of the Sherman Act. As indicated in Chapter 5, the Internet has created new opportunities for dual distribution which has increased the levels of channel conflict.

Retailers who view the channel as a partnership and abide by the law in their relations with their partners will have higher long-term profits.

The courts have not viewed dual distribution arrangements as antitrust violations. In fact, they have reasoned that dual distribution can actually foster competition. For example, the manufacturer may not be able to find a retailer to represent it in all trade areas or the manufacturer may find it necessary to operate its own retail outlet to establish market share and remain competitive with other manufacturers. The courts will apply a rule-of-reason criterion. This requires that a given practice not be viewed as absolutely legal or illegal but that the court consider all relevant factors in a realistic manner. Thus, the independent retailer suing a manufacturer for dual distribution will have to convince the court that it was competed against unfairly and competition was damaged. The retailer's best bet would be to show that the manufacturer-controlled outlets were favored or subsidized (for instance, with excess advertising allowances or lower prices) to an extent that was detrimental to the independent retailer.

Nike actively engages in dual distribution.

Exclusive Dealing

Retailers and their suppliers occasionally enter into exclusive dealing arrangements. In a **one-way exclusive dealing arrangement,** the supplier agrees to give the retailer the exclusive right to sell the supplier's product in a particular trade area. The retailer, however, does not agree to do anything in particular for the supplier; hence the term "one-way." For example, a weak manufacturer will often have to offer one-way exclusive dealing arrangements to get shelf space at the retail level. Truly one-way arrangements are legal.

A **two-way exclusive dealing agreement** occurs when the supplier offers the retailer the exclusive distribution of a merchandise line or product if in return the retailer will agree to do something for the manufacturer. For example, the retailer might agree not to handle certain competing brands. Two-way agreements violate the Clayton Act if they substantially lessen competition or tend to create a monopoly. Specifically, the courts have generally viewed exclusive dealing as illegal when it excludes competitive products from a large share of the market and when it represents a large share of the total sales volume for a particular product type.

Tying Agreements

When a seller with a strong product or service forces a buyer (the retailer) to buy a weak product or service as a condition for buying the strong one, a **tying agreement** exists. For example, a large national manufacturer with several very highly demanded lines of merchandise may try to force the retailer to handle its entire merchandise assortment as a condition for being able to handle the more popular merchandise lines. This is called a full-line policy. Alternatively, a strong manufacturer may be introducing a new product and in order to get shelf space or display space at the retail level it may require retailers to handle some of the new product before they can purchase better established merchandise lines.

Tying arrangements have been found to be in violation of the Clayton Act, the Sherman Act, and the FTC Act. Tying is not viewed as a violation per se, but it will generally be viewed as illegal if a substantial share of commerce is affected. The most serious problems involving tying arrangements are those associated with franchising. Quite often, franchise agreements contain provisions requiring the franchisee to purchase all raw materials and supplies from the franchisor. The courts generally consider tying provisions of a franchise agreement legal as long as there is sufficient proof that these arrangements are necessary to maintain quality control. Otherwise, they are viewed as unwarranted restraints of competition.[11]

Other Federal, State, and Local Laws

Several other federal laws also affect retailers, but their impact is beyond the scope of this text. One such set of these laws, which is shown in Exhibit 6.1, is extremely important today because it deals with mergers and acquisitions. As retailers seek to consolidate their operations either by selling off some unprofitable stores or by acquiring the outlets of other retailers to expand into new markets, they must consider the impact on the competitive environment.[12]

One-way exclusive dealing
occurs when the supplier agrees to give the retailer the exclusive right to merchandise the supplier's product in a particular trade area.

Two-way exclusive dealing
occurs when the supplier offers the retailer the exclusive distribution of a merchandise line or product in a particular trade if in return the retailer will agree to do something for the manufacturer such as heavily promote the supplier's products or not handle competing brands.

Tying agreement
exists when a seller with a strong product or service requires a buyer (the retailer) to purchase a weak product or service as a condition for buying the strong product or service.

LO • 5

What is the impact of various state and local laws, in addition to other federal regulations, in developing retail policies?

Our country's various trade agreements regulating the amount of importing and exporting American firms can conduct with firms in various countries, sometimes limits, or even eliminates, a retailer's ability to purchase merchandise from certain foreign countries. For example, at one extreme our country currently bans all merchandise from Iraq and Libya, while at the other extreme our membership in NAFTA attempts to reduce all barriers to trade. Also, because labor is a retailer's largest operating expense, retailers must be aware of the laws that deal with minimum wages and hiring practices. Chapter 14, Managing Human Resources, covers the major laws affecting employment and personnel decisions. Tax laws and Security and Exchange Commission (SEC) rules and regulations, which deal with the legal form of ownership (sole proprietorship, partnership, or corporation) and shareholder disclosure requirements, are also not covered in this text. Chapter 13 considers how the Americans with Disabilities Act affects the layout and design of the retailer's store.

In addition to federal laws, many state and local municipalities have passed legislation regulating retail activities. Exhibit 6.8 illustrates how state and local laws affect the retailer. Zoning laws, for example, prohibit retailers from operating at certain locations

For foreign products to come into a country, they must clear customs. This is also true of products that tourists purchase in foreign countries to bring back home.

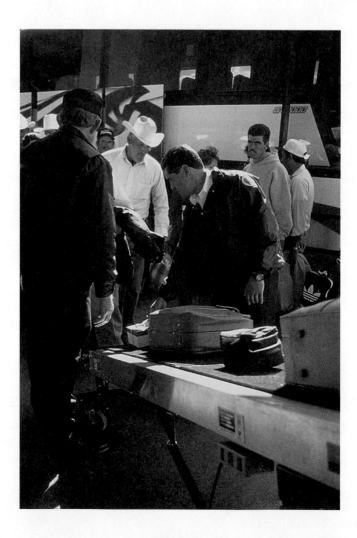

Exhibit 6.8	**State and Local Regulations Affecting Retailers**

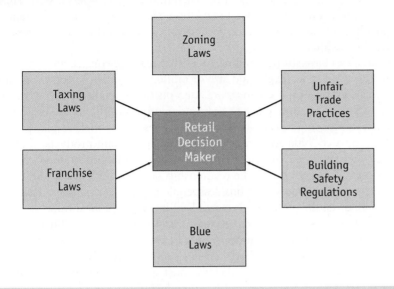

Retailers must abide by local and state laws regulating retail trade or their profitability performance will be hampered.

and require building and sign specifications to be met. Many retailers have found these codes to be highly restrictive, especially as some existing firms have been able to influence this type of legislation, thereby protecting their already established local business.

With regard to unfair trade practices laws, most states have established their own set of laws that prevent one retailer from gaining an unfair advantage over another retailer. As a general rule, "unfair trade practices" laws regulate the competitive behavior (usually relating to pricing, advertising, merchandise stocked, and employment practices) of retailers. For example, 22 states have laws against predatory pricing. The specific content of these laws varies, but usually they prohibit the retailer from seeking unfair advantages from vendors, selling merchandise below cost (or at cost plus some fixed percentage markup—6 percent is typical) with the intent of using profits from another geographic area or from cash reserves to destroy or hurt competition. These state laws are generally unclear in their definitions of selling below cost and as to the actions that can be taken (e.g., whether the retailer can give merchandise away or offer prizes or premiums without increasing an item's price as a form of price reduction).

A number of states have also introduced laws preventing both "zero down" car leases and "zero percent" financing programs that they claim mislead consumers. Also, the franchise laws in many states, for example, assume that, unless otherwise spelled out in the franchise agreement, there is an implied agreement not to locate another outlet near a current location without the current franchisee's permission. These state laws are often in conflict with federal regulations. As a result, in many instances, state laws regulating retailers have either been declared unconstitutional or amended to meet federal guidelines.

Many localities have strong building codes that regulate construction materials, fire safety, architectural style, height and size of building, number of entrances, and even elevator usage. Some local ordinances are attempts to aid retailers, such as the attempt by traffic engineers in some cities to reduce downtown traffic to under 20 miles per hour so that the consumers can observe local businesses and their display promotions. Other states enforce "blue laws" restricting the sale of certain products, such as automobiles, on Sundays. Many states have passed strong regulations on topics not covered by federal regulations governing the relationship between franchisors and franchisees in order to protect the individual businesspeople of their states. These laws require a full disclosure of all the pertinent facts involved in owning a local franchise. Many experts believe that these state franchise laws protect the current antiquated and inefficient automobile dealerships from newer, more efficient forms of competition because dealers provide 20 percent of sales tax revenues and are usually the largest advertisers in the local media. With such political clout, most state governments will make it difficult, as was discussed in the Chapter 2 E-tailing box, for discounters and Internet sellers to enter the new-car business or for Detroit to control the pricing and promotion of its own products. However, Internet businesses that serve as brokers are starting to appear. These businesses bring together purchasers with franchised dealers, who will sell the car to the purchaser at a price the Internet broker negotiates.

Finally, many state and local governments, as explained in the chapter's E-tailing box, are viewing the Internet as a cash cow. With sales of $23 billion and on-line advertising revenues of $9 billion in 2000, these taxing authorities see the Internet as a new source of tax revenue. The two pressing issues that could affect an e-retailer's future strategies are the following:

1. Who's responsible for collecting these taxes?

2. What constitutes a sufficient presence in an area that would obligate a retailer to pay taxes to that jurisdiction?

Sometimes states may pass laws that, though not fitting into any of the categories listed in Exhibit 6.8, will present problems for retailers. Two such state laws, for example, are the one requiring that only employees and not consumers may pump gas at service stations and the one requiring that all supermarkets individually price each item for sale in their stores with a sticker.

In addition, state court systems sometimes make rulings that will impact retailers across the country. For example, Supreme Courts of two states are deciding whether or not to hear cases involving injury to a customer when the retailer's employee did not follow a robber's demands as directed by the retailer's rules. Another state court is currently deciding if a retailer discriminated against a female by claiming that only men could be employed as the store's Santas. Also, various cities have passed laws governing retailing, such as the "Green River Ordinances"—named after the town in Wyoming that first passed them—restricting door-to-door selling. Other communities restrict the excessive use of garage sales, lottery promotions, and sale of obscene materials and

E-tailing

<u>Death and Taxes</u>

Mark Twain once wrote that there are only two things that are certain in life: death and taxes. After years of debate on whether Internet sales will be taxed, it seems that Mark Twain's view of taxes was right once again. Well, sort of. For e-tailers, it seems to depend on where you are located and where you operate that is going to be the sticking point of Twain's words.

The arguments for and against Internet sales being taxed both have their legitimacy. Those for Internet taxation claim that not taxing sales over the Internet creates unfair price competition between brick & mortar and e-tailers, as brick & mortar customers are required to pay sales taxes on their purchases while e-customers do not have to. Many contend that with the tremendous growth in on-line sales, vital tax revenues necessary to fund state and local government programs will be lost. On the other hand, opponents contend that taxing Internet sales will slow job growth brought forth by the Internet and reduce on-line innovation. Regardless of the side you may take, the debate is sure to continue.

In the United States, the Internet Tax Freedom Act, which will be in effect until October of 2006, sets the stage for a continued advancement of e-tailing. Simply put, the new law puts in place a number of significant rules that will help to stimulate e-tailing. First, the law placed a three-year ban on state and local governments from taxing Internet access, thus helping to keep the cost low for consumers to be on-line. Second, the law placed a three-year ban on multiple and discriminatory taxes on electronic commerce, which prevented the imposition of new tax liabilities for e-tailers and their customers. Third, it also protected from taxation those goods and services that are sold exclusively over the Internet with no comparable off-line equivalent. Fourth, it placed a ban on federal taxes on both Internet access and electronic transactions. Finally, it called on the federal government to work aggressively through the World Trade Organization (a multilateral trade organization composed of more than 130 countries) to keep electronic commerce from taxation. However, it is unknown what position the U.S. government will take as we approach 2006.

Granted, although the passage of the Internet Tax Freedom Act provides federal taxation relief, it does not bar local and state governments from taxing customers of e-tailers. In fact, almost all states have sales taxes that are applied to customers of e-tailers. Current state taxation laws for e-tailers mirror those for catalog retailers. That is to say that e-tailer customers must pay state sales taxes on sales conducted in states in which the retailers have a physical presence. So, one might think that customers at a click & mortar retailer such as Barnes & Noble, which has stores in every state, would have to pay taxes on all of their on-line sales. Well, not quite. Actually, although the chain is located in every state, barnesandnoble.com Inc. is a separate legal entity. As such, the e-tailer only has to collect taxes from those few states where it locates its warehouses. So the issue of e-tail taxation is a little complicated.

Whereas Internet taxation is complicated in the United States, the issue becomes even more complex internationally. Although the World Trade Organization has imposed a moratorium on taxing Internet transactions, the European Union is taking initial steps toward employing its value-added tax system to this new retail environment. For example, some indicate that European Union consumers may have to pay a 20 percent to 25 percent tax on products downloaded into the European Union from e-tailers in non-EU countries. Clearly, taxation of e-tail transactions will continue to be at the forefront of retailing in the 21st century.

dangerous products. In addition, states and cities might require licenses to operate certain retail businesses, such as liquor stores or massage parlors.

For further information about these various laws, a retailer should consult the local Better Business Bureau, the National Retail Federation, state and local retail trade associations, or state and local regulatory agencies.

LO • 6

How does a retailer's code of ethics influence its behavior?

Ethics in Retailing

Ethics
is a set of rules for human moral behavior.

Ethics is a set of rules for moral human behavior. These rules or standards of moral responsibility often take the form of dos and don'ts. Some retailers have an **explicit code of ethics,** which is a written policy that states what is ethical and unethical behavior. However, most often an implicit code of ethics exists. An **implicit code of ethics** is an unwritten but well understood set of rules or standards of moral responsibility. This implicit code is learned as employees become socialized into the organization and the corporate culture of the retailer.

Dollars & Sense

Retailers who abide by a strong set of ethical guidelines are more likely to achieve higher profits.

Explicit code of ethics
consists of a written policy that states what is ethical and unethical behavior.

Implicit code of ethics
is an unwritten but well understood set of rules or standards of moral responsibility.

Regardless of whether the code of ethics is explicit or implicit, it is an important guideline for making retail decisions. Shortly we will review some retail decision areas where ethical considerations are common. However, before doing so, it should be pointed out that legal behavior and ethical behavior are not necessarily the same. Unethical actions may be legal. Laws, after all, represent a formalization of behavioral standards through the political process into rules or laws. Therefore, a retailer needs to behave legally because laws represent a "formalized" set of ethical rules. In addition, retailers need to look beyond laws and engage in practices that are also ethical. One problem, though, is that "reasonable" people may disagree as to what is right and wrong behavior. For this reason, retailers should develop explicit codes of ethical behavior for their employees in order that they might have a sense of what is right and wrong.

Let's look at three decision areas where ethical considerations are needed in retailing:

1. Buying merchandise
2. Selling merchandise
3. The retailer-employee relationship

In each of these situations the retailer faces an ethical dilemma. Note that what is legal may not necessarily represent the best ethical guideline.

Ethical Behavior in Buying Merchandise

When buying merchandise, the retailer can face at least four ethical dilemmas which relate to product quality, sourcing, slotting fees, and bribery.

Product Quality   Should a retailer inspect merchandise for product quality or leave that to the customer? Although the law does not require such inspections, most retail buyers are concerned that their merchandise meets the expectations of the store's customers. As a result, some retailers have developed laboratory testing programs to verify the quality of not only their private label products but of manufacturers' brands as well.

Sourcing   Should a retailer verify the source of merchandise? A State Department document revealed that the Chinese may be exporting up to $100 million of merchandise made by prisoners, including many political prisoners, as well as counterfeiting some $800 million a year in videotapes, compact discs, and books.[13] The importation of such merchandise violates American laws, yet, most U.S. importers are unaware of this problem. In addition, though not against U.S. laws, some foreign merchandise sources use child labor or fail to pay a fair level of wages. The only way U.S. retailers can be sure that they are not buying illegal merchandise is to inspect all suppliers, down to the smallest subcontractors. However, some retailers are also having troubles with American suppliers. A program of careful vigilance to overcome such activities can be expensive and it is doubtful whether American consumers would be willing to bear the cost. Seeking to overcome such complaints, Kmart has begun to use private investigators to check out vendors to make sure they are not buying from unsavory characters.[14] Many other major American retailers have agreed to allow independent observers, including human rights officials, to monitor working conditions in their foreign factories. Consumers can check the U.S. Department of Labor's web site (http://www.dol.gov) to see if a particular retailer is involved in the program. In 2000, Nike, after years of being a target of many groups for using sweatshops, agreed to release a "complete audit of the 600 plants that manufacture its shoes and apparel—gory details and all."[15]

The issue of sourcing is of particular importance to college students, as a recent study found that $2.5 billion in college apparel (items bearing collegiate logos) had been manufactured in sweatshop factories. The University of North Carolina at Chapel Hill was the first to agree to push for humane factory working conditions from the 500 companies producing the popular sky blue UNC T-shirts and other apparel.[16]

Slotting Fees   Should a retailer demand money, commonly called slotting fees, from a manufacturer for agreeing to add a new product to its inventory? **Slotting fees** (also called **slotting allowances**) are fees paid by a vendor for space, or a slot, on a retailer's shelves, as well as for having its UPC number given a slot in the retailer's computer system. After all, if its UPC code is not in the system, individual stores could not stock the item. Retailers claim that such fees are actually a means of defraying their added expenses of adding warehouse space, replacing existing items in the store, placing the new items in the inventory control system, and as a form of insurance or a way of guaranteeing at least some profit from carrying the new item. The FTC has ruled that slotting fees, though they make a lot of vendors unhappy, are not discriminatory or anticompetitive, even though one major grocer acknowledged that the fees exceeded the retailer's costs.[17] In fact, the Internal Revenue Service even issued an "audit-issue" paper on reporting such fees for both the retailer and manufacturer. However, the U.S. Senate has begun to investigate this practice.

Slotting fees (slotting allowances)
are fees paid by a vendor for space or a slot on a retailer's shelves, as well as having its UPC number given a slot in the retailer's computer system.

Bribery   Should a retailer, or its employees, be allowed to accept a bribe? Bribery occurs when a retail buyer is offered an inducement (which the IRS considers to have a value greater than $25) for purchasing a vendor's products. Such inducements, it should be noted, are legal in many foreign countries. The reader may want to visit the document and publication section at the Transparency International web site (www.transparency.de) to see in which countries bribes are still considered part of the normal business behavior. However, in the United States, the Foreign Corrupt Practices

Act bans bribes as anticompetitive. It is, after all, hard to develop a relationship between a retailer and supplier when bribes are expected.

In the mid-1990s a JCPenney's buyer admitted to taking $1 million in bribes over several years, even though the products under question made money for Penney's. The ensuring coverage pointed out that many retailers had no formal policy on this subject. The negative consequence of this behavior has led some retailers to ban employees from accepting anything from a supplier. Wal-Mart, which by being the world's largest retailer is also the largest purchaser, has probably the strictest employee standard in the industry. Wal-Mart's employees are not allowed to accept any gifts (including samples) from vendors, not even if it is just a cup of coffee or soft drink when visiting a supplier's showroom. Kmart has gone a step further by requiring not only all its managers and buyers, but also its vendors, to sign an integrity pledge.

Ethical Behavior in Selling Merchandise

Ethics can also influence the selling process with regards to the products sold and the various selling practices that salespeople use.

Products Sold   Should a retailer sell any product, so long as it is not illegal? For example, should a convenience store operator located near a high school sell wine coolers? Should convenience stores carry cigarette paper for those few customers who prefer to roll their own and risk selling the paper to high schoolers who might use it for smoking marijuana?

Sometimes not carrying products can add to a retailer's profit. For example, Trader Joe's, a California specialty food retailer, recently analyzed all its cigarettes carried by company and brand and found only Marlboro merited the space allocated. Therefore, rather than just carry that one brand, the retailer dropped all cigarettes.[18] The case at the end of this chapter describes how the nation's second largest cigarette retailer faced this situation.

Selling Process Practices   Can a salesperson, while not saying anything wrong, be allowed to conceal from the customer all the facts? Also, should selling the "wrong" product for the customer's needs be permitted? Many retailers have ethical standards against such practices. However, as long as salespeople are paid on commission, we can expect such behavior to sometimes occur. Some highly successful retailers, such as Home Depot's Bernie Marcus, have sought to overcome this dilemma by never putting their employees at odds with their own code of ethics. Marcus has been quoted as saying, "The day I'm laid out dead with an apple in my mouth is the day we'll pay commissions. If you pay commissions, you imply that the small customer is not worth anything."[19] It should be pointed out, however, that paying commissions would be difficult in a self-service operation like Home Depot.

Ethical Behavior in the Retailer-Employee Relationship

Ethical standards can also influence the retailer-employee relationship in three ways: misuse of company assets, job switching, and employee theft.

Misuse of Company Assets   Most people would agree that stealing merchandise is illegal; but what about other types of stealing? What about an employee surfing the web or trading stock on company time? Also, what about taking an extra break or using

Home Depot employees are not paid a sales commission and thus their only interest is in serving and assisting customers. This helps discourage unethical selling techniques.

the retailer's phone for a personal long-distance call? All of these, although not subject to criminal prosecution, are forms of employee theft and should be considered when an employee develops his or her code of ethics.

Advancements in computer technology and the growth of the Internet have recently challenged one of the most treasured of American rights—the right to privacy. Most retailers have an asset that would have been unheard of a generation ago. Today's retailers have databases that contain heretofore private information about nearly every American that most consumers do not even know exists. However these databases are put together—whether collecting information from the retailer's web site or by purchasing information from state governments (e.g., driver license bureaus or voting registrars)—they do exist.

Many e-tailers, for example, not only know what purchases you made from them, but also what sections of their web site you visited. The majority of e-tailers disclose their privacy policy on their web site. Exhibit 6.9 lists the National Retail Federation's (NFR) Statement on Customer Data Privacy. In general, most of the major retailers in this country adhere to the NRF's principles. However, the shakeout in e-tailing during the early part of this decade showed just how the consumers' rights to the privacy could be violated by retailers.

Consider the case of Toysmart.com, an on-line retailer that shut down on May 22, 2000.[20] As with any company that enters bankruptcy, the creditors will want to use any of the firm's assets to settle their claims. One of the major assets of Toysmart was its database of customer information. Toysmart's web site contained the following statement: "Personal information voluntarily submitted by visitors to our site, such as name, address, billing information and shopping preferences, is never shared with a third party. All information obtained by toysmart.com is used only to personalize your experience on-line."[21] However, despite the above notice on its web site, Toysmart's database was offered for sale by the creditors in select editions of the *Wall Street Journal* on June 30, 2000.[22] Although the sale of databases is not illegal per se, both Congress and the FTC are investigating the issue of creditors rights to the use of this data.

Exhibit 6.9	National Retail Federation Principles on Customer Data Privacy

GENERAL RULE

The privacy of information collected by a retailer about its customers during the course of transactions with those customers should be maintained with the degree of confidentiality that the retailer reasonably anticipates would be expected of it by the typical shopper purchasing that type of merchandise from the retailer. Departures from this standard should be disclosed to customers at or before each time of occurrence, unless previously consented to by the customer or otherwise expressly permitted by law.

PRACTICE PRINCIPLES

Each retailer should adopt a customer privacy policy explaining its practices with respect to the information it collects about its customers.

Policies could either be corporate-wide or divisional depending upon the manner in which the company believes customers view its retail operations.

A retailer should make reasonable efforts to inform its customers of the existence of its customer privacy policies, and make the substance of such policies available, on a regular basis.

At a minimum, a customer privacy policy should allow a customer to elect whether he or she wishes to prevent the marketing of his or her name to other unaffiliated corporations, or to "opt out" of future promotional solicitations from the company(s) to which the policy applies, or both.

Retail companies should develop procedures to reasonably ensure that customer information is not accessible to, or used by, its employees or others in contravention of its policies and customer elections, and that access to personally identifiable data for non-promotional purposes is limited to those individuals with a customer servicing need to know.

Remember that consumers were told that data about them would not be sold to other parties. The question remains, what is to prevent other retailers from misusing this valuable asset and selling their databases as a means of survival?

Job Switching   Does an employee have the right to work for whomever he or she wants? Many argue that employees have a responsibility to their previous employer. The employer provided them with training and access to confidential information, such as vendor costs, customer lists, and future plans. When an employee leaves one retailer for another, the employee should respect the previous employer's right to retain the confidentiality of this information.

At the same time, the retailer should not seek to replace an employee, usually a manager or executive, just because the employee reaches the so-called 20-40-60 plateau (20 years or more with the firm; 40 years or older; and making over $60,000 a year) and replace the employee with a lower-paid, younger employee.

Employee Theft   Just as employers have a responsibility to be fair to their employees, employees must do likewise. However, many workers admit to "stealing" from their employers. Employee theft is most prevalent in food stores, department stores, and discount stores. Considering that these types of stores are usually larger in size, sales volume, and number of employees, the lack of close supervision might contribute to this problem. Some retailers, such as Wal-Mart, are trying to address this problem by offering cash bonuses just before Christmas if the store not only makes its profit goal but keeps shrinkage under a predetermined limit.

The previous discussion was not meant to be an all-inclusive list of the ethical dilemmas facing retailing today. It does, however, provide the reader with a big picture of the role of ethics in retailing.

Student Study Guide

Summary

We began this chapter by describing the multifaceted legal environment that confronts retailers in the United States. We identified constraints on retailers' activities in six broad categories: (1) pricing, (2) promotion, (3) products, (4) channel relations, (5) other federal laws, and state and local regulations and (6) ethics in retailing. Within each of these broad constraints, we summarized some specific activities that are regulated.

LO•1 Does legislation constrain a retailer's pricing policies?

With regard to pricing, which is the issue that most frequently confronts retailers, the retailer should first of all be familiar with two methods of price fixing: with other retailers (horizontal) and with channel members (vertical). In addition, the retailer must consider all the ramifications of price discrimination when purchasing merchandise. In setting retail prices, two other areas of concern are deceptive pricing and predatory pricing.

LO•2 Is there a difference between legal and illegal promotional activities for a retailer?

Regarding promotion constraints, the retailer should focus on three areas: deceitful diversion of patronage, which includes selling counterfeit or fake products; deceptive advertising, including making false claims about a product and using bait-and-switch tactics; and deceptive sales practices, which is not being completely honest in discussions about merchandise and the use of deceptive credit contracts.

LO•3 What responsibilities does a retailer have with regard to the products sold?

With regards to product constraints, the retailer should be aware of legislation dealing with product safety, product liability, and both expressed and implied warranty requirements as they relate to retailing.

LO•4 How does governmental regulation influence a retailer's behavior with other channel members?

Because all retailers are members of some type of channel, it is important to understand channel relationships in terms of the legality of territorial restrictions, dual distribution, exclusive dealing, and tying agreements.

LO•5 What is the impact of various state and local laws, in addition to other federal regulations, in developing retail policies?

In addition to the federal laws discussed in the chapter, the retailer must be aware of the impact of the various state and local laws on retailers. These laws include regulations on zoning, unfair trade practices, building safety, blue laws, and franchises.

LO•6 How does a retailer's code of ethics influence its behavior?

Laws and regulations do not cover every situation a retailer might face in the day-to-day operations of a business. In such cases, the retailer and its code of ethics will provide guidance. This is particularly important in buying merchandise, selling merchandise, and in the retailer-employee relationship.

Terms to Remember

horizontal price fixing	implied warranty of merchantability
vertical price fixing	implied warranty of fitness
price discrimination	territorial restrictions
deceptive pricing	one-way exclusive dealing
predatory pricing	two-way exclusive dealing
palming off	tying agreement
deceptive advertising	ethics
bait-and-switch advertising	explicit code of ethics
product liability laws	implicit code of ethics
expressed warranties	slotting fees (slotting allowances)

Review and Discussion Questions

LO•1 How does legislation constrain a retailer's pricing policies?

1. Deceptive pricing harms not only the consumer but also competition. Agree or disagree and explain your reasoning.

2. A federal grand jury argues that because all major supermarkets in a town are selling milk at the same price, there must be a conspiracy to fix prices. Agree or disagree and explain your reasoning.

3. Why should a retailer be familiar with the Robinson-Patman Act?

LO•2 What is the difference between legal and illegal promotional activities for a retailer?

4. Describe what is meant by the term "bait-and-switch." Is this a legal or illegal retailing tool?

5. What is deceitful diversion of patronage? Comment on its legality.

6. Explain what is meant by the term "palming off." Does palming off hurt competing retailers, consumers, or both?

LO•3 What responsibilities does a retailer have with regard to the products sold?

7. If a retail salesperson makes a misleading statement to a customer, can the retailer be held liable, even if the retailer instructed the salesperson never to make such statements?

8. What should a retailer do so that it does not violate the customer's rights under the Magnuson-Moss Warranty Act?

LO•4 How does governmental regulation influence a retailer's behavior with other channel members?

9. How could two-way exclusive dealing arrangements be harmful to the consumer and competition?

10. Discuss the concept of exclusive dealing. Are exclusive dealing arrangements in the retailer's best interest? Are they in the consumer's best interest?

LO•5 **What is the impact of various state and local laws, in addition to other federal regulations, in developing retail policies?**

11. Are state predatory laws usually effective? Why?

12. In a free market system, such as the one we have in the United States, should states be allowed to use zoning to regulate the architectural style of a retailer's building?

LO•6 **How does a retailer's code of ethics influence its behavior?**

13. Retailers should abide by the philosophy that "as long as it is legal, it is ethical." Agree or disagree and explain your reasoning.

14. A local supermarket operator, remembering that Mark McGwire used a hormone-boosting pill called andro when he hit all those home runs, read another research report on the product. However, like the ones before, this report could not find any definitive problems with the pill. Thus the pill, which is legal in the retailer's state, has great consumer appeal but has dubious effectiveness for adding strength to the human body. Is there an ethical problem, even though not a legal one, for this retailer if he or she decides to carry andro?

15. A drugstore manager is approached by a salesperson from a major pharmaceutical firm. The salesperson has a sick sister and she needs an expensive prescription drug that is manufactured by another company. Could the drugstore manager ethically trade off the free samples he has of the expensive drug the sister needs for twice their value in free samples of products that the salesperson handles? After all, because they are free samples anyway, who would be hurt by such an arrangement? Agree or disagree with the above and explain your reasoning.

16. Should retailers be allowed to sell to third parties private information about your shopping behavior (e.g., your purchase history), such as credit bureaus currently do? (Twenty years from now, would you want your own children to know what videos you rented as a college student?)

Sample Test Questions

LO•1 **Ben Cooper's Pontiac charges two different customers (one a man, the other a woman) two different prices for identical automobiles. This is in all probability a per se violation of the**

a. Clayton Act
b. your state's Unfair Trade Practices Act
c. Robinson-Patman Act
d. Sherman Act
e. this is not illegal because it involved a sale to a final consumer, not just sales between channel members

LO•2 **An example of deceitful diversion of patronage would be**

a. spreading rumors about a competitor, even if the rumors do not hurt the competitor's business
b. telling the truth about a competitor that will hurt the competitor's business
c. advertising a product at a very low price then adding hidden charges
d. putting extra large signs in your store's front window offering lower prices than your competitor next door
e. illegally using another company's trademark or brand name that results in the loss of sales for the other company

LO•3 When a customer relies on the retailer to assist the customer or to select the right goods to serve a particular purpose, the retailer is establishing

a.   an implied warranty of fitness
b.   an implied warranty of merchantability
c.   a price discrimination defense
d.   an expressed warranty of fitness
e.   an expressed warranty of merchantability

LO•4 D-A Pet Products Company has an extremely popular line of cat food. The company has recently started insisting that retailers who carry its cat food must also carry its rather overpriced cat litter. Due to its price, the litter is not a big seller, and it takes away shelf space from more profitable products. Requiring stores that stock the cat food to also stock the litter is an example of

a.   a consent agreement
b.   a tying contract
c.   unfair advertising
d.   monopolistic competition
e.   power marketing

LO•5 The most stringent laws governing franchises are typically enacted at the _____ level.

a.   federal
b.   state
c.   county
d.   local
e.   international

LO•6 Which of the following is not an ethical dilemma that a retailer faces when buying merchandise?

a.   whether the buyer believes he or she can sell the merchandise
b.   the source of the merchandise
c.   the issue of product quality
d.   whether to demand a slotting fee
e.   whether to ask for a bribe

Applications

Writing and Speaking Exercise   As assistant manager for an on-line music retailer, you have been approached by your manager to develop a competition-based pricing policy. Your manager indicates that because your market is global and pricing of CDs varies by both product and delivery costs, he would like you to develop a pricing strategy based on your global on-line competitors. Your manager believes that your firm could effectively compete on selection and service if only it could establish a pricing policy that would match competitors, thus eliminating their competitive advantage. In other words, he wants you to gather competitive intelligence from your competitors web sites to develop a pricing policy that in effect would make your CDs the exact same price (when delivery charges are included).

Prepare a response to the manager outlining your position on the potential legal and ethical implications of the strategy.

Retail Project   Each year the U.S. government's Consumer Information Center publishes the *Consumer Action* handbook. This book is designed to help consumers make informed decisions and address any problems they may have if they think they were cheated, swindled, or treated unfairly. In addition, the book lists other pamphlets and the phone numbers for all government agencies dealing with consumer issues— that is, credit, door-to-door selling, car repairs (including what to do if you purchased a "lemon"), and insurance.

You can order a copy of the handbook and get a list of all other pamphlets by writing the Consumer Information Center at P.O. Box 100, Pueblo, CO 81002 or by contacting the center on-line at (http://www.pueblo.gsa.gov).

Case

The Changing Face of Tobacco Retailers[23]

Over the past half century, Americans have become accustomed to the idea of being able to buy cigarettes at a variety of retail outlets ranging from vending machines in bars, restaurants, airports, supermarkets, convenience stores, gas stations, and discount stores. However, federal legislation may soon change the way tobacco is sold in the United States.

Wal-Mart was one of the first major retailers to address the tobacco issue. In 1990, Sam Walton admitted in a letter to a consultant that he was "still in a [quandary] on our direction for this very important issue."[24] The next year the retailer announced the banning of smoking on all Wal-Mart property, including the stores, as well as the removal of any cigarette vending machines. At the time, Walton was not aware of any vending machines, but as a precaution, he issued the "ban" order. Later, when Wal-Mart expanded into Canada by purchasing 127 Woolco stores, Walton met with the pharmacists from the newly acquired stores. They informed Walton that their job involved helping people get well, not causing health problems, which tobacco did. At their request, Wal-Mart dropped the sale of tobacco in its Canadian stores. Members of the chain's executive committee decided to continue with the sale of cigarettes after Sam Walton's death.

At the same time, various state and local agencies began to enforce age restrictions on the sale of cigarettes and other products, such as firearms, spray paint (which was used for painting gang slogans), and even glue. Wal-Mart introduced a program into its scanners that froze the cash register when the stock-keeping unit for one of these products was recorded until the clerk ascertained the age of the purchaser. As a result of this increased enforcement of the laws regulating the sale of tobacco, some retailers, especially supermarkets and drugstores, began to drop tobacco. How would this affect the sale of these legal products, which accounted for more than $60 billion in sales?

If such a change were to occur, what retailers would benefit? Some experts think that one of the retailers best prepared for cigarettes being dropped by the mass sellers is

John Roscoe's family-owned Cigarettes Cheaper chain. This 400-store operation already does $50 million in sales each year.

Cigarettes Cheaper, which only sells cigarettes in 1,200 square-foot outlets located primarily in strip malls and is second only to Wal-Mart in total cigarette sales, is a spin-off of the Roscoe's Customer Company convenience store chain. The name, Customer Company, was a reflection of Roscoe's appreciation for his consumers, and as a result he offered the lowest prices on everything in the store. His tobacco stores follow the same philosophy by charging 20 percent less on the average pack or cartoon of cigarettes.

The chain is able to charge such prices by taking advantage of every manufacturer discount available and realizing that its customers are not apt to buy just a pack or even a carton, but are more likely to purchase 10 to 12 cartons at a time. But low prices are not the only thing. Roscoe's store and similar operations have a broader range of brands and packaging than other retailers, a regular diet of promotions, and a welcoming attitude toward smokers that is not always the case elsewhere.

However, what is most impressive about Roscoe's operation are these facts:

■ No member of the family smokes, nor does Roscoe's encourage anyone to smoke.

The stores expend a great deal of effort in controlling "underage" customers. All stores have a large sign stating "No Minors Allowed Inside" and a manager could lose his or her job for violating this rule.

Many retail experts think this might be the way all cigarettes are sold in the future. What do you think?

Roscoe says his stores are just there to serve the market. Do you agree with his right to do this? Do you agree with his decision to do this?

Planning Your Own Retail Business

You are the general manager/partner for a local Ford dealership with a net worth of $1,800,000. At your regular Friday morning meeting with the salesforce, you congratulate them on being ahead of their sales quota for the year.

Things could not be better you thought to yourself as you left the meeting and returned to your office. You were going to exceed your $8.5 million sales goal for the year. Your cost of merchandise sold was expected to average 88 percent of sales and your fixed operating costs were being held to $30,000 a month. With variable cost averaging 5 percent of sales, you are expecting to produce almost a quarter million dollars in profit before taxes this year.

Just when things looked so great, your partner calls to ask if your read the article in the morning newspaper about last night's city council meeting. It seems that in order to reduce local property taxes, and keep voters happy, a council member has suggested that the city increase the sales tax by 1 percent. This tax would cover everything sold in the city, including automobiles.

Although you hate to see any type of sales tax increase, because it raises the price of your automobiles, this one in particular could present your dealership with a major problem. Just last year, several dealers representing most major domestic and foreign car manufacturers moved to a nearby suburban location, creating a sort of "car mall" where shoppers could easily move from one dealership to another and compare the various dealer offerings. One of those car mall dealers was the city's other Ford dealer. This dealer's customers would not have to pay this additional sales tax, because it appeared the suburb's government planned to keep local sales taxes at the current level and reap the benefits of seeing total retail sales increase as consumers flocked to suburban merchants to get lower prices.

What should you do? Should you absorb the additional tax to keep your prices competitive? What would this do to your profits? Or should you lobby city hall to get it to see the errors of this tax increase?

Endnotes

1. Sherman Act, 26 Stat, 209 (1890) as amended, 15 U.S.C. articles 1–7.
2. "Fakers' Paradise," *Forbes*, April 5, 1999: 49–54.
3. "Wal-Mart Wins Reversal in Trademark Lawsuit," *Wall Street Journal*, March 23, 2000: A3.
4. Fred W. Morgan and Allen B. Saviers, "Retailer Responsibility for Deceptive Advertising and Promotional Methods," A paper presented at the Retail Patronage Conference, Lake Placid, NY, May 1993.
5. In Re The Boston Beer Company, 198 F.3d 1370 (Fed Cir. 1999)
6. Morgan and Saviers, ibid.
7. *N. C. Freed Co., Inc. v. Board of Governors of Federal Reserve System* (CA2 NY) 473 F.2d 1210.
8. United States Public Law 92-573, Consumer Product Safety Act (1972).
9. Magnuson-Moss Warranty Federal Trade Commission Act, Public Law 93-637, 93rd. Congress (1975).
10. *Weaver v. Diageo*, 1999.
11. *Eastman Kodak Company v. Image Technical Services* (1992), 112 S. Ct. 2072.
12. For a detailed analysis of the changes taking place in this area of government regulation, the reader should consult: "Antitrust Enforcers Drop the Ideology, Focus on Economics," *Wall Street Journal*, February 27, 1997: A1, A8.
13. "China's Piracy Plague," *Business Week*, June 5, 2000: 44–48; "Will China Scuttle Its Pirates?" *Business Week*, August 15, 1995: 40–41; and "Copyright Pirates Prosper in China Despite Promises," *New York Times*, February 20, 1996: A1.
14. "The Detectives," *Fortune*, April 14, 1997: 123.
15. "Who Says Student Protests Don't Matter," *Business Week*, June 12, 2000: 94–96.
16. "NC Students End Sit-in on Sweatshop Issue," *Dallas Morning News*, April 24, 1999: 12A.
17. "FTC Urged to Get Tough on Retail Slotting Fees," *Advertising Age*. June 5, 2000: 1, 66.
18. Information supplied by Bob Kahn to the authors.
19. "Companies That Serve You Best," *Fortune*, May 31, 1993: 74–88.
20. "It's Layoff Time in Dot-Com Land," *Business Week*, June 12, 2000: 46–47.
21. Obtained from the Toysmart's web site on July 1, 2000.
22. This information was reported by CNBC on June 30, 2000.
23. This case is based on information supplied by Robert Kahn and William Davidson, the two individuals to whom the third edition of this textbook was dedicated.
24. Letter from Sam Walton to Robert Kahn dated July 6, 1990.

Part III
Market Selection and Location Analysis

Chapter 7
Market Selection and Retail
Location Analysis

Air travelers are a growing market segment with many needs and thus, many retailers are locating stores in airports.

Market Selection and Retail Location Analysis

CHAPTER

7

Overview

In this chapter, we review how retailers select and reach their target market through the location decision. The two broad options for reaching your target market are store-based and nonstore-based locations. The chapter's major focus is on the decision process for selecting store-based locations. We describe the various demand and supply factors that must be evaluated in each geographic market area under consideration. We conclude with a discussion of alternative locations that retailers consider as they select a specific site.

Learning Objectives

After reading this chapter, you should be able to

1. explain the criteria used in selecting a target market

2. identify the different options, both store-based and nonstore-based, for effectively reaching the retailer's target market and identify the advantages and disadvantages of business districts, shopping centers, and free-standing units as sites for retail location

3. define geographic information systems (GIS) and discuss their potential uses in a retail enterprise

4. describe the factors to be considered in identifying the most attractive geographic market for a store

5. discuss the attributes considered in evaluating retail sites within a retail market

6. explain how to select the best geographic site for a store

---

LO • 1

Explain the criteria used in selecting a target market.

Selecting a Target Market

Many retailing experts consider deciding who you want to sell to and deciding how to reach these potential customers as the most critical determinants of success in retailing. This involves the selection of a target market and evaluating alternative ways to reach this target market. Traditionally, for retailers desiring to reach a given target market this has meant selecting the best location for a store. In fact, a wise retailing executive once said that the three major decisions in retailing are location, location, and location. Although the other elements of the retail mix are also important, if the customer cannot reach your store conveniently, these elements become secondary. The easier it is to reach the store, the more store traffic a store will have and this will lead to higher sales.

Today, however, location is much broader than simply store-based location because retailers are finding alternatives to the customer traveling to a fixed-based store to purchase goods and services. For example, MacWarehouse sells computers and peripherals to households through the mail, the University of Phoenix offers an MBA on-line via a computer in the student's home or place of business, eBay has close to 6 million registered on-line members/users and records more than 2.5 million auctions on any given day, and Tupperware continues to sell most of its kitchenware via in-home parties.

As noted in earlier chapters, the Internet is becoming a major force in retailing. The equivalent of a store on the Internet is a retailer's site on the World Wide Web (WWW). When stopping at an e-tailer's web site, visitors first view the company's **home page,** which is equivalent to a storefront. From this home page a person visiting the retailer can be linked to other pages that provide more detailed information about merchandise, credit, warranties, terms of trade, and other features. The total collection

Home page
is the introductory or first material viewers see when they access a retailer's Internet site. It is the equivalent to a retailer's storefront in the physical world.

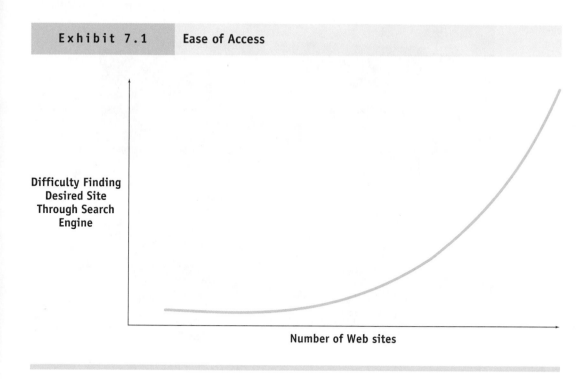

Exhibit 7.1   Ease of Access

Difficulty Finding Desired Site Through Search Engine

Number of Web sites

of all the pages of information on the retailer's web site has become known as its **virtual store.** Whereas a traditional store is located in geographic space, a virtual store is located in cyberspace.

The counterpart to location on the Internet is the "ease of access" a consumer has to the site. **Ease of access** refers to the consumer's ability to easily and quickly find a particular web site in cyberspace. To gain access to a site, a consumer can use a retailer's name (for example, www.jcpenney.com) or can use a search engine, such as Yahoo. Exhibit 7.1 illustrates that as the number of web sites increases, the difficulty finding a desired site through a search engine also increases.

Virtual store
is the total collection of all the pages of information on the retailer's Internet site.

Ease of access
refers to the consumer's ability to easily and quickly find a retailer's web site in cyberspace.

Retailers who select high-traffic geographic or cyberspace locations will be able to generate higher profits.

Regardless of whether retailers are planing a traditional store in geographic space or a virtual store in cyberspace, their first step is to develop a cost-effective way to reach the household and individual consumer that they have identified as their target market. Importantly, failure to clearly identify the target market will result in a large amount of wasted marketing expenditures.

The Limited has a well-defined target market: the moderate-income, career-oriented woman who is fashion conscious.

Market Segmentation

In Chapter 3, market segmentation was defined as a method retailers use to examine ways to segment, or break down, heterogeneous consumer populations into smaller, more homogeneous groups based on their characteristics. Because any single retailer cannot serve all potential customers, it is important that it segment the market and select a target market(s). A **target market** is that segment of the market that the retailer decides to pursue through its marketing efforts. Retailers in the same line of retail trade often pursue different target markets—for example, Ann Taylor appeals to the higher-income woman, The Limited appeals to the moderate-income woman, and Ross Dress for Less appeals to the budget-conscious female shopper. Other women's clothiers have segmented customers on other characteristics. For example, Lane Bryant, a division of The Limited, has been successful in targeting the plus-sized woman.

Target market
is the group of customers that the retailer is seeking to serve.

We are combining the topics of target market selection and location analysis because a retailer should identify its target market(s) before it decides how to best reach that target market(s). The target market can be reached through a store-based location; by this method, the consumer travels to the store, or through a nonstore retailing format in which products and services are offered at a nonstore location that is more convenient or accessible to the consumer. These are related topics because individuals of different characteristics are not randomly spread over geographic space; in fact, statistics have repeatedly demonstrated that people of similar backgrounds live nearby each other and have similar media habits, consumption habits, activities, interests, and opinions. Because of this fact, retailers such as Nordstrom know where to geographically locate their stores, and retailers such as Williams Sonoma (which has a very successful mail-order catalog for high-quality kitchenware) know which ZIP codes, geographic areas, or specific households to mail their catalogs.

Identifying a Target Market

To reach a target market successfully, three criteria should be met. First, the selected market segment should be measurable or able to be described using objective measures on which data are available, such as age, gender, income, education, ethnic group, or religion. The most commonly available objective data measure is demographic information, which the U.S. Census Bureau provides for business at little cost. Conversely, a subjective variable such as personality is more difficult to determine. For example, how can a retailer reasonably or cost-effectively measure the number of compulsive shoppers in the United States?

A second criterion is accessibility or the degree to which the retailer can target its promotional or distribution efforts to a particular market segment. Do individuals in the target market watch certain television programs, listen to certain radio programs, frequently visit certain web sites (i.e., cluster in cyberspace), or do they cluster together in neighborhoods. As we will see, the location decision is largely determined by identifying the most effective way to reach a target market. For instance, communities in cyberspace develop based upon consumer interests in specific activities, hobbies, etc. These consumer communities tend to be homogenous along the particular consumption aspect. For example, those consumers interested in backpacking exchange information on manufacturers and retailers in chat rooms resulting in unique preference structures for the virtual community when compared to those who are interested in the activity who are not part of the virtual community.

Finally, successful target marketing requires that the segment be substantial enough to be profitable for the retailer. Joe Albertson, the founder of the Albertson's supermarket chain, understood this in 1939 when he opened his first store. Albertson would drive through neighborhoods looking for diapers on clotheslines and tricycles on driveways. He knew that these were the signs of families with many mouths to feed and neighborhoods that promised future growth and therefore a place to build a grocery store. His idea must have been right, because his first store, although remodeled and expanded to meet the needs of today's customers, is still operating in the same location where it opened in 1939.[1] The chapter's Retailing: The Inside Story box describes how Albertson's is continuing to follow Joe Albertson's mission to "give the customer the merchandise they want, at a price they can afford to pay, complete with lots of tender loving care."[2]

Clearly, a retailer could develop a store to appeal to any market segment regardless of size, such as a store for fans of the Green Bay Packers, however, the retailer would have to ask itself if there were a sufficient number of Packer fans living within its trade area to make the store profitable. Although there are surely enough Packer fans in Wisconsin to support a store, a nonstore location, such as a web site on the Internet, would be a more effective way to target fans of the Green Bay Packers worldwide.

Retailers that select markets that are measurable, accessible, and substantial will be able to generate higher profit results.

Retailing: The Inside Story

Albertson's Method of Matching Stores to the Neighborhood

Albertson's annual report provides an insight as to how the supermarket chain uses segmentation through its neighborhood marketing concept to fulfill the chain's commitment to "great customer service."

Our methods today blend the science of technology and the art of human relations. Together they give us the information we need to provide customers in each neighborhood with the products and services they want. We use that information to operate each store as if it were our only store.

The first step in our neighborhood marketing process is to identify our customers. On the scientific side, demographic information tells us who lives in each neighborhood: Are most of the customers in this neighborhood married? Single? Do they have children? Are they of a particular religious or ethnic background that would indicate a need for special products?

The next step is to ask our neighbors what products and services they want in their grocery store. We ask them through community questionnaires and focus groups, and we listen carefully to their answers. We want each store to offer the right variety, the right departments and the right services for its neighborhood. For instance, a store in a neighborhood with many young families might offer destination categories such as baby care, candy, and pet care.

We also study the lifestyles — and thus, the shopping habits — of our customer. Albertson's must appeal to all types of shoppers in order to maintain its success, but statistics help us fine-tune our stores to match the demographic makeup of each neighborhood. For example, in a neighborhood with a large percentage of working moms, we might emphasize Quick Fixin' Ideas that help busy customers provide tasty and nutritious meals for their families quickly and easily. Our Quick Fixin' Ideas program allows customers to pick up meal ideas and recipes to make quickly at home or to select from a variety of meals already prepared — or both.

Such a neighborhood might also be a good candidate for an Albertson's Express fuel center, which enables customers to fill up their cars and their pantries in the same trip.

A store with a large percentage of price-conscious shoppers might put more emphasis on Albertson's Brands products. These products provide a great value, and our customers know they can expect quality at a price they can afford. Albertson's Brands products help customers stretch their food dollars further while maintaining the high quality they desire.

Albertson's is even studying cyber-customers. In the Dallas/Fort Worth area, we're testing on-line shopping over the Internet. Through our web site, customers can order groceries for home delivery and we can market directly to individuals. It's just one additional way Albertson's is providing solutions to customer needs.

Statistical tools are a great help to our Company in providing customers with the products and services they need, but we also have other ways to identify our customers and their needs. The human connections between Albertson's and the communities in which we operate help us go beyond information found in a statistic. These human connections give us special knowledge that allows us to be better friends and neighbors.

We gain this personal knowledge of the community in many ways. A store director may be an active member of the local chamber of commerce. As such, he becomes aware of upcoming community events in plenty of time to plan for, and participate in, those events. A produce manager might coach youth soccer. Because of that, she knows that the league will need refreshments for out-of-town soccer players attending a local tournament. A front-end manager may volunteer in the library of a local elementary school, thus learning about children who need donated school supplies in order to get a good start on their education.

Source: Albertson's 1998 Annual Report: 5–7.

Reaching Your Target Market

As previously noted, once a retailer identifies its target market it must identify the most effective way to reach this market. Exhibit 7.2 illustrates the different retail formats that can be used to reach target markets. Essentially there are store-based and nonstore-based retailers. **Store-based retailers** operate from a fixed store location, which requires customers to travel to the store to view and select merchandise and or services. Essentially, the retailer requires that the consumer perform part of the transportation function, which was one of the eight marketing functions discussed in Chapter 5. However, **nonstore-based retailers** reach the customer at home or at work or at a place other than a store where the customer might be susceptible to purchasing. As hinted earlier, many retailers are beginning to reach customers on the Internet.

Location of Store-Based Retailers

As shown in Exhibit 7.2, there are four basic types of locations from which a store-based retailer can select: business districts, shopping centers/malls, free-standing units, and nontraditional locations. No one type of location is inherently better than the others. Many retailers, such as McDonald's, have been successful in all four location types. Each type of location has its own characteristics relating to the composition of competing stores, parking facilities, affinities with nonretail businesses (e.g., office buildings, hospitals, universities), and other factors.

Business Districts   Historically, many retailers were located in the **central business district (CBD),** usually an unplanned shopping area around the geographic point

Store-based retailers operate from a fixed store location that requires customers to travel to the store to view and select merchandise or services.

Nonstore-based retailers intercept customers at home, at work, or at a place other than a store where they might be susceptible to purchasing.

Central business district (CBD) usually consists of an unplanned shopping area around the geographic point at which all public transportation systems converge; it is usually in the center of the city and often where the city originated historically.

Exhibit 7.2	Retail Formats for Accessing Your Target Market

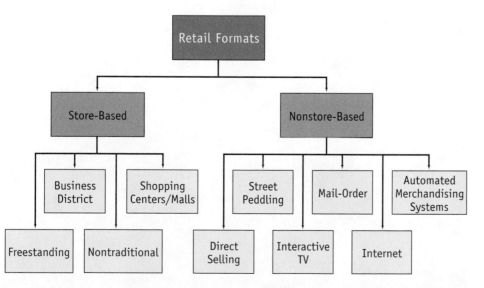

at which all public transportation systems converge. Many traditional department stores are located in the CBD along with a good selection of specialty shops. The makeup or the mix of retailers in a CBD is generally not the result of any advance planning, but depends on history, retail trends, and luck. This is beginning to change today as some communities have tried to reinvigorate their city center. To date, however, these efforts have not been too successful.

However, some towns want to protect their town center from nonlocal retailers that want to locate there. For example, in Litchfield, Connecticut, the birthplace of Ethan Allen and Harriet Beecher Stowe, many local residents protested Talbots planned entry into their town. However, Talbots, a retailer selling women's updated upscale classics, despite the local opposition, was successful in opening a store in a two-story colonial revival building.[3] Northfield, Minnesota, a town with two liberal arts colleges and remembered by some as the place where Jesse James and his gang were shot up, rejected plans by Wal-Mart and Kmart to locate there. However, in a public referendum in November 1998, the citizens approved a Target store on the edge of town. Opponents feared that the 124,000-square-foot discount store, and the businesses that would locate near it, would destroy the quaint, close-knit downtown business district that featured coffee shops, boutiques, clothing stores, and a small department store.[4]

The CBD has several strengths and weaknesses to consider. Among its strengths are easy access to public transportation, wide product assortment, variety in images, prices, and services, and proximity to commercial activities. Some weaknesses to consider are inadequate (and usually expensive) parking, older stores, high rents and taxes, traffic and delivery congestion, potentially high crime rate, and the general decaying conditions of many inner-cities. However, despite these disadvantages, Kmart recently deviated from its historical suburban location policy and opened two discount department stores in Manhattan. Despite the high costs and other disadvantages of such a location, the chain felt the high traffic and the expectation of more than $50 million in

Despite relatively high operating costs, Kmart has recognized the value of locating stores in central business districts.

annual sales were irresistible incentives.[5] Also, Staples, the office-supply superstore chain that began life as a free-standing suburban operation, now has more than two dozen Staples Express stores in downtown locations. These Express stores are only a third the size of a regular Staples, but they are successful because they satisfy the customer's "immediate need."[6]

Often, the weaknesses of CBDs have resulted in a retail situation known as inner-city retailing, which occurs when only the poorest citizens are left in an urban area. Traditionally, despite the fact that such areas annually contribute at least $85 billion, or 7 percent of all retail spending, product and service offerings in these areas have decreased, while prices have held steady or even increased. Although most consumers are aware that basketball great Magic Johnson has found success opening movie theaters in Harlem, as well as in the inner-cities of Los Angeles, Cleveland, and Houston, many are not aware of the success of other retailers in the inner-cities. Retailers, such as Dollar-General, Vons Cos., Stop & Shop, Supermarkets General, Jewel/Osco, Kroger, First National Supermarkets, A&P, American Stores, Pathmark, and even service retailers, like Sterling Optical, have used good merchandise selection and heavy public relations to find success in previously underserved inner-city areas. One of the key reasons for a retailer's success in these markets is because the retailer tailored its inventories to the special needs and tastes of inner-city residents. These retailers have also leveraged an under-utilized work force with high retention in an overall tight labor market, another factor that has helped these ventures to be successful.[7]

In larger cities, secondary business districts and neighborhood business districts have developed. A **secondary business district (SBD)** is a shopping area that is smaller than the CBD and that revolves around at least one department or variety store at a major street intersection. A **neighborhood business district (NBD)** is a shopping area that evolves to satisfy the convenience-oriented shopping needs of a neighborhood. The NBD generally contains several small stores, with the major retailer being either a supermarket or a variety store, and is located on a major artery of a residential area. An increasing number of national retail chains are finding the neighborhood business district an attractive location for new stores. This includes retailers such as Ann Taylor, the Body Shop, Starbucks, Crate & Barrel, Williams Sonoma, and Pottery Barn.

The single factor that distinguishes these business districts from a shopping center/mall is that they are usually unplanned. Like CBDs, the store mixture of SBDs and NBDs evolve partially by planning, partially by luck, and partially by accident. No one plans, for example, that there will be two department stores, four jewelry stores, two camera shops, three leather shops, twelve apparel shops, and one theater in an SBD.

Shopping Center/Mall   Ever since 1956 when Dayton's, now Target Company, opened the country's first fully enclosed shopping center, Southdale Center, in Edina, Minnesota, America has had a love affair with the shopping center.[8] A **shopping center** (or **mall**) is a centrally owned or managed shopping district that is planned, has **balanced tenancy** (the stores complement each other in merchandise offerings), and is surrounded by parking facilities. A shopping center has one or more **anchor stores** (a dominant large-scale store that is expected to draw customers to the center) and a variety of smaller stores. To ensure that these smaller stores complement each other, the shopping center often specifies the proportion of total space that can be occupied by each type of retailer. Similarly, the center's management places limits on the merchandise lines that each retailer may carry. A unified, cooperative advertising and

---

Secondary business district (SBD) is a shopping area that is smaller than the CBD and that revolves around at least one department or variety store at a major street intersection.

Neighborhood business district (NBD) is a shopping area that evolves to satisfy the convenience-oriented shopping needs of a neighborhood, generally contains several small stores (with the major retailer being a supermarket or a variety store), and is located on a major artery of a residential area.

Shopping center (or **mall**) is a centrally owned or managed shopping district that is planned, has balanced tenancy (the stores complement each other in merchandise offerings), and is surrounded by parking facilities.

Balanced tenancy occurs in shopping centers when the stores complement each other in merchandise offerings.

Anchor stores are the stores in a shopping center that are the most dominant and are expected to draw customers to the shopping center.

promotional strategy is followed by all the retailers in the center. A shopping center location can offer a retailer several major advantages over a CBD location. Among them are the following:

1. Heavy traffic resulting from the wide range of product offerings
2. Nearness to population
3. Cooperative planning and sharing of common costs
4. Access to highway and availability of parking
5. Lower crime rate
6. Clean, neat environment
7. Adequate parking space

Despite these favorable reasons for locating in a shopping center, the retailer does face several disadvantages. Among the limitations are the following:

1. Inflexible store hours (the retailer must remain open whenever the center is open and cannot be open at other times)
2. High rents
3. Restrictions as to the merchandise the retailer may sell
4. Inflexible operations and required membership in the center's merchant organization
5. Possibility of too much competition and the fact that much of the traffic is not interested in a particular product offering
6. Dominance of the smaller stores by the anchor tenant

Shopping center image, shopping center preferences, and shopping center personality all attract various subsets of consumers, giving retailers located at these centers a competitive advantage over other retailers. Therefore, it is extremely important that a retailer considering a shopping center location be aware of the makeup, image, preferences, and personality of the center under question.

As Exhibit 7.3 shows, according to the International Council of Shopping Centers, there are eight different types of shopping centers/malls, each with a distinctive function.

Shopping centers and their latter-day counterpart, the mall, have become a fixture of American life, social and economic, and are popular locations for retailers. Shopping centers and malls now account for one-half of all retail sales, excluding automobile dealerships, in the United States. Seniors take their daily exercise by walking through malls, families find malls a good source of low-cost entertainment, and teens seek out mates in malls. In many cases, the loyalties of shoppers toward a specific center/mall have over time become equal to or greater than their loyalties to a particular retailer. Surprisingly, as the Global Retailing box indicates, one type of mall, the outlet center, despite its overwhelming success in the United States, is just now entering the Canadian market.

Free-standing retailer
generally locates along major traffic arteries and does not have any adjacent retailers to share traffic.

Free-Standing Location   Another option is to be a free-standing location. A **free-standing retailer** generally locates along major traffic arteries and does not have to share traffic with any adjacent retailers that are selling competing products.

Exhibit 7.3	ICSC Shopping Center Definitions

				Typical Anchor(s)			
Type	**Concept**	**Sq. Ft. Inc. Anchors**	**Acreage**	**Number**	**Type**	**Anchor Ratio***	**Primary Trade Area****
Neighborhood Center	Convenience	30,000–150,000	3–15	1 or more	Supermarket	30–50%	3 miles
Community Center	General merchandise convenience	100,000–350,000	10–40	2 or more	Discount dept. store; supermarket; drug; home improvement; large specialty/ discount apparel	40–60%	3–6 miles
Regional Center	General merchandise fashion (Mall, typically enclosed)	400,000–800,000	40–100	2 or more	Full-line dept. store; jr. dept. store; mass merchant; disc. dept. store; fashion apparel	50–70%	5–15 miles
Superregional Center	Similar to Regional Center but has more variety and assortment	800,000*	60–120	3 or more	Full-line dept. store; jr. dept. store; mass merchant; fashion apparel	50–70%	5–25 miles
Fashion/Specialty Center	Higher-end, fashion-oriented	80,000–250,000	5–25	N/A	Fashion	N/A	5–15 miles
Power Center	Category-dominant anchors; few small tenants	250,000–600,000	25–80	3 or more	Category killer; home improvement; discount dept. store; warehouse club; off-price	75–90%	5–10 miles
Theme/Festival Center	Leisure; tourist/ oriented; retail and service	80,000–250,000	5–20	N/A	Restaurants, entertainment	N/A	N/A
Outlet Center	Manufacturers' outlet stores	50,000–400,000	10–50	N/A	Manufacturers' outlet stores	N/A	25–75 miles

Used with permission.

* The share of a center's total square footage that is attributable to its anchors

** The area from which 60–80% of the center's sales originate

Free-standing retailing offers several advantages:

1. Lack of direct competition
2. Generally lower rents
3. Freedom in operations and hours
4. Facilities that can be adapted to individual needs
5. Inexpensive parking

Global Retailing

Outlet Centers in Canada

Although very popular in the United States, outlet centers are not nearly as popular in Canada. This is in spite of the fact that most Canadians are familiar with outlet centers from visiting the U.S. Indeed, many Canadian families receive direct mail promotions from such outlet centers. Slowly, the outlet center concept is growing in Canada.

The Vaughn Mills center, a 1.4 million square foot mega-mall, opened in the fall of 2001 and was Canada's 12th outlet center. Just north of Toronto, this center brought new U.S. retailers to Canada. Many catalog stores and manufacturer's outlets have used this mall as their first entry into the Canadian market.

Outlet center development has suffered from a lack of tenant choice in Canada. In the 1990s, an outlet center mall scheduled to be the first in western Canada failed to materialize for just this reason. Planned for a location between the major city of Calgary and the popular resort town of Banff, this center could not attract enough potential retail tenants and the project was shelved.

Potential tenants in Canada are often deterred from opening such outlets due to the proximity to their regular retail formats. They fear cannibalization. Canadian retailers are slowly seeing the benefits of outlet centers. Stores such as Body Shop, Cambridge Towels, Peter Nygaard, Globo Shoes,

Danier Leather, Roots and Kodiak Country are now pursuing the outlet center format. American and international companies tend to dominate the tenant mix in most Canadian outlet centers. For example, Nike, Rockport, Guess, Levi's, Jones New York, Tommy Hilfiger, Villeroy & Boch, and Liz Claiborne are all present in outlet centers in Canada.

For consumers, the choice is currently dominated by women's wear retailers. Men's wear, childrens' wear, and department store formats are lacking. There are few department store chains in Canada, and they have not yet ventured into the outlet/clearance format.

Development of outlet centers has been concentrated in central Canada. With a larger density of population, Ontario and Quebec dominate the outlet center market. Geographic distance and a lack of density of population in other parts of Canada make the economies of scale necessary for success hard to achieve. In areas with a high density of population, such as Vancouver, other problems have deterred development. In Vancouver, land is very expensive. Competition is very close, with U.S. outlet centers easily accessible to the Vancouver population.

Source: Prepared by Professor Lynne Ricker, University of Calgary.

Free-standing retailing does have some limitations:

1. Lack of drawing power from complementary stores
2. Difficulties in attracting customers for the initial visit
3. Higher advertising and promotional costs
4. Operating costs that cannot be shared with others
5. Stores that may have to be built rather than rented
6. Zoning laws that may restrict some activities.

The difficulties of drawing, and then holding, customers to an isolated or free-standing store is the reason only large, well-known retailers should attempt it. Small retailers may be unable to develop a loyal customer base because customers may be unwilling to travel to a free-standing store that does not have a wide assortment of products and a local or national reputation. Kmart and Wal-Mart, as well as many convenience stores and gasoline stations, have used free-standing location strategies

Small local retailers are beginning to recognize the value of locating near large national chains such as Office Max. These large chains create traffic which benefits the smaller retailer.

successfully in the past. Discount appliance stores such as Best Buy and wholesale clubs such as Costco are using them today. However, when these large national chains acquire land for a free-standing store, they often acquire more than they need and then "out-parcel" (i.e., sell) the remaining land to smaller retailers. Some astute local retailers or small regional chains have found it quite attractive to buy this excess land and build stores, even at a premium price, because of the traffic a large discounter like Wal-Mart generates.

Nontraditional Locations   Increasingly retailers are identifying nontraditional locations for their stores that offer more place utility or locational convenience. Perhaps one of the oldest and best known nontraditional retail locations is the Army and Air Force Exchange Services (AAFES), which operates more than 10,000 stores in the United States and around the world on U.S. military bases. The largest of these stores are the 163 post or base exchange stores that handle 42,000 stock-keeping units (SKUs) of general merchandise.

Recognizing that a significant number of travelers spend several hours in airports and can use this time to purchase merchandise they may otherwise purchase in their local community, airport managers are looking to retail malls as a source of revenue. Due to the success of earlier versions, airports are now making retail a major part of their offering. One of the most unique airport retail malls is the one at Philadelphia International Airport. Because this airport was undergoing a major facelift at the time, retailing was not just an afterthought. As a result, the airport management could merchandise and organize in a way that made sense. The mall's 33 shops include many well-known retailers (The Gap/Gap Kids, Godiva Chocolatier, and Sunglass Hut), as well as local favorites (Philly's Finest, The Philadelphia Museum Store, and Dinardo's). Similar to other malls, it is organized around a food court.[9]

Service Retailing

Click & Mortar Banks

The old adage of "banker's hours" being the most restrictive in the industry, often 9:00 a.m. to 4:00 p.m., Monday through Friday, is melting away in the highly competitive retail banking environment. Banks, understanding the desire for convenience on the part of their clientele, have long stressed the importance of location.

To enhance location convenience to customers, banks were innovators in the movement toward the application of technology in the early 1980s through the introduction of the automated teller machine (ATM). Initially, ATMs allowed customers to make deposits and withdrawals 24 hours a day, 7 days a week, at the bank's branch offices. However, banks soon realized that location was a key element of increasing ATM usage and that through greater dispersion of their ATMs throughout the community, greater customer service could be established.

Soon, ATMs penetrated nonbanking retailers, adding to a retailer's product mix. For example, retailers such as Tesco in the United Kingdom and Wal-Mart in the United States added ATMs in their stores, allowing banks an opportunity to expand their locations while offering retailers an opportunity to broaden their product mix. Although initially banks used large-format retailers as ATM locations, soon supermarkets, convenience stores, drugstores, as well as other small-format

retailers were used. However, from the banking industry's perspective, ATMs were just the first step in banking location enhancements.

Banks next employed the technology of the Internet to expand their locations to every home equipped with a computer, thus satisfying the segment of the market that wished to complete their banking transactions on-line. The movement toward on-line banking offered the location convenience specific segments of customers enjoyed and provided banks with a broader range of location options, which added overall convenience to their retail offering. However, acknowledging that not all consumer segments desired an electronic transaction, either through an ATM or on-line, and that the location of many branch offices was inconvenient, banks began a new location strategy.

Realizing the customers' desire for location convenience and face-to-face interaction, banks began a strategy of opening branch offices in retail stores. Banks recognized that when opening a branch office in a retail store, such as a supercenter or supermarket, traffic would increase dramatically at key shopping times, such as Saturdays and Sundays, thus necessitating a revamping of their traditional hours of operation. For banking, it's all about location.

Retailers that develop stores in nontraditional locations enhance their opportunities for achieving high profit performance.

On college campuses there is an increasing number of food courts in student unions; truck and travel stops along interstate highways also are incorporating food courts; and some franchisees such as Taco Bell and Dunkin Donuts are putting small food service units in convenience stores on campuses. Georgia Tech even has a supermarket on its campus.[10] Hospitals are building emergency care clinics near where people live in the suburbs and away from the hospital, lawyers are putting in storefront offices wherever there is high pedestrian traffic, and copying services such as Kinko's are locating in major office buildings. In banking, Wells Fargo has mini-marketplaces—featuring Starbucks coffee bars, dry cleaners, delis, and postal centers—in its branches.[11] Some service retailers, however, are not as concerned with location because their services are delivered to the consumer at home. For example, plumbers, house painters, repair services, maid services, carpet cleaners, and lawn-care firms may not be concerned with their location. Travel time to the customer's location might be the only consideration involved, as the chapter's Service Retailing box illustrates.

Nonstore-Based Retailers

There is great diversity and variety among nonstore-based retailers. Perhaps the oldest form is the street peddlar who sells merchandise from a pushcart or temporary stall set up on a street. Street peddling is still common in some parts of the world such as Mexico, Turkey, Pakistan, India, and many parts of Africa and South America. But it is also seen in the United States in such places as New York City and San Francisco where peddlers sell T-shirts, watches, books, magazines, tobacco, candy, hot-dogs, and other products on street corners.

Managerial Question: Given the wide variety of locations available to target specific consumer groups, what new locations will provide the greatest opportunities for the retailers of tomorrow?

In Chapter 4, Evaluating the Competition in Retailing, we discussed several popular forms of nonstore retailing, which are depicted in Exhibit 7.2. Because retailing in the United States for the next 20 years and perhaps beyond will continue to be predominantly store based, we will focus our attention on location analysis for these retailers. However, it should be noted that some innovative retailers are using multiple retail formats to reach their target markets. For example, JC Penney not only continues to build traditional stores but also has an extensive mail-order catalog and on-line operations where different catalogs are developed to target different customer segments. In fact, most experts predict that by 2005 virtually all traditional store-based retailers will have developed multiple retail formats to reach their target markets. However, as the E-tailing box indicates, even on-line retailers may need to have a store format to complement their service offerings.[12]

Retailers who understand the need for multiple retail formats to reach their target market will be the star profit performers of the next decade.

Geographic Information Systems

LO • 3

Define geographic information systems (GIS) and discuss their potential uses in a retail enterprise.

One recent technological innovation in retailing is geographic information systems. A **geographic information system (GIS)** is a computerized system that combines physical geography with cultural geography. Physical geography is the latitude (the north/south) and longitude (east/west) of a specific point in physical space and its related physical characteristics (water, land, temperature, annual rainfall, etc.). Cultural geography

E-tailing

Do E-tailers Need a Physical Store?

Whenever Charles Schwab, the nation's number one on-line stock broker, does market research, one of the key questions asked of consumers is, "How important is a local branch office in your selection of an on-line broker?" The results are always the same—it is *not* important. As with any e-broker, customers always list as their top priorities low commissions; easy access to the broker, especially when the market is moving fast; and fast efficient problem-solving, if and when needed. The branch office question scores way down the list of options offered. Yet every time the broker opens a local office, Schwab doubles the new business it would normally get in that community. As of early 2000, Schwab had more than 300 new offices, and despite the market-research results, the e-broker planned on doubling that total over the next five years.

The brokerage firm's success with local offices particularly flies in the face of conventional Internet wisdom, which always claimed that price and convenience are king. However, in mid-2000, many e-tailers realized that e-customers, much like their physical store counterparts, wanted good customer service just as much as price. E-tailers that only sought to compete on price (such as Value America discussed in Chapter 5's Retailing: The Inside Story box), and as a result minimized fixed costs and forgot about the other elements of the retail mix, quickly found out their mistake when they ran out of cash and customers and many filed for bankruptcy. (Interestingly enough, although Schwab does 80 percent of its transactions electronically, a broker opens 70 percent of its new accounts face to face in branch offices.)

Why are brick & mortar branches so important to e-customers? Well, when you ask them, "How important is service?" or "What are your biggest frustrations?" they'll talk about web sites that are confusing or do not work or about dealing with uncaring people over an 800 number. A customer's biggest fear is having a problem and nobody to resolve it. Therefore, the local office becomes a security blanket to care and nurture the customers and their problems.

Consumers have all heard stories about web sites being down, phone calls going unanswered, and phone operators not being caring when customers do get through. Thus, even though the words "branch office" usually do not generate a positive response on market surveys, the ability to visit an office and deal with a human being is important to most customers. Therefore, Charles Schwab needs brick & mortar offices to address the fears and frustrations of its customers.

Source: Based on sections of David S. Pottruck and Terry Pearce, *Clicks and Mortar: Passion Driven Growth in an Internet Driven World* (San Francisco: Jossy-Bass, 2000), and the authors' experiences with Schwab.

Geographic information system (GIS)
is a computerized system that combines physical geography with cultural geography.

Culture
is the buffer that people have created between themselves and the raw physical environment and includes the characteristics of the population, humanly created objects, and mobile physical structures.

consists of the things that humankind has put in place on that space. To understand this, one needs to appreciate that culture is the buffer that humans have created between themselves and the raw physical environment. It includes the characteristics of the population such as its age, gender, and income and of the human-created objects placed on that space, such as fixed physical structures (factories, stores, apartment building, schools, churches, houses, highways, railroads, airports, etc.) and mobile physical structures (e.g., cars and trucks). In reality, culture includes anything that humans can put onto a physical space, which then becomes an attribute of the physical space.

For example, some areas such as Scottsdale, Arizona, become known for their very high density of golf courses; yet these golf courses were not put there by nature, but by people. Other areas become known as high-crime areas; but nature did not put crime there, people did. Recent advancements in GIS technology have allowed the retail analyst to also describe the lifestyle (activities, interests, opinions) of the residents of geographic areas. This can be quite helpful in selecting locations for stores that are highly lifestyle sensitive, such as Galyan's Trading Company. Galyan's, which is owned by The

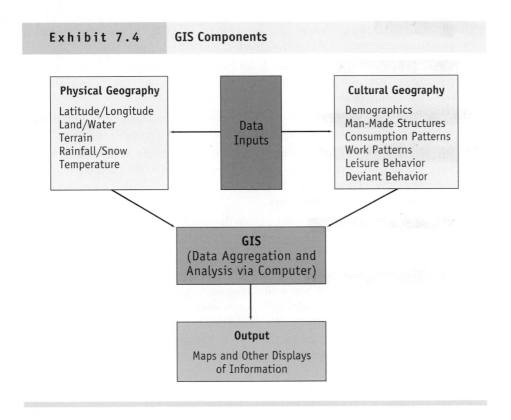

Exhibit 7.4   GIS Components

Physical Geography
- Latitude/Longitude
- Land/Water
- Terrain
- Rainfall/Snow
- Temperature

Data Inputs

Cultural Geography
- Demographics
- Man-Made Structures
- Consumption Patterns
- Work Patterns
- Leisure Behavior
- Deviant Behavior

GIS
(Data Aggregation and Analysis via Computer)

Output
Maps and Other Displays of Information

Limited, is a 100,000-square-foot category killer in the sporting goods area.[13] Exhibit 7.4 shows the key components of geographic information systems.

Thematic Maps

Historically, it was not unusual for a retailer to push pins into a map of a city where it was located. Each pin represented where a customer lived. An even more sophisticated retailer may have colored the map to represent different areas of the city in terms of income levels or ethnic composition. This was an early form of thematic mapping. **Thematic maps** are area maps that use visual techniques such as colors, shading, lines, and so on to display cultural characteristics of the physical space. Thematic maps can be very useful management tools for retailers. They can help the retailer visualize a tremendous amount of information in an easy-to-understand format. Today, thematic maps are an important feature of geographic information systems and are fully computerized, making them easy for retailers to develop.

Thematic maps use visual techniques such as colors, shading, and lines to display cultural characteristics of the physical space.

Uses of GIS

As a management technology, the GIS has a variety of important uses in retailing. Some of these more popular uses are identified as follows.

1. *Market selection.* A retailer with a set of criteria in mind, such as the demographics of its target market and the level of over- or understoring in a market, can have the GIS identify and rank-order the most attractive cities or counties or other geographic areas to consider for expansion.

2. *Site analysis.* With a particular community in mind, a GIS can identify the best possible site or evaluate alternative sites for their expected profitability.

3. *Trade area definition.* If the retailer develops a database of where its customers reside, a GIS can automatically develop a trade area map and update this daily, weekly, monthly, or annually.

4. *New store cannibalization.* A GIS can help the retailer evaluate how the addition of another store in a community can cannibalize sales of its existing stores.

5. *Advertising management.* A GIS can help the retailer allocate its advertising budget to different stores based on the market potential in their respective trade areas. Similarly, a GIS can help the retailer develop a more effective direct-mail campaign to prospective customers.

6. *Merchandise management.* A GIS can help the retailer develop an optimal mix of merchandise based on the characteristics of households and individuals within its trade area.

7. *Evaluation of store managers.* A GIS can provide an important human resource function. It can help assess how well a store manager is performing based on the trade area characteristics. Consider that two stores of the same size could be performing quite differently because of the demographics and competitive conditions in the two trade areas. Thus it would be inappropriate to either reward or punish a manager for things over which the manager has no control.

Dollars & Sense

Retailers that use GIS technology are able to improve their store location performance.

If you wish to learn more about GIS technology, you might look at some of the home pages on the Internet for firms that provide GIS services. These include the following:

> Integration Technologies at http://www.integtech.com
>
> Equifax National Decision Systems at http://www.ends.com
>
> Environmental Systems Research Institute Inc. at http://www.esri.com

Market Identification

LO • 4

What are the geographic factors to be considered in identifying the most attractive market for a store?

The location decision for store-based retailers involves three sequential steps. First, the retailer must identify the most attractive markets in which to operate. Some retailers, such as Toys"R"Us, Home Depot, Wal-Mart, and Benetton, are international, and thus when they think of adding new locations they consider the attractiveness of geographic expansion into foreign countries. Perhaps the most global of all retailers is McDonald's with more than 23,000 locations throughout the world and with plans to add more than 1,000 stores a year over the next decade. In the 1990s, retailers such as Pier 1 and Sharper Image identified Mexico as an attractive market for expansion. But most retail analysts contend that with the passage of the trade agreement with China in 2000,

China may be the most lucrative market in the early 21st century. China, after all, has the largest population of any country, and its economic status as well as its technological infrastructure are growing rapidly. Already such U.S. retailers as IGA, Home Depot, and Wal-Mart have entered China and have aggressive expansion plans. Other retailers, such as County Seat Jeans, Kmart, Kroger, and many smaller retailers, concentrate on a single country, the United States, and thus when considering new locations they evaluate the attractiveness of locations in the United States. Still other retailers concentrate on a small region, possibly a single state or city.

The second step in the retail location decision is to evaluate the density of demand and supply within each market and to identify the most attractive sites that are available within each market. Essentially, this means determining the sites most consistent with the retailer's target market and then identifying those for which the market is not already overstored or in which competition is not overly intense. The third step is the

Many U.S. firms have saturated the U.S. market and are now looking to foreign markets for store growth and expansion.

Exhibit 7.5	Selecting a Retail Location

Identify the Most Attractive Markets in Which to Operate

↓

Identify the Most Attractive Sites That Are Available Within Each Market

↓

Select the Best Site(s) Available

selection of the best site (or sites) available. This stage involves estimating the revenue and expenses of a new store at various locations and then identifying the most profitable new locations. These three steps are illustrated in Exhibit 7.5.

As stated earlier, the first step in making a good retail location decision is to identify the most attractive market or **trading area**—the geographic area from which a retailer, group of retailers, or community draws its customers—in which the retailer could locate. For instance, Dollar-General, which only now is entering larger cities, has been very successful in the past by concentrating its expansion in small towns (generally those with populations of less than 10,000) where there is less competition, easier zoning and building regulations, and lower wages and operating costs.

Trading area
is the geographic area from which a retailer, or group of retailers, or community draws its customers.

Retail Location Theories

The most attractive retail markets are not necessarily the largest retail markets. A variety of other factors need to be considered in identifying attractive markets. But to begin with, a trio of methods are especially useful for identifying the best markets.

Retail gravity theory
suggests that there are underlying consistencies in shopping behavior that yield to mathematical analysis and prediction based on the notion or concept of gravity.

Retail Gravity Theory   **Retail gravity theory** suggests that there are underlying consistencies in shopping behavior that yield to mathematical analysis and prediction based on the notion or concept of gravity. **Reilly's law of retail gravitation,**[14] named after its developer, William Reilly, dealt with how large urbanized areas attracted customers from smaller communities serving the rural hinterland. In effect, it stated that two cities attract trade from an intermediate place approximately in direct proportion to the population of the two cities and in inverse proportion to the square of the distance from these two cities to the intermediate place. That is, people will tend to shop in the larger city if travel distance is equal, or even somewhat farther, because they believe that the larger city has a better product selection, and it will be worth the extra travel.

Reilly's law of retail gravitation,
based on Newtonian gravitational principles, explains how large urbanized areas attract customers from smaller rural communities.

Two decades later, Reilly's original law was revised in order to determine the boundaries of a city's trading area or to establish a point of indifference between two cities.[15] This **point of indifference** is the breaking point at which customers would be indifferent to shopping at either city. The new formulation of Reilly's law can be expressed algebraically as

Point of indifference
is the extremity of a city's trading area where households would be indifferent between shopping in that city or in an alternative city in a different geographical direction.

$$D_{ab} = \frac{d}{1 + \sqrt{\dfrac{P_b}{P_a}}}$$

where D_{ab} is the breaking point from city A, measured in miles along the road to city B

d is the distance between city A and city B along the major highway

P_a is the population of city A

P_b is the population of city B

For example, if Levelland and Norwood are 65 miles apart and Levelland's population is 100,000 and Norwood's is 200,000, then the breaking point of indifference between Levelland and Norwood would be 26.9 miles from Levelland and 38.1 miles from Norwood. This means that if you lived 25 miles from Levelland and 40 miles from Norwood, you probably would choose to shop in Levelland because it is within your zone of indifference for Levelland and is beyond your zone of indifference for Norwood. (You might want to figure this out yourself, using Norwood as city A and Levelland as city B.)

Exhibit 7.6 shows how Reilly's law can be used to determine a community's trading area. As shown in Exhibit 7.6, city A has a population of 240,000. City B, with a population of 14,000, is 18 miles north of city A and its breaking point is 14.5 miles north of city A (point X on Exhibit 7.6). City C, with a population of 21,000, is 14 miles southwest of city A and its breaking point is 10.8 miles southwest of city A (point Z on Exhibit 7.6). Finally, city D, with a population of 30,000, is 5 miles southeast of city A and its breaking point is 3.7 miles southeast of city A (point Y on Exhibit 7.6).

Retail gravity theory rests on two assumptions: (1) the two competing cities are equally accessible from the major road and (2) population is a good indicator of the differences in the goods and services available in different cities. Consumers are attracted to the larger population center, not because of the city's size, but because of the larger amount of store facilities and product assortment available, thereby making the increased travel time and cost worthwhile. However, in its simplicity, retail gravity theory does have several limitations.

Exhibit 7.6   **Trading Area for City A**

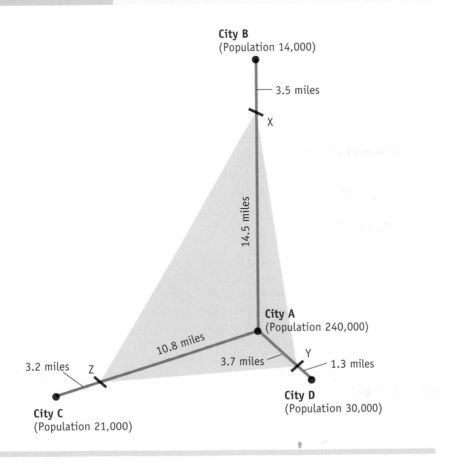

First, city population does not always reflect the available shopping facilities. For example, two neighboring cities, each with a population of 10,000 and similar demographics, would not be reflected equally if one of the cities had a shopping center with Target serving as the anchor store and the other did not. Second, distance is measured in miles, not the time involved for the consumer to travel that distance or the consumer's perception of that distance or time involved. Given our present highway system, this limitation is extremely important. Traveling 20 miles on an interstate highway to a mall located at an exit may be easier than the stop-start travel involved in going six miles through downtown traffic. Therefore, some retailers will substitute travel time for mileage. Finally, although the theory works reasonably well in rural areas, where distance is a major decision factor, it is not flawless.

Recent research on **outshopping**—that is, leaving your community to shop—from rural areas suggests that factors other than those considered by retail gravity theory are important. For example, in the 1990s Canada enacted such high sales taxes that millions of Canadians living near the border, which 70 percent of Canadians do, began to shop in the United States. As a result, the Canadian government was forced to repeal the tax.

Other factors that the retail gravity theory fails to consider include perceived differences between local and other trading centers, variety-seeking behavior, and other services provided including medical services or entertainment facilities. Also, gravity theory is less useful in metropolitan areas where consumers typically have a number of shopping choices available within the maximum distance they are willing to travel.

Saturation Theory   Another method for identifying attractive potential markets is based on retail saturation, which examines how the demand for goods and services of a potential trading area is being served by current retail establishments in comparison with other potential markets. Such analysis produces three possible outcomes:

1. **Retail store saturation** is a condition under which existing store facilities are utilized efficiently and meet customer needs. Retail saturation exists when a market has just enough store facilities for a given type of store to serve the population of the market satisfactorily and yield a fair profit to the owners.

2. When a market has too few stores to satisfactorily meet the needs of the customer, it is **understored.** In this setting, average store profitability is quite high.

3. When a market has too many stores to yield a fair return on investment, it is **overstored.**

Saturation theory, therefore, implies a balance between the amount of existing retail store facilities (supply) and their use (demand). As indicated in Chapter 4, one typically measures saturation, overstoring, and understoring in terms of the number of stores per thousand households. The consensus among retail location experts is that the United States is currently highly saturated or overstored with retail stores and thus retailers are taking a second look at some long-ignored markets, such as older downtown areas.

A possible indicator of understored versus overstored markets is the **index of retail saturation (IRS),**[16] which is the ratio of demand for a product or service divided by available supply. The IRS can be measured as follows:

$$IRS = (H \times RE)/RF$$

where IRS is the index of retail saturation for an area; H is the number of households in the area; RE is the annual retail expenditures for a particular line of trade per

---

Outshopping

occurs when a person leaves their community to shop in another community.

Retail store saturation

is a condition where there is just enough store facilities for a given type of store to efficiently and satisfactorily serve the population and yield a fair profit to the owners.

Understored

is a condition in a community where the number of stores in relation to households is relatively low so that engaging in retailing is an attractive economic endeavor.

Overstored

is a condition in a community where the number of stores in relation to households is so large that engaging in retailing is usually unprofitable or marginally profitable.

Index of retail saturation (IRS)

is the ratio of demand for a product (households in the geographic area multiplied by annual retail expenditures for a particular line of trade per household) divided by available supply (the square footage of retail facilities of a particular line of trade in the geographic area).

household in the area; and RF is the square footage of retail facilities of a particular line of trade in the area (including square footage of the proposed store). If you multiply the two terms in the numerator together (households and retail expenditures per household), you obtain dollar sales. Recalling that the denominator is square footage of retail space, it is easy to see that the IRS is essentially the sales per square foot of retail space in the marketplace for a particular line of retail trade.

> *Retailers who identify and locate in markets where the index of retail saturation is high will be able to achieve a higher profit.*

Dollars & Sense

When the IRS takes on a high value in comparison with the line of trade in other cities, it indicates that the market is understored, and therefore a potentially attractive opportunity exists. When it takes on a low value, it indicates an overstored market, which precludes the potential of a significant opportunity. Home Depot monitors its sales per square foot for a store because it recognizes if this ratio is too high that customers may not be well served and competition may be invited into the market. In fact, if sales per square foot is over $400, the company believes it is advantageous to close a thriving store and open two smaller stores. Although this practice cannibalizes the existing store, it better serves customers and avoids competition entering the market.[17] In a similar strategy, McDonald's will open more restaurants in a growing area as a proactive strategy to discourage competitors such as Carl's Jr. and Burger King from building new outlets. This also enables McDonald's to protect its market share.

As an example of how the index of retail saturation is used, consider an individual planning to open a dry cleaner in either city A or city B. This individual has the following information: Residents of both cities spend $9.28 per month on dry cleaning. The total number of households in both cities is also the same, 17,000. City A, however, has 2,000 square feet of dry-cleaning facilities, and city B has 2,500 square feet; the incoming retailer's proposed square footage is 500 square feet. Given this information and using the formula for IRS, we can find the IRS for each city:

$$\text{IRS (city A)} = 17,000 \times 9.28/(2,000 + 500) = 63.10$$
$$\text{IRS (city B)} = 17,000 \times 9.28/(2,500 + 500) = 52.59$$

Thus, based solely on these two factors of demand (number of households and average expenditure for products by each household) and one factor of supply (the square footage of retail space serving this demand), the individual would choose to locate in city A, because its value of $63.10 is higher than city B's $52.59.

As nonstore-based retailing continues to grow, retailers need to recognize that the index of retail saturation may become less useful. That is because it only incorporates store-based retailing in the supply component of the index. This does not pose a problem in the preceding dry cleaner example, but it may be a problem for apparel retailers and computer retailers because many households are using mail-order catalogs and e-tailers.

Buying Power Index   *Sales & Marketing Management* magazine annually publishes its Survey of Buying Power. This survey reports on current data for metropolitan areas, cities, and states. It provides some data that are not readily available from other sources, such as the Census Bureau. These data include retail sales for specific merchandise categories, and the area's effective buying income, total retail sales, and population.

The population, retail sales, and buying income data provide the retail manager with an overview of the potential of various trading areas. By comparing one trading area to another, the retailer can develop a relative measure of each market's potential. For each area, the retailer will develop a **buying power index (BPI)**, which is a single weighted measure combining effective buying income (personal income, including all nontax payments such as social security, minus all taxes), retail sales, and population size into an overall indicator of a market's potential. Generally, business firms use a formula for BPI that was developed by *Sales & Marketing Management*. The BPI is weighted in the following manner:

$$BPI = 0.5(\text{the area's percentage of U.S. effective buying income})$$
$$+\ 0.3(\text{the area's percentage of U.S. retail sales})$$
$$+\ 0.2(\text{the area's percentage of U.S. population})$$

It is obvious that effective buying income is the most important factor, followed by retail sales and population. This formula can be further refined by breaking down these general figures into more specific figures geared toward the consumers of the retailer's products.

For example, XYZ Corporation, a retail chain specializing in general merchandise goods, is considering expansion into one of two different trading areas. The proposed trading areas are the Alton-Granite City, Illinois, or Hamilton-Middletown, Ohio, markets. XYZ aims its general merchandise at the 25-to-34-year-old market with incomes over $35,000. Therefore, the 25-to-34-year-old group will substitute for population, the general merchandise sales will substitute for total retail sales, and households with income over $35,000 will replace effective buying income.

Using data that can be easily obtained from *Sales & Marketing Management*, XYZ can develop the BPI for each city:

$$BPI \text{ (Alton-Granite City)} = 0.5(.000386) + 0.3(.00083) + 0.2(.00012)$$
$$= .000466$$
$$BPI \text{ (Hamilton-Middletown)} = 0.5(.000717) + 0.3(.00063) + 0.2(.000112)$$
$$= .000570$$

As you can see the BPI of Hamilton-Middletown is almost 25 percent greater than that of Alton-Granite City, although the cities are nearly equal in size. Therefore, XYZ would probably choose to expand its Ohio market rather than its Illinois market.

Remember that the BPI is broad in nature and only reflects the demand levels for the two proposed trading areas, not the supply level. Therefore, it does not reflect the saturation levels of these two markets. This can be easily taken care of by dividing the BPI for each area by the area's percentage of U.S. retail selling space for general merchandise (the supply factors) to determine each area's attractiveness:

$$IRS \text{ (Alton-Granite City)} = .000466/.000452 = 1.03$$
$$IRS \text{ (Hamilton-Middletown)} = .000570/.000483 = 1.18$$

In this case the Ohio trading area is again chosen. This IRS formula does not reflect the availability of competing products or stores in nearby larger cities: Cincinnati, in the case of Hamilton-Middletown, and St. Louis, Missouri, in the case of Alton-Granite City.

Buying power index (BPI)

is an indicator of a market's overall retail potential and is composed of weighted measures of effective buying income (personal income, including all nontax payments such as social security, minus all taxes), retail sales, and population size.

Other Demand and Supply Factors   In addition to using retail gravity theory, the index of retail saturation, and the buying power index in evaluating various potential markets, the successful retailer will also look at some other demand and supply factors for each market.

Market Demand Potential

In analyzing the market potential, retailers identify certain criteria that are specific to their product line or the services they are selling. The criteria chosen by one retailer might not be of use to a retailer selling a different product line. The major components of market demand potential are as follows:

1. *Population characteristics.* Population characteristics are the most often used criteria to segment markets. Although total population figures and their growth rates are of primary importance to a retailer in examining potential markets, the successful retailer can obtain a more detailed profile of a market by examining school enrollment, education, age, sex, occupation, race, and nationality. Retailers should seek to match a market's population characteristics to the population characteristics of people who desire their goods and services.

2. *Buyer behavior characteristics.* Another useful criterion for analyzing potential markets is the behavioral characteristics of buyers in the market. Such characteristics include store loyalty, consumer lifestyles, store patronage motives, geographic and climatic conditions, and product benefits sought. These data, however, are not as easily obtainable as population data.

3. *Household income.* The average household income and the distribution of household incomes can significantly influence demand for retail facilities. Further insight into the demand for retail facilities is provided by Engel's laws. (These laws imply that spending increases for all categories of products as a result of an income increase but that the percentage of spending in some categories increases more than for others.) Thus, as average household income rises, the community will exhibit a greater demand for luxury goods and a more sophisticated demand for necessity goods.

4. *Household age profile.* The age composition of households can be an important determinant of demand for retail facilities. In communities where households tend to be young, the preferences for stores may be different from communities where the average household is relatively old. For example, older consumers spend almost four times as much at drugstores as do 30-year-olds.

5. *Household composition.* If we hold income and age constant and change the composition of the household, we will be able to identify another determinant of the demand for retail facilities. After all, households with children have different spending habits than childless households with similar incomes.

6. *Community life cycle.* Communities tend to exhibit growth patterns over time. Growth patterns of communities may be of four major types: rapid growth, continuous growth, relatively stable growth, and finally decline. The retailer should try to identify the communities that are in a rapid or continuous growth pattern, because they will represent the best long-run opportunities.

7. *Population density.* The population density of a community equals the number of persons per square mile. Research suggests that the higher the population density,

the larger the average store should be in terms of square feet and thus the fewer the number of stores that will be needed to serve a population of a given size.

8. *Mobility.* The easier it is for people to travel, the more mobile they will be.[18] When people are mobile they are willing to travel greater distances to shop. Therefore, there will be fewer but larger stores in the community. Thus in a community where mobility is high, there will be a need for fewer retailers than in a community where mobility is low.

The most attractive market areas are those in which the preceding criteria are configured in such a way that they represent maximum market potential for a particular retailer. This will vary by the type of retailer and the product lines it handles. In assessing different market areas a retailer should first establish the market demand potential criteria that characterize the desired target market it would like to attract. Exhibit 7.7 illustrates this concept with a fast-food drive-in chain that sells hamburgers, hot dogs, and drinks. This fast-food chain is a 1950s-style drive-in where people usually order burgers and drinks in their autos and in which car-hops provide service.

Exhibit 7.7 shows that the chain has determined that there are seven demographic factors that have a positive impact on fast-food restaurant sales. One of these factors may need explanation. Through research the chain has determined that its restaurants do better when at least 75 percent of the work force travels less than 14 minutes to work. When people have to travel longer to work they get tired and frustrated about being in their cars and thus are not likely to be interested in eating in their auto at a drive-in restaurant. You might examine the other six demographic factors and develop an explanation for why they would be related to the success of a fast-food drive-in restaurant. The information in Exhibit 7.7 shows the desired target market and data on the seven demographic factors for two possible communities. From analyzing this data you should conclude that community B is the most attractive market to enter from a demand potential basis.

Exhibit 7.7	**Identifying Communities with High Demand Potential for a Fast-Food Drive-In Restaurant**		
Demographic Characteristic	Desired Target Market	Community A	Community B
Population per Square Mile	over 400	375	423
Median Family Income	over $31,000	$28,024	$32,418
% Population 14–54	over 60%	48%	63%
% White Collar	over 50%	38%	54%
% People Living in 1–3 Person Units	over 70%	61%	72%
% Workforce Traveling 0–14 Minutes to Work	over 75%	49%	74%
Average Annual Household Expenditure on Eating Out	over $600	$521	$619

Market Supply Factors

In deciding to enter a new market, the successful retailer will spend time analyzing the competition. The retailer should consider square feet per store, and square feet per employee, store growth, and the quality of competition.

1. *Square feet per store.* It will be helpful if the retailer has data on the square feet per store for the average store in the communities that are being analyzed. These data will indicate whether the community tends to have large- or small-scale retailing. Of course, this is important in terms of assessing the extent to which the retailer's standard type of store would blend with the existing structure of retail trade in the community.

2. *Square feet per employee.* A measure that combines two major supply factors in retailing, store space and labor, is square feet of space per employee. A high number for this statistic in a community is evidence that each employee is able to handle more space. This could be due to either a high level of retail technology in the community or more self-service retailing. Because retail technology is fairly constant across communities, any difference in square feet per employee is most often due to the level of service being provided. In communities currently characterized by retailers as offering a high level of service, there may be a significant opportunity for new retailers that are oriented toward self-service.

3. *Growth in stores.* The retailer should look at the rate of growth in the number of stores over the past one to five years. When the growth is rapid, then, on average, the community will have better located stores with more contemporary atmospheres. More recently located stores will coincide better with the existing demographics of the community. Their atmosphere will also better suit the tastes of the marketplace, and they will tend to incorporate the latest in retail technology. All of these factors hint that the strength of retail competition will be greater when the community has recently experienced rapid growth in the number of stores. Retailers, as well as entrepreneurs, can obtain the information needed for computing the square feet per store, square feet per employee, and growth in stores from the Urban Land Institute's *Dollars and Cents of Shopping Centers*, the National Mall Monitor's *Store Retail Tenant Directory*, and Lebhar-Friedman's *Chain Store Guide*.

4. *Quality of competition.* The three preceding supply factors reflect the quantity of competition. Retailers also need to look at the strength or quality of competition. They should attempt to identify the major retail chains and local retailers in each market and evaluate the strength of each. Answers to questions such as the following would be insightful: What is their market share or profitability? How promotional and price oriented are they? Are they customer oriented? Do they tend to react to new market entrants by cutting price, increasing advertising, or improving customer service? A retailer would think twice before competing with Wal-Mart on price, Dillard's on cost control, Bloomingdale's on fashion, and Nordstrom's on service or shoe selection.

Quite often, as discussed at the beginning of the chapter, when a discounter enters a small community with an extra 80,000 to 100,000 square feet of retail space, existing small town retailers feel they cannot compete and must close down. This is undoubtedly true of the weaker of these retailers, but, despite the discounter's enormous buying advantages, small-town retailers can compete head-on with them by providing better customer service, adjusting prices on products carried by the discounters, and remaining open Sundays and evenings. Customers will appreciate the increased standard of living that the discounter's prices make possible and as a result the trading area will increase. The apparel retailer, for example, will have to cut down on basic stock items, like socks and underwear, but increase its inventory of specialty or novelty items. The sales lost on basic items will be overcome with these newer items and the larger trading area the discounter provides.

Site Analysis

LO • 5

What attributes are considered in evaluating retail sites within a retail market?

Site analysis
is an evaluation of the density of demand and supply within each market with the goal of identifying the best retail site(s).

Once retailers have identified the best potential market, the next task is to perform a more detailed analysis of the market. Only after the market is carefully analyzed can the retailer choose the best site (or sites) available. Site analysis consists of an evaluation of the density of demand and supply within each market. It should be augmented by an identification of the most attractive sites that are currently available within each market. The third and final step, site selection, will be the selection of the best possible site.

Site analysis begins by evaluating the density of demand and supply of various areas within the chosen market by census tract, ZIP code, or some other meaningful geographic factor. It continues by identifying the most attractive sites, given the retailer's requirements, available for new stores within each market. One of the advantages of using census tract data is the availability of data for census tracts published by the Census Bureau.

Census tracts are relatively small statistical subdivisions that vary in population from about 2,500 to 8,000 and are designed to include fairly homogeneous populations. They are most often found in cities and in counties of metropolitan areas—that is, the more densely populated areas of the nation.

Size of Trading Areas

Earlier we discussed the general trading area of a community. Our attention now shifts to how to determine and evaluate the trading area of specific sites within markets. In short, we will attempt to estimate the geographic area from which a store located at a particular site will be able to attract customers.

At the same time that Reilly was developing retail gravity theory to determine the trading area for communities, William Applebaum designed a technique specifically for determining and evaluating trading areas for an individual store. Applebaum's technique was based on customer spottings. For each $100 in weekly store sales, a customer was randomly selected or spotted for an interview. These spottings usually did not require much time because the interviewer only requested demographic information, shopping habits, and some pertinent consumer attitudes toward the store and its competitors. After the home addresses of the shoppers were plotted on a map, the analyst could make some inferences about trading area size and the competition.[19] Exhibit 7.8 is an example of a map generated using customer spottings.

Thus, it is relatively easy to define the trading area of an existing store. All that is necessary is to interview current customers of the store to determine where they reside. For a new store, however, the task is not so easy. There is a fair amount of conventional wisdom that has withstood the test of time about the correlation of trading area size, which can be summarized as follows:

Exhibit 7.8	Customer Spotting Map for a Supermarket

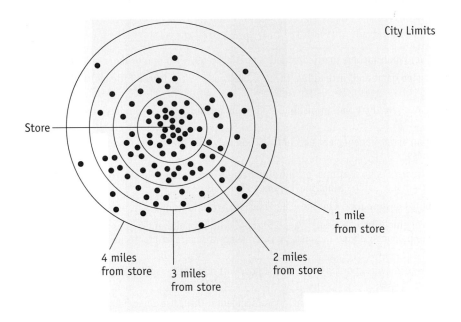

1. Stores that sell products that the consumer wants to purchase in the most convenient manner will have a smaller trading area than will stores that sell so-called specialty products.

2. As consumer mobility increases, the size of the store's trading area increases.

3. As the size of the store increases, its trading area increases, because it can stock a broader and deeper assortment of merchandise, which will attract customers from greater distances.

4. As the distance between competing stores increases, their trading areas will increase.

5. Natural and synthetic obstacles such as rivers, mountains, railroads, and freeways can abruptly stop the boundaries of a trading area.

Description of Trading Area

Retailers can access, at relatively low cost, information concerning the trading area for various retail locations and the buyer behavior of the trading area. If you go to the web sites for any of the firms providing geographical information services that were mentioned on page 242, you will be able to see how readily available this information is to the typical retailer. For example, see Equifax/National Decision Systems (http://www.ends.com).

MicroVision is a product of Equifax/National Decision Systems, which is one the nation's premier market research firms specializing in developing psychographic or lifestyle analyses of geographic areas. MicroVision is based on the old adage that birds of a feather flock together. In other words, even though the total makeup of the

Exhibit 7.9	Ten Examples of MicroVision Neighborhood Types

Neighborhood Types	Descriptors
Upper Crust	**Demographics:** Very high income married couples, age 40 to 69, with one or more children
	Lifestyles: Go casino gambling, attend live theater, play golf, write elected officials, and contribute to PBS
	Retail: Buy precious jewelry, home furnishings and improvements, coffee grinders, ice cream makers and golf clubs
	Financial: Have an asset management account, US bonds, whole life and individual medical insurance, and own a business
	Media: Read *Consumer Reports,* airline, business and science magazines; listen to classical music and news radio stations; and watch "Nightline" and news specials
	Geography: Suburbs of New York, Chicago, San Francisco, Washington, D.C.
Movers and Shakers	**Demographics:** Very high income singles, age 25 to 54, with no children, one or two adults
	Lifestyle: Recycle products, phone radio stations, do fund-raisers, participate in environmental causes and lift weights
	Retail: Order flowers by wire, purchase greeting cards, soft contact lenses, laptop PC, Honda automobile and light beer
	Financial: Have asset management account, VISA, accidental D&D, use financial planner, and have publicly traded stock
	Media: Read *Money, Consumer Reports* and *Epicurean* magazines; listen to album-oriented rock stations; and watches Friends and The Practice
	Geography: Suburban areas such as Raleigh Durham, NC; Austin, TX; Madison, WI; and Gainesville, FL
Home Sweet Home	**Demographics:** High income married couples, age 40 to 69, with one or two children
	Lifestyle: Get oil changed at quick lube shops, participate in home energy audit, go snow skiing, frequent flyer member
	Retail: Buy racquetball equipment, men's business suit, snow blower, wallpaper, gas dryer, doll accessories
	Financial: Have savings bonds, home equity line of credit, municipal bond fund, $200K in investable assets, obtained an IRA from broker
	Media: Read daily newspaper; listen to soft contemporary stations between 3 and 6 P.M.; and watch the World Series
	Geography: Suburban areas across the country, especially Hartford, CT
Great Beginnings	**Demographics:** Moderate income singles, age 18 to 39, with no children
	Lifestyle: Play billiards, go bowling, play softball, drink beer, belong to a health club, make infomercial purchases
	Retail: Buy sub-compact car, pager, water purifier, PC for on-line services, Toyota or Nissan automobile
	Financial: Have an education loan, overdraft protection, passbook account, and uses an ATM card
	Media: Read *People* magazine; listen to album-oriented rock stations; watch primetime sitcoms, Entertainment This Week, King of the Hill, and Star Trek–Next Generation (Syndicated)
	Geography: Along the East and West Coasts, especially Boston, Miami, and Seattle
Country Home Families	**Demographics:** Moderate income married couples, age 35 to 50, with two or more children
	Lifestyle: Do crafts, own a dog or cat, go bowling, camping, fishing, gardening and change their own car's oil
	Retail: Buy chain saw, electric drill, riding lawn mower, separate freezer, video camera, infant or preschooler toys

Exhibit 7.9	**continued**

Neighborhood Types	Descriptors
	Financial: Have a home equity line of credit, auto loan through a bank, IRA from an insurer, use teller and drive-through teller
	Media: Read *Popular Mechanics,* fishing and hunting magazines; listen to country stations; and watch Home Improvement, Roseanne and entertainment specials
	Geography: Northern areas, especially Bend, OR and Harrisburg, PA
Settled In	*Demographics:* Moderate income married couples, over 55, with no children
	Lifestyle: Collect coins, play the lottery, veterans club member, use utility's balanced billing program, go bowling
	Retail: Buy light beer, heavy coupon user, QVC customer, added kitchen plumbing and attic and wall insulation
	Financial: Have variable payment annuity, obtain financial advice from broker, and purchases Prudential life insurance
	Media: Read daily newspaper and *Ladies Home Journal;* listen to middle-of-the-road radio stations; and watches This Old House, Wings, The Weather Channel and Lifetime
	Geography: Primarily suburban areas around Great Lakes and Midwest
Books and New Recruits	*Demographics:* Low income singles, age 18 to 24, with no children, two to four adults
	Lifestyles: Go to barber shop, use laundromat, entertain at home, play basketball, go hunting, to the movies, and play cards
	Retail: Buy sub-compact car, designer jeans, men's sweatpants, and heavy convenience store shopper
	Financial: Bank by mail, let life insurance policy lapse, have renter's insurance, maintain a stock fund
	Media: Read *Newsweek, Glamour* and *Sports Illustrated;* listen to contemporary hits station on weekends; and watch Hard Copy, Home Improvement and Headline News
	Geography: Urban and suburban areas across the country
On Their Own	*Demographics:* Low income singles, age 18 to 39, with no children, one or two people
	Lifestyles: Go dancing, jogging, get oil changed at quick lube centers, frequently refer to the Yellow Pages, drink bourbon
	Retail: Buy compact car, women's pants suits, soft contact lenses, dress boots, answering machine, and home delivery meals
	Financial: Have renter's insurance, get financial advice from a broker, never have done business with an insurance agent
	Media: Read men's magazines; and watch primetime dramas, The Tonight Show, MTV, and Night Court (Syndicated)
	Geography: Warm weather suburbs in Nevada, Arizona, and Florida
Trying Metro Times	*Demographics:* Very low income singles, age 18 to 24 and over 70, with no children
	Lifestyle: Heavy video renters, smoke cigarettes, listen to cable radio, and play video games daily
	Retail: Eat Mexican fast-food, purchase women's designer jeans, never purchase from mail order catalog
	Financial: Get financial advice from family and friends, never used a broker, and have a loan from a consumer finance company
	Media: Read *National Enquirer,* and watch King of the Hill, South Park, Ally McBeal, and The Nashville Network
	Geography: Urban parts of Oklahoma City; Buffalo, NY; Colorado Springs

Exhibit 7.9	continued

Neighborhood Types	Descriptors
University USA	***Demographics:*** Very low income singles, age 18 to 24, with no children
	Lifestyle: Go to health club, dancing, night clubs, use quick copy services, and participate in environmental causes
	Retail: Buy imported car, heavy convenience store shopper, light grocery store shopper, eat a lot of fast-food
	Financial: Have no-interest checking account, education loan, renter's insurance, VISA card, and use phone to transfer funds
	Media: Read science, automotive, sports, music and women's fashion magazines; listen to progressive rock stations; and watch The Simpsons, MTV, Ally McBeal, King of the Hill, and Boston Public.
	Geography: College towns: Columbus, OH; Lubbock, TX; Eugene, OR

Source: MicroVision web site [http://www.ends.com] and updates by authors.

American marketplace is very complex and diverse, neighborhoods tend to be just the opposite. People tend to feel most comfortable living in areas with others who are like them. Think for a moment of the place where you are living now as a student, and of your parent's home, and you will most likely see the truth of the adage.

Consumers live in homogeneous neighborhoods for many possible reasons. One may be income, because people must be able to afford the homes. However, income alone is probably not the answer, as many types of neighborhoods have similar income levels. Factors such as age, occupation, family status, race, culture, religion, population density, urbanization, and housing types can all distinguish between very different types of neighborhoods that have similar incomes. Therefore, these other factors are usually more important for the retailer to consider than income alone.

In distinguishing between neighborhood types, MicroVision and similar products use two basic criteria. First, each type of neighborhood must be different enough from all the others to make it a distinct marketing segment. Second, there must be enough people living in each type of neighborhood to make it a worthwhile segment to retailers. Utilizing a variety of databases, including U.S. Census data and proprietary computer software, MicroVision found 50 neighborhood types in the United States. These types are distinguished from each other in many ways. Some are based primarily on income, some are family oriented, some are race oriented, some are urban, some suburban, and some rural. Most combine two or more distinguishing demographic characteristics. Exhibit 7.9 identifies ten of the 50 neighborhood types.

The names of the neighborhoods try to capture the essence of the neighborhood and provide an easy way of remembering distinctions. Also associated with the neighborhoods are demographics, lifestyle, retail opportunities, financial status, and media habits. Consider, for example, MicroVision segment 15, which is "country home families." This segment represents retail opportunities for chain saws, electric drills, riding lawn mowers, freezers, video cameras, and infant and preschooler toys. On the other hand, the more affluent MicroVision segment 1, "Upper-crust," represents retail opportunities for precious jewelry, home furnishings and improvements, coffee grinders, ice cream makers, and golf clubs.

Demand Density

The extent to which potential demand for the retailer's goods and services is concentrated in certain census tracts, ZIP-code areas, or parts of the community is called **demand density.** To determine the extent of demand density, retailers need to identify what they believe to be the major variables influencing their potential demand. One method of identifying these variables is by examining the types of customers who already shop in the retailer's present stores. The variables identified should be standard demographic variables, such as age, income, and education, because readily available data will exist on them. Let us construct an example.

A retailer is evaluating the possibility of locating in a community that has geographical boundaries as shown in Exhibit 7.10. It is composed of 23 census tracts. The community is bordered on the west by a mountain range, on the north and south by

Demand density
is the extent to which the potential demand for the retailer's goods and services is concentrated in certain census tracts, ZIP code areas, or parts of the community.

Exhibit 7.10   **Demand Density Map**

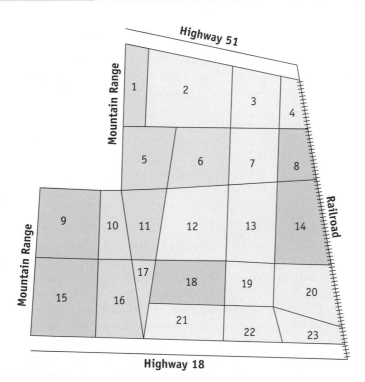

Three-Variable Demand Density Map
Variable 1 = Median income over $22,000
Variable 2 = Greater than 1,200 households per square mile
Variable 3 = Average growth in population over last 3 years
            in excess of 3 percent per year
Number of Variables Met

| 0 | 1 | 2 | 3 |

major highways, and on the east by railroad tracks. The retailer has decided that three variables are especially important in determining the potential demand: median household income of over $22,000, households per square mile in excess of 1,200, and average growth in population of at least 3 percent per year over the past three years. The thematic map in Exhibit 7.10 shows the extent to which these three conditions are met for each of the 23 census tracts in the community undergoing evaluation. Thus, you can easily visualize the density of potential demand in each tract. You should note that only three tracts (6, 10, 17) meet all three conditions.

Another method of looking at potential demand for a retailer's product could incorporate the data mentioned earlier when discussing neighborhood types. In this example, suppose a retail computer chain wanted to enter the Los Angeles market. The chain would first determine, from its own records, which MicroVision neighborhood types accounted for the largest sales in comparison to the national average of its product categories. In this case, household neighborhood types "movers and shakers" and "great beginnings" neighborhoods would be attractive locations for a computer store (see Exhibit 7.9).

Supply Density

Supply density
is the extent to which retailers are concentrated in different geographic areas of the community.

Although the demand-density map allows you to identify the area within a community that represents the highest potential demand, the location of existing retail establishments should also be mapped. This will allow you to examine the **supply density**— that is, the extent to which retailers are concentrated in different areas of the market under question.

Exhibit 7.11 shows the density of stores in the community we saw in Exhibit 7.10. Exhibit 7.11 reveals that two census tracts (10 and 17) out of the three most attractive ones have a lack of stores. Also, in the census tracts with fairly attractive demand density (two of the three conditions met), there are currently no retail outlets (see tracts 1 and 5).

Site Availability

Just because demand outstrips supply in certain geographic locations does not immediately imply that stores should be located in those locations. Sites must be available.

A map should be constructed of available sites in each community being analyzed. We have done this in conjunction with the supply-density map in Exhibit 7.11. The only available site in the top six census tracts (in terms of demand density) is in census tract 10. In tracts 1, 5, and 17, which currently have no retail outlets, no sites are available, which may explain the present lack of stores in these areas. Perhaps these tracts are zoned totally for residential use.

Although Exhibit 7.11 seems to show only one good potential site, several more may exist. Census tract 9 borders the high-density tract 10, in which there are no present stores and in which only one site is available for a new store. Tract 9, however, has two available sites. Furthermore, tract 12 has an available site that is close to the borders of tracts 11 and 17, which are both attractive but lack available sites. This same kind of analysis can be done with our retail computer chain in looking over the Los Angeles market. Some retailers have developed a checklist of all the items they want to consider during the site analysis stage. One such list is shown in Exhibit 7.12.

Exhibit 7.11   **Store Density and Site Availability Map**

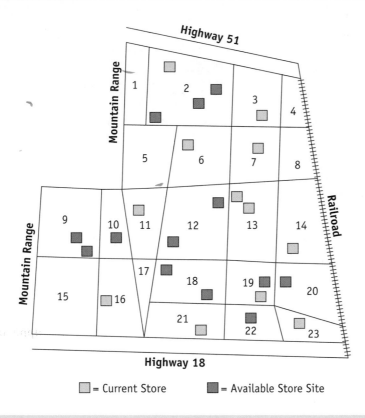

= Current Store   = Available Store Site

Site Selection Decision Process

LO • 6
How is the best geographic site selected?

On completing the analysis of each segment of the desired market and having identified the best available sites within each market, retailers are now ready to make the final decision regarding location: selecting the best site (or sites) available. Retailers are well advised to use the assistance of a real estate professional in this stage. Even if the retailers or their staff have done all the analysis to this point, the assistance of a real estate professional still should be used here. In fact, more and more large retail firms set up separate corporations to handle only their real estate transactions.

In principle, all retailers should attempt to find a **100 percent location** for their stores. A 100 percent location is a location where there is no better use for the site than the retail store that is being planned. Retailers should remember that what may be a 100 percent site for one store may not be for another. The best location for a supermarket may not be the best location for a discount department store.

How is the 100 percent location or site identified? Unfortunately, there is no best answer to this question. There is, however, general agreement on the types of things that the retailer should consider in evaluating sites: the nature of the site, traffic characteristics, type of neighbors, and the terms of purchase or lease.

100 percent location is when there is no better use for a site than the retail store that is being planned for that site.

Exhibit 7.12	Checklist for Site Evaluations

Local Demographics
  Population and/or household base
  Population growth potential
  Lifestyles of consumers
  Income potential
  Age makeup
  Educational makeup
  Population of nearby special markets, that is, daytime workers, students, and tourists, if applicable
  Occupation mix

Traffic Flow and Accessibility
  Number and type of vehicles passing location
  Access of vehicles to location
  Number and type of pedestrians passing location
  Availability of mass transit, if applicable
  Accessibility of major highway artery
  Quality of access streets
  Level of street congestion
  Presence of physical barriers that affect trade area shape

Retail Competition
  Number and types of stores in area
  Analysis of "key" players in general area
  Competitiveness of other merchants
  Number and location of direct competitors in area
  Possibility of joint promotions with local merchants

Site Characteristic
  Number of parking spaces available
  Distance of parking areas
  Ease of access for delivery
  Visibility of site from street
  History of the site
  Compatibility of neighboring stores
  Size and shape of lot
  Condition of existing building
  Ease of entrance and exit for traffic
  Ease of access for handicapped customers
  Restrictions on sign usage
  Building safety code restrictions
  Type of zoning

Cost Factors
  Terms of lease/rent agreement
  Basic rent payments
  Length of lease
  Local taxes
  Operations and maintenance costs
  Restrictive clauses in lease
  Membership in local merchants association required
  Voluntary regulations by local merchants

Nature of Site

Is the site currently a vacant store, a vacant parcel of land, or the site of a planned shopping center? Many of the available retail sites will be vacant stores. This is because 10 to 15 percent of stores go out of business each year. This does not mean that just because a men's apparel store failed in a location that a bookstore would do likewise. However, sometimes a piece of property becomes known as "jinxed" or "snakebit" because of the high number of business failures that have occurred there. Every town usually has one or more such areas and restaurants, which are one of the toughest businesses to get off the ground, seem to try these locations the most.[20] Alternatively, when the retail site that appears to be most suited to the retailer's needs is a vacant parcel of land, the retailer should investigate why it is vacant. Why have others passed up the site? Was it previously not for sale? Was it priced too high? Or is there some other reason?

Finally, the site may be part of a planned shopping center. In this case, the retailer can usually be assured that it will have the proper mix of neighbors, adequate parking facilities, and good traffic. Sometimes, of course, the center has not been properly planned, and the retailer needs to be aware of these special cases. It is difficult to succeed in a shopping center in which a high percentage of space is not rented.

Traffic Characteristics   The traffic that passes a site, whether it is vehicular or pedestrian, can be an important determinant of the potential sales at that site. However, more than traffic flow is important. The retailer must also determine whether the population and traffic are of the type desired. For example, a retailer of fine furs and leather coats may be considering two alternative sites. One site might be in the central business district and the other in a group of specialty stores in a small shopping center in a very exclusive residential area. The CBD site may generate more total traffic, but the alternative site may generate more of the right type of traffic.

The retailer should evaluate two traffic-related aspects of the site. The first is the availability of sufficient parking, either at the site or nearby. One of the advantages of shopping centers is the availability of adequate parking space. If the site is not a shopping center, then the retailer will need to determine if the parking space will be adequate. It is difficult to give a precise guideline for the space that will be needed. Generally, it is a function of four factors: size of the store, frequency of customer visits, length of customer visits, and availability of public transportation. As a rule of thumb, shopping centers estimate that there should be five spaces for every 1,000 square feet of selling space in medium-sized centers and ten spaces per 1,000 square feet in large centers.

A second traffic-related aspect the retailer should consider is the ease with which consumers can reach the store site. Are the roadways in good shape? Are there traffic barriers (rivers with a limited number of bridges, interstate highways with limited crossings, one-way streets, and heavy street use resulting in congestion limiting exits to the site)? Remember, customers normally avoid heavily congested shopping areas and shop elsewhere in order to minimize driving time and other difficulties.

Type of Neighbors   What neighboring establishments surround the site? There can be good and bad neighbors. Whether a neighbor is good or bad depends on the type of store that one is considering operating at the site. Suppose that you plan to open a children's apparel store and are considering two alternative sites. One site has a toy store and a gift shop as neighbors. The other site has a bowling alley and an adult book store as neighbors. Obviously, you know who the good and bad neighbors are.

Store compatibility
exists when two similar retail businesses locate next to or nearby each other and they realize a sales volume greater than what they would have achieved if they were located apart from each other.

However, determining the good and bad neighbors may not always be that easy, especially for an entrepreneur. A good neighboring business will be one that is compatible with the retailer's line of trade. When two or more businesses are compatible, they can actually help generate business for each other. For example, a paint store, hardware store, and auto parts store located next to one another may increase total traffic and thus benefit them all.

Research has found that retailers experience a benefit from **store compatibility.** That is, when two compatible or very similar businesses (e.g., two shoe stores) locate near each other, they will show an increase in sales volume greater than what they would have achieved if they were located apart from each other.[21] For example, when Lowes' opened a store near a Home Depot in Lewisville, Texas, the Home Depot store went from a category B to a category A store. This meant that the addition of a nearby competitor increased Home Depot's sales by 20 percent.

Some retailing experts claim that this clustering of similar retailers together dates back to the 1950s, when the choicest location for a gas station was believed to be an intersection that already had three other stations. Today, we see it with shoe stores in malls,[22] auto dealerships, furniture stores, and restaurants. Clustering of stores allows customers to walk from store to store, comparing prices, products, and service. In fact, about the only situation where compatible retailers do not achieve a greater sales volume when located in close proximity to each other is with membership retailers—that is, wholesale clubs and fitness centers. After all, consumers have already paid to use one of the retailers, so it is doubtful that they pay to shop at the other.

Exhibit 7.13 points out an interesting fact about who retailers want to locate next to when they sign leases for space. They are hoping to draw from these larger store's customers, such as what Dollar General attempts to do when it locates near a Wal-Mart store.[23] What is interesting, however, is that the combination of stores and their preferred neighbors actually increases the sales volume for both stores.

Exhibit 7.13	**If Retailers Could Select Their Neighbors**

If retailers could select their neighbors, here's who they would "want to be next to."

Retailer	Next to
Fast-food restaurant	Gasoline service station
Health food store	Fitness center, medical center
Recycled merchandise	Supercenter
Home improvement store	Supercenter
Hardware store	Wholesale club, supermarket
Zale's Jewelry	Sears, JCPenney, Mervyn's
Record Giant	Wal-Mart, Kmart
Payless Shoes	Supercenters, KinderCare
Long's Drug Stores	TJMaxx, Kmart
Cato Fashion	Kmart, Wal-Mart
Bennetton	Nordstrom, Bloomingdale's, Saks Fifth Avenue
Nursery and Crafts	Toys "R" Us, Circuit City, TJ Maxx, Marshalls

Terms of Purchase or Lease

One consideration for the retailer at this point is the lease terms. The retailer should review the length of the lease (it could be too long or too short), the exclusivity clause (whether or not the retailer will be the only one allowed to sell a certain line of merchandise), the guaranteed traffic rate (a reduction in rent if the shopping center fails to achieve a targeted traffic level), and an anchor clause (which would also allow for a rent reduction if the anchor store in a developing center does not open on time or when you open). Lease arrangements generally call for either a fixed payment, in which the rental charge is usually based on a fixed amount per month, or a variable payment, in which rent is a specified percentage of sales with a guaranteed minimum rent. It is important for the retailer to choose the one that is best.

When the retailer decides to locate in a shopping center, it usually has no other choice than to lease. However, in the case of a free-standing location, an outright purchase is often possible. Purchase and lease costs should be factored into the site's expected profitability.

Expected Profitability

The final step in site selection analysis is construction of a pro forma (expected) return on asset model for each possible site. The return on asset model comprises three crucial variables: net profit margin, asset turnover, and return on assets.

For purposes of evaluating sites, the potential return on equity is not relevant. This is because the financial leverage ratio (total assets divided by equity) is a top-management decision, which represents how much debt the retail enterprise is willing to assume. Most likely, the question of how to finance new store growth has already been answered or at least contemplated. The retailer should already have determined that it has or can obtain the capital to finance a new store. It is therefore reasonable and appropriate to evaluate sites on their potential return on assets and not return on equity.

If the retailer is to evaluate sites on their potential return on assets, it will need at least three estimates: total sales, total assets, and net profit. Each of these is likely to vary depending on the site. Sales estimates will be different for alternative sites because each will have unique trade area characteristics such as the number and nature of households and the level of competition. Estimated total assets could vary because the alternative sites will likely have different prices and the cost of construction could also vary. Finally, estimated profits could vary not only due to varying sales for the different sites but because of different operating costs. For example, some sites may be in areas where labor expenses are higher, taxes are higher, or insurance rates are higher.

Student Study Guide

Summary

Selection of a target market and determining which retail format to use to most effectively reach this market are two of the most important decisions a retailer will make. The retailer can reach potential customers through both store-based retail locations and nonstore retail formats. Geographical information systems can help the retailer gain knowledge of its potential customers and where they reside and how they behave. This can help the retailer better know how to reach its target market.

Most of the chapter discussed how to select a location for a store-based retailer. The choice of retail location involves three decisions: (1) market identification, identifying the most attractive markets; (2) site analysis, evaluating the demand and supply within each market; and (3) site selection, selecting the best site (or sites) available.

LO•1   Explain the criteria used in selecting a target market.

We began this chapter by stating that an effective target market must be one that is measurable, accessible, and substantial. Measurability deals with whether or not objective data exist on the attributes of the target market. Accessibility deals with the extent to which marketing efforts can be uniquely targeted at a particular segment of the market. Substantiability deals with the extent to which the target market is of sufficient size that it is economically worth pursuing.

LO•2   Identify the different options, both store-based and nonstore-based, for effectively reaching the retailer's target market and identify the advantages and disadvantages of business districts, shopping centers, and free-standing units as sites for retail location?

We next reviewed the four store-based location alternatives available to the retailer: the business district, the shopping center/mall, the free-standing unit, and the nontraditional store location. The business district is generally an unplanned shopping area around the geographic point where most cities originated and grew up. As the cities have grown, we witnessed an expansion of two newer types of business districts: the secondary business district and the neighborhood business district.

A shopping center or mall is a centrally owned or managed shopping district that is planned, has balanced tenancy, and is surrounded by parking facilities. It has one or more anchor stores and a variety of smaller stores. Because of the many advantages shopping centers can offer the retailer, they are a fixture of American life and account for 55 percent of all retail sales in the United States.

A free-standing retailer generally locates along major traffic arteries. There are usually no adjacent retailers selling competing products with which the retailer will have to share traffic.

The retailer also has six nonstore-based options: street peddling, mail-order, automatic merchandising machines, direct selling methods, interactive TV, and the Internet.

LO•3   Define geographic information systems (GIS) and discuss their potential uses in a retail enterprise.

Higher-quality market selection and retail location decisions can be made with the use of geographic information systems, which are computerized systems that combine physical geography with cultural geography. Not only can GIS technology be used for market selection, site analysis, and trade area definition, but it can also be used to evaluate new store cannibalization, advertising management, merchandise management, and store managers.

LO•4 What are the factors to be considered in identifying the most attractive geographic market for a store?

We began our analysis of market selection by looking at a trio of theories that can aid in the location decision. Retail gravitation theory assumes that the population of a community serves as a drawing power for the community and draws customers into its business district. The index of retail saturation reflects the total demand for the product under question with the availability of retailers to service or supply that product. The buying power index enables us to develop an overall indicator of a market's potential. We concluded our discussion on market identification by looking into other factors that could influence a community's supply (square feet per store, square feet per employee, growth in stores, and quality of competition) or demand (market population, buyer behavior, household income, age, composition, community life cycle, density, and mobility) for goods and services.

LO•5 What attributes are considered in evaluating retail sites within a retail market?

After reviewing the three location theories, we discussed the second of our three steps in the location process, site analysis, which consists of evaluating the density of demand and supply within each possible market. This process begins by determining the size, description, and density of demand and supply of various areas within the chosen market and then identifying the most attractive sites, given the retailer's requirements, available for new stores within each market.

LO•6 How is the best geographic site selected?

Finally, the retailer should conduct a site selection analysis of the top-ranking sites in each market. The goal is to select the best site or sites. Retail site analysts suggest that the following should be considered at this stage: nature of the site, traffic characteristics, type of neighbors, terms of lease or purchase, and finally the expected profitability or return on assets.

Terms to Remember

home page	trading area
virtual store	retail gravity theory
ease of access	Reilly's law of retail gravitation
target market	point of indifference
store-based retailers	outshopping
nonstore-based retailers	retail store saturation
central business district (CBD)	understored
secondary business district (SBD)	overstored
neighborhood business district (NBD)	index of retail saturation (IRS)
shopping center (or mall)	buying power index (BPI)
balanced tenacy	site analysis
anchor store	demand density
free-standing retailer	supply density
geographic information system (GIS)	100 percent location
culture	store compatibility
thematic maps	

Review and Discussion Questions

LO•1 **What criteria are used in selecting a target market?**

1. Why are the concepts of target market selection and location related?

2. What three criteria should be met to target a market successfully?

LO•2 **Identify the different options, both store-based and nonstore-based, for effectively reaching the retailer's target market and identify the advantages and disadvantages of business districts, shopping centers, and free-standing units as sites for retail location.**

3. What types of retailers would be best suited for a neighborhood shopping center?

4. Why are discount stores, such as Wal-Mart and Kmart, usually not located in shopping centers or malls?

5. Because more than half of all retail sales, excluding automobile and gasoline, occur in shopping centers and malls, can we assume that their future is bright? Support your answer.

6. What lines of retail trade do you believe will be most affected by the growth of retailing on the Internet and interactive television?

LO•3 **Define "geographic information system" (GIS) and discuss its potential uses in a retail enterprise.**

7. Why do geographic information systems include both physical and cultural geography? Give examples of physical and cultural data that may be included in a geographic information system.

8. Identify and discuss the seven uses of geographic information systems in retailing.

LO•4 **What are the factors to be considered in identifying the most attractive geographic market for a store?**

9. Is it more important for a retailer to select the proper trading area in which to locate or the correct site within the market? Explain your answer

10. What is the index of retail saturation? How is it used in making a location decision?

11. What is the buying power index? How is it used in making a location decision?

12. Calculate the buyer power indexes for the following three cities:

U.S. City	Percent of Effective Buying Income	Percent of U.S. Retail Sales	Percent of U.S. Population
Arkon City	.005	.006	.004
Binghamtown	.006	.004	.005
Cochran	.004	.005	.007

13. Compute the index of retail saturation for the following three markets. The data for department stores are as follows:

Market	A	B	C
Retail expenditures per household	$510	$575	$610
Square feet of retail space	600,000	488,000	808,000
Number of households	112,000	91,000	147,000

Based on these data, which market is most attractive? What additional data would you find helpful in determining the attractiveness of the three markets?

14. What are the two important factors in the retail gravity theory?

LO•5 **What are the attributes considered in evaluating retail sites within a retail market?**

15. Identify the factors you would consider as most important in locating a fast-food restaurant. Compare these factors with the factors you would use in selecting a site for a furniture store.

16. Explain the concepts of demand density and supply density. Why are they important to retail decision making?

17. Agree or disagree with the following statement and support your answer. When demand outstrips supply in a certain trading area, a retailer should locate there as soon as possible.

LO•6 **How is the best geographic site selected?**

18. What does store compatibility suggest about retail stores locating next to each other?

19. Why is the customer such an important factor in selecting the best site for a retail location?

Sample Test Questions

LO•1 **Which of the following is not a criterion used to successfully reach a target market?**

a. The market segment should be measurable.
b. Promotional efforts can be directed at the market segment.
c. The market segment should create high sales.
d. The market segment should be profitable.
e. Distribution efforts can be directed at the market segment.

LO•2 **Free-standing retailers offer the following advantages:**

a. lack of direct competition
b. high drawing power from nearby complementary stores
c. higher traffic than shopping malls
d. lower advertising costs
e. stores must be leased

LO•3 **Geographic information systems can be used for the following purposes:**

a. site analysis
b. trade area definition
c. advertising management
d. merchandise management
e. all of the above

LO•4 **The three sequential stages involved in selecting a location for a store-based retailer are**

a. identify the most understored markets, identify the most attractive sites that are available within each market, select the best site(s)

b. identify the most attractive markets, identify the most attractive sites that are available within each market, select the best site(s)
c. identify the most attractive markets, identify the vacant parcels of real estate within each market, select the best site(s)
d. identify the most understored markets, identify the vacant parcels of real estate within each market, negotiate terms for best site
e. identify the most attractive markets, identify the most attractive sites that are available within each market, negotiate for the lowest-priced site

LO•5   Site analysis consists of

a. analyzing density of demand
b. considering the type of neighbors
c. analyzing sources of financing for the site (i.e., debt or equity financing)
d. determining the expected profitability from operating a store at the site
e. considering the ease with which consumers can reach the site

LO•6   Which of the following is not an important consideration in selecting the best site for a new retail store?

a. nature of the site
b. traffic characteristics of the site
c. alternative investments available to the retailer
d. potential profitability of the site
e. type of neighbors

Applications

Writing and Speaking Exercise   You are doing a summer internship with Rowley Jewelers, a family-held concern located in the central business district of a resort community in southwest Missouri with a summer population of 200,000. Mac Rowley, the owner, has a problem and wants you to help him solve it. Around 10 o'clock this morning, a street vendor showed up in front of the store and began selling fake famous-name brand watches (Rolex, Ebel, Piaget) from a pushcart and suitcase for $10 to $20 each. After first asking the vendor to find another street corner and being told no, Rowley called the police to have the vendor removed. However, the police informed Rowley that street vending was not illegal. Rowley then called his city council representative, Jane Berry, explaining that he believes it was unfair for him to pay city taxes and have to compete with someone who paid no taxes. Berry told Rowley to send her a memo explaining the situation and proposing a solutions. Now Rowley wants you to write the memo for him.

Retail Project   Small as well as large retailers can benefit immensely from knowing the trade area of their store. Identify a small local retailer such as a florist, pet store, gift store, or restaurant. Contact the store owner or manager and tell them you are a student studying retailing and would like to volunteer to construct a map of the store's trade area. To do this you need to obtain the addresses of all the patrons over a one-week period and plot these on a map. Review the customer spotting map for a supermarket in Exhibit 7.8 on page 253. Develop a method to collect the needed data and construct the map of the trade area. What percent of customers are within one mile of the store? Within three miles? Within five miles?

Case The Outlet Mall

Over the past decade, Anne Wahl had watched with interest the development of factory-outlet malls. As a store manager of a regional department store chain operating in a mall, she knew that she would some day have to contend not only with the discount department store chains, but also with the manufacturers who were supplying her store as well as the outlets from some of the leading national chains. After all, Saks Fifth Avenue now has Saks Off Fifth stores, Nordstrom has the Rack, and even Neiman Marcus has its Last Call outlet stores to get rid of excess and unwanted merchandise. However, what surprised her was the rapid development of the outlet malls in recent years.

Prior to the Civil War, manufacturers began to sell at the retail level by either operating directly from their plants or by introducing small outlet stores near their plants. Still, it took more than a hundred years before manufacturers banded together and opened the first outlet shopping center near Reading, Pennsylvania, in 1972. For the next decade only two or three outlets were added each year.

Given this slow growth pattern, these outlet centers did not upset the retailers selling the manufacturers' products. Besides, the early outlet centers generally sold only "seconds," or imperfect or flawed goods, as well as overproduced merchandise. However, the economic slowdown caused manufacturers to begin opening dozens of outlets each year; as a result, almost 400 outlet centers have opened since the mid-1980s. And today's outlet malls no longer are satisfied to sell only seconds and overproduced merchandise. Now they are selling flawless products, deep in sizes and selections.

The outlet mall offers manufacturers who open stores in these malls three major advantages. First, it allows them to reach customers who normally would not purchase their brand-name products. Second, it is more profitable for a manufacturer to sell at a reduced "retail price" to the general public than it is to sell at wholesale prices to stores like Anne Wahl's. Finally, with their plants operating at less than full capacity, the manufacturers could use outlet sales to increase their production and reduce average costs.

Now Anne Wahl got the bad news in her morning paper: a land developer announced that he was beginning construction on an outlet mall featuring more than 80 manufacturers 40 miles north of Modesto, not far from Wahl's store, on an interstate highway near a resort area. Included in the press release was a list of just some of the manufacturers planning on opening stores in the new mall: Nike, London Fog, Liz Claiborne, Esprit, Van Heusen, Reebok, Levi's, Jordache, Fieldcrest Cannon, Chaus, and Eddie Bauer.

Wahl decided that early the next morning she would drive up the interstate to visit the site of the new mall. Just as she was getting out of her car at the new mall site, the land developer, Curtis Niehoff, drove up and parked beside her. Wahl went over and introduced herself to Niehoff. After some pleasantries, Niehoff stated that he assumed the reason behind Wahl's trip was that she was worried about the competition the new mall was going to provide. Wahl admitted that she was indeed worried. Niehoff then invited Wahl into his office for coffee and a chat about his plans.

Niehoff began by saying, "First, you have to understand, Anne, that we are not really going after the same target market. You are targeting the population of Modesto. We are targeting an entirely different market. For one thing, our customers will have a higher income than your market. We fully expect that by locating in this resort area, over a third of our customers will have incomes higher than $75,000. In addition, most of our customers will spend one or two full days at our mall. That's why we have triple the parking spaces of a regional mall, so that RVs and charter buses can park. In fact, our market will draw from a radius of 300 miles."

Wahl noted that this was fine and good, but she was still worried about getting into a price war with her suppliers. Once again, Niehoff tried to reassure her. "Our prices here will not be as low as you think. In fact, the wheel of retailing is taking place in all of today's new outlet malls. No longer are our stores bare-bones operators. They have added services to match that of any department store. This in turn has caused prices on this season's merchandise to rise to a point somewhere lower than your prices but above the discounters' price that you are already competing against. What our stores will offer is selection—even if some of the merchandise is last season's—and the thrill of the hunt. Also, your customers will have to consider travel time and costs when comparing your prices to ours. That's why our primary emphasis will be on the resort-area vacationer with a secondary emphasis on the interstate highway traveler." With that, Niehoff stated that he was late for a meeting and had to leave.

Driving back to Modesto, Anne Wahl was somewhat relieved at what she found out on her trip. She also felt confident that her store could compete with the outlet center. However, on arriving back at her office, she found a note stating that there would be a special meeting of all the regional mall's store managers tomorrow morning. It seems that a couple of the managers wanted everyone in the mall to ban together and "reduce, if not totally eliminate, purchases from any manufacturer who was going to open a store in the new outlet mall."

What should Wahl do?

Planning Your Own Business

The retail store you are planning has an estimated circular trade radius of five miles. Within this five-mile radius there is an average of 1,465 households per square mile. In a normal year you expect that 47 percent of these households would visit your store (referred to as penetration) an average of 3.8 times (referred to as frequency). Based on this information, what would you expect to be the traffic (i.e., number of visitors to your store per year)? (*Hint:* Traffic can be viewed as the square miles of the trade area multiplied by the household density multiplied by penetration, which is in turn multiplied by frequency.)

Once you answer this question, do some sensitivity analysis, which is an assessment of how sensitive store traffic is to changes in your assumptions about penetration and frequency. What happens if penetration drops to 40 percent or rises to 50 percent? What happens if frequency drops to 3 times annually or rises to 4.5 times annually? In this analysis only change one thing at a time and hold all other assumptions constant.

Endnotes

1. Albertson's 1998 Annual Report: 5.
2. Ibid.

3. "Of a Talbots in Litchfield (The Horror?)," *New York Times*, January 28, 1996: Section 1, p. 16.

4. "Residents Split as Target Takes Aim at Town," *Shopping Centers Today*, May 1999: 218—220.

5. "A Special K," *Discount Merchandiser*, November 1996: 24—27.

6. "Look Who's Looking Small," *Business Week*, May 17, 1999: 66—70.

7. "In The New Economy," *Inc.*, May 1999: 50; "Striking Gold in the Nation's Urban Core," *Fortune*, May 10, 1999: 152.

8. "A Mecca For Suburbanites," *U.S. News & World Report*, December 27, 1999: 49—50.

9. "Streamlined Airport Retailing Takes Off in Philadelphia," *Shopping Centers Today*, December 1998: 48.

10. "Retailing 101," *Progressive Grocer*, January 2000: 50—56.

11. "'Marketplaces' Open in Old Bank Branches," *New York Times*, May 31, 1998: 31.

12. "Returns to Sender," *Wall Street Journal*, July 17, 2000: R8.

13. "A Sporting Venture," *Business Geographics*, January 1997: 23—25.

14. William J. Reilly, *Methods for the Study of Retail Relationships* (Austin, TX: Bureau of Business Research, The University of Texas, 1929), Research Monograph, no. 4.

15. P. D. Converse, "New Laws of Retail Gravitation," *Journal of Marketing*, January 1949: 379—384.

16. Bernard LaLonde, "The Logistics of Retail Location," in William D. Stevens, ed., *American Marketing Proceedings* (Chicago: American Marketing Association, 1961): 572.

17. Home Depot, *Business Week*, February 13, 1995: 65.

18. Mobility can be viewed as both a household characteristic and a community characteristic. We chose to treat it as a community characteristic because the design of the community, the availability of public transportation, and the cost of operating an auto in any given area are determinants of mobility and are themselves characteristic of the community.

19. The essence of Applebaum's work, plus contributions from several of his students, can be found in William Applebaum and Others, in *Guide to Store Location Research with Emphasis on Supermarkets*, Curt Korhblau, ed., sponsored by the Supermarket Institute (Reading, MA: Addison-Wesley, 1968).

20. "Snakebit: Some Texas Properties Seem Immune to the Good Times," *Wall Street Journal*, August 27, 1997: T1, T3.

21. Richard L. Nelson, *The Selection of Retail Locations* (New York: F.W. Dodge, 1958): 66.

22. "Making Malls (Gasp!) Convenient," *Wall Street Journal*, February 8, 2000: B1, B4.

23. "Wal-Mart's Ankle Biters," *Forbes*, October 18, 1999: 86—92.

Part IV
Managing Retail Operations

Managing a Retailer's Finances

Overview

In this chapter, we begin by looking at how a merchandise budget is prepared
and how it is used in making plans for an upcoming merchandise season. Next
we describe the basic differences among an income statement, balance sheet,
and statement of cash flow, as well as how a retailer uses these accounting
statements in controlling its merchandising activities. Finally, we discuss the accounting inventory systems and pricing methods available to value inventory.

Learning Objectives

After reading this chapter, you should be able to

1. describe the importance of a merchandise budget and know how to prepare a six-month merchandise budget

2. explain the differences among, and the uses of, these three accounting statements: income statement, balance sheet, and statement of cash flow

3. explain how the retailer is able to value inventory

LO • 1
Why is a merchandise budget so important in retail planning and how is a merchandise budget prepared?

The Merchandise Budget

In Chapter 7 we described the role location plays in a retailer's success. Location is important and was discussed before the other elements of the retail mix because for most new retailers it is the first decision made. Also, once the retailer makes the location decision, it is difficult to change.

Another important retail mix element is merchandising, including pricing. Some experts agree that it is around merchandising that all the other retail mix elements revolve, especially if we consider chain store operators. After all, the merchandise in a JCPenney store in Muskegon, Michigan, looks much the same as one in Modesto, California. The same may be said about a Carrefour store in Buenos Aires, Argentina, or one in Paris, France. Only after these merchandising decisions are made, can retailers concern themselves with the other retail mix elements: promotion, store layout and design, and customer service. However, before we can explain how to make these merchandise decisions, we must discuss the retailer's means of controlling these activities.

A Carrefour supermarket in Toulouse, southwestern France, looks much like a supermarket in Argentina and stocks similar merchandise; except the brand names may be different.

Many people believe that the terms "retailing" and "merchandising" are synonymous. They are not. Retailing includes all the business activities that are necessary to sell goods and services to the final consumer. **Merchandising** is only one of these activities and is concerned with the planning and control involved in the buying and selling of goods and services to help the retailer realize its objectives. Success in merchandising requires total financial planning and control. This chapter is divided into three sections: the merchandise budget, retail accounting statements, and inventory valuation.

Successful retailers must have good financial planning and control of their merchandise. The retailer invests money in merchandise for profitable resale to others. A poor choice of merchandise will result in low profits or maybe even a loss. Therefore, to be successful in retailing, as in any other activity, an individual must have a plan of what is to be accomplished. In retailing, this plan of operation is called the merchandise budget. A **merchandise budget** is a plan of projected sales for an upcoming season, when and how much merchandise is to be purchased, and what markups and reductions will likely occur. The merchandise budget forces the retailer to develop a formal outline of merchandising objectives for the upcoming selling season.

Merchandising
is the planning and control of the buying and selling of goods and services to help the retailer realize its objectives.

Merchandise budget
is a plan of projected sales for an upcoming season, when and how much merchandise is to be purchased, and what markups and reductions will likely occur.

Retailers who thoroughly analyze and project all the factors in developing a merchandise budget for an upcoming season will be more profitable.

In developing the merchandise budget, the retailer must make five major merchandising decisions:

1. What will be the anticipated sales for the department, division, or store?
2. How much stock on hand will be needed to achieve this sales plan, given the level of inventory turnover expected?
3. What reductions, if any, from the original retail price must be made in order to dispose of all the merchandise brought into the store?
4. What additional purchases must be made during the season?
5. What gross margin (the difference between sales and cost of goods sold) should the department, division, or store contribute to the overall profitability of the company?

When preparing the merchandise budget, a retailer must follow four rules.

First, a merchandise budget should always be prepared in advance of the selling season. The original plan is often prepared by the buyer for a particular department to be approved by the divisional merchandising manager or the general merchandising manager. Therefore, most retail firms selling apparel and hard goods begin the process of developing the merchandise budget three to five months in advance of the budget period. This is not always the case with some specialty stores, such as music stores. A new music release is only known to the buyer about a month in advance and can be easily reordered if it goes to the top of the charts. These specialty stores also do not have to worry about markdowns because excess quantities can be returned to vendors for full credit. Generally, a firm has only two seasons a year: (1) spring/summer, usually February 1 through July 31, and (2) fall/winter, August 1 through January 31. The buyer for a particular department will usually begin to prepare merchandise budgets on or about March 1 and September 1 for the upcoming seasons.

Second, because the budget is a plan that management expects to follow in the upcoming merchandise season, the language must be easy to understand. The merchandise budget illustration contained in this chapter has only 11 items, although the number of items contained in a budget may vary due to each company's own merchandise and market characteristics. Remember, the budget serves no useful purpose if it cannot be understood by all the decision makers. Also, it must contain all the information needed for that particular retailer.

Third, the economy today is constantly changing. The merchandise budget must be planned for a relatively short period of time. Six months is the norm used by most retailers, although some retailers use a three-month, or even shorter, plan. Forecasting future sales is difficult enough without complicating the process by projecting for a time period too far into the future. The firm's general management should be concerned with long-term trends and effects on store and personnel needs. The firm's buyers are involved in the more short-term trends and effects that may influence the merchandise budget.

Fourth, the budget should be flexible enough so that changes are possible. All merchandise budgets are plans and estimates of predicted future events. However, it should be noted that competition and the consumer are not always predictable, especially in regard to fashion preferences. Thus, any forecast is subject to error and will need revisions.

Keeping in mind the preceding discussion of merchandising decisions and rules, a blank six-month merchandise budget for the housewares department of a major department store is shown in Exhibit 8.1. Do not be alarmed if Exhibit 8.1 is not clear to you at this time. In the following discussion, as well as in the next chapter, we will describe why the budget is set up in this form. Additionally, we will explain all the analytical tools used by the retailer to calculate the numbers required in developing a six-month merchandise budget or plan.

Exhibit 8.1 appears to be more confusing than it really is because each element is broken into four parts: last year, plan for the upcoming season, revised plan, and actual. This is merely a means to provide the decision maker with complete information. Last year refers to last year's sales for the period; plan for the upcoming season is what the original plan projected; revised plan is the result of any revisions caused by changing market conditions after the plan is accepted; and actual is the final results.

Exhibit 8.2 presents the same material in a simpler form. Here we only attempt to show you how and why a retailer develops a six-month merchandise plan. Exhibit 8.3 is a summary of how all the numbers in the merchandise budget are determined. Exhibit 8.2 shows the spring/summer season, February 1 to July 31, for the Two-Seasons Department Store, Department 353, with projected sales of $500,000, planned retail reductions of $50,000 or 10 percent of sales, planned initial markup of 45 percent, and a planned gross margin on purchases made of $208,750.

Determining Planned Sales

The initial step in developing a six-month merchandise budget is to estimate planned sales for the entire season and for each individual month. The buyer begins by examining the previous year's sales records. Adjustments are then made in the planning of

Exhibit 8.1   Sample Six-Month Merchandise Budget

		SIX-MONTH MERCHANDISE BUDGET Housewares Department						
		FEBRUARY	MARCH	APRIL	MAY	JUNE	JULY	Total
BOM Stock	Last Year							
	Plan							
	Revised							
	Actual							
Sales	Last Year							
	Plan							
	Revised							
	Actual							
Reductions	Last Year							
	Plan							
	Revised							
	Actual							
EOM STOCK	Last Year							
	Plan							
	Revised							
	Actual							
RETAIL PURCHASES	Last Year							
	Plan							
	Revised							
	Actual							
PURCHASES @ COST	Last Year							
	Plan							
	Revised							
	Actual							
INITIAL MARK-UP	Last Year							
	Plan							
	Revised							
	Actual							
GROSS MARGIN DOLLARS	Last Year							
	Plan							
	Revised							
	Actual							
BOM STOCK/SALES RATIO	Last Year							
	Plan							
	Revised							
	Actual							
SALES PERCENTAGE	Last Year							
	Plan							
	Revised							
	Actual							
RETAIL REDUCTION PERCENTAGE	Last Year							
	Plan							
	Revised							
	Actual							

STOCKTURN: Last Year _____ Plan _____ Actual _____
ON ORDER – BEGINNING OF SEASON _____ Plan _____ Actual _____
EOM INVENTORY FOR LAST MONTH _____ Plan _____ Actual _____
REDUCTION PERCENTAGE _____ Plan _____ Actual _____
MARKUP PERCENTAGE _____ Plan _____ Actual _____

| Exhibit 8.2 | Two-Seasons Department Store, Dept. 353, Six-Month Merchandise Budget |

	February	March	April	May	June	July	Total
1. Planned BOM Stock	$225,000	$300,000	$300,000	$250,000	$375,000	$300,000	—
2. Planned Sales	75,000	75,000	100,000	50,000	125,000	75,000	$500,000
3. Planned Retail Reductions	7,500	7,500	5,000	7,500	6,250	16,250	50,000
4. Planned EOM Stock	300,000	300,000	250,000	375,000	300,000	250,000	—
5. Planned Purchases at Retail	157,500	82,500	55,000	182,500	56,250	41,250	575,000
6. Planned Purchases at Cost	86,625	45,375	30,250	100,375	30,937.50	22,687.50	316,250
7. Planned Initial Markup	70,875	37,125	24,750	82,125	25,312.50	18,562.50	258,750
8. Planned Gross Margin	63,375	29,625	19,750	74,625	19,062.50	2,312.50	208,750
9. Planned BOM Stock-to-Sales Ratio	3	4	3	5	3	4	—
10. Planned Sales Percentage	15%	15%	20%	10%	25%	15%	100%
11. Planned Retail Reduction Percentage	10%	10%	5%	15%	5%	21.67%	10%

Planned Total Sales for the Period	$500,000
Planned Total Retail Reduction Percentage for the Period	10%
Planned Initial Markup Percentage	45%
Planned BOM Stock for August	$250,000

sales for the upcoming merchandise budget. When comparing this year's sales to last year's sales, retailers do not always compare to the exact date (i.e., comparing February 4, 2002, sales to February 4, 2001) because the dates could fall on different days of the week. For instance, as shown in Exhibit 8.4, February 4 was on a Sunday in 2001, when the retailer might be closed, and on a Monday in 2002. Rather, retailers use a retail reporting calendar, which divides the year into two seasons, each with six months as shown in Exhibit 8.4. Thus, February 4, 2002, the first Monday of the spring season, would be compared to February 5, 2001, which was the first Monday of 2001's spring seasons. In the year 2003, the first Monday of the spring season is February 3.

By using this calendar, retailers will have problems making direct comparison only once each season. Fashion/apparel retailers will be affected by the movement of Easter (April 15 in 2001, March 31 in 2002, and April 20 in 2003) when making comparisons in the spring season. Thus in 2002, because Easter is the last Sunday of March on the reporting calendar, the big apparel sales will be reported in the retailer's March sales. The following year, 2003, will see March's sales suffer in comparison. However, April apparel sales will be better, because Easter will be 15 days into the retailers' month of April and the weather will also help increase sales. During the fall season, the period between Thanksgiving and Christmas can vary in length by as much as a week. Because Thanksgiving is the fourth Thursday of November, it can fall between November 22 and 28 and as a result the number of days in the Christmas shopping season will differ from year to year. For example, in 2002 and 2003 there are four weekends and 26 and

| Exhibit 8.3 | Formulas for the Six-Month Merchandise Budget |

Determining Planned Sales for the Month

(Planned Sales Percentage for the Month) × (Planned Total Sales) = (Planned Sales for the Month)

Determining Planned BOM Stock for the Month

(Planned Sales for the Month) × (Planned BOM Stock-to-Sales Ratio for the Month) = (Planned BOM Stock for the Month)

Determining Planned Retail Reductions for the Month

(Planned Sales for the Month) × (Planned Retail Reduction Percentage for the Month) = (Planned Retail Reductions for the Month)

Determining Planned EOM Stock for the Month

(Planned BOM Stock for the Following Month) = (Planned EOM Stock for the Current Month)

Determining Planned Purchases at Retail for the Month

(Planned Sales for the Month) + (Planned Retail Reductions for the Month) + (Planned EOM Stock for the Month) − (Planned BOM Stock for the Month) = (Planned Purchases at Retail for the Month)

Determining Planned Purchases at Cost for the Month

(Planned Purchases at Retail for the Month) × (100% − Planned Initial Markup Percentage) = (Planned Purchases at Cost for the Month)

Determining Planned Initial Markup for the Month

(Planned Purchases at Retail for the Month) × (Planned Initial Markup Percentage) = (Planned Initial Markup for the Month)
                    or
(Planned Purchases at Retail for the Month) − (Planned Purchases at Cost for the Month) = (Planned Initial Markup for the Month)

Determining Planned Gross Margin for the Month

(Planned Initial Markup for the Month) − (Planned Retail Reductions for the Month) = (Planned Gross Margin for the Month)

---

27 days, respectively, between Thanksgiving and Christmas, whereas in 2001 there were five weekends and 32 days between November 22 and Christmas Day.

Even using a retail reporting calendar cannot overcome many of the uncontrollable and unexpected variables retailers encounter when forecasting sales. For example, the greatest uncontrollable variable every retailer must face is the weather. Apparel retailers in spring 2000 lost sales due to the unseasonably cool spring. This came just after warm "Indian summers" during the falls of 1998 and 1999 that hurt fall sales of sweaters and coats. In fact, 1998's fall and winter were so warm that Service Corporation International (SCI), the world's largest provider of death-care services, was forced to disappoint Wall Street with an announcement that "warm weather and a delay in the start of the flu season" negatively (at least as far as SCI was concerned) impacted the mortality rate.[1]

Exhibit 8.4	Retail Reporting Calendar

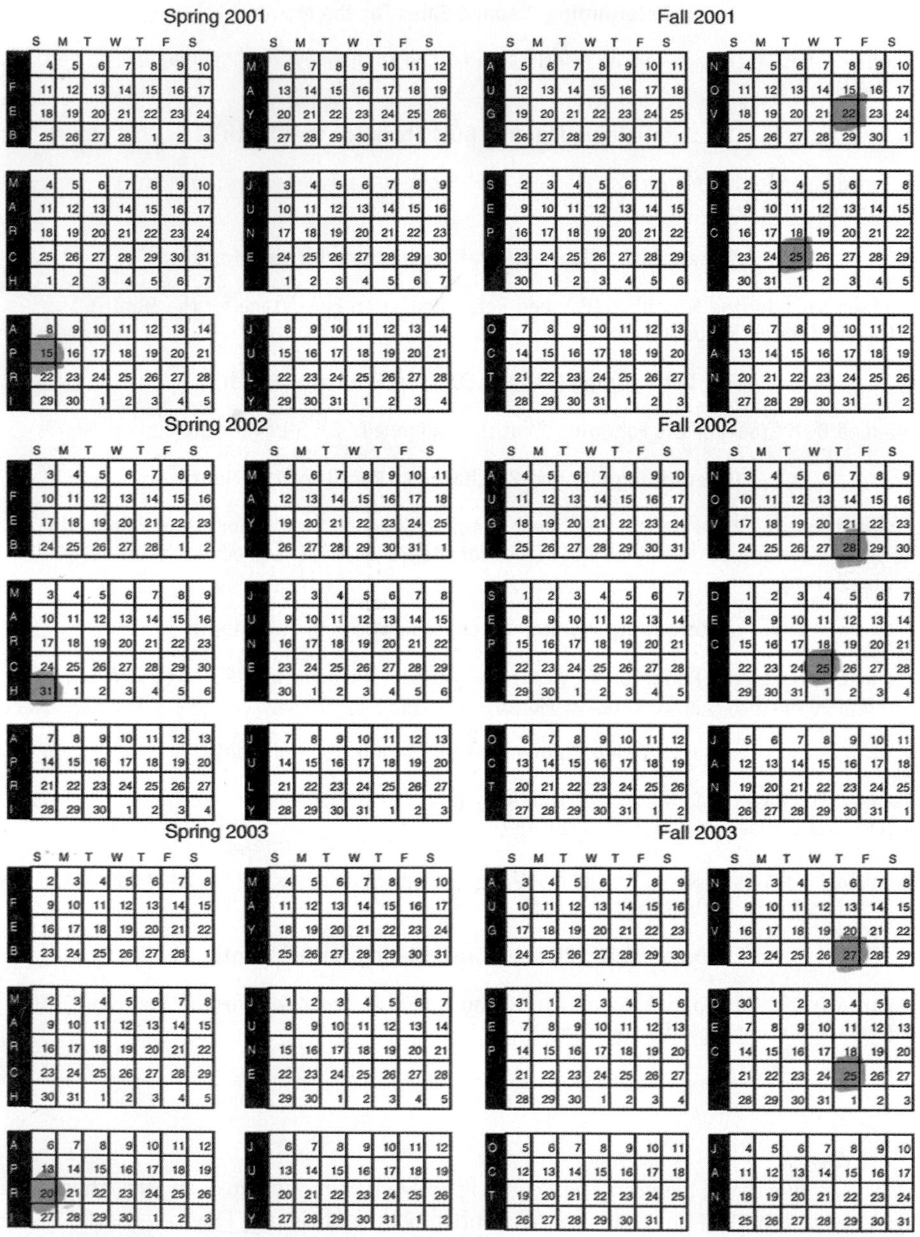

Spring 2001   Fall 2001

Spring 2002   Fall 2002

Spring 2003   Fall 2003

Sometimes the consequences of weather can really fool retailers. Recently, Texas experienced 17 straight days of 100-degrees-plus heat. Normally, tanning salons are empty during summers. However, such heat was too much for many Texans, resulting in record business for the air-conditioned tanning salons. That same summer the volume at local putt-putt courses was off nearly 70 percent. Little wonder that many large retailers, like Sears, now use long-range weather forecasts.[2]

In planning merchandise budgets, retailers must consider the sales impact of promotional events centered around holidays. Here we see a Christmas display for Laura Ashley and below an Easter display outside Macy's.

One retailer with an excellent record of forecasting sales is San Francisco-based Williams-Sonoma, best known for its Catalog for Cooks. Williams-Sonoma's secret for forecasting sales rests on its highly automated mailing lists. Its database of 4.5 million customers tracks up to 150 different pieces of information per customer. With a few simple keystrokes, the retailer can tell you what you've bought from each of its five annual catalogs (an estimated 60 percent of customers have bought from more than one), what time of the year you tend to buy, how often you buy, what category of merchandise you lean toward, and so forth. Through a complex cross-referencing of the data, Williams-Sonoma's two full-time statisticians are able to project, to plus or minus 5 percent accuracy on average, each catalog's sales.

Forecasting is most important for service retailers because their services are perishable, unlike physical products, and cannot be produced or manufactured, boxed, stored, and shelved, presenting unique forecasting problems for the retailer. In fact, services theoretically perish the moment they are produced. This perishability is not a problem when demand is steady. However, when demand fluctuates, service retailers have problems. As a result, service retailers often try to balance their demand and supply by altering their retail mix in an attempt to better manage sales. Many restaurant chains now seek to balance their supply and demand with the aid of a computer program that tracks the sales of every menu item on an hourly basis and sets cooking schedules based on the program. After consulting the printout, the restaurant's manager can determine how many baked potatoes to cook and when to put them in the oven so as to meet the expected demand. Although it is not completely accurate, the computer, according to one Texas steak house manager, bats close to 90 percent. The same program can also be used to schedule hourly employees for the restaurant as well as order merchandise. The computer program alone saves the retailer more than 25 hours a week in calculations by hand.

Return now to the example in Exhibit 8.2. After reviewing the data available, the buyer for Department 353 forecasted that $500,000 was a reasonable total sales figure for the future season. June, with a projected 25 percent of total season's sales, and April,

Williams-Sonoma uses data from its catalog sales to forecast the economic viability of a new store in a geographic area or community.

with 20 percent, are expected to be the busy months. May, with only 10 percent, is expected to be the slowest month. The remaining months will have equal sales. Since April, May, and June account for 55 percent of total sales, then February, March, and July's total must be 45 percent or 15 percent per month because they are equal. The buyer is able to determine planned monthly sales by multiplying the planned monthly sales percentage by planned total sales. Because we know February's planned monthly sales are 15 percent of the total planned sales of $500,000, February's planned sales must be $75,000 (15 percent × $500,000 = $75,000).

It is important to use recent trends when forecasting future sales. All too often some retailers in a no-growth market merely use the previous season's figures for this season's budget. This method overlooks two major influences on projected sales volume: inflation and competition. If inflation was 10 percent and no other changes occurred in the retail environment, then the retailer planning on selling the same physical volume as during the previous year should expect a 10 percent increase in this season's dollar sales. Similarly, if the exit of a competitor across town is expected to increase the number of customer transactions by 5 percent, this increase should be reflected in the budget. Suppose that last year's sales were $100,000, inflation is 10 percent, and the retailer expects its market share to increase by 8 percent, while the total market remains stable. What should your projected sales be? A simple equation used in retail planning is as follows:

$$\text{Total sales} = \text{Average sale} \times \text{Total transactions}$$

In the preceding example, average sales would increase by the 10 percent level of inflation to 1.10 times last year's sales and total transactions would increase by the 8 percent gain in market share to 1.08 times last year's total transactions for an increase in total sales of 1.188 times (or 1.10 × 1.08), resulting in a total sales increase of $18,800 or a budgeted total sales of $118,800.

Because planning future sales is the most important part of developing a merchandise budget, the retailers that do the best job of forecasting sales will be the most profitable.

Determining Planned BOM and EOM Inventories

Once the buyer has estimated the seasonal and monthly sales for the upcoming season, plans can be made for inventory requirements. To achieve projected sales figures, the merchant will generally carry stock or inventory in excess of planned sales for the period, be it a week, month, or season. The extra stock or inventory provides a merchandise assortment deep and broad enough to ensure customer sales. A common method of estimating the amount of stock to be carried is the **stock-to-sales ratio.** This ratio depicts the amount of stock to have on hand at the beginning of each month to support the forecasted sales for that month. For example, a ratio of 5:1 would suggest that the retailer have $5 in inventory (at retail price) for every $1 in forecasted sales. Planned average beginning-of-the-month (BOM) stock-to-sales ratios can also be calculated directly from a retailer's planned inventory turnover goals. For example, a retailer wants a target turnover rate of 4.0. By dividing the annual turnover rate into 12

Stock-to-sales ratio depicts the amount of stock to have at the beginning of each month to support the forecasted sales for that month.

(the number of months in a year), the average BOM stock-to-sales ratio for the season can be computed. In this case, 12 divided by 4.0 equals 3.0. Thus, the average stock-to-sales ratio for the season is 3. Generally, stock-to-sales ratios will fluctuate month to month as sales tend to fluctuate monthly. Nevertheless, it is important to always review these ratios because if they are set too high or too low, too much or too little inventory will be on hand to meet the sales target. Remember, it is just as bad to have too much inventory on hand as it is to have too little. After all, stocking up too much inventory could result in having the costs of holding that inventory outweigh the gross margins to be made on sale of the merchandise.

Retail trade associations such as the National Retail Federation (NRF) in the United States (www.nrf.com) and the Australian Retailers Association (www.ara.com.au) and others conduct surveys and publish industry average stock-to-sales ratios. For example, based on available data, the buyer for Department 353 in Exhibit 8.2 used a planned stock-to-sales ratio of 3.0 for February, April, and June, a ratio of 4.0 for March and July, and a ratio of 5.0 for May. The buyer was able to determine that $300,000 worth of merchandise was needed beginning March 1 due to a planned stock-to-sales ratio of 4.0 and planned sales of $75,000 (line 2). Two things should be noted. First, stock-to-sales ratios always express inventory levels at retail, not cost. Second, the beginning-of-the-month (BOM) inventory for one month is the end-of-the month (EOM) inventory for the previous month. This relationship can be easily seen by comparing the BOM figures (line 1) for one month with the EOM figures for the previous month (line 4).

Determining Planned Retail Reductions

All merchandise brought into the store for sale to consumers is not actually sold at the planned initial markup price. Therefore, when preparing the six-month budget, the buyer should make allowances for reductions in the levels of stock not due to sales. Generally, these planned retail reductions fall into three types: markdowns, employee discounts, and stock shortages. These reductions must be planned because as the dollar value of the inventory level is reduced, the BOM stock that is planned to support next month's forecasted sales will be inadequate unless adjustments are made this month. Therefore, a buyer must remember that reductions are part of the cost of doing business.

Dollars & Sense

Retailers who recognize that reductions are part of the cost of doing business and plan appropriately will achieve higher profits.

A small number of retailers do not include planned reductions in their merchandise budgets. They simply treat them as part of the normal operation of the store and feel they should be controlled without being part of the total budget. This gives management an understated, conservative planned-purchase figure, thereby having the effect of holding back some purchase reserve until the physical inventory reveals the exact amount of reductions. We have included planned reductions here for two reasons: (1) to reflect the additional purchases needed for sufficient inventory to begin the next month and (2) to point out that taking reductions is not bad. Too often, inexperienced retailers believe that taking a reduction is an admission of error and therefore fail to mark down merchandise until it is too late in the season. Therefore, a buyer must remember that reductions are part of the cost of doing business. Methods available to the retail buyer for minimizing retail reductions caused by retailer mistakes are discussed in Chapter 10.

It should be noted that the reductions in our six-month budget are listed as a percentage of planned sales. The buyer in our example has estimated monthly retail reduction percentages as shown on line 11. To determine planned retail reductions for March (line 3), planned monthly sales are multiplied by the planned monthly retail reduction percentage to yield the planned monthly retail reduction of $7,500 ($75,000 × 10 percent = $7,500).

Reductions are one of the major items in the merchandise budget subject to constant change. One reason is that the planned reductions may prove inadequate in light of actual conditions encountered by the retailer. If retailers delay too long in taking reductions, especially those occurring because of unexpected weather, they may be forced to take even larger price cuts later as the merchandise style depreciates even more in value. Alternatively, consider what happens when the department manager does such an effective merchandising job that not all the reduction money is needed for the period. The solution to both these dilemmas is found in the rules for developing a budget; namely, keeping it so flexible it can be intelligently administered.

Determining Planned Purchases at Retail and Cost

We are now ready to determine whether additional purchases must be made during the merchandising season. The retailer will need inventory for (1) planned sales, (2) planned retail reductions, and (3) planned EOM inventory. Planned BOM inventory represents purchases that have already been made. In the six-month merchandise budget example shown in Exhibit 8.2, the March planned purchases at retail for Department 353 are $82,500 (line 5). This figure was derived by (1) adding planned sales, planned retail reductions, and planned EOM inventory and (2) subtracting planned BOM inventory:

$$\$75,000 + \$7,500 + 300,000 - 300,000 = \$82,500$$

Once planned purchases at retail are determined, planned purchases at cost can be easily calculated. The retail price always represents a combination of cost plus markup. If the markup percentage is given, the portion of retail attributed to cost or the cost complement can be derived by subtracting the markup percentage from the retail percentage of 100 percent. Given the markup percentage is 45 percent of retail for Department 353, the cost complement percentage must be 55 percent (100 percent − 45 percent = 55 percent). Planned purchases at cost for March (line 6), must be 55 percent of planned purchases at retail or $45,375 ($82,500 × 55 percent = $45,375). Planned initial markup for March (line 7) must be 45 percent of planned purchases or $37,125 ($82,500 × 45 percent = $37,125).

Determining the Buyer's Planned Gross Margin

The buyer is accountable for the purchases made, the expected selling price of these purchases, the cost of these purchases, and the reductions that are involved in selling merchandise the buyer has previously purchased. Therefore, the last step in developing the merchandise budget is determining the buyer's planned gross margin for the period. As already discussed, the buyer, in making plans, recognizes that the initial selling price for all the products will probably not be realized and that some reductions will occur. Referring to Exhibit 8.2, the buyer's planned gross margin for February (line 8) is determined by taking planned initial markup (line 7) and subtracting planned reductions (line 3) ($70,875 − $7,500 = $63,375).

It is important for retailers to remember that the planned gross margin for a month in a merchandise budget, which is based on the purchases made that month, will not equal that month's gross margin on the retailer's financial statements, which is based on sales.

Retail Accounting Statements

LO • 2

What are the differences among, and the uses of, these three accounting statements: income statement, balance sheet, and statement of cash flow?

Successful retailing also requires sound accounting practices. The number and types of accounting records needed depend on management's objectives. Large retailers generally require more detailed information usually based on merchandise lines or departments. Smaller retailers may be able to make firsthand observations on sales and inventory levels and make decisions before financial data are available. For example, a Chinese retailer owning and operating a 100-square-foot store can easily use observation to obtain a general idea of the store's inventory. Still, the small retailer should consult the accounting records to confirm personal observations.

Properly prepared financial records provide measurements of profitability and retail performance. In addition, they show all transactions occurring within a given time period. However, these financial records must provide the manager not only with a look at the past but also with a look into the future so the manager can plan. Financial records not only indicate if a retailer has achieved good results; they also indicate what growth potential and problem areas lie ahead:

1. Is some merchandise line outperforming or underperforming the rest of the store?
2. Is the inventory level adequate for the current sales level?
3. Is the firm's debt level too high (does the firm owe too much money)?
4. Are reductions, including markdowns, too high a percentage of sales?
5. Is the gross margin adequate for the firm's profit objectives?

These are a few of the questions that the financial data must answer for the retailer. The authors know of one company where merchandise line "X" was generating an annual profit of $800,000, and merchandise line "Y" was losing money at the rate of $600,000. Management was totally unaware of the situation and was just happy to be making $200,000! Management was astounded when a little accounting work revealed the true situation.

Let's look at the three financial statements most commonly used by retailers: the income statement, the balance sheet, and the statement of cash flow.

All retailers, small or large, need to regularly prepare an income statement, balance sheet, and statement of cash flow to be able to monitor the financial health of their businesses.

Income Statement

The most common financial statement a retailer prepares is the income statement (also referred to as the profit-and-loss statement). The **income statement** provides a summary of the sales and expenses for a given time period, usually monthly, quarterly, seasonally, or annually. Comparison of current results with prior results allows the retailer to notice trends or changes in sales, expenses, and profits. Also, the mere fact that a retailer reports increased earnings each year and the income statement looks great should not lead one to believe that everything is fine. As the E-tailing box points out, financial statements may not always reflect the true nature of the business.

Income statements can be broken down by departments, divisions, branches, and so on, enabling the retailer to evaluate each subunit's operating performance for the period. Exhibit 8.5a shows the basic format for an income statement and Exhibit 8.5b shows the income statement for TMD Furniture.

Income statement is a financial statement that provides a summary of the sales and expenses for a given time period, usually a month, quarter, season, or year.

Exhibit 8.5a	Retailers' Basic Income Statement Format

Gross Sales		$_____
— Returns and Allowances	$_____	
Net Sales		$_____
— Cost of Goods Sold	$_____	
Gross Margin		$_____
— Operating Expenses	$_____	
Operating Profit		$_____
± Other Income or Expenses	$_____	
Net Profit Before Taxes		$_____

Exhibit 8.5b	Sample Income Statement

TMD Furniture, Inc.
Six Month Income Statement
July 31

				Percentage
Gross Sales			$393,671.79	
Less: Returns and Allowances			16,300.00	
Net Sales			$377,371.79	100%
Less: Cost of Goods Sold				
Beginning Inventory		$ 98,466.29		
Purchases		218,595.69		
Goods Available for Sales		$317,061.98		
Ending Inventory		103,806.23	213,255.75	56.5%
Gross Margin			$164,116.04	43.5%
Less: Operating Expenses				
Salaries & Wages:				
Managers	$18,480.50			
Selling	17,755.65			
Office	7,580.17			
Warehouse & Delivery	6,685.99	50,502.31		
Advertising		$ 15,236.67		
Administration and Warehouse Charge		800.00		
Credit, Collections and Bad Debts		1,973.96		
Contributions		312.50		
Delivery		1,434.93		
Depreciation		5,398.56		
Dues		23.50		
Employee Benefits		566.26		
Utilities		3,738.74		
Insurance		3,041.75		
Legal and Auditing		1,000.00		
Mds. Service & Repair		1,439.16		
Miscellaneous		602.00		
Rent		9,080.00		
Repairs & Maintenance		1,576.99		
Sales Allowances		180.50		
Supplies, Postage		1,135.40		
Taxes:				
City, County & State	$ 2,000.00			
Payroll	3,902.90	5,902.90		
Telephone		1,520.09		
Travel		404.92		
Warehouse Handling Charges		12,216.86	118,088.00	31.3%
Operating Profit			$ 46,028.04	12.2%
Other Income:				
Carrying Charges		$ 3,377.48		
Profit on sale of parking lot		740.47	4,117.95	1.1%
Net Profit Before Taxes			$ 50,145.99	13.3%

Gross sales are the retailer's total sales including sales for cash or for credit. **Returns and allowances** are reductions from gross sales. Here the retailer has made a financial adjustment for customers because they have become dissatisfied with their purchases and returned the merchandise to the retailer. Because these reductions represent cancellations of previously recorded sales, the gross sales figure must be reduced to reflect these cancellations.

Net sales, gross sales less returns and allowances, represent the amount of merchandise the retailer actually sold during the time period.

Cost of goods sold is the cost of merchandise that has been sold during the period. Although this concept is easy to understand, the exact calculation of the cost of goods sold is somewhat complex. For example, like their own customers, retailers may obtain some return privileges or receive some allowances from vendors. Also, there is the issue of determining how inventory levels will be carried on the company's books. This will be fully discussed in the next section of this chapter.

Gross margin is the difference between net sales and cost of goods sold or the amount available to cover operating expenses and produce a profit.

Operating expenses are those expenses that a retailer incurs in running the business other than the cost of the merchandise (e.g., rent, wages, utilities, depreciation, and insurance).

Not only must retailers consider GAAP regulations, but they must also take into account Internal Revenue Service (IRS) rulings. The IRS recently provided a tax break for retailers when it ruled that retailers may now estimate inventory shrinkage (the loss of merchandise through theft, loss, and damage).[3] This will enable retailers to reduce ending inventory and thus taxable earnings. Prior to this ruling, which results from court cases involving Kroger and Target, the IRS did not permit retailers to estimate shrinkage from the last physical inventory to the end of the retailer's tax year, usually the end of January. Because it is not feasible for most retail chains to count all their inventory in one day in late January, most chains check inventory on a rotating basis throughout the year and can now estimate their losses without being challenged by the IRS.

Operating profit is the difference between gross margin and operating expenses.

Other income or expenses includes income or expense items that the firm incurs, though not in the course of its normal retail operations. For example, a retailer might have purchased some land to use for expansion and after careful deliberation, postponed the expansion plans. Now, the retailer rents out that land. Because renting land is not in the normal course of business for a retailer, the rent received would be considered other income.

Net profit is operating profit plus or minus other income or expenses. Net profit is the figure on which the retailer pays taxes and thus is usually referred to as net profit before taxes.

Most retailers actually divide the income statement into two sections: the first, or top half, being those elements above the gross margin total and the second, or bottom half, being those elements below the gross margin total. Sales and cost of goods sold are essentially controllable by the buying functions of the retail organization. In more and more retailing operations today, the buying organization is separated from the management of the operating expenses that are shown below gross margin. Some retailers use the terms "top line" (sales), "gross" (gross margin), and "bottom line" (operating profit) when referring to the key elements of their income statement.

Finally, it is important to point out that just as they do in the reporting of revenues, Generally Accepted Accounting Principles (GAAP) allow for variations in how retailers report certain expenses. Pre-opening expenses, for example, can be expensed as they occur, during the month the store opens, or capitalized and written off over several

---

Gross sales
are the retailer's total sales including sales for cash or for credit.

Returns and allowances
are refunds of the purchase price or downward adjustments in selling prices due to customers returning purchases, or adjustments made in the selling price due to customer dissatisfaction with product or service performance.

Net sales
is gross sales less returns and allowances.

Cost of goods sold
is the cost of merchandise that has been sold during the period.

Gross margin
is the difference between net sales and cost of goods sold.

Operating expenses
are those expenses that a retailer incurs in running the business other than the cost of the merchandise.

Operating profit
is gross margin less operating expenses.

Other income or expenses
includes income or expense items that the firm incurs which are not in the course of its normal retail operations.

Net profit
is operating profit plus or minus other income or expenses.

E-tailing

All Accounting Statements Are Not the Same

Revenue recognition has always been a chronic sore point for the Securities and Exchange Commission (SEC) in the agency's efforts to protect investors. For example, in the late 1990s many investors failed to understand how e-tailers presented their financial statements in such a manner that the retailers were able to boost revenues. (At the time, when most e-commerce companies were not yet profitable; they were trading at multiples of their net revenue.) Priceline, Amazon, iVilliage, and eBay were just some of the e-tailers that embraced such accounting practices to increase revenues. The accounting practices were not illegal, but they were extremely aggressive. The SEC reasoned that if investors did not understand how these companies were reporting revenues and profits, their chances of making money in the stock market over the long run were next to impossible.

Although the aggressive accounting tactics these companies employed caused a great deal of concern at the SEC, under the current generally accepted accounting principles (GAAP) the e-tailers were doing nothing wrong. Still, the SEC was concerned that the e-tailers were inclined to use some specific tactics to inflate their revenues. After all, a small increase in the "top line" can send the company's stock price soaring upward and trigger bonuses to management.

One tactic cited by the SEC used by many Internet retailers was reporting the gross sales price of merchandise instead of the net sales price. This may not sound significant, but if e-tailers like Priceline were required to report their net sales revenues, their revenues for 1999 would have dropped from $152 million to $18 million. This is because Priceline did not reduce its sales price by the cost of the hotel rooms, airline tickets, and rental cars it eventually sold to customers. Priceline's logic behind the accounting system it used was the fact that the company maintained the full risk of ownership of the tickets and should therefore be allowed to report the gross bookings.

Barter transactions are still another area of concern at the SEC. The problem is that bartering revenue for advertising space on the web makes up a significant portion of many of these companies' reported revenues. These transactions are required to be recorded at book value, but determining the value of a web site's ad space can be very difficult because often no cash is exchanged. Therefore, e-retailers have been able to pump up revenues by simply increasing the proposed fair value of these transactions.

All companies know that freebies, coupons, and discounts are an excellent way to attract customers, but some Internet years. Advertising can be written off when the ad runs or when payment is made. Store fixtures can be depreciated over 5 years or 40 years. Thus, when comparing the financial statements of different retailers, it is important to know how each retailer treated these and other expenses. Not only are there differences in the way U.S. retailers can report revenues and expenses, but, as described in the Global Retailing box, there are differences in the way retailers in different countries can report their financial performances.

Balance Sheet

Asset
is anything of value that is owned by the retail firm.

The second accounting statement used in financial reporting is the balance sheet. A balance sheet shows the financial condition of a retailer's business at a particular point in time, as opposed to the income statement which reports on the activities over a period of time. The balance sheet identifies and quantifies all the firm's assets and liabilities. The difference between assets and liabilities is owner's equity or net worth. Comparison of a current balance sheet with that from a previous time period enables a retail analyst to observe changes in the firm's financial condition.

retailers have found ways to avoid showing the effects these promotions have on revenues. When these Internet retailers provide merchandise at a discount, they book the sale at full price instead of the discounted price. These may not have an effect on net income, but it does make the companies revenues look much more appealing.

Fulfillment costs are the costs incurred for warehousing, packaging, and shipping products. Many e-retailers, including Amazon.com and eToys, showed these costs as marketing expenses, whereas traditional businesses book these expenses as cost of sales. The purpose of not showing these expenses as cost of sales is to keep the expenses from cutting into the company's profit margin and thus leading the average investor to believe the company is more profitable than it actually is.

One final area of SEC concern is "auction accounting." Auction houses are required by GAAP to recognize income from listing fees over the period the item is on the auction block. However, eBay and other Internet auction sites booked the listing revenue as soon as it is received. Also, these companies booked transaction fees as soon as they are received, when they should have been booked once the transaction had been completed and the product had been mailed to the bidder. Consequently, Internet retailers that are employing these accounting practices are prematurely recognizing revenue in order to improve the top line of the income statement.

Although the SEC is looking into changing the way e-retailers are accounting for revenues, investors must be aware of the aggressive tactics these companies are using. As more and more people begin to invest in technology stocks in a quest for superior financial returns, they need to be informed about the accounting practices these companies are using so they can make an informed decision about the future profitability of the company.

E-tailers were not the only retailers who may have overinflated their incomes. In 1998, the SEC forced wholesale club retailers to adopt a more conservative accounting policy for membership fees. The SEC maintained that when customers pay a fee to a wholesale club, such as BJ Wholesale, Sam's Club, or Costco, the fees represent the right to shop there for a given period of time. Therefore, if the club offers "full refunds" to unhappy customers, these fees should not be recognized as income when received, but only as the membership term expires.

Source: The authors acknowledge the help of Nicole Bowers, Texas Tech University, in the preparation of this box.

A typical balance sheet format is illustrated in Exhibit 8.6. As Exhibit 8.6a shows, the basic equation for a balance sheet is

$$\text{Assets} = \text{Liabilities} + \text{Net worth}$$

Hence both sides always must be in balance with each other. Exhibit 8.6b shows the balance sheet for TMD Furniture.

An **asset** is anything of value that is owned by the retail firm. Assets are broken down into two categories: current and noncurrent.

Current assets include cash and all other items that the retailer can easily convert into cash within a relatively short period of time (generally a year). Besides cash, current assets include accounts receivable, notes receivable, prepaid expenses, and inventory. **Accounts and/or notes receivable** are amounts that customers owe the retailer for goods and services. Frequently, the retailer will reduce the total receivables by a fixed percentage (based on past experience) to take into account those customers who may be unwilling or unable to pay. **Prepaid expenses** are those items, such as trash

Current assets
are assets that can be easily converted into cash within a relatively short period of time (usually a year or less).

Accounts and/or notes receivable
are amounts that customers owe the retailer for goods and services.

Prepaid expenses
are those items for which the retailer has already paid, but the service has not been completed.

Global Retailing

Accounting Rules Vary by Country

The International Accounting Standards Committee (IASC) has been working toward achieving uniformity in accounting principles since 1973. The organization has grown tremendously to represent 143 organizations in 104 countries. Presently, the IASC has issued 40 international accounting standards (IASs). These standards address a number of topics, including goodwill, inventory valuation, and business combinations.

The treatment of goodwill, which is the premium over book value that a purchaser pays when it acquires another company, varies greatly between different countries. According to international accounting standards, goodwill should be amortized over a period of 5 to 20 years. However, the IASC strongly recommends that companies use the 5-year period for amortization. Several countries have complied with this standard. Some of them include Australia, Mexico, Spain, Japan, and Brazil. However, there is still a great deal of variation between other countries. Great Britain and Switzerland allow companies to immediately expense goodwill, whereas Italy, Germany, and Hong Kong allow companies to choose whether they want to immediately expense goodwill or amortize it over a period of 5 to 20 years. The United States and Canada permit the amortization of goodwill over a 40-year period. France does not provide a maximum number of years that goodwill can be amortized over, and China has not yet addressed the treatment of purchased goodwill.

The problem with such wide variations in the area of goodwill is that it makes the comparison of financial statements very difficult. For example, if a U.S. corporation purchases a business in Great Britain, the goodwill must immediately be expensed. This will have a severe negative impact on the profitability of the business in the first year. However, if a corporation in Great Britain purchases a business in the United States, it will be allowed to amortize goodwill over 40 years, which will have little effect on the financial statements of the company in the first year of business.

In 1991, the IASC issued exposure draft E32 that would have eliminated LIFO (last in, first out) as an alternative method of valuing inventory. The IASC argued that the LIFO method did not assign the most current costs to ending inventories and therefore distorted the balance sheet. However, due to public sentiment, the IASC reversed its E32 position and has continued to allow LIFO as an alternative method of valuing inventories. This was good news to the United States

and other countries that used the LIFO method, because revaluing their inventories with the FIFO (first in, first out) or weighted average method would have resulted in higher ending inventory values and a higher tax liability.

The IASC has also addressed accounting for business combinations. IASC provided two methods for accounting for mergers and acquisitions. The purchase method of accounting for business combinations effectively reports the earnings of two separate businesses as one business through the use of consolidated financial statements. The net assets of the acquired company are carried on these statements at their cost to the acquiring company. The other method of accounting for mergers and acquisitions is the pooling of interests method. This method may only be used when the transaction is principally an exchange of voting common shares or if all of the net assets and operations of the two entities are combined into one entity.

The pooling of interests method effectively reports the earnings of only one business, and the net assets of the acquired company are carried on the combined entity's financial statements at their premerger value. Currently, Canada, Germany, and the United States follow this IAS. Belgium, Australia, France, and Hong Kong only allow companies to use the purchase method, whereas companies in Japan generally use the pooling of interests method. The reporting requirements of each country essentially result in a difference in the valuation of the acquired company's net assets. The pooling of interests method will typically result in a lower net asset figure than the purchase method.

Currently, standards issued by the IASC are not mandatory unless a particular country adopts them. This explains the wide variation in reporting requirements. However, every day more countries realize the need for uniform accounting principles in international financial reporting. As the awareness of this need intensifies, the IASs will hopefully influence the standards adopted in leading industrial countries.

Still, although U.S. retailers may complain about GAAP and IRS rules, it could be worse. The *Wall Street Journal* recently reported that a Chinese premier reminded Chinese taxpayers that "tax evasion can result in death by execution."*

Source: *"It Could Be Worse," Wall Street Journal, April 3, 1999: A1.
*The authors acknowledge the help of Nicole Bowers, Texas Tech University, in the preparation of this Global Retailing box.

Exhibit 8.6a — Retailers' Basic Balance Sheet Format

Current Assets			Current Liabilities		
Cash	$_____		Accounts Payable	$_____	
Accounts Receivable	$_____		Payroll Payable	$_____	
Inventory	$_____		Current Notes Payable	$_____	
Prepaid Expenses	$_____		Taxes Payable	$_____	
Total Current Assets		$_____	Total Current Liabilities		$_____
Noncurrent Assets			Long-term Liabilities		
Building (less depreciation)	$_____		Long-term Notes		
Fixtures and Equipment			Payable	$_____	
(less depreciation)	$_____		Mortgage Payable	$_____	
Total Noncurrent Assets		$_____			
Goodwill		$_____	Total Long-term Liabilities		$_____
			Net Worth		
			Capital Surplus	$_____	
			Retained Earnings	$_____	
			Total Net Worth		$_____
Total Assets		$_____	**Total Liabilities** and **Net Worth**		$_____

Exhibit 8.6b — Sample Balance Sheet

TMD Furniture, Inc.
Balance Sheet
July 31

Current Assets			Current Liabilities		
Cash	$ 11,589		Accounts Payable	$57,500	
Accounts Receivable	71,517		Payroll Payable	$ 1,451	
Inventory	103,806		Current Notes Payable	$14,000	
			Taxes Payable	$ 1,918	
Total Current Assets		186,912	Total Current Liabilities		$ 74,869
Noncurrent Assets			Long-term Liabilities		
Building (less depreciation)	$ 61,414		Long-term Notes Payable	$52,750	
Fixtures and Equipment			Mortgage Payable	$38,500	
(less depreciation)	$ 11,505				
Total Noncurrent Assets		72,919	Total Long-term Liabilities		$ 91,250
Goodwill		100	Net Worth		$ 93,812
Total Assets		$259,931	**Total Liabilities** and **Net Worth**		$259,931

collection or insurance, for which the retailer has already paid but the service has not been completed. **Retail inventories** comprise merchandise that the retailer has in the store or in storage and is available for sale.

Noncurrent assets are those assets that cannot be converted into cash in a short period of time (usually 12 months) in the normal course of business. These noncurrent

Retail inventories
comprise merchandise that the retailer has in the store or in storage and is available for sale.

Noncurrent assets
are those assets that cannot be converted to cash in a short period of time (usually 12 months) in the normal course of business.

or long-term assets include buildings, parking lots, the land under the building and parking lot, fixtures (i.e., display racks), and equipment (i.e., air conditioning system). These items are carried on the books as cost less accumulated depreciation on everything except the land. Depreciation is necessary because most noncurrent assets have a limited useful life; the difference between the asset and depreciation is intended to provide a more realistic picture of the retailer's assets and prevent an overstatement or understatement of these assets. However, as every retailer has learned, the value of real estate property can fluctuate greatly over time.

Although noncurrent assets and fixed assets are important in retailing, the high profit retailer recognizes that current assets (primarily inventory) are usually more critical to achieving outstanding profit performance.

Goodwill
is an intangible asset, usually based on customer loyalty, that a retailer pays for when buying an existing business.

Total assets
equal current assets plus noncurrent assets plus goodwill.

Liability
is any legitimate financial claim against the retailer's assets.

Current liabilities
are short-term debts that are payable within a year.

Accounts payable
are amounts owed vendors for goods and services.

Long-term liabilities
are debts that are due in a year or longer.

Total liabilities
equal current liabilities plus long-term liabilities.

Net worth,
often called **owner's equity,** is total assets less total liabilities.

Some retailers also include goodwill as an asset. **Goodwill** is an intangible asset, usually based on customer loyalty, that a retailer pays for when buying an existing business. Usually the dollar value assigned to goodwill is minimal.

Total assets equal current assets plus noncurrent assets plus goodwill.

The other part of the balance sheet reflects the retailer's liabilities and net worth. A **liability** is any legitimate financial claim against the retailer's assets. Liabilities are classified as either current or long term.

Current liabilities are short-term debts that are payable within a year. Included here are accounts payable, notes payable that are due within a year, payroll payable, and taxes payable. **Accounts payable** are amounts owed vendors for goods and services. Payroll payable is money due employees on past labor. Taxes due the government (federal, state, or local) are also considered a current liability. Some retailers also include interest due within the year on long-term notes or mortgages as a current liability.

Long-term liabilities include notes payable and mortgages not due within the year. **Total liabilities** equal current liabilities plus long-term liabilities.

Net worth (also called **owner's equity**) is the difference between the firm's total assets and total liabilities and represents the owner's equity in the business. The figure reflects the owner's original investment plus any profits reinvested in the business less any losses incurred in the business and any funds that the owner has taken out of the business.

In actuality, the balance sheet does not reflect all the retailer's assets and liabilities. Specifically, such items as store personnel can be an asset, or a liability, to the business. These items might not appear on the balance sheet but are extremely important to the success of a high-performance retailer. Other items that could be either assets or liabilities, although not in the strict accounting sense, are goodwill, customer loyalty, and even vendor relationships. Each of these items can contribute to the success or failure of a retailer.

The mere fact that a retailer reports increased earnings each year and the balance sheet looks great should not lead one to believe that everything is fine. As the Retailing: The Inside Story box points out, in very rare cases, financial statements can be fraudulent. However, a careful analysis of the statements should have warned people about one of the largest frauds in retailing history.

Retailing: The Inside Story

Maybe Somebody Should Have Examined the Books a Little Closer*

Since its beginnings in the early 1980s, retail analysts believed that Phar-Mor Inc., a Youngstown, Ohio, operator of 310 deep-discount drugstores, could do no wrong. Phar-Mor's concept of relying on sharp buyers to pounce on manufacturer's special deals was well positioned for the value-conscious consumer of the 1990s. Bargain hunters flocked to its stores and sales exceeded $3 billion in 1991. Consequently, most retail analysts expected Phar-Mor to continue its rapid growth into the 21st century. Even Sam Walton wondered how Phar-Mor could make money with the prices it charged.

However, everything changed in July 1992 when the company fired two key executives and announced that its books had been falsified by $500 million—the largest retail fraud ever uncovered. The fraud began as a scheme to inflate lower than expected earnings by overstating payments, reportedly as much as $25 million, made by large vendors such as Gibson Greetings Inc. and Rubbermaid Inc. The vendors made these payments in exchange for an "exclusive supply agreement" covering specific time periods. For example, Rubbermaid created a large "Everything Rubbermaid" department for each store and Gibson, as an exclusive supplier, was promised an expanded greeting card department.

Actually, this is just one of the ways retailers can improve their performance by "cooking the books" and with the aid of the computer it may actually be easier to do than when all accounting was done manually. For example, buyers have always been under great pressure to produce profits. The following is an illustration to show how easily an unscrupulous retailer, such as Phar-Mor, can take advantage of the firm's use of the computer to produce phony profits.

Most retailers appreciate the computer's help in tracking sales, controlling inventory, and developing work schedules; what many are not aware of is its ability to produce nonexisting profits, which Phar-Mor was able to do. Consider the following two cases.

Under the Old System (Precomputer)

A buyer purchases 1,000 camper shorts at $15 to sell at $29.95. After the first week, the buyer notices that none of the shorts were sold, so the buyer realizes his or her mistake and marks them down to $13.88 and has the stockers mark each pair of shorts with the new price. On the general ledger the buyer takes a reduction of $16,070 (1,000 × $16.07). During the first week at the new price, 100 shorts are sold. The price of $13.88 would remain until the buyer lowered the price again. (Remember, it would be difficult to have the buyer increase the price, because the $13.88 stickers would probably still show. In addition, the labor costs would be high.) Anyway, the inventory on hand for the shorts would now be $12,492 (900 × $13.88).

With a New Computer System

The same facts as above exist, except that after selling the 100 pairs of shorts, the buyers realizes that the "annual inventory" is about to be taken. The buyer may wonder, "What should I do if I want a bonus? How about cooking the books."

The buyer simply reenters the original selling price of $29.95 in the computer and changes the price on the shelf. (Remember, with the new computer system, the buyer does not have to re-mark each item.) Now our inventory would be $26,955 (900 × $29.95).

By simply changing the price in the computer, the buyer increased profits by $14,463 (900 × the markdown of $16.07) and there is no way an outside auditor would detect the phony profit. After all, the auditors will check the count and the price in the computer's price look-up (PLU) and find both to be correct.

The buyer/department manager/store manager and even the divisional merchandise manager would all get a bigger bonus based on the phony computer entry.

Now they just have to find a way to make up for this phony entry before next year's inventory. This was Phar-Mor's undoing.

*For a detailed analysis of the issues involved in this case, see "Finding Auditors Liable for Fraud," *The CPA Journal,* July 1997: 14–21.

Based on an idea given the authors by Robert Kahn.

Statement of Cash Flow

A third financial statement that retailers can use to understand their business is the statement of cash flow. A statement of cash flow lists in detail the source and type of all revenue (cash inflows) and the use and type of all expenditures (cash outflows) for a given time period. When cash inflows exceed cash outflows, the retailer is said to have a positive cash flow; when cash outflows exceed cash inflows, the retailer is said to be experiencing a negative cash flow. Thus the purpose of the statement of cash flow is to enable the retailer to project the cash needs of the firm. Based on projections, plans may be made either to seek additional financing if a negative flow is projected, or to make other investments if a positive flow is anticipated. Likewise, a retailer with a positive cash flow for the period might be able to take advantage of "good deals" from vendors.

Retailers who do the best job of managing cash flow will be more profitable.

A statement of cash flow is not the same as an income statement. In a statement of cash flow, the retailer is only concerned with the movement of cash into or out of the firm, whereas an income statement reflects the profitability of the retailer after all revenue and expenses are considered. Consider the example of TMD Furniture for the month of August as shown in Exhibit 8.7a.

Exhibit 8.7a	Sample Cash Flow Statement

TMD Furniture, Inc.
Cash Flow Statement
July 31

Cash Sales	$15,450	
Collection of Accounts Receivable	24,998	
Refund on State Taxes	97	
Total Cash Inflow		$40,545
Cash Outflow		
Rent	$1,513	
Purchases at Cash	5,750	
Salaries	8,483	
Utilities	1,450	
Advertising	2,300	
County Taxes	173	
Supplies	921	
Telephone	150	
Paying Off Accounts Payable	20,632	
Paying Off Notes Payable	7,000	
Total Cash Outflow		$48,372
Total Cash Flow		($7,827)

Exhibit 8.7b	Typical Cash Inflow and Outflow Categories

Cash Inflow	Cash Outflows
Cash sales	Paying for merchandise
Collecting accounts receivable	Rent expenses
Collecting notes receivable	Utilities expenses
Collecting other debts	Wages and Salary expenses
Sale of fixed assets	Advertising expense
Sale of stock	Insurance premiums
	Taxes
	Interest expenses
	Supplies and other expenses
	Purchase of other assets
	Paying off accounts payable
	Paying off notes payable
	Buying back company stocks
	Paying dividends

August is a slow month for furniture sales as many customers are taking vacations, and as a result TMD is expecting sales of only $40,000 for the month. However, only $15,450 of that amount will be for cash and TMD expects to collect $24,998 on its account receivables. Along with a tax refund check due from the state for $97, TMD has projected a cash inflow of $40,545 for August. However, because August is the month that several notes and accounts payable are due, TMD Furniture is expecting to have to pay out $48,372 during August. This will result in a negative cash flow for the month of $7,827. TMD has prepared for this by having cash on hand (as reported on the July 31 balance sheet) of $11,589.

However, many retailers forget about cash and realize the difference between cash flow and profit only after the coffers are empty. In the case of TMD Furniture, paying off the notes and accounts payable had no effect on the income statement. Likewise, the statement of cash flow only considered that part of purchases that were paid for with cash, not those placed on account. These credit purchasers had no direct effect on the cash flow. Exhibit 8.7b lists the typical retailer's cash inflow and outflow items. It should be noted that retailers that decide to use major credit cards, instead of handling their own credit operations, are able to convert sales much more quickly to cash because they do not need to wait for customers to pay for their purchases—some other party such as a bank assumes this financing function.

Although the statement of cash flow is generally not considered as important as the income statement, more and more retailers are becoming aware of its importance. In fact, the number one cause of retailing bankruptcies in recent years has been cash flow problems. A retailer can be growing quickly and be profitable yet fail due to inadequate cash flow.

The lack of a sufficient cash flow is not limited to those large troubled chains you hear about in the news. The Service Retailing box, for example, describes how recent legal changes have reduced the cash flow of retailers selling extended service protection (ESP) warranties. Likewise, many a small entrepreneur has come up with a brilliant idea for a retail operation only to fail. The entrepreneur's problems usually started by overestimating revenues and underestimating costs resulting in a negative cash flow. By not making sure they had enough cash on hand to withstand the rocky first two

Service Retailing

New Rules for ESPs

Today most independent retailers, especially those that also provide appliance service, are relying on third-party administers (TPAs) to administer and back their service contracts on older products and their in-house extended service protection (ESP) programs. These ESPs, which are sold on 20 percent of all new major appliances and 25 percent of all consumer electronics, have long been attractive to retailers because almost 60 percent of such contracts is actually profit, especially since competition from discounters has lowered the margins on many of the products.

Today state governments are taking a greater interest in protecting the public from underfinanced service contract programs. Most states now require that all service contracts be backed by insurance. If escrow accounts are used as alternatives to insurance, some states require that the proceeds from contract sales after paying expenses, such as commissions and administration fees, be deposited in a bank for up to 10 years before sellers can realize the profit from the sale.

These rules hit hard the in-house programs of appliance retailers, who in the past, usually placed just 50 to 75 percent of each contract sale after expenses in escrow accounts.

Funds for these and other policies sold at the same time remained in such accounts for the duration of the contracts to pay the claims. However, as contracts expired, dealers withdrew the remaining funds as profits.

The states felt that these escrow systems had two weaknesses. If contract prices were not kept current with actual service costs and the frequency of covered product failures, the escrow account could be depleted easily. Likewise, if contract sales on new products declined but renewals on older policies remained high, the fund would not have enough money in escrow for the length of the service contracts to cover claims for the more failure-prone older products. In both cases, the contract program could become bankrupt.

The government remedies to assure that all ESP claims would be fulfilled created new problems for small retailers' in-house programs. With relatively low contract sales, small dealerships could not get insurance coverage priced to allow continued contract sales at competitive prices. Additionally, the 10-year escrow requirement in use by most states not only prevented retailers from immediately claiming earned profits, it also created cash flow problems. The Internal Revenue Service (IRS) demanded immediate tax payments on sales revenues the retailers could not touch legally for years.

Source: This box was suggested by Marvin Lurie, North American Retail Dealer Association, and is used with his permission.

years of starting up a business, most retailers are assuring themselves failure. No wonder more than a quarter of all new retail operations fail during the first two years. In fact, according to one of the author's mentors, the first thing to look for when examining a retailer's financial records to determine its ability to survive is accounts payable—government payroll taxes. It seems that when retail firms get into a cash bind, they tend to postpone payments to the government so that they can pay their suppliers and employees. After all, they can always pay the taxes later. Unfortunately, the government does not always agree with such thinking.[4]

LO • 3
How does a retailer value its inventory?

Inventory Valuation

Due to the many merchandise lines carried, inventory valuation is quite complex. Yet the retailer must have information such as sales, additional purchases not yet received, reductions for the period, gross margin, stock shortages, and inventory levels in order operate profitably.

There are two major decisions that a retailer must make with regard to valuing inventory: (1) which accounting inventory system to use and (2) which inventory pricing method to use.

Accounting Inventory System

Two accounting inventory systems are available for the retailer: (1) the cost method and (2) the retail method. We will describe both methods on the basis of the frequency with which inventory information is received, difficulties encountered in completing a physical inventory and maintaining records, and the extent to which stock shortages can be calculated.

The Cost Method   The **cost method** of inventory valuation provides a book valuation of inventory based solely on the retailer's cost including freight. It looks only at the cost of each item as it is recorded in the accounting records when purchased. When a physical inventory is taken, all the items are counted, the cost of each item is taken from the records or the price tags, and the total inventory value at cost is calculated.

One of the easiest methods of coding the cost of merchandise on the price tag is to use the first 10 letters of the alphabet to represent the price. Here A = 1, B = 2, C = 3, D = 4, E = 5, F = 6, G = 7, H = 8, I = 9, and J = 0. A product with the code HEAD has a cost of $85.14. The cost method is useful for those retailers who sell big-ticket items and allow price negotiations by customers. Sales personnel can know from the code how much room there is for negotiation to cover the cost of the merchandise plus operating expenses.

The cost method of inventory valuation does have several limitations:

1. It is difficult to do daily inventories (or even monthly inventories).
2. It is difficult to cost out each sale.
3. It is difficult to allocate freight charges to each item's cost of goods sold.

The cost method is generally used by those retailers with big-ticket items and a limited number of sales per day (i.e., a jewelry store selling expensive rings or an antique furniture store), where there are few lines or limited inventory requirements, infrequent price changes, and low turnover rates.

The Retail Method   The **retail method** of inventory values merchandise at current retail prices. It overcomes the disadvantages of the cost method by keeping detailed records of inventory based on the retail value of the merchandise. The fact that the inventory is valued in retail dollars makes it a little more difficult for the retailer to determine the cost of goods sold when computing the gross margin for a time period.

There are three basic steps in computing an ending inventory value using the retail method: calculation of the cost complement, calculation of reductions from retail value, and conversion of the adjusted retail book inventory to cost.

STEP 1. CALCULATION OF THE COST COMPLEMENT   Inventories, both beginning and ending, and purchases are recorded at both cost and retail levels when using the retail method. Exhibit 8.8 shows an inventory statement for Whitener's Sporting Goods for the fall season.

In Exhibit 8.8, the beginning inventory is shown at both cost and retail. Net purchases, which are the (total purchases less merchandise returned to vendors, allowances, and discounts from vendors) are also valued at cost and retail. Additional

---

Cost method
is an inventory valuation technique that provides a book valuation of inventory based solely on the retailer's cost of merchandise including freight.

Retail method
is an inventory valuation technique that values merchandise at current retail prices, which is then converted to cost based on a formula.

Exhibit 8.8	Inventory Available for Whitener's Sporting Goods Sale, Fall Season	

	Cost	Retail
Beginning Inventory	$199,000	$401,000
Net Purchases	70,000	154,000
Additional Markups		5,000
Freight-in	1,000	
Total Inventory Available for Sale	$270,000	$560,000

markups are the total increases in the retail price of merchandise already in stock, which were caused by inflation or heavy demand and are shown at retail. Freight-in is the cost to the retailer for transportation of merchandise from the vendor and is shown in the cost column.

Using the information from Exhibit 8.8, the retailer can calculate the average relationship of cost to the retail price for all merchandise available for sale during the fall season. This calculation is called the cost complement:

$$\text{Cost complement} = \text{Total cost valuation/Total retail valuation}$$
$$= \$270,000/\$560,000 = .482$$

Because the cost complement is .482, or 48.2 percent, 48.2 cents of every retail sales dollar is composed of merchandise cost.

STEP 2. CALCULATION OF REDUCTIONS FROM RETAIL VALUE   During the course of day-to-day business activities, the retailer must take reductions from inventory. In addition to sales, which lower the retail inventory level, retail inventory levels can be lowered by retail reductions. These reductions include markdowns (sales, reduced prices on end-of-season, discontinued, or damaged merchandise), discounts (employee, senior citizen, student, religious, etc.), and stock shortages (employee and customer theft, breakage). Markdowns and employee discounts can be recorded throughout an accounting period, but a physical inventory is required to calculate stock shortages.

In Exhibit 8.8, it was shown that Whitener's had a retail inventory available for sale of $560,000 for the upcoming fall season. This must be reduced by actual fall season sales of $145,000, markdowns of $12,000, and discounts of $2,000. This results in the ending book value of inventory having a retail level of $401,000, as is shown in Exhibit 8.9.

Once the ending book value of inventory at retail is determined, a comparison can be made to the physical inventory to compute the actual stock shortages; if the book value is greater than the physical count, a stock shortage has occurred. If the book value is lower than the physical count, a stock overage has occurred. Shortages are due to thefts, breakages, overshipments not billed to customers, and bookkeeping errors, which is the most common cause. These errors result from the failure to properly record markdowns, returns, discounts, and breakages. Many retailers have greatly

Exhibit 8.9	Whitener's Sporting Goods Ending Book Value at Retail, Fall Season		
		Cost	Retail
Inventory Available for Sale at Retail			$560,000
Less Reductions:			
Sales		$145,000	
Markdowns		12,000	
Discounts		$ 2,000	
Total Reductions			159,000
Ending Book Value of Inventory at Retail			$401,000

reduced their original shortage estimate by reviewing the season's bookkeeping entries. A stock overage, an excess of physical inventory over book inventory, is usually the result of bookkeeping errors, either miscounting during the physical inventory or improper book entries. Exhibit 8.10 shows the results of Whitener's physical inventory and the resulting adjustment.

Because a physical inventory must be taken in order to determine shortages (overages) and retailers only take a physical count once or twice a year, shortages (overages) are often estimated in merchandise budgets as shown in Exhibits 8.1 and 8.2. As a rule of thumb, retailers may estimate monthly shortages between 1/2 to 3 percent.

STEP 3. CONVERSION OF THE ADJUSTED RETAIL BOOK INVENTORY TO COST   The final step to be performed in using the retail method is to convert to cost the adjusted retail book inventory figure in order to determine the closing inventory at cost. The procedure involved here is to multiply the adjusted retail book inventory ($398,000 in the case of Whitener's) by the cost complement (.482 in the Whitener's example):

$$\text{Closing inventory (at cost)} = \text{Adjusted retail} \times \text{Cost complement book inventory}$$

$$= \$398,000 .482 = \$191,836$$

Although this equation does not yield the actual closing inventory at cost, it does provide a close approximation of the cost figure. Remember that the cost complement

Exhibit 8.10	Whitener's Sporting Goods, Stock Shortage (Overage) Adjustment Entry, End of Fall Season		
		Cost	Retail
Ending Book Value of Inventory at Retail			$401,000
Physical Inventory (at retail)			398,000
Stock Shortages			$ 3,000
Adjusting Ending Book Value of Inventory at Retail			$398,000

	Cost	Retail
Exhibit 8.11 — Whitener's Sporting Goods Income Statements August 1–January 31		
Sales		$145,000
Less: Cost of Goods Sold:		
Beginning Inventory (at Cost)	$200,000	
Purchases (at Cost)	70,000	
Goods Available for Sale	$270,000	
Ending Inventory (at Cost)	191,836	
Cost of Goods Sold		78,164
Gross Margin		$66,836
Less: Operating Expenses		
Salaries	$ 30,000	
Utilities	1,000	
Rent	19,000	
Depreciation (Fixtures + Equipment)	2,200	
Total Operating Expenses		52,200
Net Profit Before Taxes		$14,636

is an average. Now that ending inventory at cost has been determined, the retailer can determine gross margin, as well as net profit before taxes if operating expenses are known. We will discuss expenses in more detail later. In the Whitener's example, let's use $12,000 for salaries, $1,000 for utilities, $9,000 for rent, and $2,200 for depreciation. This is shown in Exhibit 8.11.

The retail method has several advantages over the cost method of inventory valuation. Among these advantages are the following:

1. Accounting statements can be drawn up at any time. Inventories need not be taken for preparation of these statements.

2. Physical inventories using retail prices are less subject to error and can be completed in a shorter amount of time.

3. The retail method provides an automatic, conservative valuation of ending inventory as well as inventory levels throughout the season. This is especially useful in cases where the retailer is forced to submit insurance claims for damaged or lost merchandise.

A major complaint against the retail method is that it is a "method of averages." This refers to the fact that closing inventory is valued at the average relationship between cost and retail (the cost complement), and that large retailers offer many different classifications and lines with different relationships. This disadvantage can be overcome by computing cost complements for individual lines or departments.

Another limitation is the heavy burden placed on bookkeeping activities. The true ending book inventory value can be correctly calculated only if there are no errors in recording beginning inventory, purchases, freight-in, markups, markdowns, discounts, returns, transfers between stores, and sales. As noted earlier, many of the retailers' original shortages have later been determined to be bookkeeping errors. Most retailers today use the retail method of inventory valuation, which was created in the early 1900s.

Inventory Pricing Systems

Two methods of pricing inventory are FIFO and LIFO. The FIFO (first in, first out) method assumes that the oldest merchandise is sold before the more recently purchased merchandise. Therefore, merchandise on the shelf will reflect the most current replacement price. During inflationary periods this method allows "inventory profits" (caused by selling the less expensive inventory earlier rather than the more expensive newer inventory) to be included as income.

The LIFO (last in, first out) method is designed to cushion the impact of inflationary pressures by matching current costs against current revenues. Cost of goods sold are based on the costs of the most recently purchased inventory, whereas the older inventory is regarded as the unsold inventory. The LIFO method results during inflationary periods in the application of a higher unit cost to the merchandise sold and a lower unit cost to inventory still unsold. In times of rapid inflation most retailers use the LIFO method, resulting in lower profits on the income statement, but also lower income taxes. Most retailers also prefer to use LIFO for planning purposes, because it accurately reflects replacement costs. In addition, the Internal Revenue Service only permits a retailer to change its method of accounting once.

Let's study an example of the effect of the LIFO and FIFO methods of inventory valuation on the firm's financial performance. Suppose you began the year with a total inventory of 15 fax machines, which you purchased on the last day of the preceding year for $300 each. Thus, if the fax machines were the only merchandise you had in stock, your beginning inventory was $4,500 (15 × $300). Suppose also that during the year you sold 12 fax machines for $700 each for total sales of $8,400, that in June you purchased 8 new fax machines (same make and model as your old ones) at $325, and that in November you bought 4 more at $350. Thus, your purchases were $2,600 in June and $1,400 in November for a total of $4,000, and you would still have 15 fax machines in stock at year end. Under the LIFO inventory approach, your ending inventory would be the same as it was at the beginning of the year ($4,500), because we would assume that the 12 fax machines sold were the 12 purchased during the year. However, using the FIFO approach, you would assume that you sold 12 of the original $300 fax machines and had 3 left. These 3 fax machines, along with June's and November's purchases, result in an ending inventory of $4,900 [(3 × $300) + (4 × $350)]. Now let's see how these approaches can affect your gross margins.

	LIFO	FIFO
Net sales	$8,400	$8,400
Less: Cost of goods sold		
Beginning inventory	$4,500	$4,500
Purchases	4,000	4,000
Goods available	$8,500	$8,500
Ending inventory	4,500	4,900
Cost of goods sold	4,000	3,600
Gross margin	$4,400	$4,800

FIFO
stands for first in, first out and values inventory based on the assumption that the oldest merchandise is sold before the more recently purchased merchandise.

LIFO
stands for last in, first out and values inventory based on the assumption that the most recently purchased merchandise is sold first and the oldest merchandise is sold last.

Managerial Question: Retailers are given a choice as to whether to use the LIFO or FIFO method. Given such a choice, would it make a difference in the selection of a method if the retailer were privately owned versus being a publicly traded company?

Student Study Guide

Summary

LO•1 **Why is a merchandise budget so important in retail planning and how is a merchandise budget prepared?**

The purpose of this chapter has been to introduce you to the major financial statements and their importance in retail planning. We began our discussion with the six-month merchandise budget. This statement projects sales, when and how much new merchandise should be ordered, what markup is to be taken, what reductions are to be planned, and the target or planned gross margin for the season. The establishment of such a budget has several advantages for the retailer:

1. The six-month budget controls the amount of inventory and forces management to control markups and reductions.
2. The budget helps to determine how much merchandise should be purchased so that inventory requirements can be met.
3. The budget can be compared with actual or final results to determine the performance of the firm.

We concluded our discussion of the six-month merchandise budget by showing how each of the figures are determined. We illustrated how to estimate sales, inventory levels, reductions, purchases, and gross margin.

LO•2 **What are the differences among, and the uses of, these three accounting statements: income statement, balance sheet, and statement of cash flow?**

The second section of this chapter explained how the retailer uses three important accounting statements: the income statement, the balance sheet, and the statement of cash flow. The income statement gives the retailer a summary of the income and expenses incurred over a given time period. A balance sheet shows the financial condition of the retailer at a particular point in time. The statement of cash flow lists in detail the source and types of all revenue and expenditures for a given time period.

LO•3 **How does a retailer value its inventory?**

The final section of this chapter described two decisions a retailer must make with regards to inventory record keeping: the accounting system (cost or retail) and whether to use the LIFO or FIFO pricing method.

The cost system is the simplest, but the retail system is the most widely used because of these advantages:

1. Accounting statements can be drawn up at any time.
2. Physical inventories using retail prices are less subject to error and can be completed in a shorter amount of time.
3. The retail method provides an automatic, conservative valuation of ending inventory as well as inventory levels throughout the season.

The FIFO method assumes that the oldest merchandise is sold before the more recently purchased merchandise, making merchandise on the shelf more accurately reflect the replacement price. During inflationary periods this method allows "inventory profits" to be included as income. The LIFO method is designed to cushion the impact of inflationary pressures by matching current costs against current revenues. Cost of goods sold are based on the costs of the most recently purchased inventory, whereas the older inventory is regarded as the unsold inventory. In times of rapid inflation most retailers use the LIFO method, resulting in lower profits on the income statement, but also lower income taxes. Most retailers also prefer to use LIFO for planning purposes, because it accurately reflects replacement costs.

Terms to Remember

merchandising
merchandise budget
stock-to-sales ratio
income statement
gross sales
returns and allowances
net sales
cost of goods sold
gross margin
operating expenses
operating profit
other income or expenses
net profit
asset
current assets
accounts and/or notes receivable

prepaid expenses
retail inventories
noncurrent assets
goodwill
total assets
liability
current liabilities
accounts payable
long-term liabilities
total liabilities
net worth (or owner's equity)
cost method
retail method
FIFO
LIFO

Review and Discussion Questions

LO•1 Why is a merchandise budget so important in retail planning and how is a merchandise budget prepared?

1. What are the components of a merchandise budget?
2. What rules should be used in developing a merchandise budget?
3. It costs money to carry inventory, yet retailers must carry an amount of inventory in excess of planned sales for an upcoming period. Why?
4. What is a stock-to-sales ratio?
5. Why should a retailer be allowed to change its merchandise budget after the start of a season? If changes can be made, what would cause such changes?
6. A retailer, who last year had sales of $120,000, plans for an inflation rate of 5 percent and a 4 percent increase in market share. What should planned sales for this year be?
7. The number of transactions is expected to decline 2 percent, but because of inflation, average sales will be increased by 4 percent. If sales last year were $100,000 what will they be this year?

LO•2 What are the differences among, and the uses of, these three accounting statements: income statement, balance sheet, and statement of cash flow?

8. In what ways are the balance sheet and the income statement different? How do retailers use these two financial statements?

9. What is the difference between a statement of cash flow and an income statement?

10. You are working as a loan officer at a local bank. Earlier today, a former high school classmate came to see you about a loan for the family's retail business. After looking over the store's financial statements you notice that the store is posting a strong net income growth but has had a negative cash flow for the past two years. Should this concern you?

11. The Toy Shoppe is trying to determine its net profit before taxes. Use the following data to find The Toy Shoppe's net profit:

Rent	$ 25,000	Salaries	$ 60,000
Purchases	$150,000	Sales	$420,000
Ending inventory	$120,000	Utilities	$ 40,000
Beginning inventory	$110,000		

12. A hardware store with sales for the year of $200,000 and other income of $23,000 has operating expenses of $40,000. Its cost of goods sold is $95,000. What is its gross margin, its operating profit, and its net profit in dollars?

LO•3   How does a retailer value its inventory?

13. List the advantages and disadvantages the retail method of inventory valuation has over the cost method.

14. Define FIFO and LIFO and the reasons for using one or the other.

15. Why is it difficult to determine the exact value of inventory when preparing financial statements?

Sample Test Questions

LO•1   Which one of the following factors is not found on a six-month merchandise budget?

a. planned gross margin
b. current liabilities
c. planned sales percentage
d. planned BOM stock
e. planned purchases at retail

LO•2   The _____ provides the retailer with a picture of the organization's profit and loss situation.

a. expense report
b. index of inventory valuation
c. statement of cash flow
d. income statement
e. statement of gross margin

LO•3   The total cost valuation of a retailer's inventory is $120,000, whereas the total retail valuation of sales was $200,000. Approximately how much of every retail sales dollar is made up of merchandise cost?

a. 12 cents
b. 40 cents
c. 60 cents
d. $1.20
e. $1.50

Applications

Writing and Speaking Exercise

Dressing Up the Balance Sheet   Retailers, especially small retailers, learned a long time ago that lenders judge the worth and creditability of a business by the firm's financial statements. Thus, many retailers make their statements look as good as possible. Retailers engage in a number of questionable activities to window-dress their books.

First, because ratio analysis is probably the most common way lenders analyze a balance sheet, retailers try to improve their ratios in a number of ways. Some attempt to improve the current ratio (current assets divided by current liabilities) by paying off current debt before the review. For example, suppose a retailer has $20,000 in cash, $30,000 in other current assets, and $25,000 in current liabilities, for a current ratio of 2:1. If $12,500 of the cash is used to reduce debt, however, the ratio improves significantly to 3:1. The same thing occurs when a retailer exchanges long-term debt for short-term debt. Another method is to have the retailer borrow against receivables from a bank or a finance company. Retailers normally issue a payment to the lender for any collection on these receivables. As a result, on the day the retailer collects from a customer, the retailer's bank balance is impressive. The next day, however, it is anemic again.

Another method troubled retailers use to improve their balance sheet is to have the lending institution agree to a slower repayment schedule, enabling the retailer to build up its cash balance.

As a retail consultant you have been asked to address these tactics at a meeting of the local retail merchants association. Before developing your presentation, you must decide if these methods are legal? Also, are they ethical?

Retail Project   Go to the library and look at the most recent annual reports for four or five of the Top 25 Retailers listed in on the inside cover of this book. (If you are using the Internet, go to the retailer's home page or to http://finance.yahoo.com. Next enter the retailer's name or stock symbol. Then click "profile.") Using the financial data from these reports, compare the net cash flow to the net income for each of the retailers you chose and explain the reason for the differences.

Case   Dolly's Place

Last year, after years of teaching retailing/merchandising at the local university, Dolly Loyd decided to retire and return to her first love—running an intimate apparel store. Because she used to run such a department for a major retail chain before teaching, she kept up with the current trends in the industry. Loyd gained the support of an ex-high school classmate who after making millions with an Internet startup financed her new endeavor.

Today Loyd is beginning to make plans for the upcoming fall season. Loyd anticipates planned sales of $300,000 for the fall season based on a planned initial markup of 50 percent. Within the season, planned monthly sales are projected to be as follows: 15 percent in August and September, 10 percent in October, 20 percent in November, 30 percent in December, and 10 percent in January. To ensure a profitable season, trade association records were consulted. The records indicated: (1) the stock-to-sales ratios need to be 3.5 for August, 3.0 for September, 4.0 for October, 3.0 for November, 2.5 for December, and 4.0 for January; (2) reductions can be planned at 10 percent for the first four months, 20 percent for December and 30 percent for January; and (3) with Valentine's Day approaching, an inventory of $180,000 will be necessary to begin the spring season. Complete a six-month merchandise budget for Dolly Loyd.

Dolly's Place Six-Month Merchandise Budget	Date: May 15 Season: Fall						
Fall/Winter	**Aug**	**Sept**	**Oct**	**Nov**	**Dec**	**Jan**	**Seasonal Total**
1. Planned BOM[a] Stock							
2. Planned Sales							
3. Planned Retail Reductions							
4. Planned EOM[b] Stock							
5. Planned Purchases @ Retail							
6. Planned Purchases @ Cost							
7. Planned Initial Markup							
8. Planned Gross Margin							
9. Planned BOM Stock/Sales Ratio	3.5x	3.0x	4.0x	3.0x	2.5x	4.0x	—
10. Planned Sales Percentage	15%	15%	10%	20%	30%	10%	100%
11. Planned Retail Reduction	10%	10%	10%	10%	20%	30%	15%

Planned total sales for the period $300,000

Planned total retail reduction

Percentage for the period

Planned initial markup percentage

For the period   50%

Planned BOM Stock for *February* $180,000

Note: All dollar signs have been deleted from the merchandise budget grid.

[a]BOM refers to beginning of the month

[b]EOM refers to end of the month

Planning Your Own Small Business You are unsure of what level of sales to forecast for your new drugstore, which you plan to open on New Year's Day. Consequently, you have decided to make some assumptions. You believe that it is reasonable to assume that your trade area will encompass about 25 square miles. The city planning department has told you that within this area the population density is 2,857 people per square mile. You conservatively estimate that 20 percent of these individuals will visit your store an average of four times annually and that 85 percent will purchase something on a typical visit. You expect them to spend an average of $25 per visit to your store. Information you have received from industry sources suggest that drugstores do more business in the fall and winter than in the spring and summer. In fact, you expect sales during each of the months of November, December, January, and February to be 10 percent of your annual volume. The remaining eight months will share equally the 60 percent of remaining sales. You believe that for your business to be profitable you need to have a beginning of month inventory to sales ratio of 3.0 for October through November and 2.5 for the remaining months. You want to plan your beginning of month inventory for each of the next 12 months. You also want to begin the first month of your second year of business with $250,000 in inventory at retail prices.

Endnotes

1. Service Corporation press release dated February 23, 1999.
2. "Corporate America Loves The Weather," *U.S. News & World Report*, April 13, 1998: 8—49.
3. IRS Revenue Procedure 97-37.
4. Based on information supplied by Robert Kahn.

Merchandise Buying and Handling

Overview

In this chapter, we explain the planning that retailers must do regarding their merchandise selection. We also analyze how a retailer controls merchandise to be inventoried. The selection of, and negotiations with, vendors is also discussed, as well as the security measures used when handling the merchandise.

Learning Objectives

After reading this chapter, you should be able to

1. explain the differences between the four methods of dollar merchandise planning used to determine the proper inventory stock levels needed to begin a merchandise selling period

2. explain how retailers use dollar merchandise control and describe how open-to-buy is used in the retail buying process

3. describe how a retailer uses unit stock planning and model stock plans in determining the makeup of a merchandise mix

4. describe how a retailer selects proper merchandise sources

5. describe what is involved in the vendor-buyer negotiation process and what terms of the contract can be negotiated

6. discuss the various methods of controlling loss through shrinkage, vendor collusion, and theft

Dollar Merchandise Planning

LO • 1

What is the difference between the four methods of dollar merchandise planning used to determine the proper inventory stock levels needed to begin a merchandise selling period?

There is an old retailing adage that "goods well bought are half sold." In this chapter, we look at merchandise management—that is, the merchandise buying and handling process and its effect on a store's performance.

Merchandise management is the analysis, planning, acquisition, handling, and control of the merchandise investments of a retail operation. *Analysis* is used in our definition because retailers must be able to correctly identify their customers before they can determine the needs and wants of the consumer in order to buy the correct merchandise. *Planning* occurs because merchandise must be purchased six to twelve months in advance of the selling season. The term *acquisition* is used because, with the exception of service retailers, merchandise needs to be bought from others, either distributors or manufacturers. In addition, all retailers, even those selling only services, must acquire the equipment and fixtures needed to complete a transaction. Proper *handling* assures that the merchandise is where it is needed and in the proper shape to be sold. *Control* of the large dollar investments in inventory is important to ensure an adequate financial return on the retailer's merchandise investment.

Merchandise management
is the analysis, planning, acquisition, handling, and control of the merchandise investments of a retail operation.

In fact, many retailing experts agree that it was the failure to properly manage merchandise that caused The Gap, one of the most successful retail operations for over a decade, to recently stumble. First, the chain failed to change its merchandise as the consumer changed. Second, the merchandise selections in the chain's three divisions, Gap, Old Navy, and Banana Republic, actually confused customers and resulted in an internal cannibalization of customers.

Whatever career path you decide to take in retailing, you cannot avoid some contact with the firm's merchandising activities. This is because merchandising is the day-to-day business of all retailers. As inventory is sold, new stock needs to be purchased, displayed, and sold once again. Clearly then, as we explained in Chapter 8, merchandising, though only a subfunction of retailing, is its heartbeat. Therefore, retailers that do a superior job at managing their inventory investment will be the most successful. If a retailer's inventory continues to build up, then the retailer either has too much money tied up in inventory or is not making the sales it was expecting and is heading for trouble. Likewise, a retailer who is frequently out of stock will quickly lose customers. Now you know why the business trade press and retailers take such an interest in retail inventory levels as retailers approach different seasons. For example, Christmas, which traditionally accounts for 25 to 30 percent of annual sales, can be ruined by the lack of inventory to support sales. On the other hand, if the inventory is not sold, the costs involved in carrying excess inventory can force the retailer into taking extra markdowns, besides having to pay interest on the inventory investment.

Because inventory is the largest investment that retailers make, high-profit retailers use the gross margin return on inventory model when analyzing the performance of their inventory. **Gross margin return on inventory** (GMROI) incorporates into a single measure both inventory turnover and profit. It can be computed as follows:

(Gross margin/Net sales) $\times$ (Net sales/Average inventory at cost)
$$= \text{(Gross margin/Average inventory at cost)}$$

Here the gross margin percentage (gross margin/net sales) is multiplied by net sales/dollars invested in inventory to get the retailer's gross margin dollars generated for each dollar invested in inventory. Net sales is typically computed on an annual or 12 month basis. (Note, sales/dollars invested in inventory is not the same as inventory turnover. Inventory turnover measures sales/inventory at retail. In the GMROI equation, we are using inventory at cost to reflect our investment in carrying the merchandise.) Thus, if a particular item has a gross margin of 45 percent and sales per dollar of inventory investment of 4.0, its GMROI would be $1.80 ($.45 $\times$ 4). That is, for each dollar invested in inventory, on average the retailer obtains $1.80 in gross margin annually. Gross margin dollars are used to first pay the store's operating expenses (both fixed and variable) with the remainder being the retailer's profit.

> **Gross margin return on inventory**
> is gross margin divided by average inventory at cost; alternatively it is the gross margin percent multiplied by (net sales divided by average inventory investment).

Retailers that use the GMROI model when planning inventory and evaluating inventory decisions will be more profitable.

Dollars & Sense

Before we continue our discussion of merchandise management, you may want to review earlier chapters. Because all retailing activities are aimed at serving the customer's needs and wants at a profit, you may want to review Chapter 3 on the customer. Likewise, because merchandise management is concerned with the acquisition of inventory from other channel members, you may also want to review Chapter 5 on the behavior of the different channel members.

As we pointed out in Chapter 8, successful merchandise management revolves around planning and control. Because it takes time to buy merchandise, have it delivered, record the delivery in the company records, and properly display the merchandise, it becomes essential to plan. Buyers need to decide today what their stock requirements will be weeks, months, a merchandising season, or even a year in advance.

As planning occurs, then it is only logical that control be exercised over the merchandise dollars or units that the retailer plans on purchasing. A good control system is vital. After all, if the retailer carries too much inventory, the costs of carrying that inventory might outweigh the gross margin to be made on the sale, especially if the retailer is forced to reduce the selling price. After concluding our discussion on the dollar amount of inventory needed for stock requirements, the remainder of this chapter looks at the other merchandising decisions facing the retailer: the dollar amount available to be spent, the unit or type of goods to be purchased, choosing and evaluating merchandise sources, handling vendor negotiations, handling the merchandise in the store, and evaluating merchandise performance.

Service Retailing

Planning the Merchandise Mix for a Water Park

No matter where you live in the world, one of the ultimate summertime favorites is water. As the temperature rises, young and old try to beat the heat by finding their way to water. Whereas going to beaches and pools have been favorite pastimes, one type of retailer that has gained considerable popularity is the water park. With raging raft rides, heralding water slides, and lazy rivers to float in, it is no wonder that these service retailers have become a central element in summertime fun. However, have you ever stopped to think of the merchandise mix that these water parks offer?

For instance, your typical water park caters to a variety of target markets, including small children and their parents, teenagers, as well as young adults. Thus, a water park retailer must develop an optimal merchandise mix of attractions, rides, and facilities to satisfy a diverse clientele.

First let's look at the attractions and rides. A number of typical rides come to mind when one thinks of a water park. For instance, most water parks have a number of different types of water slides. There are enclosed slides (32 inches wide), unenclosed slides (38 or 42 inches), slides that can also carry inner tubes (54-inch open and 54- and 56-inch enclosed), slides that can carry multiperson inner tubes (84 inches), and family raft slides (120 inches). There are also speed slides and multidrop slides, as well as children's flat bottom slides and children's flumes and water coasters. Next, most parks have a wave pool; most probably have a children's water play area, as well as some sort of slowly flowing river that people can float on in inner tubes. Further, a number of changing areas, restrooms, concession stands or restaurants, as well as merchandise facilities are necessary. To make a successful water park, how many of each of these attractions, rides, and facilities should there be?

Just like any other retailer, successful water parks operate based on careful demand forecasting. In this case both the demand for the park (by each market segment matched to attraction type) must be calculated and estimates of capacity for each ride must be assessed to determine the optimal mix. For example, let's start with a simple estimate of 40,000 people a day. Of these customers, 50 percent will be teenagers and young adults and 50 percent will be families. That means that during a day, 20,000 teenagers and young adults and 20,000 people in family groups will be at the park. Well, not exactly; demand at a water park is not uniform. Rather, let's say that 60 percent of customers arrive between 9 and 11 a.m., 20 percent arrive between 11 a.m. and 1 p.m. and 20 percent arrive after 1 p.m. The average stay is slightly longer than 6 hours. As such, first estimate the average number of people who are at the park at any one time in each segment. Remember, having rides too full results in long lines and dissatisfied customers, whereas having too many rides leads to overcapacity and wasted resources.

Given the estimates on demand for each ride, the retailer must next determine the capacity of each ride as well as the supportive facilities. For example, the 54-inch enclosed slide, which is popular with teenagers and young adults, will accommodate approximately 600 people per hour, whereas the enclosed 32-inch slide, often used more by children, will accommodate approximately 360 riders per hour. The speed slides, as well as the 38-inch open slides, used mostly by teenagers and adults, will accommodate 360 people per hour. In terms of facilities, what capability should the changing rooms and restrooms be designed to accommodate? As you can see, determining the merchandise mix for a service retailer such as a water park is a highly complex issue. However, with careful planning success is highly likely.

Buyers, working with upper management, are responsible for the dollar planning of merchandise requirements. In the previous chapter, we described the various factors that must be considered in making the sales forecast, the first step in determining inventory needs. Once planned sales for the period in question have been projected, buyers are then able to use any one of four different methods for planning dollars invested in merchandise: basic stock, percentage variation, weeks' supply, and the stock-to-sales ratio method.

Although our discussion in this chapter focuses on retailers who sell tangible goods, the same basic principles may be applied to service retailers, with one exception. Whereas tangible products are first produced, then sold, and then consumed, services are first sold, then produced and consumed simultaneously. Thus service retailers are prevented from stockpiling their inventories in anticipation of future demand. Given the inability to stockpile inventories, service retailers must pay special attention to forecasting demand. In addition, as shown in the Service Retailing box, these retailers must adjust their retailing mix and make preparations, especially regarding personnel, to satisfy their customers' wants.

Basic Stock Method

The **basic stock method** (**BSM**) is used when retailers believe that it is necessary to have a given level of inventory available at all times. It requires that the retailer always has a base level of inventory investment regardless of the predicted sales volume. In addition to the base stock level, there will be a variable amount of inventory that will increase or decrease at the beginning of each sales period (one month in the case of our merchandise budget) in the same dollar amount as the period's sales are expected to increase or decrease. The BSM can be calculated as follows:

Average monthly sales for the season
    = Total planned sales for the season/Number of months in the season

Average stock for the season
 = Total planned sales for the season/Estimated inventory turnover rate for the season

Basic stock = Average stock for the season − Average monthly sales for the season

Beginning-of-month (BOM) stock at retail = Basic stock + Planned monthly sales

Basic stock method (BSM) is a technique for planning dollar inventory investments and allows for a base stock level plus a variable amount of inventory that will increase or decrease at the beginning of each sales period in the same dollar amount as the period's expected sales.

To illustrate the use of the basic stock method, let's look at the planned sales for Department 353 of Two-Seasons Department Store, shown in Exhibit 8.2. Assume that the inventory turnover rate for the six months, or the number of times the average inventory is sold, for the season is 2.0.

Average monthly sales for the season	= Total planned sales/Number of months
	= \$500,000/6 = \$83,333
Average stock for the season	= Total planned sales/Inventory turnover
	= \$500,000/2 = \$250,000
Basic stock	= Average stock − Average monthly sale
	= \$250,000 − \$83,333 = \$166,667
BOM @ retail (February)	= Basic stock + Planned monthly sales
	= \$166,667 + \$75,000 = \$241,667
BOM @ retail (March)	= \$166,667 + \$75,000 = \$241,667
BOM @ retail (April)	= \$166,667 + \$100,000 = \$266,667
BOM @ retail (May)	= \$166,667 + \$50,000 = \$216,667
BOM @ retail (June)	= \$166,667 + \$125,000 = \$291,667
BOM @ retail (July)	= \$166,667 + \$75,000 = \$241,667

It is obvious that $166,667 of basic stock is added to each month's planned sales to arrive at the BOM stock. In those cases where actual sales either exceed or fall short of planned sales for the month, the retailer can easily adjust the amount of overage or shortfall to bring the next month's BOM stock back in line by buying more or less stock. Therefore, the basic stock method works best when a retailer has a low turnover rate (that is, less than 6 times a year) or if sales are erratic.

Percentage Variation Method

Percentage variation method (PVM)
is a technique for planning dollar inventory investments that assumes that the percentage fluctuations in monthly stock from average stock should be half as great as the percentage fluctuations in monthly sales from average sales.

A second commonly used method for determining planned stock levels is the **percentage variation method (PVM).** This method is used when the retailer has a high yearly turnover rate (that is, 6 or more times a year). The percentage variation method assumes that the percentage fluctuations in monthly stock from average stock should be half as great as the percentage fluctuations in monthly sales from average sales.

BOM stock = Average stock for season $\times \frac{1}{2}$
$$\times\ [1 + (\text{Planned sales for the month/Average monthly sales})]$$

Because the PVM utilizes the same components as the BSM, we can use the data from the previous example.

$$\text{BOM (February)} = \$250,000 \times \tfrac{1}{2}[1 + (\$75,000/\$83,333)] = \$237,500$$
$$\text{BOM (March)} = \$250,000 \times \tfrac{1}{2}[1 + (\$75,000/\$83,333)] = \$237,500$$
$$\text{BOM (April)} = \$250,000 \times \tfrac{1}{2}[1 + (\$100,000/\$83,333)] = \$275,000$$
$$\text{BOM (May)} = \$250,000 \times \tfrac{1}{2}[1 + (\$50,000/\$83,333)] = \$200,000$$
$$\text{BOM (June)} = \$250,000 \times \tfrac{1}{2}[1 + (\$125,000/\$83,333)] = \$312,500$$
$$\text{BOM (July)} = \$250,000 \times \tfrac{1}{2}[1 + (\$75,000/\$83,333)] = \$237,500$$

Weeks' Supply Method

Weeks' supply method (WSM)
is a technique for planning dollar inventory investments that states that the inventory level should be set equal to a predetermined number of weeks' supply, which is directly related to the desired rate of stock turnover.

A third method for planning inventory levels is the **weeks' supply method (WSM).** Generally, the WSM formula is used by retailers such as grocers in which inventories are planned on a weekly, not monthly, basis and where sales do not fluctuate substantially. It states that the inventory level should be set equal to a predetermined number of weeks' supply. The predetermined number of weeks' supply is directly related to the stock turnover rate desired. In the WSM, stock level in dollars varies proportionally with forecast sales. Thus, if forecast sales triple, then inventory in dollars will also triple.

To illustrate the WSM, let's return to our earlier problem and use the following formulas:

Number of weeks to be stocked
  = Number of weeks in the period/Stock turnover rate for the period
Average weekly sales
  = Estimated total sales for the period/Number of weeks in the period
BOM stock   = Average weekly sales $\times$ Number of weeks to be stocked

Thus,

Number of weeks to be stocked $= 26/2 = 13$

Average weekly sales $\quad = \$500,000/26 = \$19,231$

BOM stock $\quad\quad\quad\quad = \$19,231 \times 13 = \$250,000$

Having determined the number of weeks' supply to be stocked (13 weeks) and the average weekly sales (\$19,231), stock levels can be replenished on a frequent or regular basis to guard against stockouts.

Stock-to-Sales Method

The final method for planning inventory levels, and the one we used in Chapter 8, is the **stock-to-sales method (SSM).** This method is quite easy to use but requires the retailer to have a beginning-of-the-month stock-to-sales ratio. This ratio tells the retailer how much inventory is needed at the beginning of the month to support that month's estimated sales. A ratio of 2.5, for example, would tell retailers that they should have two and one-half ($2\frac{1}{2}$) times that month's expected sales on hand in inventory at the beginning of the month.

Stock-to-sales ratios can be obtained from internal or external sources. Internally, the statistics can be obtained if the retailer has designed a good accounting system and has properly stored historical data so that they can be readily retrieved. Externally, the retailer can often rely on retail trade associations, such as the Menswear Retailers Association, or national groups, such as the National Retail Federation (NRF) in the United States, the Australian Retailers Association, the Retail Merchants Association of New Zealand, the German Retail Association, the Japan Retail Association, or the Hong Kong Retail Management Association. These and other trade associations collect stock-to-sales ratios from participating merchants and then compile, tabulate, and report them in special management reports or trade publications.

However, these ratios should only be used as a guide to how much inventory to have on hand at the beginning of each month. Successful chain store retailers have long known that even stores located nearby each other require not only different merchandise mixes, but also different inventory levels per sales dollars. This is a reflection of the store's trading area, layout, and competition. However, inventory turnover remains a key factor in a retailer's financial performance. Planned average beginning of the month stock-to-sales goals can be easily calculated using turnover goals. If you divide the number of months in the season by the desired inventory turnover rate, an average BOM stock-to-sales ratio for the season can be computed. For example, if you desired an inventory turnover rate of 2.0 (4.0 annually) for the upcoming six-month season, your average BOM stock-to-sales ratio would be 3.0 ($6/2.0 = 3.0$).

Stock-to-sales method (SSM) is a technique for planning dollar inventory investments where the amount of inventory planned for the beginning of the month is a ratio (obtained from trade associations or the retailer's historical records) of stock-to-sales.

Retailers who realize that the various dollar merchandise plans are not hard and fast rules to be followed at all times for all stores will have higher profits.

LO • 2

How does a retailer use dollar merchandise control and open-to-buy techniques in the retail buying process?

Open-to-buy

refers to the dollar amount that a buyer can currently spend on merchandise without exceeding the planned dollar stocks.

Dollar Merchandise Control

Once the buyer has planned the dollar amount of merchandise to have on hand at the beginning of each month (or season), it becomes essential that the buyer does not make commitments for merchandise that would exceed the dollar plan. In short, the dollars planned for merchandise need to be controlled. This control is accomplished through a strategy called the open-to-buy approach. **Open-to-buy (OTB)** represents the dollar amount that a buyer can currently spend on merchandise without exceeding the planned amount of merchandise dollar stocks discussed previously. When planning for any given month (or season), the buyer will not necessarily be able to purchase a dollar amount equal to the planned dollar stocks for that month (or season). This is because there may be some inventory already on order but not yet delivered. To illustrate this point more succinctly, let's compute the OTB for an upcoming month.

Assume that at the beginning of February the buyer for Department 353 of the Two-Seasons Department Store (Exhibit 8.2) had already ordered, but had not yet received, $15,000 worth of merchandise at retail. Keeping planned EOM stock at $300,000 and planned reductions for February at 10 percent of planned sales, the buyer's planned purchases for February will remain $157,500. However, the open-to-buy totals for the month will only be $142,500 at retail because we are now accounting for that $15,000 of merchandise already ordered but not yet received. The computations would look like this:

1. Planned sales for February	+ 75,000
2. Plus planned reductions for February	+ 7,500
3. Plus end-of-month (EOM) planned retail stock	+$300,000
4. Minus beginning-of-month (BOM) stock	−225,000
5. Equals planned purchases at retail	$157,500
6. Minus commitments at retail for current delivery	−15,000
7. Equals open-to-buy results	$142,500

The OTB figure should not be set in stone because it can be exceeded. Consumer needs are the dominant consideration. If sales exceed planned sales, additional quantities should be ordered above those scheduled for purchase according to the merchandise budget. This should not, however, be a common occurrence. If this is the case, the sales planning process is wrong. Either the buyers are too conservative in estimating sales or they are buying the wrong merchandise. In any case, the buyer, along with management, should always determine the causes of OTB adjustments. Some common buying errors include the following:

1. Buying merchandise that is either priced too high or too low for the store's target market
2. Buying the wrong type of merchandise (i.e., too many tops and no skirts) or buying too much "trendy fashion" merchandise
3. Having too much or too little basic stock on hand
4. Buying from too many vendors
5. Failing to identify the season's hot items early enough in the season

6. Failing to let the vendor assist the buyer by adding new items or new colors to the mix (all too often, the original order is merely repeated, resulting in a limited selection)

Merchandise planning is a dynamic process subject to many changes. Consider the implications that could arise in planning your stock levels as a result of (1) sales for the previous month being lower or higher than planned, (2) reductions being either higher or lower than planned, and (3) shipments of merchandise being delayed in transit. Understanding the consequences of each of these situations can show you the interrelationship of merchandising activities with the merchandise budget. Such occurrences make retailing a challenging and exciting career choice. The appendix to this chapter examines in detail the unique challenges facing a fashion goods buyer.

Unit Stock Planning

LO • 3

How does a retailer use unit stock planning and model stock plans in determining the makeup of a merchandise mix?

The dollar merchandise plan is only the starting point in merchandise management. Once the retailer has decided how many dollars can be invested in inventory, the dollar plan needs to be converted into a unit plan. After all, on the sales floor, items, not dollars, are sold. The retailer must then determine which assortment of items will constitute the merchandise mix.

Optimal Merchandise Mix

Exhibit 9.1 shows the three dimensions of the optimal mix: variety, breadth, and depth. Each of these dimensions needs to be defined; however, we need first to define merchandise line or category. A **merchandise line** consists of a group of products that are closely related because they are intended for the same end use (all televisions), are sold to the same customer group (junior miss clothing), or fall within a given price range (budget women's wear). Today, for example, over 90 percent of grocery retailers use the term **category management** to refer to their management of categories, or lines, as a strategic business unit.[1] That is, a supermarket buyer using category management, would no longer be concerned with GMROI for just the Tide or Cheer detergent. Today, that buyer would be concerned with the GMROI for the entire detergent line or category. For that buyer, the line or category is his or her strategic business unit.

Variety   The **variety** of the merchandise mix refers to the number of different lines the retailer stocks in the store. For example, department stores have a large variety of merchandise lines. Some have more than 100 departments, carrying such lines as menswear, women's wear, children's clothing, infant's wear, toys, sporting goods, appliances, cosmetics, and household goods. On the other hand, Office Depot, a specialty chain, carries only one basic merchandise line: office supplies. In the middle of these two would be a retailer like Sportsmart, which sells a complete range of sporting goods.

Breadth   **Breadth,** also called assortment, refers to the number of merchandise brands that are found in the merchandise line. For example, a supermarket will have a large amount of breadth, or assortment, in the number of different brands of mustard that it carries: six or seven national or regional brands, and a private brand. A 7-Eleven

Merchandise line is a group of products that are closely related because they are intended for the same end use (all televisions); are sold to the same customer group (junior miss clothing); or fall within a given price range (budget women's wear).

Category management refers to the management of merchandise categories, or lines, rather than individual products, as a strategic business unit.

Variety refers to the number of different merchandise lines that the retailer stocks in the store.

Breadth (or assortment) also is the number of merchandise brands that are found in a merchandise line.

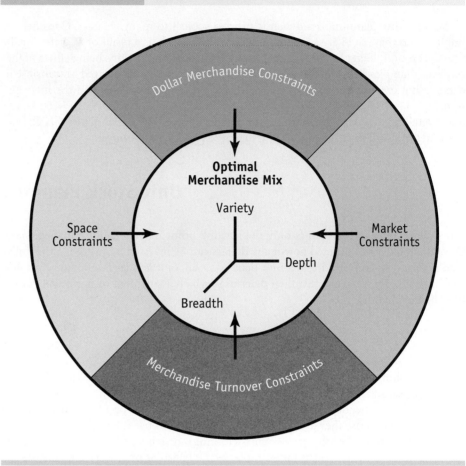

Exhibit 9.1   **Dimensions of and Constraints on Optimal Merchandising Mix**

Dollar Merchandise Constraints

Optimal Merchandise Mix

Variety

Space Constraints

Market Constraints

Depth

Breadth

Merchandise Turnover Constraints

convenience store, however, will offer very little breadth in that it will generally carry only one or two brands in any merchandise line.

Breadth is especially a problem for retailers selling private-label brands. Retailers need to achieve a proper balance between their own private labels and the national brands. However, sometimes a powerful manufacturer may try to tie some of its merchandise lines together. That is, if the retailer carries one product, the retailer must carry the manufacturer's entire product line. But because private-label brands, as noted in Chapter 4, offer retailers a lower cost and a higher gross margin, retailers generally do not want to carry the manufacturer's complete line. A **battle of the brands** occurs when retailers, in determining the breadth of the product assortment, have their own products competing with the manufacturer's products for shelf space and control over display location. One of the consequences of the battle of the brands is that many retailers are now stocking either one or both of the top brands in a product line or category and their own private brand. As a result, many "third tier" brands have been left off the store's shelves.

Battle of the brands occurs when retailers have their own products competing with the manufacturer's products for shelf space and control over display location.

Most supermarkets are able to offer considerable depth in their merchandise mix.

Depth Merchandise depth refers to the average number of stock-keeping units (SKUs) within each brand of the merchandise line. In our preceding example, the supermarket manager must decide on which sizes and types of French's mustard to carry. The convenience store will probably only carry the regular nine-ounce jar of French's. Depth is an acute problem today because all too often retailers are constrained in the number of SKUs they can carry by the following four factors.

Depth
is the average number of stock-keeping units within each brand of the merchandise line.

A convenience store, such as this one in Japan, is not able to offer much depth in its merchandise mix.

Constraining Factors

Research indicates that the merchandise mix can, in addition to satisfying customer wants, actually shape those wants and impact whether and what customers purchase.[2] Exhibit 9.1 details the four constraining factors that may restrict the retailer's design of the optimal merchandise mix. Remember, just as the trading areas for each store in a chain are different, the optimal mix is different for every store. Merchandise mix decisions are a blend of financial plans that consider the retailer's dollar and turnover constraints, combined with the store's space constraints as well as the constraints caused by the actions of the competition.[3]

Dollar Merchandise Constraints   There are seldom enough dollars to emphasize variety, breadth, and depth. If the retailer decides to emphasize variety, it would be unrealistic to expect the retailer also to have a lot of breadth and depth.

For instance, assume for the moment that you are the owner/manager of a local gift store. You have $70,000 to invest in merchandise. If you decide that you want a lot of variety in gifts (jewelry, crystal, candles, games, cards, figurines, ashtrays, clocks, and radios), then you obviously could not have much depth in any single item, such as crystal glassware.

Some retailers try to overcome this dollar constraint by shifting the expense of carrying inventory back on the vendor. When a retailer buys a product on **consignment**, the vendor retains the ownership of the goods, usually establishes the selling price, and is paid only when the goods are sold. Or the retailer might try to get **extra dating,** where the vendor allows the retailer some extra time before paying for the goods. For example, most textbook publishers either sell their books on consignment or give the bookstores an extra 60 days in which to pay. In this way, your campus bookstore orders its books in early July for an early August delivery. The bookstore then sells the books in late August or early September. However, because the books were sold on consignment, or with extra dating, the bookstore does not have to pay the publisher until October.

Space Constraints   The retailer must also deal with space constraints. If the retailer wants to emphasize depth or breadth, space is necessary. If the retailer wants to stress variety, it is also important to have enough empty space to separate the distinct merchandise lines. For example, consider a single counter containing cosmetics, candy, fishing tackle, women's stockings, and toys. This would obviously be an unsightly and unwise arrangement. As more variety is added, empty space becomes necessary to allow the consumer to clearly distinguish among distinct product lines.

Retailers, especially in the grocery business, have been able to turn this space constraint into an advantage by charging the manufacturers "slotting fees," which were discussed in the Ethics section in Chapter 6, to carry their products.

Merchandise Turnover Constraints   As the depth of the merchandise increases, the retailer will be stocking more and more variations of the product to serve smaller and smaller segments. Consequently, inventory turnover will deteriorate and the chances of being out of stock will increase. One does not have to minimize variety, breadth, and depth to maximize turnover, but one must know how various merchandise mixes affect inventory turnover.

Market Constraints   Market constraints should also affect decisions on variety, breadth, and depth of the merchandise mix. The three dimensions have a profound

Consignment
is when the vendor retains the ownership of the goods and usually establishes the selling price; it is paid only when the goods are sold by the retailer.

Extra dating
is when the vendor allows the retailer extra time before payment is due for goods.

The high cost of retail space in some communities severely constrains the retailer's merchandise mix.

effect on how the consumer perceives the store, and consequently on the customers the store will attract. The consumer perceives a specialty store as one with limited variety and breadth of merchandise lines but considerable depth within the lines handled. An individual searching for depth in a limited set of merchandise lines such as formal menswear will thus be attracted to a menswear retailer specializing in formal wear. On the other hand, the consumer perceives the general merchandise retailer such as Target as a store with lots of variety and breadth in terms of merchandise lines, but with more constrained depth. Therefore, someone who needs to make several purchases across several merchandise lines, and who is willing to sacrifice depth of assortment, would be more attracted to the general merchandise retailer.

The constraining factors make it almost impossible for a retailer to emphasize all three dimensions. However, if you are going to lose customers, lose the less profitable ones by properly mixing your merchandise in terms of variety, breadth, and depth within the dollar, space, turnover, and market constraints.

Managerial Question: How can retailers overcome these constraints to provide greater value, especially in comparison to their competition, for the consumer?

Model Stock Plan

Model stock plan
is a unit stock plan that shows the precise items and quantities that should be on hand for each merchandise line.

After you decide the relative emphasis to be placed on the three dimensions of the merchandise mix, you need to decide what merchandise lines and items to stock.[4] Units are planned using a model stock plan. The **model stock plan,** which is always used with fashion items, gives the precise items and quantities that should be on hand for each merchandise line. A separate model stock plan needs to be compiled for each line of merchandise.

Exhibit 9.2 shows a hypothetical menswear retailer attempting to develop a unit plan for men's shirts. It has already conducted a dollar plan and has allocated $35,000 at retail for men's shirts. Because the average retail price of a shirt for the store is $35, 1,000 shirts will be stocked. The model unit plan will reveal how many shirts of each kind the retailer should keep in stock. Although the exhibit only shows the breakdown within one attribute (casual shirts), the same procedure would be followed for all types of shirts.

Identify Attributes   The first thing the menswear retailer should do is attempt to identify what attributes the customer considers in purchasing shirts. Exhibit 9.2 shows that the retailer has identified six attributes: (1) type of shirt (dress, casual, sport, or work), (2) size, (3) sleeve length, (4) collar type, (5) color, and (6) fabric. Are any key attributes left out? What about price? If customers shop for shirts by price, then price should also be a product attribute.

Identify Levels   The second step is to identify the number of levels under each attribute. The retailer in Exhibit 9.2 has selected four types of shirts to stock, four sizes, two sleeve lengths, two collar types, four colors, and two fabrics.

In relation to the first two steps in the construction of a model stock plan, a basic principle of merchandise management can be identified: Stocking requirements grow explosively as more product attributes and expanded levels are offered on each attribute. If the retailer offers four shirt types, four sizes in each type, two sleeve lengths, two collar styles, four colors, and two fabrics, then it will have to stock 512 shirts (4 × 4 × 2 × 2 × 4 × 2), just to stock one unit of each. More important, if the retailer now decides to offer two price points instead of one, the stocking requirements double to 1,024 items. But this example assumes that only 1,000 shirts can be stocked. Obviously, the retailer has a problem if it wants to feature six or seven attributes and several levels on each attribute.

The preceding discussion illustrates the need for a basic trade-off in merchandise management. As more attributes are featured, the probability increases that a product on hand will match the customer's needs and purchasing power. However, there is a cost associated with increasing this probability, the cost of carrying the additional

Exhibit 9.2	Partial Model Unit Plan for Men's Shirts

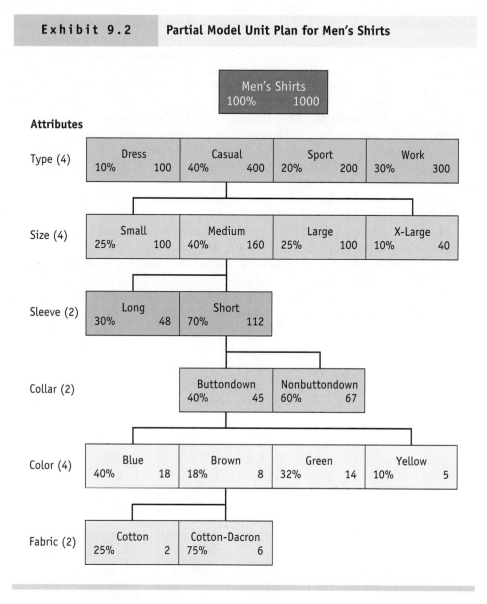

Attributes

Men's Shirts
100%   1000

Type (4)
Dress	Casual	Sport	Work
10% 100	40% 400	20% 200	30% 300

Size (4)
Small	Medium	Large	X-Large
25% 100	40% 160	25% 100	10% 40

Sleeve (2)
Long	Short
30% 48	70% 112

Collar (2)
Buttondown	Nonbuttondown
40% 45	60% 67

Color (4)
Blue	Brown	Green	Yellow
40% 18	18% 8	32% 14	10% 5

Fabric (2)
Cotton	Cotton-Dacron
25% 2	75% 6

inventory. At some point, the carrying cost of the additional inventory required to increase the probability of purchase is greater than the profit obtained from those additional unit sales. Successful retailers know that they will have to allow some customers to walk out of their store empty-handed.

The more profitable retailers realize that between a fifth and a sixth of the average retailer's inventory is either obsolete or not needed by the store's target customers and will work to overcome this problem.

Dollars & Sense

Allocate Dollars or Units   The third step in developing the model stock plan is to allocate the total dollars or units to the respective item categories. There is an optimum allocation if the model unit plan has recommended quantities for each item that are in direct proportion to market demand patterns. If the plan reflects this optimum, then by comparing actual stocks with model stocks one can easily determine if the stocks are out of balance. The more actual stocks mirror the model stock plan, the more the stocks will be in balance; and balanced stocks maximize sales potential. Stocks that are out of balance cause customers to walk out of the store without the item they came to purchase. Worse yet, the customer might purchase a product that is not well suited to his or her needs. Over the long run, this may hurt the retailer's business.

But how can a retailer determine that the recommended quantities for each item are in direct proportion to market demand patterns? The most useful thing to do is to analyze past sales records. Exhibit 9.3 shows the sales experience of our hypothetical menswear retailer in reference to the last 500 shirts sold. This exhibit, derived from past sales records, shows the demand density for different types and sizes of shirts. This simple analysis forms the basis of planning unit stocks in the model plan. Changing the data in Exhibit 9.3 to percentage form, we can see that 10 percent of our sales were for dress shirts, 40 percent for casual shirts, 20 percent for sport shirts,

Exhibit 9.3   **Sales Analysis of Men's Shirts**

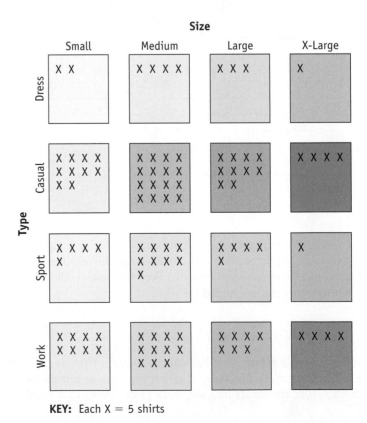

KEY: Each X = 5 shirts

and 30 percent for work shirts. Furthermore, of the casual shirts, 25 percent were small, 40 percent medium, 25 percent large, and 10 percent extra large. The percentage derived from such a sales analysis can then be used in the model stock plan (Exhibit 9.2). Thus, in this example, past sales are used to indicate future demand density. Therefore, of the 1,000 shirts we plan to stock, 100 will be dress shirts, 400 casual shirts, 200 sport shirts, and 300 work shirts. These numbers are obtained simply by multiplying the 1,000 shirts by the percentage obtained in the sales analysis. In the past, 10 percent of the shirts sold were dress shirts, so we will plan to stock 100 dress shirts, which is 10 percent of 1,000. A similar procedure is conducted to determine how many to stock in each size, sleeve length, collar type, color, and fabric.

Retailers who analyze past sales records but also become aware of changing market conditions when purchasing merchandise will be more profitable.

Dollars & Sense

Retailers should not always allow past sales results to determine future stocking patterns. Consider, for example, how relying on past records to determine what sizes to purchase would have produced a problem because women's sizes have increased in recent years. In fact, the only women's apparel sizes to experience a sales growth in recent years were the larger sizes. Retailers, manufacturers, and even fashion magazines realize that over a third of all women wear a size larger than 14. Plus sizes now generate $25 billion in annual sales as these customers want style and quality. Today's successful retailers are disregarding past sales records and offering larger selections of plus sizes featuring the latest looks, including the same designer-made fitted dresses and coats that slimmer women wear. Retailers such as Saks, Bloomingdale's, and Macy's are experiencing record sales for this market by lavishing prime floor space and advertising dollars on the plus sizes.

Special Problems with New Stores

So far we have ignored the problems individuals have when opening their first store. Entrepreneurs, whether brick & mortar or on-line types, have no past sales records to rely on. In this situation, does one only use intuition and creativity in developing a model stock plan? Certainly not. Of the three analytical steps discussed earlier, the first two pertain as much to the new entrepreneur as to any existing retailer. However, for the third step, one will not have any historical sales records to study. Here the retailer can still use analytical skills by obtaining trade or other external sources on consumer purchasing patterns. For example, grocery retailers, especially the on-line types described in the E-tailing box in Chapter 3, could consult the Towne-Oller Index, which measures actual sales and the sales rank of each product and shows the number of different products needed to meet the demand of a certain percentage of the buying public for that particular product line. For instance, one might see that if 80 percent of the demand preferences for mouthwash is the desired goal, the four leading brands would need to be stocked.

In addition, creative skills are as important for entrepreneurs opening their first store as they are for buyers going back to the market to restock existing stores. The creative buyer, for example, would recognize that there might be savings gained by stocking fewer brands of a product, such as canned green beans, that does not really evoke strong brand preferences and carrying a greater selection of products, such as ice cream, that evokes strong preferences. Here, even though the retailer does not have the desired brand of green beans and the customer is forced to purchase a less-preferred brand, the customer will forgive the retailer when he or she sees the large selection of the more important product category—ice cream. Likewise, the creative retailer is more apt to not follow the "prescribed" rules of thumb that all its competitors follow but come up with new ideas to gain an advantage over the competition.

Retailers who use analytical and creative skills when selecting merchandise for resale will be more profitable.

Conflicts in Unit Stock Planning

Unit stock planning is an exercise in compromise and conflict. The conflict is multidimensional because not everything can be stocked. The conflicts are summarized as follows:

1. Maintain a strong in-stock position on genuinely new items while trying to avoid the 90 percent of new products that fail in the introductory stage. The retailer will want to have on hand the types of new products that will satisfy customers. If the consumer is sold a poor product, it hurts the retailer as much as, if not more than, the manufacturer. The problem becomes one of screening out poor products before they reach the customer. Any screening device, however, has error; the retailer might end up stocking some losers and turning down winners. Thus a basic conflict arises; but even the best of buyers will make a mistake sometimes and be forced to use markdowns to unload slow-selling merchandise. The chapter's E-tailing box describes how the Internet can assist the retail buyer in evaluating new products.

2. Maintain an adequate stock of the basic popular items while having sufficient inventory dollars to capitalize on unforeseen opportunities. Many times, if the retailer fills out the model stock with recommended quantities, there is little, if any, money left over for the super buy that is just around the corner. But if the retailer holds out that money and cuts back on basic stock, customers may be lost and that super buy may never surface. For this reason, it is important that retailers realize that they should never be out of stock on staples and best-selling products.

3. Maintain high merchandise turnover goals while maintaining high margin goals. This is perhaps the most glaring conflict. Usually, items that turnover more rapidly have thinner profit margins. Therefore, trying to build a unit plan that will accomplish both objectives will surely be challenging.

4. Maintain adequate selection for customers while not confusing them. If customers are confronted with too many similar items, they will not be able to make up their minds and they may leave the store empty-handed and frustrated. On the other hand, if the selection is inadequate, the customer will again leave

E-tailing

Using Cyberspace to Gather Data

Suppose a household goods buyer at the local department store is wondering if there is a demand for left-handed cooking gadgets. Given that as baby boomers age they spend more time entertaining at home, the buyer assumes that the 13 percent of Americans who are left-handed will want special equipment to match that of their right-handed counterparts to aid in developing their gourmet skills. However, before making any rash merchandising decisions, the buyer decides to surf the net for some more information.

The buyer begins with on-line newsgroups. Before leaving the office one Friday night, the buyer searches the Usenet listings using the key words *food, cooking, left,* and *gourmet.* Finding no groups for gourmet, only four for cooking, but nearly eighty for food, the buyer posts a short message on a busy discussion group called "rec.food.cooking" asking people what left-handed cookware they would like to see sold at local stores. Under *left,* the buyer finds several possible information sources, with the busiest being "alt.lefthanders." Here the buyer posts the same message.

Next the buyers goes to the Yahoo! search engine. One of the five matches under the word *left-handed* is for Southpaw Pineapple, a gift store catering to left-handers. The buyer spends the next 15 minutes before heading home visiting this store's web site to check out what this retailer is offering.

On returning to work the following Monday morning, the buyer finds only six responses to her messages from the "rec.food.cooking" group. One of the replies is from a women who used to own a left-handed specialty store in St. Louis. The women lists what items were hot sellers and what items were slow movers. She also provides the names and phone numbers of seven other stores carrying such cookware across the country. The five other replies ask for combinations of cooking mitts, cheese grater, a can-opener, and scissors for left-handers. There were no other responses to the message.

Based on this quick cyberspace search, the household buyer decides to rethink her idea about stocking left-handed cookware.

empty-handed. Thus, a delicate balance needs to be struck between too little and too much selection.

5. Maintain space productivity and utilization while not congesting the store. Take advantage of buys that will utilize the available space, but avoid buys that cause the merchandise to spill over into the aisles. Unfortunately, some of the best buys come along when space is already occupied.

As should be readily evident at this point, unit stock planning is no easy task. Equally challenging is the selection of vendors from whom to buy the merchandise.

Selection of Merchandising Sources

> **LO • 4**
> **How do retailers select proper merchandise sources?**

After deciding on the type and amount of inventory to be purchased, the next step is to determine where the retailer is to obtain the merchandise. All too often people have misconceptions about how retailers choose and negotiate with vendors. In reality, with proper planning and control, it can be a very rewarding experience, especially when your customers react positively to your merchandise selection. However, no matter how rewarding your buying experience is, it will also be grueling. Not only must the retail buyers determine what merchandise lines to carry, but the buyers also must select

When buyers go to market they must be well prepared so they can successfully negotiate with vendors.

the best possible vendor to supply them with these items and then must be able to negotiate the best deal possible with that vendor.

Unless the retailer owns a manufacturing or wholesale operation, when selecting a merchandise source, the retailer must consider many criteria. These criteria are dependent on the retailer's type of store and merchandise sold. Generally the following criteria, which may vary across merchandise lines, should always be considered: selling history, product quality, consumers' perception of the manufacturer's reputation, reliability of delivery, trade terms, projected markup, after-sale service, transportation time, distribution center processing time, inventory carrying cost, country of origin, fashionability, and net-landed cost.[5] Country of origin is becoming a more important issue every day, as governments use trade agreements to limit the amount of merchandise that can be imported from various countries and consumers rebel against sweatshops and the use of child labor in certain countries. Often retailers check out the Council on Economic Priorities web site (www.cepnyc.org), which ranks more than 200 consumer product manufacturers on workplace issues, in addition to product safety, quality, and price. However, some people are beginning to question retailing's role in policing this sourcing problem, which was also covered in the Ethics section in Chapter 6.

Even things as minor as the number of units in a pack can be a significant factor in choosing a vendor. Wal-Mart, for example, asked a vendor to ship protractors (remember those from your grade school days?) in packs of 10 instead of 80. Working with vendors this way allowed the retail chain to only increase inventories by 4 percent while increasing sales by over 12 percent. The $1.4 billion saved by such vendor negotiations was now available for other uses.[6]

Likewise, in cases where a manufacturer offers to co-op some expense, for example, advertising or display support, the amount of price reduction has been shown to have a significant effect on the purchase decision.[7] Some retailers also check to see whether the same merchandise will be made available to a nearby competitor; in such cases, it may be advantageous for the retailer to consider using a private label or not purchasing the merchandise. Toys "R" Us was accused by the FTC of stifling price competition by threatening not to stock certain toys if the vendors also sold them to discounters. The discounters, which try to offer lower prices by only carrying the "hottest" toys, claim that some vendors would not sell them the "hot" toys for fear of losing business to Toys "R"–Us, which has just under 20 percent of toy sales in the United States. The FTC claims that such action allows Toys "R" Us to maintain high margins.[8]

Recent research concludes that the use of private-label brands indicates that private branding (1) increases as the perceived consequences of making a buying mistake decrease, (2) increases when the different brands in the category are perceived to vary more in their quality, and (3) decreases if the category benefits are deemed to require actual trial or experience instead of being assessable through search of package label information.[9]

One of a retailer's greatest assets when dealing with a vendor is the retailer's past experiences with that vendor. Whether you are a small retailer doing all the buying yourself or a new buyer for a large chain, you should always approach vendors with two important pieces of information: the vendor profitability analysis statement and the confidential vendor analysis. The **vendor profitability analysis statement** (see Exhibit 9.4) lists the record of all purchases you made the previous year, the discount granted you by the vendor, transportation charges paid, the original markup, markdowns, and finally the season-ending gross margin on that vendor's merchandise. It is the positive relationship with a supplier described in the vendor profitability tables that may encourage a retail buyer to try that vendor's new product. Still, while Mattel is a strong player in the toy market, it may not have been big enough to get many toy buyers to purchase what turned out to be the most successful doll in toy market history back in

Vendor profitability analysis statement is a tool used to evaluate vendors and shows all purchases made the prior year, the discount granted, the transportation charges paid, the original markup, markdowns, and finally the season-ending gross margin on that vendor's merchandise.

Exhibit 9.4   Two-Seasons Vendor Profitability Analysis

| Vendor Name | Purchases | | Discount and Anticipation % | Freight % | Markup % Landed Loaded | Markdown | | Gross Margin Percentage | Vendor No. |
	Cost	Retail				$	%		
Anderson Sports	62,481	129,861	7.1	1.4	50.7	20,211	15.6	46.2	273359
Jack Frost, Inc.	26,921	53,962	8.0	1.3	49.4	3,233	6.0	50.5	818922
Sue's Fashions	25,572	51,930	8.1	1.8	49.9	6,667	12.8	47.1	206284
Jana Kantor Asso.	14,022	29,434	8.0	.8	52.0	481	1.6	55.1	050187
Pierce Mills	12,761	25,438	9.5	1.7	49.8	7,858	30.9	33.1	132886
Ray, Inc.	2,196	4,416	8.0	1.8	49.4	754	17.1	43.8	148296
Dusty's Place	2,071	4,332	8.0	1.3	51.6			55.4	662411
Lady Carole	1,050	2,100	8.0	2.1	48.9			52.9	676841
Jill Petites	740	1,584	10.4	.5	54.2	640	40.5	29.2	472977
Andrea's	198	410	8.0	.8	51.1			55.0	527218

Cost: your cost
Retail: your original selling price
Discount and anticipation %: discount received for early payments
Freight %: your shipping expenses
Markup % Landed Loaded: [Retail selling price − (Cost + Freight)]/Retail selling price
Markdown: Amount original selling price is reduced
Gross Margin %: [Actual selling price − (Cost + Freight − Discount and Anticipation)]/Actual selling price

Global Retailing

Barbie's Secret Past

Confidential vendor analysis is identical to the vendor profitability analysis but also provides a three-year financial summary as well as the names, titles, and negotiating points of all the vendor's sales staff.

1959. As the Global Retailing box describes, the concept behind Barbie was not something Mattel wanted to promote to the buyers.

The **confidential vendor analysis** (see Exhibit 9.5) lists the same companies as in the profitability analysis statement, but it also provides a three-year financial summary as well as the names, titles, and negotiating points of all the vendor's sales staff. This last piece of information is based on the notes taken by the buyer after the previous season's buying trip.

Based on the information obtained in the previous two reports, some retailers classify vendors into five categories.

Class A vendors are those from whom the retailer purchases large and profitable amounts of merchandise.

Class A vendors. These are the vendors from whom the retailer purchases large and profitable amounts of merchandise. The retailer may distinguish these vendors from others by purchasing a certain minimum quantity from them. These vendors and the retailer work together as partners.

Barbie, whose full name is Barbie Millicent Roberts, is a direct descendent from Lilli, a 1940s German calling card for sex. Back in the late 1950s, Ruth Handler, Barbie's inventor and a Mattel cofounder, was trying to convince her husband, another Mattel partner, that the company should produce a grownup looking doll for little girls. Most of the dolls on the market at the time were of the baby type. On a trip to Germany, she saw the doll of her imagination. It was called "Lilli" and was just what Handler envisioned that Mattel should produce for America's girls.

However, it turns out that the German doll had a different target market. It was a present brought by a young man, along with a bouquet of flowers or a bottle of wine, to a prospective date's house as a signal that he was interested in more than just dinner! Nevertheless, in 1959 Mattel, at Handler's urging, introduced Lilli to America as Barbie. It was named after Handler's own daughter Barbara. (Ken, by the way, was named after her son.)

The motivation research, conducted by Ernst Dichter, one of the leading experts at the time, only added more to Barbie's checkered past. Dichter's focus groups determined that the best promotional approach was to tell mothers that Barbie would teach their daughters how to dress and coif in order to get a husband. Also, Mattel paid an unheard of amount — $500,000 — to sponsor the entire season of Disney's *Mickey Mouse Club* television show.

Of course, as Professor Stan Hollander points out, the early ad pitch may have led to Barbie's 1970s disgrace when feminists charged the doll with every crime against womanhood from illegal measurements (leading to unrealistic body images among both sexes) to indecent exposure.*

However, a better question may be "Had retail buyers back in 1959 and 1960 known about Barbie's German ancestor, would they have purchased the doll for their stores?" Barbie may have never reached the point where anyone cared.

Today, Barbie, with a wider face to make her less waif-thin, has made a triumphant comeback (worldwide 2000 sales of $1.6 billion). She is more career oriented in today's market — her wardrobe-minded family exists side by side with Teacher Barbie, Vet Barbie, and even a "limited-issues" of Millennium Celebration Barbie and Barbie for President. (At Barbie.com there is a full list of all the Barbies available.) A new advertising campaign targets different versions of Barbie to specific age groups, particularly older girls whose interest in the doll had waned. Little wonder, the average girl today has 10 Barbie dolls.

Source: *"Barbie's Checkered Past," *Retrospectives in Marketing*, Stan Hollander, ed., Michigan State University, November 1998: 2. Used with permission.

Retailers who maintain and review both a vendor profitability analysis and a confidential vendor analysis statement before going to market will be more profitable.

Class B vendors. These are the vendors who generate satisfactory sales and profits for the retailer. They occasionally develop a strong product offering for the retailer.

Class C vendors. These are the vendors who carry outstanding lines but do not currently sell to the retailer. This is the type of vendor that the store buyer desires as a supplier.

Exhibit 9.5   Confidential Vendor Analysis

Trip Dates _Fall Market_ City _Dallas_ Buyer's Name _Cooper_ Dept. Name _Women's Wear_ Dept. No. _491_

Vendor/Address Phone No./Floor No.		Volume History 200X	200X	200X	Markup History 200X	200X	200X	Markdown History 200X	200X	200X	Vendor Executives & Titles	Remarks
West Texas Blouse	Spring	590.5	719.4	330.8	47.5	47.7	46.7	2.4	5.3	4.4	Larry Wilcox (VP)	Cash Discount
	Fall	1002.8	706.7		47.3	47.5		3.4	7.8		Julie Davin	Prone to co-op
	Year	1593.3	1426.1		47.4			3.1			Ted Rombach	ads
	Objectives:											
	Results As of 5/22:											
Flatland Fashions	Spring	224.5	230.2	210.8	47.7	50.0	47.2	6.5	8.5	3.8	Joe Hall (P)	
	Fall	175.8	230.5		47.3	47.6		17.0	9.0		Richard Reel	Will deal on
	Year	400.3	460.7		47.5	48.8		11.1	8.7			transportation
	Objectives:											
	Results As of 5/22:											
Southern	Spring	-0-	42.3	50.7		48.4	45.4	-0-	9.1	4.2	Jackie Poteet (SM)	
	Fall	37.0	69.2		47.1	42.3		7.7	7.8		Boonie Hanley	"Quantity"
	Year	37.0	112.5		47.1	44.7		7.7	8.2		Carol Little	
	Objectives:											
	Results As of 5/22:											
Gallo	Spring	21.7	195.0	55.6	46.9	50.0	48.3	1.3	0.2	1.2	Ruth Wilson (P)	
	Fall	-0-	13.9		-0-	46.7		-0-	2.0		John Murphy	Easier of the
	Year	21.7	33.4		46.9	48.6		1.3	0.9			two
	Objectives:											
	Results As of 5/22:											

Class B vendors are those that generate satisfactory sales and profits for the retailer.

Class C vendors are those that carry outstanding merchandise lines but do not currently sell to the retailer.

Class D vendors are those from whom the retailer purchases small quantities of goods on an irregular basis.

Class E vendors are those with whom the retailer has had an unfavorable experience.

Class D vendors. These are the vendors from whom the retailer purchases small quantities of goods on an irregular basis. Because of the expense of the small orders, it is doubtful if the purchases from these vendors produce any profits for either the retailer or the vendor.

Class E vendors. These are the vendors with whom the retailer has had an unfavorable experience. Only after the approval of top store officials can orders be placed with these vendors.

Even buyers who do not go to market, but have the vendors come to them, evaluate their vendors. For years, many grocers felt that firms like Procter & Gamble treated retailers poorly. These grocers needed the many products that P&G manufactured, but they did not like P&G's "we win, you lose" attitude, which forced retailers to purchase the complete line of P&G products to earn merchandising money. P&G was a class B vendor, at best. Recently, however, P&G has developed a program in which it helps all its customers in developing their merchandise plans for the next months and no longer requires grocers to purchase slow-moving products.[10] This new attitude of "let's both win" has seen many supermarket managers reevaluate P&G as a class A vendor. P&G knows that it can only be as successful as its retailers let it be.

After selecting the vendor(s), the retailer still must decide on the specific merchandise to be bought. Some products, such as the basic items for the particular department in question, are easy to purchase. Other products, especially new items, require more careful planning and consideration. Retailers should concern themselves with several key questions. Among them are the following:

1. Where does this product fit into the strategic position that I have staked out for my department?
2. Will I have an exclusive with this product or will I be in competition with nearby retailers?
3. What is the estimated demand for this product in my target market?
4. What is my anticipated gross margin for this product?
5. Will I be able to obtain reliable, speedy stock replacement?
6. Can this product stand on its own, or is it merely a "me-too" item?
7. What is my expected turnover rate with this product?
8. Does this product complement the rest of my inventory?

Vendor Negotiations

LO • 5

What is involved in the vendor-buyer negotiation process and what terms of the contract can be negotiated?

The climax of a successful buying plan is the active **negotiation,** which involves finding mutually satisfying solutions for parties with conflicting objectives, with those suppliers whom you have identified as suitable supply sources. The effectiveness of this buyer-vendor relationship depends on the negotiation skills of the buyer and the economic power of the firms involved.

The retail buyer must negotiate price, delivery dates, discounts, shipping terms, and return privileges. All of these factors are significant because they affect both the firm's profitability and cash flow.

Manufacturers, as well as retailers, have in recent years become increasingly aware of the cost of carrying excess inventory. Likewise, both parties have also become more concerned with the time value of money and its resulting effect on the firm's cash flow. Because both parties to the negotiation process are aware of these cost factors and are trying to shift these costs to the other party, most negotiations do produce some conflict. However, successful negotiation is usually accomplished when buyers realize that the vendors are really their partners in the upcoming merchandising season. Both the buyer and vendor are seeking to satisfy the retailer's customers better than anybody else. Therefore, buyers and vendors must resolve their conflicts and differences of opinion, remembering that negotiation is a two-way street and a long-term profitable relationship is the goal. After all, the vendor wants to develop a long-term relationship with the retailer as much as the retailer does with its customers.

Negotiation
is the process of finding mutually satisfying solutions when the retail buyer and vendor have conflicting objectives.

What can be negotiated? There are many factors to be negotiated (prices, freight, delivery dates, method of shipment and shipping costs, exclusivity, guaranteed sales, markdown money, promotional allowances, return privileges, and discounts) and life is simplest when there are not surprises. Therefore, the smart buyer leaves nothing to chance and discusses everything with the vendor before purchase orders are signed. The buyer and seller, together, work out the upcoming merchandising plans using the buyer's merchandise budget and planned turnover. Therefore, the buyer and seller should seek to make negotiations a win-win situation where both sides win and neither feels like a loser, such as P&G and its retailers are doing today. The essence of negotiation is to trade what is cheap to you but valuable to the other party, for what is valuable to you but cheap to the other party.

Dollars & Sense

The retailer who puts all the upcoming areas of negotiations and previous agreements with the vendor in writing before going to market will be more profitable.

The smart buyer puts all the upcoming areas of negotiations and previous agreements in letter form and sends it out before going to market. This helps to eliminate any misunderstandings afterward. Price, of course, is probably the first factor to be negotiated. Buyers should attempt to purchase the desired merchandise at the lowest possible net cost. However, although the vendor is the buyer's partner, the buyer should not expect unreasonable discounts or price concessions. The buyer can try to bring about a price concession that is legal under the Robinson-Patman Act.

The buyer must be familiar with the prices and discounts allowed by each vendor. This is why past records are so important. However, the buyer must remember that his or her bargaining power is a result of his or her planned purchases from the vendor. As a result, a large retailer may be able to purchase goods from a vendor at a lower price than a small "mom-and-pop" retailer. Five types of discounts can be negotiated.

Trade Discount

Trade discount
is also referred to as a functional discount and is a form of compensation that the buyer may receive for performing certain wholesaling or retailing services for the manufacturer.

A **trade discount,** sometimes referred to as a **functional discount,** is a form of compensation that the buyer may receive for performing certain wholesaling or retailing services for the manufacturer. In as much as this discount is given for the performance of some service, the size of the discount will vary with that service. Thus variations in trade discounts are legally justifiable on the basis of the different costs associated with doing business with various buyers.

Trade discounts are often expressed in a chain, or series, such as "list less 40-20-10." Each figure in the chain of discounts represents a percentage reduction from the list price of an item. Assume that the list price of an item is $1,000 and that the chain of discounts is 40-20-10. The buyer who receives all these discounts would actually pay $432 for this item. The computations would be as follows:

List price	$1,000
Less 40%	−400
	600
Less 20%	−120
	480
Less 10%	−48
Purchase price	$ 432

To illustrate how the various chains of discounts permit a vendor to compensate the members of the distribution channel for their marketing activities, let's look at the preceding example. Assume that the manufacturer sells through a channel system that includes manufacturers' agents, wholesalers, and small retailers. The purchase price of $432 is accorded to the manufacturers' agent who negotiates a sale between the manufacturer and the service wholesaler. The manufacturers' agent then charges the service wholesaler $480 for the item, thus realizing $48 for rendering a number of marketing activities. The service wholesaler, in turn, charges a retailer $600 for the item, thus making $120. The retailer then sells the item at the suggested list price of $1,000, thus making $400 in gross margin to cover expenses and a profit.

Trade discounts are legal where they correctly reflect the costs of the intermediaries' services. Sometimes, large retailers want to buy directly from the manufacturer and pay only $432, instead of $600. If this action is anti-competitive and enables the large retailer to undercut the competition, it would be illegal, unless one of the three defenses of the Robinson-Patman Act explained in Chapter 6 can be applied.

Quantity Discount

A **quantity discount** is a price reduction offered as an inducement to purchase large quantities of merchandise. Three types of quantity discounts are available:

1. **Noncumulative quantity discount:** a discount based on a single purchase
2. **Cumulative quantity discount:** a discount based on total amount purchased over a period of time
3. **Free merchandise:** a discount whereby merchandise is offered in lieu of price concessions

Noncumulative quantity discounts can be legally justified by the manufacturer if costs are reduced because of the quantity involved or if the manufacturer is meeting a competitor's price in good faith. Cumulative discounts are more difficult to justify, because many small orders may be involved, thereby reducing the manufacturer's savings.

For an example of how a quantity discount works, consider the following schedule:

Order Quantity	Discount from List Price
1 to 999	0%
1,000 to 9,999	5%
10,000 to 24,999	8%
25,000 to 49,999	10%

If a retailer, which had already purchased 500 units, wanted another 800 units, it would have to pay list price if the vendor uses a noncumulative policy. However, the retailer would receive a 5 percent discount on all purchases if the vendor uses a cumulative pricing policy.

Quantity discount
is a price reduction offered as an inducement to purchase large quantities of merchandise.

Noncumulative quantity discount
is a discount based on a single purchase.

Cumulative quantity discount
is a discount based on the total amount purchased over a period of time.

Free merchandise
is a discount whereby merchandise is offered in lieu of price concessions.

Quantity discounts might not always be in the seller's best interest and should always be viewed by the buyer as an invitation for further negotiations. Consider the following price schedule published by IBM for a computer:[11]

Quantity	Unit Price
1–19	$5,795
20–49	$5,099
50–149	$4,636
150–249	$4,486

Let's say that as a buyer for a retail chain, you want 18 of these computers and your cost is $104,310 (18 × $5,795). But 20 would only cost $101,980 (20 × $5,099). What do you do?

You actually have four choices:

1. Tell IBM to ship 20 computers at $5,099, and you keep the extra 2.
2. Tell IBM to ship you 18 computers at $5,099 and have IBM keep the other 2.
3. Order 20 but tell IBM to ship you only 18 and to credit you for two computers at $5,099 each.
4. Negotiate a purchase price.

Whenever quantity discounts are offered, buyers should always check to see if by ordering more, the total purchase price may be lower.

Many times, retailers can make a quick profit from utilizing quantity discounts by selling the extra merchandise to a diverter to sell in a gray market. The diverter, which is not an authorized member of the marketing channel but still functions as an intermediary, will be able to purchase these goods cheaper from the retailer than it can from the manufacturer and sell this excess merchandise to other retailers. However, many authorized retailers are upset when diverters provide other retailers with such merchandise. Some retailers have dropped cosmetic lines when Kmart, where most of its cosmetics are diverted, started to carry the line. In addition, Costco has a vice-president of "diverting" who purchases more than $200 million worth of merchandise from unauthorized vendors.[12]

Consider the previous retailer that needed only 18 computers and purchased 20 computers. Here the retailer sold the two computers to a diverter for $3,500 each. As a result, the retailer was better off by $9,330 than it would have been had it bought only 18 computers at $5,795 each (18 × $5,795 = $104,310; 20 × 5,099 = $101,980 − $7,000 = $94,980). The diverter could now profit by selling these two computers to another retailer for $4,000 each.

Today diverters are important members of the retailer's channel, especially in the grocery and computer fields. However, as pointed out in Chapter 5, not all manufacturers or retailers feel the same way about them. Nonetheless, it was the manufacturers' pricing policies that enabled diverters to function economically. The chapter's Retailing: The Inside Story box describes how computer manufacturers have tried to keep their products out of the gray market.

Promotional discount
is a discount provided for the retailer performing an advertising or promotional service for the manufacturer.

Promotional Discount

A third type of discount available is a **promotional discount** that is given when the retailer performs an advertising or promotional service for the manufacturer. For

Retailing: The Inside Story

Can Manufacturers Stop Diverters?

There does not appear to be any way that manufacturers can stop the spread of diverters if they continue to use quantity discounts. What was once confined to the supermarket industry has now spread through the electronics industry, into department stores via the cosmetic goods channels, and even to automobile dealers.

Let's consider some of the strategies computer manufacturers have used in the past to prevent their current channel members from acting as diverters, and ways diverters have gone around them.

Maintenance/Field Service

Manufacturers feel that "only we can sell and maintain the product." They believe that by not giving out the shop repair manual they can force customers to return to authorized dealers for repair and warranty. Obtaining the manual is usually no problem, however, because many suppliers provide one directly to customers. Diverters often throw in a manual to close a deal. Remember, if the manufacturer cannot control inventory and prices, how can it expect to control a manual, especially with all the photocopiers around?

Distributor Training

The manufacturer may only train repair people at its headquarters. Here the diverter simply hires a trained person away from an authorized dealer or subcontracts the dealer to moonlight.

Warranty/Guaranty Agreements

Often the warranty is voided if the product is purchased at an "unauthorized dealer." This is easy to overcome. Does the buyer know or care who authorized dealers are? If the product breaks down, the buyer will hold the manufacturer responsible. Besides, most products experience problems only after the warranty expires.

Cash Rebates Directly to the Customer

This is a potentially effective countermeasure. If the manufacturer makes a point of advertising the rebate widely, those diverters that do not have the rebate card or whose place of purchase will prevent the manufacturer from honoring the card will be forced to explain this to the customer, jeopardizing the sale.

Some diverters will either honor the rebate directly from their profits or simply not carry the line during the rebate time period. After all, no manufacturer will continue such a program indefinitely. Some diverters send in the card for the customer and list the authorized dealer they themselves purchased the product from.

Cumulative Discounts and Year-End Bonuses and Deleting the Channel Members Who Do Not Cooperate

Although these two ideas might make sense for manufacturers at first, unfortunately the Federal Trade Commission (FTC) would consider such actions a means of price control or fixing, restraint of trade, and collusion.

Thus, about the only thing a manufacturer can do to prevent diverters from becoming unauthorized members of its channel is to stop using quantity discounts.

Retailers who understand how to negotiate the various discounts, especially quantity discounts, to their advantage will be more profitable.

example, a vendor might offer a retailer 50 extra jeans if the retailer (1) purchases 1,250 jeans during the season and (2) runs two newspaper advertisements featuring the jeans during the season. One of the main reasons that manufacturers offer such discounts is because the rates newspapers charge local retailers are often lower than the rates charged national manufacturers. These discounts are legal as long as they are available to all competing retailers on an equal basis.

Seasonal Discount

Seasonal discount
is a discount provided to retailers if they purchase and take delivery of merchandise in the off season.

Retailers can earn a **seasonal discount** if they purchase and take delivery of the merchandise in the off-season (e.g., buying swimwear in October). However, this does not mean that all seasonal discounts result in the purchase of merchandise out of season. Retailers in resort areas often take advantage of these discounts because swimwear is never out of season for them. As long as the same terms are available to all competing retailers, seasonal discounts are legal.

Cash Discount

Cash discount
is a discount offered to the retailer for the prompt payment of bills.

The final discount available to the buyer is a **cash discount** for prompt payment of bills. Cash discounts are usually stated as 2/10, net 30, which means that a 2 percent discount is given if payment is received within 10 days of the invoice date and the net amount is due within 30 days.

Although the cash discount is a common method for encouraging early payment, it can also be used as a negotiating tool by delaying the payment due date. This future-dating negotiation may take many forms. Several of the most common are as follows:

End-of-month (EOM) dating
allows the retailer to take a cash discount and the full payment period to begin on the first day of the following month instead of on the invoice date.

1. **End-of-month (EOM) dating** allows for a cash discount and the full payment period to begin on the first day of the following month instead of on the invoice date. End-of-month invoices dated after the 25th of the month are considered to be dated on the first of the following month.

Middle-of-month (MOM) dating
allows the retailer to take a cash discount and the full payment period to begin on the middle of the month.

2. **Middle-of-month (MOM) dating** is similar to EOM except the middle of the month is used as the starting date.

Receipt of goods (ROG) dating
allows the retailer to take a cash discount and the full payment period to begin when the goods are received by the retailer.

3. **Receipt of goods (ROG) dating** allows the starting date to be the date goods are received by the retailer.

4. **Extra dating (Ex)** merely allows the retailer extra or free days before the period of payment begins.

Extra dating (Ex)
allows the retailer extra or interest-free days before the period of payment begins.

5. A final discount form to be considered, but which is not widely used today, is anticipation. **Anticipation** allows a retailer to pay the invoice in advance of the expiration of the cash discount period and earn an extra discount. However, anticipation is usually figured at an annual rate of 7 percent, which is below the current cost of money.

Anticipation
allows the retailer to pay the invoice in advance of the end of the cash discount period and earn an extra discount.

Many vendors have eliminated the cash discount because retailers, especially department stores, have been taking 60 to 120 days to pay and still deduct the cash discount. In fact, many vendors are requiring new accounts to pay up front, until credit is established.

Delivery Terms

Delivery terms are another factor to be considered in negotiations. They are important because they specify where title to the merchandise passes to the retailer and whether the vendor or buyer will pay the freight charges and who is obligated to file any damage claims. The three most common shipping terms are as follows:

1. **Free on board (FOB) factory.** The buyer assumes title at the factory and pays all transportation costs from the vendor's factory.
2. **Free on board (FOB) shipping point.** The vendor pays the transportation to a local shipping point, but the buyer assumes title at this point and pays all further transportation costs.
3. **Free on board (FOB) destination.** The vendor pays all transportation costs and the buyer takes title upon delivery.

Free on board (FOB) factory
is a method of charging for transportation where the buyer assumes title to the goods at the factory and pays all transportation costs from the vendor's factory.

In-Store Merchandise Handling[13]

LO • 6

What methods are available to the retailer for controlling loss through shrinkage, vendor collusion, and theft?

The retailer will need to have some means of handling incoming merchandise. For some types of retailers (e.g., a grocery store), this need will be significant and frequent; for others (e.g., a jeweler), it will be relatively minor and infrequent. A retailer with a frequent and significant amount of incoming merchandise needs considerable planning of merchandise receiving and handling space. To illustrate, consider that a full-line grocery store will need to build receiving docks to which 40-to-60-foot semitrailers can be backed up. Similarly, space may be needed for a small forklift to drive between the truck and the merchandise receiving area to unload the merchandise. Subsequently, the merchandise will need to be moved from the receiving area, where it will be counted and marked, to a storage area, either on the selling floor or in a separate location.

The point at which incoming merchandise is received can be a high-theft point. The retail manager needs to design the receiving and handling area in order to minimize this problem. Several types of theft will be mentioned in the following discussion. Some involve the retail employees themselves, others involve outsiders.

Vendor collusion includes the types of losses that occur when the merchandise is delivered. Typical losses involve the delivery of less merchandise than is charged for, removal of good merchandise disguised as old or stale merchandise, and stealing other merchandise from the stockroom or off the selling floor while making delivery. This type of theft often involves both the delivery people and the retail employee who signs for the delivery with the two splitting the profit.

Employee theft occurs when employees steal merchandise where they work. Although no one knows for sure how much is stolen annually from retailers, because all shrinkage statistics are based only on apprehensions, as many as 30 percent of American workers admit to stealing from their employers, even if it is only small items like a pen or pencil. Although some of the stolen goods come from the selling floor, a larger percentage is taken from the stockroom to the employee lounge and lockers, where it is kept until the employees leave with it at quitting time. Employee theft, which amounts to more than $800 per apprehension, is most prevalent in food stores, department stores, and discount stores. Considering that these types of stores are usually larger in size, sales volume, and number of employees, the lack of close supervision might contribute to this problem. Exhibit 9.6 shows 50 ways that an employee can steal from a bar.

Free on board (FOB) shipping point
is a method of charging for transportation in which the vendor pays for transportation to a local shipping point where the buyer assumes title and then pays all further transportation costs.

Free on board (FOB) destination
is a method of charging for transportation in which the vendor pays for all transportation costs and the buyer takes title on delivery.

Vendor collusion
occurs when an employee of one of the retailer's vendors steals merchandise as it is delivered to the retailer.

Employee theft
occurs when employees of the retailer steal merchandise where they work.

Merchandise handling in retail enterprises is a significant point where theft by employees can occur.

Customer theft
is also known as shoplifting and occurs when customers or individuals disguised as customers steal merchandise from the retailer's store.

Customer theft is also a problem; in fact over a dozen shoppers are caught for every case of employee theft, although the average amount of merchandise recovered has a value of less than $50. Stealing merchandise from the stockroom and receiving area may be easier than taking it from the selling floor for several reasons. First, much of the stockroom merchandise is not ticketed, so it is easier to get it through electronic antishoplifting devices. Second, once the thief enters the stock area, there is very little antitheft security. Most security guards watch the exits and fitting rooms. Third, there is usually an exit in the immediate area of the stockroom through which the thief can carry out the stolen goods. Some retailers have wired these exits to set off an alarm when opened without a key, helping to reduce thefts somewhat. Another innovative retailer, after determining that employees were hiding merchandise in the compressed, discarded, and baled boxes that were left out as trash, started using a special spiked baler that punches holes in boxes to damage any stolen merchandise.[14]

The retailer must be aware that there is an excellent opportunity for receiving, handling, and storage thefts to occur. Therefore, steps should be taken to help cut down on these crimes. The retailer cannot watch the employees every minute to see whether or

Exhibit 9.6	50 Things Bar Owners Should Be on the Lookout For

1. The "Phantom Register" trick: just set up an extra register in bar for use only during busy times. The income from this register is not totaled on master tape and funds are skimmed by the bartender.

2. Serve and collect while register is being read between shift changes.

3. Claim a phony walk-out and keep money received from customer.

4. Pick up customer's cash when he or she isn't paying attention.

5. Fake a robbery of the night deposit on way to bank. It is difficult for owners to prove this fake occurred.

6. Add phantom drinks to a customer's "running tab."

7. The "Phantom Bottle" ploy: here the bartender brings his or her own bottle of liquor onto shift and pockets cash from its sale.

8. The "Short Pour" trick: just pour less than shot to cover "give away" liquor costs.

9. Don't ring up any sale and keep the cash.

10. The "Short-ring" trick: here the bartender under-rings the correct price of item and pockets the difference.

11. The "Free-Giveaway" trick: bartender gives drinks to friends in anticipation of larger tips.

12. Mislead the owner regarding the number of draft beers that can be poured from a keg.

13. Undercharge for drinks with the anticipation of a larger tip.

14. Reuse register drink receipts.

15. Trade drinks to the cook for meals.

16. Add water to liquor bottle to maintain inventory.

17. Substitute lower-priced liquor when asked for call brands.

18. Being in collusion with the delivery person, selling "stolen" products that he or she provides, and splitting the profit.

19. Ask for kickbacks from liquor distributor.

20. Dispensing and registering one shot on computerized dispenser system, while short-shoting the liquor into two glasses.

21. Short-changing a customer when he or she is a "little under the weather" and claim it was a "honest" mistake if caught.

22. Claim a returned drink: extra drink produced and can be sold by bartender.

23. When bar is selling both liquor to go and by the drink, count missing bottles as "to go sale."

24. The "Owner Is a Jerk" ploy: here, the bartender is the only person in charge of liquor pick-up, check-in, and stocking.

25. Complimentary cocktail or wine coupons from hotel room sold by maids to bar personnel, which they can place in register for cash.

26. Add two different customer drinks together and charge both, claiming misunderstanding in who was purchasing the round.

27. Ringing food items on liquor key to cover high liquor cost percent.

28. Selling "after-shift drinks" to customers, not having them consumed by other employees.

continued

Exhibit 9.6 **continued**

29. Not pouring enough liquor into blended fruit drinks to cover other shortages.
30. Having customer sign credit card voucher in advance and then overcharge the ticket.
31. Claiming opening bank was short.
32. Total out register in midshift. Start new tape. Cashier keeps both new tapes and cash.
33. Incorrect "over-ring" or "void" of register.
34. Making sales during tape changes.
35. Mistotaling the amount on the credit card or change the amount after customer leaves.
36. Taking money from the game machines or jukeboxes.
37. Accumulating the guest checks to ring up after customer leaves so as to change the amount or leave out items.
38. Run credit card through twice.
39. Selling empty kegs and returnable bottles to an off-premise retailer.
40. Place the tip jars next to cash register — easy to place cash in tip jar and ring "no sale" for register activity.
41. Falsifying cumulative register readings and "losing" tape.
42. Adding extra hours to your time card and splitting it with the shift manager.
43. Help the shift manager claim a fictitious employee on payroll.
44. Taking home food or liquor or fake a burglary.
45. Taking funds from vending machines.
46. Ringing up sales at happy hour prices, but charging regular bar prices to the customer when he or she is keeping receipts.
47. Servers charging for happy hour hors d'oeuvres and bar snacks.
48. Holding back bank deposits for a couple days and investing or borrowing money or just don't deposit money (or lesser amount) and keep difference.
49. Bartender handwriting bar tabs and ringing up lesser amounts on the register.
50. Wrapping booze into garbage can for later retrieval.

not they are honest, but some surveillance is helpful. However, the retailer must consider the employee's and customer's right to privacy versus the retailer's right to security. Legislation is currently being considered by several states that, if approved, would allow the use of electronic monitoring, by video and audio systems, only when advance notice is given. In effect, workers and shoppers must be informed when they are being monitored.

The amount of storage space the retailer needs is related to the physical dimensions of the merchandise and the safety stock level needed to maintain the desired rate of stock turnover. For example, furniture is bulky and requires considerable storage space; and grocery items turn over frequently, so more merchandise is needed than can be displayed on the shelves. This excess inventory causes retailers to have to stack boxes and cartons on the floor of the stockroom. Excess inventory, therefore, can lead to cluttered stockrooms and warehouses and invites theft. In most cases, having an excess

Customer theft or shoplifting is a major problem and expense in all lines of retailing. Often the costs of shoplifting can make the difference between a marginally profitable and a high profit retailer.

number of boxes in storage is both inefficient and costly, when the retailer is probably paying employees anywhere from $5 to $15 per hour to keep the storeroom in order. Thus, in most cases, some type of equipment will be used to increase productivity in this area. For instance, rather than having the employees carry incoming merchandise, numerous types of carts are made especially for this purpose. Also, instead of stacking the cartons and boxes directly on the floor of the stockroom where they must remain packed and risk being damaged, the merchandise can be unpacked, checked, inventoried, and ticketed, then placed on shelves or in bins until needed. By doing this, one can increase the amount of merchandise stored per square foot by decreasing the amount of packing material. As noted earlier, a tidy, well-ordered stock area is less tempting to dishonest employees. Trash compactors can be helpful by compressing the packing clutter.

Although much theft results from in-store merchandise handling, retailers must also be aware of how theft in transit may influence their ability to have the appropriate amount of merchandise on hand. Therefore, retailers must be able to not only plan to have the appropriate amount of merchandise on hand to meet the customers' demand, but also ensure that the merchandise planned for the store shelves actually arrives. Whether a retailer outsources its logistics or employs its own transportation force, ensuring that the merchandise makes it from the warehouse to the retail floor is critical for success.

So what can happen to merchandise in transit you ask? Hijacking. While a significant amount of shipment hijacking does occur in the United States, the global playing field can be fraught with peril. Consider, for instance, the case of a truck carrying a load of consumer electronics bound for Paraguay. Deep in the heart of the Brazilian jungle the driver realizes that the road ahead is blocked. As the truck comes to a stop the driver realizes that his truck is about to be hijacked. Luckily he has with him an off-duty Brazilian police officer to help protect the shipment. The police officer exits the cab of the truck, and immediately the driver can sense a gleam of familiarity between his security officer and one of the bandits. It seems that the bandit is also a police officer. After a brief discussion the truck is allowed to move on, with its shipment. Although this may seem to be fiction, it is actually a true story. And although this was a shipment of consumer electronics, other high-value products, such as apparel, perfume, cigarettes, and alcohol, are subject to hijacking. Whether on land, sea, or air, hijacking is unfortunately a relatively common occurrence in the retail supply chain.

The probability of theft in transit varies considerably from region to region. Whereas relatively few shipments are hijacked in Canada, the United States, Western Europe, and the Middle East, highjacking in regions such as Eastern Europe, Latin America, Russia, and Southeast Asia is more common. Deteriorating economic conditions in these regions have led to increased organized crime activity, resulting in increased theft of cargo. For many people in these regions, hijacking one shipment of consumer electronics can generate more cash than the average person in these regions makes in a lifetime.

Although statistics related to the theft of cargo destined for retailers is difficult to obtain because few companies want to publicize their security problems, losses due to hijacking, and the resulting disruption to retail operations are a major concern. However, losses due to hijacking are preventable, or at least avoidable to a degree. Here are some tips that retailers and their supply chain partners can employ to minimize the threat of hijacking:

1. Eliminate the retailer's name from the side of containers carrying the cargo. For consumer electronics companies such as Best Buy, putting their name on the truck, signaling to all that a shipment of consumer electronics is inside, is tantamount to saying, "steal me."

2. Install electronic monitoring devices on all shipment vehicles. Whether one is shipping by land, sea, or air, being able to track the container the merchandise is shipped in can help to determine its location when hijacked.

3. Carefully screen all internal transportation personnel as well as third-party logistics personnel in each global market. Given that these personnel are under loose supervision due to the nature of their jobs, higher security standards are critical.

4. Hire security personnel for each shipment. It is much easier for a single person to collude with others than it is for multiple people to conspire to steal.

As retailers continue to expand globally, the risks involved in international hijacking will continue to grow. However, by implementing a few security measures, retailers can minimize disruptions to their supply of merchandise and thereby increase the level of customer satisfaction by minimizing stockouts.

Student Study Guide

Summary

Merchandise management is the analysis, planning, acquisition, and control of inventory investments in a retail enterprise. An understanding of the principles of merchandise management is essential to good retail management. A major part of merchandise management is planning. The retailer needs to plan, first, the dollars to invest in inventory and, second, the units of merchandise to purchase with these dollars. These two forms of planning are called dollar merchandise planning and unit stock planning.

LO•1 What is the difference between the four methods of dollar merchandise planning used to determine the proper inventory stock levels needed to begin a merchandise selling period?

In the section on dollar merchandise planning, we discussed how the basic stock (which is used when retailers believe that it is necessary to have a given level of inventory available at all times, plus a variable amount of inventory that is tied to forecasted sales for the period), percentage variation (which assumes that the percentage fluctuations in monthly stock from average stock should be half as great as the percentage fluctuations in monthly sales from average sales), weeks' supply (where the beginning inventory level should be set equal to a predetermined number of weeks' supply), and stock-to-sales (where the retailer wants to maintain a specified ratio of inventory to planned sales) inventory methods can be used in retailing today.

LO•2 How does a retailer use dollar merchandise control and open-to-buy techniques in the retail buying process?

Once the buyer has planned the dollar merchandise to have on hand at the beginning of each month (or season), it becomes essential that the buyer does not make commitments for merchandise that would exceed the dollar plan. In short, the dollars planned for merchandise need to be controlled by an open-to-buy technique. OTB represents the dollar amount that a buyer can currently spend on merchandise without exceeding the planned dollar stocks discussed previously.

The OTB figure should not be set in stone because it can be exceeded. Consumer needs are the dominant consideration. If sales exceed planned sales, additional quantities should be ordered above those scheduled for purchase according to the merchandise budget.

LO•3 How does a retailer uses unit stock planning and model stock plans in determining the makeup of a merchandise mix?

The dollar merchandise plan is only the starting point in determining a merchandise line, which consists of a group of products that are closely related because they are intended for the same end use, are sold to the same customer group, or fall within a given price range. Once the retailer has decided how many dollars can be invested in inventory, the dollar plan needs to be converted into a unit plan.

However, there seldom will be enough dollars to emphasize all three inventory dimensions: variety, breadth, and depth. Therefore, retailers must select a merchandise mix that appeals to the greatest number of profitable market segments.

LO•4 How do retailers select proper merchandise sources?

In addition to deciding what and how much to purchase, successful merchandise management must also consider vendor selection and negotiations. In this section, we reviewed the major factors (selling history, product quality, consumers' perception of the manufacturer's reputation, reliability of delivery, trade terms, projected markup, quality of merchandise, after-sale service, transportation time, distribution center processing time, inventory carrying cost, country of origin, fashionability, and net-landed cost) that are important in the selection of a vendor and how a buyer prepares for a buying trip.

LO•5   What is involved in the vendor-buyer negotiation process and what terms of the contract can be negotiated?

The climax of a successful buying plan is the active negotiation, which involves finding mutually satisfying solutions for parties with conflicting objectives, with those suppliers whom you have identified as suitable supply sources. The effectiveness of this buyer-vendor relationship depends on the negotiation skills of the buyer and the economic power of the firms involved. The retail buyer must negotiate price, delivery dates, discounts (trade, quantity, promotional, seasonal, and cash), delivery terms, and return privileges. All of these factors are significant because they affect both the firm's profitability and cash flow.

LO•6   What methods are available to the retailer for controlling loss through shrinkage, vendor collusion, and theft?

We concluded the chapter with a discussion on in-store merchandise handling as a means to control losses by theft.

Terms to Remember

merchandise management	class E vendors
gross margin return on inventory	negotiation
basic stock method (BSM)	trade discount
percentage variation method (PVM)	quantity discount
weeks' supply method (WSM)	noncumulative quantity discount
stock-to-sales method (SSM)	cumulative quantity discount
open-to-buy technique	free merchandise
merchandise line	promotional discount
category management	seasonal discount
variety	cash discount
breadth (or assortment)	end-of-month (EOM) dating
battle of the brands	middle-of-month (MOM) dating
depth	receipt of goods (ROG) dating
consignment	extra dating (Ex)
extra dating	anticipation
model stock plan	free on board (FOB) factory
vendor profitability analysis	free on board (FOB) shipping point
confidential vendor analysis	free on board (FOB) destination
class A vendors	vendor collusion
class B vendors	employee theft
class C vendors	customer theft
class D vendors	

Review and Discussion Questions

LO•1   What are the differences between the four methods of dollar merchandise planning used to determine the proper

inventory stock levels needed to begin a merchandise selling period?

1. If your annual turnover rate is 10 times, which inventory stock level method would you use and why?

2. Herb's Hardware is attempting to develop a merchandise budget for the next 12 months. To assist in this process, the following data have been developed. The target inventory turnover is 4.8 and forecast sales are as follows:

Month	Forecast Sales
1	$27,000
2	26,000
3	20,000
4	34,000
5	41,000
6	40,000
7	28,000
8	27,000
9	38,000
10	39,000
11	26,000
12	28,000

Develop a monthly merchandise budget using the basic stock method (BSM) and the percentage variation method (PVM).

LO•2 How do retailers use dollar merchandise control and how is the open-to-buy approach used in the retail buying process?

3. What problems can occur to buyers who use the open-to-buy approach if they misjudge planned sales?

4. What does the term "open-to-buy" (OTB) mean? How can it be used to control merchandise investments?

5. A buyer is going to market and needs to compute the OTB. The relevant data are as follows: planned stock at end of March, $319,999 (at retail prices); planned March sales, $149,999; current stock-on-hand (March 1), $274,000; merchandise on order for delivery, $17,000; planned reductions, $11,000. What is the buyer's OTB?

LO•3 How does a retailer use unit stock planning and model stock plans in determining the makeup of a merchandise mix?

6. What are the major constraints in designing the optimal merchandise mix?

7. How can merchandise lines have too much breadth, yet not enough depth?

8. Manufacturers of so-called third-tier brands argue that they are being squeezed out of many stores by the major brands. Do you agree with that assessment? Why?

LO•4 How does a retailer select proper merchandise sources?

9. What do you think is the most important criterion in selecting a vendor? Why?

10. Why should a new buyer look over the previous buyer's "confidential vendor analysis" before going to market?

LO•5   **What is involved in the vendor-buyer negotiation process and what terms of the contract can be negotiated?**

11. If a vendor ships you $1,000 worth of merchandise on April 27 with terms of 3/20, net 30 EOM, how much should you pay the vendor on June 8?

12. How does a cash discount differ from a trade discount?

13. A retailer purchases goods that have a list price of $5,000. The manufacturer allows a trade discount of 40-25-10 and a cash discount of 2/10, net 30. If the retailer takes both discounts, how much is paid to the vendor?

14. How can cumulative quantity discounts be considered to be anticompetitive?

LO•6   **What methods are available to the retailer for controlling loss through shrinkage, vendor collusion, and theft?**

15. Why is the receiving room such a high theft area for retailers?

16. Should the retailer's right to security take precedence over the employee's and the customer's right to privacy when retailers set up an electronic monitoring system in their stores to curb losses from theft?

Sample Test Questions

LO•1   **Determine the buyer's BOM for August, using the percentage variation method, based on the following information: planned sales for August = $170,000; average monthly sales = $142,000; average stock for the season = $425,000.**

a. $466,900
b. $390,000
c. $254,400
d. $425,000
e. $453,800

LO•2   **The open-to-buy concept provides information about how much the buyer can order at**

a. the beginning of a merchandising period
b. the middle of a merchandising period
c. the end of a merchandising period
d. anytime during the merchandising period
e. anytime a vendor fails to ship merchandise on time

LO•3   **Which of the following factors is not a constraint on the retailer's optimal merchandise mix?**

a. space
b. merchandise turnover
c. legal
d. dollar merchandise
e. market

LO•4   **A vendor profitability analysis statement**

a. is a vendor's financial statement that is made available to all retailers
b. is a retailer's analysis of the profitability of the different vendors and their lines from the prior year

c. is a schedule maintained by the retailer, which shows each vendor's initial data for new lines, shipment of orders, and gross margins

d. is a retailer's financial statement used by the vendor for determining credit limits

e. contains a list of who provided the retailer with discounts during the prior three years

LO•5 **A cumulative quantity discount is based on**

a. a single purchase

b. the total amount of merchandise purchased over a period of time

c. the total amount of merchandise purchased since you began dealing with a vendor

d. the amount of free merchandise a vendor is offering

e. cumulative discounts are only offered if a buyer is purchasing more than 50,000 units

LO•6 **Which two parties are usually involved in losses due to vendor collusion?**

a. delivery people and customers

b. retail employee signing for the delivery and delivery person

c. vendor sale representative and retail employee signing for the delivery

d. customers and vendor sales representative

e. vendor sales representative and the retailer's accountant

Applications

Writing and Speaking Exercise   It is early September and the local economy is starting to slow, which will affect sales in your department. As the store's newest buyer (you moved into your current position in early March), you do not want to make any merchandising mistakes in your first Christmas season. Today you receive a memo from the president stating, "I would rather lose sales than get stuck with a tremendous overhang of merchandise and end up giving it away come December. So cut back your OTB by 25 percent." After reading this memo several times, you decide to respond to the president. What will your response say?

Retail Project   In the chapter, we mentioned that before going to market you can check out the Council on Economic Priorities (CEP) web site (www.cepnyc.org), which ranks consumer products manufacturers, as well as retailers, on several workplace issues. In addition, the web site also looks at several other issues relating to corporate social responsibility: charitable giving, community outreach, disclosure of information, environment, family benefits, and the advancement of minorities and women.

Go to this web site and examine for yourself how the CEP grades each one of these issues. Do you agree or disagree with the statement that retail buyers should examine this web site before going to market so as to not purchase merchandise from manufacturers on the dishonor roll? Or should retailers merely check out this web site to be prepared for any future problems involving manufacturers of products that they are selling? Finally, are some of these issues more important than others?

Case   Responsibilities in the Retail Supply Chain

For years, American regulators have worried that the low-cost merchandise that was so popular with consumers was being made by political prisoners in China. However, the real worry may be closer to home. Many of this country's garment manufacturers supplying the biggest retailers rely on small subcontractors to cut and assemble the clothing that they sell to the retailers. Competitive pressures from countries with lower labor costs has caused a resurgence in what was once thought to be a 100-year-old problem: sweatshop conditions to keep costs down. Highly publicized raids on small factories have turned up unsafe conditions, subminimum wages, and violations of overtime requirements across the country.

The goods manufactured were headed for major U.S. retailers. The Labor Department called on retailers to combat sweatshop conditions by policing their suppliers and the suppliers' subcontractors. With more than 20,000 domestic subcontractors and declining budgets, the government is hard pressed to police these small firms that often open and close, and rename their operations, with great speed to avoid detection.

However, retailers are not legally responsible for labor violations of their suppliers' subcontractors and they may legally sell such goods. The Labor Department is hoping that bad publicity, such as the announcement of the major retailers selling items manufactured in these plants, will get retailers involved, and it has asked retailers to make unannounced spot checks on these firms. Unfortunately, the announcement of such a "hit list" did not seem to affect consumer behavior. Besides, the cost would be too great for all size retailers. Sears alone uses 10,000 direct suppliers, each with its own subcontractors. This complex network makes it difficult to determine which firm actually makes goods for a retailer. Retailers also claim to lack the legal expertise to detect labor code violations, and their contracts are not written to perform these factory inspections. In addition, tough competition makes the expense of this supervision difficult to pass along to customers.

While conceding the cost factor, the Labor Department still wants retailer cooperation. Contracts, spokespeople for the department claim, can be written to include random spot checks. Experts can be hired. The Labor Department feels that retailers with large orders from manufacturers should be able to force subcontractor compliance.

The divisional merchandise manager has asked you for a recommendation on how the firm should address this issue. How do you respond?

Planning Your Own Retail Business   Judy Cox is in the process of developing the merchandise budget for her family clothing store, which she will be opening next year. She has decided to use the basic stock method of merchandise budgeting. Planned sales for the first half of next year are $635,000, and this is divided as follows: February = 9 percent, March = 10 percent, April = 15 percent, May = 21 percent, June = 22 percent, and July = 23 percent. Planned total retail reductions are 9 percent for February and March, 4 percent for April and May, and 12 percent for June and July. The planned initial markup percentage is 48 percent. Cox desires the rate of inventory turnover for the season to be two times. Also, she wants to begin the second half of the year with $400,000 in inventory at retail prices.

Develop a six month merchandise budget for Judy Cox.

Endnotes

1. "Category Management Can Work—Really," *Progressive Grocer*, May 1997: 5a.

2. Itamar Simonson, "The Effect of Product Assortment on Buyer Preferences," *Journal of Retailing*, Fall 1999: 347–370.

3. "A Blueprint for Local Assortment Management," *Chain Store Age*, February 1997: 27–34.

4. For a detailed discussion of this model, see Stephen Smith, Narendra Agrawal, and Shelby McIntyre, "A Discrete Optimization Model for Seasonal Merchandise Planning," *Journal of Retailing*, Summer 1998: 193–221.

5. "Finding Gold in the Supply Chain Stream," *Chain Store Age*, January 1997: 164.

6. "Managing for Results," *Wal-Mart's 1998 Annual Report*: 14.

7. Rockney G. Walters, "An Empirical Investigation into Retailer Response to Manufacturer Trade Promotion," *Journal of Retailing*, Summer 1989: 253–272.

8. "Can Toys"R"Us Get on Top of Its Game?" *Business Week*, April 7, 1997: 124–128; and "Is "Toys-R-Us" Playing Fair?" *U.S. News & World Report*, March 17, 1997: 53.

9. Rajeev Batra and Indrajit Sinha, "Consumer-Level Factors Moderating The Success of Private Label Brands," *Journal of Retailing*, Summer 2000: 175–191.

10. "P&G to Stores: Keep the Dented Crisco Cans," *Wall Street Journal*, March 21, 1997: B1.

11. The following example is based on "Unauthorized Channels of Distribution: Gray Markets," by Roy Howell, Robert Britney, Paul Kuzdrall, and James Wilcox, *Industrial Marketing Management* (1986): 257–263. Used with permission of the authors.

12. "Inside the Cult of Costco," *Fortune*, September 6, 1999: 185–190.

13. For a more complete discussion of loss prevention, the reader should consult *The Ernst & Young/IMRA Survey of Retail Loss Prevention Expenses and Trends* in the most recent January issue of *Chain Store Age*.

14. "Anti-Theft Balers," *Chain Store Age Executive*, February 1999: 82.

Apparel Merchandising's Unique Role in Retailing

by

Dr. Mary Ann Eastlick

University of Arizona

One of the most exciting and lucrative areas of retailing is ready-to-wear apparel. This is evidenced by the variety of retailers that offer fashion apparel ranging from traditional department and specialty retailers such as Macy's, Neiman-Marcus, and The Gap to discounters like Wal-Mart and Kmart.

Individuals interested in working in apparel retailing should be familiar with the differences involved in retailing fashion and nonfashion merchandise. Although fundamentals of retailing are the same across product and service classes, several characteristics of fashion goods can create a need for distinct approaches in conducting business. For example, special planning and control methods are used to monitor constant changes in fashion trends and predict consumer demand.

The purpose of this appendix is to describe several approaches used by apparel retailers to deal with unique characteristics of fashion products. In doing so, fashion is defined and described in relation to its life cycle and factors that influence its adoption and diffusion.

What Characterizes Apparel as Fashion?

The term *fashion* is often associated with apparel and accessories. In reality, it can be applied to a variety of products, services, and forms of human behavior,[1] such as apparel, furniture, architectural styles, tastes in food and restaurants, and preferences for different video games.

Two guidelines are used to identify objects as *fashion*:

1. whether aesthetic and emotional appeals are used in evaluating the object and
2. if the object is accepted by a sizable segment of consumers.

One characteristic common to fashion objects is that sensory subjective criteria including visual images, scents, tastes, sounds, and tactile feelings influence purchase and use decisions. Excellent examples of these aesthetic and emotional appeals are provided in messages communicated by fashion advertisements. Whereas a company like Calvin Klein promotes apparel that conveys a sensual or daring image, another, like DKNY or

Armani, emphasizes a sophisticated, refined appeal. Image-creating properties such as these can be important considerations when retailers predict product demand. Compared to functional properties like quality and price, these subjective characteristics are more difficult to observe, measure, and quantify.

Objects are not technically defined as fashion until they begin to experience acceptance by a sizable group of consumers. Acceptance implies that the use of a product is considered socially appropriate by one's reference groups (friends, family, coworkers, classmates, fraternity brothers, etc.). Given the variety of consumer segments that exist, what might be perceived as fashion by some groups will not be seen that way by others. Retailers need to recognize which products are considered fashionable by consumers in their target market.

Stages of Fashion Adoption: The Fashion Life Cycle

The process by which fashion is introduced, reaches widespread consumer acceptance, then eventually falls from popularity and becomes obsolete is an important consideration when predicting product demand. Although these stages correspond closely to the introduction, growth, maturity, and decline stages of retail life-cycle theory, the description of each phase for fashion stresses the important influence of social acceptance on the duration and shape of the life cycle. With fashion-oriented merchandise, the five-stage life cycle shown in Exhibit 9A.1 is used:

1. Fashion leadership
2. Increasing social visibility
3. Conformity within and across social groups
4. Social saturation
5. Decline and obsolescence[2]

| Exhibit 9A.1 | Five-Stage Fashion Life Cycle |

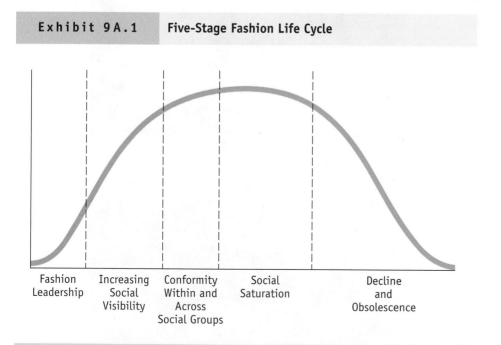

In the first phase of the fashion life cycle, a new fashion is introduced to the consumer via change agents. Change agents are typically leaders of social groups such as prominent personalities, celebrities, or members of the social elite. Following initial introduction, acceptance of the fashion within and across social groups continues to grow until reaching a state of mass conformity then saturation. At this time, consumers start to lose interest in the fashion, its acceptance begins to decline, and it eventually becomes obsolete.

The Fashion Life Cycle and a Store's Fashion Image

One way that retailers establish their fashion image is by associating their store with merchandise at one or more stages of the life cycle. For example, those retailers that sell fashion apparel in the first two stages of the cycle make up the "high fashion market," which consists of both one-of-a-kind and ready-to-wear designer apparel created by prominent European, U.S., and East Asian design houses such as those of Armani, Dior, and Marc Jacobs. Specialty department stores like Saks Fifth Avenue and Neiman-Marcus and designer boutiques are examples of upscale U.S. retailers selling high fashion. These stores can command premium prices for their merchandise because of the status associated with the prestige brand-name lines they carry and the superior quality and service they offer. In recent years, however, consumer demand for expensive, high

DKNY focuses its fashion design efforts on the high-fashion market and thus retailers that carry DKNY fashion can project a high-fashion image.

fashion apparel has been declining in the United States. High fashion design houses and retailers are turning to new, affluent consumer markets in parts of the world such as Asia,[3] ready-to-wear apparel, and other fashion products for new business opportunities.

The majority of apparel sold in the United States is *mass fashion,* which is made up of apparel that is in the middle of the life cycle (i.e., conformity within and across social groups). These styles are often adaptations or "knock-offs" of those offered by prominent designers. Examples of retailers involved in the mass fashion business include most traditional department and specialty chain stores, such as Dillard's, JCPenney Co., Bloomingdale's, The Limited, and Ann Taylor; promotional department stores like Mervyn's; and discounters like Target and Kmart. Competition among retailers in the mass fashion market is intense because these retailers are currently operating at overcapacity, the consumers they target have become very value and price oriented, and the costs of raw materials used to make the apparel are increasing.[4]

Mass fashion retailers attempt to differentiate themselves from their competitors by their product, price, and service offerings. A few mass fashion retailers including upscale department and specialty stores like Lord & Taylor and Talbot's are able to position themselves to appeal to upper-end, affluent consumers by offering "bridge" and better fashion lines and specialized customer services. *Bridge* lines have a fashion image somewhere between those of high and better fashions and are often the ready-to-wear lines of high fashion design houses such as DKNY and Ann Klein II. *Better lines* have an image just above that of mass fashion and include lines like Tommy Hilfiger, Liz Claiborne, and Jones New York. Considering the fashion life cycle, elements of bridge and better fashions (i.e., style, design details, color, or fabric) place these fashion lines in growth phases of their life cycles (i.e., stages that correspond to the fashion life stage of increasing social visibility).

Mass fashion retailers also seek to differentiate themselves from their competitors by developing private label merchandise to be sold exclusively by their stores. They either work with designers or celebrities and product developers from resident buying offices and apparel manufacturing firms or employ their own development and design personnel to create this merchandise. For example, Wal-Mart and Kmart have successfully used celebrity private labels such as the Kathie Lee Gifford and Jaclyn Smith lines, respectively, to increase their market share in the mass fashion business. Others like Talbot's maintain the image of their own Talbot's brand.

Fashion apparel in the social saturation stage of the life cycle is usually sold by *closeout* retailers, which specialize in buying the entire inventory or excess inventory of manufacturers or retailers going out of business. Sometimes, in addition to selling excess production of current styles or sizes, outlet stores also offer slow-selling fashions from previous seasons at extremely low prices.

Merchandise in the last stage, decline and obsolescence, has little demand, even at extremely low prices. Therefore, such merchandise is usually given away to charitable organizations and thrift shops.

Fashion Adoption and Diffusion

The extent of consumer acceptance determines the manner and speed at which fashion moves through the stages in its life cycle. Acceptance rates are influenced by economic, social, political, psychological, and lifestyle factors, and it is important that retailers understand these theories. Several theories are used to explain how these factors affect fashion adoption and diffusion.[5]

Downward Flow Theory

Advocates of the *downward flow* (or *trickle-down*) *theory* claim that fashion is first introduced by exposure from the upper socioeconomic classes. Diffusion occurs as the fashion is adopted by successively lower social classes who are attempting to imitate social classes above them and compete for social status. As adoption gradually diffuses to lower classes, the upper class differentiates itself by turning to new fashions. This theory is not widely used to explain contemporary fashion adoption and diffusion because it proposes that wealthy fashion clientele and their fashion designers dictate fashion to other consumers.

Collective Selection Theory

The *collective selection theory* proposes that most fashion diffuses horizontally across social groups through social interactions and interpersonal influences. It states that initial adoption and acceptance of a fashion can occur almost simultaneously across socioeconomic classes because of both mass production and the mass communication of consumer information.

This theory is widely accepted as being most applicable to contemporary fashion adoption. It is often used to explain why similar fashion styles are offered by diverse groups of retailers at a variety of price ranges. Collective selection also explains the increased speed at which fashion travels through its life cycle. For example, communication technologies, such as the Internet, have enabled some mass fashion retailers to copy designer fashions and make them available for sale before the designers' originals are even produced.[6]

Subcultural Leadership Theory

Another common theory of fashion adoption and diffusion is the *subcultural leadership theory,* which recognizes the influence of subcultural groups such as youth, street gangs, and ethnic groups on the mass population. The theory advocates that fashion may flow in an outward direction through the social classes or from a subcultural group to the mass population. This manner of fashion adoption was highly evident in the 1960s and 1970s as fashions worn by youth (such as the use of jeans for everyday apparel) were accepted by the mass population. The adoption of the "grunge" look introduced by 1990s rock groups to youth is also explained by the subcultural leadership theory.

Communication Models

Another important group of theories used to describe fashion adoption are known as communication models. These *communication models* describe the influence of mass media and interpersonal communications on the adoption process. Communication models also recognize the role of fashion change agents including innovators, opinion

The grunge fashion look evolved from a distinctive subculture.

leaders, and innovative communicators who provide visual and verbal communication about new fashions.

One communication model emphasizes the symbolic meanings that consumers attach to their possessions.[7] This approach is consistent with an emerging theme of contemporary research on consumer behavior called hedonic or symbolic consumption. When applied to fashion products, this model focuses on relationships between an individual's self-image, social identity, and the images communicated through use of various fashion objects.

Other similar research proposes that retail patronage motives for hedonically consumed products like fashion rely more on symbolic than on tangible features of such products.[8] As information is gained from this field of research, fashion retailers may benefit from a better understanding of the symbolic and aesthetic product characteristics that motivate fashion consumers.

Understanding Fashion Adoption

Just as changes in social, economic, technological, and political conditions cause changes in the retailer's strategies, operations, or managerial decisions, these environmental factors also stimulate new fashion trends. Knowledge of fashion adoption theories can be useful for predicting how new fashions will diffuse through society and making retail mix decisions to promote their acceptance. The following two examples illustrate these points.

Influence of Technology on Fashion Distribution

New technologies, such as mass customization and e-tailing, have the potential to radically change the manner in which fashion products are produced and distributed to consumers. A futuristic view of mass customization involves the use of imaging devices capable of scanning an individual customer's body. The image then will be stored and can serve as an electronic paper doll on which garments from racks or in electronic picture form can be superimposed on the body image. Items can then be custom-made by manufacturers who will use the body image as an electronic pattern.[9] These fashions may be sold through both store and e-tailers. To encourage mass market acceptance of these new manufacturing and retailing methods, companies will need to identify opinion leaders to promote their benefits as well as the innovators and early adopters who will use them.

Use of Change Agents

The U.S. consumer is increasingly value oriented and has developed a more functional attitude toward clothing purchases. These social and economic trends create new growth opportunities for discounters like Wal-Mart and moderately priced department stores such as Sears and JCPenney. A variety of strategies including well-known brands, reputable private-label programs, and celebrity endorsements are being successfully employed to target new markets and have contributed to a growing apparel business for these retailers at the expense of both department and specialty stores.

Unique Challenges of Retailing Fashion

The symbolic properties of fashion goods combined with the complex social interactions that influence their adoption and diffusion create unique challenges for fashion retailers. Among these challenges are managing products with short product life cycles, broken life cycles, and symbolic and aesthetic characteristics that can be difficult to identify.

Short Product Life Cycles

Fashion trends change constantly because they result from social, economic, political, and technological conditions influencing consumer behavior. Therefore, life cycles for fashion products tend to be relatively short. When changes in fashion are gradual or evolutionary, they can be monitored and managed more easily than when changes occur rapidly.

Although fashion goods move through their life cycles at varying rates, there is evidence that fashion, like most other products, is also experiencing increasingly shorter product life cycles. One explanation for more rapid changes in fashion trends is the increased speed at which information on new fashions is disseminated to consumers through mass media and other electronic communication technologies.

Shortened product life cycles mean that retailers must pay careful attention to product demand. If a particular fashion experiences accelerated sales growth, a retailer must not only have sufficient inventory available to meet increased demand, but must also be able to recognize whether the product is a fad or is entering the decline stage of its life cycle. In either case, saturation among consumers will follow quickly. Excess inventory may then be difficult to sell, resulting in a loss to the retailer. Merchandise information systems that use computerized inventory management to effectively manage the time between the manufacturing of a product and its sales, similar to those employed by stores like Dillard's and Sears Roebuck and Co., are becoming essential for fashion retailers.

Although short product life cycles are generally considered a phenomena reserved for fashion products, business analysts report that virtually all types of businesses are experiencing reduced lead times for new product development and shorter product life cycles. Consequently, all types of retailers may eventually have to become more "fashion oriented" with respect to their merchandising decisions.

Broken Product Life Cycles

Many classifications of fashion goods are subject to temporary interruptions in their life cycles. There are three distinct reasons for broken cycles: seasonal, catastrophic, and revolutionary. Seasonal breaks, which are normally due to changing climactic conditions, are the most common reason for a life cycle interruption. Catastrophic events, such as wars, and fashion revolutions are not as common and are beyond the scope of this appendix.

For apparel, changing weather patterns create needs for different clothing styles and fabrications. Also in most regions of the country, custom dictates the use of different colors and fabrics based on the season of the year. Consequently, demand for seasonal fashion products is not continuous throughout the life of the product. For some products, the life cycle can stop at the end of a season and start again the next time the season begins. For others, the life cycle may only span the length of a season. The fashion industry has geared its distribution efforts to these seasonal shifts in demand. For women's apparel, suppliers produce up to five seasonal collections: spring, summer or transition, fall I, fall II, and resort or holiday. For menswear, there are typically two to four seasonal lines produced depending on whether the supplier produces tailored menswear or sportswear.

Symbolic and Aesthetic Consumption Properties

Fashion products convey meanings about a user to others in his or her social group that play an important role in the decision to purchase or, for that matter, discard a fashion. The meanings communicated by fashion are based on subjective criteria and emotional responses that come from within an individual. They are not readily observable and may be difficult to identify.

Consumer preferences for products displaying designer names like Gucci or Dior or licensed cartoon characters like Mickey Mouse provide evidence of the importance of symbolism and emotional appeal present in fashion goods. That consumers discard usable fashions out of boredom or because they are perceived to be outdated is another indicator of the importance of symbolism. Often, there is little relationship between price and value measured in objective terms like quality, dependability, and service.

Adapting Retail Practices

Although fashion retailers operate in a manner that is substantially similar to nonfashion retailers, they find it necessary to adapt specific practices to address needs created by distinct characteristics of fashion goods. This section describes several of these practices including identifying consumer segments and creating buying and assortment plans. The impact of technological advances on buying and controlling merchandise is also discussed.

Identifying Consumer Fashion Segments

Chapter 2, Retail Strategic Planning and Operations Management, addressed the importance of accurately identifying a viable target market and selecting appropriate retail mix strategies. Because competition among fashion retailers is very intense, effective consumer segmentation is essential to survival.

Research has shown the long-term level of involvement in fashion to be very effective for differentiating segments of fashion consumers.[10] Differences in fashion involvement are related to variations in the importance given merchandise price, quality, service, and fashionability. Demographic and socioeconomic characteristics, preferences for different fashion information sources, shopper orientations, lifestyles, and store choice also vary by level of fashion involvement. In addition, fashion involvement is predicted to be useful for identifying segments of fashion consumers with different attitudes toward the symbolic properties of fashion goods.

Another way to effectively segment fashion consumers is to target segments with unique fashion needs. Special groups such as plus-size women, big and tall men, and pregnant women are all examples of niches targeted by both fashion retailers and manufacturers.

Developing Assortment Plans

A common goal of retailers is offering a merchandise assortment balanced to consumer demand. Because demand for fashion changes constantly, maintaining a balanced fashion assortment is of major importance to fashion retailers.

Separate assortment plans are developed for both basic and fashion merchandise categories. Basic or staple categories include goods whose product attributes are similar from one selling season to the next, whereas the attributes of fashion categories are highly susceptible to change. Merchandising decisions related to these attributes (i.e., styles, design features, colors, fabrics, etc.) for fashion categories need to be monitored closely and revised to take advantage of new fashion trends.

Technological advances in information systems have greatly enhanced the fashion retailer's ability to plan and maintain balanced assortments. Some fashion retailers are able to augment their traditional merchandise information system with information from their customer databases. Fashion retailers like Talbot's, Saks Fifth Avenue, and Bloomingdale's use their customer databases to identify and build loyalty among active customers by marketing to their individual needs. In turn, these retailers use purchase profiles developed from their databases to plan and maintain their merchandise assortments.

Retailer-Supplier Relationships

All retailers are finding that establishing closer working relations with suppliers is essential for survival. Because of keen competitiveness in the fashion business and increased segmentation of consumer markets, fashion retailers are placing increasing importance on developing the supplier relationships pointed out in Chapter 5, Channel Behavior. Partnerships, especially those utilizing quick response (QR) systems, are of particular importance to retailers that sell fashion goods.

For fashion retailers that have adopted quick response, the benefits have exceeded initial expectations. Whereas basic assortments are automatically replenished by the vendor when they reach minimum stock levels, fashion assortments are monitored very closely by buying personnel. This permits detailed analysis of the performance of a product by important attributes such as size, style, and color and enables a buying staff to respond more precisely to consumer demand for changing fashion trends. As a result of using quick response, fashion goods retailers report dramatic increases in sales and turnover and decreases in markdowns.

The effectiveness of quick response also influences the manner in which some of the large retailers purchase merchandise. Many now have buying teams that are responsible for establishing master basic and model stock plans and developing an approved vendor list. Vendors are now selected not only on factors like product quality, price, and delivery schedules but also on their capabilities for "partnershiping" using quick response.

The use of merchandise planners or coordinators, a relatively new middle management position created by upscale fashion retailers and manufacturers, provides evidence of the importance of selling partnerships for retailers and vendors. These positions are found in either large department and specialty retailers like Mervyn's and Macy's or collection manufacturers such as Polo, Nautica, Liz Claiborne, and Perry Ellis. Planners are employed to track collection sales and other merchandise performance information, assist in buying and reordering merchandise, and present selling seminars. They provide suppliers with increased consumer exposure and offer assistance in analyzing their business with a supplier and monitoring fashion trends.

Summary

Fashion retailing is a very dynamic business due not only to distinct characteristics associated with the product class but also to complex social interactions that influ-ence fashion adoption and diffusion. Factors related to unique characteristics of fashion products including constant change that results in short life cycles and a tendency to experience broken life cycles were described. Difficulties in identifying the important symbolic and aesthetic properties of fashion goods were also discussed.

Retailers have adapted several practices for identifying target consumers and planning and controlling fashion assortments to address the special problems in merchandising fashion goods. In addition, advances in selling partnerships with suppliers augment a fashion retailer's ability to analyze consumer demand and improve productivity and financial performance.

Endnotes

1. George B. Sproles, *Fashion Consumer Behavior Toward Dress* (Minneapolis, MN: Burgess, 1979): 5.

2. Ibid., 5–8.

3. "French Fashion Loses Its Primacy as Women Leave Couture Behind," *Wall Street Journal*, August 29, 1995: A1, A9.

4. "Out of Fashion, Many Women Lose Interest in Clothes, to Retailers Dismay," *Wall Street Journal*, February 28, 1995: A10; and "Consumers Draw the Line in Fashion," *Fortune*, May 1, 1995: 21.

5. George B. Sproles, "Behavioral Science Theories of Fashion," in Michael R. Solomon, ed., *The Psychology of Fashion* (Lexington, MA: D. C. Heath, 1983): 55–70; and Susan B. Kaiser, *The Social Psychology of Clothing* (New York: Macmillan, 1985): 332–338.

6. "Fashion Knockoffs Hit Stores before Originals as Designers Seeth," *Wall Street Journal*, August 8, 1994: A1, A4.

7. Richard A. Feinberg, Lisa Mataro, and Jeffrey Burroughs, "Clothing and Social Identity," *Clothing and Textiles Research Journal*, Fall 1992: 18–23; Russell Belk, Melanie Wallendorf, and John F. Sherry Jr., "The Sacred and the Profane in Consumer Behavior: Theodicy on the Odyssey," *Journal of Consumer Research*, June 1989: 1–13; Elizabeth C. Hirschman and Morris B. Holbrook, "Hedonic Consumption: Emerging Concepts, Methods, and Propositions," *Journal of Marketing*, Summer 1982: 92–101.

8. Hirschman and Holbrook: 95–97.

9. "Garment Scanner Could Be a Perfect Fit," *Wall Street Journal*, September 20, 1994: B1, B6.

10. Jonathan Gutman and Michael Mills, "Fashion Life Style, Self Concept, Shopping Orientation, and Store Patronage: An Integrative Analysis," *Journal of Retailing*, Summer 1982: 64–86; Charles W. King and Lawrence J. Ring, "Market Positioning across Retail Fashion Institutions: A Comparative Analysis of Store Types," *Journal of Retailing*, Spring 1980: 37–55; and Lawrence J. Ring, "High-End Fashion Positioning", in William R. Darden and Robert F. Lusch, eds., *Patronage Behavior and Retail Management* (New York: Elsevier Science, 1983): 165–178.

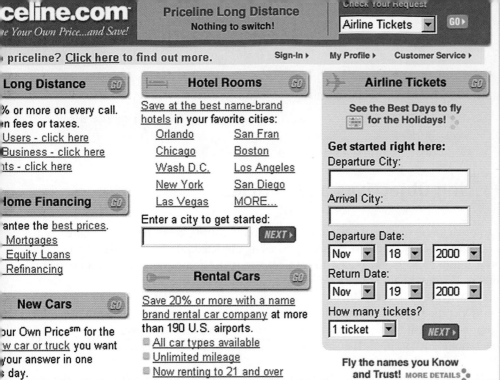

Priceline.com has revolutionized retail pricing by allowing the customers to name their own prices. The potential customer will then wait, usually one business day, to learn if any seller will provide the product or service at that price.

Merchandise Pricing

Overview

In this chapter, we examine the retailer's need to make pricing decisions. We begin with a discussion of the impact of a firm's objectives on its pricing policies. After reviewing several strategies, we look at why initial markups and maintained markups are seldom the same. We also discuss how a retailer establishes an initial markup. We conclude this chapter with a discussion of why and how a retailer takes markdowns during the normal course of business.

Learning Objectives

After reading this chapter, you should be able to

1. discuss the factors to be considered when establishing a retailer's pricing objectives and policies

2. describe the differences between the various pricing strategies available to the retailer

3. describe how retailers calculate the various markups

4. discuss why markdown management is so important in retailing, as well as some of the errors that cause markdowns

---

LO • 1
What factors should be considered when establishing a retailer's pricing objectives and policies?

Pricing Objectives and Policies

Although most retailers have gotten savvy about cutting costs, few have figured out how much money they have passed up by using outdated pricing strategies and tactics. As a result, retailers today tend to routinely overprice some products and underprice others. Pricing should not be a difficult decision, if retailers have been performing their other activities correctly. Pricing, as we pointed out in our Retail Strategic Planning and Operations Management Model (Exhibit 2.3), is an interactive decision made in conjunction with the firm's mission statement, its goals and objectives, its strategy, its operational management (i.e., merchandise planning, promotional mix, customer services, facilities, and people.

Pricing, as pointed out in Chapter 1's Service Retailing box on golf course pricing, does present more difficult decisions for retailers of services. This higher degree of difficulty exists because services are intangible, not easily stored, and cannot be returned to the vendor for credit. A movie theater running a hit movie during a blizzard will have the same fixed costs for being open as it would on any other night. The theater manager cannot resell the empty seats at a later date or increase attendance on the night of the blizzard by reducing ticket prices. It is no coincidence that service retailers, beginning with airlines, then hotels, and even now golf courses were the first to get "smart" in making their pricing decisions.[1]

Interactive Pricing Decisions

As shown in Exhibit 10.1, decisions regarding pricing objectives should be interactive with other retail decisions. Specifically, the decision to price an item at a certain level should interact with the retailer's decisions on lines of merchandise carried, location, promotion, credit, customer services, the store image the retailer wishes to convey, as well as the legal constraints discussed in Chapter 6.

Merchandise   Retailers should not set prices without carefully analyzing the attributes of the merchandise being priced. Does the merchandise have attributes that differentiate it from comparable merchandise at competing retailers? What is the value of these attributes to the consumer? Consider, for example, the menswear retailer who has purchased 100 men's suits for the fall selling season. What are the attributes of these suits (size, color, type of fabric, cut or style, brand label, quality of workmanship, quality of fabric)? How does the consumer value these attributes? Is a Giorgio Armani label more valuable than a Stanley Blacker label or a Hart-Shafner Marx label? Is good workmanship worth more? Are better-quality fabrics worth more? The answers to these questions are not easily determined; they depend on the retailer's market and how the retailer makes the consumer aware of these differences in the various merchandise lines.

Merchandise selection presents the retailer with another decision: the range of prices to be made available to the consumer. Remember, the retailer's controllable element of price can be either the cost of goods sold or the gross margin that is added to

Exhibit 10.1	**Interaction between a Retailer's Pricing Objectives and Other Decisions**

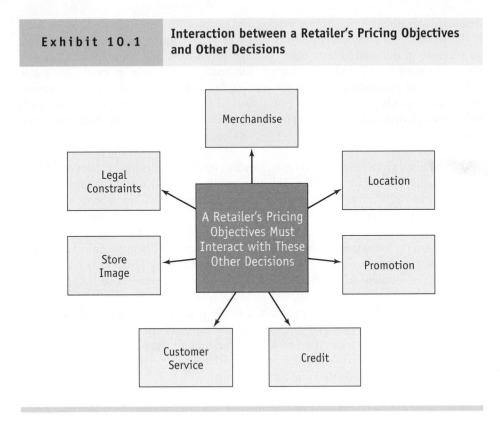

the cost. The retailer, in deciding to buy an item to sell at a specific price, may either purchase lower-cost merchandise and have a high gross margin to offset the higher expenses needed to sell at that price, or purchase more expensive goods and reduce the gross margin and expenses in order to sell at a given price.

Location   The location of the retail store, as we discussed in Chapter 7, has a significant effect on prices that can be charged. The closer the store is to competitors with comparable merchandise and customer service, the less pricing flexibility the retailer has. The distance between the store and the customer is also important. Generally, if the retailer wants to attract customers from a greater distance, it must either increase its promotional efforts or lower prices on its merchandise. This is because of the increasing travel costs (expressed in both time and dollar amounts) consumers incur when they are located farther from the store. Travel costs cut into the amount the customer is able or willing to pay for the merchandise, thus forcing the retailer to lower prices to attract those customers. For example, the lowest prices for many brand-name products can usually be found at factory outlet malls, yet these locations usually have the highest travel costs. Thus, for many consumers it is cheaper to purchase the merchandise at a nearby retailer. However, catalog and on-line retailers break down location barriers providing a national and worldwide presence. Thus, pricing for these retailers is balanced between price increases for providing greater convenience to customers with price decreases which create higher volume and the ability to spread overhead over this higher volume.

Promotion   The next chapter illustrates how promotion can increase demand for the retailer's merchandise. This chapter, however, shows how pricing can influence demand. This does not mean that pricing and promotion decisions are independent. If the retailer promotes heavily and is also very price competitive, the result may be an increase in demand greater than the high promotion and lower price strategies would produce independently. Imagine, for example, the retailer establishing low prices but not promoting them in the marketplace. How would consumers know of the price cuts? Or imagine heavy promotion but no cut in prices. Obviously, each will generate demand, but the interactive and cumulative effect of both would be much greater.

Credit   For a given price level on merchandise, retailers selling on credit, even if they are only using bank cards, are often able to generate greater demand than retailers not selling on credit. Conversely, retailers selling merchandise on credit may be able to charge slightly higher prices than retailers not selling on credit and still generate the same demand as noncredit retailers. That credit-granting retailers can charge higher prices is seen by the action of some retailers offering special discounts for cash-paying customers. This is an attempt to eliminate the 1.5 to 4.5 percent that credit card companies charge retailers on credit card purchases and shift the credit costs back on the customers actually using the credit.

Although most U.S. retailers maintain a single pricing policy for credit and cash payments (i.e., you pay the same with credit or cash), many retailers in other countries do not. In some cases, prices marked are cash prices and thus customers are charged more if they decide to pay using credit. Alternatively, when prices marked are credit prices, consumers can get a discount for paying with cash.

E-tailers targeting teens, who account for nearly $150 billion in retail sales annually, have a special problem with regards to credit because on-line purchases require a credit card. Teen retailers, such as Delia, are trying to overcome such problems through the use of third-party web sites, such as icanbuy.com and RocketCash.com. These web sites allow parents to set up accounts that their children can use to make purchases at participating e-tailers.

Customer Services   Retailers that offer many customer services (delivery, gift wrapping, alterations, more pleasant surroundings, sales assistance) tend to have higher prices. A decision to offer many customer services will automatically increase operating expenses and thus prompt management to increase retail prices to cover these additional expenses. However, such a policy may result in higher profits. Consider women's dresses. Customer service used to be common in department stores that took 50 to 60 percent initial markups, but pricing pressure by discounters caused department stores to respond by cutting markups and service. Women purchasing dresses began to feel neglected in department stores, especially when they had to start paying for alterations. Specialty stores have picked up on this and as a result offer the consumer greater assistance in selecting and trying on a dress, something unheard of in the low-price stores. Another example of a retailer justifying a higher price by offering outstanding service is No Kidding. This small toy store in an affluent suburb just west of Boston cannot compete with the retail megamarkets on either price or variety. Therefore, it does not carry the extremely popular items, such as Barbie, Nintendo, or the latest SonyPlaystation that everybody else discounts. Rather, No Kidding carries items that cannot be found in the bigger stores. However, what enables No Kidding to produce a profit at a time when most small toy shops fail is the makeup and behavior of its sales staff. This well-informed staff is mostly made up of moonlighting teachers who can discuss the finer points of play and inform the purchaser what is developmentally correct for a child of a certain age. In addition, the store wraps gifts at no charge, accepts returns without a re-

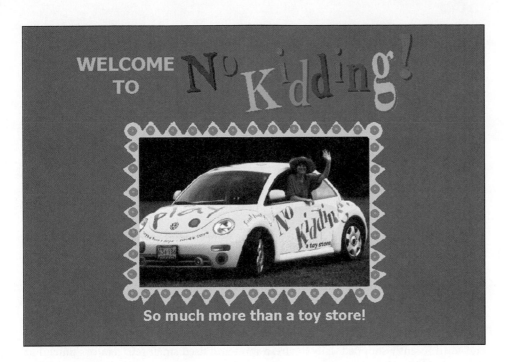

Retailers that offer higher levels of customer service have more pricing flexibility. No Kidding offers hard-to-find toys and employs a highly informed and helpful sales staff which help to justify its higher prices.

ceipt, and donates part of its profits to local schools and public television.[2] In fact, many consumers are willing to pay more for extra service. Consequently, it is important to remember that customer service decisions interact strongly with pricing decisions.

It is also important to note that service standards vary greatly by country. For example, Japan has extremely high service standards in their retail operations. In Japan, gift-wrapping is customary and retailers commonly accept merchandise for return even after the product has been well used. Alternatively, many countries throughout the world do not accept returns no matter what the reason. In these retail operations, once the product is sold it is no longer the retailer's concern—truly a buyer beware situation. Given differences in service levels, retailers must adapt pricing levels accordingly.

Store Image   One of the cues a customer uses in determining a retailer's image is the retailer's prices. If not offset by a poor location with poor service and merchandise selection, prices aid the customer (either consciously or unconsciously) in developing an image of the store. If an exclusive, high-fashion store, such as Nordstrom, started to discount its merchandise heavily, such as JCPenney currently does, it simply would not be the same store in the eyes of the customers. The merchandise, store decor, and personnel may remain unchanged, but the change in pricing strategy will significantly alter the overall store image. Thus, pricing policies and strategies interact with store image policies and strategies.

Legal Constraints   Though not an interactive decision, pricing decisions must only be made after examining the impact of the legal environment. This is especially true if state laws are involved and the retailer wants to operate in more than one state where these laws may be different. As pointed out in Chapter 6, a retailer may not set a price in collusion with a competitor, may not offer different prices in markets with the intent of driving a competitor out of business, may not sell below cost, and may not claim or imply in any ads that a price has been reduced unless it really has.

The other environmental factors discussed in Part 2 (consumer behavior, competitor behavior, and channel relationships), should also be considered when the retailer is developing its overall pricing and market strategy. Still, pricing decisions are easy to make in the United States when compared to some other countries' retail environments. For example, reducing prices hardly seems controversial, but it can be in Japan where it challenges a monopolistic system of distribution that has long been in place.

The United States has laws against vertical monopolies and other restraints of trade to ensure fair competition. American consumers can buy from a full-price retailer or they can use a discounter. American discounters depend on bulk purchase discounts from manufacturers, rapid inventory turnover, inexpensive real estate, and price-conscious shoppers who are willing to perform some marketing channel functions themselves.

However, the densely populated Japanese market does not work like the one in the United States. Japan's distribution system is not set up for discounters. Japan has nearly the same number of retail stores as the United States does, 1.6 million, but it has only half the population of the U. S. Many retailers in Japan are small mom-and-pop outlets. Supporting Japan's vast system of retailers is a multilayered network of 500,000 wholesalers who supply their customers with goods and credit. The system is expensive, but it is well suited to a country whose consumers lack personal transportation and until recently shopped daily for fresh food and used small refrigerators much like those used in college dorm rooms. Wholesalers compose a major link in the traditional system of *keiretsu*, the vertical monopoly of market distribution used by large manufacturers to suppress competition and keep fixed prices high.

Pricing Objectives

A retailer's pricing objectives should be in agreement with its mission statement and merchandising policies. Some objectives may be profit oriented, some may be sales oriented, and some may be to leave things just the way they are. However, by beginning with the proper pricing objectives, the retail manager can establish pricing policies that will complement the store's other decisions and assist in attracting the desired target customers.

Target return objective
is a pricing objective that states a specific level of profit, such as percentage of sales or return on capital invested, as an objective.

Profit-Oriented Objectives   Many retailers establish the objective of achieving either a certain rate of return or maximizing profits.

Target Return   A **target return objective** sets a specific level of profit as an objective. This amount is often stated as a percentage of sales or of the retailer's capital investment. A target return for a supermarket might be 2 percent of sales.

Profit maximization
is a pricing objective that seeks to obtain as much profit as possible.

Profit Maximization   A **profit maximization** objective seeks to obtain as much profit as possible. Some people claim that this pricing policy "charges all the traffic will bear."

Retailers know that if they follow such a policy, they are inviting competitors to enter the market. However, in some cases, a retailer may have a temporary monopoly and want to take advantage of it. The first video rental stores, knowing that others would follow shortly, often charged high rental fees, only to lower them when competition, such as Blockbuster, entered the market. This is **skimming,** or trying to sell at the highest price possible before settling on a more competitive level. Other retailers may take

Skimming
is a pricing objective in which price is initially set high on merchandise to skim the cream of demand before selling at more competitive prices.

Global Retailing

Although Markups Can Be Greater, Profits Can Be Lower

One of the most challenging issues for retailers as they expand globally is the widely divergent underlying factors influencing profits. As one might imagine, one of the greatest factors affecting profits is a retailer's ability to achieve its desired markup (selling price-cost). Thus, setting an effective selling price is critical. This necessitates taking into account local competition, the retailer's global price positioning, as well as differences in local taxes and other factors. However, even when retailers are able to obtain their desired selling price, underlying profits may diminish. For example, one European retailer was able to achieve its desired selling price with its European operations. However, in relation to its worldwide operations, its European operations had significantly lower profits. Why? Labor and land costs.

Labor and land costs are just two of the critical factors influencing a retailer's profits in its international operations. First, let's take a look at how labor costs influence profits. Labor is typically a significant share of costs for retailers. In the United States, most retailers employ a large number of unskilled workers at low wages. Alternatively, in other countries, such as France, labor can be a significant cost for the retailer due to the country's negotiated wages, which are often two to three times those in the United States. The significant difference in underlying labor costs necessitates a retailer to adjust its overall retail mix. Although simply raising prices would seem to be one manner of paying for higher labor costs, increased local prices may change the retailers position in the market. For example, Toys "R" Us realized that in order to maintain its price positioning and achieve its desired level of profits in France, it was necessary to reduce its labor force by one-third.

Second, the availability and resulting cost of real estate differs drastically from country to country. For example, for years Tokyo has maintained the world's highest property values. Therefore, global retailers, such as the United Kingdom's the Body Shop, need to make critical decisions regarding underlying cost adjustments to maintain pricing consistency. How, for example, should the Body Shop adjust its overall retail mix when land costs in Tokyo are 10 times as high as in other markets? Some might argue that the retailer could just pass the higher costs on to its customers as all retailers in the local market have similar real estate costs and therefore it can maintain its price positioning relative to local competition. Ignoring the obvious global price positioning inconsistency this would create, there is another concern. Although significant price adjustments might have been effective 20 years ago, today in an age of print catalogs and e-tailing, a one-price pricing policy would surely cannibalize the local brick & mortar retailer. For instance, if the Body Shop were to increase its local prices in Tokyo significantly, many Japanese customers would simply purchase their product from the Body Shop's print catalog, thus lowering the Tokyo brick & mortar's profits.

As you can now imagine, pricing for a global retailer is fraught with challenges. Balancing global corporate profits while adjusting to local competitive pricing pressures and maintaining a consistent global image and retail position in the face of widely diverse underlying costs creates challenges to global success.

---

the opposite approach and use **penetration,** which seeks to establish a loyal customer base by entering the market with a low price.

As our Global Retailing box illustrates, pricing aimed at achieving a certain profit objective is even more difficult for retailers competing globally.

Sales-Oriented Objectives Sales-oriented objectives seek some level of unit sales, dollar sales, or market share, but do not mention profit. Two of the types most commonly used in retailing are growth in market share and growth in dollar sales.

Although both of these objectives are common with retailers today, especially with smaller retailers, the achievement of either does not necessarily mean that profits will

Penetration
is a pricing objective in which price is set at a low level in order to penetrate the market and establish a loyal customer base.

also increase. After all, if a retailer lowers prices, gross margin will go down and sales may improve, but the retailer may not make more money.

Status Quo Objectives Retailers who are happy with their market share and level of profits sometimes adopt status quo objectives, or "don't rock the boat" pricing policies. Many supermarkets gave up on the extra profits and increases in market share that "double coupons" might have brought because they were afraid of what competitive actions would have resulted. It should be noted that such pricing actions as double couponing are not always effective and profitable. Many times, especially when other retailers match the promotion, it's only the retailer's regular customers who use them.

Also, some retailers prefer to compete on grounds other than price. Convenience stores, for example, seldom match the prices of nearby supermarkets. Still, sometimes retailers, such as McDonald's and Burger King, who want the consumer to focus on factors such as quality of food, service, and locational convenience, instead of price, are forced to drop prices in the face of mounting competition just to maintain status quo market share.

Managerial Question: Should the pricing objectives of a retailer's brick & mortar, catalog, and e-tailing operations be the same?

Pricing Policies

Pricing policies are rules of action, or guidelines, that ensure uniformity of pricing decisions within a retail operation. A large retailer has many buyers who are involved in pricing decisions. By establishing the store's overall pricing policies, the top merchandising executives provide these buyers with a framework for adopting specific pricing strategies for the entire organization.

A retail store's pricing policies should reflect the expectations of its target market. Very few retailers can appeal to all segments of the market. Low- and middle-income consumers are usually attracted to low-priced discount stores. The middle-class market often shops at moderate-priced general merchandise chains. Affluent consumers are frequently drawn to high-priced specialty stores that provide extra services. Only supermarkets are able to cross the various income lines, and even then there is some basis for segmentation. Successful retailers carefully position themselves in a market and then direct their specific pricing strategies toward satisfying their target market. Many times the proper pricing policies influence consumers to patronize one store over another.

In establishing a pricing policy, retailers must decide whether they should price above market levels, at market levels, or below market levels.

Above-market pricing policy
is a policy where retailers establish high prices because nonprice factors are more important to their target market than price.

Pricing above the Market Some retailers, either by design or circumstance, follow an **above-market pricing policy.** Certain market sectors are receptive to high prices because nonprice factors are more important to them than price. Some retailers such as Nordstrom offer such outstanding service that it has minimal price competition. Other retailers, such as small neighborhood drugstores and hardware stores, are forced to price above the market because of their high cost structure and low sales volume. Some other conditions that permit retailers to price above market levels involve merchandise offerings, services provided, convenient locations, and extended hours of operation.

Merchandise Offerings   Some consumers will pay higher-than-average prices for specialty items, for an exclusive line, or for unusual merchandise. Prestige retailers, such as Gucci or Neiman Marcus, carry high-priced specialty items. An exclusive line, such as Christian Dior, permits higher-than-average prices. Unusual merchandise, such as one-of-a-kind gifts in Neiman Marcus' annual Christmas catalog, is normally not price compared because no competitor carries similar merchandise.

Services Provided   In many communities, there are service-oriented merchants with a loyal group of customers who are willing to pay higher prices to obtain an array of services ranging from wardrobe counseling to delivery. Nordstrom's clerks have a habit of doing special things like dropping off purchases at a customer's home, sending thank you notes to customers, or even ironing a newly purchased shirt so the customer can wear it that day. These services put Nordstrom in a nonprice-competitive sector of retailing.

Convenient Locations   The convenient location of gift shops in hotels and airline terminals allows them to charge high prices. Knowing that consumers value time, fast-food retailers select sites adjacent to residential areas. Retailers in metropolitan office buildings often charge premium prices not only because of their accessible locations but because of their higher rents. In addition, consumers have no other place to shop. For example, at many airports a stranded, hungry flyer has to eat lunch there, or not eat. There are no other alternatives.

Extended Hours of Operation   By remaining open while other stores are closed, some merchants are able to charge higher-than-average prices. Service plazas on interstate highways justify their higher prices by never closing. However, e-tailers, competing against brick & mortar, brick & click, and other e-tailers, typically do not increase prices as a result of extended hours of operation.

Pricing at Market Levels   Most merchants want to be competitive with one another. The retailer's use of comparison shoppers—that is, having employees visit competitive retail outlets in order to compare prices—stems from this basic premise. Competitive pricing involves a **price zone,** a range of prices for a particular merchandise

Price zone
is a range of prices for a particular merchandise line that appeals to customers in a certain market segment.

Nordstrom prices above the market, however, this upscale retailer provides many extra services. Here we see longtime doorman, George Singleton, opening the door for a customer while waving to another, at Nordsrtom's flagship department store in downtown Seattle.

line that appeals to customers in a certain demographic group, such as Kmart selling women's tops for $9.99 to $19.99. Dillard's does not need to match the prices of Kmart. However, Macy's should establish prices that are on a similar level with its competitor, Bloomingdale's. At the other end of the price spectrum, Kmart should be competitively priced with Wal-Mart and Target. Pricing at market levels is extremely important for e-tailers given the ease of on-line price comparisons.

The size of a retail store affects its ability to compete on a price basis. Small retailers usually pay more for their merchandise and have higher expenses as a proportion of sales than larger retailers. Although small retailers have joined voluntary cooperative chains to reduce their expenses through quantity discounts, they continue to experience a cost disadvantage. For these reasons small retailers, such as mom-and-pop grocery stores and convenience stores, often stress convenience and service strategies rather than price in their retailing mix. Even in this case, the price cannot be too far out of line.

Below-market pricing policy

is a policy that regularly discounts merchandise from the established market price in order to build store traffic and generate high sales and gross margin dollars per square foot of selling space.

Pricing below the Market   Because there is a large market sector buying mainly on a price basis, a **below-market pricing policy** is attractive to many retailers such as discounters and warehouse clubs. For retailers to consistently price below the market and be profitable, they must concentrate on generating gross margin dollars per square foot of space, not the gross margin percentage. After all, profitability is not directly related to the gross margin percentage of the product sold but to the amount of gross margin per unit sold times the number of units sold. Such retailers must always try to increase the sales per square foot of store space as they are compelled to reduce their markups. In the on-line retail world, Amazon.com is well known for buying wisely and operating on lower margins than brick & mortar retailers.

eBay's introduction of the cyber-auction and Priceline.com's "name your own price" policy has led many to believe that all retailers will soon be forced to sell below market. (Never mind that it is impossible for everybody to sell below the average price.) Buyers and sellers around the world could use cyberspace to know what the "market will bear" and that it would be hard to charge a higher price than the lowest competitor. But this has not happened yet.[3] Amazon.com may charge lower prices than most brick & mortar stores for books, but its prices remain substantially above those of other on-line retailers. However, Amazon.com has a larger market share than all the low-price competitors combined. In fact, this probably means that although price is important, the low-price retailer must also convey trust and brand awareness to the consumer, which is a message America's two below-market leaders, Amazon.com (on-line) and Wal-Mart (brick & mortar), have sent the consumer.

In addition to buying wisely, which may include closeouts and seconds, below-market stores stock fast-selling merchandise, curtail customer services, and operate from modest facilities. Also, some of them stock private-label brands extensively and enhance their low-price image by promoting the price differences between their private brands and comparable national brands. That some retailers are successful with such a policy is evident by the fact that many local retailers, especially restaurants, now use supercenters as their suppliers.

LO • 2

What are the various pricing strategies available to the retailer?

Specific Pricing Strategies

Various pricing strategies are adopted by the traditional brick & mortar retailers in their effort to achieve certain pricing objectives. The pricing strategies should be in accord with the other components of the store's retail mix: location, promotion, display,

E-tailing

Pricing Strategies in an On-Line World

The Internet has created a dynamic world for retailers. One area of e-tailing that has dramatically changed from the traditional brick & mortar world is pricing. To better understand on-line pricing, one can examine a number of on-line pricing strategies currently in use.

To begin with, e-tailers are experimenting with numerous pricing strategies. For instance, most retailers, such as Amazon.com or Gap.com, maintain a one-price pricing strategy whereby all goods are offered at a set price. By employing this strategy, e-tailers are able to maintain consistency across markets. However, one challenge of the one-price strategy is its inflexibility when it comes to meeting different regional demand conditions. For example, although an e-tailer may be able to obtain a higher margin in the Los Angeles market than in the Kansas City market, a one-price strategy necessitates an e-tailer to determine its overall optimal price given national demand characteristics.

A second popular pricing strategy that has grown in importance is the auction pricing strategy. Although not new to the world of retailing, allowing consumers to bid for products and services has led to one of the most popular on-line pricing strategies to date. E-tailers set a floor price under which they will not sell the product and allow consumers to bid based on the value they place on the product or service. By allowing customers to bid for products and services, customer satisfaction increases and margins can, in some cases, be maximized. E-tailers, such as eBay, Amazon.com, and the Sharper Image, as well as many small on-line auction retailers, have implemented an auction strategy successfully.

A twist on the auction pricing strategy is the reverse auction. Using a reverse auction strategy, an e-tailer acts as an intermediary through which customers can indicate their desire to purchase a product or service. Then producers compete to offer the best price.

A similar strategy that has proved itself successful through Priceline.com is the "name your own price" strategy. The e-tailer using this strategy allows customers to determine the price they are willing to pay for a specific product or service. This information is then transferred to a number of select suppliers who determine if they are willing to accept the consumer's price.

Demand aggregation pricing is also an emerging on-line pricing strategy. Demand aggregation allows consumers to band together to negotiate better prices with retailers. Under this pricing strategy, the e-tailer actually negotiates a set price reduction schedule with sellers based on the number of consumers it can aggregate to purchase a specific product. For example, let's say that a Sharp 4-Head VCR has a manufacturer's suggested selling price of $130 and sells at a brick & mortar retailer for around $100. A consumer could go to an e-tailer such as Amazon.com to get the VCR for about $80. At a demand aggregation retailer, such as Mercata.com, the price may be $70 initially. However, as more and more people indicate a desire to purchase the product, the price will fall even more. Thus, in the end, although the customer was willing to pay $70 for the VCR, after all of the demand is aggregated (over a specified time period) the final price may be $55. Thus, by getting more people to buy the product, the price drops.

Though not exhaustive in terms of on-line pricing strategies, these examples provide insight into some of the most popular ones. However, the Internet is continually evolving and with it e-tailing pricing strategies are sure to as well. What new on-line pricing strategies may be just around the corner?

service level, and merchandise assortment. The chapter's E-tailing box describes some of the pricing models that e-tailers are using.

Customary Pricing

Customary pricing occurs when a retailer sets prices for goods and services and seeks to maintain those prices over an extended period of time. Candy bars, newspapers, movies, and vending machine products are all items that use customary pricing. For

Customary pricing is a policy in which the retailer sets prices for goods and services and seeks to maintain those prices over an extended period of time.

such products, retailers, such as movie theaters with their $8 ticket prices, seek to establish prices that customers can take for granted for long periods of time.

Variable Pricing

Variable pricing
is a policy that recognizes that differences in demand and cost necessitate that the retailer change prices in a fairly predictable manner.

Variable pricing is used when differences in demand and cost force the retailer to change prices in a fairly predictable manner. Flowers tend to be higher priced when demand is greater around Mother's Day and Valentine's Day. It is a common practice for most resorts to increase their rates on premium rooms in June, a busy wedding time. Tuesday and Wednesday nights tend to have lower demand for movies, so many theaters offer $2 specials on those nights. Fresh fruits tend to sell for less during their growing seasons, when the retailer's costs are down. Also, many restaurants offer the same meal at lunch as for dinner but with a discounted lunch price (often 10 percent to 20 percent lower) to increase demand.

Flexible Pricing

Flexible pricing
is a policy that encourages offering the same products and quantities to different customers at different prices.

Flexible pricing means offering the same products and quantities to different customers at different prices. Retailers generally use flexible pricing in situations calling for personal selling. The advantage of using flexible pricing is that the salesperson can make price adjustments based on the customer's interest, a competitor's price, a past relationship with the customer, or the customer's bargaining ability. Most jewelry stores and automobile dealerships use this pricing policy, although not all customers like it. Other retailers vary their prices by giving discounts to special consumer groups such as senior citizens and the clergy. Even some employee groups (for example, credit unions) have negotiated price discounts with selected retailers.

Flexible pricing can increase costs as customers begin to bargain for everything, or find that they paid more than a friend did for the same product. That is why the one-price policy is so popular in the United States.

One-Price Policy

One-price policy
is a policy that establishes that the retailer will charge all customers the same price for an item.

Under the **one-price policy,** a retailer charges the same price for an item to all customers. A one-price policy may be used in conjunction with customary or variable pricing. All people buying the same CD at a local retailer will pay the same price. Roland Hussey Macy, the founder of Macy's Department Store, is credited for adopting the one-price policy, but recently the authors have found evidence that a Sacramento retailer, Weinstock & Lubin, was using this policy in 1875, nearly four decades before Macy's.[4] This policy meant efficiency and fairness in handling customer transactions in a large store, where the selling activity is delegated to salespersons who have varying degrees of loyalty to the retailer. If salespeople were permitted to bargain over price, customers who are shrewd and assertive could conceivably negotiate terms that are unprofitable to the retailer.

A one-price policy, therefore, speeds up transactions and reduces the need for highly skilled salespeople. Most catalog operators adopt a one-price policy because they are forced to retain their prices until the expiration date of the catalog, which can be six months from its issuance.

Today, some automobile manufacturers, such as GM, who already has had success with this policy in its Saturn division, are encouraging their dealers to adopt the

The Saturn division of GM has generally been successful with its one-price policy for selling automobiles.

one-price policy as a means of regaining market share. For example, suppose that GM determines that most buyers of the Pontiac Grand Am SE want an FM/AM radio with CD player, antilock brakes, dual airbags, air conditioning, tilt steering wheel, and power door locks. By packaging all these options together, the dealers can sell the car for $15,995 which is substantially less than what the buyer would have paid buying all these "extras" separately. Also, GM hopes that the use of this one-price policy gives its dealers a competitive advantage over a similarly equipped Honda Accord LX or Toyota Camry DX. However, such a pricing policy will only work if all the dealers voluntarily agree to stick to the plan. Otherwise, the flexible price dealer will know the price it has to beat.

Price Lining

To simplify their pricing procedures and to aid consumers in making merchandise comparisons, some retailers establish a specified number of price lines or price points for each merchandise classification. Once the price lines are determined, these retailers purchase goods that fit into each line. This is called **price lining.** For example, the price lines for men's slacks could be limited to $29.95, $49.95, and $69.95. The monetary difference between the price lines should be large enough to reflect a value difference to consumers. This makes it easier for a salesperson to either trade up or trade down a customer. **Trading up** occurs when a salesperson moves a customer from a lower-priced line to a higher one. **Trading down** occurs when a customer is initially exposed to higher-priced lines but expresses the desire to purchase a lower-priced line.

Retailers select price lines that have the strongest consumer demand. By limiting the number of price lines, a retailer achieves broader assortments, which leads to increased sales and fewer markdowns. For example, a retailer who stocks 150 units of an item and has 6 price lines would have an assortment of only 25 units in each line. On the other hand, if the 150 units were divided among only 3 price lines, there would be 50 units in each line.

Price lining
is a pricing policy that is established to help customers make merchandise comparisons and involves establishing a specified number of price points for each merchandise classification.

Trading up
occurs when a retailer uses price lining and a salesperson moves a customer from a lower-priced line to a higher one.

Trading down
occurs when a retailer uses price lining, and a customer initially exposed to higher-priced lines expresses the desire to purchase a lower-priced line.

Many retailers of athletic footwear use price lining to provide customers ample choices within each price line and major value differences in each successively higher priced line.

When retailers are limited to certain price lines, they become specialists in those lines. This permits them to concentrate all their merchandising and promotional efforts on those lines, thus defining more clearly their store image. In addition, they direct their purchases to vendors who handle those lines. The vendors, in turn, provide favored treatment to their large-volume retailing customers. Other advantages of price lining include buying more efficiently, simplifying inventory control, and accelerating inventory turnover. From the shopper's perspective, it is easy to shop when price lining is used, because differences are perceived among the various price points.

An analysis of a store's best-selling price lines is essential prior to making any decision to alter them. Generally the middle-priced lines should account for the majority of sales. When the bulk of sales occurs at the extremes of the price lines, a retailer should take corrective actions. These include altering the assortments in the present price lines, changing the price lines, redirecting the salespersons' efforts, developing more effective promotions, or adjusting the total marketing mix to a new target market.

Odd Pricing

Odd pricing
is the practice of setting retail prices that end in the digits 5, 8, 9 — such as $29.95, $49.98, or $9.99.

The practice of setting retail prices that end in the digits 5, 8, or 9—such as $29.95, $49.98, or $9.99—is called **odd pricing.** A quick look at retail advertisements in newspapers will reveal that many retailers use an odd-pricing policy. Retailers feel that odd prices produce significantly higher sales. The effectiveness of the use of certain rather common odd-numbered prices based on the theory that $9.99 sounds lower to the customer than $10 and 99 cents sounds better than $1 has never been proven with any conclusive research.[5] Another theory suggests that the use of an odd price means the price is at the lowest level possible, thus encouraging the customer to purchase more units.

Still, a more plausible explanation for the adoption of odd-numbered pricing might go back to the early part of the 20th century before there was a sales tax. In those days, when merchandise was priced at even dollars, it was very easy for salesclerks to pocket either an occasional one-, five-, or ten-dollar bill or gold piece because they did not have to make change for the customer. When Marshall Field caught on to this, he devised the first odd-numbered pricing system to stop the practice. Field ruled that, "We'll charge 99 cents instead of even dollars. This will force the clerks to ring up the sales, open the cash register, put the money in and give the customer a receipt and change." Maybe this explains why despite the lack of supportive research, odd-pricing is such a standard in retailing today.

Because odd prices are associated with low prices, they are typically used by retailers who sell either at prices below the market or at the market. Retailers selling above the market, such as Neiman Marcus and Nordstrom, usually end their prices with even numbers that have come to denote quality. These retailers would likely sell an item for $90.00 rather than $89.99. Prestige-conscious retailers are not seeking bargain hunters as customers.

Multiple-Unit Pricing

With **multiple-unit pricing** the price of each unit in a multiple-unit package is less than the price of each unit if it were sold individually. Grocery retailers use multiple-unit pricing extensively in their sales of cigarettes, light bulbs, candy bars, and beverages. Apparel retailers often sell multiple units of underwear, hosiery, and shirts.

Retailers use multiple-unit pricing to encourage additional sales and to increase profits. The gross margin that is sacrificed in a multiple-unit sale is more than offset by the savings that occur from reduced selling and handling expenses. Generally multiple-unit pricing can be effectively employed for items that are either consumed rapidly or used together.

Multiple-unit pricing occurs when the price of each unit in a multiple-unit package is less than the price of each unit if it were sold individually.

Multiple-unit pricing is popular in supermarkets where many products sold are consumed rapidly and thus, the customer is receptive to buying more of the product than they immediately need.

Bundle Pricing

Bundling
occurs when distinct multiple items, generally from different merchandise lines, are offered at a special price.

Bundling generally involves selling distinct multiple items offered together at a special price. Here the perceived savings in cost or time for the bundle justifies the purchase. Many travel agencies use bundling for their vacation packages, by packaging airfare, hotel, transfers, and meals together. The example of GM's one-price policy for its Grand Am discussed earlier could also be an example of bundle pricing. Before Congress recently deregulated the telecommunications industry, consumers had to shop separately for local, long distance, paging, cable television, Internet access, and cellular service. While the so-called major telecommunications companies were busy trying to meet the various state and federal requirements to bundle these services together, the previously unknown Frontier Corp. became an industry leader by offering all of these together a year before everybody else did.

As mentioned in Chapter 3's Service Retailing box, bundle pricing can involve tying in a service with the product. Today, a small number of retailers are testing a form of bundling to encourage customers to patronize their establishments by providing baby-sitting services gratis or for a small fee.

For example, research by some movie theaters found that the main obstacle encountered by many parents in coming to the movies was the baby-sitting situation. As a result, some theaters now offer either "Monday Night Is Baby's Night" for babies, or child care centers for children aged 2 to 8. This later bundling program seems to be going over well with parents who previously could only think about attending PG movies.

Grocery stores and physical fitness centers are also testing the addition of child care facilities. Such action shows that retailers are getting more oriented toward their customers' needs, especially those times when child and adult activities really diverge (adult versus kiddie movies and getting a workout). Some parents, especially single parents, feel that some errands and tasks can be sharing activities, particularly trips to the grocery store. However, these parents also are aware that most of the time, youngsters get bored with sitting in a shopping cart.

Nevertheless, the future of these facilities is still unclear. Over the past decade, several for-profit child care centers in shopping malls have gone out of business because of the unpredictable feast-or-famine nature of demand. These centers have to be staffed at all times for anyone who walks in. As a result, centers, even those charging a fee, must have some subsidy from the sponsoring retailer or mall association to make a go of it, and the establishments have to look at child care as an amenity. Thus, the question remains, will consumers without children want to subsidize those with children through higher prices? Or will those with children be willing to pay the price?

Leader Pricing

Leader pricing
is when a high-demand item is priced low and is heavily advertised in order to attract customers into the store.

In **leader pricing** a high-demand item is priced low and advertised heavily in an effort to attract consumers into a store. The items selected for leader pricing should be widely known and bought frequently. In addition, information should be available that will permit consumers to make price comparisons. National brands of convenience goods, such as Crest toothpaste, Mitchum antiperspirant, Maxwell House coffee, and Coca-Cola, are often designated as leader items.[6]

Leader pricing is usually part of a promotional program that is directed to increase store traffic. A successful program will increase sales for all areas of a store. In many instances, the price of the leader item is reduced only for a special promotion. There are retailers, such as supermarkets, however, who regularly feature leader items.[7] Today,

Service Retailing

On-Line Services Help Consumers Find the Best Price

Price is a key shopping element. Comparing prices in the brick & mortar world was usually not worth the hassle. Going from retailer to retailer often took all day long, thus costing a consumer more in terms of their time than it actually saved them in money. In an on-line world, price is consistently ranked as consumers' number 1 reason for shopping on-line. However, even in the on-line world, comparing prices between e-tailers often takes all afternoon, clicking through one e-tailer's web site after another. Even then, consumers are never sure that they have checked all of the retailers that they need to. Enter a new breed of service retailers who have simplified everything from buying books to acquiring shipping services. Enter the world of on-line price comparison services providing consumers value by saving them time and money.

On-line price comparison retailers deal in information. These retailers — such as www.cdpricecompare.com, www.surfformusic.com in the music industry, www.dollarflowersroses.com and www.123-flowers.com in the flower industry, or www.iship.com for your shipping needs — collect pricing information from a wide variety of retailers and provide it to consumers in an easy-to-understand comparison format. Take for instance if you were in the mood for the latest Billboard number 1 album. Instead of going to www.cdnow.com, www.amazon.com, www.buy.com, www.barnesandnoble.com,

www.mymusic.com, www.musicuniverse.com, and so on to find the best price, you simply go to www.cdcompareprice.com and type in the title of the album. With one simple click, you get a comparison of the availability of the CD through the various on-line retailers with their prices clearly displayed. For example, the latest Billboard number 1 CD may be $14.94 at one on-line retailer but only $9.90 at another. A price savings of $5.04. The key to success for these on-line service retailers is in the faith that consumers put in them that they are in fact getting the best deal on-line.

Thus, retailers such as www.flowersandroses.com offer consumers a chance to compare flower prices across a wide range of on-line flower companies, such as Pro Flowers, Great Flowers, FlowerFarm, Flower.com, FlowersFast, FTD, florist.com, Flowers USA, 1-800-Flowers, Silk World, and PC Flowers and Gifts. Given the wide coverage of the market, consumers gain confidence in their purchase decision.

The service these on-line retailers provide consumers is invaluable. However, from the standpoint of on-line retailers, positioned on price, it means an increase in pressure to maintain operational efficiencies that will continually maintain the lowest prices, thus truly increasing the competitive on-line environment. Once again, the on-line world is reshaping retailing as we know it.

many convenience stores use gasoline as a leader. These retailers reduce their gas price by a penny or two, just enough to get the customer into their store. Once in the store, customers are exposed to fast-food sandwiches, groceries, fresh produce, beverages, and even fresh flowers. In such stores, the inside operations contribute over 70 percent of the store's gross margin dollars and subsidize the gasoline business. For those customers who just want gas, these stores have pay-at-the-pump facilities.

A retailer using leader pricing should carefully evaluate its usefulness. If consumers are limiting their purchases to only the leader items, then the policy is ineffective. Because the leader items may be sold at or near a retailer's cost, higher-markup items must also be sold to generate a profit for the retailer. An item that is sold below a retailer's cost is known as a **loss leader.** For example, every Thanksgiving many supermarkets sell turkeys at a loss in hopes of attracting consumers to their stores and making a profit on the rest of their purchases.

The pricing actions of discounters using below-market pricing have forced manufacturers into changing their pricing strategies, thus endangering another group of retailers' use of leader pricing. The use of **everyday low prices (EDLP)** has propelled Wal-Mart to the top spot in retail sales. Retailers using EDLP want vendors to offer

Loss leader
is an extreme form of leader pricing where an item is sold below a retailer's cost.

Everyday low prices (EDLP)
is when a retailer charges the same low price everyday throughout the year and seldom runs the product on sale.

them constant prices throughout the year by phasing out virtually all deep discounts and offering them the same low price every day. For example, instead of selling retailers a case of peanut butter for $20 one week and offering it on sale the next week for $15, they want it priced at $18 every week. This would limit the ability of leader pricers, such as supermarkets, to continue their use of "high-low pricing." **High-low pricing** involves the use of high everyday prices and low leader specials on featured items for their weekly ads. An example of a nonfood retailer using high-low pricing is JCPenney, which has regularly scheduled sales every week.

The use of leader pricing by e-tailers, when price is often the major criteria, has caused problems for consumers. After all, checking all those web sites for the best price takes time. This, as the chapter's Service Retailing box describes, has enabled a new type of service retailer to fill that gap.

High-low pricing involves the use of high everyday prices and low leader "specials" on items typically featured in weekly ads.

Bait and Switch Pricing

The practice of advertising a low-priced model of a shopping good, such as a television or a computer, to lure shoppers into a store is called **bait-and-switch pricing.** Once the shoppers are in the store, a salesperson tries to persuade them to purchase a higher-priced model. Bait-and-switch pricing, which was discussed in detail in Chapter 6, is considered by the Federal Trade Commission to be an illegal practice when the low-priced model used as bait is unavailable to shoppers, or as some in the industry describe as being "nailed to the floor."

Bait-and-switch pricing is a practice where a low-priced model of a shopping good, such as an automobile or refrigerator, is used to lure shoppers into a store and then the salesperson attempts to persuade them to purchase a higher-priced model.

Private-Label Brand Pricing

A private-label brand item often can be purchased by a retailer at a cheaper price, have a higher markup percentage, and still be priced lower than a comparable national brand. Private brands also permit the retailer a large degree of pricing freedom because consumers find it difficult to make exact comparisons between private brands and national brands of similar goods. Marks & Spencer, Mervyn's, Sears, Kmart, and others price their private brands below the market. A retailer can use private labels to differentiate itself and its merchandise from competitors. At a time when everybody seems to be selling the same things, retailers are using their own store's image as an advantage by developing their own exclusive private labels. Studio B, one of Bloomingdale's private labels, offers a trouser-and-vest outfit for $116. A look-alike designer-name outfit would cost more than $300. Zellers, a division of The Hudson Bay Company, has relied on private labels to respond to Wal-Mart's invasion of its Canadian market. With its motto—"The Lowest Price Is the Law"—Zellers uses private labels to give it exclusivity and quality, especially in apparel where 80 percent of its line is private.[8]

LO • 3

How does a retailer calculate the various markups?

Using Markups

A retail buyer should be able to calculate rapidly whether a proposed purchase will provide an adequate markup or gross margin. The markup can be expressed in dollars or as a percentage of either the selling price or the cost of the good. There are times, however, when a retail buyer needs to compute the markdown, which is a reduction in the selling price of the goods. Markdowns are made in order to move certain merchandise, especially when the color or size assortments are no longer complete.

Calculating Markup

To calculate the selling price (or retail price), the retailer should begin with the following basic markup equation:

$$SP = C + M$$

where C is the dollar cost of merchandise per unit, M is the dollar markup per unit, and SP is the selling price per unit.

Thus, if the retailer has a cost per unit of $16 on a calculator and a dollar markup of $14, then the selling price per unit is $30. In other words, **markup** is simply the difference between the cost of the merchandise and the selling price, which is the same as gross margin.

This markup is intended to cover all of the operating expenses (wages, rent, utilities, promotion, credit, etc.) incurred in the sale of the product and still provide the retailer with a profit. Occasionally, a retailer will sell a product without a markup high enough to cover the cost of the merchandise in order to generate traffic or build sales volume. For instance, many e-tailers began by expecting high turnover to allow them to be profitable. However, low margins coupled with low traffic caused many to close before volume could make up for their low margins. However, this chapter is only concerned with using markup to produce a profit on the sale of each item.

Markup
is the selling price of the merchandise less its cost, which is equivalent to gross margin.

Markup Methods

Markup may be expressed as either a dollar amount or as a percentage of the selling price or cost. It is most useful when expressed as a percentage of the selling price because it can then be used in comparison with other financial data such as the previous year's sales results, reductions in selling price, and even the firm's competition. The equation for expressing markup as percentage of selling price is as follows:

$$\text{Percentage of markup on selling price} = (SP - C)/SP = M/SP$$

Although some businesses, usually manufacturers or small retailers, express markup as a percentage of cost, this method is not widely used in retailing because most of the financial data the retailer uses are expressed as a percentage of selling price. Nevertheless, when expressing markup as a percentage of cost the equation is as follows:

$$\text{Percentage of markup on cost} = (SP - C)/C = M/C$$

Several problems occur when we attempt to equate markup as a percentage of selling price with markup as a percentage of cost. Because the two methods use different bases, we really are not comparing similar data. However, there is an equation to be used to find markup on selling when we know markup on cost:

Percentage of markup on selling price = Percentage of markup on cost/(100% + Percentage of markup on cost)

Likewise, when we know markup on selling price we can easily find markup on cost:

Percentage of markup on cost = Percentage of markup on selling price/(100% − Percentage of markup on selling price)

The preceding equations are conversions, converting percentage markup on cost to percentage markup on selling price, or vice versa. Exhibit 10.2 shows a conversion table

Exhibit 10.2	Markup Conversion Table		

Markup Percentage on Selling Price	Markup Percentage on Cost	Markup Percentage on Selling Price	Markup Percentage on Cost
4.8	5.0	32.0	47.1
5.0	5.3	33.3	50.0
8.0	8.7	34.0	51.5
10.0	11.1	35.0	53.9
15.0	17.7	36.0	56.3
16.7	20.0	37.0	58.8
20.0	25.0	40.0	66.7
25.0	33.3	41.0	70.0
26.0	35.0	42.8	75.0
27.3	37.5	44.4	80.0
28.0	39.0	47.5	90.0
28.5	40.0	50.0	100.0
30.0	42.9	66.7	200.0

for markup on cost and markup on selling price. Let's go back to our original example of the calculator and see how easy it is to determine markup on selling price when we know the markup on cost and vice versa.

The retailer purchased the calculator for $16 and later sold it for $30. The difference between the selling price and the cost is $14. This $14 as a percentage of selling price (markup on selling price) is 46.7 percent ($14/$30). This same $14, however, represents 87.5 percent ($14/$16) of the cost (markup). In this example, if all we knew was that the calculator had an 87.5 percent markup on cost, we could determine that this was the same as a 46.7 percent markup on selling price:

Percentage of markup on selling price = Percentage of markup on cost/(100% + Percentage of markup on cost) = 87.5%/(100% + 87,5%) = 46.7%

Likewise, if we knew we had a 46.7 percent markup on selling, we could easily determine markup on cost:

Percentage of markup on cost = Percentage of markup on selling price (100% − Percentage of markup on selling price) = 46.7%/(100% − 46.7%) = 87.5%

Exhibit 10.3 gives you the total picture of the relationships between markup on cost and markup on selling price. In Exhibit 10.3, you can see that dollar markup does not change as the percentage changes on cost or selling price. Dollar markup is presented as a percentage of a different base, cost, or selling price.

Exhibit 10.3	Relationship of Markups Expressed on Selling Price and Cost

Exhibit 10.4 reviews the basic markup equations.

Using Markup Formulas when Purchasing Merchandise

Although quite simple in concept, the basic markup formulas will enable you to determine more than the percentage of markup on a particular item. Let us work with the markup on selling price formula to illustrate how an interesting and frequently occurring question might be answered. If you know that a particular type of item could be sold for $8 per unit and that you need a 40 percent markup on selling price to meet

Exhibit 10.4	Basic Markup Formulas

$$\% \text{ Markup on Selling Price} = \frac{\text{Selling Price} - \text{Cost}}{\text{Selling Price}} = \frac{\text{Markup}}{\text{Selling Price}}$$

$$\% \text{ Markup on Cost} = \frac{\text{Selling Price} - \text{Cost}}{\text{Cost}} = \frac{\text{Markup}}{\text{Cost}}$$

Finding % Markup on Cost when % Markup on Selling is Known:

$$\% \text{ Markup on Cost} = \frac{\% \text{ Markup on Selling Price}}{100\% - \% \text{ Markup on Selling Price}}$$

Finding % Markup on Selling Price when % Markup on Cost is Known:

$$\% \text{ Markup on Selling Price} = \frac{\% \text{ Markup on Cost}}{100\% + \% \text{ Markup on Cost}}$$

Finding Selling Price when Cost and % Markup on Cost Are Known:

$$\text{Selling Price} = \text{Cost} + \% \text{ Markup on Cost (Cost)}$$

Finding Selling Price when Cost and % Markup on Selling Price Are Known:

$$\text{Selling Price} = \frac{\text{Cost}}{(1 - \% \text{ Markup on Selling Price})}$$

your profit objective, then how much would you be willing to pay for the item? Using our equation for markup on selling price, we have

$$\text{Percentage of markup on selling price} = (SP - C)/SP$$

$$40\% = (\$8 - C)/\$8$$

$$C - \$4.80$$

Therefore, you would be willing to pay $4.80 for the item. If the item cannot be found at $4.80 or less, it is probably not worth stocking.

Likewise, if a retailer purchases an item for $12 and wants a 40 percent markup on selling price, how would the retailer determine the selling price? Returning to our original equation (SP = C + M), we know that SP = C + .40SP because markup is 40 percent of selling price. If markup is 40 percent of selling price, cost must be 60 percent because cost and markup are the complements of each other and must total 100 percent. Thus if

$$60\% \ SP = \$12.00$$

(divide both sides by 60 percent), then

$$SP = \$20.00$$

Initial versus Maintained Markup

Up to this point we have assumed that we have been able to sell the product at the price we initially set when the product arrived at the store. We have assumed that the initial markup (the markup placed on the merchandise when the store receives it) is equal to the maintained markup or achieved markup (the actual selling price less the cost). Because in many cases the actual selling price for some of the firm's merchandise is lower than the original selling price, the firm's maintained markup is usually lower than the initial markup. Thus, maintained markup differs from initial markup by the amount of reductions:

$$\text{Initial markup} = (\text{Original retail price} - \text{Cost})/\text{Original retail price}$$

$$\text{Maintained markup} = (\text{Actual retail price} - \text{Cost})/\text{Actual retail price}$$

Five reasons can account for the difference between initial and maintained markups. First, is the need to balance demand with supply. Because most markup formulas are cost oriented rather than demand oriented, adjustments in selling prices will occur. This is especially true when consumer demand changes and the only way for retailers to reduce their inventory and make their merchandise salable is by taking a markdown or reduction in selling price. A second reason is stock shortages. Shortages can occur from theft by employees or customers, or by mismarking the price when merchandise is received or sold. In either case, the selling price received for the goods will be less than the price carried in the inventory records. In fact, clerical error probably accounts for more stock shortages than theft. Third, there are employee and customer discounts. Employees are usually given some discount privileges after they have worked for the firm for a specified period of time. Also, certain customer groups (i.e., religious and senior citizen groups) may be given special discount privileges.

Fourth, is the cost of alterations. Some fashion apparel items require alterations before the product is acceptable to the customer. Although men's clothing is often altered free of charge, there is usually a small charge for altering women's wear. Nevertheless, this charge usually does not cover all alteration costs and therefore alterations are actually a part of the cost of the merchandise.

A fifth and final reason that initial markup may be different from maintained markup is cash discounts. Manufacturers or suppliers offer retailers cash discounts to encourage prompt payment of bills. Cash discounts taken reduce the cost of merchandise and therefore make the maintained markup higher than the initial markup. This is just the opposite of the first four factors.

Some large retailers ignore cash discounts in calculating initial markup because the buyer may have little control over whether or not the discount is taken. The reason for this is that achieving discounts through prompt payment is thought to be the result of financial operations rather than merchandising decisions, and therefore the buyer should not be penalized if the discounts are not taken.

Planning Initial Markups

As the previous discussion illustrates, retailers do not casually arrive at an initial markup percentage. The initial markup percentage must be a carefully planned process. Markups must be large enough to cover all of the operating expenses and still provide a reasonable profit to the firm. In addition, markups must provide for markdowns, shortages, employee discounts, and alteration expenses (all of these together are referred to as total reductions), which reduce net revenue. Likewise, cash discounts taken, which increase net revenue, must be included.

Initial Markup Equation   To determine the initial markup, use the following formula:

Initial markup percentage = (Operating expenses + Net profit + Markdowns
                           + Stock shortages + Employee and customer discounts
                           + Alteration costs − Cash discounts)/(Net sales
                           + Markdowns + Stock shortages
                           + Employee and customer discounts)

We can simplify this equation if we remember that markdowns, stock shortages, and employee and customer discounts are all retail reductions from stock levels. Likewise, gross margin is the sum of operating expenses and net profit. This produces a simpler formula:

Initial markup percentage = (Gross margin + Alteration costs − Cash discounts
                           + Reductions)/(Net sales + Reductions)

Because some retailers record cash discounts as other income and not as a cost reduction in determining initial markup, the formula can be simplified one more time:

Initial markup percentage = (Gross margin + Alteration costs
                           + Reductions)/(Net sales + Reductions)

Regardless of which of the three formulas is used, the retailer must always remember the effect of each of the following items when planning initial markup: operating expenses, net profits, markdowns, stock shortages, employee and customer discounts, alteration costs, cash discounts taken, and net sales.

At this point, a numerical example might be helpful. Assume that a retailer plans to achieve net sales of $1 million and expects operating expenses to be $270,000. The net profit goal is $60,000. Planned reductions include $80,000 for markdowns, $20,000 for merchandise shortages, and $10,000 for employee and customer discounts. Alteration costs are expected to be $20,000, and cash discounts from suppliers are expected to be $10,000. What is the initial markup percentage that should be planned? What is the cost of merchandise to be sold?

The initial markup percentage can be obtained by using the original equation:

$$\text{Initial markup percentage} = (\$270{,}000 + \$60{,}000 + \$80{,}000 + \$20{,}000 \\ + \$10{,}000 + \$20{,}000 - \$10{,}000)/(\$1{,}000{,}000 \\ + \$80{,}000 + \$20{,}000 + \$10{,}000) = 40.54\%$$

The cost of merchandise sold can also be found. We know that the gross margin is operating expenses plus net profit ($330,000). This gross profit is equivalent to net sales less cost of merchandise sold, where cost of merchandise sold includes alteration costs and where cash discounts are subtracted. Thus, in the problem at hand, we know that $1 million less cost of merchandise sold (including alteration costs and subtracting cash discounts) is equal to $670,000. Because the alteration costs are planned at $20,000 and cash discounts at $10,000, the cost of merchandise is equal to $660,000 ($670,000 − $20,000 + $10,000).

We can verify our result by returning to the basic initial markup formula: asking price minus cost divided by asking price. The asking price is the planned net sales of $1 million plus planned reductions of $110,000 ($80,000 for markdowns, $20,000 for shortages, and $10,000 for employee and customer discounts). The cost is the cost of merchandise before the alteration costs and prior to cash discounts, or $660,000. Using the basic initial markup formula, we obtain ($1,110,000 − $660,000)/$1,110,000, or 40.54 percent. This is the same result we achieved earlier.

The preceding computations resulted in a markup percentage on retail selling price for merchandise lines storewide. Obviously, not all lines or items within lines should be priced by mechanically applying this markup percentage, because the actions of competitors will affect the prices for each merchandise line. Thus, the retailer will want to price the mix of merchandise lines in such a fashion that it obtains a storewide markup percentage. To achieve this, some lines may be priced with considerably higher markups and others with substantially lower markups than the storewide average that was planned using the initial markup planning equation. It will be helpful to explore some of the common reasons for varying the markup percentage on different lines or items within lines.

Markup Determinants   In planning initial markups, it is useful to know some of the general rules of markup determination. These are summarized as follows:

1. As goods are sold through more retail outlets, the markup percentage decreases. On the other hand, selling through few retail outlets means a greater markup percentage.
2. The higher the handling and storage costs of the goods, the higher the markup should be.
3. The greater the risk of a price reduction due to the seasonality of the goods, the greater the magnitude of the markup percentage early in the season.
4. The higher the demand inelasticity of price for the goods, the greater the markup percentage.

Although these rules are common to all retail lines, there are others that are unique to each line of trade and are only learned through experience in the respective lines, such as how much to markup produce in a supermarket during different seasons.

Markdown Management

Although retailers would prefer to have their initial markup (the markup placed on the merchandise when the store receives it) equal to the maintained markup (the actual selling price less the cost), this seldom happens. **Markdowns,** which are reductions in the price of an item taken in order to stimulate sales, and other reductions result in a firm receiving a lower price for its merchandise than originally asked. The markdown percentage is the amount of the reduction divided by the original selling price:

Markdown percentage = Amount of reduction/Original selling price

Thus maintained markup (sometimes referred to as "gross margin" or just plain "gross") is the key to profitability because it is the difference between the actual selling price and the cost of that merchandise.

For effective retail price management, markdowns should be planned. In principle they need to be planned because pricing is not a science with high degrees of precision, but an art form with considerable room for error. If retailers knew everything they needed to know about demand and supply factors, they could use the science of economics to establish a price that would maximize profits and ensure the sale of all the merchandise. Unfortunately, retailers do not possess perfect information about supply and demand factors. As a result, the entire merchandising process is subject to error, which then makes pricing difficult. Four basic errors can occur: (1) buying errors, (2) pricing errors, (3) merchandising errors, and (4) promotion errors.

Markdown
is any reduction in the price of an item from its initially established price.

Buying Errors

Errors in buying occur on the supply side of the pricing question. They result as the retailer buys the wrong merchandise or buys the right merchandise in too large a quantity. The merchandise purchased could have been in the wrong styles, sizes, colors, patterns, or price range. Too large a quantity could have been purchased because demand was overestimated or a recession was not foreseen. Whatever the cause of the buying error, the net result is a need to cut the price to move the merchandise. Often the resulting prices are below the actual cost of the merchandise to the retailer. Thus, buying errors can be quite costly. As a consequence, you might expect that the retail manager would wish to minimize buying errors. However, this is not the case. The retailer could minimize buying errors by being extremely conservative. It could buy only what it knew the customer wanted and what it could be certain of selling. Then buying errors would be minimized, but at the expense of lost profit opportunities on some riskier types of purchase decisions. Recall that when we reviewed the determinants of markups we mentioned that the greater the risk of potential price reductions the higher the markup percentage. This is simply another way of recognizing that taking a gamble on some purchases that represent buying errors can be profitable if initial markups are high. Review the most common errors made by buyers discussed in Chapter 9.

Retailing: The Inside Story

Sears' Youngest Buyer

A good friend of one of the authors is a toy buyer for a major retailer. Several years ago, she was caught by surprise during the Christmas season by the popularity of Tickle-Me-Elmo. As she later explained, "How was I to know that Rosie O'Donnell was going to plug that doll on her television show?" Still, this buyer was better suited to understanding what kids would like and not like because she took her grandchildren with her when she went to market.

Yes, guessing the success or failure of Christmas toys is a risky business. Years ago, when many of the readers were kids, one manufacturer, Coleco, made a big Christmas bet on an inexpensive computer. Only as an afterthought did the firm's press releases mention that among the new toys being introduced was a doll named Chattie Cathy. Well, the doll was an overwhelming success, the computer was a failure, and the company was soon out of business.

Apparel retailers have long been aware of the fact that predicting what teenagers will want and what they will shun, as well as which items will be fads and which will last, is even more risky than buying Christmas toys. Therefore, some retailers are making use of a new breed of "expert buyer." For example, Sears Roebuck's vice-president for children's apparel, Greg Sandfort, recently left most $5.5 million buying spring apparel decisions to a 9-year-old girl. This was despite the fact that he had 21 years in the clothing business.

Sandfort was betting that Morgan Brittany Dolly of Cumberland, Maryland, could tell his buyers what "tween" girls (those between children and junior sizes) will wear. Sears was hoping that this strategy, like buyers taking their children and grandchildren to the market with them, was a better way to spot trends than using a focus group, which tends to confirm buyers' decisions and can be influenced by an outspoken member of the focus group.

How and why did Sears choose Miss Dolly? Well, she was chosen from 3,000 kids who sought the job on a Sears web site the previous summer. Her essay on the upcoming season's fashions was judged the best and in addition to the trip to the market, her pay included a family trip to New York and a $1,000 shopping spree. (Choosing the fashions was really "awesome.")

Her favorite picks included zip-up vests, bell-bottoms, hipsters, khaki pants, animal prints, handkerchief-style tops, Indian beads, and some reversible skirts. She nixed anything pink and what many believe would be the season's hottest item scoop-neckline tops. "I'm an active girl," she pointed out. "They might slip off the shoulder." (By the way,

---

Chapter 3's discussion of demographics mentioned that many times, baby boomers are a retailer's buyer for products aimed at Gen-X or Gen-Y consumers. These groups are not only different in age but in their buying behavior, making it difficult for retailers to prevent buying errors unless they make a well-considered effort. The chapter's Retailing: The Inside Story box describes a unique approach Sears used to overcome this problem.

Pricing Errors

Errors in pricing merchandise can be another cause of markdowns. Errors occur when the price of the item is too high to move the product at the speed and in the quantity desired. The goods may have been bought in the right styles, at the right time, and in the right quantities, but the price on the item may simply be too high. This would create purchase resistance on the part of the typical customer.

during the week, she sported a less trendy style: her school uniform.)

Most of the vendors were taken aback when they first saw the youngster. However, all agreed that she was very polished for a 9-year-old and had tons of charisma.

How did her selections do? According to Mike Dagne, divisional merchandise manager for Sears, Morgan had a strong batting average and she definitely added some newness to the Sears assortments through her fashion choices. "Morgan's selections helped raise the level of our fashion offerings," said Dagne. Among Morgan's picks, reversible skirts and animal prints were hot items."

Source: Based in part on an author's investment in Coleco and on information supplied by Sears.

Most retail buyers have professional training and many years of experience. However, 9-year-old Morgan Brittany Dolly broke that rule by successfully advising Sears of what girls would wear.

An overly high price is often relative to the pricing behavior of competitors. Perhaps, in principle, the price would have been acceptable, but if competitors price the same item substantially lower, then the original retailer's price becomes too high.

Merchandising Errors

Although many new retailers believe that carrying over seasonal or fashion merchandise into the next merchandising season is the most common merchandise error, it really isn't. The buyer's failure to inform the sales staff about how the new merchandise relates to the current stock, ties in with the store's image, and satisfies the needs of the store's target market is the most common merchandising error. A key merchandising error is the failure to keep the department manager and salesforce informed about the new merchandise lines, so that these goods will be available to the customer. Too many times, the new merchandise is left in the storeroom or the salespeople are not informed on the key features of the new item, and thus the customer will never be able to become excited about the new merchandise. Another merchandising error is the improper handling of the merchandise by the sales staff or ineffective visual presentation of the merchandise. Mishandling errors could be failure to stock the new merchandise behind old merchandise whenever possible or simply misplacing the merchandise. All too often a slow seller is a "lost" bundle of merchandise.

Promotion Errors

Finally, it is often the case that even when the right goods were purchased in the right quantities and were priced correctly, the merchandise fails to move as planned. In this situation, there is most often a promotion error. The consumer has not been properly informed or prompted to purchase the merchandise. The advertising, personal selling, sales promotion activities, or in-store displays were too weak or sporadic to elicit a strong response from potential customers.

Markdown Policy

Retailers will find it advantageous to develop a markdown timing policy. In almost all situations, retailers will find it necessary to take markdowns; but the crucial decisions become when and how much of a markdown to take. In principle, there are two extremes to a markdown timing policy: early and late.

Early Markdown Policy   Most retailers who concentrate on high inventory turnover pursue an early markdown policy. Markdowns taken early speed the movement of merchandise and also generally enable the retailer to take less of a markdown per unit to dispose of the goods. One of the author's bosses taught him early in his retailing career that "The first markdown is the cheapest to take. Therefore, once you take it, do not look back." In other words, when you as a buyer make a merchandising error, take your loss early and do not look back because taking that early markdown will allow the dollars obtained from selling the merchandise to be used to help finance more salable goods. At the same time, the customer seems to benefit, because markdowns are offered quickly on goods that some consumers still think of as fashionable and the store has the appearance of having fresh merchandise. For example, the best women's apparel shoppers usually visit their favorite store three to four times a month. Thus, it is important for the retailer to always have the appearance of presenting fresh merchandise. Many fashion retailers use the following set of rules when taking early markdowns.

- After the third week, mark it down 25 percent from the original price.
- After the seventh week, mark it down 50 percent from the original price.
- After the eleventh week, mark it down 75 percent from the original price.
- After the sixteenth week, sell it to an outlet store or give it to charity.

Another advantage of the early markdown policy is that it allows the retailer to replenish lower-priced lines from the higher ones that have been marked down. For instance, many women's wear retailers will regularly take slow-moving dresses from higher-priced lines and move them down to the moderate- or lower-priced lines. Other retailers mark goods down at regular intervals until the merchandise is sold. In effect, this represents a markdown, even though it is not recognizable by the consumer.

Late Markdown Policy   Allowing goods to have a long trial period before a markdown is taken is called a late markdown policy. This policy avoids disrupting the sale of regular merchandise by too frequently marking goods down. As a consequence, customers will learn to look forward to a semiannual or annual clearance, in which all or most merchandise is marked down. Thus, the bargain hunters or low-end customers will be attracted only at infrequent intervals.

Regardless of which timing policy a retailer follows, it must plan for these reductions. Markdowns are not always the result of buyer errors. They may simply be the selling of merchandise that is late in the season and before larger markdowns must be taken. Remember, when preparing a merchandise budget, the retailer must estimate reductions for that time period.

Amount of Markdown   An issue related to the timing of markdowns is their magnitude. If the retailer waits to use a markdown at the last moment, then the markdown should probably be large enough to move the remaining merchandise. This, however, is not the case with an early markdown. An early markdown only needs to be large enough to provide a sales stimulant. Once sales are stimulated, the retailer can watch merchandise movement; when it slows, the retailer can provide another stimulant by again marking it down. Which is the more profitable strategy depends on the situation. One rule of thumb for markdowns is that prices should be marked down at least 25 percent in order for the consumer to notice. However, the markdown percentage should vary with the type of merchandise, time of season, and competition.

Often retailers are able to have their suppliers supplement their markdown losses with "markdown money," or some other type of price reductions. Here's how it works: Let's say Acme Clothing Company delivers 100 sweaters to Judy's Dress Shop at the wholesale price of $40 each. Judy in turn plans to take her customary markup of 50 percent on the selling price in order to sell each sweater for $80, thus producing a gross margin of $4,000.

However, after three months Judy still has 50 of the sweaters in stock, which she puts on sale for $50 each in order to move the merchandise. After selling the remaining sweaters, Judy's gross margin was only $2,500: [(50 × $80) + (50 × $50) − (100 × $40)].

The following month Judy goes to market and visits the Acme showroom. Judy wants Acme to pay her the $1,500 she lost in taking the markdowns on their sweaters. Judy threatens Acme with a loss of future orders if it does not cover her losses. Does this sound fair to you?

Actually, this type of scenario happens quite frequently when buyers go to market. Buyers maintain that manufacturers should share in the responsibility when the merchandise does not sell as promised. Buyers claim that if the supplier cannot deliver the gross margin desired, there is no reason to order from that supplier again. From the retailer's standpoint, when the manufacturer contributes markdown money, the manufacturer is really asking for a second chance to prove the salability of its lines. This markdown money could be in the form of cash payment or of a discount on future purchases.

Now let's look at how the maintained markup percentage is determined. A retailer purchases the calculator, used in an earlier example, for $16 with the intent of selling it for $25 (an initial markup of 36 percent). However, the calculator did not sell at that price and the retailer reduced it to $20 in order to sell it. This would result in a maintained markup of 20 percent:

$$\text{Maintained markup} = (\text{Actual selling price} - \text{Cost})/\text{Actual selling price}$$
$$= \$4/\$20 = 20\%$$

The following formula can also be used to determine the maintained markup percentage:

$$\text{Maintained markup percentage} = \text{Initial markup percentage}$$
$$- [(\text{Reduction percentage})(100\%$$
$$- \text{Initial markup percentage})]$$

where

$$\text{Reduction percentage} = \text{Amount of reductions/Net sales}$$

In the preceding example,

$$\text{Maintained markup percentage} = 36\% - [(\$5/\$20) \times (100\% - 36\%)]$$
$$= 36\% - 16\% = 20\%$$

Student Study Guide

Summary

LO•1 What factors should be considered when establishing a retailer's pricing objectives and policies?

Pricing decisions are among the most frequent a retailer must make. They cannot be made independently, because they interact with the merchandise, location, promotion, credit, customer service, and store image decisions the retailer has already made, as well as the federal and state legal constraints.

The pricing objectives the retailer ultimately sets must also agree with the retailer's mission statement and merchandise policies. These objectives can be profit oriented, sales oriented, or seek to maintain the status quo.

After establishing its pricing objectives, the retailer must next determine the pricing policies to achieve these goals. These policies must reflect the expectations of the target market.

LO•2 What are the various pricing strategies available to the retailer?

Among the strategies discussed were customary pricing, variable pricing, flexible pricing, one-price policies, price lining, odd pricing, multiple-unit pricing, bundle pricing, leader pricing, bait pricing, and private-label brand pricing.

LO•3 How does a retailer calculate the various markups?

The basic markup equation states that, per unit, the retail selling price is equal to the dollar cost plus the dollar markup. Markups can be expressed as either a percentage of the selling price or as a percentage of the cost to the retailer. Because the initial selling price that the retailer puts on a newly purchased item may not be attractive enough to sell all the inventory of that item, the price may need to be reduced. When we talk of actual selling prices versus initial selling prices, we are discussing the difference between an initial and a maintained markup.

Initial markups should be planned. Next, the initial storewide markup percentage can be determined by using operating expenses, net profit, alteration costs, cash discounts, markdowns, stock shortages, employee and customer discounts, and sales. The retailer must recognize that not all items can be priced by mechanically applying this markup percentage. Some lines will need to be priced to yield a considerably higher markup and others, a substantially lower markup. The initial markup is seldom equal to the maintained markup because of three kinds of reductions: markdowns, shortages, and employee and customer discounts.

LO•4 Why is markdown management so important in retailing?

Because the retailer does not possess perfect information about supply and demand, markdowns are inevitable. Markdowns are usually due to errors in buying, pricing, merchandising, or promotion. Because markdowns are inevitable, the retailer needs to establish a markdown policy. Early markdowns speed the movement of merchandise and also allows the retailer to take less of a markdown per unit to dispose of the merchandise. Late markdowns avoid disrupting the sale of regular merchandise by too frequent markdowns. The best policy from a profit perspective depends on the particular situation involved.

Terms to Remember

target return objective	trading up
profit maximization	trading down
skimming	odd pricing
penetration	multiple-unit pricing
above-market pricing policy	bundling
price zone	leader pricing
below-market pricing policy	loss leader
customary pricing	everyday low pricing
variable pricing	high-low pricing
flexible pricing	bait-and-switch pricing
one-price policy	markup
price lining	markdown

Review and Discussion Questions

LO•1 What factors should be considered when establishing a retailer's pricing objectives and policies?

1. How does a store's location affect the price it can charge?

2. How can promotion decisions influence the demand for a retailer's product line?

3. Is a profit maximization objective fair to a retailer's customers?

4. When should a skimming pricing objective be used?

5. What is the major objection to a retailer using a sales-oriented pricing objective?

6. Could a retailer use an above-market pricing policy with private-label products?

LO•2 What are the various pricing strategies available to the retailer?

7. Would you prefer to buy a car from a dealer using a flexible or a one-price policy? Why?

8. Do you think odd pricing is really effective?

9. What type of store would be most likely to use leader pricing?

10. What is EDLP? What type of retailer is most likely to use this pricing policy?

LO•3 How does a retailer calculate the various markups?

11. Compute the markup on selling price for an item that retails for $19.95 and costs $11.20.

12. Complete the following:

	Dress Shirt	Sport Shirt	Belt
Selling price	$30.00	$24.95	$12.50
Cost	18.00	14.35	7.50
Markup in dollars	_____	_____	_____
Markup percentage on cost	_____	_____	_____
Markup percentage on selling price	_____	_____	_____

13. A buyer buys 28 raincoats at $342 per dozen. If the department markup on selling price is 52.5 percent, what should be each raincoat's retail price?

14. If the markup on cost is 56 percent, what is the markup on selling price?

15. Which is more important to a retailer, initial or maintained markup?

16. Can an initial markup ever be equal to the maintained markup? Explain.

17. Assume that a retailer plans to achieve a net sales of $1.5 million and expects operating expenses to be $375,000. The net profit goal is $100,000. Planned reductions include $88,000 for markdowns, $38,000 for merchandise shortages, and $14,000 for employee and customer discounts. Cash discounts from suppliers are expected to be $30,000. At what percentage should initial markups be planned?

18. Intimate Apparel wants to produce a 12 percent operating profit this year on sales of $460,000. Based on past experiences the owner made the following estimates:

Net alteration expenses	$800	Employee discount	$3,400
Markdowns	27,000	Operating expenses	215,000
Stock shortages	4,200	Cash discounts earned	2,100

Given these estimates, what average initial markup should be asked for the upcoming year?

19. What are some of the key determinants used in determining markup percentage?

LO•4 Why is markdown management so important in retailing?

20. Why should a retailer plan on taking markdowns during a merchandising season?

21. Somebody once said "Good buyers never have to take markdowns." Do you agree with that statement? Explain your answer.

22. Given the following information, what is the maintained markup percentage? Planned sales = $300,000; planned initial markup = 40 percent; planned reductions = $36,000.

Sample Test Questions

LO•1 What word best describes the relationship between a retailer's pricing decisions and the merchandise, location, promotion, credit, services, image, and legal decisions that retailers must make?

a. independent
b. separate
c. interactive
d. competitive
e. multifaced

LO•2 If a retailer is offering the same products and quantities to different customers at different prices, the retailer has what kind of pricing policy?

a. two-price
b. customary
c. flexible
d. leader
e. variable

LO•3 **If a retailer buys a product for $25 and sells it for $45, what is the markup percentage if the markup is based on the selling price?**

a. 44.4 percent
b. 80 percent
c. 75 percent
d. 100 percent
e. 55.5 percent

LO•4 **An item was marked down to $19.99 from its original retail price of $29.99. What is the reduction percentage for this item?**

a. 33.3 percent
b. 25 percent
c. 50 percent
d. 41.3 percent
e. 66.7 percent

Applications

Writing and Speaking Exercise   You have just been hired to be the merchandise manager of a small chain (four stores) of women's apparel stores. The chain caters to working women, and five of its six buyers have less than a year's experience. In looking over the records, you notice that these buyers have been late in taking markdowns. As a result, the chain's profits have suffered. In talking with the buyers, you detect a sense of fear in taking markdowns. They believe that a markdown is an admission of an error in their buying decisions and that if they make too many errors, their jobs will be in jeopardy. You decide to write the buyers a memo regarding markdowns. What will you say?

Retail Project   On your next trip to a mall, visit all the anchor stores and leading apparel stores. Look around at displays and notice if they are having sales. Now, based on the amount of merchandise on sale and the amount of reductions, determine if each store is using an early or late markdown policy. Explain your reasoning for each store, and especially explain the reasoning for differences between the stores. (*Note:* You can also do this project for different e-tailers.)

Case   Lone Star Department Store

Part A   The buyer for the women's sweater department has purchased wool sweaters for $37, and she wants to sell them at a 47 percent markup on selling price. At what price should each sweater be sold?

Part B   The buyer for men's shirts has a price point of $25 and requires a markup of 40 percent. What would be the highest price he should pay for a shirt to sell at this price point?

Part C   The buyer for housewares hopes to achieve net sales of $1,000,000 for the coming year. Operating expenses are $190,000 and retail reductions are $80,000. Management has set a profit goal of $110,000. What should the initial markup percentage be?

Part D   The women's dress department wants to produce an 18 percent operating profit on forecasted sales of $600,000. The divisional merchandise manager has made the following estimates:

Alterations	$1,800	Operating expenses	$150,000
Stock shortages	3,000	Markdowns	55,000
Employee discounts	1,500	Cash discounts earned	400

Based on this information, what initial markup percentage will be needed?

Planning Your Own Retail Business

The on-line retail operation you recently opened is doing well but you are uncertain of your pricing strategy. Currently the typical customer purchases four items at an average price of $11.71 for an average transaction size of $46.84. The cost of goods is 60 percent of sales, which yields a gross margin of 40 percent. You are considering lowering prices by 10 percent across the board so you can better compete with other music e-tailers. If you lower prices by 10 percent, you believe that the average items purchased per customer would rise by 25 percent. Assuming your assumptions are correct, should you lower prices by 10 percent across the board? If not, do you have an alternative pricing strategy to propose?

Endnotes

1. "The Power of Smart Pricing," *Business Week*, April 10, 2000: 160–162.
2. "A Small Toy Store Manages to Level the Playing Field," *Wall Street Journal*, December 20, 1996: A1, A8.
3. For a complete discussion of this subject, see Erik Brynjolfsson and Michael Smith, "Frictionless Commerce? A Comparison of Internet and Conventional Retailers," *Management Science*, April 2000.
4. Based on material found in the Robert Kahn Collection, University of Oklahoma.
5. Zarrel V. Lambert, "Perceived Prices as Related to Odd and Even Price Endings," *Journal of Retailing*, Fall 1975: 13–21, 78; and "Strategic Mix of Odd, Even Prices Can Lead to Increased Retail Profits," *Marketing News*, March 7, 1980: 24.
6. For a more complete discussion of a store manager's ability to use this strategy, see Joel E. Urbany, Peter R. Dickson, and Alan Sawyer, "Insights Into Cross- and Within-Store Price Search: Retailer Estimates Vs. Consumer Self-Reports," *Journal of Retailing*, Summer 2000: 243–258.
7. For a more complete discussion of grocery pricing, see James Binkley and John Connor, "Grocery Market Pricing and the New Competitive Environment," *Journal of Retailing*, Summer 1998: 273–294.
8. "Zellers Fights Back," *Discount Merchandiser*, January 1996: 24–30.

To reach the youth market, retailers, such as Old Navy, employ quirky advertisements aimed at the idiosyncrasies of their target market. These ads allow Old Navy to set themselves apart from other retailers.

Advertising and Promotion

Overview

Promotion is a major generator of demand in retailing. This chapter focuses on the role of advertising, sales promotion, and publicity in the operation of a retail business. Retail selling, another important element of promotion, is discussed in Chapter 12. Our discussion is directed at describing how retailers should manage their firm's promotional resources.

Learning Objectives

After reading this chapter, you should be able to

1. name the four basic components of the retailer's promotion mix and discuss their relationship with other decisions

2. describe the differences between a retailer's long-term and short-term promotional objectives

3. list the six steps involved in developing a retailer's advertising campaign

4. explain how retailers manage their sales promotion and publicity

---

LO • 1

What are the four basic components of the retailer's promotion mix and how are they related to other retailer decisions?

The Retail Promotion Mix

By making their targeted customers aware of current offerings, retailers use promotion to generate sales. This does not mean that sales cannot occur without using promotion. Some sales will always take place even if the retailer does not spend any money on promotion. For example, households close to a retailer may shop there strictly for convenience and a passersby might occasionally visit the store for an impulse purchase. Most retailers, however, use a combination of location, price levels, displays, merchandise assortments, customer service, and promotion as a means to generate store traffic and sales.

Retailers make trade-offs between the elements of the retailing mix. Some retailers, such as Dallas-based Gadzooks with 340 stores in 33 states, operate in high-rent prime mall locations and seldom advertise. Gadzooks, which sells popular brand apparel and accessories to teens aged 14 to 18, prefers to use these prime mall locations to generate customer traffic. With the exception of its end-of-summer/back-to-school and winter holiday promotions, most of Gadzooks' other promotional expenses are made in combination with other mall merchants utilizing the mall's co-op promotional campaigns. Wal-Mart is another retailer that spends only a small percentage of its sales on promotion. Wal-Mart believes that lower prices are more effective than location and heavy promotional expenditures in generating traffic levels. Thus, although direct promotional expenditures are not always a prerequisite to generating sales, they are a means of achieving sales above those that could be obtained merely from offering a lower price, having a better location, or offering outstanding service. After all, without promotion, how would consumers be aware of these retail offerings. Therefore, many of today's high-performance retailers use **promotion** to bring traffic into their stores, move the traffic to the various selling areas of the store, and entice the traffic into purchasing merchandise.

Promotion
is a means that retailers use to bring traffic into their stores, and it includes advertising, sales promotion, publicity, and personal selling.

Types of Promotion

Promotion has four basic components: advertising, sales promotion, publicity, and personal selling. Collectively, these components constitute the retailer's promotion mix. Each component is defined as follows and will be discussed from a managerial perspective.[1]

Advertising
is paid, nonpersonal communication through various media by business firms, nonprofit organizations, and individuals who are in some way identified in the advertising message and who hope to inform or persuade members of a particular audience; includes communication of products, services, institutions, and ideas.

1. **Advertising** is "paid, nonpersonal communication through various media by business firms, nonprofit organizations, and individuals who are in some way identified in the advertising message and who hope to inform and/or persuade members of a particular audience; includes communication of products, services, institutions, and ideas." Retail advertising's function is primarily to inform potential buyers of the problem-solving utility of a retailer's offering, with the objective of developing consumer preferences for a particular retailer. Retailers most commonly use the following advertising media: the Internet, newspapers, radio, television, and printed circulars.

Advertising and sales promotion are frequently used in retailing to increase store traffic and sales.

2. **Sales promotions** "involve the use of media and non-media marketing pressure applied for a pre-determined, limited period of time at the level of consumer, retailer or wholesaler in order to stimulate trial, increase consumer demand, or improve product availability." The most popular sales promotion tools in retailing are premiums, frequent buyer programs, coupons, in-store displays, contests and sweepstakes, product demonstrations, and sampling.

3. **Publicity** is "non-paid-for communications of information about the company or product, generally in some media form." Popular examples are Macy's Thanksgiving Day Parade and local retailers supporting various civic and educational groups.

4. **Personal selling** is "selling that involves a face-to-face interaction with the consumer." Personal selling and other services provided by retailers, which will be discussed in detail in the next chapter, occur when the retailer's promotional efforts cause a shopper to reach a specific selling area.

All four components of the retailer's promotion mix need to be managed from a total systems perspective—that is, they need to be blended effectively to achieve the retailer's promotion objectives and reinforce each other. If the advertising conveys quality and status, so must the sales personnel, publicity, and sales promotion. Otherwise, the consumer will receive conflicting or inconsistent messages about the retailer, which will result in confusion and loss of patronage.

Sales promotion
involves the use of media and nonmedia marketing pressure applied for a predetermined, limited period of time at the level of consumer, retailer, or wholesaler in order to stimulate trial, increase consumer demand, or improve product availability.

Publicity
is non-paid-for communications of information about the company or product, generally in some media form.

Personal selling
involves a face-to-face interaction with the consumer with the goal of selling the consumer merchandise or services.

Retailers who integrate their promotional efforts with the other elements of the retailing mix will be higher profit performers.

Dollars & Sense

The management of promotional efforts in retailing must also fit into the retailer's overall plan. Promotion decisions relate to and must be integrated with other management decisions, such as location, merchandise, credit, cash flow, building and fixtures, price, and customer service. For example, consider the following:

1. There is a maximum distance consumers will travel to visit a retail store. Thus, a retailer's *location* will help determine the target for promotions. Retailers should direct their promotional dollars first toward households in their **primary trading area,** the area where the retailer can serve customers, in terms of convenience and accessibility, better than the competition, and then to **secondary trading areas,** areas where a retailer is still competitive despite a competitor having some locational advantage. However, e-tailers who are in every sense global in presence must determine specific areas, whether they be countries or communities, in which to focus their promotional efforts.

2. Retailers need high levels of store traffic to keep their *merchandise* rapidly turning over. Promotion helps build traffic.

3. A retailer's *credit customers*, such as Neiman Marcus's InCircle members, who on average charge more than $3,000 a year, are more store loyal and purchase in larger quantities. Thus, they are an excellent target for increased promotional efforts. Although the increased use of MasterCard, Visa, and Discover cards has impacted this retail advantage in recent years, many retailers have overcome this problem by developing their own co-branded cards.

4. A retailer confronted with a temporary *cash flow* problem can use promotion to increase short-term cash flow.

5. A retailer's promotional strategy must be reinforced by its *building and fixtures* decisions. Promotional creativity and style should coincide with building and fixture creativity and style. If the ads are exciting and appealing to a particular target market, so should the building and fixtures. For example, Nike's promotion emphasizes athletics. As such, it is no small wonder that Nike created Nike Town retail facilities complete with basketball courts and running tracks.

6. Promotion provides customers with more information. That information will help them make better purchase decisions, because risk is reduced. Therefore, promotion can actually be viewed as a major component of *customer service.*

The retailer that systematically integrates its promotional programs with other retail decision areas will be better able to achieve high-performance results. One retailer even developed a set of basic promotional guidelines that all retailers should follow when using promotion. These guidelines are as follows:

- Try to utilize only promotions that are consistent with and will enhance your store image.

- Review the success or failure of each promotion to help in developing better future promotions.

- Wherever possible, test new promotions before making a major investment by using them on a broader scale.

- Use appeals that are of interest to your target market and that are realistic to obtain. For example, double couponing offers everybody an award, whereas a sweepstakes has only one winner.

Primary trading area is the geographic area where the retailer can serve customers, in terms of convenience and accessibility, better than the competition.

Secondary trading area is the geographic area where the retailer can still be competitive despite a competitor having some locational advantage.

- Make sure your objectives are measurable.
- Make sure your objectives are obtainable.
- Develop total promotional campaigns, not just ads.
- The lower the rent, the higher the promotional expenses generally needed.
- New stores need higher promotional budgets than established stores.
- Stores in out-of-the way locations require higher promotional budgets than stores with heavy traffic.[2]

Promotion in the Channel

The retailer is not the only member of the marketing channel that uses promotion. Manufacturers also invest in promotion for many of the same reasons retailers do — that is, to move merchandise more quickly, to speed up cash flow, and to better retain customer loyalty. However, the promotional activities of the retailer's channel partners may sometimes conflict with the retailer's. There are three major differences in the way retailers and manufacturers use promotion:

1. *Product image versus availability.* The manufacturer's primary goal is to create a positive image for the product itself and differentiate it from competing products. For example, when introducing a new product, a manufacturer will attempt to explain how the product works. Retailers, on the other hand, are primarily interested in announcing to their customers that they have the product available for purchase at a convenient location.

2. *Specific product benefits versus price.* Manufacturers generally do not care where customers make their purchases, just so long as they buy the manufacturer's product. That is why manufacturers promote the benefits of their products. Retailers, on the other hand, do not care which brand the customer purchases. (Remember retailers carry products from many different manufacturers.) Retailers just want the customer to make the purchase in their store. Thus, in addition to availability, retailers feature the product's price in their ads.

3. *Focused image versus cluttered ads.* In comparison to manufacturers, most retailers carry a larger variety and breadth of products, whereas manufacturers produce a greater depth than most retailers carry. Thus, retail ads, which are usually geared toward short-term results, tend to be more cluttered with many different products as opposed to manufacturer ads that focus on a single product theme.

Retailers who realize that there are major differences in the way retailers and manufacturers use promotion will be more profitable than those who do not understand these differences.

Dollars & Sense

Sometimes a lack of promotional harmony by channel members results from other factors. Consider the case of the automobile channel. Assume that an increase in inflation has slowed the country's rate of real economic growth and as a result, the country's auto sales are 10 percent lower than last year. The manufacturer believes that this recession will be short-lived and therefore does not want to get into a price war by offering any price rebates or other special promotions from the factory. However, the automobile dealers believe that the recession will be fairly prolonged. They feel that advertising by the manufacturer should be increased and that special allowances should be given for increased local advertising. They would also like to see the manufacturer tie in this increased advertising program with a cash rebate from the factory. Because the manufacturer and dealer have different beliefs about the economy's future, this could lead to serious problems between them.

A second possible source of problems is when the channel members feel that another channel member's promotional campaign is a mistake. For example, Benetton, the Italian clothing manufacturer, has a history of creating conflict within its channel. Ads featuring a dead Bosnian soldier, an AIDS patient, and a nun and priest in an intimate pose have divided opinions and infuriated some retail franchisees for years. A recent controversial campaign has pushed the issue of free speech and advertising once again. This time, some believe Benetton has gone too far. Benetton's 2000 ad campaign, titled "Death Row," featured U.S. death row prisoners and their stories. Although Benetton intended to make a statement regarding capital punishment, the ads infuriated some retailers. For instance, U.S. retailer Sears Roebuck & Company decided to ban Benetton clothing from its stores after the campaign began.

Another source of problems among channel members over promotional policies occurs when the manufacturer seeks, through the use of promotion, to attract a high-quality, high-price, high-status image to its brand, while the retailer wants to be known as the price leader and advertises "I will not be undersold!" This recently occurred when Nissan introduced a new campaign that sought to develop a positive brand image for its line of cars, but dealers said that the campaign did not help them sell cars.[3] Here the manufacturer's and the retailer's promotional efforts were not interwoven and again a serious conflict developed between them. Such different perceptions show why it is important for retailers to develop the cooperative relationship with their suppliers discussed in Chapter 5 so that the conflict can be resolved.

Benetton's use of controversial advertisements frequently creates conflict within the marketing channel and has led to some retailers refusing to sell Benetton clothing.

Promotional Objectives

LO • 2

What are the differences between a retailer's long-term and short-term promotional objectives?

To efficiently manage the promotion mix, retail managers must first establish their promotion objectives. These promotional objectives should flow from the retailer's overall objectives discussed in Chapter 2. They should be the natural outgrowth of the retailer's operations management plans. As such, all promotion objectives should ultimately seek to improve the retailer's financial performance, because this is what strategic and operating plans are intended to accomplish.

Exhibit 11.1 shows how promotion objectives should relate to financial performance objectives. As this exhibit shows, promotion objectives can be established to help improve both long- and short-term financial performance.

Long-Term Objectives

Institutional advertising is an attempt by the retailer to gain long-term benefits by selling the store itself rather than the merchandise in it. By doing this, the retailer is creating a positive image for itself in the consumer's mind. Retailers using institutional ads generally seek to establish two long-term promotion objectives: creating a positive store image and promoting public service.

Institutional advertising is a type of advertising in which the retailer attempts to gain long-term benefits by promoting and selling the store itself rather than the merchandise in the store.

Creating a Positive Store Image
The first objective is intended to establish or reinforce, in the consumer's mind, the positive store image the retailer wants to convey relative to its competitors. Here, the retailer is seeking to gain that differential advantage by providing a clear positive image that is distinctive from other retailers. By providing such an image, the retailer hopes to develop a long-term relationship with the customer. Two of the most successful retailers in this area have been Neiman Marcus and Nordstrom. Today when consumers think of these retailers, they perceive elegantly designed store layouts featuring the top names in fashion backed by excellent service and a helpful, knowledgeable sales staff. Promotion directed at fulfilling this objective

Exhibit 11.1   **Possible Promotion Objectives in Retailing**

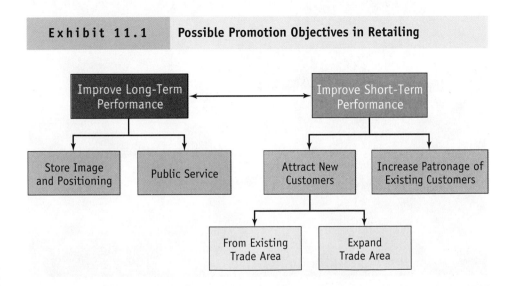

will have its major effect on improving the retailer's long-term financial performance. However, as you might expect, this type of promotion will also assist the retailer in the short run, such as when a consumer is seeking to purchase a gift for a special friend and the retailer's ad suggests that "perfect gift" idea. After all, promotional efforts of a store have been found to be a key predictor of store choice when a consumer is gift shopping.

Public Service Promotion   The second long-term objective is directed at getting the consumer to perceive the retailer as a good citizen in the community. Retailers may sponsor public service advertisements to honor local athletes and scholars as well as provide cash and merchandise to local charities. For example, some retailers offer meeting rooms for use by local civic organizations; some supermarkets have begun publishing consumer newsletters with health, cooking, safety, and beauty tips, whereas others provide public service announcements and sponsor programs on public television stations. Target is an excellent example of this. Target sponsors a number of public service activities at both the national and local levels. For instance, at the national level every time a guest makes a pharmacy or health product purchase at Target, a donation is made to St. Jude Children's Research Hospital. Target and its employee volunteers are also active at the local level. For instance, Target volunteers help to build playgrounds at local schools.

Short-Term Objectives

Promotional advertising is a type of advertising in which the retailer attempts to increase short-term performance by using product availability or price as a selling point.

Promotional advertising, on the other hand, attempts to bolster short-term performance by using product availability or price as a selling point. The two most common promotional objectives are increasing the patronage of existing customers and attracting new customers.

Today's retailers take a serious interest in giving back to the community through volunteer programs.

Increased Patronage from Existing Customers   Increased patronage is probably one of the most common promotion objectives found in retailing. Simply stated, promotion expenditures should be directed at current customers to encourage them to make more of their purchases at the retailer's store. In other words, promotion attempts to make present customers more store loyal. Amazon.com, for example, in an effort to increase patronage from existing customers, offers a wide range of coupons. Within a few days of making a purchase of books, for instance, one of the authors received a $50 coupon to purchase garden supplies from Amazon. Amazon.com's use of coupons to cross-sell is a clear attempt to increase patronage from current customers.

Attraction of New Customers   A second major short-term promotion objective is to increase the number of customers that can be attracted to the store. One approach is to try to attract new customers from the retailer's primary trading area. There are always some households within the primary trading area that, for a variety of reasons, do not patronize the retailer. Perhaps they do their shopping at a retailer close to their place of employment or perhaps they simply do not think that the retailer's store is attractive to their tastes. Maybe they once had a bad experience while shopping there and vowed never to return. A second approach to gaining new customers is to attempt to expand the trading area by attracting customers from the secondary trading area. Here the retailer might want to consider using different media so as to expand the geographic coverage of its promotional efforts. A third type of new customer is the customer just moving into the retailer's market area. Mobile consumers, for instance, are generally more prone to use national retailers, because they are familiar with the stores, unless local retailers use promotions to inform them of their offerings.

Interdependence

The two-way arrow in Exhibit 11.1 suggests that although promotion objectives can be established to improve either long- or short-term financial performance, programs designed to achieve either objective will benefit the other as well. Promotion efforts to build long-term financial performance will begin to have an effect almost immediately, but also will have a cumulative effect over time. Similarly, efforts to promote short-term financial performance will carry over to affect the long-term future of the retailer.

Steps in Planning a Retail Advertising Campaign

LO • 3
What are the six steps involved in developing a retailer's advertising campaign?

What is involved in planning a retail advertising campaign? As discussed in Chapter 2, the elements of the retailer's advertising campaign are just a part of the company's overall strategy. A retailer's advertising campaign is a six-step process:

1. Selecting advertising objectives
2. Budgeting for the campaign
3. Designing the message
4. Selecting the media to use
5. Scheduling the ads
6. Evaluating the results

Selecting Advertising Objectives

The advertising objectives should flow from the retailer's promotion objectives, but should be more specific because advertising itself is a specific element of the promotion mix. The objectives should be chosen only after the retailer considers several factors that are unique to retailing:

1. *Age of store.* New stores or stores seeking to rebuild a poor image need more advertising.
2. *Store location.* Stores in poor locations need more advertising.
3. *Types of goods sold.* Retailers selling high-image fashion goods generally require more advertising than discounters normally use. These high-fashion retailers also need greater personal selling support in order to increase inventory turnover.
4. *Level of competition.* The greater the level of competition, the more advertising and other promotional activities are needed.
5. *Market area size.* The size of the market often dictates the type and extent of the media that can be used. Also, the larger the market, the greater the need for promotional activities.
6. *Supplier support.* Suppliers may provide advertising and other promotional support that will enable the retailer to reduce its expenditures for those activities.

The specific objectives that advertising can accomplish are many and varied and the one(s) chosen depend on the target market the retailer is seeking. Examples of common objectives used by retailers include the following:

- Make consumers in your trading area aware that you offer the lowest prices (Wal-Mart's "Always Low Prices").
- Make newcomers in your trading area aware of your existence (the "welcome wagon" coupons given to new residents of the area).
- Make customers aware of your large stock selection (Nordstrom's promising the shopper a free shirt if the retailer is out of stock on the basic sizes).
- Making a specific target market aware of your product offering (JCPenney's "At least part of you is comfortable" campaign, showing teens in awkward personal situations and suggesting that they at least seek the comfort of a pair of Arizona Jeans).
- Increase traffic during slow sales periods (Subway sandwich shop's "Two-for-One Tuesdays").
- Move old merchandise at the end of a selling season (the after-Christmas clearance sales that many retailers use).
- Strengthen your store's image or reputation (Neiman Marcus's famous Christmas catalog that generates news stories around the world when the catalog is mailed to customers).
- Identify your store with the nationally advertised brands that it sells (Dillard's featuring Tommy Hilfiger clothing in its ads).
- Reposition the image of your store in the minds of consumers (the Holiday Inn example discussed later in the chapter).

- Cultivate new customers (any of the one-day discounts that a customer gets for opening a charge account with the retailer).
- Make consumers think of you first when a need for your products occurs, especially if the product or service is not commonly purchased (1-800-FLOWERS or the St. Louis service retailer's easy-to-remember jingle "For a hole in your roof or a whole new roof—Frederick Roofing").
- Retain your present customers (any of the airlines' frequent-flyer programs).
- Get customers who previously shopped at your store, but no longer do, to return to your store (the JCPenney "I Love Your Style" campaign).

Although the ultimate goal of almost every advertising campaign is to generate additional sales, you will notice that increasing sales was not listed above as an advertising objective. That is because other elements of the retail mix, that are outside of advertising's control, could negatively impact sales. The retailer could have, for example, selected the wrong merchandise for its target customers, charged too high a price for the merchandise in comparison to the competition, or improperly displayed the merchandise in the store. Therefore, since increasing sales is usually beyond the total control of just the advertising campaign, advertising should not be held solely accountable for increasing total sales.

Regardless of the objective chosen, the advertising must be aimed at a specific market segment and be measurable over a given time period. For example, Holiday Inn recently sought to reposition itself. The object of the chain's "On the Way" campaign was directed at middle-age business travelers and pointed out that Holiday Inn today is not the same boring place as their parents took them to when they were kids. The ads conveyed the message that Holiday Inn was a completely remodeled operation that catered to the needs of the business traveler. Thus, a good description of this campaign's objective would be "to increase the level of positive feelings among middle-age business travelers about Holiday Inn by 30 percent over the next six months."

Budgeting for the Campaign

A well-designed retail advertising campaign requires money that can be spent on other areas (e.g., more merchandise or higher wages for employees). The retailer hopes that the dollars spent on advertising will generate sales that will in turn produce added profits, which can then be used to finance the other activities of the retailer.

When developing a budget, the retailer should first determine who is going to pay for the campaign—that is, will the retailer be the sole sponsor or will it get co-op support from other retailers or the manufacturer?

Retailer-Only Campaigns If a retailer decides to do the campaign alone, the retailer generally uses one of the following methods to determine the amount of money to be spent on the advertising campaign: the affordable method, the percentage-of-sales method, or the task and objective method.

1. *The affordable method.* Many small retailers use the **affordable method** by allocating all the money that they can afford for advertising in any given budget period. This may lead to an inadequate appropriation or to a budget that is not

Affordable method
is a technique for budgeting advertising in which all the money a retailer can afford to spend on advertising in a given time period becomes the advertising budget.

related to actual needs. The logic of this approach suggests that advertising does not stimulate sales or profits, but rather is supported by sales and profits. However, some retailers have little choice but to use this approach. A small retailer cannot go to the bank and borrow $100,000 to spend on advertising. This is unfortunate, because the small retailer might benefit more from advertising than from additional inventory or equipment. Thus, we can see that although the affordable method may not be ideal in terms of advertising theory, it is certainly defensible given the financial constraints that confront the small retailer.

Percentage-of-sales method

is a technique for budgeting in which the retailer targets a specific percentage of forecasted sales as the advertising budget.

2. *Percentage-of-sales method.* In the **percentage-of-sales method** of budgeting for advertising, the retailer targets a specific percentage of forecasted sales to be used for advertising. The percentage of sales that should be used is frequently determined by industry data or the retailer's past experience. Industry data, such as that shown in Exhibit 11.2, are often published by trade associations. These figures are averages, however, and do not reflect the unique circumstances and objectives of a particular retailer. A more suitable guide to the level of advertising appropriations is the retailer's past sales experience. The average percentage of advertising expenditures to sales for the past several years can be applied to the current year.

One of the weaknesses of the percentage-of-sales method is that the amount of sales becomes the factor that influences the advertising outlay. In a correct cause-and-effect relationship, the level of advertising should influence the amount of sales. In addition, this technique does not reflect the retailer's advertising goals. One of the author's early retail mentors said that he "never saw business so bad that he couldn't buy all of it he wanted." By that he meant that when business slowed and all his competitors reduced their ad budgets, this retailer would then increase his ad expenditures. Without the clutter of competitor ads, consumers became more aware of his ads and his sales increased, despite the general sales slowdown affecting the other local merchants.

Another weakness of this method is that it gives more money to departments that are already successful and fails to give money to departments that with a little extra money could be successful. Percentage of sales does, however, provide a controlled, generally affordable amount to spend, and if spent wisely, it may work out well in practice. Most retailers, especially the smaller ones, do not use ad agencies and lack the sophistication required to adequately implement the task and objective approach. A percentage-of-sales guideline allows the retailer to follow objectives in an affordable, controlled manner. If the dollars are carefully applied in appropriate amounts over the year in such a way that they relate to expected sales percentages in each month, the percentage-of-sales method can work well.

Task and objective method

is a technique for budgeting in which the retailer establishes its advertising objectives and then determines the advertising tasks that need to be performed to achieve those objectives.

3. *Task and objective method.* With the preceding budgeting methods, advertising seemed to follow sales results. With the **task and objective method,** the logic is properly reversed; advertising leads to sales or some other measure of financial performance. Basically, the retailer establishes its advertising objectives and then determines the advertising tasks that need to be performed to achieve those objectives. Associated with each task is an estimate of the cost of performing the task. When all of these costs are totaled, the retailer has its advertising budget. In short, this method begins with the retailer's advertising objectives and then determines what it will cost to achieve those objectives.

Exhibit 11.2	Advertising Expenditures as a Percentage of Sales

Line of Trade	Ad Dollars As Percentage of Sales
Apparel and accessory stores	3.8
Auto and home supply stores	0.6
Building materials, hardware, garden	2.5
Catalog, mail-order houses	9.1 •2.
Computer and software stores	0.2
Department stores	4.3
Drug and proprietary stores	0.4
Eating places	3.8
Electronic parts, equipment	0.9
Family clothing stores	3.4
Furniture stores	9.4 •1.
Grocery stores	1.2
Hardware, plumbing, and heat equipment	4.4
Hobby, toy, and game shops	3.3
Home furniture and equipment stores	2.8
Lumber and other building materials	0.5
Miscellaneous general merchandise stores	6.4 3.
Miscellaneous shopping goods stores	3.6
Radio, TV consumer electronic stores	3.7
Record and tape stores	1.0
Retail stores	5.9 • 4
Shoe stores	3.0
Variety stores	1.5
Women's clothing store	5.6 5.

Source: From *Advertising Ratios & Budgets,* published by Schonfeld & Associates. Used with their permission.

Exhibit 11.3 gives an example of the task and objective method. Notice that the retailer has five major advertising objectives and a total of 11 tasks to perform to accomplish these objectives. The total cost of performing these tasks is $99,020. Although the task and objective method of developing the advertising budget is the best of the three methods from a theoretical and managerial control perspective, it is still not totally adopted by all retailers because it is difficult to implement.

Many of the major retailers use a combination of the percentage-of-sales method, which they use to keep pace with competitors, and the task and objective method, which reflects the different tasks they must accomplish to reach their objectives. Thus, as shown in Exhibit 11.4, although the percentages for close competitors are similar, they are still different because of circumstances relating to the other elements of the

	Exhibit 11.3	Task and Objective Method of Advertising Budget Development	

	Objective and Task	Estimated Cost
Objective 1:	Increase traffic during dull periods.	
Task *A:*	15 full-page newspaper advertisements to be spread over these dates: February 2–16; June 8–23; October 4–18	$22,500
Task *B:*	240, 30-second radio spots split on two stations and spread over these dates: February 2–16; June 8–23; October 4–18	4,320
Objective 2:	Attract new customers from newcomers to the community.	
Task *A:*	2,000 direct-mail letters greeting new residents to the community	1,000
Task *B:*	2,000 direct-mail letters inviting new arrivals in the community to stop in to visit the store and fill out a credit application	1,000
Task *C:*	Yellow-Page advertising	1,900
Objective 3:	Build store's reputation.	
Task *A:*	weekly 15-second institutional ads on the 10 P.M. television news every Saturday and Sunday	20,800
Task *B:*	one half-page newspaper ad per month in the home living section of the local newspaper	9,500
Objective 4:	Increase shopper traffic in shopping center.	
Task *A:*	cooperate with other retailers in the shopping center in sponsoring transit advertising on buses and cabs	3,000
Task *B:*	participate in "Midnight Madness Sale" with other retailers in the shopping center by taking out 2 full-page newspaper ads — one in mid-March and the other in mid-July	3,000
Objective 5:	Clear out end-of-month, slow-moving merchandise.	
Task *A:*	run a full-page newspaper ad on the last Thursday of every month	18,000
Task *B:*	run 3, 30-second television spots on the last Thursday of every month	14,000
Total advertising budget		$99,020

retail mix. For example, in a recent year Payless Cashways spent 1.2 percent of its sales on advertising, while rivals Lowes and Home Depot spent 0.6 percent and 0.5 percent; Sears spent 4.4 percent, while Penney's spent 3.3 percent; Target spent 2.3 percent and Kmart spent 1.3 percent, while Wal-Mart spent 0.4 percent.[4]

Co-Op Campaigns   Although most retail advertising is paid for solely by the retailer, sometimes manufacturers and other retailers may pay part or all of the costs for the retailer's advertising campaign.

Vertical cooperative advertising allows the retailer and other channel members to share the advertising burden. For example, the manufacturer may pay up to 40 percent of the retailer's cost for advertising the manufacturer's products up to a ceiling of 4 percent of annual purchases by the retailer from the manufacturer. If the retailer spent $10,000 on advertising the manufacturer's products, then it could be reimbursed 40 percent of this amount (or $4,000) as long as the retailer purchased at least $100,000 from the manufacturer during the previous year.

There is a strong temptation among retailers to view vertical co-op advertising money as free. Retailers forget, however, that good advertising, like a good investment, should increase revenues from customers, not just from vendors—that is, even if the supplier is putting up 50 percent of the expense, the retailer must still pay the other 50

Vertical cooperative advertising

occurs when the retailer and other channel members (usually manufacturers) share the advertising budget. Usually the manufacturer subsidizes some of the retailer's advertising that features the manufacturer's brands.

Exhibit 11.4	Advertising Expenditures as a Percentage of Sales for Some Leading Retailers

Line of Trade	Ad Dollars As Percentage of Sales
Building materials & hardware	
Home Depot, Inc.	0.5
Lowe's	0.6
Payless Cashways	1.2
Department stores	
Dillards	4.4
May Department Stores	3.8
JCPenney Co.	3.3
Sears Roebuck & Co	4.4
Family clothing stores	
Abercrombie & Fitch	3.5
American Eagle Outfitters, Inc	3.1
Grocery stores	
Albertsons	1.5
Great Atlantic & Pacific Tea Co	1.4
Kroger Co	1.1
Pathmark Stores Inc	0.5
Publix Super Markets Inc	1.1
Safeway Inc	1.4
Winn-Dixie Stores Inc	1.2
Variety stores	
Dollar General	5.3
Dollar Tree Stores Inc.	10.1
Family Dollar Stores	0.4
Kmart Corp	1.5
Target Corp	2.3
Wal-Mart Stores	0.5
Women's clothing store	
Charming Shoppes	2.5
Dress Barn Inc	1.3
Limited Inc	7.6
Talbots Inc	6.2

Source: From *Advertising Ratios & Budgets,* published by Schonfeld & Associates. Used with their permission.

percent. In addition, because the supplier often exercises considerable control over the content of the advertising and its objectives may be different than the retailer's, retailers actually may be paying 50 percent of the supplier's cost of advertising rather than vice versa. Also, suppliers know that it is a common media practice to offer local retailers a discount on rates relative to national advertisers. Thus, suppliers often use local retailers to get them this discount on their ads.

Retailers must, therefore, decide whether they can get a better return on their money with vertical co-op dollars or by paying all advertising costs themselves which may enable them to better achieve their objectives.

Retailers can be more profitable if they pass up some co-op promotional deals.

Horizontal cooperative advertising

occurs when two or more retailers band together to share the cost of advertising usually in the form of a joint promotion of an event or sale that would benefit both parties.

Horizontal cooperative advertising is when two or more retailers band together to share the cost of advertising. Significantly, this tends to give small retailers more bargaining power in purchasing advertising than they would otherwise have. Also, if properly conducted, it can create substantially more store traffic for all participants. For example, retailers in shopping malls often jointly sponsor multiple-page spreads in newspapers promoting special events such as "Santa Land" or "Moonlight Madness" sales, and downtown merchants usually jointly sponsor "Sidewalk Days" or "Downtown Days" sales. That these events are good traffic generators is shown by the many malls that have recently turned a very slow shopping night (Halloween) into a very successful "Dead Night." By having a store-to-store program that provides a safe place for trick-or-treating, a mall can pull significantly more people into each retailer's store than the retailers operating individually could expect to do at the same cost.

However, sometimes these horizontal co-op programs can produce unexpected negative results. Doral Chenoweth, a nationally recognized consultant on mall promotions, was once asked to list all the bad mall promotions known to mankind. His response was that it would take a thousand pages just to list them, and that was not counting his own. Chenoweth's "three all-time bad mall promotions" all involved animal acts and two resulted in lawsuits.

Number one, and the only one not generating a lawsuit, involved a Michigan mall in the early 1970s, when *Flipper* (the dolphin) was a top children's television show. The mall had Flipper appear in a big pool in the parking lot. Of course, there were many so-called Flippers available for rent at the time, and the mall's marketing director decided to save money and use the cheapest one, a 15-year-old dolphin named Max. You can imagine what happened when, at high noon after the big buildup that attracted thousands of youngsters, Max flipped into the pool and suddenly died of a heart attack. At least the mall got some publicity out of this sad event when a newspaper columnist suggested the mall should then have had a sale on fish sandwiches.

An Ohio mall sought to draw customers to its grand opening with a live bear act. A small boy standing too close was mauled and nearly killed in front of everybody. Wire services had a field day with photos. At least everybody in the trading area now knew the mall was open for business.

Even such tame animal acts like petting zoos are too risky in our present lawsuit-minded society. Consider the Minnesota mall where a billy goat escaped from its pen and ran through the mall. During the chase, two elderly patrons fell into a planter and sued the mall.

Maybe that's why Chenoweth joins David Letterman, when advising mall marketing managers, in saying "always avoid stupid pet tricks."

Designing the Message

The next step in developing an advertising campaign is to design a creative message and select the media that will enable the retailer to reach its objectives. In reality, these decisions are made simultaneously. Creative messages cannot be developed without knowing which media will be used to carry the message to the target market. This text, however, will cover media selection after discussing how retailers design their message.

Creative decisions are especially important for retailers because their advertising messages usually are seeking an immediate reaction from the consumer and have a short life span. The development of such messages is one of retailing's major failings. By merely covering up the retailer's name in ads used in your local newspaper or tuning out the retailer's name in a broadcast ad, you will realize that all too often retailers lack originality in their ads—the ads will all look/sound the same.

Creative retail ads should seek to accomplish three goals:

1. Attract attention and retain attention
2. Achieve the objective of the advertising strategy
3. Avoid having any errors, especially legal ones

Accomplishing these goals is an extremely difficult task in today's marketplace given the consumer's limited attention span. With newspaper and magazine readership declining and the increased use of the remote control to "surf the tube" during television commercial breaks, it is becoming more and more difficult for retailers to find a unique way to break through the competitive clutter to get the consumer's attention and then to hold it.

In 2000, *Advertising Age* gave the Best of the Show award for commercials to the online job-search site, Monster.com, a service retailer, for its Super Bowl ad. The ad, which was a parody of the then very popular Nike-esque aspirational montages, featured children talking about what they wanted to be when they grew up. In the Monster.com ad, however, they uttered a litany of employment humiliations. All the children began their statements with the familiar Nike "When I grow up," only to conclude with such statements as these:

"I wanna file . . . all day."

"I want to claw my way up to middle management."

"I want to be replaced on a whim."

"I want to brown nose."

"I want to be forced into early retirement."

Before the Super Bowl, Monster.com's traffic was running around 1.5 million unique visitors per month. For the remainder of the year, it averaged more than 2.5 million per month.[5] Although Monster.com did an outstanding job of attracting and holding attention, a major problem for all advertisers is "when do we replace an ad?" In 2000, for example, Tricon Global Restaurants' Taco Bell chain dropped its popular chihuahua from its ads. Dinky, who will always be remembered for saying "Yo quiero Taco Bell," was replaced when the chain's sales fell flat. The chain later claimed that it was planning a major global expansion and felt some Latin American consumers might find the Dinky ads offensive. However, *Advertising Age* pointed out that the falling sales problem probably was not the dog's fault, but was due to the fact that Taco Bell had only introduced one new product—which failed in test markets—in the previous year.[6] The public still watched the dog, but without new products, they had no reason to increase their visits to Taco Bell. Still other advertising executives claim that Dinky was an example of the creative idea, the dog, overwhelming the strategy of making consumers aware of the chain's product offerings.[7] Another highly rated retailer ad that was recently discontinued was the "Softer Side of Sears" promotion. Here Sears wanted to use a new campaign—"Sears: The Good Life at a Great Price. Guaranteed."—to focus on the broad range of products and services at Sears and to move away from women's apparel, where it had not been strong in the past and where it was more difficult to compete. The ad was discontinued due to its ineffectiveness of repositioning Sears in the marketplace. In addition, Sears' overall strategy to reposition itself within the marketplace also failed.

Dollars & Sense

Retailers who realize the importance of creative decisions in their advertising will have higher long-term profits.

Although Taco Bell's Dinky became a celebrity in its own right, other retailers use real people. Kmart, for example, has successfully used Martha Stewart in its ads to attract attention from middle-aged adults, while Old Navy has employed Morgan Fairchild, Carrie Donovan, and "Magic the dog" in quirky ads to gain the attention of the youth market. Small local retailers often use big, bold copy offering something exciting in their print ads to get attention. Other retailers use a combination of one or more of the common advertising appeals to gain attention. These appeals are profit, fear, pleasure, vanity, convenience, romance, admiration, and health.

Managerial Question: Should a retailer change its advertising campaign every year so that consumers do not get bored with it?

However, even after the retailer gets the consumer's attention, the retailer must hold on to that attention. After all, if consumers have already seen or read the ad, why should they view it again. Some common approaches that retailers use to gain repeated viewing include the following:

Lifestyle	Shows how the retailer's products fit in with the consumer's lifestyle
Fantasy	Creates a fantasy for the consumer that is built around the retailer's products
Humorous	Employs humor that relates to using the retailer's products
Slice-of-life	Depicts the consumer in everyday settings using the retailer's products
Mood/Image	Builds a mood around using the retailer's products

Finally, before using the ad, the retailer should pretest it with both consumer groups and legal experts for errors. For example, Burger King recently ran a national television ad featuring a bookish-looking boy playing a cello badly. After being zapped by a cartoon character, the boy is taken to a Burger King for a Whopper and is transformed into a skilled electric-guitar player. Music teachers began complaining to Burger King at once, and some even picketed outside Burger King restaurants. By failing to pretest the ad, Burger King never realized that it could offend these teachers. Likewise, in the Holiday Inn campaign mentioned earlier, the chain's first ad of this campaign was dropped after only one airing. In it, a former male, Bob Johnson, returns to his high school reunion as a transsexual and nobody is able to recognize him/her. Holiday Inn hoped this would reinforce the campaign's main message of "the renovations at Holiday Inn." Unfortunately, many viewers found the ad offensive and it was dropped at once. Both of these mistakes could have been detected during a pretest. The Global Retailing box shows that American retailers are not the only ones who sometimes fail to pretest or proof their promotions.

Although these errors are serious enough in nature, they should not present the retailer with legal problems. That does not mean the retailer is not in danger of violating some laws with its ads, even if it is not trying to deceive the consumer. Chapter 6 discussed some of the various federal laws governing retail advertising. All too often the

Global Retailing

International Promotion Mistakes

There are usually significant differences between domestic and foreign retail markets. Nowhere have international retailers had more problems than with regard to promotional activities. However, the real errors in international promotion usually result from retailers trying to write signs and instructions in a foreign language and not checking these signs for errors. Sometimes, poor knowledge of the customer's language results in unintentional but highly interesting promotions. Consider the following errors by foreign retailers trying to translate ads into English:

- Airline counter in Copenhagen: We take your bags and send them in all directions.
- Tokyo bar: Special cocktails for ladies with nuts.
- Mexico City discount store: American well speaking here.
- Paris dress shop: Dresses for street walking.
- Hong Kong dentist: Teeth extracted by latest Methodists.
- Rome laundry: Ladies, please leave your clothes here and spend the afternoon having a good time.
- French hotel: Please leave your values at the front desk.
- Athens hotel: We expect our visitors to complain daily at the office between the hours of 9 and 11 a.m.

- Tokyo hotel: The flattening of underwear is the job of the chambermaid—to get it done, turn her on.
- Paris hotel: Splendid views, and a French widow in every room.
- Bangkok dry cleaner: Drop your trousers here for best results.
- Men's room at a Mexican golf course/resort: Guests are requested not to wash their balls in the hand basins.
- Amsterdam hotel: You are encouraged to take advantage of our chambermaids.
- Swiss restaurant: Special today . . . no ice cream.
- Hong Kong tailor shop: Order your summer suit now. Because of big rush we execute customers in strict rotation.
- Stockholm furrier: Fur coats made for ladies from their own skin.
- Newspaper ad for donkey rides in Thailand: Would you like to ride on your own ass?

Still even native Americans have trouble with English, consider this sign on a Philadelphia clothing store: Semi-Annual Clearance Sale! Savings Like These Only Come Once a Year, or the Concord, California, florist advertising a Pre-Grand Opening Clearance.

retailer runs into trouble with local laws. Some states, for example, limit promotions involving games of chance, others regulate the use of ads with price comparisons among retail stores, and others regulate the use of certain words in the description of merchandise. For example, the Pennsylvania Human Relations Commission has issued guidelines against the use of the following words in real estate ads because they may discriminate among consumer groups: *bachelor pad, couple, mature, older seniors, adults, traditional, newlyweds, exclusive, children,* and *established neighborhood.*

Internationally, individual countries, or in some cases groups of countries such as the European Union, set specific guidelines for advertising content that must be adhered to. For instance, in the European Union, advertising with or directed at children or young people is generally allowed. However, the ad must not directly encourage children or young people to buy a product and must not exploit their inexperience and credulity. It must not cause them any physical or mental harm. Broadcasts that could cause minors physical or mental harm must be transmitted between 11 p.m. and 6 a.m.

Selecting the Media To Use

Today's retailer has many media alternatives from which to select. In the past, retailers generally categorized media as either print (which included newspaper, magazines, and direct mail) or broadcast (which lumped radio and television together). Now, however, retailers are beginning to classify media from a managerial perspective by recognizing that newspapers and television are mass media alternatives aimed at a total market, whereas radio, magazines, direct mail, and the Internet can be more easily targeted toward specific markets.

Newspaper Advertising The most frequently used advertising medium in retailing is the newspaper for the following reasons. (1) Most newspapers are local. This is advantageous because most retailers appeal to a local trading area. (2) A low technical skill level is required to create advertisements for newspapers. This is helpful for small retailers. (3) There is only a brief time period between when the copy for a newspaper ad is written and when the ad will appear. Because some retailers do a poor job of planning and because they tend to use advertising to respond to crises (poor cash flow, slackening of sales, need to move old merchandise), the short lead time for placing newspaper ads is a significant advantage.

Retail newspaper advertising also has its disadvantages, including the following: (1) the fact that a consumer was exposed to an issue of a newspaper does not mean the consumer read or even saw the retailer's ad; (2) the life of any single issue of a newspaper is short—it's read and subsequently discarded; (3) the typical person spends relatively little time with each issue, and the time spent is spread over many items in the newspaper; (4) newspapers have poor reproduction quality, which leads to ads with little appeal; and (5) if the retailer has a specific target market, much of its advertising money will be wasted, because newspapers tend to have a broad appeal. In fact, seldom does the retailer's target market match the circulation of any newspaper. Despite these disadvantages, newspapers continue to be the number 1 form of advertising for retailers. Many of the large brick & mortar retailers, such as Wal-Mart, Target, Sears, Mervyn's, and Kmart, as well as e-tailers, such as Mercata.com, Petsmart.com, and Buy.com, use newspapers to deliver their own centrally produced inserts.

Television Advertising Today retailers, such as Sears and Penney's are turning to television advertising as a means of creating an image or position in the marketplace.[8] Research suggests that, over time, pictures retain their effects on consumer memory and evaluation to a greater extent than the verbal messages from media such as radio. However, television advertising is expensive. A half-dozen well-designed television ads may use up the total ad budget. In addition, for the small or even intermediate-sized retailer, a television ad would reach well beyond its trading area. A final disadvantage of television advertising is that competition is high for the viewer's attention. During advertising periods, the viewer may take a break and leave the room, may be exposed to several ads, or may use the remote control to "surf" to other channels. "Surfing the tube" has become a significant problem recently as most viewers have remote controls and the number of channels available has increased from as few as three or four in some markets in the 1970s to the more than 500 that are now available on many cable systems. Such an increase in channel availability may cause retailers to view television advertising not so much as a mass audience approach but as one that can be targeted to specific markets.[9]

In spite of the preceding drawbacks, television advertising can be a powerful tool for generating higher sales. The American public spends more time relaxing in front of the television than in any other recreational activity. Television has broad coverage; over 98 percent of homes in the United States have at least one television set. These sets offer the retailer a vehicle in which both sight and sound can be used to create a significant perceptual and cognitive effect on the consumer. It should be noted that television penetration rates differ across the world and therefore its usefulness as a media to reach consumers can differ as well.

Further, the widespread development of cable television has made television attractive to small, local retailers. Local cable operators have been selling advertising on cable channels, which is quite competitive with that of newspaper advertising. However, retailers just starting to use television advertising may be hard pressed to find a niche because so many others have already been seeking to fill niches too. The point to remember, as mentioned earlier, is to sell both the products and store image at the same time. Cable television has also provided a new means of television advertising—24-hour shopping channels.

Radio Advertising   Many retailers prefer to use radio because it can target messages to select groups. In most communities there are five to ten or more radio stations, each of which tends to appeal to a different demographic group. Retailers can use radio, through the use of proper variations in volume and types of sounds, to develop distinctive and appealing messages and to introduce a store and its image to current and potential customers. In short, radio offers retailers a lot of flexibility. Also, many radio audiences develop strong affection and trust for their favorite radio announcers. When these announcers endorse the retailer, the audience is impressed.

Radio advertising also has its drawbacks. Radio commercials, especially the uncreative ones, are not easily saved or referred to again like print media ads. In fact, some media experts claim that radio's lack of creativity is a major shortcoming. All too often ad agencies and radio stations lack the creativity to help local retailers. The CBS radio network, claiming the last truly great radio campaign was Motel 6's "And we'll leave the light on for you," recently hired top creative people to stimulate better radio commercials at both the national and local levels.[10] In addition, radio is frequently listened to during work hours or driving to and from work (drive time) and tends, over time, to become part of the background environment. Also, because radio is nonvisual, it is impossible to effectively demonstrate or show the merchandise that is being advertised. Finally, radio signals tend to cover an area much larger than a retailer's trading area. Therefore, a good portion of the retailer's advertising dollars may be wasted.

Magazine Advertising   Relatively few local retailers advertise in magazines, unless the magazine has only a local circulation. Nationally based retailers such as JCPenney's will allocate some of their advertising budget to magazines. Usually, the retail ads that these retailers place in magazines are institutional.

Magazine advertising can be quite effective. In relation to newspapers, magazines perform well on several dimensions. They have a better reproduction quality; they have a longer life span per issue; and consumers spend more time with each issue of a magazine than a newspaper. For example, magazines have the unique quality of being shared among family and friends, thus extending the reach of the advertisement. An added benefit is that featured articles in a magazine can put people in the mood for a particular product class. For example, a feature article on home remodeling in *Better Homes and Gardens* can put people in a frame of mind to consider purchasing wallpaper, carpeting, tiling, draperies, paint, and other home improvement items. The major disadvantage of using magazines is that the long lead time requirements prevent price appeal advertising, as well as the lack of urgency in its messages.

Direct Mail   Direct marketing can be a powerful addition to the retailer's promotional strategy. With direct mail, the retailer can precisely target its message at a particular group as long as a good mailing list of the target population is available. Bloomingdale's, for example, uses a customer database to select targeted recipients for each of its roughly 300 annual catalog and promotional mailings. In addition, direct mail provides retailers a personal contact with individual consumers who share certain valued characteristics. Thus, although all of Bloomingdale's customers receive the Christmas catalog, only those recently purchasing a men's suit will receive a postcard promoting a sale on shirts and ties. Such messages can reach the consumer without the competition noticing. Finally direct-mail results can generally be easily measured, thus providing the retailer with important feedback information.

On the negative side, direct-mail advertising is relatively expensive per contact or message delivered. Also, the ability to reach the target market totally depends on the quality of the mailing list. If the list is not kept current, advertising dollars will be wasted. For example, the University of Phoenix regularly sends one of the authors a direct mail advertisement suggesting that he could further his career prospects if he obtained a bachelor's degree in business. Given that the author already has a Ph.D. in business, is this an example of wasted ad dollars? A related problem is the incidence of unopened or unexamined mail, especially when it is addressed to "occupant" or is mailed using third-class postage.

Another negative pertains to electronic direct mail or spam. Although most Americans tolerate direct mail solicitations, the infestation of unsolicited e-mail irritates nearly everyone. At the present time, spamers and consumer groups are trying to settle this issue out of court without infringing on the spamers' right to free speech and their ability to conduct business. However, it appears only the courts will be able to settle this issue.[11]

The Internet   The Internet is playing an important promotional role for retailers. With current estimates of more than 55 million unique users, projections indicate that the Internet will have more than 200 million users in the next few years. Although we have discussed the various aspects of selling on-line throughout this text, we have not specifically addressed the use of the Internet by retailers as a promotional media.

A key aspect of the Internet is its ability to provide customers with information. The communication elements of advertising, sales promotion, and public relations are all strategic options a firm can use when communicating with its various publics. For example, a firm may wish to provide on-line customers with samples of its advertising on its web site, such as Merrill Lynch (www.ml.com) or the Gap (www.gap.com). Or a firm may wish to use sales promotions, such as on-line coupons like those sometimes used by Harold's (www.harolds.com), a clothing retailer, or Amazon.com. A retailer can also use its web site to share specific information on good works through press releases or bylined articles, to confirm sound financial fundamentals to investors or potential investors, or to explain its environmental position and community involvement, a path taken by both the Walt Disney Company (www.disney.com) and Target (www.target. com). In essence, the Internet provides a platform for a retailer to employ a relatively low-cost integrated marketing communications mix. Thus, the retailer increases shareholder value by enhancing its image, by providing customers with a

The Southwest Airlines Internet site is designed to provide information and to communicate with all its relevant public. In addition, Southwest Airlines promotes use of its site by offering double frequent flyer credits when flights are booked on the Internet.

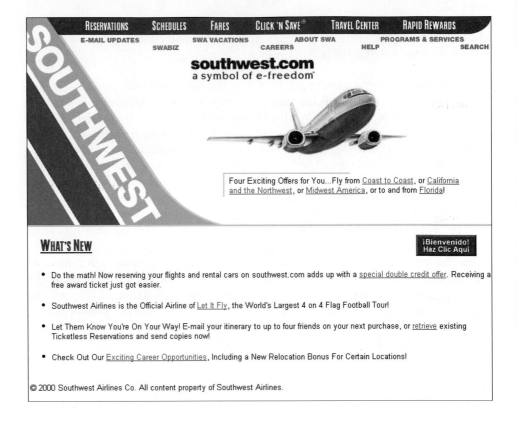

variety of highly specialized information. For example, Southwest Airlines (www.ifly-swa.com) utilizes its web site to provide a fully integrated marketing communication mix. Southwest offers on-line ticketing, investor information, and advertising, as well as sales promotions and public relation materials, thus effectively communicating with all of its relevant publics.

Miscellaneous Media   The retailer can advertise using media other than those previously identified, including the yellow pages, outdoor advertising,[12] transit advertising (on buses, cabs, subways), electronic information terminals, specialty firms such as the welcome wagon, and shopping guides (newspaper-like printed material, but with no news). Each of these options is usually best used to reinforce other media and should not be relied on exclusively unless the retailer's advertising budget is minimal. Most retailers look upon these media vehicles as geared more toward particular product advertising by manufacturers. However, that does not mean a retailer cannot make use of them.

Retailers who understand the advantages and disadvantages of the various media will be higher profit performers.

Media Selection

To select the best media, the retailer needs to remember the strengths and weaknesses of each medium and needs to determine the coverage, reach, and frequency of each medium being considered.

Coverage refers to the theoretical maximum number of consumers in a retailer's target market that can be reached by a medium—not the number actually reached. For example, if a newspaper is circulated to 70 percent of the 20,000 households in a retailer's trading area, then the theoretical coverage is 14,000 households.

Reach, on the other hand, refers to the actual total number of target customers who come into contact with the ad message. Another useful term is **cumulative reach,** which is the reach achieved over a period of time.

Frequency is the average number of times each person who is reached is exposed to an advertisement during a given time period.

Different media can be evaluated by combining knowledge on the cost of ads in a medium and the medium's reach and cumulative reach. The most commonly used methods for doing this are the **cost per thousand method (CPM)** and **cost per thousand—target market (CPM-TM).** The most appropriate way to compute the CPM is to divide the cost for an ad or series of ads in a medium by the total number of people viewing the ad. For example, if a newspaper ad cost $500 and was distributed to 38,200 households, then the CPM is $13.09 [($500/38,200) × 1,000)]. However, the ad may only have reached 13,860 customers in the retailer's target market, the cost per thousand for the target market is $36.08 [($500/13,860) × 1,000]. As you can see, CPM-TM only measures members of the retailer's target market who are reached by the ad.

Comparing CPM and CPM-TM for different media vehicles can also provide information on the effectiveness of the media. For example, let's compare billboard to cable television advertising. Let's say that billboard and cable both cost $1,000 a month and each also reach 1 million consumers. Here the CPM for both is $1.00. However, given the focused nature of cable, the retailer may reach 900,000 in its target market, thus having a $1.11 CPM-TM. The billboard, however, only reaches 500,000 of the retailer's targeted customers and as a result the retailer has a CPM-TM of $2.00. Comparing CPM-TMs we can see that cable television, with its $1.11 CPM-TM, is more effective than the billboard, with its CPM-TM of $2.00, for the retailer. Thus, a medium such as cable television may cost more based on CPM, but if it has a significantly better CPM-TM, it may be the better buy.

Lastly, **impact** refers to how strong an impression an advertisement makes and how well it ultimately leads to a purchase. As a result of the increase in media alternatives and consumers spending a stable amount of time on the various media, CPM-TMs had a five-fold increase in the 1990s.

Scheduling the Ads

When should a retailer time its advertisements to be received by the consumer? What time of day, day of week, week of month, and month of year should the ads appear? No uniform answer to these questions is available for all lines of retail trade. Rather, the retailer should consider the following conventional wisdom:

1. Ads should appear on, or slightly precede, the days when customers are most likely to purchase. If most people shop for groceries on Thursday through Saturday, then grocery store ads might appear on Wednesday and Thursday.

Coverage
is the theoretical maximum number of consumers in the retailer's target market that can be reached by a medium and not the number actually reached.

Reach
is the actual total number of target customers who come into contact with an advertising message.

Cumulative reach
is the reach that is achieved over a period of time.

Frequency
is the average number of times each person who is reached is exposed to an advertisement during a given time period.

Cost per thousand method (CPM)
is a technique used to evaluate advertisements in different media based on cost. The cost per thousand is the cost of the advertisement divided by the number of people viewing it, which is then multiplied by 1,000.

Cost per thousand— target market (CPM-TM)
is a technique used to evaluate advertisements in different media based on cost. The cost per thousand per target market is the cost of the advertisement divided by the number of people in the target market viewing it, which is then multiplied by 1,000.

Impact
refers to how strong an impression an advertisement makes and how well it ultimately leads to a purchase.

2. Advertising should be concentrated around the times when people receive their payroll checks. If they get paid at the end of each month, then advertising should be concentrated at that point.

3. If the retailer has limited advertising funds, it should concentrate its advertising during periods of highest demand. For example, a muffler repair shop would be well advised to advertise during drive time on Thursday and Friday when the consumer is aware of his or her problem and has Saturday available for the repair work.

4. The retailer should time its ads to appear during the time of day or the day of the week when it will obtain the best CPM-TM. Many small retailers have found the advantages of late-night television.

5. The higher the degree of habitual purchasing of a product class, the more the advertising should precede the purchase time.

Many retailers use advertising to react to crises, for example, an unexpected buildup of inventory due to slow sales. Of course, if this is the situation, the timing of ads is not planned in advance. This, however, is an ineffective method of scheduling retail advertising. The rules above are only suggestions based on conventional wisdom. Sometimes a retailer, depending on the situation, may use a different scheduling plan to make the best use of its money. For example, earlier in the chapter it was mentioned that one of the author's mentors suggested advertising when others were not advertising and not advertising so much as to get lost in the crowd when others were advertising.

Evaluating the Results

Will the advertising produce results? It depends on how well designed the ads are and how well the advertising decisions were made. A consistent record of good retail advertising decision making can be made only if the retailer effectively plans its advertising program.

Some retailers try systematically to assess the effectiveness and efficiency of their advertising. **Advertising effectiveness** refers to the extent to which the advertising has produced the result desired (i.e., helped to achieve the advertising objective). **Advertising efficiency** is concerned with whether the advertising result was achieved with the minimum financial expenditure.

The effectiveness or efficiency of a retailer's advertising can be assessed on a subjective basis. Simply ask yourself: Are you satisfied with the results produced? Do you believe you achieved those results at the least cost? Most, but not all, ineffective advertising is due to the retailer committing at least one of ten common errors:

1. The retailer may be bombarding the consumer with so many messages and sales that any single message or sale tends to be discounted. A retailer that has a major sale every week tends to wear out its appeal.

2. The advertising may not be creative or appealing. It may be just more "me too" advertising in which the retailer does not effectively differentiate itself from the competition.

3. The advertisement may not give customers all the information they need. The store hours or address may be absent because the retailer assumes that everyone

Advertising effectiveness is the extent to which the advertising has produced the result desired.

Advertising efficiency is concerned with whether the advertising result was achieved with the minimum financial expenditure.

already knows this information. Or, information may be lacking on sizes, styles, colors, and other product attributes.

4. The advertising dollars may have been spread too thinly over too many departments or merchandise lines.

5. There may have been poor internal communication among salesclerks, cashiers, stock clerks, and management. For example, customers may come to see the advertised item, but salesclerks may not know the item is on sale or where to find it, and cashiers may not know the sale price. Worse yet, for a variety of reasons, the advertised product may not be available when the consumer seeks to purchase it.

6. The advertisement may not have been directed at the proper target market.

7. The retailer did not consider all media options. A better buy was available, but the retailer did not take the time to find out about it.

8. The retailer made too many last-minute changes in the advertising copy, increasing both the cost of the ad and chances for errors.

9. The retailer took co-op dollars just because they were "free" and therefore thought to represent a good deal.

10. The retailer used a medium that reached too many people not in the target market. Thus, too much money was spent on advertising to people who were not potential customers.

Management of Sales Promotions and Publicity

LO • 4
How do retailers manage their sales promotion and publicity?

Retailers also use sales promotions, which provide some type of short-term incentive, and publicity to increase the effectiveness of their promotional efforts. The role of sales promotions and publicity in the retail organization should be consistent with and reinforce the retailer's overall promotional objectives.

Role of Sales Promotion

Sales promotion tools are excellent demand generators. Many can be used on relatively short notice and can help the retailer achieve its overall promotion goals. Furthermore, sales promotions can be significant in helping the retailer differentiate itself from competitors. Retailers have long known that consumers change their shopping habits and brand preferences to take advantage of sales promotions, especially those that offer something special, different, or exciting.

Retailers must remember that, because all stores are able to shop the same vendors, merchandise alone does not make a store exciting. In-store happenings of sales promotion can generate excitement. Many retailers fail to recognize that the role of sales promotions is quite large and may represent a larger expenditure than advertising. They do not recognize this because of their poor record-keeping systems. They know the cost of advertising because most of that is paid to parties outside the firm. However, the cost of sales promotions often includes many in-store expenses that the retailer does not trace to promotion activities. If these costs were properly traced, many retailers would discover that sales promotions represent a sizable expenditure. Therefore, promotions warrant more attention by retail decision makers than is typically given.

Types of Sales Promotion

As a rule, high-performance retailers break sales promotions into two categories: those where they are the sole sponsors and those involving a joint effort with other parties. These are shown in Exhibit 11.5.

Sole-Sponsored Sales Promotions   Just like advertising, sales promotions are an expense to the retailer that may or may not be shared with others. With sole-sponsored sales promotions, the retailer has complete control over the promotion, but is also completely responsible for the costs. Although there may be some overlap in the sponsorship of these promotions, retailers generally consider these sales promotions to be sole sponsored:

Premiums
are extra items offered to the customer when purchasing promoted products.

Contests and sweepstakes
are sales promotion techniques in which customers have a chance of winning a special prize based on entering a contest in which the entrant competes with others, or a sweepstakes in which all entrants have an equal chance of winning a prize.

Frequent buyer programs
are a form of sales promotion program in which buyers are rewarded with special rewards, which other shoppers are not offered, for purchasing often from the retailer.

1. **Premiums** are extra items offered to the customer when purchasing a promoted product. Premiums are used to increase consumption among current consumers and persuade nonusers to try the promoted product. Generally the retailer is solely responsible for such programs, although some exceptions may occur. An example of a successful premium is when McDonald's gives away a free toy, such as a Teenie Beanie Baby, with the purchase of a Happy Meal.

2. **Contests and sweepstakes,** which face legal restrictions in some states, are designed to create an interest in the retailer's product and encourage both repeat purchases and brand switching. Although, such programs produce only one grand prize winner, the selection of a prize that will appeal to a large segment of the market and the addition of smaller prizes make such promotions very popular with consumers. Many local restaurants use weekly drawings not only to generate business but also to track their customers. As the Retailing: The Inside Story box describes, one retailer used a simple little Halloween pumpkin decoration contest to generate both awareness and business.

3. **Frequent buyer programs** are still rapidly growing as retailers begin to appreciate the importance of combining this promotion with their database system to

Exhibit 11.5   **Types of Sales Promotions**

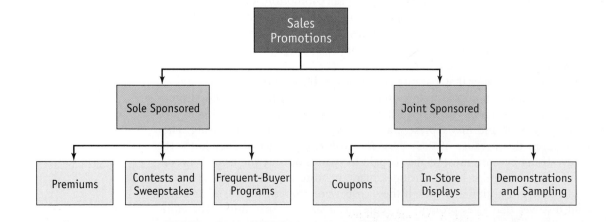

Retailing: The Inside Story

The Pumpkin Promotion

T&M Appliance & TV of Clinton, Missouri, population 1,500, ran a Halloween pumpkin sales promotion contest that produced record sales of 207 units, up 60 percent from the 130 monthly average, and it cost T&M less than $500.

The way the contest worked was that customers came into the store in early October to get a free pumpkin to carve. They came back with their entry on October 26 or 27, and returned once again to see all the entries and vote for their favorite for the People's Choice award. They came back a fourth time after the October 29 judging during the Moonlight Madness costume contest and parade on Main Street to pick up their pumpkin.

The major expense for the contest was $250 in prize money. The store purchased 150 pumpkins for $95. Attractively designed and well-written orange flyers cost $75, and store decorations such as straw bales cost $35 for a grand promotion cost of $455.

The pumpkins made a great display in the store for Moonlight Madness. A half-page of the store's regular full-page newspaper ad was devoted to the contest. T&M plans to make this promotion an annual event.

T&M recommends these helpful hints to retailers considering a similar promotion.

- Have flyers printed in September.
- When all the pumpkins are gone, tell customers they still can enter with their own pumpkin.
- Put finished pumpkins on paper plates when they are on display in the store—they will leak.
- Start giving away the pumpkins early in October— every day they are in a customer's home will remind the customer of the store.
- Take promotional flyers to the local library, day care centers, and public schools.
- Keep a list of customers who receive pumpkins and those who return them.
- Put the carved pumpkins throughout the store so customers will see all the store's merchandise.
- Coordinate the promotion with other holiday promotions in the store's area.
- Phone the local newspapers to print photos and stories about the promotion.

Source: Based on information supplied by Marvin Lurie of the North American Retail Dealers Association.

---

solidify their relationship with the customer. Neiman Marcus, for example, offers a free trip for two to London when the customer purchases $125,000 on their Neiman Marcus credit card. In addition, the retailer offers smaller rewards starting with membership in its InCircle Club when the customer's purchases reach $3,000. Piggly Wiggly's, a grocery chain in the southeast, credits its Pig's Favorite loyalty card with protecting its customer base from attack by supercenters and another regional grocer. According to the chain's director of loyalty marketing, "If either of those operations is getting any of our business, it is not our top customers."[13] In fact, as the chapter's Service Retailing box indicates, many consumers have become so loyal to some frequent shopper/flyer programs that they sometimes pass on bargains available at other retailers.

Jointly Sponsored Sales Promotions   Jointly sponsored sales promotions offer retailers the advantage of using "other people's money" (OPM). Although in some cases such promotions require the retailer to relinquish some control, the cosponsor's monetary offering to the retailer more than makes up for it. Retailers generally consider the following promotions to be jointly sponsored:

Service Retailing

The Millennium's New Addiction: Frequent Flyer Consumers

The room is small and relatively dimly lit. To the side of the room are refreshments—not much, just some coffee and pastries. They are something of an after-dinner snack for the small group that meets every Tuesday night. A circle of chairs in the center of the room denotes the traditional support group structure. As the meeting comes to order a man stands and begins.

"Hi. My name is Andrew and I am a frequent flyer mile junkie. I just can't stop myself. I consider myself a relatively intelligent person. Or at least I thought I was. Maybe I am. I'm not quite sure anymore. But one thing that I have come to realize is that I may have gone too far. That is why I am here. I will do almost anything to gain frequent flyer miles. I have a credit card that I pay $50 a year just to use. Why? Because I get frequent flyer miles when I charge with it. It's crazy. I stay at particular hotels simply because I get frequent flyer miles on my airline at that hotel. When comparing air travel arrangements for an upcoming trip, I realized I could get a direct flight on one airline, or I could fly my frequent flyer airline but would have to change planes. In total the trip on my favorite airline would take an extra three hours each way. My decision was to take my favorite airline. I rationalized that I could get some work done in the airport. Yeah, right. I now eat cereal for breakfast. Why? My airline is having a promotion with a cereal manufacturer and they are putting coupons on the box. I have enough boxes of cereal to last me a lifetime.

"My addiction has also caused me to change my perspective in a number of ways. For instance, I have a new hero now. Not Tiger Woods or anyone most of you would have heard of. His name is David Phillips. Mr. Phillips is a king in the frequent flyer world. Actually, many just call him the pudding guy. In 1999 he found a promotion between an airline and Healthy Choice. The promotion included coupons on Healthy Choice products where you could get 500 or 1,000 miles for purchases. He knew that he could really make out if he could find a very low-cost Healthy Choice product. What was it? Pudding. And after an investment of $3,000 he had earned himself 1.25 million frequent flyer miles. In 2000 he added another 1 million miles by flying to ten Latin American cities. A deal he indicated was even better than the pudding. He clearly knows how to take advantage of a sales promotion."

Andrew is not alone. Many have fallen in love with frequent flyer promotions. In fact, frequent flyer programs are one of the most popular service promotions going today. Some say it is the feeling of getting something for nothing, or something for something you already do like purchasing on a credit card, that drives these people. How do the airlines see it? Profits. Realize that in most cases the miles are never redeemed.

As such, the current realized cost to the airlines is minimal (although the unrealized cost is somewhat high). Further, the joint promotions, such as the Healthy Choice promotion that David Phillips leveraged, did not cost the airline anything. The airline actually sells the frequent flyer miles to other companies for a few cents a mile, which adds up to more than the airline makes on a standard round-trip sale. The airlines are not really giving anything away for free. Thus, from the airline's perspective, frequent flyer programs increase patronage by customers such as Andrew and make money from the joint programs like the one with Healthy Choice. One industry expert estimates that the airline industry actually clears about $2 billion a year through their frequent flyer promotions. Not a bad promotion for a service retailer.

Source: Note: David Phillips is real, but Andrew is a composite based on individuals known to the authors.

1. **Coupons** offer the retail customer a discount on the price of a specific item. In 1997 American manufacturers offered consumers more than 269 billion money-off coupons worth more than $180 billion. Although only 2 percent of these coupons are redeemed, this represents a windfall worth more than $500 million to retailers because they receive, on average, a 10-cent coupon handling fee from the manufacturers. Some manufacturers, such as Procter & Gamble, have been

testing various programs to lower everyday prices and discontinue coupons. However, this move has met strong consumer, retailer, newspaper (they make big money on coupons also), and political opposition.

Other manufacturers are testing the use of the Internet for coupon delivery. By going to the Cool Savings' web site (www.coolsavings.com) consumers can get coupons for a number of major products. The manufacturer benefits by getting vital demographic information on the consumer and is able to track redemption rates on all coupons issued.

2. **In-store displays** are promotional displays that seek to generate traffic, advertise, and encourage impulse buying. Such displays offer manufacturers a captive audience for their products in the retailer's store. (Remember, the retailer does not care which brand the customer purchases, just as long as the purchase is made in its store.) As a result, the manufacturer is willing to pay for the right to "rent" the space necessary for this display from the retailer. Chapter 13 provides a greater discussion on in-store displays.

3. **Demonstrations and sampling** are in-store presentations or showings intent on reducing the consumer's perceived risk of purchasing a product. These presentations or showings on the ease, convenience, or product superiority are paid for by the manufacturer at a price that is usually higher than the retailer's cost for providing that service.

Joint demonstrations and sampling promotions do not have to just be with the retailer's suppliers or other retailers. Every spring, retailers, especially malls, invite landscapers and other lawn care experts on to their grounds to promote their own merchandise and services. Consumers are just getting ready to prepare their lawns for the summer and love the convenience of being able to visit with all the lawn experts at one location. In addition to bringing merchandise for sale, many of these lawn professionals also bring samples of their work to place either in the mall hallways or in the parking lot. This is really a case of using OPM because the retailer and malls do not have to use their money for this promotion; the lawn care folks are willing to do it as a form of self-promotion.

Coupons
are a sales promotion tool in which the shopper is offered a price discount on a specific item if the retailer is presented with the appropriate coupon at time of purchase.

In-store displays
are promotional fixtures of displays that seek to generate traffic, highlight individual items, and encourage impulse buying.

Demonstrations and sampling
are in-store presentations with the intent of reducing the consumer's perceived risk of purchasing a product.

Evaluating Sales Promotions

As Exhibit 11.6 indicates, sales promotions are intended to help generate short-term increases in performance. As such, they should be evaluated in terms of their sales and profit-generating capability. As with advertising, sales promotions can also be evaluated with sophisticated mathematical models. However, the development and use of such models is usually not cost-effective. A simpler approach is to monitor weekly unit volume before the sales promotion and compare it to weekly unit volume during and after the promotion.

Publicity Management

Publicity was defined at the outset of this chapter as non-paid-for communications of information about the company or products, generally in some media form. However, this definition is actually misleading. In many instances publicity is purchased. An example of this may be the health reports on your local television news program. Although sometimes these are in fact publicity, other times they may be part of the health

Exhibit 11.6	What Sales Promotion Should and Should Not Be Used For

Tasks That Sales Promotions Are Capable of Accomplishing

Get consumers to try a new product

Stimulate the sales of mature products

Neutralize competitive advertising and sales promotions

Encourage repeat usage by current users

Reinforce advertising

Tasks That Sales Promotions Are Incapable of Achieving

Change the basic nonacceptance of an undesired product

Compensate for a poorly trained sales force

Give consumers a compelling reason to continue purchasing a product over the long-run

Permanently stop an established product's declining sales trend

provider's promotional contract with the station.[14] Even when the retailer does not directly pay for publicity, it can be very expensive to have a good publicity department that plants the commercially significant news in the appropriate places. It may be even more expensive to create the news that is worth reporting. For example, even though Macy's Fourth of July fireworks display in New York, Domino's sponsoring a car in the Indianapolis 500 race, and McDonald's Ronald McDonald Houses all create favorable publicity, they are expensive.

Recently, many manufacturers and even retailers have paid money to have the naming rights to various sports venues. Whether the money could be better spent in other ways is debatable, especially in view of the misfortune the Lowe's home improvement chain has had. In 1999, Lowe's paid $35 million to change the name of the Charlotte Motor Speedway to Lowe's Motor Speedway for 10 years. In one of the first events at the newly named Lowe's, an Indy Racing League race, debris from a wreck flew into the crowd killing some fans. Four months later two Lowe's stores were pipe-bombed in an apparent retaliation. In 2000, another 100-plus NASCAR fans were injured when a pedestrian bridge at Lowe's collapsed following a Winston Cup race. Weeks later, a "staged" explosion during a Memorial Day observance, just before the start of another NASCAR race, caused minor injuries to some more fans. These events generated a couple thousand newspaper and television stories across the country, and all mention Lowe's. *Sports Illustrated* even commented that "when you pay to name a facility and then your name and image are part of negative situations, it's almost like turning lemonade back into lemons."[15]

Several years ago, Dallas restaurateur Dee Lincoln, cofounder of Del Frisco's Double Eagle Steakhouse, made great use of publicity when she paid a record $80,000 for a 1,309-pound Maine-Anjou crossbreed at Denver's National Western Stock Show. An opposing bidder said at the time her winning bid was accepted, "Lady, you must either be really crazy or have too much money." Well Dee Lincoln is not crazy. What Lincoln wanted and got was hundreds of thousands dollars worth publicity for her high-quality steakhouses, the newest of which had just opened in Denver. In addition to having her name or picture in all the Denver media, as the show's highest bidder Lincoln got to perform other highly visible duties for the remainder of the cattle show.[16]

We will not pursue a detailed discussion of publicity management, because most retailers do not formally have a publicity department or even a person in charge of publicity. Rather, let us mention that publicity (like other forms of promotion) has its strengths and weaknesses. Perhaps the major advantages are that it is objective and credible and appeals to a mass audience. The major disadvantages are that publicity is difficult to control and time. Except for annual events, such as a charity fund-raiser, publicity may be hard to plan, and if it is planned, the cost can become exorbitant. In addition, as the chapter's E-tailing box describes, sometimes retailers can experience bad publicity in the form of false rumors that spread like wildfire across the Internet.

Other times, events such as the one Lowe's experienced are beyond the retailer's control and can generate negative publicity. For example, consider how Jack in the Box initially failed to properly handle the negative publicity resulting from a breakout of e. coli bacteria in one of its restaurants in the early 1990s. Although the chain did all the right things regarding consumer safety (it suspended hamburger sales, recalled all hamburgers from its distribution system, increased the cooking time of its meat products, and started work on a new distribution and preparation system that would surpass all industry standards), it failed on the public relations front. The chain waited a week before accepting responsibility when it should have expressed concern—as well as letting people know all the facts as the chain knew them—immediately. As a result, the press had a field day because it really did not know the whole story and rumors spread around the country for months. The chain's sales dropped for the next two years and the restaurant in one of the author's towns closed down after e. coli stories continued to appear in the press. Today, however, Jack in the Box, with the help of a new ad campaign featuring Jack himself, has used PR to turn its business around. Today, whenever an e. coli outbreak occurs, which is two or more times a year, the Jack in the Box PR department refers reporters to trade press articles about the chain's food-safety innovations. The retailer has learned a valuable lesson in that all companies will someday experience a crisis that nobody wants to deal with, but must be able to communicate about before things really get out of hand.[17]

Retailers who prepare for various types of negative publicity in advance will be more profitable.

If publicity is formally managed, it should be integrated with other elements of the promotion mix. In addition, all publicity should reinforce the store's image.

E-tailing

Cookies and Complaints

Have you received this e-mail message?

FWD: Free Neiman Marcus Cookie Recipe

This is a true story. Please forward it to everyone that you can. You will have to read it to believe it.

My daughter and I had just finished a salad at Neiman Marcus Cafe in Dallas and decided to have a small dessert. Because both of us are such cookie lovers, we decided to try the "Neiman Marcus Cookie." It was so excellent that I asked if they would give me the recipe and the waitress said with a small frown, "I'm afraid not."

"Well" I said, "would you let me buy the recipe?"

With a cute smile, she said yes. I asked how much and she responded, "Only two-fifty; it's a great deal!"

I said with approval, "Just add it to my tab." Thirty days later, I received my Visa statement from Neiman Marcus and it was for $285. I looked again and remembered I had only spent $9.95 for two salads and about $20 for a scarf. As I glanced at the bottom of the statement, it said, "Cookie Recipe — $250."

That's outrageous!

I called Neiman's accounting department and told them that the waitress said it was "two-fifty," which clearly does not mean "two hundred and fifty dollars" by any *possible* interpretation of the phrase. Neiman Marcus refused to budge. They would not refund my money, because according to them, "What the waitress told you is not our problem. You have already seen the recipe — we absolutely will not refund your money at this point." I explained to her the criminal statutes which govern fraud in Texas. I threatened to refer them to the Better Business Bureau and the state's attorney general for engaging in fraud. I was basically told, "Do what you want, we don't give a damn, and we're not refunding your money."

I waited a moment, thinking of how I could get even, or even try to get any of my money back. I just said, "Okay, you folks got my $250, and now I'm going to have $250 worth of fun." I told her that I was going to see to it that every cookie lover in the United States with an e-mail account has a $250 cookie recipe from Neiman Marcus . . . for free.

She replied, "I wish you wouldn't do this."

I said, "Well you should have thought of that before you ripped me off," and slammed down the phone on her. So, here it is! Please, please, please pass it on to everyone you can possibly think of. I paid $250 dollars for this. I don't want Neiman Marcus to ever get another penny off of this recipe.

(Recipe may be halved):

- 2 cups butter
- 4 cups flour
- 2 tsp. baking soda
- 2 cups granulated sugar
- 2 cups brown sugar
- 5 cups blended oatmeal (measure oatmeal and blend in blender to a fine powder)
- 24 oz. chocolate chips
- 1 tsp. salt
- 18 oz. Hershey bar (grated)
- 4 eggs
- 2 tsp. baking powder
- 3 cups chopped nuts (your choice)
- 2 tsp. vanilla

Cream the butter and both sugars. Add eggs and vanilla; mix together with flour, oatmeal, salt, baking powder, and soda. Add chocolate chips, Hershey bar, and nuts. Roll into balls and place two inches apart on a cookie sheet. Bake for 10 minutes at 375 degrees. Makes 112 cookies. Have Fun!

This is not a joke — this is a true story. Ride free citizens! This isn't some stupid chain letter either. Pass it on. If you don't, you won't die or get dumped. You'll just do the world an injustice. Thanx.

Probabilities suggest that you have received this message. But is the story true? No. Actually, the same story/recipe has been spread about Mrs. Fields Cookies. In fact, Neiman Marcus will provide the recipe free to anybody and the retailer has even put the real recipe, which is different from the one in the e-mail letter, for the chocolate chip cookie on its own web site (www.neimanmarcus.com).

Only in rare circumstances do retailers ever find out who started false rumors about them, such as with Neiman Marcus or Mrs. Fields. In the past, there have been rumors about snakes being found in overcoats, a fast-food chain using worms in its hamburgers, and a global furniture retailer selling a cactus filled with a nest of deadly spiders. You probably have heard many of these, as well as many others. Have you ever noticed though that the events told in the stories never actually happened to the person sending you the e-mail, but rather to some "friend of a friend"?

For retailers to be able to handle these falsehoods, they must first be aware of them. As such, it is important for retailers to maintain a systematic program of monitoring the on-line rumor mill. For many retailers, simply checking general web sites such as UrbanLegends (www.urbanlegends.com) or Angry.net may be effective. After all, once the rumor is known, appropriate remedies can be developed. However, some (ex)customers get so mad at retailers that they develop web sites targeted directly at the retailer, which begin with their own complaints and soon generate both valid complaints and somewhat questionable happenings, which, whether true or not, contribute to a negative public perception of the retailer. The most common names for these so-called complaint URLs are ihate(retailer's name).com or (retailer's name)sucks.com. In other cases, individuals have created web sites that work on misspellings of the retailer's name. Examples include Untied Airlines: The Most Unfriendly Skies (www.untied.com), which is aimed at United Airlines, and Allsnake (www.allsnake.com), which targets Allstate Insurance. As a result, successful retailers who want to prevent such behavior have adopted a four-prone attack plan:

1. Buy the URLs for their name followed by the word "sucks.com" or preceded by the word "ihate."
2. Locate the web site's creator and determine why he or she is mad. If possible, apologize and then fix the problem before it irritates others.
3. Tell your side of the story on your web site, as Neiman-Marcus has done.
4. When all else fails, take the hate site creators to court. Many will back away from a costly court battle. Although the retailer may lose if the consumer can successfully mount a First Amendment defense, the court will find in favor of the retailer that can prove it has been the victim of libel or slander.

Student Study Guide

Summary

LO•1 What are the four basic components of the retailer's promotion mix and how are they related to other retailer decisions?

A retailer's promotion mix comprises advertising, sales promotions, publicity, and personal selling. All four components need to be managed from a total systems perspective and must be integrated not only with each other but with the retailer's other managerial decision areas such as location, merchandise, credit, cash flow, building and fixtures, price, and customer service. In addition, the retailer must realize that its promotional activities may be in conflict with the way other channel members use promotion.

LO•2 What are the differences between a retailer's long-term and short-term promotional objectives?

A retailer's promotional objectives should be established to help improve both long- and short-term financial performance. Long-term, or institutional, advertising is an attempt by the retailer to gain long-term benefits by selling the store itself rather than the merchandise in it. Retailers seeking long-term benefits generally have two long-term promotion objectives: creating a positive store image and promoting public service.

Short-term, or promotional, advertising attempts to bolster short-term performance by using product availability or price as a selling point. The two most common promotional objectives are (1) increasing the patronage of existing customers and (2) attracting new customers.

LO•3 What are the six steps involved in developing a retailer's advertising campaign?

A retailer's advertising campaign is a six-step process: (1) selecting advertising objectives, (2) budgeting for the campaign, (3) designing the message, (4) selecting the media to use, (5) scheduling the ads, and (6) evaluating the results.

The advertising objectives should flow from the retailer's promotion objectives and should consider several factors that are unique to retailing, such as the store's age and location, the merchandise sold, the competition, the size of the market, and the level of supplier support. The specific objectives that advertising can accomplish are many and varied and the ones chosen depend on these factors.

When developing a budget, retailers must decide whether they can get a better return on their money with vertical co-op dollars or by total sponsorship of advertising seeking to achieve their objectives. In budgeting advertising funds, retailers tend to use the affordable method, the percentage-of-sales method, or the task and objective method. Although most retail advertising is paid for solely by the retailer, sometimes manufacturers and other retailers may pay part or all of the costs for the retailer's advertising campaign. For example, vertical cooperative advertising allows the retailer and other channel members to share the advertising burden while horizontal cooperative advertising is when two or more retailers band together to share the cost of advertising.

Retailers must develop a creative retail ad that accomplishes three goals: attracts and retains attention, achieves its objective, and avoids having any errors. Some of the common approaches that retailers use to gain repeated viewing include showing how the retailer's products fit in with the consumer's lifestyle, creating a fantasy for the consumer that is built around the retailer's products, having the campaign built around humor that relates to using the retailer's products, depicting the consumer in everyday settings using the retailer's products, and building a mood around using the retailer's products. Before using any ad, the retailer should pretest it with both consumer groups and legal experts for errors.

Once the budget is established, it should be allocated in such a way that it maximizes the retailer's overall profitability. In determining allocations, retailers can choose from a variety of media alternatives, primarily newspapers, television, radio, magazines, direct mail, and the Internet. Each medium has its own advantages and disadvantages. To choose among the media, the retailer should know their strengths and weaknesses, coverage and reach, and the cost of an ad.

After the retailer selects a medium, it must decide when the ad should appear. Although the right time for an ad to appear will vary among retailers, conventional wisdom suggests that the ads should (1) appear on, or slightly precede, the days when customers are most likely to purchase, (2) be concentrated around the times when people receive their payroll checks, (3) be concentrated during periods of highest demand, (4) be timed to appear during the time of the day or the day of the week when the best CPM (or CPM-TM) will be obtained, and (5) precede the purchase time, especially for habitually purchased products.

Advertising results can be assessed in terms of efficiency and effectiveness. Effectiveness is the extent to which advertising has produced the result(s) desired. Efficiency is concerned with whether the result was achieved with minimum cost.

LO•4 How do retailers manage their sales promotion and publicity?

Retailers use sales promotions, which provide some type of short-term incentive, and publicity to increase the effectiveness of their promotional efforts. The role of sales promotions and publicity in the retail organization should be consistent with and reinforce the retailer's overall promotion objectives.

Sales promotion tools are excellent demand generators. Many can be used on relatively short notice and can help the retailer achieve its overall promotion goals. Retailers usually break sales promotions into two categories: those where they are the sole sponsors (premiums, contests and sweepstakes, and frequent buyer programs) and those involving a joint effort with other parties (coupons, displays, and demonstrations and sampling).

Although retailers may not pay for publicity directly, the indirect cost can be quite significant. Most retailers do not have formal publicity departments or directors, but some of the more progressive retailers do. The major advantage of publicity is that it is objective, credible, and appeals to a mass audience. The major disadvantage is that publicity is difficult to control and schedule.

Terms to Remember

promotion	affordable method
advertising	percentage-of-sales method
sales promotion	task and objective method
publicity	vertical cooperative advertising
personal selling	horizontal cooperative advertising
primary trading area	coverage
secondary trading area	reach
institutional advertising	cumulative reach
promotional advertising	frequency

cost per thousand method (CPM)   premiums
cost per thousand-target market   contests and sweepstakes
  (CPM-TM)   frequent buyer program
impact   coupons
advertising effectiveness   in-store displays
advertising efficiency   demonstrations and sampling

Review and Discussion Questions

LO•1 **What are the four basic components of the retailer's promotion mix and how are they related to other retailer decisions?**

1. Why should a retailer highlight price and not product features in its ads for national branded products? Should the same rules be applied for private-label products?

2. How could the promotional efforts of other members of a retailer's channel affect the retailer's promotional decisions?

LO•2 **What is the differences between a retailer's long-term and short-term promotional objectives?**

3. Explain how a long-term promotional objective can affect the firm over the short term.

4. Should the promotional objectives for Neiman Marcus be the same as those for Penney's or your hometown's local department store? Explain your answer.

LO•3 **What are the six steps involved in developing a retailer's advertising campaign?**

5. What factors unique to retailing should be considered before selecting an advertising objective? Which one of these factors is most important?

6. From the creative standpoint, it is said that a retail ad should accomplish three goals. What are these goals?

7. Describe the three methods available to the retailer for determining the amount to spend on advertising? Which one is the best one to use? Which one is most commonly used by small retailers?

8. What is cooperative advertising? When should it be used?

9. What methods should a retailer use in making the media selection decision?

10. How should an advertising campaign be evaluated?

11. An old proverb claims that "Doing advertising without planning is like running a giant manure spreader; your advertising department throws words out the back faster than you can shovel money in the front." Do you agree or disagree with this statement? Explain your reasoning.

12. Throughout the chapter, the importance of aiming all promotions toward the retailer's target market was stressed. Yet one retail expert recently observed that even the most sophisticated supermarket manager tends to advertise, not to its target market, but to everybody in its trading area. This expert claimed all one had to do to observe this was to look at the weekly one- or two-page ads a supermarket runs. These ads with all their price cuts should prove that supermarket managers have no clear strategy. Agree or disagree with this statement and support your reasoning.

LO•4 How do retailers manage their sales promotion and publicity?

13. What is sales promotion? How is it different from advertising?

14. What is publicity? Isn't this always free to the advertiser? How does publicity fit into a retailer's promotional efforts?

15. You own a small chain of music stores, Ben's House of Music, serving three nearby towns. Earlier this morning an employee came into your office and said that while surfing the web last night he came across a web site called Ihatebenshouseofmusic.com. What should you do?

Sample Test Questions

LO•1 Which of the following areas should not be taken into consideration when formulating a retailer's promotional strategy?

a. the retailer's credit customers
b. the price level of the merchandise
c. merchandise/inventory levels
d. the retailer's building and fixtures
e. the retailer's net worth

LO•2 The two objectives of institutional advertising include:

a. creating a positive store image and public service promotion
b. increasing patronage from existing customers and attracting new customers
c. publicity and sales promotions
d. advertising a sale and generating store traffic
e. using "other people's money" and using "co-op" money

LO•3 Which of the following should not be part of The Campus Shoppe's advertising campaign's objectives. The Campus Shoppe desires to increase

a. awareness of its two locations
b. sales among incoming freshmen
c. sales to 40 percent
d. sales over the next three months.
e. All the above belong in the retailer's advertising objectives.

LO•4 Consumer premiums are considered to be a form of:

a. joint-sponsored sales promotion
b. publicity that utilizes OPM
c. advertising
d. personal selling
e. sole-sponsored sales promotion

Applications

Writing and Speaking Exercise   While doing your summer internship with P&B Appliances, your boss, Jim Kenderdine, tells you that he has been approached by Sony with a co-op advertising offer on large-screen televisions, but he was wondering if his limited advertising money could better be spent on advertising cell phones, especially with the college students coming back in the fall. He wants you to advise him on this problem.

Kenderdine has $5,000 that he can spend on advertising either Sony televisions or cell phones. With regards to the televisions, Sony has offered to pay 50 percent of the cost of several television and newspaper ads. This would allow P&B to purchase $10,000 of advertising for a $5,000 investment. No co-op deal is being offered by the supplier of the cell phones, but cell phones are fast becoming a popular item among college students, and Kenderdine believes the store could benefit substantially from $5,000 in advertising.

Kenderdine believes that with the additional advertising, sales of the large-screen TVs, which have a 50 percent gross margin, would increase from $80,000 to $110,000 for the month. Cell phones, however, while having a 60 percent gross margin, only are planned to generate sales of $18,000. Kenderdine believes that with $5,000 (the amount P&B would have to pay with the Sony deal) of key radio and campus newspaper ads he could increase cell phones sales volume to $60,000.

Given this information, prepare a memo for Kenderdine with your recommendation.

Retail Project   Find two current advertisements using the same medium (newspaper, television, radio, Internet, etc.) that you believe are effective in achieving their objectives and two that you do not believe are effective.

Explain what you feel each ad's objectives were and why you categorized them as you did. In reviewing the ineffective ads, was something wrong with the creative design? Did they fail to hold the consumer's attention? Did they use the wrong medium to reach their intended market? How would you improve these ads?

Case

The New Advertising Campaign[18]

O'Haran's Furniture is located in north central Dallas, Texas. The store was founded by Thom O'Haran, an Irish immigrant, in 1901 and has been operated since 1977 by his granddaughter, Ruth Reel, and her husband, Dick. As one of the area's most successful merchants, last month Reel was elected to replace Mort Ettinger, the owner of several local Dairy Queen franchises, as president of the North Central Business Roundtable (NCBR). Due to the close-knit relationship of the area's business community that Ettinger developed over the past decade, the job of president has until recently been largely ceremonial.

The event that has changed the nature of the job was a series of advertisements that ran on local television stations featuring the area's only hospital, General Medical, and its prenatal program. For nearly 15 months, the residents of the entire Dallas/Fort Worth Metroplex have watched and shared the joy as Billy Ray Smith and his wife, MaryJo, first found out they were going to have a baby and—with the proper prenatal care at General Medical—delivered a healthy eight-pound boy. Not only did the ads show General Medical in a favorable light, but they also reflected on the neighboring business community.

The ads, which began last year, were first-person accounts of the pregnancy. In the first ad MaryJo related to viewers how she told Billy Ray he was about to become a father. Later ads, which were updated monthly, showed the doctor at General Medical telling MaryJo the baby was going to be a healthy boy, the couple painting the baby's room at their home, the couple taking birthing classes, and the couple doing all the other things new parents do. Finally, earlier this year the entire metroplex rejoiced as the ads showed little Bubba Smith being born. In fact, more than a hundred residents sent cards and gifts to the couple and baby in care of the hospital.

Now, however, the ads are a source of problems for Ruth Reel and the other NCBR officers. While planning the roundtable's annual business awards dinner, the officers decided to honor General Medical for its contributions to the area's business community. As part of the award ceremony, the roundtable also wanted to present Billy Ray, MaryJo, and little Bubba with gift certificates from local merchants.

That's when the bad news first hit. Bubba was really a baby girl named Jennifer Ann and Billy Ray and MaryJo were not a couple, but actors from Waco. In fact, MaryJo not only was not married to Billy Ray; she never was pregnant. One of the local radio stations picked up on the false pregnancy story and soon all the television and radio stations, as well as the newspaper, were saying "Shame on you, General Medical." One radio station went so far as to call the ads deceptive and asked for the attorney general to investigate. Others began questioning General Medical's ethics. More than a dozen expectant mothers who had planned to use General Medical for their delivery asked their doctors if they could switch hospitals.

Now some of the local merchants were worrying that the unfavorable publicity being cast on General Medical would reflect on them. A few even wanted General Medical kicked out of the NCBR.

1. Were the ads deceptive?
2. Were the ads unethical?
3. What should Ruth Reel do to handle this situation?

Planning Your Own Retail Business

Your Uncle Nick has agreed to sell you his supermarket where you have worked for seven years after graduating from college. Uncle Nick is 72 years old and is ready to step down from day-to-day management.

After operating the Crest Supermarket on your own for six months you begin to analyze how you can increase store traffic and consequently annual sales and profitability. During a recent trip to the Food Marketing Institute convention you ran across several successful grocers. Some of them competed largely on price where others competed more on promotion and advertising.

You have decided to pursue a heavy promotion-oriented strategy. Consequently you have budgeted to increase advertising by $20,000 monthly or $240,000 annually and to also have a weekly contest where you give away $100 in groceries to 25 families. This will cost you ($52 \times 100×25) $130,000 annually.

Currently, Crest Supermarket serves a trade area with a two-mile radius where the density of households is 171 per square mile. Seventy percent of these households shop at Crest an average of 45 times per year. Of those that visit Crest, 98 percent make a purchase, which averages $24.45. Crest operates on a 25 percent gross margin.

You estimate that with your new promotion program the radius of Crest's trade area will increase to 2.5 miles. Assume that all other relevant factors remain constant (171 households per square mile, 70 percent of households shopping Crest, 98 percent closure rate, $24.45 average transaction size, 25 percent gross margin percent). Is the planned promotion program and investment of an additional $370,000 annually a profitable strategy?

Hint: Assume the trade area is circular and thus its size in square miles can be computed as pi (22/7) times the radius of the circle squared. The total square miles of the trade area can be multiplied by the number of households per square mile to obtain total households in the trade area. This in turn can be multiplied by the percent that shop at Crest, which in turn can be multiplied by the average number of trips annually to Crest, which will yield total traffic. This traffic statistic can be multiplied by the percent of visitors that make a purchase, which will yield total transactions. You should be able to figure out the rest of the computations on your own that are needed to determine if the promotional strategy is profitable.

Endnotes

1. The definitions of the four types of promotion used in this section are from *Dictionary of Marketing Terms* (Chicago: American Marketing Association, 1988) and are reprinted with permission of the American Marketing Association.

2. This list was developed by the late Louis Bing, Bing Furniture Company, Cleveland, Ohio.

3. "McDonald's Dual Ad Campaign Leading to a Single Result: Trouble," *Advertising Age*, March 10, 1997: 24; and "Nissan's Ad Campaign Was a Hit Everywhere But in the Showrooms," *Wall Street Journal*, April 8, 1997: A1, A14.

4. The above information was provided by Schonfeld & Associates, Inc., and is used with the firm's written permission.

5. "Monster.com: Best of the Show," *Advertising Age*, May 29, 2000: s2–s3.

6. "It's Easy to Blame a Chihuahua, but Taco Bell's Got Bigger Woes," *Advertising Age*, July 24, 2000: 26; and "Tricon Agencies Brace For Shakeup," *Advertising Age*, July 17, 2000: 1, 66.

7. "Beasts' TV Careers Rise, Fall," *Lubbock Avalanche Journal*, July 29, 2000: 8C.

8. "Penney's Touts Fashion to Regain Edge from Sears," *Advertising Age*, March 10, 1997: 6.

9. "Narrowcasting TV Spots by Area No Longer a Dream," *Advertising Age*, April 14, 1997: S2; and "Making a Stand in Bid for Upscale TV Viewers," *Advertising Age*, April 14, 1997: S24.

10. "King of All Radio," *Fortune*, April 14, 1997: 110–114.

11. "Opponents Seek Compromise on SPAM," *Dallas Morning News*, July 29, 2000: 2F.

12. For a detailed description of the current status of outdoor advertising, see "Road Show: The New Face of Billboards," *Business Week*, May 8, 2000: 75–90.

13. "Pigging Out," *Chain Store Age*, July 1999: 77–82.

14. "The Corruption of TV Health News," *Business Week*, February 28, 2000: 66–68.

15. "Lowe's Can't Catch a Break," *Sports Illustrated*, June 12, 2000: 80.

16. Based on an idea from Alan Peppard's column in the February 8, 1997, issue of the *Dallas Morning News* and conversations with Lincoln and her staff.

17. "Coming Clean," *Forbes*, May 17, 1999: 156, 160

18. The names and events in this case are fictional and not to be confused with any real events.

Customer service is a function of customer expectations. When lodging at an expensive, high-quality hotel, a customer has different expectations than he or she would at a Motel 6. Thus, the services offered need to be appropriately adjusted.

Customer Services and Retail Selling

CHAPTER

12

Overview

In this chapter, we demonstrate how customer services, including retail selling, generate additional demand for the retailer's merchandise. We also examine the determination of an optimal customer service level. We conclude the chapter by looking at the unique managerial problems that retailers must address.

Learning Objectives

After reading this chapter, you should be able to

1. explain why customer service is so important in retailing
2. describe the various customer services that a retailer can offer

3. explain how a retailer should determine which services to offer

4. describe the various management problems involved in retail selling, salesperson selection, training and evaluation

5. describe the steps involved in the retail selling process

LO • 1

Why is customer service so important in retailing?

Customer Service

The old rules about customer loyalty are obsolete. Today's customers are tired of making a series a wishes (see the shopper's wish list in Exhibit 12.1) before embarking on their planned purchases. Now customers define loyalty on their terms, not the retailer's. Little wonder then, the average firm loses half of its customers every five years.[1] And as Exhibit 12.2 illustrates, even those customers that continue to shop with a particular retailer are not always loyal. Without exception, high-quality service must be a fact of life for all retailers.

High-quality service is defined as delivering service that meets or exceeds customers' expectations. In this definition there is no absolute level of quality service, but only service that is perceived as high quality because it meets and exceeds the expectations of customers. For example, suppose a consumer has lunch at a restaurant at which he or she expects to have slow service and is served in 10 minutes. The next day at lunch, the same consumer eats at another restaurant that he or she expects to have fast service and again is served in 10 minutes. Even assuming that other factors such as cleanliness, friendliness, and food quality are the same, this consumer might report the service quality to be better in the first restaurant, because the 10-minute service was faster than expected, and report lower service quality in the second restaurant, because the 10-minute service was slower than expected. On an absolute basis, the service was the same in each case—good food in 10 minutes—but the customer's evaluation was different due to different expectations. Just the opposite may be expected at dinner. Here you will want to enjoy the time you are having with friends and family and 10-minute service may be perceived as an unsatisfactory rush job.

High-quality service is the type of service that meets or exceeds customers' expectations.

Exhibit 12.1	**A Shopper's Wish**

Please . . .

- Let me find a parking place near the store
- Do not let me pay too much
- Have the sales staff pretend that they care
- Do not make me have to return anything
- Get me in and out as fast as possible
- Do not make me have to wait in line to make my purchase
- Let this experience be "somewhat" enjoyable
- Do not make me have to deal with "other" obnoxious shoppers

Exhibit 12.2	The Cross-Shopping Trend

Percent of Consumers Who Shop for Sporting Goods Most at . . .

Also Shop At . . .	Department	JCPenney	Sears	Discount	Chain	Specialty	Local	Mfg-owned	Pro	Outlet	Non-store
Department	100	43	39	38	43	44	42	59	51	43	38
JCPenney	43	100	59	40	37	40	44	44	45	35	42
Sears	32	49	100	34	28	32	32	40	39	32	36
Discount	74	82	84	100	77	77	78	75	76	79	83
Chain	55	48	43	48	100	57	54	67	51	51	53
Specialty	60	55	54	52	62	100	65	71	73	56	53
Local	44	46	41	40	45	50	100	54	57	43	47
Mfg-owned	17	12	14	10	15	15	14	100	25	14	16
Pro	14	13	13	10	11	15	15	25	100	13	14
Outlet	48	40	44	44	45	48	45	57	53	100	50
Non-store	22	24	25	23	23	22	25	32	28	25	100

Source: "Sportstyle Cross-Shopping: The Disloyal Consumer." *A Special Report from Sportstyle and Kurt Salmon Associates.* Used with permission from Kurt Salmon Associates.

In an attempt to offer the high-quality service expected and to reduce customer defections, retailers are now engaging in relationship retailing programs.[2] **Relationship retailing** includes all the activities designed to attract, retain, and enhance customer relationships. No longer will retailing be driven by the expansion of large, homogeneous chains offering only low prices. Profitable retailers of the future will be those that concentrate on building long-term relations with loyal customers by promising and consistently delivering high-quality products, complemented with high-quality service, shopping aids to ease the purchase process, and using honest prices to build and maintain a reputation for absolute trustworthiness. Loyal customers, after all, are less price conscious and are less prone to shop other retailers selling the same merchandise mix. In addition, a study by the U.S. Office of Consumer Affairs revealed that it costs a retailer five times as much money to attract a new customer as it does to get a former customer to return.[3] As a result, today's retailers are not trying to maximize the profit on each transaction, but are instead seeking to build a mutually beneficial relationship with their customers, even to the point of dropping unprofitable customers.[4] The new operating maxim for retailers is: "Proper management of relationships will produce a satisfied customer who will become a repeat customer, and repeat customers produce long-term profits." Leo Shapiro, a well-known retail consultant, claimed that the "dollars that walk out of a store every day to be spent at a competitor's store represent the most immediate, major source of potential sales and profit growth."[5] The late Robert Kahn, another retail consultant, often argued that just reducing the amount of customer defections by as little as 10 percent can often double a retailer's profits.

Relationship retailing comprises all the activities designed to attract, retain, and enhance long-term relationships with customers.

High-profit retailers are those who realize that the longer a customer stays with a retailer, the more profitable that customer is to the retailer's operations.

High-performance retailers can develop these relationships with their customers by offering two benefits:

1. *Financial benefits* that increase the customer's satisfaction, such as the frequent purchaser discounts or product upgrades already offered by some supermarkets, airlines, and hotels.

2. *Social benefits* that increase the retailer's social experience with the customer. For example, Nordstrom's employees not only drop notes to their frequent shoppers; they maintain a file on each customer that lists family members, their birthdays, preferences, and sizes. Thus, no customer is a stranger more than once to a Nordstrom salesperson.

The impact model of retailing (Exhibit 12.3) is based on retailing's three most basic tasks: getting consumers from your trading area into your store, converting these consumers into loyal customers, and doing so in the most efficient manner possible. Chapter 7 described how retailers determine their trading area and the earlier chapters of Part IV, Chapters 8 through 11, discussed the first task: how retailers budget for and select their merchandise, then price and promote this merchandise. Likewise, Chapter 8 covered the third task by describing the basic method available to retailers for controlling inventory cost. The next two chapters will discuss the second and most important

Exhibit 12.3	**Three Basic Tasks of Retailing**

1 Get Consumers into Your Store   **2** Convert Them into Customers   **3** Operate as Efficiently as Possible

Source: Based on *Management Horizon's* Impact Model of Retailing. Used with permission.

task—converting the consumer from your trading area who has decided to give your firm a chance into a loyal (and thus profitable) customer.

Due to all the cost cutting following the recent span of consolidation and retrenchment by retailers during the 1990s, this second task is even more difficult. Retailers today are so standardized in either their physical layout or web site design, with each one carrying the same merchandise styles and colors, that customers cannot tell them apart. More important, many retailers have an indifferent and undertrained salesforce. As a result, there is a complete breakdown of what is essential for a successful retailer: exciting merchandise, backed up by outstanding service, and personal selling that generates loyal customers. In recent years, the intense competition from discounters caused many retailers to lower customer service levels as a means of staying price competitive. These retailers felt that reduced service levels would lower their operating costs thus allowing increased price competitiveness. No wonder that the shopping experiences for most customers have not always met their expectations, resulting in an unsatisfying experience.[6]

Retailers must differentiate themselves by meeting the needs of their customers better than the competition. Thus, retailers have again come to realize that customer service is a strength. Instead of frustrating the customer by not having the necessary stock on hand or the proper selling support on the sales floor, today's profitable retailers realize that customer service is a major demand generator for their merchandise. However, it is important that retailers also remember that when you encourage your customers to establish high expectations, the slightest disappointment in service can be a catastrophe. Even Nordstrom, the retailer most famous for its outstanding service, cannot please all its customers all the time. One study quoted an unhappy customer as saying, "Never during our visit did she ask me how much money I wanted to spend, who my favorite designers were . . . or what fashion pet peeves I had."[7] Although Nordstrom really did not make any mistakes, the high service retailer failed to live up to the very high expectations that it trained its customers to expect. After all, this is the retailer who has an on-line operation that carries some 20 million pairs of shoes from more than 60 manufacturers so as to never disappoint a customer.[8] Not having those items in stock when customers want them predictably lowers customer service and the resulting levels of satisfaction.

Customer service consists of all those activities performed by the retailer that influence (1) the ease with which a potential customer can shop or learn about the retailer's offering, (2) the ease with which a transaction can be completed once the customer attempts to make a purchase, and (3) the customer's satisfaction with the transaction. These three elements are the pretransaction, transaction, and posttransaction components of customer service. Some common services provided by retailers include alterations, fitting rooms, delivery, gift registries, check cashing, in-home shopping, extended shopping hours, gift wrapping, charge accounts, parking, layaway, and merchandise return privileges. It must be remembered that none of these services are altruistic offerings; they are all designed to entice the customers with whom the retailer is seeking to develop a relationship.

Retailers should design their customer service programs around pretransaction, transaction, and posttransaction elements of the sale in order to obtain a differential competitive advantage. After all, in today's world of mass distribution, most retailers have access to the same merchandise and, therefore, retailers can seldom differentiate themselves from others solely on the basis of merchandise stocked. The same can be said regarding location and store design advantages. Retailers can, however, obtain a high degree of differentiation through the satisfaction of customers as a result of their customer service programs.

Customer service consists of all those activities performed by the retailer that influence (1) the ease with which a potential customer can shop or learn about the store's offering, (2) the ease with which a transaction can be completed once the customer attempts to make a purchase, and (3) the customer's satisfaction with the transaction.

A retail shopping experience is more than negotiating your way through the retailer's store, web site or catalog, finding the merchandise you want, interacting (or not interacting) with the staff, and paying for the merchandise. It also involves your actions before and after the transaction. Therefore, serving the customer before, during, and after the transaction can help to create new customers and strengthen the loyalty of present customers. If customer service before the transaction is poor, the probability of a transaction occurring declines. If customer service is poor at the transaction stage, the customer may back out of the transaction. If customer service is poor after the transaction, the probability of a repeat purchase at the same store declines. The customer who visits a retailer and finds that the level of service is below expectations or that the product is out of stock will become a **transient customer.** This transient, or temporary, customer will seek a retailer with the level of customer service he or she thinks is appropriate. At any given moment, for all lines of retail trade, there are a significant number of transient customers. The retailer with a superior customer service program has a significant advantage in turning these transients into loyal customers. Thus, customer service can play a significant role in building a retailer's sales volume.

Customer service cannot happen all by itself, but must be integrated into all aspects of retailing. That is why the profitable retailers of the future will know that the demand for their merchandise is not just price elastic, as economists would have us believe, but also *service elastic.* This means that an increase in service levels of 1 percent will result in a more than 1 percent increase in sales.

Transient customer
is an individual who is dissatisfied with the level of customer service offered at a store or stores and is seeking an alternative store with the level of customer service that he or she thinks is appropriate.

Merchandise Management

One of the best ways a retailer can serve a customer is by having in stock the merchandise that the customer wants. Few things are more disturbing to a customer than to make a trip to a store for a specific item only to discover that the item is out of stock. That is why Nordstrom offers its customers a free dress shirt if it is ever out of stock on any of the basic sizes. It wants the customers to be confident of finding any style, color, or size. The better the store is at allocating inventory in proportion to customer demand patterns, the better the customer will be served.

Building and Fixture Management

Retailers' decisions regarding building and fixtures can also have a significant effect on how well the customer is served. For example, consider how the following building and fixture dimensions might influence customer service: heating and cooling levels, availability of parking space, ease of finding merchandise, layout and arrangement of fixtures, placement of restrooms and lounge areas, location of check-cashing counters, complaint and returns desks, level of lighting, and width and length of aisles.

This list is not comprehensive; it is intended merely to provide evidence for the proposition that customer service considerations need to be taken into account in building and fixture decisions.

Promotion Management

Promotion provides customers with information that can help them make purchase decisions. Therefore, retailers should be concerned with whether the promotion programs they develop help the consumer. The following questions can help the retailer assess whether its promotion is serving the consumer:

1. Is the advertising informative and helpful?
2. Does the advertising provide all the information the customer needs?
3. Are the salespeople helpful and informative?
4. Are the salespeople friendly and courteous?
5. Are the salespeople easy to find when needed?
6. Are sufficient quantities available on sales promotion items?
7. Do salespeople know about the ad and what's being promoted and why?

This list is not comprehensive, but rather is intended only to show that customer service issues need to be considered in designing promotional programs.

Price Management

Price management also influences how well the customer is served. Are prices clearly marked and visible? Is pricing fair, honest, and straightforward? Are customers told the true price of credit? These questions suggest that the pricing decision should not be isolated from the retailer's customer service program.

Credit Management

The management of credit, both in-house and bankcard credit, should also be integrated into the customer service program. Credit, along with the retailer's layaway

Credit cards have become a major form of payment. Few retailers can survive if they do not accept credit cards.

Retailing: The Inside Story

Using Customer Services to Capture a Market

Thirty-nine-year old Chris Zane, who while still a high school student purchased the bike shop where he worked, is now the largest independent bicycle dealer in the New Haven market. How did he do it? By offering the best customer service in the market.

Nearly 20 years ago, Zane launched his first serious assault on his competitors by offering one-year service guarantees (covering parts and labor on all routine service) when everyone else was only promising 30-day guarantees. As competitors matched this posttransaction service guarantee, he simply increased his until he was offering a two-year guarantee. Then he learned that some dealers in other markets were offering five-year service guarantees. Figuring that five years is the life of most bikes, he started offering a lifetime of free service.

In reality, this lifetime guarantee was a safe bet for Zane based on percentages. Most customers will use the guarantee during the first year they have the bike. Actually, just 25 percent come back after that. Zane figured his liability for lifetime free service would be minuscule, even by making it retroactive.

The guarantee soon became the foundation of his business. When an individual came in with a six-year-old pump that had worn out, Zane gave him a new one. Why should Zane do this?

Because he understood what a customer's lifetime of business would be worth. For example, the guy with a $60 pump had a premium model. This was a chance to have the customer fall in love with Zane's shop. Because Zane had a good relationship with the manufacturer, he knew he could send the broken pump back and get credit, no questions asked, so the cost of the return was zero. The potential payoff, however, was big enough that even if Zane had been forced to absorb the cost of the pump (about $30), it still would have made economic sense for him to take it back.

Within months, the individual had already come back twice and spent $200 on accessories (a $100 net to Zane), and Zane was betting that he would get the first shot at the sale when it came time for the customer to buy a new premium bike. At an average cost of $400 for a bike, with a 35 percent margin, Zane stood to make another $140 and that did not include the intangibles. Such a customer will probably spread the word to other serious and heavy-spending biking enthusiasts—Zane's ideal prospects.

In addition, Zane also found a transaction service that not only made customers happy, but also went straight to his bottom line. One day, Zane was talking to a customer who was in the cellular phone business and learned that although distributors charged approximately $225 for a telephone, the phone

plans, is a significant aid in that it both encourages customer loyalty and helps customers purchase merchandise. A retailers' credit policies influence customers' perception of how well they are being serviced. Some retailers, such as Holiday Inn, have recently begun issuing their own cobranded credit cards. They hope that these cards, in addition to increasing loyalty to the retailer and generating credit-transaction profits, will add to the retailer's database so that the retailer can improve future promotions. For example, Holiday Inn's Visa card provides cardholders membership in its Priority Club, which translates to free food and drinks at regular Holiday Inns and credits toward free stays at any of its locations.

A Recap

Integration with the elements of the retailer's retail mix is important when retailers develop their customer service programs. Much of what has already been discussed in this book, somehow, either directly or indirectly, relates to one of the three broad company would actually pay a $250 commission for each activation. Zane called Bell Atlantic immediately, proposing that his bike shop become a retailer. He wanted to give away a phone to anyone who bought a bike—a value-added incentive for customers that would actually earn him a net profit of $25. Bell Atlantic saw the bike shop as an alternative channel of distribution, making Zane the first retailer in the area to offer free phones. He activated 500 phones the first year, which earned him $12,500, plus another $25 per phone in co-op-advertising allowances. His profits are larger today, because the cost of phones fell to about $165, but commissions have remained the same.

Although Zane's transaction and posttransaction services were his best selling tools, they sometimes made customers suspicious of his prices. Zane knew his prices were competitive, but customers wanted to find that out for themselves. So he started advertising a 90-day-price-guarantee program (a pretransaction service): if a customer found the same bike anywhere in Connecticut for less, Zane would give that customer the difference plus 10 percent. His sales went up 54 percent the first year, compared with his normal 25 percent growth rate, and he handled 20 percent more customers.

However, such guarantees also present a downside. Zane's service guarantee, for example, has limited his opportunity for growth. Shortly, after he initiated the guarantee, he was forced to drop a line of bicycles because the warranty work was killing his profits. Although the manufacturer covered the cost of parts, Zane was obliged to provide free labor, and the number of repairs was too great given his low margins. With a lifetime of free service on every bike sold looming ahead of him, he dropped the brand.

Attention to detail is an integral part of Zane's basic business philosophy, but it's also critical to his survival. Wal-Mart is coming to town, as is Ski Market, a category-killer sporting-goods store. "When a category killer comes in you have to have all your programs in place," says Zane. "You have to work to be as strong as they are and kill them where they're weak. And customer service is where they're weakest."

Zane is not, in fact, comfortable with merely serving his niche, as a good specialty retailer probably ought to be. He wants to lure customers from Wal-Mart and believes that the giant's presence will actually help him because "there will be more inexpensive bikes out there that need to be fixed." Soon he'll have a better point-of-sale computer system that will help him track customers more effectively and do more targeted marketing.

Source: Based on information supplied by Chris Zane and used with his permission.

---

categories of customer service: pretransaction, transaction, and posttransaction. Successful retailers view customer service as a means of gaining an advantage in competition with other retailers. As a result, even discounters are beginning to empower all their employees, not just management, to do whatever is reasonable to take care of the customer. The Retailing: The Inside Story box describes how one small independent bike dealer became a force in the industry by emphasizing customer service.

The more profitable retailers integrate customer service decisions with their merchandise, promotion, building and fixtures, price, and credit management decisions.

<table>
<tr><td>

LO • 2

What are the various customer services that a retailer can offer?

</td></tr>
</table>

Common Customer Services

Much of the discussion on location, merchandise, pricing, and promotion in previous chapters had implications for serving the customer. However, many of the more popular types of customer services have not been mentioned or have received sparse coverage. Let us review some of them.

Pretransaction Services

Pretransaction services are services provided to the customer prior to entering the store.

The most common **pretransaction services,** which are provided to the customer prior to entering the store, are convenient hours and information aids. Each of these makes it easier for the potential customer to shop or to learn of the retailer's offering.

Convenient Hours   The more convenient the retailer's operating hours are to the customer, the easier it is for the customer to visit the retailer. Convenient operating hours are the most basic service that a retailer should provide to its customers. Retailers must determine what their customers want and weigh the cost of providing those wants against the additional revenues that would be generated. If your target customers, because of their work schedules, want longer hours, the retailer should do so, provided it is profitable. Some retail entrepreneurs are now serving their time-deprived customers with round-the-clock food service, auto-repair services, and medical services. Some merchant groups have started banning together to start a concierge service at the local commuter train station which, for a fee paid by the merchants, will return video rentals, handle their dry cleaning, pick up prescriptions, and do other shopping chores for the commuter.

A retailer's operating hours also depend on the competition. If a competitor is willing to stay open until 9 p.m. six nights per week to serve customers, it would probably not be wise to close every night at 6 p.m. unless a lease provision requires it. As one illustration, many brick & mortar retailers are transforming themselves into brick & click retailers to compete with retailers who offer the most convenient hours, 24-7.

Retailers must also remember that many local and national laws, which were described in Chapter 6, may restrict the ability of retailers to set their hours of operations. For example, some states employ blue laws to restrict some types of retailers from operating on Sundays. For example, in Oklahoma and Texas new car dealers cannot be open on Sunday. Internationally, as illustrated in the chapter's Global Retailing box, retailers are undergoing tremendous changes in operating hour regulation.

Information Aids   As already mentioned, the retailer's promotional efforts help to inform the customer. Many retailers offer customers other information aids that help them enter into intelligent transactions. Today, for example, with the click of a mouse consumers can not only search for products or services, but more importantly, they can determine what choices are available in local stores, the location of specific stores, and information on how to get there.[9] Consumers can also get information about a retailer's return policies, credit policies, merchandise availability, and even merchandise prices on the web site of most major retailers. There are even web sites where consumers experience firsthand a virtual walk through the store. Other web retailers, such as the GAP (www.gap.com) or Lands' End (www.landsend.com), let con-

Global Retailing

Competition Is Changing the Shape of Retail Laws in Germany

For years, the most restrictive retail laws in Europe have been those in Germany. However, increased global competition is having a significant effect on the retail landscape with varied results. To understand the present situation it is important to understand a little about German retail history. Retail laws in Germany have actually changed very little from the early 1930s. In an attempt to protect the small mom-and-pop retailer from larger retailers and keep order in the marketplace, several types of laws were enacted, laws that did the following:

- Limited when products could be put on sale
- Banned unlimited guarantees
- Outlawed retailers from providing complementary gifts to customers with purchases
- Restricted the retailer's operating hours

This last set hurt retailers the most. For example, as recently as 1995, stores were required to close at 6:30 p.m. on weekdays (except Thursday, on which stores were allowed to remain open until 8:30 p.m.), at 2 p.m. on Saturday, and were not allowed to open on Sundays. As such, many consumers would rush into stores at 1:30 p.m. on Saturday afternoon as retailers were required by law to close at 2 p.m., not to open again until Monday morning. Small shopkeepers and labor unions fiercely opposed any change to the retail laws. They claimed that longer hours would increase their underlying op-

erating costs, which would result in a rise in the general cost of merchandise. For many mom-and-pop retailers, any change in operating hours would necessitate the primary owners working longer days simply to stay open, as they do not have any other employees. To complicate the matter, working hours are written into union contracts thus necessitating contract renegotiation whenever there is a change to retail operating hours.

Although many consumers can understand the small retailer's position, they desire the same level of customer service by global retailers. As such, many German consumers desiring better store hours have gone shopping in neighboring countries such as Holland, Belgium, and France where the retailing laws are less restrictive and shopping is more convenient. The growth of cross-national shopping excursions was evident in the decline of German retail sales in the mid-1990s.

In partial response to changing consumer demands and the decline in the retail sector, the German government loosened, to some extent, the restrictive retailing laws. For example, by mid-2000 retailers were allowed to operate until 8 p.m. on weekdays and 4 p.m. on Saturdays, but they were still required to remain closed on Sundays. As such, German retailers are forced to operate under restrictive customer service conditions, necessitating differentiation on other aspects of the retail mix, as well as continuing to compete with retailers in neighboring countries.

sumers move images of the latest fashions around on the screen to get a feel for how the different outfits will mix and match.

In addition, retailers regularly offer demonstrations that instruct the customer on how to use, operate, or care for a product. For example, as a means of getting away from price competition, the Dorothy Lane Market in Dayton has a reputation for pampering its upscale customer base. One of its stores offers weekly cooking classes. Customers can also pick out recipes off stacks of cards and placards in the wine section that describe the various wines and with which meal to serve them. Not surprisingly, retailers that offer these demonstrations can increase their market share because many customers are afraid to buy a new item without first knowing how to use it. If the store offers classes or specific instruction on the use of a product, the customer will be less resistant to trying and ultimately purchasing the product. For many items that are technologically

One element of retailing that is lacking in the on-line environment is the ability to try on apparel. Innovative on-line retailers, such as Landsend.com, employ on-line cyber modeling to enhance the customer's shopping experience.

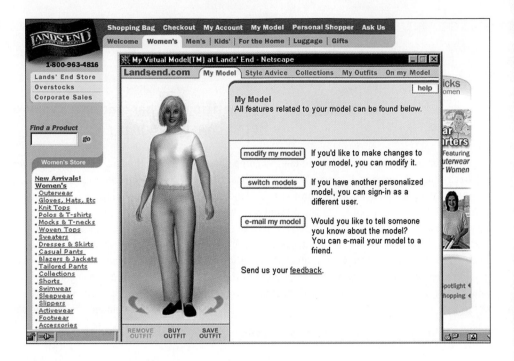

sophisticated or represent significant departures from traditional ways of doing something, the customer will tend to buy from the retailer that offers instruction.

Some firms also offer booklets that provide useful consumer information. In this regard, Sears provides its customers with many informational booklets including *Floor Coverings: Their Selection and Care, Kitchen Planning Basics, How to Select Furniture, How to Select Hand and Power Tools,* and *a Fabric Care Manual.* These booklets can be important sources of pretransaction information to the consumer. During the summer months, nurseries and lawn care retailers provide lawn and gardening tips on local radio and television shows.

Transaction Services

Transaction services are services provided to customers when they are in the store shopping and transacting business.

In the past, retailers believed that transaction services meant having salespeople who would personally take care of an individual customer. But for the profitable retailers of the future, the term **transaction services** will mean getting customers out of the store as fast as possible with the conveniences they seek once they have made their purchases. The most important transaction services are credit, layaway, gift wrapping and packaging, check cashing, personal shopping, merchandise availability, personal selling, and the sales transaction itself. These services facilitate transactions once customers have made a purchase decision.

Credit   One of the most popular transaction-related services offered by retailers is consumer credit. Offering credit can be of great service to the customer because it enables one to shop without the need to carry large sums of money. In addition, it allows the customer to buy now and pay later. Credit can be a benefit to the retailer also: it increases sales by increasing impulse buying as well as the purchase of expensive items. Of course, in-house credit can decrease profits if the credit policy is too lenient.

Layaway   When the retailer offers a layaway service, the customer can place a deposit (usually 20 percent) on an item, and in return the retailer will hold the item for the customer. The customer will make periodic payments on the item and, when it is paid for in full, can take it home. In a sense, a layaway sale is similar to an installment credit sale; however, the retailer retains physical possession of the item until the customer pays for it.

A negative aspect of using layaways is that many items are never picked up by the customer. The retailer then has to return a "dated" item to regular inventory where a markdown, which is usually larger than the first customer's initial payment, is required.

Gift Wrapping and Packaging   Customers are typically better served if their purchase is properly wrapped or packaged. The service may be as simple as putting the purchase into a paper bag/sack or as complex as packaging crystal glassware in a special shatterproof box to prevent breakage.

The retailer must match its wrapping service to the type of merchandise it carries and its image. A discount grocer or hardware store does quite well by simply putting the merchandise into a paper sack. Specialty clothing stores often have dress and suit boxes that are easy for customers to carry home. Some upscale retailers are even putting the purchased merchandise in decorated shopping bags or prewrapped gift boxes. This reduces considerably the number of packages that must be gift wrapped.

Many larger department stores and most gift shops offer a gift-wrapping service. Usually there is a fee for gift wrapping unless the purchase price exceeds some limit, usually $10 or $25. Other retailers also offer a courtesy wrap, which consists of a gift box and ribbon or a store paper that identifies the place of purchase. This type of wrap is not only a goodwill gesture, but also a form of advertising.

Check Cashing   Most retailers offer some form of check-cashing service. The most basic type of check-cashing service consists of allowing customers to cash a check for the amount of purchase. Most retailers now have on-line acceptance systems on

Layaway plans are a popular customer service for lower income households which use these plans to finance purchases.

their registers, which make check cashing as easy as using a credit card. Other retailers provide their customers with an identification card that entitles them to pay for merchandise with a personal check. More liberal check-cashing retailers allow qualified customers to cash checks for amounts in excess of the purchase price, usually not for more than $20. This practice has resulted in some supermarket chains becoming the biggest check-cashing operators in some cities, bigger than the banks.

Personal Shopping   The recent changes in family lifestyles have left many Americans without enough time to accomplish all they need and want to do. Other shoppers hate browsing in stores more than they hate doing household chores. Successful retailers have sought to aid these consumers with personal shopping services. **Personal shopping** is the activity of assembling an assortment of goods for a customer. This can be as varied a service as picking out clothing, filling a nonstore order (many retailers now offer key customers an 800 phone number or a web site location), assembling a supply of groceries and sending them to the customer's home, or selecting a wedding gift. Personal shopping services are one of the best ways to build a relationship with the customer.

Personal shopping
occurs when an individual who is a professional shopper performs the shopping role for another; very upscale department and specialty stores offer personal shoppers to their clients.

Merchandise Availability   Merchandise availability as a service simply relates to whether the customers can easily find the items they are looking for. Three causes exist for the customer being unable to find an item: the item can be out of stock, it is not located where the customer needs it, or the customer does not know what is really needed. The retailer can minimize out-of-stock conditions by good merchandise management, although some out-of-stock situations are inevitable. The retailer can increase the customer's ability to locate a needed item in the store by having a well-designed layout, in addition to proper in-store signing, displays, and helpful and informative employees. The problem of not knowing what is really needed is more difficult to overcome. Although most major retailers have a bridal registry, both in-store and on-line (for example, the phone number for Chicago's Marshall Field's registry is 1-800-2-I DO I DO), Sears has introduced a program covering all its product lines for all occasions, such as Mother's Day, Father's Day, Christmas, and birthdays.[10]

Merchandise availability is an element of customer service that many retailers take for granted, but they should not. When customers do not find items they are looking for in a store—regardless of the cause—they will remember their bad experiences and will in all probability tell their friends.

Personal Selling   Another important transactional service that retailers can offer is a strong, customer-oriented retail salesforce. A good job of personal selling, resulting in a need-satisfying experience, or even the use of suggestive selling, if done well, will greatly enhance customer satisfaction. One study found that 73 percent of the time when a customer reported having the "best-ever shopping experience," there was salesforce involvement. The same study also pointed out the dangers of ineffective sale personnel because 81 percent of the time when a customer reported having the "worst-ever shopping experience," there was direct employee involvement.[11] Personal selling is discussed in detail later in this chapter.

Sales Transaction   The final service to be discussed is the sales transaction itself. Some discount retailers are making headway by seeking to invoke a positive, personal touch by having a "greeter" welcome customers when they enter the store. Specialty retailers, such as Home Depot, Neiman Marcus, and L.L. Bean, offer excellent service. In a similar manner, many older malls are seeking to improve both their sales and their unsafe image with their own greeter programs. North Ridge Mall in Salinas, California, for example, has an Ambassador Corps—a group of employees whose job is greeting customers at their cars, driving them around in golf carts, and offering a wide range of other services, including information on merchandise availability, prices, store location, and the names of key employees. These ambassadors contact more than 35,000 customers each month and as a result, these customers spend almost $20 more per visit than the mall's other customers.[12] Most retailers, however, do very little to establish a differentiation on which to build customer loyalty. At these stores, good service, at the transaction stage, simply means keeping checkout lines short and accepting credit cards so customers do not leave frustrated. Retail managers that have failed to improve their transaction processes probably view service as a cost to be controlled, so as not to negatively impact their year-end bonus, and not as something that will increase demand.

Probably, the two most overlooked problems regarding transaction services are having clean restrooms and minimizing the dwell time. The majority of all shopping experiences should be recreational and entertaining. This is especially true for retailers selling nonessential products such as books. As such, the retailer should never do anything to drive the consumer away, as Leonard Riggio, the feisty CEO of Barnes & Noble, has recognized with a strategy that offers customers Starbucks coffee, comfy chairs, the clubby atmosphere, and, yes, public restrooms.[13] Sam Walton believed that his restrooms should be the best in town so that a woman will never want to leave his store to rush home to use the bathroom. In fact, whenever Sam would visit a store, he and his wife, Helen, always checked the restrooms.[14]

Dwell time refers to the amount of time a consumer must spend waiting to complete a purchase. Such time greatly influences the customer's expectations and evaluations of the retailer. Although customers understand that certain waiting periods are required, especially for services, which cannot be produced ahead of demand, there must be the perception that the line or waiting time is moving.

It may seem like a simple thing, but for any retailer serving hundreds of customers daily the decision on how to line them up can have a major impact on customer satisfaction. This decision affects all retailers ranging from the U.S. Post Office to fast-food operations to hotels to banks. Currently, most retailers are moving away from multiple lines and opting for the single, serpentine line. This type of line, which was first made popular at amusement parks, got its name because of its long, snakelike shape. After all, with multiple lines customer frustration builds up as other lines move faster versus the single focus offered by the serpentine line. In recent years, as the frustration of waiting to complete the transaction increases, the dwell time has become a threat to retailers, according to a study by America's Research Group. According to the study, 83 percent of women and 91 percent of men say that long waits, what they call "register rage," has caused them to stop patronizing a particular store.[15] Similar frustrations with completing transactions can occur trying to make a purchase on-line also, often due to technical difficulties. In fact, recent estimates indicate that over 65 percent of e-tailing shopping carts are abandoned.[16]

Dwell time
refers to the amount of time a consumer must spend waiting to complete a purchase.

Posttransaction Services

The relationship between the retailer and the consumer has become more complex in today's service-oriented economy. The nature of many products, such as computers, automobiles, and travel and financial services, require an extended relationship between the retailer and the consumer. The longer this period of time can be extended by

E-tailing

E-tailers' Two Major Posttransaction Problems

According to a recent study about on-line retailers, two of the three major concerns of consumers who are shopping on-line are slow delivery and handling returns. (The other concern is the inability to see and touch items before the purchase.) These concerns are particularly important if e-tailers want to attract repeat business. It seems that e-tailers with the biggest problems are those with little experience in catalog retailing and those who hand the function off to outside companies that are not closely supervised for quality control.

Two of the major benefits promised by on-line retailers are lower prices and convenience. Convenience was meant to be the fact that the consumer could shop from his or her home or office 24 hours a day, 7 days a week, and expect delivery within a reasonable time. However, the ease and speed of ordering products on-line has raised expectations for an equally speedy delivery and return.

For example, the same customer who would wait for ten days for a catalog order will begin to complain only three days after placing an on-line order. Actually, 70 to 80 percent of all on-line customers will make more than one where-is-my-order (WISMO) call to an 800-number, at a cost to the e-tailer of $2.80 to $7 each. Little wonder that Land's End finds the extra cost for UPS's second-day delivery worth it. Further damaging the image of e-tailers is the fact that several major e-retailers recently paid $1.5 million in fines for failing to properly notify on-line shoppers about shipping delays during the 1999 holiday season—the season when e-tailing was supposed to come of age. CDnow, KBkids.com, Macys.com and Toysrus.com were among the e-retailers that violated the Federal Trade Commission's mail-and-telephone-order rule mandating that goods be shipped on time. (When a date is not promised, shipment must occur within 30 days. If the merchant cannot ship as promised, shoppers must be told and a new shipping date set so a customer can accept the delay or cancel the order.) However, most experts believe that this is one of the easiest problems for retailers to overcome.

With regards to returns, which may be the biggest problem for on-line merchants, it is not the number of returns that is the problem, but how they are handled. Delayed exchanges or mishandled returns are the biggest complaints. Consumers especially dislike having to pay high return postage and the inability to return the item to a nearby store.

Retail consultants such as Marvin Rothenberg believe Internet shoppers would buy more on-line if they could return items more easily. As a result, some on-line retailers are

---

Posttransaction services are services provided to customers after they have purchased merchandise or services.

taking care of the customer's satisfaction with the product after the transaction is completed, the greater the chances are that future sales will result. The most common **posttransaction services,** which are provided after the sale has been made, are complaint handling, merchandise returns, merchandise repair, servicing, and delivery. Posttransaction services are especially important for on-line retailers as emphasized in the chapter's E-tailing box.

Complaint Handling   Customer dissatisfaction is undoubtedly the major source of customer complaints and it occurs when the customer's experience with a retailer's product or service fails to live up to expectations. The proper handling of customer complaints can mean a big difference in retail performance. Interacting with customers is a sensitive issue because it involves employees who make human errors dealing with customers who make human errors. In essence, this doubles the chance of misunderstanding and mistakes between the two parties. Unfortunately, these mistakes and misunderstandings often lead to a poor image of the retailer. Therefore, it is essential that retailers try to solve customer complaints. If retailers solve the customer's problem, then the customer is being served.

copying catalog retailers in offering free shipping and returns. However, many brick & clicks still do *not* allow on-line ordered items to be returned to their brick & mortar locations. In contrast, the Gap and Macy's accept store returns of merchandise purchased on-line. Estee Lauder allows the return of Clinique merchandise to stores that carry its products if the store allows this policy.

According to figures from the National Retailing Federation (NRF), an average of $5 is returned from every $100 of Internet sales. This compares to an average of 5 to 7 percent for the average direct marketing retailer, and 6 percent for traditional retailers. However, these statistics are somewhat misleading because a large percentage of Internet sales are CDs and books, which generally have low return rates.

Return rates for products like clothing are much higher. According to a study by UPS, approximately 35 percent of on-line clothing sales are returned. Bluefly.com, which closely controls its returns, has an average return rate of 20 percent. This on-line retailer of clothing and housewares uses an outside firm to handle these operations but manages the process closely. After a customer calls to return the item, the item is shipped back at the company's expense via UPS (the proper packing slip is enclosed with each order). The customer's

account is credited within a week of the customer's sending it. Bluefly repackages and restocks items that are returned in perfect condition; otherwise Bluefly discards or repairs the item for discount sale.

Other retailers are trying to better educate customers by providing them with more information about the item and responding to other possible questions or problems. Companies such as Land's End allow the customer to view an item from all sides and request a customer's measurements so that they can provide the best fit. Furniture.com also allows viewing from all angles and offers a design option that permits a customer to see how the furniture fits with the customer's current furniture. E-mail or spoken conversations with design consultants are also options, as are free swatches. Customers can hold the furniture for a week before returning it — without added shipping cost. The only catch is that customers get a credit, not a refund.

Source: Based on information supplied by the National Retail Federation (NRF), Marvin Rothenberg, and Jan Owens, as well as "E-retailers Fined for Holiday Shipping Woes," *USA Today*, July 27, 2000: 1B; "Returns to Sender," *Wall Street Journal*, July 17, 2000: R8; and "The Home Delivery Supply Chain: Where the Clicks Meet the Road," *Global Online Retail Report*, January 2000: 59–62.

High performance retailers place a very high emphasis on responsive complaint handling systems. They recognize the cost of fixing mistakes is less than the cost of an unhappy customer.

There are several ways of handling and solving customer complaints. However, regardless of the method used, the "Six Rules to Follow When Handling a Customer's Complaint," shown in Exhibit 12.4, should be followed. For a large retailer, the central complaint department is most efficient. Here, a staff that is specifically trained for this task hears all customer complaints. This method leaves the salesforce free to do its job and allows the customer to deal with someone who has the authority to act on most complaints. Many large retailers have even started to use 800 numbers to address

Exhibit 12.4	**Six Rules to Follow When Handling a Customer's Complaint**

Acknowledge the importance of the customer. Before the customer even begins to explain his or her problem, acknowledge that the customer is important by telling him or her that you are there to help. Try to ease the customer's frustration.

Understand the customer's problem. Ask all the questions needed to completely understand the situation. Determine the responsibilities of each party and what went wrong. Do not assign any fault at this stage.

Repeat the problem (as you understand it) to the customer. Without interrupting the customer, paraphrase the problem as you understand it.

Think of all possible solutions. Using your creative powers, think of all possible, even wild, solutions that could remedy the problem.

Agree on the solution. Determine the solution that is fair to both parties and then have both parties agree to it.

Above all, make sure the customer leaves feeling as you would want to feel if you were the customer. If you would not be satisfied with the solution if you were the customer, start over. Remember, it is better to lose a little now than to take a chance on losing a customer for life.

customer complaints; this way, the retailer can properly handle these complaints with little effort on the part of the customer.

Some retailers have the individual salesperson handle the complaint. They believe that a friendly, sympathetic attitude exhibited by the salesperson will have a positive effect on future sales, especially if the complaint is about a product rather than the retailer or salesforce. This method does, however, have several disadvantages. First, the individual salesperson often does not have the authority to settle problems. As a consequence, it is usually necessary to call in someone else to take care of the complaint and usually the customer must state the problem once again. A second drawback of this system is the fact that a salesperson that is listening to a past customer complaining cannot serve present customers who, incidentally, are overhearing the complaints.

Other retailers are making an all-out effort to stop complaints before they occur. Ohio's Sun Television & Appliances has hired an outside marketing firm to do daily computerized price checks on all comparable merchandise. If somebody beats Sun's price within 30 days of any customer's purchase, the customer automatically gets a check in the mail for the difference.[17] Other retailers seek to stop complaints before they happen with the use of guarantees. Costco, for example, has what many consider the greatest guarantee in retailing. Its "diamond guarantee" promises to pay a member $100 if a stone it sells is appraised for less than double the Costco price.[18]

Regardless of the complaint-handling system, the retailer needs to remember three things when handling complaints. The customer deserves courteous treatment, a fair settlement, and prompt action. Remember, even if the sale is lost, the customer need not be lost. The proper handling of complaints has substantial paybacks for the smart retailer. Sometimes, however, the customer makes it difficult for even the best salesperson to handle a complaint and make the customer happy. Luckily there is an on-line support group for front-line employees. Through www.customerssuck.com employees can share and vent their frustrations regarding unruly and sometimes simply plain stupid customers. For example, while it may seem like an innocent question, asking an employee dressed in a polyester pirate costume at the local Fish & Chips place "Do you work here?" is tantamount to abusing the employee. Or what answer do customers really expect to get when they ask, "Can I ask you a question?" Although salespeople sometimes wish they could yell no, they know that it would not be most appropriate.

Then there are the customers who seem clueless. For example, what is the best way to deal with a customer who apparently does not understand the concept of the product they are buying. "I work at the complaint desk for one of those warehouse hardware stores," one salesperson reported on the web site. "One night as I was about to go off shift this guy comes up to the counter mad as heck. It seems that he bought a soaker hose (the ones with all the holes in them to irrigate your lawn, etc.) and when he hooked it up it leaked all over the place. He then proceeded to exchange it for another one. After he left we were in hysterics and the news went through the store in a matter of minutes. But the funny thing is he was back the next day with the same complaint (and madder than before if that was possible). It seems he did not need a soaker hose at all but just liked the color."

Other customers want to return products after they have been used. For example, one customer service representative of a hardware store indicates that one of the most commonly returned items is a plunger. "It would not be so bad, but usually they come back in a plastic bag just after they have been used."

Merchandise Returns   The handling of merchandise returns is an important customer service, sometimes making the difference between profit and loss. The return policy can range from "no returns, no exchanges" to "the customer is always right." Retailers need to decide if they want either of these extreme policies or a more moderate one. Few services build customer goodwill as quickly as a fair return policy. On the other hand, the return service is probably the most widely abused service by American consumers. Thus, it is important that the retailer's return policy be consistent with its image.

Depending on the item returned, there could be a substantial loss due to the time the item was out of stock. Beach or patio furniture, for example, would not sell as well in the winter, and a returned snow shovel would be in low demand in the summer. Because of this delay, returned merchandise is often stored until the proper season or sold at a reduced price. Reducing the price is also common practice if the merchandise has been used. There is also an opportunity cost—the foregone interest or return on investment dollars to be made. This money is tied up in merchandise that is in the possession of the customer but has not been paid for and will be returned.

With losses approaching $1 billion due to return fraud, retailers are now beginning to put limits on their return policy because of abuses by consumers. For example, several computer retailers serving college markets now require the product to be returned within 60 days of purchase. This is because a number of college students have been found to want to return laptops at the end of a term. Wal-Mart has abandoned its open-ended return policy and set a 90-day limit. Under Wal-Mart's old policy the retail chain once replaced a thermos that had not been manufactured since the early 1950s, ten years before the first Wal-Mart opened. Nordstrom, which in the past would accept back hundreds of pairs of shoes during the prom season, is now refusing to take back dresses when the sales tags have been removed. What's more, the chain now puts the tags in conspicuous places where they cannot be covered up with a sash, shawl, or belt. Probably the most abused return policy is when electronic retailers get back large-screen television sets the Monday after the Super Bowl. To best assess money-back guarantee programs, retailers should estimate the salvage value of returned merchandise, the probability of mismatching the product to consumers, transaction costs of returning merchandise, and the consumer value of product trial.

Servicing and Repair   Any new product with more than one moving mechanical part is a candidate for future servicing or repair. In fact, even items without moving parts such as clothing, coffee tables, and paintings are candidates for repair. Retailers who offer merchandise servicing and repair to their customers tend to generate a higher sales volume. If the work they perform is good, they can also generate repeat business. For example, if the service department of a TV and appliance store has a reputation for doing good work at fair prices, customers will not only purchase TVs at the store but will also purchase radios, stereos, and washers.

Repair servicing, along with delivery, is perhaps one of the most difficult customer services to manage. Although good repair service can stimulate additional sales, many customers will never be satisfied because it is difficult to schedule appointments. In today's urban environment, it is virtually impossible for retailers to schedule a repair call or deliveries even within a three-hour time frame. There's traffic, parking, plus the inability to figure time needed until the repair or service personnel arrive. These factors often make it difficult for today's two-wage-earner families to be home when the retailer's personnel arrive. These disgruntled customers then tell their friends, relatives, and acquaintances of their experiences.

Delivery   Delivery of merchandise to the customer's home can be a very expensive service, especially because of the high cost of energy. Nonetheless, the benefits derived from providing delivery may be worth the expense if the merchandise and customer characteristics warrant it. For example, when consumers think of delivery, they usually think of Domino's Pizza. When Thomas Monaghan started the company, pizza already enjoyed widespread popularity. He soon realized that success could come by focusing on fast, free delivery, something no one else did.[19] Retailers such as florists can also

Retailers that develop a reputation for knowledgeable service and sales personnel can help to build long-term relationships with customers and thus, sales.

offer free delivery (which is actually absorbed in slightly higher prices), or they can charge the customer a small fee to help offset the cost.

Determining Customer Service Levels

It is not easy to determine the optimal number and level of customer services to offer. Theoretically, however, one could argue that a retailer should add customer services until the additional revenue that is generated by higher service levels is equal to the additional cost of providing those services. In the short run, cutting back on costly customer services usually increases profits. However, such action may present serious long-run problems as customers shop elsewhere for better services.

It is difficult to decide what specific customer services to offer in order to increase sales volume. Exhibit 12.5 lists six factors to be considered when determining the customer services to offer: the retailer's characteristics, the services offered by the competition, the type of merchandise handled, the price image of the retailer, the income of the target market, and the cost of providing the service. It is the retailer's job to study these six areas to arrive at the service mix that will increase long-run profits by keeping present customers, enticing new customers, and projecting the right type of image. Above all else, retailers must remember to be realistic and not expect to satisfy the wants and needs of all customers. No strategy could be less profitable than trying to satisfy everybody. What the retailer is really trying to do is to use its sales staff as the conduit between the vendor's expectations and the customer's expectations, as shown in Exhibit 12.6.

Exhibit 12.5	Factors to Be Considered When Determining Customer Services to Offer

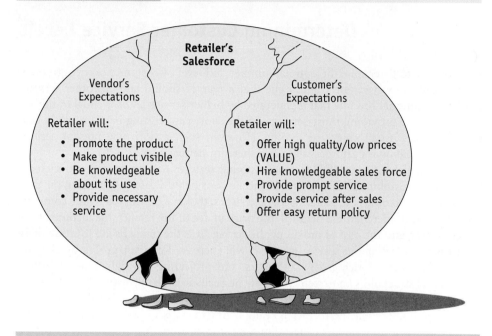

| Exhibit 12.6 | How the Retailer's Salesforce Meets the Expectations of Both Vendors and Customers |

Retailer's Salesforce

Vendor's Expectations

Retailer will:

- Promote the product
- Make product visible
- Be knowledgeable about its use
- Provide necessary service

Customer's Expectations

Retailer will:

- Offer high quality/low prices (VALUE)
- Hire knowledgeable sales force
- Provide prompt service
- Provide service after sales
- Offer easy return policy

Retailer's Characteristics

Retailer's characteristics include store location, store size, and store type. It is especially important to look at these three characteristics when considering adding a service.

Services offered in the downtown area of a large city would probably be different from those offered by a similar store in a suburban shopping center. For example, a drugstore in the downtown area might offer free delivery of prescriptions as a service to its clientele. This service would be of great benefit to city dwellers without cars and businesspeople who do not want to spend time waiting at the drugstore for a prescription. This same service in a suburban shopping center would not be as important. This druggist might get a better return on investment by offering such services as check cashing, credit, and plenty of free parking rather than free delivery of prescriptions.

The size and type of store also determine which services to offer. A major department store would offer a different assortment of services than a supermarket. There would also be a difference between a large and small store of the same type, or a brick & mortar, click & mortar, and e-tailer as well.

Competition

The services offered by competitors have a significant effect on the level and variety of customer services offered. A retailer must also offer these services, or suitable substitutes, or offer lower prices.

Suppose there are three clothing stores of the same general type, price range, and quality within a given area. Store A and store B offer free gift wrapping, standard alterations, bankcard credit, and a liberal return policy. Store C, on the other hand, offers only standard alterations and has an exchange-only return policy. Customers who are shopping for gifts will generally prefer stores A and B to store C because they can be confident that whatever they purchase will ultimately be just right. It can even be gift wrapped there at the store. If the gift is not suitable, the receiver can exchange it or even get a cash refund. In this situation, store C can do two things to compete: add services or lower prices.

Type of Merchandise

The merchandise lines carried can be an indication of the types of services, especially personal selling, to offer. The principal reason is that certain merchandise lines benefit from knowledgeable sales personnel; for example, would you want a less-than-knowledgeable salesperson to assist you in purchasing an engagement ring for the woman of your dreams? Or worse yet, would you want your boyfriend buying your engagement ring at a self-service discounter? In addition, other products benefit from offering complimentary services: bicycles and free assembly, major appliances and delivery, women's and men's suits and alterations, and sewing machines and free sewing lessons.

Price Image

Customers usually expect more services from a retailer with a high-price image than from a discounter. When a customer perceives a retailer as having high prices, it also sees the retailer as possessing an air of luxury. Therefore, the services rendered by this retailer should also carry the image of luxury or status. Some of the typical high-price image services include personal shopping, a home design studio, free gift wrapping, free delivery, and free alterations.

On the other end of the scale, discounters need not offer luxury services, because customers who shop there are seeking low prices and not fancy customer services. A discounter or one with a low-price image might offer such basic services as free parking, layaway, bankcard credit, and convenient store hours.

Target Market Income

The higher the income of the target market, the higher the price that consumers will pay. The higher the prices consumers will pay, the more services the retailer can profitably provide. Some customers may expect more services than retailers can afford, but retailers must avoid the strong temptation of providing costly services to such consumers. In the long run, the retailer will have to raise prices to pay for the services and then it will quickly lose its share of low-income customers.

Cost of Services

It is important that retailers know the cost of providing a service so that they have an idea of how much in additional sales they will need in order to pay for the service. For example, a customer service expected to increase costs by $20,000 per year for a store operating on a gross margin of 25 percent would have to stimulate sales by at least ($20,000/0.25) or $80,000. In this sense, customer services are evaluated in a manner

Retail stores with a high-price image communicate a feeling of luxury and they create higher customer expectations for special services.

similar to promotional expenditures. The key criterion becomes the financial effect of adding or deleting a customer service. As a result, one national retailer recently started charging for its catalog after decades of providing it for free. Research determined that although nearly 20 percent fewer customers got the catalog, those that got it felt that they had an investment ($5) in the catalog. As a result, these customers increased their purchases by 25 percent.

Another way of expressing the cost of having poor service is to examine what the costs would be if a store does not offer good service. If a 100-store supermarket chain alienated only one customer per day per store, the chain would lose $94.9 million in annual revenue. This is based on the assumption that grocery business is repeat business and that the real cost is the $50 a customer spends weekly.

Managerial Question: How can e-tailers differentiate themselves from other e-tailers, brick & click retailers, and brick & mortar retailers based on service assortment?

Retail Sales Management

LO • 4

What are the various management problems involved in retail selling, salesperson selection, and training and evaluation?

Retail salespeople and the service they provide are major factors in consumer purchase decisions. For example, when the retail salesperson is rude or is not helpful, customers often walk out of the store empty handed. The salesperson is a major determinant of a retailer's image. When the salesperson is available, friendly, and helpful, customers are often influenced to enter into a transaction with the retailer. The management of the retail salesforce plays a crucial role in the success or failure of retail operations.

Types of Retail Selling

In many retail settings, the employees are called salespersons or order takers. For example, consider the role of salespeople in a typical fast-food restaurant such as McDonald's, Burger King, or Wendy's. Most order takers simply ask the customers, "Can I take your order?" Little if anything related to the actual sale occurs. Similarly, in a discount department store such as Kmart, Target, or Wal-Mart, salespeople may show a customer where a specific product is or, if the product is not on the shelf, may go to the storeroom to attempt to locate the item. However, seldom do they attempt to sell merchandise or demonstrate its use. In fact, one discounter's policy is to provide "next-to-no-sales-help." Discounters "do not want to get into the business of person-to-person selling." Retailers employing order takers are appealing to those customers who want value instead of service. Perhaps they should be referred to as retail clerks. Nonetheless, one must recognize that these order takers can influence demand, especially in a negative manner. If you stand at the counter of a McDonald's and no one asks you for your order, you may get frustrated and leave the store without making any purchase.

Retail employees who are most appropriately labeled salespersons should be order getters as well as order takers. Order getters have conversations with prospective purchasers for the purpose of making a sale. They inform, guide, and persuade the customer to culminate a transaction either immediately or in the future. For example, in many restaurants the determination of whether the customer will order a dessert is related to the relationship they have established with their host or hostess.

The degree of emphasis the retailer places on its employees' being order getters depends on the line of retail trade and the retailer's strategy. Retailers that concentrate on the sale of shopping goods (e.g., automobile dealers, furniture retailers, computer retailers, and appliance retailers) want their salespeople to be both order getters and order takers. In lines of retail trade where convenience goods are predominantly sold (gasoline service stations and grocery retailers), the role of the salesperson (or what many may call the retail clerk) is that of an order taker. In terms of strategic orientation, it is generally true that retailers with high margins and high levels of customer service place more emphasis on order getting. Those with low margins and a low customer service policy tend to emphasize order taking. Clearly, however, regardless of the line of retail trade or the retailer's strategic thrust, all retail enterprises must carefully evaluate the role of the salesperson in helping to generate demand.

Salesperson Selection

Selecting retail salespeople should involve more than casually accepting anyone who answers an ad or walks into the retail establishment seeking a job. In fact, the casualness with which many retailers have selected people to fill sales positions is one cause of poor productivity.

Criteria   To select salespeople properly, retailers must decide on their hiring criteria. What is expected from retail salespeople? Are retailers looking for a salesforce that has low absenteeism or the ability to generate a high volume of sales? Are they seeking other qualities? Are they seeking a combination of factors? Unless retailers know what they are looking for in salespeople, they will not acquire a salesforce that possesses the proper qualities.

However, good results are not only dependent on the salesperson's characteristics but also on how satisfied the salesperson is with the job and how the sales job was designed.

Retail selling jobs should be designed to have high levels of variety (the opportunity to perform a wide range of activities), autonomy (the degree to which an employee determines the work procedures), task identity (the degree to which an employee is involved in the total sales process), and feedback from supervisors and customers.

Predictors   Once retailers determine the hiring criteria, they must then identify the potential predictors to meet the chosen criteria. The most commonly used predictors in selecting retail salespeople are demographics, personality, knowledge and intelligence, and prior work experience. We discuss the criteria for selecting managerial trainees later in the chapter.

DEMOGRAPHICS   Depending on the specific line of retail trade, demographic variables can be important in identifying good retail salespeople. For example, a music store appealing to teens will probably benefit from having retail salespeople under 30 years of age. A high-fashion women's apparel store appealing to 30- to 50-year-old, career-oriented, and upwardly mobile women would probably not desire 18-year-old salespeople from lower-class backgrounds. Interestingly enough, a study by J.D. Power & Associates of over 33,000 new car buyers has shown that women salespersons scored higher or at least equal to men in 13 of the 15 categories evaluated. The two items where men scored best were knowledge of "models and features" and "competitive vehicles." Women, however, score substantiality higher in "sincerity," "honesty," and "concern for the buyer's needs."[20] Obviously, there are exceptions to each of the preceding cases, but the essential point is that demographics play an important role in the retail sales process.

PERSONALITY   An applicant's personality can reflect on his or her potential as a retail salesperson. The retailer would most likely prefer salespeople who are friendly, confident, consistent, and understanding of others. These personality traits can be

Women auto salespeople have become much more popular. Research has shown that women auto salespeople are perceived as more honest and trustworthy.

identified either through a personal interview with the applicant or by personality inventory tests. In most lines of retail trade the personal interview is sufficient.

KNOWLEDGE AND INTELLIGENCE   Many products that retailers sell are technically complex. Consider, for example, computers, televisions, microwave ovens, 35-mm cameras, and 10-speed bicycles. Salespeople with knowledge of these products are better able to sell them. Similarly, to be able to respond to customer inquiries in a logical fashion, retail employees need to possess a level of education and intelligence compatible with the job description.

EXPERIENCE   One of the most reliable predictors of success as a salesperson is prior work experience, especially selling experience. If applicants have performed well in prior jobs, there is a good chance that they will perform well in the future. However, many applicants for retail selling jobs are young and have no prior work experience of any magnitude. These applicants are better assessed on their personal character and apparent ambition, drive, and work ethic.

Salesperson Training

After salespeople are selected, they will need some form of training. This is true even if they have selling experience. In these training programs, retailers have to explain their own policies to the trainees. Furthermore, retailers may believe that inexperienced salespeople should become familiar with and knowledgeable about the retailer's merchandise, the different customer types they may have to deal with, and the selling strategies available for different customer choice criteria. Even order takers need training in greeting customers, thanking customers, and using a point-of-sale terminal. For example, one of McDonald's greatest challenges when entering foreign countries is training the employees to be friendly.

Probably the most important item the retailer can train the new sales staff about is common customer courtesy. One national discounter insists that all its sales staff carry the following "crib sheet" about being customer friendly with them at all times they are on the sales floor.

Customer friendly means

Smiling

Greeting the customer

Being as helpful as you would want somebody to be to you

Using the customer's name (if possible)

Saying "thank you"

The importance of being customer friendly can be seen from studies in the medical field. These studies found that the doctor's competence and prescribed method of treatment played a very small role in determining if a malpractice suit would be filed. Rather it was the interpersonal skills that the doctor used with the patient that was the determining factor.[21]

Retailer's Policies   In most situations, the interface between the customer and retailer takes place through the salesperson. It is thus important for the salesperson to become familiar with the retailer's policies, especially those that may involve the customer directly. Some of these policies relate to merchandise returns and adjustments, shoplifting, credit terms, layaway, delivery, and price negotiating. In addition, the retail salesperson should be knowledgeable about work hours, rest periods, lunch and dinner breaks, commission and quota plans, nonselling duties, and standards of periodic job evaluation. Sales employees should also be informed about criteria used for promotion and advancement within the retail enterprise.

Merchandise   If the merchandise includes shopping goods, the retailer will want to familiarize its salespeople with the strengths and weaknesses of the merchandise. This allows salespeople to assist customers in shopping for the best goods to meet their needs. It also suggests that the salesperson should become knowledgeable of the competitor's merchandise offerings and their strengths and weaknesses.

Increasingly, retail salespeople need to be familiar with the warranty terms on merchandise the retailer handles and also the serviceability of the merchandise. This implies that the salesperson should know something about the reputation of each manufacturer the retailer represents. Exhibit 12.7 lists in greater detail the specific information that a retailer generally expects its salesperson to know about its products.

Customer Types   Many retailers have recognized that an important way to increase customer satisfaction is by having their salespeople identify and respond to certain customer types.[22] Various customer types are described in Exhibit 12.8. By knowing how to handle each of these customers, the salesperson can generate additional sales. Too many times retailers tend to dwell on handling the machinery of a job rather than the feelings of a customer. One retail clerk, who should get on-line at the customerssuck.com web site discussed earlier in the chapter, said this about her training program: "The computer training was real good. I know how to do all this technical stuff, but nobody prepared me for dealing with all these different types of people."

Customer Choice Criteria   The retail salesperson should also learn how to identify the customer's choice criteria and how to respond to them.[23] There are four choice criteria situations: (1) the customer has no active product choice criteria; (2) the customer has product choice criteria but they are inadequate or vague; (3) the customer has product choice criteria but they are in conflict; and (4) the customer has product choice criteria that are explicit and well defined. For each situation, there is an appropriate selling strategy that the salesperson should learn.

NO ACTIVE PRODUCT CHOICE CRITERIA   The best sales strategy when the customer does not have a prior criteria set is to educate the customer on the best choice criteria and possibly how to weigh them. For example, a prospective customer enters an automobile dealership to purchase a used automobile but does not know what criteria to use in selecting the best car. The salesperson may present convincing arguments on why the customer should consider four criteria in the following order of importance: warranty, fuel economy, price, and comfort. Once the salesperson and customer agree on this list, they can work together at finding the used car that best fits the criteria.

INADEQUATE OR VAGUE CHOICE CRITERIA   When the criteria are inadequate or vague, the range of products that will satisfy them is often wide. Perhaps the easiest thing for the salesperson to do is to show that a particular product fits a customer's choice criteria. Because the choice criteria is vague, this would not be difficult and little

Exhibit 12.7	Summary of Merchandise Information Needed by Salespersons

Uses of the Product
Primary and secondary uses
Suitability
Versatility

How to Use the Product
How to operate it, wear it, prepare it, eat it, apply it, assemble it, display it, place it

How to Care for the Product
How to handle and adjust the product
How to clean the product
How to store the product
How to oil and grease the product
How to refrigerate the product

Appearance of the Product
Beauty
Style
Ensemble possibilities

Services Available with the Product
Credit terms
Shipping terms
Speed and cost of delivery
Transportation methods

How the Product Will Perform
Durability
Degree of color performance
Shrinkage or stretchage (in case of textiles)
Breaking strength
Resistance to water, wind, wear, heat, light
Cost of upkeep

How the Product Is Made
Size
Weight
Weave (in case of textiles)
Finish
Handmade or machine made
Pressed, molded, stamped, inlaid, etc.
Conditions under which goods are made
Packaging

Background of the Product
History of the article
History of the manufacturer
History of its uses
History of competing articles
Rarity
Prestige

Source: Kenneth H. Mills and Judith E. Paul, *Successful Retail Sales* (Englewood Cliffs, NJ: Prentice-Hall, 1979): 82–83. Reprinted with permission of the publisher.

Exhibit 12.8	Various Customer Types

Characteristics	Basic Types	Recommendations
Doesn't trust any salesperson. Resists communication as they have a dislike of others. Generally uncooperative and will explode at slightest provocation.	**Defensive** 	Avoid mistaking their silence for openness to your ideas. Stick to basic facts. Tactfully inject product's advantages and disadvantages.
Intense, impatient personality. Often interrupt salespersons and have a perpetually "strained" expression. Often driven and successful people who want results fast.	**Interrupter**	Don't waste time, move quickly and firmly from one sales point to another. Avoid overkill since they know what they want.
Confident in their ability to make decisions and stay with them. Open to new ideas but wants brevity. Highly motivated by self-pride.	**Decisive** 	No canned presentations. The key is to assist. Don't argue or point out errors in their judgement.
They worry about making the wrong decision, therefore, they tend to postpone all decisions. Want salesperson to make decision for them.	**Indecisive**	Avoid becoming frustrated yourself. Determine as early as possible the need and concentrate on that. Avoid presenting customer with too many alternatives. Start with making decisions on minor points.
Friendly, talkative types who are enjoyable to visit with. Many have excess time on their hands (e.g., retirees). They usually resist the close.	**Sociable** 	You may have to wait out these customers. Listen for points in conversation where you can interject product's merits. Pressure close is out. Subtle friendly close needed.
Quick to make decision. Impatient, just as likely to walk out as they were to walk in.	**Impulsive** 	Close as rapidly as possible. Avoid any useless interaction. Avoid any oversell. Highlight product's merits.

actual selling may be involved. However, the customer may have trouble believing that the product the salesperson selected is the best one to meet his or her needs. The customer may therefore choose to shop around at other locations.

If the sales clerk is interested in building repeat business and customer goodwill and has a wide range of products to sell, a preferable strategy would be to help the customer define his or her problem in order to arrive at a set of choice criteria. The customer and sales clerk can work together in defining the criteria of a good product and then select the product that best fits the criteria.

CHOICE CRITERIA IN CONFLICT   Prospective customers with choice criteria that are in conflict frequently have trouble making purchase decisions. There are two basic ways in which choice criteria can be in conflict. First, the customer may want a product to possess two or more attributes that are mutually exclusive. For example, a person purchasing a mountain bike may wish it to be of high quality and low price. This person will quickly find that these two attributes do not exist in common. The best strategy in this situation is for the salesperson to play down one of the attributes and play up the other. A second way the choice criteria could be in conflict is when a single attribute possesses both positive and negative aspects. Consider a person thinking of purchasing a high-performance automobile. High-performance automobiles have both positive aspects (status, speed, and pleasure fulfillment) and negative aspects (high insurance rates and low mileage per gallon). For this type of conflict, the best selling strategy is to enhance the positive aspects and downplay the negative aspects.

EXPLICIT CHOICE CRITERIA   When the customer has well-defined, explicit choice criteria, the best selling strategy is for the salesperson to illustrate how a specific product fits these criteria. "The sales clerk guides the customer into agreeing that each attribute of his product matches the attributes on the customer's specification. If, at the end of the sales talk, the customer does not agree to the sales clerk's proposition, he appears to be denying what he has previously admitted."[24]

Evaluation of Salespeople

Evaluation of salespeople seeks to determine each salesperson's value to the firm. That determination is important as a basis for salary adjustments, promotions, transfers, terminations, and sales reinforcement. The retailer should develop a systematic method for evaluating both individual salespeople and the total sales staff. Rather than subjectively evaluating performance, the manager should develop performance standards for its sales staff.

Performance Standards   Several standards can be developed to measure a salesperson's performance. Some standards apply only to individual efforts, whereas others assess both individual and total salesforce effort.

CONVERSION RATE   The **conversion rate** is the percentage of all shoppers who make a purchase—that is, those shoppers who are converted into customers. This is a measure of the salesforce's performance, not the performance of the individual salesperson.

A poor conversion rate can have a variety of causes. Perhaps there were not enough clerks on hand when customers needed them. This could have resulted in a high degree

Conversion rate
is the percentage of shoppers that enter the store that are converted into purchasers.

of unassisted searching and long customer waiting times, with many customers exiting the store without making a purchase. Or the number of sales clerks could have been adequate to handle the flow of customers, but the salespeople may not have done a good selling job. A poor selling job could have several causes, such as the clerk giving inadequate product information to the customer, disagreeing or arguing too strongly with the customer, demonstrating the product poorly, having an unfriendly attitude, or giving up on the sale too early. However, all of these factors are really related to poor training, which is the underlying reason for poor sales. Also, a low conversion rate may have been due to factors beyond the salesperson's control, such as inadequate merchandise levels. The important point is that when a substandard conversion rate exists, the retailer should identify the causes and remedy the situation, because even a small increase in the conversion rate can have a major impact on retail sales.[25]

A consultant, Marvin Rothenberg, studied what happened in four chains operating a total of 68 department stores. He found that 131,328,000 sales opportunities a year (that is, 2.4 million shoppers who averaged 1.9 shopping visits per month going into 2.4 departments per trip) produced only 38 million sales transactions. Thus, 93 million department store shopping visits resulted in no sale.

In fact, 49 million of the department store shoppers who made no purchase did not even have contact with a salesperson or a cashier. Another 44 million had contact with a salesperson but did not buy anything. And among these two segments of 93 million shoppers already in the department stores, 28 million came in with the intent of making a specific purchase! In total, 71 percent of all the department store shopping visits resulted in shoppers either having no contact with sales personnel or having the wrong kind of contact (in that it was unproductive) and as a result made no purchase. No wonder Rothenberg, in another study, found that one-third of customers who entered a store with the expressed intent of making a specific purchase walked out without making any purchase. It is obvious that a small increase in converting these nonpurchasing consumers into customers could increase sales dramatically, even if the shopper is only in the store as a means to combat loneliness.

For example, if these retailers did nothing more than just contact half the 49 million customers who had no sales contact, and if the conversion rate among this group was only half what it was among those who had contact, the number of sales transactions, currently 38 million, would increase by 15 percent (half of 49 million who had no contact multiplied by half of the conversion rate for those who had contact equal 5.6 million more sales transactions). That's an opportunity to add 15 percent to sales by doing nothing more than what is already being achieved when customers contact a salesperson. Yet for many retailers this is a lost opportunity as they either do not want to or do not know how to train their sales staff in the proper methods of servicing a customer. Worse yet are those retailers who want to cut back on operating expense and therefore do not have the necessary number of sales personnel on duty. Either way, the retailer is missing out on a great opportunity to increase sales.

High salesperson productivity is one of the hallmarks of high-performance retailers. These retailers do a better job selecting, training, and evaluating their salespeople.

SALES PER HOUR Perhaps the most common measure of a salesperson's or salesforce's performance is sales per hour. Sales per hour is computed by dividing total dollar sales over a particular time frame by total salesperson or salesforce hours.

When employing this measure, remember that standards should be specific to the group or person being evaluated for a particular time period. For example, in a department store the sales per hour of selling effort cannot be expected to be the same for the toy department as for the jewelry department. Nor could one expect the same sales per hour during July and December, because of the heavy Christmas demand for toys and jewelry. In some lines of retail trade, particularly those selling high-ticket items such as automobiles, the key performance measure is gross profit generated per salesperson.

USE OF TIME Standards can be developed for how salespeople should spend their time. A salesperson's time can be spent in four ways:

1. Selling time is any time spent in assisting customers with their needs. This would be time spent talking, demonstrating, writing sales receipts, or assisting the customer in other potentially revenue-generating ways.

2. Nonselling time is any time spent on nonselling tasks such as marking merchandise or straightening up the merchandise.

3. Idle time is time the salesperson is on the sales floor but is not involved in any productive work.

4. Absent time occurs when the salespeople are not on the sales floor. They may be at lunch, in the employee lounge, in another part of the store, or in some inappropriate place.

The retailer may develop standards for each of these ways to spend time. For example, the standard time allocation may suggest that salespeople spend 60 percent of their time selling, 28 percent of their time on nonselling activities, 5 percent idle, and 7 percent absent. Any deviation from these standards should be investigated and corrective measures should be taken if necessary.

Data Requirements To establish proper standards of performance the retailer needs data. What are good standards for the conversion rate? Sales per hour? Time allocation? Only data will help answer these questions. For brick & mortar retailers, data can come from retail trade associations, consulting firms, or the retailer's own experience. However, the on-line retailer has a decisive advantage in terms of data as the retailer's web site records all unique users who actually visit the web site.

Once the retailer obtains the data on which to base standards, it must collect additional data continually or at least periodically on actual performance. For example, an increasing number of retailers today are always surveying their customers and use other programs, such as mystery shoppers, to evaluate their salespeople. In fact, a whole service industry specializing in mystery shopping has developed for retailers to employ as detailed in our Service Retailing box. The results of mystery shopper surveys, along with the employee's actual conversion rate, sales per hour, and time allocation, must be contrasted to their respective standards. If the actual data differ significantly from the standard, an investigation of the cause is warranted. Both favorable and unfavorable variances should be investigated, because you may learn just as much from unusually good performance as from unusually poor performance.

Service Retailing

Mystery Shopping Programs Ensure Your Drink Order Is Made Just Right

The increasing competitive pressure to deliver high quality customer service among retailers has created a whole industry of quality assessment specialists. Mystery shoppers, who are also referred to as phantom or anonymous shoppers, help retailers monitor the implementation of their policies and the preparedness of their employees for the unexpected. In a typical mystery shopping experience, an anonymous trained researcher engages the retailer's staff, either in their brick & mortar store, over the telephone, or on the Internet, and seeks to complete a required task (such as purchasing a product or making a customer service inquiry). The shopper then completes a detailed report on the various aspects of the shopping experience. This report covers such topics as the cleanliness of the store shelves, the friendliness of the retail salespeople, and their ability to solve the shopper's problem. The details provided in the report are as objective as possible and focus primarily on the facts of the experience. For example, mystery shoppers report the exact amount of time until they are greeted in the store, verbatim conversations with employees, the length of time they waited in line to purchase their products, and physical appearance of displays in each aisle of the store. As such, a key element of a mystery shopper is a keen memory, as no notes can be taken during the retail shopping experience, but can only be recorded once the mystery shopper is clear of the retailer's presence.

Clearly, an advantage of mystery shoppers to retailers is that they provide an independent assessment of the retailer's customer service operations rather than relying on employees for customer service assessments. As such, all retail sectors can benefit from independent assessment of their service quality that is provided through mystery shopping programs. Whether one speaks of clothing retailers, hotels, restaurants, or financial services, mystery shopping can help retailers, or their channel partner, assess the experience of a retailer's customers. Such data provides valuable information on the retailer's particular strengths and weaknesses. For example, one well regarded liquor manufacturer wanted to ensure the quality of training that its retailers maintained regarding the preparation of its product. As such, they hired a market research firm to send out their mystery "drinkers" to ensure that the gin and tonics served used branded glasses, swizzle sticks, and ice buckets, thus, guaranteeing the perfect gin and tonic.

While such shoppers were once used by retailers to identify employees who were lax in their responsibilities with customers, the general demeanor of mystery shopping programs has changed considerably. Today, the most successful mystery shopping programs are aimed at identifying areas for retail improvement. Rather than focusing on any specific employee's shortcomings in the customer service experience, retailers are using the data from mystery shopping research to develop more effective training and employee reward programs to heighten their level of service.

The demand for mystery shoppers by retailers throughout the world is evidenced by the fact that it has spawned a whole new segment of market research. In fact, the demand for mystery shoppers has grown so strong that top market research firms, such as NOP, Taylor Nelson Sofres, and Research International have all begun to offer these services to their clients. As one can imagine, the service of assessing service is a key area of strategic retail importance as customers continue to demand increasingly higher levels of service quality.

Source: Based on Adam Finn and Ujwal Kayande, "Unmasking a Phantom: A Psychometric Assessment of Mystery Shopping," *Journal of Retailing,* Summer 1999: 195–217 and the authors' experiences with mystery shoppers.

The Retail Sales Process

LO • 5

What steps are involved in the retail selling process?

There are several basic steps that occur during the retail selling process. The length of time that a salesperson spends in each one of these steps depends on the product type, the customer, and the selling situation. Exhibit 12.9 details the process model.

Exhibit 12.9	**Selling Process in the Retail Environment**

Step 1 — Prospecting
Who can benefit from your product
a. Finding Prospects.
b. Qualifying prospects, (determining whether a prospect has the ability, buying power, and willingness to make a purchase).

Step 2 — Approach
The first 15 seconds are the key as they set the *mood* for the sale.
a. Never say "May I help you?"
   A single "Hello," "Good morning," or "What may I show you?" makes the customer realize that you are glad they are in your store.
b. Determine as early as possible the customer's needs.
   Listen — *What you hear* is more important than anything you could possibly tell your customer. Ask a few well-chosen questions — What do I need to know?
   1. Product needed or problem to be solved.
   2. User of the product (tell me about so-and-so).

Step 3 — The Sales Presentation
Getting the customer to want to buy your product/service
a. Pick the right price level.
   If uncertain — ask "Is there a price range you have in mind?" Remember, you can't pick out the *right product* for the uncertain customer if the price is wrong.
b. Pick the right product.
   Match user and need with product. Show the customer at least two items.
c. Show the merchandise in an appealing manner.
   1. Make the merchandise stand out.
   2. Show the item so that its good points will be seen.
   3. Let the customer handle the merchandise.
   4. Stress the features of the product.
   5. Explain the benefits of these features.
   6. Appeal to the customer's emotions.
d. Help the customer decide.
   1. Handle objections.
   2. Replace unneeded items.
   3. Watch for unconscious clues.
   4. Stress features and benefits of "key" product.

Step 4 — Closing The Sale
Reaching an agreement
a. What is going on in the customer's mind.
b. Four effective ways to close.
   1. Make the decision for the customer.
   2. Assume the decision has already been made.
   3. Ask the customer to choose.
   4. Turn an objection around.

Step 5 — Suggestion Selling
Follow-up leads to other sales.

Successful retail salespeople do a better job at prospecting, approaching, sales presentation, and closing the sale and suggestion selling, which in turn results in higher retailing profitability.

Dollars & Sense

Prospecting

Prospecting is the search process of finding those who have the ability and willingness to purchase your product. Prospecting is particularly important when the store is full of customers. A salesperson should be aware that good prospects generally display more interest in the products than poor prospects who are "just looking." Salespeople should take advantage of the behavioral cues shown in Exhibit 12.8.

Approach

The salesperson may meet hundreds of customers a day, but the customer is only going to meet the salesperson once that day. Therefore, it is extremely important that the first 15 seconds set the mood for the sale. Never begin the sales presentation with "May I help you?" or any other question to which the customer may respond negatively. A simple good morning (afternoon, evening) or any other greeting acknowledging the customer's presence should do. Nordstrom, long recognized for its outstanding service, has its salesforce use an item the customer is wearing as an approach, if something better is not evident.

The key to a successful approach is discerning as soon as possible the customer's needs by asking the right questions and listening. What the salesperson hears about the customer's problem or need is more important than anything the salesperson can possibly contribute at this point. Ideally, the salesperson should ask a few well-chosen questions to find out more about the customer's need or the problem to be solved. The salesperson should also find out if the user of the product is a different individual than the customer. Remember, the salesperson should ask only as many questions as needed and let the customer do the talking.

Sales Presentation

Once the initial contact has been established and the salesperson has listened to the customer's problems and needs, the salesperson is in a position to present the merchandise and sales message correctly. How the salesperson presents the product or service depends on the customer and the situation. The key, however, is to get the customer to want to buy the product or service. The salesperson can begin by determining the right price range of products to show the customer. Showing the customer an item that is priced too high or too low will generally result in a lost sale. If uncertain, the salesperson should ask the customer about his or her desired price range.

Next, the salesperson should pick out what he or she believes will be the right product or service to satisfy the customer's needs. The salesperson should be careful not to show the customer too many products so as to avoid confusing the customer.

The salesperson should tell the customer about the merchandise in an appealing way, stressing the features that are the outstanding qualities or characteristics of the product. The customer should be encouraged to handle the merchandise. The salesperson can then help the customer decide on the product or service that best fulfills the customer's needs. The salesperson should address any objection that the customer might have, replace the unneeded items, and continue to stress the features and benefits of the product the customer seems most interested in. Training and retraining are ongoing activities for all successful retailers.

Closing the Sale

Closing the sale is a natural conclusion to the selling process. However, for most sales-persons, closing the sale is the most difficult part of the selling process. Remember, the salesperson is there to help the customer solve a problem, so the salesperson should not be afraid to ask for the sale. The key to closing the sale is for the salesperson to determine what is going on in the customer's mind. Exhibit 12.10 lists some of the signals a salesperson should be on the lookout for at this stage of the selling process. If the sales-person waits too long, or is too impatient, in completing this step, the customer will be gone before the salesperson realizes it. There are four effective ways to close a sale: (1) make the decision for the customer, (2) assume that the decision has been made and ask if the sale will be cash or charge, (3) ask the customer to select the product, and (4) turn an objection around by stressing a positive aspect of the product. For example, a salesperson might suggest that although the initial cost of a product might be high, its longer life span will reduce total cost.

Closing the sale is the action the salesperson takes to bring a potential sale to its natural conclusion.

Suggestion Selling

An effective salesperson continues to sell even after the sale has been completed. An additional sale is always possible. The salesperson should find out if the customer has any other needs or if the customer knows of anybody else with needs that can be solved with the salesperson's product line. A good example of the follow-up would be the salesperson selling a Valentine's gift to a college student for his girlfriend and asking if he can help him with a gift for his mother. However, suggestion selling can also decrease a consumers satisfaction with the retailer as some customers view suggestion selling as an annoyance.

Exhibit 12.10	**Some Closing Signals the Salesperson Should Be on the Lookout For**

The customer reexamines the product carefully.

The customer tries on the product (i.e., trying on a sport coat or strapping on a wristwatch).

The customer begins to read the warranty or brochure.

The customer makes the following statements:
  I always wanted a compact disc player.
  I never realized that these were so inexpensive.
  I bet my wife would love this.

The customer asks the following questions:
  Does this come in any other colors?
  Do you accept Discover cards?
  Can you deliver this tomorrow?
  Do you have a size 7 in this style?
  Do you accept trade-ins?
  Do you have any training sessions available?
  Do you have it in stock?
  What accessories are available?
  Where would I take it to get it serviced?
  Is it really that easy to operate?

Student Study Guide

Summary

LO•1 **Why is customer service so important in retailing?**

This chapter emphasizes that customer service is a key revenue-generating variable for the retailer. To properly manage the customer service decision area, the retailer needs to build a relationship with the customer by integrating customer service with merchandise, promotion, building and fixtures, price, and credit management. Only an integrated customer service program will allow the retailer to achieve maximum profits.

LO•2 **What are the various customer services that a retailer can offer?**

Customer services are classified into pretransaction, transaction, and posttransaction services. Pretransaction services make it easier for a potential customer to shop at a retailer's location or learn about the retailer's offering. Common examples are convenient hours and informational aids. Transaction-related services make it easier for the customer to complete a transaction. Popular transaction-related services are consumer credit, gift wrapping and packaging, check cashing, personal shopping, merchandise availability, personal selling, and the transaction itself. Posttransaction services influence the customer's satisfaction with the merchandise after the transaction. The most frequently encountered are handling of complaints, merchandise returns, servicing and repairing, and delivery.

LO•3 **How should a retailer determine which services to offer?**

Conventional wisdom suggests that in establishing the mix of customer services the retailer should consider six factors: retailer's characteristics, competition, type of merchandise, price image, target market income, and cost of the service.

LO•4 **What are the various management problems involved in retail selling, salesperson selection, and training and evaluation?**

This chapter also illustrates the role of managing the retail salesperson. Regardless of whether sales clerks are primarily order getters or order takers, they play an important role in the demand for a retailer's products. However, the role played by the order getter is obviously more important in this regard.

The criteria to be used in the selection of a selling staff and its training program was discussed. The section ended by discussing ways to evaluate the performance of retail salespeople.

LO•5 **What steps are involved in the retail selling process?**

The retail selling process consists of five steps: prospecting, approach, presentation, close, and suggestion selling. The length of time a salesperson spends on each step depends on the product type, customer, and selling situation.

Terms to Remember

high-quality services	dwell time
relationship retailing	posttransaction services
customer service	transaction services
transient customer	conversion rate
pretransaction services	prospecting
personal shopping	closing the sale

Review and Discussion Questions

LO•1 Why is customer service so important in retailing?

1. Retailers with high levels of customer service, because of the extra costs involved, are usually less profitable then retailers with low service levels. Agree or disagree and defend your point of view.

2. If retailers are losing half of their customers every five years, why can't they identify these lost customers and go after them? Does the size of the store make any difference? Also, is it easier for on-line retailers to do this than for brick & mortar types?

3. Do customers at different retail formats demand the same type of service? Explain the reasoning behind your answer.

LO•2 What are the various customer services that a retailer can offer?

4. How are a brick & mortar retailer's customer service problems related to an on-line retailer's decisions? Are not the problems the same for both retailers? Explain your answer.

5. Is complaint handling more important for brick & mortar retailers or on-line retailers? What do you feel accounts for the differences between these two types of retailers?

LO•3 How should a retailer determine which services to offer?

6. How would the type of customer affect the level of customer service a retailer should offer?

7. Should a retailer seek to meet or exceed a competitor's level of customer service?

LO•4 What are the various management problems involved in retail selling, salesperson selection, and training and evaluation?

8. Develop a list of predictor variables you would use to screen applicants for a sales position in (a) a jewelry department in a high-prestige department store, (b) a used-car dealership, (c) a health club, and (d) an antique shop.

9. How can a small retailer evaluate the performance of its two salespeople?

10. A retail discount department store chain has analyzed the annual sales per salesperson in 20 of its stores nationwide. The sales per salesperson range from a low of $91,000 to a high of $134,000. Develop the list of factors that might help to explain this wide variation.

LO•5 What is involved in the retail selling process?

11. What should retail salespeople know about consumer behavior?

12. What should retail salespeople know about customer choice criteria?

13. Provide examples of suggestion selling in a discount store.

14. Someone once said that "selling is selling regardless of the product or service being sold." Do you agree with this statement? Defend your position.

15. Why is selling so much more important for service retailers than it is for retailers selling physical products?

Sample Test Questions

LO•1   A transient customer is a consumer who visits a retailer

a. and finds the item desired in a matter of minutes
b. only when his or her regular retailer is closed
c. that does not meet his or her customer service expectations
d. while on vacation
e. and then visits all the other retailers in the neighborhood

LO•2   Merchandise availability is an example of a(n)

a. cost of sales
b. pretransaction service
c. operating cost
d. posttransaction service
e. transaction service

LO•3   Which of the following is not a factor in determining the service level to offer?

a. income of target market
b. price image of the retailer
c. services offered by the competition
d. firm's management structure
e. retailer's characteristics

LO•4   Which one of the following factors is not one of the elements that need to be considered when designing a sales job?

a. feedback from supervisors
b. the number of complaints a salesperson should have to handle
c. the amount of variety involved
d. the appropriate degree of autonomy
e. the level of task identity present

LO•5   What is the first step that a salesperson should take during the sales presentation?

a. Inform the customer about the merchandise in an appealing manner.
b. Select the right product or service that he or she believes will satisfy the customer's needs.
c. Greet the customer.
d. Help the customer to decide on the product that best fulfills the customer's needs.
e. Determine the right price range of products.

Applications

Writing and Speaking Exercise   You have just taken a summer job at your uncle's pest control firm. On your first day on the job, your uncle asks you to help him solve a major problem that has been bothering him for some time.

No-Pest, the name of your uncle's firm, has been a successful family-run business operating in a mid-western city of 75,000 for more than 50 years. In fact, most of the city's mortgage bankers insist on using No-Pest for their termite inspections before granting a mortgage. In addition, a poll in the local newspaper cited No-Pest as the Reader's Choice Award winner for being the best exterminator in the city. Still, although many consumers use No-Pest for their termite problems, less than a third take advantage of the firm's extended warranty. And the vast majority of those drop the warranty after the first or second year.

At a recent trade meeting, your uncle heard that the national average for the extended service guarantee was over 50 percent and that most of those users kept their warranty for more than five years. Your uncle provided you with these facts to aid you in solving his problem. The No-Pest termite control process, which cost $1,000 for a typical house, involves drilling holes for chemicals completely around the house and in the house where water pipes emerge from the ground. For a smaller fee, usually around $200, No-Pest will just treat the infected area and hope the termites don't return or spread throughout the house. The warranty plan involved annual visits to the house to look for termites and the charge was 10 percent of the original cost, usually $100 per year. The two other services No-Pest performs are spraying the lawn for fleas and ticks, ($60) and spraying the interior of the house for insects ($40).

That first afternoon, you went with your uncle while he made his first warranty check at the home of Barbara Healy. Your uncle arrived at Healy's home just after 1 p.m. and spent approximately 10 minutes looking over her home, inside and outside, for possible signs of termites. After he was sure that there were no signs of infestation, he presented Healy with an updated warranty covering the next 12 months and collected her check. Healy, while writing out the check, made some comments about paying $100 for such a little bit of time and wondered aloud if she could continue the program. As you were leaving, Healy asked what would happen if she discontinued the warranty and termites later appeared. Your uncle explained that there would be no need to completely redo the entire house, just the infected area for the $200 fee. When you and your uncle got into the truck, he said that he expected that Healy would drop the service next year.

Given what you learned in this chapter about high-quality service and retaining the customer, you decide to prepare a memo discussing the advantages and disadvantages of several alternative strategies he could use, indicating their short–term and long–term impact on profit and their likely effect on customer satisfaction.

Retail Project   As you are approaching graduation it occurs to you that you need a new suit for interviewing. In considering your retail alternatives you decide to compare on-line clothing retailers with brick & mortar stores.

Determine the differences in the amount of time involved in shopping between the two retailers, the time it would take for you to obtain the clothing from each, and price. Which would you choose to use?

Case   **Tech-No-Tronics**

Tech-No-Tronics is a 10-store retail operation that carries various lines of personal computers, printers, word processing software packages, and related products such as carrying cases and resume paper. Tech-No-Tronics focuses on meeting the needs of middle-income consumers.

Five Tech-No-Tronics stores are located in areas that are the homes of large community colleges or mid-sized universities. Management believes that approximately 70 percent of the sales in these stores are accounted for by individuals who attend these schools at some level (i.e., traditional undergraduates, continuing education, graduate students, etc.), students' parents, and members of the schools' staffs.

The other five stores are situated in downtown business districts. The downtown stores primarily attract young professionals who work in the area and are technically unsophisticated.

Tech-No-Tronics' philosophy is to help the "average Joe or Jane" purchase his or her first computer as painlessly as possible. Management wants the stores' image and products to reflect this user-friendly objective.

Based on this information, answer the following questions:

1. What factors would management want to consider when selecting potential Tech-No-Tronics salespeople? What kind of a person would Tech-No-Tronics want to employ? Why?

2. Discuss some pretransaction and posttransaction services that may be of particular importance to Tech-No-Tronics customers.

Planning Your Own Retail Business

Franklin's Jewelers, a family business your grandfather started in 1952, had annual sales last year of $453,250. Your parents, who purchased this business from your grandfather in 1981, have asked you to help them develop a strategy to improve sales. Because you plan to open a second Franklin's Jewelers store upon graduation, with your family's support, you want to use this opportunity to impress your parents with your business and retail marketing skills.

In reviewing the store's records you were surprised to find that a record had been kept of how many shoppers visited the store on a daily basis. For the most recent year you computed that there were 14,000 visitors and that 2,590 of these made a purchase. You also have spent the last few weeks observing the salespeople (including your parents) make sales presentations. Your observation is that they do a good job of approaching shoppers and making a sales presentation; however, they are weak and passive on closing a sale. You also have observed that the salespeople make little effort to cross-sell merchandise.

Your recommendation is to have a local professor who teaches a course in personal selling conduct a sales training workshop. This two-day workshop would cost $2,500. After consulting with the professor, you both believe the training should produce an increase in average transaction size of $25 and an increase in the conversion rate of 5 percent.

Based on the preceding information, show the impact on annual sales of the proposed training program.

Endnotes

1. "Learning from Customer Defections," *Harvard Business Review*, March/April 1996: 56–69.

2. For a detailed discussion of this topic, see Pratibha Dabholkar, David Shepherd, and Dayle Thorpe, "A Comprehensive Framework for Service Quality: An Investigation of Critical Conceptual and Measurement Issues through a Longitudinal Study," *Journal of Retailing*, Summer 2000: 139–173.

3. "After All You've Done for Your Customers, Why Are They Still *Not Happy*?" *Fortune*, December 11, 1995: 178–182.

4. "Why Service Stinks," *Business Week,* October 23, 2000: 118–128.

5. Leo J. Shapiro, "How to Increase Sales by 20 Percent without Attracting Any New Customers," *International Trends in Retailing*, December 1998: 37–49.

6. University of Michigan's American Customer Satisfaction Index at www.bus.umich.edu/research/nqrc. This survey is updated quarterly.

7. "Americans Can't Get No Satisfaction," *Fortune*, December 11, 1996: 186–194.

8. "Filling Big Shoes," *Forbes*, November 15, 1999: 170–172.

9. "Retailers Harness Internet Mapping Services to Generate Store Traffic," *Stores*, January 2000: 114–116.

10. "Sears Rolls Out Gift Registry to 800 Mall Stores," *Advertising Age*, February 24, 1997: 3, 83.

11. SIRS presentation at National Retail Federation (NRF) Annual Convention 2000, January 18, 2000.

12. "Mall 'Ambassadors' Dispel Bad Image," *Shopping Centers Today*, September 1996: 21.

13. "Speaking Volumes," *Dallas Morning News*, April 16, 2000: 1H, 5H.

14. Based on a letter from Sam Walton to Robert Kahn, dated June 5, 1991.

15. "Big Retailers Try to Speed Up Checkout Lines," *Wall Street Journal*, March 13, 2000: B1.

16 "Clinching the Holiday E-Sale," *Wall Street Journal,* October 9, 2000: B1.

17. "The Latest Weapon in the Price Wars," *Fortune*, July 7,1997: 200.

18. "Inside the Cult of Costco," *Fortune*, September 6, 1999: 185–190.

19. Domino's press release, dated September 25, 1998.

20. "Customers Like Buying Cars from Women, Survey Finds," *USA Today*, November 8, 1994: B1.

21. W. Levinson et al., "Physician-Patient Communication. The Relationship with Malpractice Claims among Primary Care Physicians and Surgeons," *JAMA*, February 19, 1997: 553–559; Gerald B. Hickson et al., "Obstetricians' Prior Malpractice Experience and Patients' Satisfaction with Care," *JAMA*, November 23/30, 1994: 1583–1587; and Stephen S. Entman et al., The Relationship between Malpractice Claims History and Subsequent Obstetric Care," *JAMA*, November 23/30, 1994: 1588–1591.

22. For a more complete discussion of this subject, see Arun Sharma and Michael Levy, "Categorization of Customers by Retail Salespeople," *Journal of Retailing*, Spring 1995: 71–82.

23. Much of the following is based on John O'Shaughnessy, "Selling as an Interpersonal Influence Process," *Journal of Retailing*, Winter 1971–1972: 32–46.

24. O'Shaughnessy, ibid.: 41.

25. The following information was provided the authors by Marvin J. Rothenberg and is used with the written permission of Marvin J. Rothenberg, Inc., Retail Marketing Consultants, Ft. Lee, N.J.

Store Layout and Design[1]

Overview

In this chapter, we discuss the place where all retailing activities come to-gether—the retail store. The store can be the most meaningful form of commu-nication between the retailer and its customers. Most important, the store is where sales happen, or fail to happen. We will see that with all its hundreds of elements, the store has two primary roles: creating the proper store image and increasing the productivity of the sales space. We identify the most critical ele-ments in creating a successful retail store and describe the art and science of store planning, merchandise presentation, and design.

Learning Objectives

After reading this chapter, you should be able to

1. list the elements of a store's environment and define its two primary objectives

2. discuss the steps involved in planning the store

3. describe how various types of fixtures, merchandise presentation methods and techniques, and the psychology of merchandise presentation are used to increase the productivity of the sales floor

4. describe why store design is so important to a store's success

5. explain the role of visual communications in a retail store

---

LO • 1

What are the elements of a store's environment?

Introduction to Store Layout Management

The previous chapter discussed how customer service and personal selling can be used to develop a relationship with the customer. This chapter discusses another method retailers can use to initiate and continue this relationship—the retail store itself. Stanley Marcus, the legendary chairperson-emeritus of Neiman Marcus, once told a group that every morning he expected to see the following headline in the Dallas Morning News: "Shopper Found Dead in Local Store; Cause of Death—Boredom."[2] He was trying to get the group to realize the importance of getting customers excited about coming into their store. In this economy of time-poverty, this is particularly important when

Allen Questrom, Chairman and CEO of JCPenney, recognized that store design, layout, and atmosphere are critically important. He once said, "We sell discretionary merchandise. We have to sell theater and excitement."

customers enter the store with a negative attitude/emotion because they have other things they would rather be doing.[3] Time poverty has impacted retailers in other ways. A recent study by Procter & Gamble found that Americans now spend only 21 minutes shopping for groceries and 20 minutes preparing the meal. (By the way, only a generation ago, the average preparation time was over an hour.) However, the increased use of market segmentation, discussed in detail in Chapter 3, whereby retailers break down heterogeneous consumer populations into smaller, more homogeneous groups based on each population's characteristics, has had the effect of making shopping more confusing and less exciting for these time-pressed shoppers.[4] Allen Questrom, the chairman and CEO of JCPenney, noted the importance of making shopping easy and exciting, as was evident when he said, "We sell discretionary merchandise. We have to sell theater and excitement."[5]

In fact, no other variable in the retailing mix influences the consumer's initial perception of a brick & mortar retailer as much as the store itself. Profitable retailers today are spending a great deal of time and effort making sure the right things happen in their stores, and that their targeted customers enter these stores, shop, and spend money. Simply put, for retailers the store is "where the action is." Although this chapter is concerned with the physical store, the same factors may be used to develop an e-tailer's "virtual store." For a short illustration of layout in a virtual store, see the chapter's E-tailing box.

Although a store is composed of literally thousands of details, its two primary objectives around which all activities, functions, and goals in the store revolve are **store image** and **space productivity.** However, before discussing these two objectives, it is important to identify the elements (shown in Exhibit 13.1) that compose the store environment, each of which will be discussed in detail in this chapter.

Store image
is the overall perception the consumer has of the store's environment.

Space productivity
represents how effectively the retailer utilizes its space and is usually measured by sales per square foot of selling space or gross margin dollars per square foot of selling space.

Exhibit 13.1	Elements That Compose the Store Environment

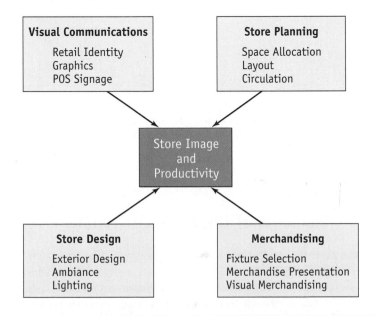

E-tailing

Store Design without the Store

The virtual world is a new world. For e-tailers, the constraints of print catalogs and the physical brick & mortar world are no more. E-tailers face an incredible challenge in today's evolving virtual world. What should a web site look like? How should it be structured? What should it include? And, most of all, how can an e-tailer turn browsers into buyers? Unfortunately, there is no magic checklist that an e-tailer can use to transform its web site into an e-tailing powerhouse, no reliance on a specific technology, site structure, or the like for instant success. Most consumers spend less than 5 seconds at a web site the first time they visit. As such, there is a limited window of opportunity to capture the attention of an on-line user. Although there is no strict list of do's and don'ts, as the on-line rules are constantly changing, a few underlying fundamentals have been identified that can drive repeat visits and encourage purchasing. Here are a few elements to consider when designing an e-tailing site:

- *Keep content current.* On-line consumers browse frequently and therefore it is very important to update information on the site continually; this includes merchandise presentation as well as stock rotation. Two aspects of content should be considered: merchandise presentation and description.

Merchandise presentation: The web offers e-tailers a plethora of merchandise presentation options. No longer limited to gondolas in the physical world, e-tailers can provide consumers with 3D presentations, which allow consumers a full view of merchandise. Some types of merchandise, such as music or movies, avail themselves to on-line product trials to enhance the consumer experience, whereas apparel can be demonstrated through cyber-modeling whereby virtual images of a customer can be input and the customer can "try on" the clothes. The key to successful on-line merchandise presentation is to optimize the technology while minimizing download time for the consumer.

Merchandise description: Write in web-ease. Consumers on-line scan information as opposed to reading it. Writing for the web means keeping the information short and concise with creative use (not overuse) of font styles and sizes. Use text descriptions to catch the consumer's eye and draw her or him to the merchandise.

- *Make the site easy and enjoyable to use.* Ease of use is a primary concern for on-line consumers. Ease of use means that users with little or no experience either on-line or with your product category should easily be able

High-profit retailers, whether operating traditional stores or virtual stores, place a heavy emphasis on designing their physical facilities or web site so as to enhance image and increase productivity.

Elements of the Store Environment

The first decision the retailer must make in planning a store is how to allocate the scarce resource, space. Next, the retailer must create a store layout, which shows the location of all merchandise departments and the placement of circulation aisles to allow customers to move through the store. The merchandise presentation must be, as discussed earlier, exciting so as to catch and hold customers' attention, be easy to understand, and encourage shoppers to browse, evaluate, and buy. Therefore, the to move about the site and find the information they desire. Much like signage in a brick & mortar world, e-tailers must clearly show the way for on-line consumers. The enjoyability factor of a web site is directly related to its ease of use but extends further into the atmospherics of the site. The use of colors, shading, sounds, and so on all add to the consumer's experience. As such, e-tailers must determine what experience they wish their customers to have and then design the atmospherics of the site to match.

- *Be considerate of download time.* Although many e-tailers are connected to the Internet through high-speed modems, most of the e-tailer's potential customers are not. Fancy graphics can slow download time and create speed bumps for potential customers. A slow download time often stimulates the customer to move to a competitor.
- *Structure an on-line community where consumers can interact with one another or contribute to the site's content.* The virtual world allows for new methods of integrating customers into a retailer's business. Offering potential consumers an opportunity to become involved in the site can build a loyal clientele.

The web offers opportunities for retailers to interact with consumers in new and innovative ways. Profitable retailers take advantage of the technological possibilities. An e-tail site should not be designed to replicate either a retailer's print catalog or brick & mortar store, but it should be designed to keep pace with the evolving technology.

These are just a few of the elements that an e-tailer can use to enhance the on-line experience of potential customers and thus transform a browser into a buyer. Unfortunately, turning browsers into buyers is not as easy as you might think. For instance, in the brick & mortar world once a consumer has selected merchandise (by, for example, putting it in his or her shopping cart), there is a high likelihood that the consumer will be purchasing the product. Conversion rates, which were discussed in the previous chapter, are not so good for many e-tailers. As pointed out in the previous chapter, 65 percent of shopping carts are abandoned on-line. As such, e-tailers must also develop secure and easy processes for customers to purchase on-line. Although privacy and security are of paramount importance to customers, many on-line shopping carts are abandoned simply because the consumer becomes frustrated with the e-tailer's checkout process.

presentation of the merchandise is a critical factor in the selling power of a store and has a significant effect on the store image. A bookstore with a high percentage of face-outs, for example, can create the image of being a specialty book boutique that carries a limited selection of exclusive titles and is therefore a rather pricey place to shop. A bookstore with virtually all spine-outs is often perceived as cramming in a huge selection of titles sold at low prices. So merchandise presentation is a critical factor in determining both store image and productivity.

Most shoppers are accustomed to noticing the layout and design of a store, which comprises all elements affecting the human senses of sight, sound, smell, and touch. An effective store layout and design, including the storefront, creates a comfortable environment that enhances the merchandise and entices shoppers to browse and buy. Not to be overlooked is in-store lighting, which not only helps create the proper image but draws customers' eyes around the store and onto merchandise. Likewise, in-store graphics such as art, photography, and signs form an important visual communication link between the store and its customers by providing much needed information on how to shop in the store. The chapter's Retailing: The Inside Story box describes how supermarket managers have perfected the art of laying out and designing their stores.

The method by which a bookstore arranges books on a shelf, either spine in or face out, can have a major influence on the store image.

Sometimes retailers tend to forget the lessons in the Retailing: The Inside Story box. For example, many managers ignore their own 25-25-50 rule on endcaps. This rule states that 25 percent of all endcaps should be advertised sale merchandise that the customer will seek out and another 25 percent should be unadvertised sale items that will cause the customer to be alert when looking at an endcap. The remaining 50 percent should be regular priced seasonal or impulse merchandise. Retailers tend to violate this rule when manufacturers offer money for the right to set up their own displays. Although the managers will gain a short-term profit by renting out most of their endcap space, they often destroy the long-term profits that a well-defined endcap policy generates.

Objectives of the Store Environment

The two primary objectives of creating the desired store image and increasing space productivity amount to a simple description of the three basic tasks of retailing described in Exhibit 12.3:

- Get consumers into the store (*market image*)
- Convert them into customers buying merchandise once inside the store (*space productivity*)
- Do this in the most efficient manner possible

The retailer must constantly balance these first two elements of the model, as they are sometimes at odds.

Developing a Store Image   The starting point in creating this image is, of course, the merchandise carried in the store, along with the retailer's promotional activities, customer service, and salesforce. The store itself also serves a critical role in creating and reinforcing the desired store image.

Retailing: The Inside Story

Consumer Behavior: Supermarket Style

Although no one knows how many supermarket managers took a consumer behavior class in college, these managers surely understand how and why consumers behave the way they do in supermarkets.

Observe

Most consumers not only are right-handed, they think right-headed.

- Thus, because supermarkets make more money on their store's private-label brands, due to their higher margins, they stock the store brands to the right of the name brands so that the consumer has to reach across the store brand to get the name brand.
- Likewise, supermarkets display the higher gross margin merchandise on the right side of an aisle, as gauged from the predominant direction of cart traffic.
- Because 90 percent of all customers entering a store turn right, that area is the most valuable for the store. Thus, it is no accident that produce, a deli, or a bakery is the first section that customers reach. That is because they can see, feel, and smell the merchandise. This in turn will get their mouths watering and make them hungry. Any supermarket manager will tell you that the best customer is a hungry customer.

Most consumers think neatness counts.

- Thus, merchants sometimes try to make their point-of-purchase displays look like a mess. These so-called "dump displays," which are affectionately known by some grocers as "organized chaos," are deliberately arranged in a haphazard fashion so the items inside look cheap and are, therefore, a great bargain. The same thought process works for merchants leaving out open cartons piled on top of another. Usually the items are not on sale, they merely look "hot," or are such a great deal that the retailer cannot keep the merchandise in stock.
- For the same reason, handwritten (as long as they are legible) signs create the impression of recently lowered

prices (i.e., there has not been time to get the printed signs). Thus, even though they do not always look great, handwritten signs move the merchandise faster than standard printed signs.

Most consumers are likely to focus on a large central display.

- The point-of-purchase displays at the end of each supermarket aisle that are known in the trade as endcaps are usually the focus of a customer's attention as he or she wheels a cart through the store. Thus, a smart retailer knows to follow the 25-25-50 rule.

Consumers are creatures of habit and when something is out of place they become more sensitive to their environment.

- While supermarket managers make regularly scheduled display changes for staple items, such as cake mixes, salad dressings, and cereals, they do not want to move the items to new locations because that may upset time-pressed customers. However, by changing shelf displays of these staples, the grocer draws the attention of the customer and thereby increases the chances of an impulse sale.

There is a little bit of greed in every one of us.

- Supermarket managers may put a limit on the purchase of a sale item, such as saying, "Limit 4 to a Customer." Not only will consumers think that the limit restrictions mean it's a great deal, but they will often buy the limit, even if they do not need that many.
- Similarly, many customers get so excited by finding a great price on a staple like peanut butter, they fail to notice that the item's complementary products, in this case jelly and bread, may have had their prices increased.

Source: The authors acknowledge the assistance of Paul Adams, Fleming Companies, and the late Robert Kahn with this box.

To illustrate the importance of store image, consider for a moment the words "7-Eleven." For most people, these words represent more than just two numbers. Together, they form the name of one of the most familiar American retailers, a chain with more than 4,000 convenience stores.

The thoughts and emotions this logo evokes in customers constitute 7-Eleven's store image. Regardless of what its managers would like its market image to be, regardless of what image they have tried to create, the store's actual image exists only in the minds and hearts of consumers. Many factors influence that image.

First, the name itself has a great influence. If the stores were called "8-Twelve," we all might have a different image in our heads. (The name was created in 1946 to stress the stores' operating hours, 7 a.m. to 11 p.m. every day, then unheard of in retailing.)[6] The rhythm and rhyme of *seven* and *eleven* allow the name to roll easily off our tongues and be more memorable, even if the customer does not shoot craps. (Remember, in craps a 7 or an 11 on the shooter's first roll is a winner.) The orange and green colors of the logo suggest to us certain things about the chain's quality. The storefront, historically a large black mansard roof, conveys a heavy, masculine appearance, and the windows plastered with price savings signs suggest a promotional environment. When you walk in the store, a buzzer warns clerks of entering shoppers, suggesting a concern about safety and theft. The smell of cheese nachos and the sight of sausages and hot dogs rolling around on the hot dogger create a certain atmosphere. Even the uniforms worn by the store clerks leave an impression, which joins all other impressions on the five senses to create 7-Eleven's store image in our minds. The consumer's image of a store is, therefore, a combination of out-of-store factors; location (Chapter 7), advertising, and publicity (Chapter 11) plus the dozens of in-store variables perceived by the consumer.

Recently, in fact, 7-Eleven has conducted experiments to change its store image to that of a high-quality food service provider. Managers have altered not only the merchandise mix but such store variables as colors, layout, light levels, and aisle widths to affect the consumer's perception of a 7-Eleven store.

This is why planning the store environment is so important to a retailer. Although advertising and other promotional activities are important in establishing a desired store image, the store itself makes the most significant and lasting impression on our collective consciousness and it is here that the retailer must focus great energy on creating the right image.

This effort is complicated by the knowledge that consumers are extremely fickle, able to change their feelings about retailers at any time for little substantive reason, and the fact that today there are more stores than ever vying for limited consumer dollars. It is not surprising that image engineering—the ability to create and change a store's image—becomes more important every day for a retailer's survival.

Increasing Space Productivity   The store's image attracts customers. However, when the customers are visiting the store or its web site, the retailer must also convince them to make a purchase. Therefore, a store environment must increase its space productivity, a goal that is summarized in a simple but powerful truism in retailing: *The more merchandise customers are exposed to, that is presented in an orderly manner, the more they tend to buy.* After all, the typical shopper in a department store goes into only two or three shopping areas per trip. Through careful planning of the store environment, the retailer can encourage customers to flow through the entire store, or at least more shopping areas, and see a wider variety of merchandise. The proper use of in-store advertising and displays will let the customer know what's happening in other shopping areas and encourage a visit to those areas. Conversely, however, the store does not want to have merchandise pushed into every conceivable nook and cranny of the store so that customers cannot get to it.

High-profit retailers design their stores to expose shoppers to as much merchandise as possible, displayed in a safe and orderly manner, creating an uncongested shopping environment.

Dollars & Sense

Many retailers are focusing more attention on in-store marketing, based on the theory that marketing dollars spent inside the store, in the form of store design, merchandise presentation, visual displays, or in-store promotions, should lead to significantly greater sales and profit increases than marketing dollars spent in advertising and other out-of-store vehicles such as public relations and promotions. After all, it is easier to get a consumer who is already in your store to buy more merchandise than planned, than to get a new consumer to come into your store.

One factor that detracts from space productivity is shrinkage, or the loss of merchandise through theft, loss, and damage. It is called **shrinkage** because retailers usually do not know what happened to the missing merchandise, only that their inventory level in the store has somehow shrunk. Even stores that move customers through the entire space and effectively use in-store marketing techniques to maximize sales can fall victim to high shrinkage. Remember, when a store sells an item for $1.29, it earns only a small percentage of that sale, perhaps ranging from 35 to 60 cents. When that item is stolen, lost, or damaged, however, the store loses the cost of that $1.29 item, maybe 69 cents, in the case of a $1.29 item, and this loss is deducted from the store's overall sales. Shrinkage ranges from 1 to 4 percent of retail sales. Although this may seem like a small number, consider that the after-tax profit for many retailers is little more than 4 percent, so high shrinkage alone can make the difference between a profit and a loss.

Therefore, to enhance space productivity, retailers must incorporate planning, merchandise presentation, and design strategies that minimize shrinkage by avoiding hidden areas of the store that shoplifters can take advantage of, and reduce the number of times merchandise must be moved, during which damage and loss can occur.

Shrinkage
represents merchandise that cannot be accounted for due to theft, loss, or damage.

Store Planning

LO • 2
What is involved in store planning?

Planning an effective retail store is like planning an effective piece of writing, and moving through a store as a customer is much like reading through an article or a chapter in a book. The words are like the merchandise, which are there for you to review, understand, and consume. Just as a book needs more than words to make sense, a store needs more than merchandise to be shopable.

The store's layout and design is like the organization of chapters, sections, and subsections in this book. Grouping the words and thoughts into mental chunks makes the book easier to digest and understand. Unless a store specializes in only one product type, for example candles, if that store is not broken into departments and categories it would be impossible for a consumer to shop there effectively. The books would be mixed in with the shovels, the CDs would be mixed in with the garden plants, and the consumer would not know where to begin.

Signs and graphics are like the headlines and punctuation, which give you cues to understanding the organization of both a book and the merchandise in a store. Without headlines and subheadlines, this chapter would be a stream of words, very difficult and, even worse, boring to read and understand. Similarly, without signs, a store would seem like an endless sea of racks and merchandise, difficult to understand and shop.

Finally, the photos, exhibits, charts, and boxes in this book are the equivalent of a retailer's visual displays and focal points, or areas where the merchandise is pulled off the shelf or racks and displayed in theatrical vignettes, which successful retailers use to break up the store space, illustrate merchandise opportunities in the store, and visually demonstrate how certain merchandise goes together or can work in the consumer's life. Like photos and exhibits in a book, these visual displays elaborate on the text, or the bulk of merchandise on the racks, to make statements.

Most importantly, a retail store and a piece of writing are similar in the way they affect the consumer. Many writing coaches teach aspiring writers that each time an uncommon word is used or a punctuation mark is missing, the reader hits a speed bump in the writing and must mentally pause to consider what the author means to convey. After hitting three speed bumps, readers may conclude that the writing is too difficult to understand and quit reading.

It is the same in a retail store. All cues must work subliminally to organize the merchandise and guide the shopper effortlessly through the store. Each time shoppers become a bit confused as to where they are, where they need to go, how much an item costs, or where certain merchandise is, they become frustrated. The shopper may not consciously react to the first or second instance of frustration, but eventually the shopper may walk out, concluding that the store is too hard to shop. Exhibit 13.2 is one retailing expert's list of warning signs that managers should be on the lookout for, because each warning sign indicates a speed bump waiting to drive customers away from a store.

Most shoppers cannot consciously identify the elements of a good store, but certainly they know when these elements are missing. We have all experienced the feeling that a store seems to "really have it together." It's easy to shop, fun, and exciting; the merchandise is easy to understand; the associates seem friendly. You conclude that this store is a "good shop" and, with any luck, you are completely oblivious to the thousands of little details that have guided you through the shopping experience.

In retailing, the term **floorplan** indicates where merchandise and customer service departments are located, how customers circulate through the store, and how much

Floorplan
is a schematic that shows where merchandise and customer service departments are located, how customers circulate through the store, and how much space is dedicated to each department.

Exhibit 13.2   **These Warning Signs May Indicate a Space Problem**

Open spaces on the selling floor, even if the product is on hand

Cluttered and disorganized aisles, hallways, and stockrooms

Excessive time required to put away new receipts

Insufficient staging space for large shipments of advertised products

Sales associates continually required to leave the sales floor to locate additional merchandise

Poor utilization of vertical space and excessive time required retrieving products stored on high shelves

Sales lag expectations for specific locations where space or fixtures are a known issue

Off-site storage or multiple stockrooms required for a single commodity space is dedicated to each department. The floorplan, which is based around the predicted demands of the store's targeted customer, serves as the backbone of the store and is the fundamental structure around which every other element of the store environment takes shape. Some retailers, such as Target and Wal-Mart, analyze the data from their scanners with the demographics of the store's trading area when developing a floorplan. The retailers then structure the merchandise to the needs of each store. In addition, the retailers place merchandise in key strategic locations. For example, H.E.B. Grocery Company places the jelly next to the peanut butter, facial tissues next to the cold medicines, and chocolate syrup next to the ice cream. (Next time you are in a supermarket, see if it locates such items together.) Other retailers, know that toys and movies are kid magnets and thus display snacks right next to them. Another rule a retailer must follow is to think of the age of the consumer. For example, a retailer should never put a child's toy way up on the top shelf where kids cannot reach it or denture cream on the bottom shelf where seniors cannot easily bend down and get it. One retailing format that is an exception to such rules is the warehouse club. Costco, for example, uses crazy product positioning as part of its selling formula. The retailer has found that putting toothpaste next to golf clubs and cereals next computer tables not only increases impulse purchasing but provides customers with a "thrill of the hunt" psychological lift when they find something. Besides, such positioning tends to make customers more alert as to what is available. Therefore, the store's layout and design, including merchandise location, must be carefully planned to meet the retailer's merchandising goals, make the store easy to understand and shop, and allow merchandise to be presented effectively. The chapter's Service Retailing box illustrates how the overall design of a retailer, in this case a service retailer that most consumers do not want to use, can have a significant psychological impact on customers.

Allocating Space

The starting point for developing a floorplan is analyzing how the available store space, usually measured in square footage, should be allocated to various departments. This space allocation can be based on mathematical calculation of the returns generated by different types of merchandise. However, before describing this process, we must understand the various types of space in the store.

Types of Space Needed   Shoppers are most familiar with the sales floor, but this is not the only element in a retail store with which the planner must contend. There are five basic types of space needs in a store: (1) back room; (2) office and other functional spaces; (3) aisles, service areas, and other nonselling areas of the main sales floor; (4) wall merchandise space; and (5) floor merchandise space. The retailer must balance the quest for greater density of merchandise presentation with the shopability and functionality of the store. Because space is the retailer's ultimate scarce resource, rarely can the retailer achieve all of its desired goals. Rather, most retailers find themselves compromising on one or more dimensions, carefully weighing the priorities, strategic goals, and special constraints. In reviewing each of these categories of space, keep in mind that the goal is to make the largest portion possible of the space available to hold merchandise and be shopable.

BACK ROOM   To operate virtually any type of retail store, some space is required as back room, which includes the receiving area to process arriving inventories and the

Service Retailing

Partial-Casket Displays: The Newest Things at Funeral Homes

Over the past decade, a small team of retailing experts has quietly entered the arcane world of funeral services. A retail consultant, while in England, stumbled on a new means of handling one of the most difficult decisions a family must ever face—deciding on a casket for a loved one. The English concept was to just show partial caskets, thereby freeing up space to show more products. Returning to the United States, the consultant used focus groups to improve the use of the quarter-casket concept. As a result, purchasing a casket at funeral homes using this method is now a lot like shopping at any other local retailer. Gone are the intimidating rows of coffins in the funeral home's back room. Instead, corners of caskets, with prices clearly marked, extend out from walls—cheap to one side, expensive to the other—kind of like cabinet samples at a hardware store. This merchandising method makes it easier for families to buy a casket for a loved one.

This new display method not only makes the buying experience less of a crisis, but also gets consumers to choose a more premium box. The quarter-casket system works because it "abstracts" the very object being sold, in part because the caskets remain closed. To examine the lining, shoppers pull out little drawers below the shelves that reveal swatches of material similar to what they would see when buying a sofa. Utilizing this new method of displaying caskets enables mourners to avoid the discomfort of seeing a number of full-size boxes. In fact, most customers never see a complete casket until they come back for the service. This concept has been found to reduce stress on the survivors.

Like retailers everywhere, operators of the nation's 22,000 funeral homes have been searching for ways to increase profit. In view of recent Federal Trade Commission rulings requiring the full disclosure of all pricing, they have barely managed to hold their own against the on-line and discount casket retailers. However, funeral homes do have a built-in advantage because mourners usually want one-stop services, so they tend to buy everything at the funeral home where the body will be viewed.

This partial-casket strategy has been described as a clever blend of Wal-Mart (neat rows of accessible product) and Starbucks (premium pricing for perceived premium value) that not only eases the transaction for consumers, but has raised the average sale by $200 to $400 per coffin. After all, as is the case with any merchandise display, when customers understand the display and are presented with a wider range of options, they tend to spend money at their comfort level, which means they want to be in the middle of the price range.

The new display rooms can show 30 or even 40 casket styles versus the average of 18 that fit into traditional casket rooms. The displays load up on selections in the $2,000-to-$3,000 range, where customers tend to buy caskets and where they can choose from more midrange units lined up in logical price progressions. So it's easy for customers to identity a feature or material they like in one of these caskets—and then comfort themselves by spending an additional $200 or $400, rather than the more typical $1,000 price jumps they used to face.

The new rooms also offer more price points in the upper-end caskets, which makes, say, solid cherry caskets a more inviting alternative to the even higher priced walnut and mahogany models.

The casket company behind this new display method is York Caskets of Houston. "We had to reinvent ourselves," says Fred Turner, the York Group's marketing chief. The York Group reports that its first 50 displays showed an average gain of $438 per funeral since they were installed in 1997. The next batch of 175 showed a $300 to $400 gain. Many funeral home operators, however, balk at the initial price of $25,000 to $125,000, depending on room size and features. Nevertheless, with York's guaranteed 24-hour delivery from nearby warehouses, the funeral homes no longer have a major investment in caskets.

Source: Based on material supplied by Fred Turner of The York Group, Inc.

The redesign of casket display rooms has more than doubled the number of caskets that can be displayed.

stockroom to store surplus merchandise. The percentage of space dedicated to the back room varies greatly depending on the type of retailer, but the amount of space is shrinking for all types. Historical back room percentages have ranged from nearly 50 percent in some department stores to as little as 10 percent in some small specialty and convenience stores. General-merchandise stores have historically dedicated about 15 to 20 percent of their store space to the back room. The need to squeeze more sales out of expensive retail space, coupled with new distribution methods allowing smaller, more frequent merchandise deliveries from suppliers (called quick response inventory or efficient consumer response, depending on the industry involved), have allowed retailers to shrink their back rooms, with department stores cutting back to about 20 percent and others cutting back to 5 percent or less.

Some recent retail formats, such as warehouse clubs, have only receiving areas but virtually no back room stock capacity. In these stores, the store fixtures are usually large "warehouse racks" that carry shopable inventory at reachable heights (up to 84 inches) and carry large palettes or cartons of excess inventory at higher levels. These racks can go as high as 15 feet.

Warehouse clubs are taking advantage not only of the width and depth of the store but also of the height. In other words, although retailers pay expensive rents for their store space, as measured in square footage, the store and the merchandise can be stacked as high as possible at little additional cost using the *cubic* footage of the store. The ability of shoppers to reach does limit the height at which shopable merchandise can be stacked, but it does not limit the use of this high space to carry excess inventory. The same inventory carried in the back room would consume additional square footage, either causing higher rent or reducing the amount of shopable space. Essentially, the sales floor doubles as the back room. Most important, this stocking method visually creates a dramatic low-cost image in the store, which can be advantageous to value-oriented retailers but detrimental to fashion or high-end retailers.

OFFICES AND OTHER FUNCTIONAL SPACES Every store must contain a certain amount of office and other functional space. This often includes a break room for associates, a training room, offices for the store manager and assistant managers, a cash office, bathroom facilities for both customers and employees, and perhaps other areas. Though necessary, the location of such functional spaces receives a lower priority than the location of the sales floor and stockroom. Often they are located on mezzanines over the front of the store, over the back stockroom, or in side spaces too small to be stockrooms.

AISLES, SERVICE AREAS, AND OTHER NONSELLING AREAS   Even on the main sales floor, some space must be given up to nonselling functions, the most obvious of which is moving large numbers of shoppers through the store. The retailer's first step, particularly in larger stores, is to create main aisles through which shoppers will flow on their way through the store, and secondary aisles that draw customers back into the merchandise. These aisles must be wide enough to accommodate peak crowds, and in large stores they may be as wide as 15 feet. The amount of space dedicated to aisles can be significant. For instance, a 15-foot aisle running around the perimeter of an 80,000-square-foot store (the size of a typical discount store) may consume 12,000 square feet, or 15 percent of the entire space!

In addition to aisles, space must be given to dressing rooms, layaway areas, service desks, and other customer service facilities that cannot be merchandised. Although the retailer always attempts to minimize the amount of nonmerchandisable space, customer service is an equally important part of a store and should not be short-changed.

FLOOR MERCHANDISE SPACE   Finally, we come to the store space with which we as shoppers are most familiar, the floor merchandise space. Here, many different types of fixtures are used to display a wide variety of merchandise. Generally speaking, retailers use so-called bulk fixtures on the floor to carry large quantities of merchandise. But increasingly, retailers are realizing that the best goal is not just to cram the largest possible amount of merchandise on the floor, but to attractively and effectively display the largest amount customers can understand and shop.

WALL MERCHANDISE SPACE   The walls are one of the most important elements of a retail store. They serve as fixtures holding tremendous amounts of merchandise, as well as serving as a visual backdrop for the merchandise on the floor.

Space Allocation Planning   To determine the most productive allocation of space, the retailer must first analyze the profitability and productivity of various categories of merchandise. According to one study, around 20 percent of the average retailer's inventory is either obsolete or not wanted by the retailer's target market.[7] Such a number indicates the importance of analyzing the profitability and productivity of all merchandise.

There are several methods for measuring these variables. Regardless of the method used, the results must somehow relate some type of profitability performance measure (e.g., net sales, net profit, or gross margin) to the amount of space used in the store in order to get a productivity figure to use in determining the best allocation of the square footage. Two situations may cause a retailer to perform these tasks: revising the space allocation of an existing store and planning a new store.

IMPROVING SPACE PRODUCTIVITY IN EXISTING STORES   A retailer that has been in business for some time can develop a sales history on which to evaluate merchandise performance, refine space allocations, and enhance space productivity. One easy measure to use is the **space productivity index,** which compares the percent of the store's total gross margin dollars for a particular merchandise category to its percentage of space utilized. An index rating of 1.0 would be an ideal department size. If the index is greater than 1.0, the product category is generating a larger percentage of the store's gross margin than the percentage of store space it is using, and consideration should be given to allocating additional space to this category. If the index falls below 1.0, the product category is under-performing relative to other merchandise and should be considered for a reduction in space allocation. The merchandise productivity analysis shown in Exhibit 13.3 indicates that in this store, softlines (apparel and apparel accessories) categories, with an index of 1.29, are performing very well and perhaps should

Space productivity index is a ratio that compares the percentage of the store's total gross margin that a particular merchandise category generates to its percentage of total store selling space used.

Exhibit 13.3	Merchandise Productivity Analysis

Category	Total Sales	Sale as % Total	Total Sq. Ft.	Sq. Ft. % Total	Sales per Sq. Ft.	Total G.M. $	G.M. $ % Total	Space Productivity Index
Softlines								
Juniors	259,645	3.9	1,602	2.9	162.08	211,497	4.57	1.58
Dresses	47,829	0.7	608	1.1	78.67	33,426	0.72	0.66
Misses	512,458	7.7	3,702	6.7	138.43	429,403	9.29	1.39
Womens	170,819	2.6	1,934	3.5	88.33	148,899	3.22	0.92
Boys	184,485	2.8	2,542	4.6	72.58	144,866	3.13	0.68
Mens	751,604	11.3	3,591	6.5	209.30	603,330	13.05	2.01
Infants	204,983	3.1	1,658	3.0	123.63	142,545	3.08	1.03
Toddlers	47,829	0.7	497	0.9	96.24	43,261	0.94	1.04
Girls	191,318	2.9	2,542	4.6	75.27	157,573	3.41	0.74
Lingerie	273,311	4.1	2,431	4.4	112.43	262,548	5.68	1.29
Accessories	245,980	3.7	1,602	2.9	153.55	238,735	5.16	1.78
Jewelry	129,823	1.9	829	1.5	156.60	123,484	2.67	1.78
Total Softlines	3,020,084	45.2	23,537	42.6	128.31	2,539,566	54.92	1.29
Hardlines								
Domestics	498,792	7.5	4,531	8.2	110.08	407,745	8.82	1.08
HBA	464,628	7.0	1,989	3.6	233.60	153,153	3.31	0.92
Housewares	457,795	6.8	3,591	6.5	127.48	254,979	5.51	0.85
Cosmetics	75,160	1.1	608	1.1	123.62	55,913	1.21	1.00
Tobacco	140,187	2.1	221	0.4	634.33	37,349	0.81	2.02
Candy	144,944	2.2	387	0.7	374.53	88,179	1.91	2.72
Sporting Goods	184,485	2.8	2,652	4.8	69.56	129,948	2.81	0.59
Stationery	307,475	4.6	2,763	5.0	111.28	254,150	5.50	1.10
Furniture	75,160	1.1	1,547	2.8	48.58	60,333	1.30	0.47
Home Entertainment	601,284	9.0	2,265	4.1	265.47	255,973	5.54	1.35
Toys	300,642	4.5	2,431	4.4	123.67	143,429	3.10	0.70
Seasonal	145,333	2.2	2,652	4.8	54.80	90,168	1.95	0.41
Hardware/Paint	163,986	2.5	2,100	3.8	78.09	111,274	2.41	0.63
Pet Supplies	13,666	0.2	55	0.1	248.47	13,094	0.28	2.83
Auto Accessories	81,993	1.2	1,271	2.3	64.51	29,227	0.63	0.27
Total Hardlines	3,655,480	54.8	29,061	52.6	125.79	2,084,914	45.08	0.86
Non-Selling	—	—	2,652	4.8	—	—	—	—
Total Scores	6,675,564	100.0	55,250	100.0		4,624,480	100.00	1.00

be given more space, and hardlines (nonapparel products), with an index of .86, are under-performing and should be considered for downsizing.

Of course, as with all financial analysis, the space productivity index is simply a tool to help management make decisions, not a decision-making formula. Even though a certain category may have a low index, senior management may retain its full space because a new buyer has just been hired or because the category is an important image builder. A high-index category might not be given more space if management expects a hot fashion trend to cool off soon and believes the space productivity index for that category will drop accordingly.

SPACE ALLOCATIONS FOR A NEW STORE   When a retailer is creating a new store format, no productivity and profitability data are available on which to base the allocation of space. In these situations, the retailer bases space allocation on industry standards, previous experience with similar formats, or, more frequently, the space required to carry the number of items specified by the buyers. Recently, Kroger, for example, used information obtained from existing stores to revamp its beverage section at new locations. In its newer stores, one side of a 48-foot-long aisle was committed to bottled waters and New Age drinks—some 150 different types. At the same time Kroger reduced the space normally allocated for the traditional colas. Once a detailed assortment plan has been created, typical stock levels are estimated based on minimum and maximum quantities. The retailer can then determine the amount of shelf space required to carry this merchandise. By determining the space for each item, then for each category, then for each department, the retailer can develop the floorplan for the store. As you can imagine, optimizing a store's space is a grueling process.

Robert Kahn, the late editor of *Retailing Today,* liked to tell the story of when he was a director of and consultant to Wal-Mart. He explained to Sam Walton that one of the problems with retailers was that they thought the best ways to get higher sales per square foot (which they recognized was an important factor in store profitability, because the higher sales would reduce fixed operating expenses as a percentage of sales) were to run more ads and add more merchandise displays. Thus, retailers at the time reduced their aisle space and stacked the merchandise so high that many customers either could not reach the top or were afraid to touch the display.

Kahn, however, had his own ideas about the customer's behavior in the store and explained that there was a better formula for higher sales per square foot:

Sales per square foot $= f$ (Number of customers)

$\times$ (The length of time they spend in the store)

Therefore, according to Kahn's theory, retailers should concentrate on the time customers spend in the store, not how much merchandise they are exposed to. Based on this concept, Kahn outlined four things that Wal-Mart should do:

1. There should not be any aisle in which a customer could not comfortably pass another customer with a cart without having to ask that customer to move.
2. The restrooms should be the best in town so that a customer will never want to rush home to use the bathroom.
3. Forget the old retail adage that if a customer is sitting down, he or she isn't shopping. Put at least one bench in each store, in the alcove at the front door.
4. In all large stores put a coffee stand catty-corner from the snack bar so that customers could recharge themselves in order to spend more time and money shopping.

All four ideas seemed to agree with Sam Walton's concept that a retailer was a failure if after getting customers to come into the store, the retailer did not do everything possible to satisfy all their needs and not force them to go elsewhere for merchandise.

As an experiment, Wal-Mart built 10 new 85,000-square-foot stores and 10 new 115,000-square-foot versions. The stores had identical amounts of fixtures and merchandise. The larger stores used the extra 30,000 square feet for wider aisles, extra space at the checkouts, and tried to project an open, friendlier image. For example, the new restrooms, which were checked every two hours for cleanliness, had tile, not cement, floors; diaper changing shelves in both the men's and women's restrooms; and easy-to-clean vinyl covered walls. Also, 8 to 10 benches were placed in the main aisles. However, Wal-Mart dropped Kahn's coffee bar idea.

The first indication of the success of the larger stores was that their parking lots were always full because shoppers were spending so much more time in the stores. Sales figures showed that the larger stores not only had higher sales but were also producing higher sales per square foot of store space than the smaller stores—despite all that "wasted" aisle space. Wal-Mart did not know exactly what the customers were doing in these larger stores, just that they were spending more time and money. As a result, Wal-Mart went with the larger-store model and increased from five to six the parking spaces per 1,000 square foot of store space.

Kahn used the experience as the basis for his work in 1998 as an expert witness supporting a suit by two disabled individuals under the American with Disabilities Act (ADA). The case involved the R. H. Macy & Company, which purchased an O'Connor & Moffat store in San Francisco during the 1940s. Despite three expansions, the store still had inadequate-sized aisles. Macy's, along with the California Retailers Association, and its own expert witnesses, claimed that "It's pretty basic in retail. Inventory per square foot drives sales per square foot, which drives profit." Kahn used the Wal-Mart experience to demonstrate that a "reduction in non-aisle space permitted greater access to merchandise, which in turn leads to an increase in sales. If Macy's was correct, why did not all retailers eliminate all aisles and stack merchandise to the ceiling to maximize profit?"[8] Despite the rather general guideline of the ADA, it is important that retailers not lose sight of the fact that disabled persons represent 21 percent of the entire U.S. population. Today, profitable retailers need to understand the relationship between "the store needs and objectives and those of disabled customers."[9]

Circulation

The circulation pattern not only ensures efficient movement of large numbers of shoppers through the store, exposing them to more merchandise, but it also determines the character of the store. Disney Stores, for example, are designed not only to communicate the fun and excitement of the theme parks and famous characters but also to get customers to walk to the video wall at the back of the store. After all, chances are good that when the customers get to the video wall, they will return using a different route. This will expose them to more merchandise and increase the chance of a sale. Four basic types of layout are in use today—the free flow, grid, loop, and spine—each of which is described in the following discussion. Shoppers have been trained to associate certain circulation patterns with different types of stores, so in reading these descriptions, try to think of how they are used in different stores you shop and the store image they evoke in your mind.

Clint Eastwood's Mission Ranch in Carmel, California, was sued by a customer who claimed the facility was not fully accessible to her wheelchair.

Free-flow layout
is a type of store layout in which fixtures and merchandise are grouped into free-flowing patterns on the sales floor.

Free Flow   The simplest type of store layout is a **free-flow layout** (Exhibit 13.4), in which fixtures and merchandise are grouped into free-flowing patterns on the sales floor. Customers are encouraged to flow freely through all the fixtures, because there are usually no defined traffic patterns in the store. This type of layout works well in small stores, usually smaller than 5,000 square feet, in which customers wish to browse through all of the merchandise. Generally, all the merchandise is of the same type, such as all fashion apparel, perhaps categorized only into tops and bottoms. If there is a greater variety of merchandise (for instance, men's and women's apparel, bedding, and health and beauty aids), a free-flow layout fails to provide cues as to where one department stops and another starts, confusing the shopper.

Grid layout
is a type of store layout in which counters and fixtures are placed in long rows or "runs," usually at right angles, throughout the store.

Grid   Another traditional form of store layout is the **grid layout,** in which the counters and fixtures are placed in long rows or "runs," usually at right angles, throughout the store. In a grid layout (Exhibit 13.5), customers circulate up and down through the fixtures, and, in fact, the grid layout is often referred to as a maze. The most familiar examples of the grid layout are supermarkets and drugstores.

In stores where customers wish to browse, such as in this Disney Design Store, the free-flow layout works well.

| Exhibit 13.4 | **Free-Flow Layout** |

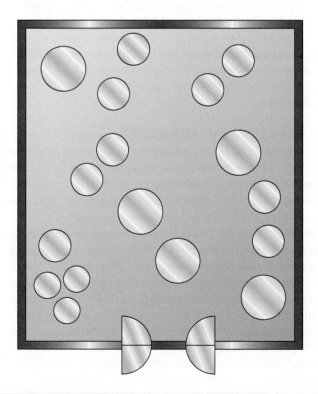

Exhibit 13.5	Grid Layout

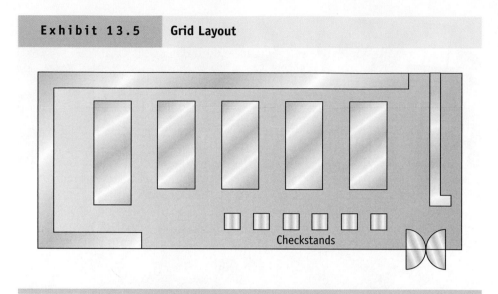

Checkstands

The grid is a true "shopping" layout, best used in retail environments in which the majority of customers wish to shop the entire store. In supermarkets, for instance, many shoppers flow methodically up and down all the fixture runs, looking for everything they might need along the way. However, if the shopper wishes to find only several specific categories, the grid can be confusing and frustrating because it is difficult to see over the fixtures to where other merchandise is located (especially today, as fixtures have become higher). For example, Service Merchandise places discounted Black & Decker power tools at the rear of the store to lure customers into purchases of high-margin jewelry located near the entrance.[10] Supermarkets move customers through the entire store by placing the meats, dairy goods, and other frequently purchased items at the rear of the store. However, the retailers must be careful, because forcing customers to do this when they do not want to may frustrate customers and lead some to go elsewhere for merchandise.

Loop layout

is a type of store layout in which a major customer aisle begins at the entrance, loops through the store — usually in the shape of a circle, square, or rectangle — and then returns the customer to the front of the store.

Loop   Over the past 15 years, the **loop layout** (sometimes called a racetrack layout) has become popular as a tool for enhancing the productivity of retail stores. A "loop," as shown in Exhibit 13.6, provides a major customer aisle, which begins at the entrance, loops through the store, usually in the shape of a circle, square, or rectangle, and then returns the customer to the front of the store. Although this seems like a simple concept, the loop can be a powerful space productivity tool.

The major benefit of the loop layout is that it exposes shoppers to the greatest possible amount of merchandise. An effective circulation pattern must first guide customers throughout the store to encourage browsing and cross-shopping. Along the way, shoppers must be able to easily see and understand merchandise to the left and right, so ideally the main aisle should never stray more than 60 feet from any merchandise. The way to simultaneously accomplish these two goals is to create a main circulation loop that mirrors the configuration of the outside walls of the store and is never more than 60 feet from the outside wall. In larger stores, the interior island of the loop can itself be too large to easily see across, and internal walls may be created to shorten sightlines to merchandise.

Exhibit 13.6	Loop Layout

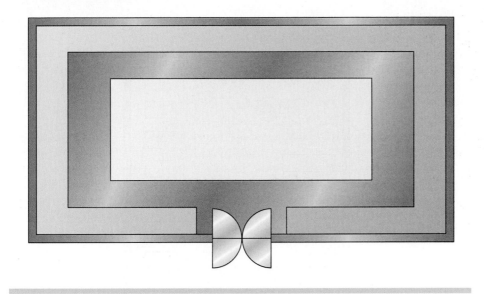

Spine   The **spine layout,** which is shown in Exhibit 13.7, is essentially a variation of the free-flow, grid, and loop layouts and combines the advantages of all three in certain circumstances. A spine layout is based on a single main aisle running from the front to the back of the store, transporting customers in both directions. On either side of this spine, merchandise departments branch off toward the back or side walls. Within these departments, either a free-flow or grid layout can be used, depending on the type of merchandise and fixtures in use. The spine is heavily used by medium-sized specialty stores, either hardlines or softlines, ranging in size from 2,000 to 10,000 square feet. Often, especially in fashion stores, the spine is subtly set off by a change in floor coloring or surface and is not perceived as an aisle, even though it functions as such.

Spine layout
is a type of store layout in which a single main aisle runs from the front to the back of the store, transporting customers in both directions, and where on either side of this spine, merchandise departments using either a free-flow or grid pattern branch off toward the back side walls.

Shrinkage Prevention

When planning a store's layout and design, the prevention of shrinkage due to theft, damage, and loss must be considered. Some layouts minimize a retailer's vulnerability to shoplifters. One of the most important considerations when planning the layout is visibility of the merchandise. Most shoplifting takes place in fitting rooms, blind spots, aisles crowded with extra merchandise, or behind high displays. Fitting rooms, one of the most common scenes of the shoplifting crime, should be placed in visible areas, which can be monitored by associates. Historically, display fixtures have been kept no higher than eye level, to allow store associates to monitor customers in other aisles. Recently, mass merchandisers have found that increased sales from the greater merchandise intensity of higher fixtures outweighs the increase in shoplifting due to reduced visibility. This depends greatly on merchandise type, however. Expensive items that are easily placed into pockets and handbags, such as compact discs, are high-theft items and are usually kept on low fixtures to discourage shoplifting. The manager's office and

Exhibit 13.7	Spine Layout

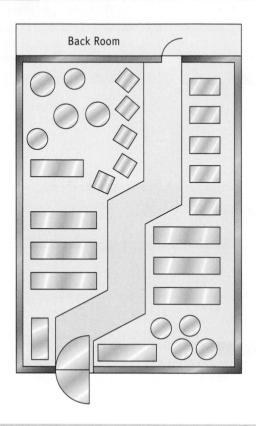

other security windows can be an excellent deterrent to shoplifting if they are placed in an obvious area above the sales floor level, where managers can easily see the entire store. Electronic security systems, including sensor tags and video cameras, have become very popular and are usually located in a highly visible location to serve as a deterrent.

Planning Fixtures and Merchandise Presentation

LO • 3

How are the various types of fixtures, merchandise presentation methods and techniques, and the psychology of merchandise presentation used to increase the productivity of the sales floor?

Retailing is theater, and in no area is that more true than in merchandise presentation. Recently retailers have been increasing their emphases on merchandise presentation, as competition has grown and stores try to squeeze more sales out of existing square footage. There are two basic types of merchandise presentation, visual merchandising and on-shelf merchandising. In thinking of retailing as "theater," as JCPenney's Questrom suggested at the beginning of the chapter, visual merchandising is analogous to the stage props that set scenes and serve as backdrops.

Merchandise presentation is a complex activity best learned on the retail floor. Although this text will not attempt to teach the art and science of merchandise presentation, you should be familiar with a number of basic components of merchandise presentation and their potential impact on store image and sales, including fixture type and selection and certain techniques and methods of on-shelf merchandising.

On-shelf merchandising, which describes the merchandise that is displayed on and in counters, racks, shelves and fixtures throughout the store, represents the stars on our theater stage. This is the merchandise that the shopper actually touches, tries on, examines, reads, understands, and hopefully buys. Therefore, on-shelf merchandising must not only present the merchandise attractively; it must display the merchandise in a manner that is easy to understand and accessible to the shopper. Further, it must be reasonably easy to maintain, with customers themselves able to replace merchandise so it is equally appealing to the next shopper. It must not be so overwhelming that the customer is afraid to touch the merchandise. As a result of getting more than 25,000 complaints a year regarding injuries from falling merchandise, Wal-Mart has sought to reduce the level of merchandise carried in every store. After all, despite the efforts of top management, many managers still falsely believe the best way to improve sales (and their year-end bonuses) is to put as much merchandise as possible into the store.

On-shelf merchandising is the display of merchandise on counters, racks, shelves, and fixtures throughout the store.

Fixture Types

Store fixtures fall into three basic categories: hardlines, softlines, and wall fixtures.

Hardlines Fixtures   The workhorse fixture in most hardlines departments is known as the gondola, so named because it is a long structure consisting of a large base, a vertical spine or wall sticking up as high as eight feet, fitted with sockets or notches into which a variety of shelves, peghooks, bins, baskets, and other hardware can be inserted. The basic gondola can hold a wide variety of merchandise by means of hardware hung from the vertical spine. If you think of your last trip to a discount store or supermarket, the long, heavy duty fixtures fitted predominantly with shelves are gondolas. In addition to the gondola a few other types of fixtures are in common use today: tables, large bins, and simple flat-base decks. These fixtures are commonly used in promotional aisles to display advertised or other special value merchandise.

Softlines Fixtures   The bulky gondola is inappropriate for fashion-oriented softlines merchandise. A large array of fixtures have been developed to accommodate the special needs of softlines, which often are hung on hangers. As shown in Exhibit 13.8, the four-way feature rack and the round rack are the two fixtures most heavily used today. These smaller, more specialized fixtures have replaced the straight rack, a long pipe with legs on each end from which rows of apparel were hung, which for generations was the most prevalent softlines fixture. Although it held a great quantity of garments and was easy to maintain, the straight rack provided few opportunities to differentiate one style or color of garment from another, which merchants have found is the key to selling more. A straight rack is like the hanger rod in your closet, and if you think of what you see when you open your closet, it is nothing more than sleeves. You know your own clothes, so sleeves are enough to tip you off to what the rest of the garment looks like. When you are shopping, however, the more of the garment you are exposed to, and the more varieties of size, silhouette (shape), and color, the more you are going to buy. So merchants prefer "face out" presentations over "sleeve out" presentations. Of course, face-outs take up more space than sleeve-outs, so it is impractical to face out all or even a high percentage of the total merchandise on the floor.

The round rack is known as a **bulk or capacity fixture** and is intended to hold the bulk of merchandise without looking as heavy as a long straight rack of merchandise.

Bulk or capacity fixture is a display fixture that is intended to hold the bulk of merchandise without looking as heavy as a long straight rack of merchandise.

Exhibit 13.8	Four-Way Feature Rack and Round Rack

Feature fixture

is a display that draws special attention to selected features (e.g., color, shape, or style) of merchandise.

Although it is smaller than the straight rack, it too allows only sleeve-outs unless fitted with special hardware. The four-way rack, on the other hand, is considered a **feature fixture,** because it presents merchandise in a manner that features certain characteristics of the merchandise (such as color, shape, or style). The ingenious design also allows it to hold a large quantity of merchandise on the hanger arms behind the four face-outs. However, to be easily shopped, all the merchandise on one arm must be the same type of garment with variations only in color and size. When poorly merchandised so that the front garment does not match those behind it, the four-way leaves the customer in the same quandary as the straight rack.

Wall Fixtures   The last type of fixtures are those designed to be hung on the wall. To make a store's plain wall merchandisable, it is usually covered with a vertical skin that is fitted with vertical columns of notches, similar to those on the gondola, into which a variety of hardware can be inserted. Shelves, peghooks, bins, baskets, and even hanger bars can be fitted into wall systems. Hanger bars can be hung parallel to the wall, much like your closet bar, so that large quantities of garments can be "sleeved out," or they can protrude perpendicularly from the wall, either straight out (straight-outs) or angled down (waterfalls), to allow merchandise to be faced out. The primary quality to remember about wall systems is that walls can generally be merchandised much higher than floor fixtures. Whereas on the floor, round racks are kept to a maximum of 42 inches so that customers can easily see over them to other merchandise, garments can be hung on the wall as high as customers can reach, which is generally

Blockbuster Video displays new releases along the wall from virtually bottom to ceiling. This clearly communicates that Blockbuster Video emphasizes new releases, which incidentally, rent for a premium.

about 72 inches. This allows walls to be "double hung" with two rows of garments, or even "triple hung" with smaller children's apparel. Therefore, walls not only hold large amounts of merchandise, but also serve as a visual backdrop for the department.

Merchandise Presentation Planning

As we have just discussed, retailers use a large array of fixtures and hardware. This may seem to present an endless variety of ways to merchandise product, but there are essentially six methods of merchandise presentation:

1. *Shelving.* The majority of merchandise is placed on shelves that are inserted into gondolas or wall systems. Shelving is a flexible, easy-to-maintain merchandise presentation method.
2. *Hanging.* Apparel on hangers can be hung from softlines fixtures, such as round racks and four-way racks, or from bars installed on gondolas or wall systems.
3. *Pegging.* Small merchandise can be hung from peghooks, which are small rods inserted into gondolas or wall systems. Used in both softlines and hardlines, pegging gives a neat, orderly appearance, but can be labor intensive to display and maintain.
4. *Folding.* Higher-margin or large, unwieldy softlines merchandise can be folded and then stacked onto shelves or placed on tables. This can create a high-fashion image, such as when bath towels are taken off peghooks and neatly folded and stacked high up the wall.
5. *Stacking.* Large hardline merchandise can be stacked on shelves, the base decks of gondolas, or "flats," which are platforms placed directly on the floor. Stacking is easily maintained and gives an image of high volume and low price.

6. *Dumping.* As discussed in the Retailing :The Inside Story box earlier in the chapter, large quantities of small merchandise can be dumped in bins or baskets inserted into gondolas or wall systems. This highly effective promotional method can be used in softlines (socks, wash cloths) or hardlines (batteries, grocery products, candy), and creates a high-volume, low-cost image.

The method of merchandise presentation can have a dramatic impact on image and space productivity. Different merchandise presentation methods have been shown to strongly influence buying habits and stimulate consumers to purchase more. There is a certain "psychology of merchandise presentation," which must be carefully considered in developing merchandise presentation schemes. Less than 20 percent of store shoppers make an impulse (unplanned) purchase, and these purchases are made by only 60 percent of the shoppers who actually entered the store with an intent to make a specific purchase. Thus, 40 percent of the shoppers who enter a store to make a purchase are "wasted" because of a failure by the store to use merchandise presentation to generate additional purchases.[11] This is why department store design incorporates a gauntlet of goodies to stimulate impulse buys. For example, cosmetics, usually the store's most profitable department, is always near the main entrance. Typically, the department is leased to cosmetic companies who use their own salespeople to sell the perfume, lipstick, and eye shadow. The other high-impulse items (e.g., hosiery, jewelry, handbags, and shoes) are usually nearby while the "demand" products (e.g., furniture) are on upper floors. After all, these stores would be unprofitable if they failed to induce a significant amount of impulse buying.

Many consumers believe that most innovations of modern retailing began in the United States. This, however, is not the case. The first retail chain can be traced back to 1672 in Japan. Today, the House of Mitsui is the sixth largest company in *Fortune* Magazine's Global 500. The chapter's Global Retailing box traces the development of the department store almost 40 years before Sears entered the mail-order business and more than 60 years before Sears became a chain store operator.[12]

The following are a number of key psychological factors to consider when merchandising stores:

1. *Value/fashion image.* One of merchandise presentation's most important psychological effects is to foster an image in the customer's mind of how trendy, exclusive, pricey, or value oriented the merchandise is. For each of the merchandise presentation methods mentioned previously, we discussed its effect on price image. By changing the merchandise presentation method, we can change the perception of our towel display from common, high-volume, high-value to an exclusive selection of high-fashion merchandise, which presumably will be at higher prices.

2. *Angles and sightlines.* Research has shown that as customers move through a retail store, they view the store at approximately 45-degree angles from the path of travel, as shown in Exhibit 13.9, rather than perpendicular to their path. Although this seems logical, most stores are set up at right angles because it is easier and consumes less space. Therefore, merchandise and signage often wind up being at a 90-degree angle to the main aisle. Exhibit 13.9 also shows how four-way feature racks can be more effectively merchandised by being turned to meet the shoppers' sightlines head on.

3. *Vertical color blocking.* To be most effective, merchandise should be displayed in vertical bands of color wherever possible. As customers move through the store,

Global Retailing

The World's First Department Store: Boucicaut's Bon Marche

In 1852, Aristide Boucicaut and a partner started a small shop in Paris selling fabric. Boucicaut began to experiment with all kinds of new ideas. His partner became concerned with all of Boucicaut's wild ideas and sold his share back to Boucicaut stating, "I prefer to leave you to continue your experiments alone." By 1863, Boucicaut had "invented" the department store. He called it Bon Marche, which translates to "Good Market." Before that time much fabric, general merchandise, and food was sold by peddlers and in small specialty shops. The markups in Bon Marche were lower, but its volume was higher. He stopped the time-honored practice of haggling over price. The price was fixed. (It would be another two decades before the "one price only" policy was adopted in the United States by Sacramento merchant David Lubin.) There was no obligation to buy. You could come and look. He also began the practice of full refunds. Boucicaut also learned the art of delegation. He simply could not be in all the departments of his store.

What Boucicaut developed, worked; it was a miracle. Sales the first year were half a million francs; by 1860, they were 5 million francs. Just 18 years after he started, in 1870, Bon Marche's sales were 20 million francs. Copies of this phenomenon were fast to develop in Europe and the United States. A. T. Stewart in New York City was the first American department store founded in 1862. The first English department store was Whitely's, which though founded in 1823 was only converted to a true department store in 1871.

The department store became a fact of life in Europe and North America. Technology played a vital role in the success of the department store. The printing shops had just become automated. Now, more than just a few copies of a newspaper could be printed for daily circulation. Street railways had been developed so that people could travel longer distances to shop. Then, the electric light improved the illumination of interior spaces. The use of second and higher floors was made possible through another new gadget, the elevator. The combination of the entrepreneurial genius and a flood of technical developments made for a revolutionary success. After all, electricity was as revolutionary in those days as the computer is today.

Source: Michael J. O'Connor, "Global Marketing: A Retail Perspective," *International Trends in Retailing*, December 1998: 22. Quoted with the written permission of Arthur Andersen, the publisher. Additional information was obtained from the Robert Kahn Collection of Retailing History, University of Oklahoma.

their eyes naturally view a "swath" approximately two feet in height, parallel to the floor, at about eye level. This is shown in Exhibit 13.10. This visual swath of merchandise will be viewed as a rainbow of colors if each merchandise item is displayed vertically by color (i.e., the vertical columns represent different colors and within these colors could be different sizes). This method of merchandise presentation will create such a strong visual effect that shoppers will be exposed to more merchandise and this in turn will increase sales. In addition, when shopping for clothing, customers most often think first of color. Thus, they can easily find the column of color on display and locate their size.

Selecting Fixtures and Merchandise Presentation Methods[13]

Proper fixtures emphasize the key selling attributes of merchandise while not being overpowering. Although it is not always possible to follow, a good guideline for selecting fixtures is to *match the fixture to the merchandise, not the merchandise to the fixture.*

Exhibit 13.9	45-Degree Customer Sightline

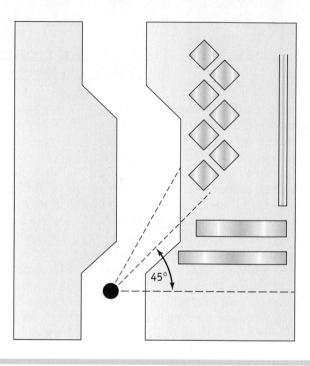

This means you should only use fixtures that are sensitive to the nature of the merchandise, but all too often, retailers are forced to put merchandise on the wrong fixture.

Consider intimate apparel, for instance. This is a fast-selling, high-margin merchandise category that can enhance a retailer's image in fashion merchandising. Though retailers entering into this business might be tempted to place intimate apparel on existing shelves of a gondola, they would be well served to consider special fixtures to enhance the delicate qualities of intimate apparel. In fact, the large, metal, bulky appearance of the gondola will overpower the small, delicate intimate apparel and therefore reduce sales potential. More delicate fixtures made of softer materials will enhance sales. Similarly, it would not make sense to bulk stack fragile merchandise, because the weight of items might damage those lower in the stack. It would not make sense to peghook large, bulky items, because they take up too much room and might be too heavy for the peghook.

Visual Merchandising

Visual merchandising is the artistic display of merchandise and theatrical props used as scene-setting decoration in the store.

The second type of merchandise presentation, **visual merchandising,** is the artistic display of merchandise and theatrical props used as scene-setting decoration in the store. Although on-shelf merchandising must be tastefully displayed to encourage shopping, a store with just on-shelf merchandising would be boring. In fact, many low-price stores contain little visual merchandising, and indeed they do appear more boring than

Exhibit 13.10　　**Vertical Color Blocking**

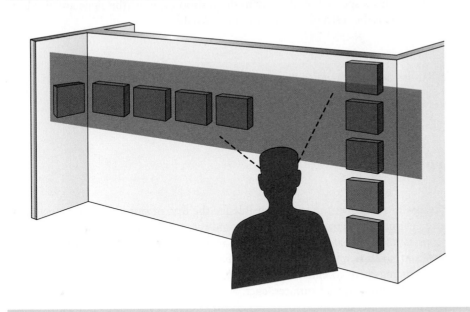

their upscale cousins in fashion retailing, which concentrate heavily on visual merchandising displays, or "visuals" as they are often called.

An effective visual merchandising display has several key characteristics. Visual displays are not typically associated with a shopable fixture, but are located in a focal point, feature area, or other area remote from the on-shelf merchandising and perhaps even out of the customer's reach. Its goal is to create a feeling in the store conducive to buying merchandise.

Another characteristic of visual merchandising is its use of props and elements in addition to merchandise. In fact, visuals do not always include merchandise—they may just be interesting displays of items somehow related to the merchandise offering or to a mood the retailer wishes to create. It may be a wooden barrel, a miniature airplane, or a mock tree with autumn leaves. Visuals are like the illustrations and design elements in a book that make it interesting and tell you whether this is an upscale, serious shopping experience, a frivolous, fun shopping experience, or a down and dirty, low-price shopping experience.

To be most effective, however, visuals should incorporate relevant merchandise. In apparel retailing, mannequins or figure forms are used to display merchandise as it might appear on a person, rather than hanging limply on a hanger. This helps the shopper visualize how these garments will enhance her or his appearance. Good fashion visuals include more than just one garment, to show how tops and bottoms go together and how belts, scarves, and other accessories can be combined to create an overall fashion look. This is called accessorization. When successful, visuals help the shopper translate the merchandise presentation from "garments on a rack" to "fashionable clothes that will look good on me."

The retailer should be careful in setting visuals to make sure that the displays do not create walls that make it difficult for shoppers to reach other areas of the store. In addition, the retailer should give careful consideration to the placement of such signs. A very popular fast-food restaurant recently changed its sign placement. It originally had the signs for its specials on the way to the restrooms. Now the signs are visible as the customers exit the restrooms and are more relaxed.[14]

Managerial Question: How do fixtures and merchandise presentation interact to influence consumers in different types of retailers?

<table>
<tr><td>

LO • 4

Why is store design so important to a store's success?

</td></tr>
</table>

Store Design

Store design is the element most responsible for the first of our two goals in planning the store environment: creating a distinctive and memorable store image. Store design encompasses both the exterior and the interior of the store. On the exterior, we have the storefront, signage, and entrance, all of which are critical to attracting passing shoppers and enticing them to enter. On the inside, store design includes the architectural elements and finishes on all surfaces, such as wall coverings, floor coverings, and the ceiling. There are literally hundreds of details in a store's design, and all must work together to create the desired store ambiance, which is the overall feeling or mood projected by a store through its aesthetic appeal to human senses.

Ambiance
is the overall felling or mood projected by a store through its aesthetic appeal to human senses.

Storefront Design

If the retail store can be compared to a book, then the storefront, or store exterior, is like the book cover. It must be noticeable, easily identified by passing motorists or mall shoppers, and memorable. The storefront must clearly identify the name and general nature of the store and give some hint as to the merchandise inside. Generally, the storefront design includes all exterior signage and the architecture of the storefront itself. In many cases, the storefront includes display windows, which serve as an advertising medium for the store. Store windows must catch the attention of passing shoppers, enticing them inside the store. Therefore, windows should be maintained in exciting visual displays that are changed frequently, are fun and exciting, and reflect the merchandise offered inside.

Interior Design

Unless you have ever been responsible for redecorating a house or room, you may be unaware of the dozens of design elements that go into a physical space. We can break interior design into two types of elements: the finishes applied to surfaces and architectural shapes. Think of all the elements from the floor to the ceiling. First, we have some type of floor covering placed over either a concrete or wood floor—at the least paint, but more frequently vinyl floor covering, carpet, ceramic tile, or marble. Each of these surfaces leaves a different impression on the shopper. An unpainted concrete floor conveys a low-cost, no-frills environment. Vinyl floor covering makes another statement, which, depending on its quality, sheen, color, and design pattern, can vary from very downscale to very upscale. Carpet suggests a homelike atmosphere conducive to selling apparel. Ceramic tile and especially marble suggest an upscale, exclusive, and probably expensive shopping experience.

Retailers even have more options for covering the walls, from paint and wallpaper to hundreds of types of paneling. The ceiling must also receive a design treatment, whether it is finished drywall (a very upscale image because it is expensive to do), a suspended ceiling (very common and economical, though not distinctive), or perhaps even an open ceiling with all the pipes and wires above painted black (which suggests a low-price warehouse approach). Then, there are thousands of types of moldings that can be applied to the transitions from floor to wall to ceiling and hundreds of architectural design elements that can be incorporated.

Lighting Design

Another important, though often overlooked, element in a successful store design is lighting. Retailers have come to understand how lighting can greatly enhance store sales. One of the keys to success for Blockbuster Video was its move away from the 100-watt bulbs that its competitors used to brighter lights. Department stores, on the other hand, have found that raising lighting levels in fashion departments can actually discourage sales, because bright lighting suggests a discount store image. Brighter in-store lighting also influences shoppers to examine and handle more merchandise in a wine store.

Lighting design, however, is not limited to simple light levels. Contemporary lighting design requires an in-depth knowledge of electrical engineering and the effect of light on color and texture. Not only have retailers learned that different types and levels of lighting can have a significant impact on sales (for example, less lighting implies elegance);[15] in addition, the types of light sources available have multiplied quickly. Today, there are literally hundreds of light fixtures and lamps (bulbs) from which to choose.

Many retailers, probably because of the increasing risk of accidents or lawsuits, are actually using too much outdoor lighting today. Lighting is measured in foot-candles. One foot-candle is a unit of illuminant equal to one lumen per square foot. Research has found that customers in urban areas feel safest in parking lots lighted by five foot-candles, whereas those in suburban parking lots prefer three foot-candles. (By comparison, one foot-candle lights most roadways and full moonlight is 1/100th of one foot-candle.) However, most businesses, especially gas stations, restaurants, and convenience stores, are now lighting at 100 to 150 foot-candle levels. This not only substantially increases costs but causes "light pollution" for the neighborhood.[16]

Sounds and Smells: Total Sensory Marketing

Effective store design appeals to all human senses of sight, sound, smell, and touch. Obviously, the majority of design activity in a retail store is focused on affecting sight. For example, have you ever gone into a Wal-Mart store and had the greeter say "Hello" to you? Sam Walton's wife, Helen, suggested the idea of the greeter as a way to put customers in a better mood and to convey a feeling of warmth toward the retailer. However, Sam Walton soon came to realize another benefit of the greeter, it slowed the customer down as they entered the store. The first 20 feet inside a store is a decompression chamber for customers as they adjust to the different lighting and climate of the store. Not only did the sight of the greeter allow Wal-Mart to convey a positive message, but as the customer slowed down to return the greeting more merchandise was noticeable at the front of the store. Research has shown that the other senses can be important too, and many retailers are beginning to engineer the smells and sounds in their stores.

Despite some recent academic research to the contrary,[17] smell is believed to be the most closely linked of all the senses for memory and emotions. Retailers hope that its use as a key in-store marketing tool will put consumers in the "mood." Victoria's Secret has deployed potpourri caches throughout its store, and in fact now sells them, to create the ambiance of a lingerie closet. The Walt Disney Company uses the smell of fresh baked cookies on Main Street in the Magic Kingdom to relax customers and provide a feeling of warmth. The Knot Shop, a men's tie store catering to female shoppers buying ties as gifts, employs scent tiles impregnated with leather and tobacco scents to create the ambiance of a men's store, with the goal of making female customers feel that this is the type of store in which their male friend or spouse would buy his own tie.

Retailers have piped music (e.g., Muzak) into their stores for generations, believing that a musical backdrop will create a more relaxing environment and encourage customers to stay longer.[18] Increasingly, music is being perceived as a valuable marketing tool, because the right music can create an environment that is both soothing and reflective of the merchandise being offered. For example, a jeans retailer might play hip-hop over baggies and classic rock over the Dockers. Researchers believe that while the tempo of music affects how long shoppers stay in a store, the type of music may be just as influential on how much they purchase.[19] For instance, although classical music is soothing and has been shown to encourage customers to shop longer[20] and select more expensive merchandise,[21] it may be inconsistent with the desired ambiance of a trendy fashion store catering to college-age women. Today, some retailers are experimenting with placing advertisements in with the background music. Other retailers have found a different use for this canned music. A shopping mall in Australia plays Bing Crosby music to drive out the kids who want to hang out there after school. In addition, the mall uses pink fluorescent lights, which supposedly highlight pimples. The NSW train service in Australia uses canned music at stops in high-crime areas to keep the undesirable element away.[22]

Profitable retailers employ exterior designs that pull shoppers into the store and interior designs that stimulate sales.

Visual Communications

LO • 5

What is the role of visual communications in a retail store?

The previous chapter was devoted to the retail selling process. However, sales associates cannot always be available to assist customers, particularly in this era of increased competitive pressure and reduced gross margins, which has caused many retailers to cut costs by reducing their sales staffs. Even department stores, which staked their reputations on high levels of personal customer service, have had to reduce their service levels and learn to rely on alternative service strategies. How then can retailers provide good selling communications and high customer service while controlling labor costs?

The answer is visual communications in the form of in-store signage and graphics. Retailers can plan the store environment to incorporate signs, large photopanels, and other visual devices that serve as silent salespersons, providing shoppers with much needed information and directions on how to shop the store, evaluate merchandise, and make purchases. Because these visual communications are inanimate objects that stay permanently in place, they require only a one-time installation cost, low maintenance, and can always be relied on to perform their function, the same way, for every shopper. Unlike sales associates, visual communications are never late for work, are never in a bad mood, and never mistreat customers. Of course, neither are they as effective as a good sales associate, who provides the personal touch that makes customers feel welcome and comfortable. But when carefully balanced with personal service, visual communications, with their reliability and low cost, can create an effective selling environment and are therefore becoming an important tool in the store designer's toolbox.

Earlier, we likened a retail store to a well-written book. Visual communications are akin to the headlines, subheads, illustrations, and captions that give the reader direction and illustrate the written descriptions. Without visual communications, a store would be like a newspaper full of words but no headlines, a jumbled, incomprehensible mess of merchandise. An effective visual communications program includes a range of messages, from those large and bold in nature, used sparingly to provide cues to the gross organization of the space, to the smaller, more specific and plentiful messages that describe actual merchandise. A visual communications program includes the following important elements.

Name, Logo, and Retail Identity

The first and most visible element in a comprehensive visual communications program is the retailer's identity, composed of the store name, logo, and supporting visual elements. The name and logo are seen not only on the storefront and throughout the store, but also in advertising and all communications with the consumers, and therefore they must be catchy, memorable, and, most of all, reflect the retailer's merchandising mission. Historically, many retail companies have taken the name of their founders, as is the case with most department stores. That practice has fallen out of vogue, however, as retailing has become a game of crafty store images and catchy retail identities. A founder's name rarely captures the merchandising spirit of a company as well as names such as Bath & Body Works, Home Depot, and Toys "R" Us. With advertising messages bombarding customers more than ever and the effectiveness of each message waning, retailers have found it necessary for their names to be highly distinctive, as well as descriptive of their unique offerings.

Once a name has been chosen, a logo is developed to visually portray the name in a creative and memorable manner. Again, the key is to keep the logo simple and easy to understand at a glance, while making it exciting enough to leave a lasting image in the customers' minds. The logo is often accompanied by taglines that provide more description of the store concept, such as "Fashions for the Home." Kmart, for example, changed its logo to the big red "K" in an effort to reflect its move into an upscale environment and away from its old polyester and blue-light image.

The logo's most prominent placement is on the outside of the store. This is critical to attracting customers and creating high store traffic. Another reason why the store

Kmart, by redesigning its logo and store signage, created a more contemporary look.

name and logo should be succinct and descriptive is because this important role is often played to motorists passing by at 45 miles per hour.

Institutional Signage

Once inside the store, the first level of visual communications is known as institutional signage, or signage that describes the merchandising mission, customer service policies, and other messages on behalf of the retail institution. This signage is usually located at the store entrance to properly greet entering customers and at service points such as the service desk, layaway window, and cash registers. In addition, some retailers place institutional signage throughout the store, to reinforce special policies such as customer service several times during the shopping trip. This signage might include messages such as "Lowest Price Guaranteed" or "All Major Credit Cards Accepted."

Directional and departmental signage are large signs that are usually placed fairly high, so they can be seen throughout the store.

Category signage are smaller than directional and departmental signage and are intended to be seen from a shorter distance; they are located on or close to the fixture itself where the merchandise is displayed.

Directional, Departmental, and Category Signage

Directional and departmental signage serve as the highest level of organization in an overall signage program. These signs are usually large and placed fairly high, so they can be seen throughout the store. They help guide the shopper through the shopping trip and locate specific departments of interest. Not all stores use directional signage, particularly smaller store environments where it is not necessary, but virtually all stores larger than 10,000 square feet in size use some type of departmental signage. Once a shopper locates and moves close to a particular department, category signage is used to call out and locate specific merchandise categories. **Category signage** is usually smaller in size, because it is intended to be seen from a shorter distance and is located on or close to the fixture itself. For instance, the departmental sign might say "Sporting Goods" and be two feet high, six feet wide, and hang from the ceiling. On the other

Note how this customer service sign is in very large letters and placed high so it can be seen from many areas of the store.

hand, category signage might be only six inches high and two feet wide, affixed to the top of the gondola, and read "Hunting," "Tennis," or "Fitness."

Point-of-Sale (POS) Signage

The next level of signage is even smaller, placed closer to the merchandise, and known as **point-of-sale signage,** or POS signage. Because POS signage is intended to give details about specific merchandise items, it usually contains more words and is affixed directly to fixtures. POS signage may range in size from 11 by 17 inches to a 3-by-5-inch card with very small words describing an item. Always, however, the most important function of POS signage is to clearly state the price of the merchandise being signed.

POS signage includes a set of sign holders used throughout the store, along with a variety of printed signs that can be inserted into the hardware. Store associates mix and match the signage and hardware as directed by management, so that POS signage changes frequently. Special POS signs for sales, clearance, and "as advertised" specials are often a different color than the normal price signage to highlight these special values.

Point-of-sale signage is relatively small signage that is place very close to the merchandise and is intended to give details about specific items.

Lifestyle Graphics

Visual communications encompass more than just words. Many stores incorporate large graphics panels showing so-called lifestyle images in important departments. These photo images portray either the merchandise, often as it is being used, or simply images of related items or models that convey an image conducive to buying the product. In a high-fashion department, lifestyle photography might show a scene of movie stars arriving at a nightclub in very trendy fashions, suggesting that similar fashions are available in that department. In sporting goods, a lifestyle image might show an isolated lake surrounded by autumn colored trees, with mist rising off the water and the sun rising in the background.

Retailers must be careful when choosing lifestyle photography, for as the saying goes, "beauty is in the eye of the beholder." One person's lifestyle is not necessarily another's, so lifestyle photography must be kept general in nature so as to be attractive to the majority and offensive to none. Increasingly, photopanels and lifestyle imagery, which can be expensive to create, are being provided free of charge to retailers by merchandise vendors who are looking to gain an advantage for their products on the retail floor.

Retailers can use visual communications, such as institutional signage, directional and departmental signage, category and POS signage, and lifestyle graphics, to communicate more effectively with shoppers and increase space productivity.

Student Study Guide

Summary

LO•1 What are the elements of a store's environment?

In this chapter, we focused on the retail store, a key factor influencing the consumer's initial perception of the retailer. It must effectively convey the image desired by the retailer and provide a shopping environment that is conducive to high sales. The guiding principle in effective store planning, merchandise presentation, and design is that the more merchandise customers are exposed to, the more they tend to buy. This depends largely on planning the name, logo, and visual appearance of the store to convey a desired market positioning image. Although retailers work diligently to influence their images, true store image is an amalgam of all the messages consumers receive, from advertising, to stories they hear from friends, to the store itself.

LO•2 What is involved in store planning?

Store planning refers to developing a plan for the organization of the retail store. First, the retailer must decide how to allocate the available square footage among the various types of space needed. This is usually accomplished by conducting a mathematical analysis of the productivity of various merchandise categories. By comparing the sales or gross margin produced by various categories with the space they use, the retailer can develop a plan for the optimal allocation of available space. Next the floorplan is created, showing the placement and circulation patterns of all merchandise departments. Finally, thought must be given as to how the floorplan can aid in reducing shrinkage.

LO•3 How are the various types of fixtures, merchandise presentation methods and techniques, and the psychology of merchandise presentation used to increase the productivity of the sales floor?

Fixture selection and merchandise presentation are critical to exposing customers to the maximum amount of merchandise. There are many types of store fixtures, as well as specific methods of merchandise presentation, which have been shown to maximize merchandise exposure and lead to increased sales. Particularly, there is a psychology of merchandise presentation, which utilizes customer's natural shopping behaviors and adopts merchandise presentation to match them. In addition to maximizing sales, fixture selection and merchandise presentation must conform to operational constraints and be easy to maintain.

LO•4 Why is store design so important to a store's success?

The most visible element of the store is the design of its storefront and interior decor. The storefront or exterior must be eye-catching, inviting, and reflective of the merchandise offered inside. The interior design must be comfortable, put the shopper in the proper buying mood, and provide a backdrop that enhances but does not overpower the merchandise. The store designer must always remember that shoppers are there to look at the merchandise, not to admire the store design.

LO•5 What is the role of visual communications in a retail store?

A successful selling environment is based on effective visual communications with the retailer's customers. Because shoppers require information even when sales associates are not available, visual communications must be used throughout the store to provide direction, specific information, and prices. A visual communications program begins with the store name and logo and includes a range of interior signage that walks the customer through the buying experience.

Finally, literally hundreds of details are applied in a successful retail store, and all must be carefully coordinated to create a cohesive, targeted store image that reflects the retailer's mission.

Terms to Remember

store image	on-shelf merchandising
space productivity	bulk or capacity fixture
shrinkage	feature fixture
floorplan	visual merchandising
space productivity index	ambiance
free-flow layout	directional and departmental signage
grid layout	category signage
loop layout	point-of-sale signage
spine layout	

Review and Discussion Questions

LO•1 What are the elements of the a store's environment?

1. Discuss the two primary objectives of the store environment and how these are achieved.

2. Discuss some of the constraints retailers face when trying to change their market position.

3. What is merchandise presentation and how does it impact sales?

4. What is the simple but powerful truism in retailing that store planners can use as a guide to increasing the space productivity of a store environment? Does this truism also hold for e-tailers? Why? or why not?

5. Why are retailers focusing increasingly on in-store marketing? Discuss some in-store marketing strategies and their effect on customers.

LO•2 What is involved in store planning?

6. What lessons can store planners draw from an effectively written book?

7. Discuss the various types of space in a retail store, describing the role of each.

8. Describe the space allocation planning process. How is this different for a new store as opposed to an existing store?

9. Identify the four main types of store layouts, discussing their differences and impact on customers.

LO•3 How are the various types of fixtures, merchandise presentation methods and techniques, and the psychology of merchandise presentation used to increase the productivity of the sales floor?

10. In the theater of retailing, discuss the differences between the "props and visual backdrops" and the "stars."

11. Discuss the different uses of bulk or capacity fixtures and feature fixtures.

12. If retail space is such a scarce resource, why shouldn't an apparel retailer always use the "sleeved out" approach so as to stock more merchandise in the limited available space?

13. What is the psychology of merchandise presentation and how is it used? Can it be used by e-tailers?

LO•4   Why is store design so important to a store's success?

14. What are the goals of interior and exterior design?

15. Why is lighting design important to store planners?

16. Can sounds and smell influence store performance?

LO•5   What is the role of visual communications in a retail store?

17. What are the goals of visual communications?

18. How are the different types of visual communications used and what is their effect on customers?

19. Why isn't the founder's name a good choice for the name of a retail store?

Sample Test Questions

LO•1   The two primary objectives of the store environment are

a. effective sales management and creating a distinctive ambiance
b. creating the store image and increasing space productivity
c. creative merchandise presentation and effective store traffic control
d. maximizing impulse purchase opportunity and effective shelf space allocation
e. maintaining market share and effective merchandise control

LO•2   The goal of store layout and design in store planning should be to

a. maximize customer access to high-profit items
b. evenly divide floor space between the five functional areas of a retail store
c. make the store easy to understand and shop and allow the merchandise to be effectively presented
d. allow for the rapid restocking of valuable shelf space in low-turnover merchandise categories
e. design a store that maximizes back room stock capacity

LO•3   The psychology of merchandise presentation refers to the fact that

a. different merchandising methods can strongly influence the store's image and its sales
b. psychologists should always be hired as merchandisers
c. merchandise presentation teaches consumers how to shop effectively
d. social factors strongly influence shopping behavior
e. shoppers can be classified according to psychological tests

LO•4   Store design does all but which of the following:

a. it is responsible for creating a distinctive and memorable store image
b. it maximizes sales transactions per customer visit
c. it includes the architectural elements and finishes on all surfaces
d. it seeks to attract passing shoppers and entice them to enter the store
e. it encompasses the store's exterior and interior

LO•5   **Which of the following is not part of a visual communications program?**

a. store name and logo
b. institutional signage
c. directional and category signage
d. lifestyle graphics
e. television advertising

Applications

Writing and Speaking Exercise   You have just been made the new assistant manager of Value Sports Center. One of your first duties at this all-sports equipment retailer is to help the manager design the prototype for the new megasized store that you will be moving to next year. Your job is to prepare a memo stating what type of circulation flow the store should use, where the various departments should be located in the box-shaped building of 35,000 square feet, and what can be done to reduce shrinkage. Be sure to include in your memo how the layout might change as the calendar changes.

Retail Project   Let's look more closely at some of the attributes that often influence supermarket choice decisions. Nine frequently cited attributes are the following:

1. Competitive prices

2. Choice of national versus private labels

3. Physical characteristics (including decor, layout, and floor space)

4. Fast checkouts

5. Produce quality

6. Convenience (including hours, location, ease of entrance and parking, ease of finding items)

7. Services (including credit, delivery, return policy, and guarantees)

8. Store personnel (including helpfulness, friendliness, and courtesy)

9. Advertised specials in stock

For your assignment you are to rank these attributes in order of importance to you. After ranking them, take the most important attribute and assign it the value of 10, take the second most important attribute and assign it the value of 9. Continue to do this for your top five attributes with your fifth attribute getting a value of 6.

Now visit two supermarkets or supercenters and assign a value (1 being very poor, 10 being very good) to the stores' performance on your five attributes. Next multiply your rank value by their performance value for each attribute and sum the total. Is the store with the highest total points your favorite? If there is a difference, why?

If you were planning to shop on the Internet, what "store" attributes would be the most important to you for clothing?

Case   The Image Shoppe

The Image Shoppe is housed in a vast warehouse-type building. Adjacent to the store is a large suburban mall that is the home of three full-service department stores, a large discount store, and an array of specialty and shoe stores. The Image Shoppe primarily features merchandise for young adults, from middle income families, and targets consumers in that age bracket, along with their parents.

Six months ago Lori Greenly bought The Image Shoppe from John Meyers. Meyers had organized and operated the store in a very haphazard manner. As merchandise arrived, he or other employees simply placed the goods wherever space was available, which led to the dissolution of distinct departments or areas. There is little or no storage space in the building, so Meyers usually placed all stock on the selling floor, even if it meant stacking merchandise to the ceiling or putting goods on the top of shelves or other fixtures.

The display fixtures being used currently had been collected over the years, usually bought from defunct retail operations or discount suppliers. Posters, banners, and sports memorabilia hang throughout the store in attempts to make the young shoppers feel at ease. Meyers had usually piped the local Top 40 radio station through the store's intercom system.

After several months of observation, Greenly believes some drastic changes must take place. She sees The Image Shoppe as having become, unintentionally, a discount department store. The image and atmosphere projected by the layout, displays, and merchandise do not sufficiently attract the desired clientele. Greenly does not feel that The Image Shoppe conjures up the picture of up-to-date fashions and current trends in apparel in the minds of the local high school or college students. Actually, a greater percentage of the sales are accounted for by lower-income adults.

Greenly has found through research that three of the specialty stores in the mall have increased their sales by over 25 percent in the past year, whereas sales at The Image Shoppe have decreased by at least that much. In addition, one of the full-service department stores has launched a complete promotional campaign and merchandising strategy designed to attract members of The Image Shoppe's desired target market.

In addition to decreasing sales and the declining "quality" of the customers, The Image Shoppe also suffers from a high shrinkage rate due to shoplifting. During the time that Greenly has been at the helm, the percentage of merchandise shoplifted in terms of sales has increased by 2 percent each month. With the store's current setup, it is difficult to police all possible areas that may be vulnerable to theft, all of the time. The stereo and jewelry sections have been hardest hit. Most of those items are displayed in a self-service style for the convenience of the customers.

Greenly is firm in her belief that The Image Shoppe should attempt to reestablish itself as a local leader in current fashions, target young adults from the middle-income bracket, and continue to operate as a junior department store. Her vision is that The Image Shoppe will become the area's department store version of The Limited or The Gap.

1. What other elements of the retail mix will Lori Greenly want to consider in her attempts to create the appropriate image for The Image Shoppe? Give examples of how selling space layout decisions and decisions concerning other elements of the retail mix might interact.

2. Detail a layout that would help Greenly achieve her goals. Include descriptions of types of fixtures to be used, space allocations, and so on.

3. What actions could Greenly take when designing a revamped layout to decrease the amount of shoplifting activity that takes place within The Image Shoppe?

Planning Your Own Retail Business   After graduation from college, you opened a swimwear store on South Padre Island. You called your store the Zig Zag. The building you located is 400 square feet and had been vacant for 18 months. Because of the limited amount of start-up capital you had to invest in the business, you moved into the building without remodeling either its exterior or interior.

During the first year, the Zig Zag had 13,400 visitors of which 3,350 made a purchase. The average transaction size was $38. The Zig Zag operates on a gross margin of 55 percent and has annual fixed operating expenses of $30,000. Variable costs were 15 percent of sales. The two primary fixed expenses are rent of $1,100 a month and salaries of $1,200 a month. You keep all profits in the business to reinvest in inventory and other immediate business needs.

Because your first year was profitable, you are now considering remodeling the store. Your landlord will not help with these expenses. To paint the exterior would cost $1,400. With regards to the interior, you are thinking of tiling the floor in a zigzag pattern, which will cost $1,600. In addition, new lighting and some new fixtures would cost $4,000.

You believe these changes will increase traffic by 10 percent and that your closure or conversation rate will increase to 30 percent. Will your proposed changes pay for themselves the first year?

Endnotes

1. The authors want to acknowledge the assistance of Randall E. Gebhardt, our coauthor on *Retail Marketing*, for his early input into this chapter.

2. Stanley Marcus in a speech to the Spring ACRA Meeting, Dallas, TX, April 17, 1993.

3. Haim Mano, "The Influence of Pre-Existing Negative Affect on Store Purchase Intentions," *Journal of Retailing*, Summer 1999: 149–172.

4. Neil Stern, "Supermarkets at the Crossroads: The Ultimate Three-Part Store," *International Trends In Retailing*, June 1997: 57–68.

5. "Federated, Macy's Head for Alter and Big Alterations," *Wall Street Journal*, November 18, 1994: B4.

6. Alan Liles, *Oh Thank Heaven! The Story of The Southland Corporation* (Dallas, TX: The Southland Corporation, 1977).

7. John Rutherford, the director of Kmart's Vendor Relations, in a speech titled "The Evolution of Profitability" given at the University of Arizona Southwest Retail Center's 4th Annual Global Retail Symposium, March 5, 1999.

8. Based on conversations with Robert Kahn.

9. Carol Kaufman-Scarborough, "Reasonable Access for Mobility-Disabled Persons Is More Than Widening the Door," *Journal of Retailing*, Winter 1999: 479–508.

10. "I Screwed It Up," *Forbes*, December 6, 1993: 144.

11. The above material was provided for the authors' use by Marvin J. Rothenberg of Marvin J. Rothenberg Inc., Ft. Lee, N.J.

12. Michael J. O'Connor, "Global Marketing: A Retail Perspective," *International Trends in Retailing*, December 1998: 19–35; and "The Global 500," *Fortune*, July 24, 2000: F-1.

13. For a more detailed discussion of this topic, the reader should consult the latest edition of Martin M. Pegler's *Stores of the Year*, published by Retail Reporting Corporation, New York.

14. Based on an example in Paco Underhill's *Why We Buy: The Science of Shopping* (New York: Simon & Schuster, 2000).

15. "Blinded by the Light," *Progressive Grocer*, August 2000: 57–58.

16. Ibid.

17. Paula Fitzgerald Bone and Pam Scholder Ellen, "Scents in the Marketplace: Explaining a Fraction of Olfaction," *Journal of Retailing*, Summer 1999: 243–262.

18. Charles Areni and David Kim, "The Influence of Background Music on Shopping Behavior: Classical versus Top-Forty Music in a Wine Store," *Advances in Consumer Research*, 1993: 336–340.

19. Gordon C. Bruner II, "Music, Mood, and Marketing," *Journal of Marketing*, October 1990: 94–104.

20. Ronald E. Milliman, "Using Background Music to Affect Behavior of Supermarket Shoppers," *Journal of Marketing*, Summer 1982: 86–91.

21. Charles Areni and David Kim, "The Influence of Background Music on Shopping Behavior: Classical versus Top-Forty Music in a Wine Store," *Advances in Consumer Research*, 1993: 336–340.

22. Based on information supplied by Charles Areni, James Cook University, August 2000.

Part V
Retail Administration

Chapter 14
Managing Human Resources

Salespeople are one of the
most critical, but often
overlooked or under-
emphasized, human resources
in retailing.

Managing Human Resources

Overview

In this chapter, we examine the role that human resources plays in retail firms.
We show that to carry out a retail strategy successfully, it is necessary not only
to have the proper number and mix of human resources, but to have them empowered to serve the customer. Thus, retail managers must plan for human resources, they must acquire human resources, they must train and develop human
resources, they must evaluate the employees' performances, and, finally, they
must compensate human resources.

Learning Objectives

After reading this chapter you should be able to

1. list and explain the steps involved in planning human resources

2. describe the process involved in hiring employees

3. discuss how retailers manage existing employees

4. describe the various methods retailers can use in compensating their employees

LO • 1

What steps are involved in planning human resources?

Planning for Human Resources

In our discussion of retail planning in Exhibit 2.3, we described the role of operations management, which is concerned with maximizing the efficiency of the retailer's use of resources. In this chapter we look at one, if not the most important, of those retail resources: human resources. Human resources make things happen. After all, the most profitable retailers have already organized their operations around the customer and allow these customers to interact with the retailer (i.e., the employees) in whatever manner is most convenient.[1] It is important that retailers remember that customers typically do not care who owns a retail store; they just want their questions answered, their problems solved, and the money for their purchases taken by the "first person they see." For many retailers, labor productivity has not risen over the past two decades. These retailers appear to be caught in a vicious circle in which the relatively low wages they offer salespeople have attracted low-quality employees, which tends to perpetuate the low wage–low quality cycle. In fact, it might even be argued that Americans have developed utter contempt for the retail clerk. Not all retailers are in this vicious circle, many have gotten out by investing time and money in their employees.

Nordstrom employees, for example, who are known and respected for their service around the world, make a great deal of money on commission by both knowing their merchandise and knowing how to take care of the customer. Home Depot employees, although not on commission, are paid an above-average wage to provide outstanding customer service. However, what really sets these two retailers' employees, as well as the employees of other high-performance retailers, apart from their counterparts is that they have been empowered by their employers to take care of the customer. **Empowerment** simply means the employee has the power to make things right for the customer. An empowered retail employee does the following:

Empowerment
occurs when employees are given the power in their jobs to do the things necessary to satisfy and make things right for customers.

1. Seeks to understand the customer's problem
2. Desires to develop a relationship with the customer
3. Understands the value of customer loyalty
4. Is allowed or encouraged by management to solve the customer's problem

The more profitable retailers empower their employees to solve customer problems.

Nordstrom employees have a reputation for customer care and service.

The profit impact of empowering employees in retailing is dramatic. Providing good customer service or using suggestion selling can often be the difference between success and failure for many retailers. Because retailers operate on a very low net profit margin, even a small increase in salesforce productivity—be it measured in sales per employee hour or gross margin per employee hour—would, in most part, directly translate into an improvement in store profits. Consequently, retailers are now trying to improve labor's productivity, especially that of the salesforce, by training and using empowerment. An additional benefit of empowerment is that it leads to greater customer satisfaction and higher self-esteem among employees, which in turn reduces employee turnover. Before being able to empower their employees, retailers must first decide what human resources are needed to achieve their firm's goals and objectives. Next, retailers must make sure that only the right types of employees are hired, that they are managed properly, and that they are fairly compensated for their efforts. These activities will be the focus in this chapter.

Task Analysis

The starting point for a retailer's human resources planning is task analysis. **Task analysis** involves simply identifying all of the tasks the retailer needs to perform and breaking those tasks into jobs. Retailers need to follow four steps: *identifying the functions* within the marketing system that retailers need or wish to perform, *identifying the tasks* that need to be performed within each function, *mapping the tasks into jobs*, and *developing the job description and job specifications*.

Task analysis
is the process of identifying all the tasks that the retailer needs to perform and breaking those tasks into jobs.

Marketing Functions   Chapter 5 stressed the retailers' need to view themselves as a part of a larger marketing system. Retailers are but one institution in a marketing channel, which, as a system, must perform eight marketing functions: buying, selling, storing, transporting, sorting, financing, information gathering, and risk taking. Because the eight functions can be shifted and divided, no single institution in the marketing channel will typically perform all of the functions.

The starting point for good human resource planning is for the retailer to decide which and how much of the eight marketing functions it will perform. As retailers assume more functions, they will require more human resources. For instance, when compared to a small retailer, the large chain retailer may do the following:

1. Perform more of the buying function by having buying offices in major cities throughout the world
2. Perform more of the selling function by heavily advertising and promoting merchandise on TV and radio and in newspapers and magazines
3. Perform more of the storage function by operating its own warehouses
4. Perform more of the transportation function by having its own trucks
5. Perform more of the sorting functions by buying in large quantities and breaking bulk and in some cases doing its own packaging
6. Perform more of the financing function by establishing a subsidiary to finance consumer purchases or by helping to finance small manufacturers
7. Perform more of the information-gathering function tracking customer purchases and developing a department of consumer research and long-range planning
8. Perform more of the risk-taking function by designing and developing specifications for products and then contracting with manufacturers to produce them

Identifying Tasks   Once retailers have established the amount of each marketing function to perform, they must identify all of the tasks that will need to be performed. Functions are broad classifications of activities; tasks are specific activities. For example, selling is a function that may involve the tasks of customer contact, customer follow-up, advertising in newspapers, and pricing merchandise.

Exhibit 14.1 provides a list of typical tasks that most retailers perform, ranging from transporting goods to cleaning the floor and windows of the store.

Mapping Tasks into Jobs   The third step involves the mapping of tasks into jobs. Retailers want a job to be composed of a relatively similar set of tasks. Because most retail tasks are not similar, retailers will need to find those tasks that are most similar and group them together. The smaller the retail firm, the less this will be possible. In a mom-and-pop store, the owner does everything from purchasing supplies and merchandise, preparing financial statements, contacting customers, to even washing windows.

As stores grow in size and add more employees, specialization can occur. As a retailer grows, the tasks of granting credit, billing customers, paying bills, and preparing financial statements will be placed in the hands of an accounting or financial clerk, while the tasks of handling customer complaints, repairing and altering merchandise, and gift wrapping may be placed in the hands of a director of customer services. When the retailer was smaller, these two sets of tasks may have been handled by the same person, even though they were not similar in nature. At the other extreme, if the retailer gets large enough, each task may be performed by a separate individual and ultimately there may be many employees handling a single task. For instance, Sears needs

Exhibit 14.1	**Typical Tasks Performed by Retailers**		
Searching for merchandise	Pricing merchandise	Supervising employees	Forecasting sales
Packaging	Following up on customers	Displaying merchandise	Doing customer research
Gift wrapping	Handling customer complaints	Contacting customers	Preparing press releases
Advertising		Transporting inbound merchandise	
Purchasing supplies	Cleaning store	Transporting outbound merchandise	Preparing financial statements
Purchasing merchandise	Controlling inventory		Storing merchandise
Granting credit	Hiring and firing employees	Paying bills	Preparing merchandise statistics
Billing customers	Training employees	Handling cash	
Building merchandise assortments	Selling	Altering merchandise	Maintaining the store
		Repairing merchandise	Providing store security

hundreds of employees just to bill customers and thousands more just to purchase merchandise.

Development of Job Descriptions and Job Specifications   Once the tasks have been mapped into jobs, job descriptions and job specifications should be developed so that human resource managers know what skills are required to do the job and the kind of training that should be provided to the employee. Employees prefer working for employers with explicit job descriptions. For example, if an employee's code of conduct states that theft of any type from the firm is a misdeed and the employee's job description makes it a responsibility to report such theft by others, then employees seem to be more willing to report such incidences than if it was not listed as a responsibility.

Job descriptions and specifications also can help determine the sources that should be used to recruit applicants, the selection procedures that should be used to evaluate applicants, and the training and development that should be given new employees in order to maximize performance.

Long-Range and Short-Range Analysis

Retailers generally use two different time frames in planning their human resource needs. On a long-range time horizon (one to five years), the major focus is on the retailer's projected growth in sales volume and number of stores. Frequently, the growth in sales and number of stores depends on the availability of good human resources. In analyzing long-range growth trends, retailers should pay particular attention to the speed and predictability of sales growth, the geographical dispersion of growth, and the amount of growth related to line-of-trade diversification.

Most retailers, however, are more concerned with the short-range time frame. This is anything less than one year and in many cases may be weekly, monthly, or seasonal. Historically, for example, one of the most time-consuming and difficult jobs for retail managers was the weekly labor schedule, which took 6 to 10 hours a week to complete. Today, with the aid of computer programs such as Labor Day from Timecorp Systems,

To successfully compete and attract employees, some retailers offer special benefits such as exercise classes.

SuperSked from Management Robotics, Smart Scheduler from Kronos, People-Planner from Information Marketing Businesses, and Staff Works from SAP Campbell, most retailers have reduced this chore to less than a hour. The use of these programs free managers to make better use of their time.[2]

It is also wise for the managers to analyze any recurring seasonal trends. If retailers always do strong business during the noon hour or the Christmas season, they should plan to have adequate human resources during these periods. Periodic and predictable increases in short-run demand for human resources can be handled either by utilizing part-time employees or by having existing employees participate in job sharing. Part-time employees for peak periods such as the noon hour or weekends and Christmas can help retailers serve more customers. One way of attracting good part-timers is to send out stuffers to your charge account holders, those customers who already use and probably like the store, offering part-time employees not only the standard employee discount privileges but extending the discount to friends and family members, and trying to make the work experience fun. For example, Macy's West offers aerobics classes to all associates and provides free lunches on sale days.[3] Although these peak business rushes can often be handled by having existing employees share jobs, such as having managers waiting on customers, or by having some employees work overtime, using overtime is not a long-term solution. At 60 hours a week, a worker's performance declines by 25 percent.[4]

Dollars & Sense

Retailers that best schedule employees (supply of labor) to match the flow of shoppers (demand) will achieve higher profit levels.

Hiring the Right Person for the Job

LO • 2

What is the process for hiring employees?

Retailers must remember that human resources are acquired in a competitive marketplace. Good employees are not waiting around to be hired, and seldom will they come pounding at your door. In fact, when good workers or managers are looking for employment, they will seldom think of contacting retail firms, simply because of the reputation many retailers have for low starting wages. Therefore, retailers must aggressively seek out and recruit good employees; in so doing, they must compete with other industries for labor resources.

Sources

What avenues can retailers use to obtain human resources? The seven sources shown in Exhibit 14.2 are the most common: competitors, walk-ins, employment agencies, schools and colleges, former employees, advertisements, and recommendations.

Retailers sometimes have to resort to using a different type of labor pool in order to match personnel with business demand. For example, Best Western International, when faced with a shortage of reservation takers, once had to turn to a most unconventional source of employees—the Arizona Department of Corrections, which was seeking productive and profitable work for its inmates.[5] Today, other retailers, such as Home Depot, Target, Mervyn's, and Lowe's, are using software programs to gather application forms and then sort, organize, and screen applicants while they are in the store on a shopping trip. Using signage, the retailer encourages customers to use computer-equipped kiosks in the store to apply for a job. Once the application is completed, the data are transmitted to a processing center where the name and social security number are matched. The applicant's other information is compared against a preestablished "success" profile for new hires. The data are then transmitted back to the retailer where the manager can interview the applicant before he or she leaves the store.[6]

Screening and Selection

Regardless of the specific source, all job applicants should be subject to a formal screening process to sort the potentially good from the potentially bad employees. As with any judgment process, some mistakes will happen. But fewer errors occur when employers use a screening process.

Retailers tend to vary in the amount of screening they use although, in principle, four screens are utilized: application forms, the personal interview, testing, and references. The total applicant pool for a particular job is progressively reduced as the applicants are subjected to each screen.

Application Blanks   As a matter of procedure, all applicants should be asked to fill out an application form. The application form should capture, conveniently and compactly, the individual's identity, training, and work history that will relate to his or her performance of the job tasks. Title VII of the Civil Rights Act of 1964 prohibits employers from discrimination in employment on the basis of race, color, religion, sex, or national origin; the Age Discrimination in Employment Act of 1967 (ADEA) prohibits employers from discrimination in employment on the basis of age; and the Americans

Exhibit 14.2	Sources of Retail Employees

Competitors. Competitors are the most common source for middle to upper management personnel, particularly when the retailer does not have someone to promote from within the firm due to geographic or line-of-trade conditions.

Walk-ins. Often a source for clerical, sales, and custodial positions, but seldom for managerial or supervisory employees. Walk-ins are most frequent during periods of high unemployment, when retailers need additional human resources least.

Employment Agencies. All states provide public employment services, which are typically available free of charge to both job seekers and employers. They are a reasonable, if not good, source for unskilled employees. At the same time, they are an excellent source for minority, handicapped, and veteran employees. This can help retailers meet their commitment to help achieve a specific policy of equal employment opportunities for all persons.

Private employment agencies, which may charge either the hiring company or the applicant a fee, are generally a much better source for managerial and white-collar employees, especially top executives. Two examples are Retail Executive Search, Inc., based in Chicago and Retail Recruiters based in New York City. Both are good sources for suitable candidates for top management retail positions.

Schools and Colleges. High schools that have Distributive Education Clubs of America (DECA) chapters provide an excellent source for operating-level employees. Many such employees have the basic talent, skills, and ambition to become shift managers or assistant department managers within a one- or two-year period.

Junior-college graduates, because of their college training, can begin in some low-level supervisory roles, such as assistant night manager of a store.

Four-year college graduates, and in some cases MBAs, expect and receive higher starting salaries due to educational experiences that enable them to move quickly into management positions.

Former Employees. Since retail organizations are always changing, there may come a time when a position is open for which a former employee would be excellent. It is not uncommon for a person to leave one retail organization as an assistant buyer to take a job as a sales rep for a supplier or as a buyer at another retail organization and then return to the initial retailer several years later as divisional merchandise manager.

Advertisements. Advertisements are a good source for sales clerks, cashiers, and janitors and occasionally buyers and managers. This is especially true when a retailer is entering a new geographic area and wants to make sure that employees at other retail firms in the area are aware that the new retailer is really interested in obtaining personnel with knowledge of the local market and not merely transferring existing personnel.

Recommendations. Current employees and vendors may have acquaintances or friends with an interest in applying for the jobs that are open. This source is good for filling jobs at all levels in the organization. Sales clerks as well as store managers, vice-presidents, and sales reps may know others seeking employment at a variety of ranks or positions.

with Disabilities Act of 1990 (ADA) prohibits employers from discrimination in employment on the basis of handicap/disability. Thus, the employer is effectively prohibited from asking any questions whose answer could be used to discriminate between two different groups of applicants. For example, if it could be shown that a certain group has a higher chance of having an arrest record or that this group changes residences more often than the average applicant, then questions concerning such information would be illegal. After all, such questions could be used to discriminate and normally do not elicit data indicative of likely job performance. Remember, an

Home Depot uses kiosks with computer terminals to help promote employment with the firm and get a good source of applicants.

employer should only ask questions that are pertinent to the applicant's ability to perform the job in question. Very rarely, exceptions may be made where a question about religion, sex, or national origin (but never race or color) can be asked because it is a **bona fide occupational qualification** (BFOQ) that is reasonably necessary to the narrow operation of a particular enterprise.[7]

Bona fide occupational qualification is a qualification that potential employees should have in order to be able to perform certain narrow job functions for a particular retailer.

Moreover, laws and regulations in many states also prohibit discrimination on other bases, such as having made workers' compensation claims in the past, marital status, ancestry, arrest record, credit record, prior accidents on the job, disabilities unrelated to ability, and so on. Some questions, such as those pertaining to weight and height, should only be used with caution. According to recent federal court decisions; employers, such as a hospital or swimming pool, may refuse to hire an overweight person when the applicant's weight will hamper his or her ability to perform the required work. The individual may not use the ADA as a defense, because according to the courts, being overweight is *not* a disability. However, the employer will not have a valid defense if that employer refuses to hire an overweight person because of that person's appearance. Therefore, before asking any question on their employment application, many retailers now check the EEOC's web site (http://www.eeoc.gov) or a commercial web site, such as http://www.smartbiz.com. After all, this is generally not an area where most retailers have a high level of expertise. Exhibit 14.3 shows some examples of legal and illegal questions that retailers have used. Retailers should make every effort to avoid using questions that are illegal.

From the list of qualified applicants who filled out applications, the retailer must select the best possible subset of candidates for each job.

Personal Interview   Those applicants who possess the basic characteristics needed to perform the job should be personally interviewed. This important step allows the retailer to assess how well qualified the applicants are for the job. By its very nature an interview is subjective, but in a well-structured interview one can obtain information or at least gain insight into the attitudes, personality, motives, and job aspirations of the interviewee.

Exhibit 14.3	**Legal and Illegal Questions for Employment Applications**

Legal Screening Devices

Are you over 18?

Is there anything that would prevent you from being transferred to another city? (If the job entails a transfer.)

Do you currently use, or have you in the past used, another name?

What do you feel are your major strengths (weaknesses)?

Are you a U.S. citizen or an alien authorized to accept permanent employment in the United States?

Where do you live?

Can you perform the functions involved with or without reasonable accommodation?

Do you have any physical disability that would prevent you from performing this particular job? If so, what, if any, reasonable accommodations could be made to enable you to perform the job?

Where have you worked previously?

Illegal Screening Devices

How old are you?

Are you over 18 and under 70?

List the names and dates of all schools attended. (Start with high school)

Do you prefer being called Miss, Mrs. or Ms.?

What is the name of your pastor or rabbi?

How many days were you sick last year?

Are you married?

Does stress ever affect your ability to be productive?

How many dependents do you have?

What languages, besides English, do you speak fluently?

What social organizations are you currently a member of?

Other than the usual holidays, would you be absent for any religious holidays?

What medications are you currently taking?

Do you have any relatives working for the firm?

Where does your spouse work?

How long have you lived at your current residence?

Have you ever been arrested?

Have you ever filed for workmen's compensation?

Do you have a disability?

Have you ever had a serious illness?

How much alcohol do you drink per week?

Many interviewers overlook the fact that the interview should be a two-way communication process. Not only does the retailer want to gather information about the applicant, but the applicant may desire information about the retailer. Allowing time for the applicant to ask questions is essential if the retailer is competing for the talents of highly desired applicants. In fact, part of the interview time may actually be used by the interviewer to try to sell the applicant on working for the retailer as well as honestly explaining what the job entails so as not to lead to job dissatisfaction or possible legal complications based on misunderstandings.

As mentioned earlier in the chapter, many retailers are now using the computer to both attract applicants and gather information about the applicant during the interview phase. Home Depot, for example, starts the interview at its in-store kiosks with a short video describing the company, the work environment, and what kind of hours the applicant will be expected to work. Applicants are also told about the process, which includes a drug test and a series of general and personal questions.[8]

Testing Sometimes formal tests will be administered to those applicants who received favorable ratings in their personal interviews. These tests may look for certain characteristics, such as intelligence, interests, leadership potential, personality traits, or honesty. Home Depot mentioned in the previous paragraph, also uses its kiosks to test the applicant. After all, more information can be obtained about the applicant this way, and it is cheaper to obtain. Also, because the responses were made to the computer directly rather than on paper or given to the interviewer, respondents have reported that they felt the information was more readily subject to instant checking and verification with other databases. Thus, to avoid potential embarrassment, applicants were more truthful. As a result, these tests have an excellent record at picking out the low-integrity applicants and in screening out the kind of irresponsible and counterproductive behavior that drives bosses crazy: disciplinary problems, disruptiveness on the job, chronic

Application blanks, personal interviews, and testing are all used to screen applicants for retail positions.

Retailing: The Inside Story

An Ambiguous Lexicon for Job Recommendations

Every once in a while, a person requests a letter of recommendation from a previous employer, professor, or family friend about whom the letter writer has serious reservations. Does the writer send a moderately favorable letter and live with his or her conscience or write a frank, unfavorable letter and risk a lawsuit when the person finds out about it? (Remember, under certain circumstances, such letters are no longer confidential.)

Professor Robert J. Thornton at Lehigh University has developed the following guidelines for handling such a dilemma.

To describe a candidate who is not particularly industrious, here is what the writer can say (and what the writer really meant):

- "You will be very fortunate to get this person to work for you." (She's not very industrious.)
- "He could not have done a better job for us if he had tried." (He's not only incompetent, but he's lazy as well.)
- "I think it's safe to say that his true interests were lying in the stockroom." (He used to sneak naps there.)
- "No job is too much for this man to handle." (He just can't seem to deal with any kind of responsibility.)
- "She works effortlessly." (She doesn't expend much energy.)

- "You will never catch him asleep on the job." (He's too crafty to get caught.)
- "He always found his work challenging." (It was hard for him to get going.)
- "She doesn't think twice about attacking a difficult problem." (In fact, she doesn't think about it at all.)
- "He spared no effort in his work." (He did as little as possible.)

To describe a candidate who is incompetent:

- "I recommend this man with no qualifications whatsoever." (He's woefully inept)
- "I understand that she would very much like to work with you if possible." (She just can't seem to get herself moving, though)
- "No amount of praise would suffice for the job that he's done for us." (He's bungled everything he ever tried to do.)
- "Her former buyer was always raving about her work." (Her mistakes nearly drove him insane.)
- "He would always ask if there was anything he could do." (And we would always ask ourselves the same question.)
- "He has completed his schooling, and is now ready to strike out in a career." (I expect his batting average to be .000.)

tardiness, and excessive absenteeism. A big advantage of this system for Home Depot is that prior to its use the retailer hired only one or two of thirty or more applicants who completed the application/interview process. Now, the figure may be as high as twenty out of thirty.[9]

Other assessments used by retailers include drug tests and credit checks with local credit bureaus. In fact, although only about 25 percent of all employers check out an applicant's credit history, most of those that do are retailers.[10] Retailers sometimes check for prior workers' compensation claims. However, because each state has different laws regarding what may be checked or tested, the retailer should consult with a local attorney before using them. In addition, some tests could violate the applicant's rights if he or she is not advised of such inquiries ahead of time and given the opportunity to consent, or if the tests run afoul of the antidiscrimination laws designed to protect minorities and the disabled. Besides, in many cases these tests have been found not only to violate the applicant's rights but also to give error-ridden information about the applicant.

- "I wouldn't hesitate to give her an unqualified recommendation." (She just doesn't have the skills for the job.)

To describe a person who has no ambition:

- "Once she got started on a project she wouldn't stop until it was finished." (It's the only thing she actually did in all the years she was with us.)
- "He couldn't care less about the number of hours he had to put in." (We just wish he could have cared more about them.)
- "He is not the type to run away from responsibility." (He'll walk very quickly though.)
- "From the moment he arrives at work, he is ready to go." (. . . home.)
- "She didn't think much of the extra time she had to work." (In fact, she didn't do much thinking during her regular work hours.)

For the person who has mediocre work habits or credentials and should never be hired:

- "Waste no time in making this candidate an offer of employment." (She's not worth further consideration.)

- "All in all, I cannot recommend this person too highly." (He has lackluster credentials.)
- "You can't offer this man too high a salary." (You're better off saving your money.)
- "We were forever asking him for new ideas." (We were sick and tired of the old ones.)
- "She has made immeasurable contributions to our firm." (Far too minor to be measured.)

In addition, Thornton also demonstrates the use of the "questionable" or "missing" comma. Which applicant would you hire?

- "He won't do anything, which will lower your high regard for him" or "He won't do anything which will lower your high regard for him."
- "The job required very few skills, which he lacked" or "The job required very few skills which he lacked."

Source: Based on material in Robert Thornton's *Lexicon of Intentionally Ambiguous Recommendations*, 2nd ed.(Central Point, OR: Almus Publications, 1998). Used with the written permission of Professor Robert Thornton.

References   As a general rule, retailers should not ask for or check the references the applicant has provided until the applicant has been screened or filtered through the preceding stages. If references were obtained and verified on all initial applicants, the cost would be excessive.

Negligent hiring is one of the hottest issues in current employment law. The premise is that an employer can be held responsible for an employee's unlawful actions if it did not reasonably investigate an employee's background and then placed the employee in a position where he or she caused harm to a customer. When references are obtained and checked, the retailer should try to assess the honesty and reliability of the applicant. The reason for leaving the prior place or places of employment should also be investigated. The retailer should be interested in finding out what type of person will vouch for the prospective employee. Although most references that an applicant provides can be expected to give a neutral or favorable recommendation (if they give one at all), the reference check does give the retailer a means to verify the accuracy and completeness of the application. Also, as a point of information, many retailers have found greater success using telephone interviews instead of asking for written replies. This method enables retailers to gather more complete and honest evaluations than do letters, even if it is only in what the reference does not say about the applicant. The chapter's Retailing: The Inside Story box points out one of the major problems faced by people who write letters of recommendation.

One final comment on checking references: the retailer must tread carefully here to avoid breaking federal and state laws. The personnel manager will be well advised to visit the firm's legal staff yearly to determine the firm's and the applicant's legal rights. New laws are regularly being enacted in the courts, Congress, and state legislatures.

Managing Existing Employees

LO • 3

How do retailers manage existing employees?

Once an employee is hired, the retailer must prepare programs for training the employee to meet current or future job requirements, evaluating employees, and motivating them. After all, in an economy with a low unemployment rate, if an employee does not like something about the job, it's training, or even his or her coworkers, that employee can easily go elsewhere. Therefore, the most critical job for retailers today is retaining current employees.[11] A recent study of the supermarket industry by the Coca-Cola Retailing Research Council found, for example, that the median retention rate of hourly supermarket employees was 97 days—that is, one-half of all new supermarket hires terminate their employment within 97 days of starting work.[12] The study further found that the cost (including both direct and opportunity cost, which are described in Exhibit 14.4) of replacing this hourly employee was $4,291 for a union store and $3,372 for a nonunion store.[13] In all, employee turnover costs the average supermarket almost $190,000 annually in direct and opportunity costs.[14] Turnover is thought to be an even more serious problem in specialty stores because they typically hire part-timers at entry-level positions.

Managerial Question: Your store is understaffed and after reviewing the current applications on file, you do not find any good applicants available. Should you hire someone who does not meet your standards and risk having to replace him or her within a couple of months or should you have your present staff continue to work overtime?

The preceding study also found that employer practices fostering close working relationships made a significant impact on improving the retention rate of hourly employees.[15] Therefore, one of the most important tasks for retailers today is developing a teamwork attitude among its employees in an effort to reduce turnover.

Teamwork
seeks to stress the importance of overall department (store, division, or company) performance by working toward team versus individual achievements.

Teamwork

Teamwork seeks to stress the importance of overall department (store, division, or company) performance by working toward team versus individual achievements. Federated Department Stores has taken the approach that teams do not need bosses to lead them. The chain's management feels that the employees can work better leading

Exhibit 14.4	Various Types of Employee Turnover Costs

Direct: These costs are reflected on the retailer's financial statements.

- Cost of recruiting applicants
- Cost of evaluating applicants (including interviews, reference checks, and any testing)
- Cost of training classes (including management's time)
- Pay (including benefits) during period when new employee is taking training course
- Part of supervisor's pay (including benefits) to cover costs spent helping new employee during first few weeks of job

Indirect: These activities cause a reduction in the firm's revenue. Thus, while they are not shown on the retailer's financial statements, they are still a cost.

- Loss of customers that were "loyal" to former employee
- Lost sales resulting from the lack of product knowledge during the initial time of job
- Lost sales and potential profits missed from alienated customers resulting from inexperience in retail selling
- Decrease in employee morale caused by the departure of an employee
- The effect of the employees' lower morale on customers

themselves and managing their own time, functions, and responsibilities. After all, the people who know the business best are the empowered employees. Team members, working in merchandising, store management, marketing, finance, and logistics, work in concert with each other to define their roles based on the knowledge and talent of each member. Members are compensated based partly on the overall team's performance, the individual's contribution to the team, and the individual's value based on his or her knowledge and skills to the team.[16] Such compensation plans have been found to be extremely important to Generation Xers, the group which now makes up the largest number of retail associates.[17]

Retailers that are able to develop a team-oriented attitude among their employees and management will achieve higher profit levels.

Dollars & Sense

Self-service retailer Best Buy, which is engaged in a heated battle with Circuit City and its highly trained commission-oriented salesforce, recently changed its incentive program. As an experiment, Best Buy is now testing the use of "team" commissions in its appliance department.[18] Wal-Mart has long used such a teamwork approach by offering bonuses to all employees based on their store's profits and shrinkage total. In fact, many retail experts credit Wal-Mart's partnership program as a major contributing factor behind its success.[19]

Training and Developing Employees

Retailers wanting the best return on their human resource investment should provide training and development for both new and existing employees. Training and development are consistent with the concept of human resource planning.

Training is not a "one-time happening" however. Retailers today view training as a process of continuing education. For example, as shown in the chapter's Global Retailing box, McDonald's invests a great deal of money in training to maintain its lead as the world's leading fast-food retailer. Thus, as an individual's responsibilities increase, so do the training and development. Employees are taught not just technical skills but administrative and people skills as well. Each phase of development is built on the training that has preceded it and includes training in merchandising, operations management, motivation, decision making, problem analysis, and time management.

In addition to developing a pool of future managers and assisting employees with present duties, training and development programs enable the employees to know where they are and how they are doing. Generation Xers, in particular, want to be challenged and encouraged to use different skills. If they feel the job is more compelling, they will be more apt to view retailing as part of their long-term personal growth strategy.[20] Retail managers must remember that a career in their field is different than careers in other business fields. In the beginning it is like a pyramid, with the employee becoming increasingly specialized toward the goal of being a buyer—the ultimate specialist. Afterward, the goal is to increase breadth, not specialty, so as to become a store or division manager.

Today, as shown in the chapter's Service Retailing box, there is a new type of training tool available to retailers. On-line training is one of the fastest growing ways of training employees and it is used by many of the smaller retailers who cannot afford to have a complete training staff.

Retailers that invest in training and developing both new and existing employees will achieve higher profit levels.

Evaluating Employees

Performance appraisal and review is the formal, systematic assessment of how well employees are performing their jobs in relation to established standards and the communication of that assessment to employees. Employees place a great deal of importance on appraisals, and the way the appraisal system operates affects morale and organizational climate in significant ways. Moreover, the appraisal system also has an impact on other human resource processes, such as training and development, compensation, and promotion.

Informal appraisals tend to take place on an ongoing basis within the retail firm as supervisors evaluate their subordinates' work on a daily basis and as subordinates appraise each other as well as their supervisors. However, the formal, systematic appraisal of an individual is likely to occur at certain intervals throughout the year or when the employee is being considered for a wage increase, a promotion, a transfer, or an opportunity to improve job skills.

Retailers of all sizes should try to use objective criteria for the appraisal and review process wherever possible. Exhibit 14.5 presents a form for the objective review and appraisal of salespeople. However, not every item that the retailer might want to evaluate can be quantified. Larger retail operations use a committee, frequently consisting of the vice-president of human resources/personnel and one or two other executives, to evaluate each employee. Some retailers, especially smaller ones, sometimes forego the formal evaluation process and judge a salesperson on the basis of dollar sales, number of transactions, errors, on-time performance, ratio of returned merchandise, and customer complaints.

It is important to recognize several key factors in conducting performance appraisals. First, the process should be an ongoing affair, not just a periodic review. Regularly scheduled review times should not keep supervisors from appraising or coaching their subordinates whenever necessary. Second, employees seek feedback, or information about how well they are doing their jobs, and this feedback should be provided on a timely and relevant basis. Third, the person doing the review should know what the job being reviewed entails and what the performance standards are. Many times employees can become upset with the review process when the reviewer is not aware of problems and limitations of the job under review. Fourth, different supervisors are likely to rate personnel with different degrees of leniency or severity. Therefore, not only should the person making the review understand the performance standards, but at least two people should make the review. Finally, research has shown that the particular method of reviewing the employee does not matter. Retailers have found success in various types of measures including the rating scale, checklist, free-form essay, and rankings.

Motivating Employees

Human resource management goes beyond selecting, training, and compensating employees. It also involves motivating them to improve current performance. A successful retailer today must constantly motivate all employees to strive for higher sales figures, to decrease expenses, to communicate company policies to the public, and to solve problems as they arise. This is achieved through the proper use of motivation.

Motivation is the drive that a person has to excel at the activities he or she undertakes, such as a job. Several theories on motivation have been developed. These can be

Performance appraisal and review
is the formal, systematic assessment of how well employees are performing their jobs in relation to established standards and the communication of that assessment to employees.

Motivation
is the drive that a person has to excel at activities, such as a job, he/she undertakes.

Global Retailing

Training for Global Operations: A Degree in Hamburgerology

Training takes on a different tone and different challenges when global retailers are involved. Global retailers are subject to multiple legal systems and a variety of worker regulations, not to mention the difficulties created through cultural differences. So how can a retailer who is successful in one country expand successfully into many countries? For a little insight on how one of the world's leading food service retailers has accomplished this task, here is the story of the evolution of one of the greatest global retail training centers: McDonald's.

Hamburger University

Hamburger University, which is the centerpiece of an extensive training-oriented organization, sits in Oak Brook, Illinois, just outside of Chicago. Developed in 1961 in the basement of a restaurant, Hamburger U sets the standard for global retail training centers. From the beginning McDonald's believed that training was the key to success. From the basement of that restaurant back in 1961 to its leading-edge training facility of today, equipped with the latest technology, video cameras, computers, audio-response keyboards, and a huge team of translators that translate lessons into 26 languages, McDonald's continues to lead the industry in global training.

Hamburger U, which awards the degree of "bachelor's of hamburgerology," is part of a total training system for McDonald's worldwide. Prior to entering Hamburger U, international managers are taught the essentials of running a franchise in regional training classes in Japan, Germany, England, and Brazil. At the regional training centers, managers participate in four classes aimed at improving franchisee skills. Thus, by the time a manager reaches the Oak Brook campus, he or she has already completed at least 2,000 hours of training. At Hamburger U the emphasis is on the keys to success in the burger business. Quality customer services, consistency of product and service, methods of improving profitability, and employee motivation are just a few of the areas Hamburger U emphasizes in its training.

McDonald's is clearly a world leader in retail food service. Through its top-notch training programs, McDonald's has been able to Americanize much of the world. Now, McDonald's has turned its training on itself, moving from training to learning in an area where the retailer has been lacking: integrating the knowledge of local franchisees into its existing knowledge base. For example, in terms of product offerings, although McDonald's has always been good at adapting its menu to local tastes—for example offering bulgogi burgers in South Korea or teriyaki sauce in Japan—the company often failed to integrate many of the non-American ideas into its global operations. However, recent efforts to learn from franchisees have led to successes. One of the first attempts to do this was the McFlurry. The McFlurry, an ice cream dessert developed in

---

Content theories
refer to theories on motivation that ask, "What motivates an individual to behave?"

Process theories
refer to theories on motivation that ask, "How can I motivate an individual?"

divided into **content theories**, which ask, "What motivates an individual to behave?" and **process theories,** which ask, "How can I motivate an individual?" Among the content theories we will discuss are Maslow's hierarchy of needs, Herzberg's two-factor theory of motivation, and McGregor's Theory X and Theory Y. In our discussion of the process theories we will look at two of the most widely used: expectancy theory and goal setting.

Content Theories   Abraham Maslow, a noted psychologist, developed a **hierarchy of needs model,** which is shown in Exhibit 14.6, which suggests that people have different types of needs and that they satisfy lower-level needs before moving to higher levels. The first level is the basic physiological need, which can be satisfied by the employee's cash wages. Once employees become content at this level, they become concerned with safety and security needs. Retailers have satisfied these needs with such

McDonald's established Hamburger University to train employees and franchisees to deliver high quality and consistent levels of customer service.

Canada, is now offered in more than 35 countries. However, products are only one area in which McDonald's is trying to learn from its franchisees. Integrating the successful processes and practices of local franchisees, while challenging, presents great opportunities to McDonald's as a global organization. For McDonald's the key has been training. Expanding this to training and learning is sure to be a strategy that will lead to future successes.

benefits as security patrolled parking locations. The third level of needs, that of belongingness and social needs, can be satisfied with "employee or salesperson of the month" awards. A similar approach can be used at the fourth level of needs, esteem, with fancier offices and job titles. The highest need level is self-actualization or "becoming all you can be." Here retailers can provide seminars to help broaden the horizons of employees. Maslow's hierarchy thus provides retailers with ideas that can appeal to the basic needs of their employees.

Offering another perspective on motivation was **Herzberg's two-factor theory,** which suggested that two factors motivate individuals: hygiene factors and motivators. Hygiene factors are extrinsic to the individual and can be organizationally determined. Examples of hygiene factors in a retail setting are pay, verbal praise, and special name badges. Motivators, on the other hand, are intrinsic to the individual and include the feeling of self-accomplishment or the desire to excel.

Hierarchy of needs model
theorizes that individuals have lower-level physiological and safety and security needs, which are first satisfied before higher-level needs of belongingness or social esteem and self-actualization are pursued.

Service Retailing

Retail Training: From CD-ROMs to On-line

Retail training is one of the fastest growing service sectors in the retail trade. Retailers today recognize that the difference between mediocre and premier retailing firms is determined to a great extent by the skills their employees possess. As such, these retailers are investing heavily in the training of both their front-line employees and their retail executives. Service providers are leveraging technology from CD-ROMs and on-line sources to provide small mom-and-pop retailers as well as large global retail chains efficient and effective training. Two specific areas have dominated the retail sector: product knowledge and general business skills.

One of the keys to retail sales success is the knowledge retail associates possess relating to the products that the retailer offers. Traditionally, retail product knowledge training was conducted through product brochures, videos, or in the most intensive and expensive training, on-site vendor workshops. However, service firms such as KnowYourStuff.com and Channel Reps. Inc. are changing the nature of retail training. For instance, Channel Reps Inc., a leading retail training firm, has provided on-site training for firms such as CompUSA and Best Buy on behalf of vendors such as Lucent Technologies and Hitachi PC Corp. Although extremely effective, Channel Reps began leveraging its training expertise in early 1998 by offering a modified version of its on-site training on-line, termed Retail University. By the year 2000, Channel Reps had tens of thousands of registered users learning about vendors products and taking hundreds of thousands of tests a year to assess retail associate product knowledge. As such, Channel Reps works in conjunction with both retailers and retail vendors, thus providing both with an independent assessment of employee product knowledge. Similarly, KnowYourStuff.com brings manufacturers together with retailers for product-related information. With KnowYourStuff.com, manufacturers place their training

material on-line. The manufacturers' retail partners have access to the site 24 hours a day, seven days a week. As the sales associates of a retailer work through the on-line training materials, consisting of lessons, quizzes, and the like, retail management can assess the employee's grasp of the material and determine areas of needed improvement. Although on-line training offers a clear convenience advantage, the independent assessment and ability of retail associates to repeat lessons until they have mastered them is a key area to continual improvement.

A second aspect for training that retailers are taking advantage of relates to general business skills. Employee training for general business skills not only makes for more effective retailer associates, but it also can protect the retailer. For example, one of the greatest areas of on-line training currently is sexual harassment awareness. Training retail employees not only makes for a better workplace, it also can protect the retailer from legal liability. That is to say, a retailer can require all of its employees to complete an on-line training course in sexual harassment awareness. The requirement of such a course demonstrates that the retailer addresses these types of issues within the workplace, thus helping to minimize legal liabilities. Clearly, as retailers continue to recognize the importance of employee training for competitive positioning, providers of on-line training will become more and more important. The key to these service providers is maintaining top-quality programs that allow both manufacturers and retailers the opportunity to develop and assess retail associate skill levels.

The best training and development program devised is useless unless management adopts a philosophy of complete support. In the past, many retail executives got so tied up in merchandising concerns, they forgot about human resources—a big mistake.

Thus, Maslow's and Herzberg's theories as to what motivates an individual to behave are quite similar. Herzberg's hygiene factors are basically Maslow's two lower-level needs (physiological and safety) and motivators are his top two levels (esteem and self-actualization). Maslow's third level of need, belonging, can fit into either of Herzberg's two categories depending on the situation.

Exhibit 14.5	Criteria Used in the Appraisal and Review Process

Merchandise Procedures:	Employee's accuracy in counting and inventorying merchandise.	*Product- Merchandise Knowledge:*	Knowledgeable of design, style, and construction of merchandise group.
	Prevents merchandise shrinkage due to mishandling of merchandise.		Knowledgeable of special promotions and/or advertised sale items.
	Keeps merchandise in a neat and orderly manner on sales floor.		Knowledgeable of material (fabrics), color coordination, and complementary accessories related to returned merchandise.
	Knows the design and specification of warranties and guarantees of the merchandise groups.	*Store Policy:*	Provides accurate and complete paperwork related to returned merchandise.
	Gets merchandise on sales floor quickly after merchandise arrival.		Provides accurate and complete paperwork related to work schedules.
Customer Service Ability:	Provides courteous service to customers.		Provides accurate and complete paperwork for cash and credit transactions.
	Handles customer complaints and/or service problems as indicated by store procedure.		Shows up on time for work, sales meetings, and training sessions.
	Follows proper procedure concerning merchandise returns and lay-aways when conducted through credit transactions.		Accurately follows day-to-day instructions of immediate supervisor.
	Suggests add-on or complementary merchandise to customers.		Employee's overall job-related attitude.
Sales Ability:	Has strong ability to close the sale.		
	Promotes sale of merchandise items having profit margins.		
	Acts as a resource to other departments or other salespeople needing assistance.		
	Works well with fellow workers in primary merchandise department.		

Source: Robert P. Bush, Alan J. Bush, David J. Ortinau, and Joseph F. Hair, Jr., "Developing a Behavior-Based Scale to Assess Retail Salesperson Performance," *Journal of Retailing,* Spring 1990: 119–136.

A third content theory was McGregor's Theory X and Theory Y. **Theory X** assumes that employees must be closely supervised and controlled and that economic induce- ments (salaries and commissions) will provide the means of influencing employees to perform. This theory assumes that employees need to be induced or coerced to work because they are inherently lazy. **Theory Y,** on the other hand, assumes that employees

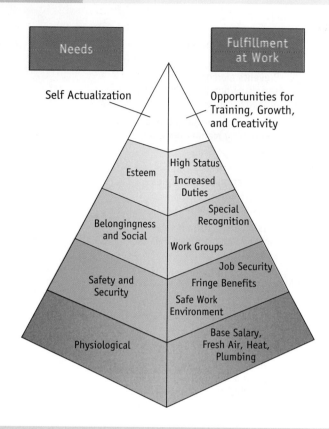

| **Exhibit 14.6** | **How Retailers Can Use Maslow's Hierarchy of Needs** |

Herzberg's two-factor theory
argues the two factors encourage people to work hard: hygiene factors, which are extrinsic to the individual, and motivators, which are intrinsic to the individual.

Theory X
is a theory of management that views employees as unreliable and thus must be closely supervised and controlled and given economic inducements to perform properly.

Theory Y
is a theory of management that views employees as self-reliant and enjoying work and thus can be empowered and delegated authority and responsibility.

Expectancy theory
suggests that an employee will expend effort on some task because the employee expects that the effort will lead to a performance outcome that will lead in turn to a reward or bonus that the employee finds desirable or valued.

are self-reliant, enjoy work, and can be delegated authority and responsibility. Over the past decade, many different retailing employee groups have foregone wage increases for a share of management. These employee-managed retail stores have generally experienced an increased organizational effectiveness, thus supporting Maslow's, Herzberg's, and the Theory Y contention that money alone is not a primary motivator.

Process Theories   On the other side of content theories are process theories that are concerned with how to motivate a salesperson to behave in the retailer's best interest.

Expectancy theory addresses the relationship between effort, performance, and organizational outcomes. It assumes that employees know this relationship and that this knowledge influences them to behave in one way or another. More specifically, expectancy theory states that an employee's (for instance, a salesperson) motivation to expend effort on some task depends on whether (1) the salesperson expects that the effort will lead to a sale (performance), (2) the sale will likely lead to a reward or bonus (outcome), and (3) the reward or bonus is desirable (valued). Obviously the critical consideration is how much value the salesperson attaches to the reward or bonus, be it cash, prizes, promotions, fancier offices, increased job status, better conditions, or a greater sense of achievement. Expectancy theory appears to provide a logical answer to the question "How do I motivate staff?" For instance, if a salesperson likes to travel and thinks he or she can reach quota, he or she will work hard to win a trip.

Goal setting is a way to obtain the firm's objectives that depend on inducing a person to behave in the desired manner. The goals must be attainable; too difficult a goal, such as an increase in sales of 50 percent, will not motivate a salesperson because the chances of achieving the target are slim. Likewise, too easy a goal, such as a 1-percent increase, is often de-motivating and unchallenging. The time frame is also important. Too long a time frame is generally de-motivating. Just as you would put off a term paper due in four months, the salesperson might do the same with a year-long sales goal. A 10 percent increase in yearly sales might be broken down into either the two seasons or 12 months, with changes made at stated intervals based on market conditions.

Remember, it is the retail manager's job to motivate employees in a manner that yields job satisfaction, low turnover, low absenteeism, and high performance results.

Goal setting
is the process in which management and employees establish goals that become the basis for performance appraisal and review.

Human Resource Compensation

What methods can retailers use in compensating their employees?

As all businesspeople know, human resources are not free goods. They are expensive, and in retailing their cost typically represents 50 percent of operating expenses. We will not discuss here how to control labor expenses but merely highlight some important aspects about compensating human resources.

Compensation is one of the major variables in attracting, retaining, and motivating human resources. The quality of employees that can be attracted, whether as sales clerks or executives, is directly proportional to the compensation package offered. The better the human resource, the higher the price. Naturally, other things besides compensation are important to employees. According to a recent report by Deloitte & Touche's Human Resource Strategies Group, "more flexible, portable benefits systems with fewer links to age and service" are desired by today's retail associates. In addition, these benefits should be compatible with the employee's lifestyle choices.[21]

Competitive compensation is just as important to retaining good employees as it is to attracting them. In this regard, the retailer needs to realize that if it invests more money in training and developing employees, these employees will actually increase in value, not only to the retailer, but also to competitors who may try to hire them. Thus, as the retailer invests money to train and develop employees, it must also make a commitment to provide them with more compensation, or the retailer will be training and developing employees for its competitors.

Here the term **compensation** includes direct dollar payments (wages, commissions, bonuses) and indirect payments (insurance, vacation time, retirement plans). Compensation plans in retailing can have up to three basic components: a fixed component, a variable component, and a fringe benefit component. The **fixed component** typically is composed of some base wage per hour, week, month, or year. The **variable component** is often composed of some bonus that is received if performance warrants. Sales clerks may be paid a bonus of 10 percent of sales above some established minimum; department managers may receive a bonus based on the profit performance of their department. Workers in restaurants often receive tips, a variable component that the retailer does not control. Finally, a **fringe benefit package** may include such things as health insurance, disability benefits, life insurance, retirement plans, the use of automobiles, and financial counseling.

Compensation
includes direct dollar payments (wages, commission, bonuses) and indirect payments (insurance, vacation time, retirement plans).

Fixed component
typically is composed of some base wage per hour, week, month, or year.

Variable component
is often composed of some bonus that is received if performance warrants.

Fringe benefit package
is a part of the total compensation package offered to many retail employees and may include health insurance, disability benefits, life insurance, retirement plans, child care, use of an auto, and financial counseling.

Each of the three components helps the retailer to achieve a different human resource goal. The fixed component helps to ensure that employees have a source of income to meet their most basic financial obligations. This helps to fulfill the employees' physiological needs. The variable component allows the retailer to offer employees an incentive for higher levels of effort and commitment, which helps to fulfill a belongingness and social need among employees for special recognition in return for high performance. The fringe benefit component allows the retailer to offer employees safety and security. Retail employees have a need to be protected and cared for when they are faced with difficult times or when they become too old to provide for themselves. Also, certain employees (especially executives) have a need for prestige and status.

The best combination of fixed, variable, and fringe compensation components depends on the person, the job, and the retail organization. There is no set formula. Some top retail executives prefer mostly salary, others thrive on bonuses, still others would rather have more pension benefits. The same holds for sales clerks. Therefore, the compensation package needs to be tailored to the individual. We now focus our attention on compensation of the salesforce, but the same principles apply to managers.

Common Types of Compensation Programs for Salesforce

Retail salesforce compensation programs can be conveniently broken into three major types: (1) straight salary, (2) salary plus commission, and (3) straight commission. Each of these methods has its advantages and disadvantages.

Straight Salary   In the straight salary program, the salesperson receives a fixed salary per time period (usually per week) regardless of the level of sales generated or orders taken. However, over time, if the salesperson does not help generate sales or take enough orders, he or she will likely be fired for not performing adequately. Similarly, over time, if the salesperson helps to generate more than a proportionate share of sales or fills more than a proportionate number of orders, the retailer will be unable to retain the employee without a raise.

Many small retailers use this compensation method, because they typically assign tasks such as stock rearranging, merchandise display, and other nonselling duties to their salespeople. Therefore, if the employees were paid on a commission basis they would spend little if any time on their nonselling duties, and the retail organization would suffer. Many promotional and price-oriented chain stores whose salespeople are merely order takers use the straight salary method because the salesperson is not much of a causal factor in generating sales. Also, most clerks and cashiers, as well as other lower-level retail personnel are almost always paid straight salaries.

The salesperson may view this plan as attractive because it offers income security or as unappealing because it gives little incentive for extraordinary effort and performance. Thus, for this method (which is also the easiest plan for the employee to understand) to be effective it must be combined with a periodic evaluation so that superior salespeople can be identified and singled out for higher salaries.

Salary Plus Commission   Sometimes the salesperson is paid a fixed salary per time period plus a percentage commission on all sales or on all sales over an established quota. Because merchandise lines and items can vary in terms of gross margins, some retailers pay commissions on gross margin dollars generated. The fixed salary is

E-tailing

E-tailers Take Compensation to New Heights

There is no other word to describe it: exodus. In droves, well-positioned, highly paid retail executives working for established retailers began leaving their firms to join dot-com startup e-tailers during the late 1990s. For many, the move to e-tailers necessitated a significant reduction in salary and a significant increase in the number of hours worked. So why were retailing execs willing to do this? There were two reasons: professional challenge and stock options.

Clearly, for many retail executives the new professional challenges offered by e-tailing was a significant draw. E-tailing provided the perfect venue for many retail execs to demonstrate their highly developed retail skills applied to this new technological retailing area, as well as develop many new skills, thus reviving their enthusiasm for retailing. However, there is no denying the fact that the lure of stock options was enormous.

For retail execs, moving to the dot-com world offered the potential to be a millionaire because of the stock options offered by the dot-com firms. E-tailers, unlike traditional retailers, offer many of their new retail execs stock options (an option to purchase a specific amount of stock at an agreed-upon price). For example, let's say that a retail exec is making $180,000 with a traditional retailer. However, an e-tailer comes along and offers the exec $50,000 plus stock options. The stock options work something like this. Let's say that the e-tailers stock is trading for $25 per share. The new exec is allowed to purchase 25,000 shares of stock anytime within the next five years for $5 per share. Thus, if the exec were to start working and then purchase his or her 25,000 shares at $5 and sell them for $25, the exec would make $20 per share for a total of $500,000. However, let's say that the exec does not cash out his or her options right away. In a few years, once the e-tailer has become successful, each share is now worth $125. If the exec were to cash out at this point the exec would make $120 per share or $3 million.

Although stock options have been a major element in recruiting retail execs from traditional retailers, recent uncertainty in the ability of e-tailers to become profitable has meant that for many execs who defected the traditional retail marketplace, the financial future is grim. Continuing with the preceding example, let's say that one year after the exec joins the e-tailer, the stock is trading for $4 per share. Now the shares are, for the most part, worthless and the executive has taken a $130,000 cut in pay and is now working 16 hours a day rather than 10. It is the old risk and reward paradigm at work. If one wishes great rewards, one must take great risks. When many e-tail stocks took a turn for the worse in 2000, stock options were no longer the draw they once were for e-tailers wishing to draw on the talents of retail execs working for traditional retailers. At this point, the future is uncertain. Surely there will be very successful e-tailers who will help make millionaires out of their executives. For retail execs considering the move, the key issue is selecting the right e-tailer to join.

lower than that of the salesperson working on a straight salary plan, but the commission structure gives one the potential to earn more than the person on the straight salary plan. In fact, most salespeople on the salary plus commission program earn more than their counterparts on a straight salary program.

This plan gives the employees a stable base income—and thus incentive to perform nonselling tasks—but it also encourages and rewards superior effort. Therefore, it represents a good compromise between the straight salary and the straight commission programs. In many cases, top management generally receives a salary and a bonus based on overall store or department performance.

The chapter's E-tailing box describes a variation of the salary plus commission plan whereby some Internet retailers are offering employees ownership interest as compensation.

Straight Commission   Income of some salespeople is limited to a percentage commission on each sale they generate. The commission could be the same percentage on all merchandise or it could vary depending on the profitability of the item. Retail salespeople working on a straight commission typically receive commissions of 2 percent to 10 percent of the selling price.

The straight commission plan provides substantial incentive for retail salespeople to generate sales. However, when the general business climate is poor, retail salespeople may not be able to generate enough volume to meet their fixed payment obligations (mortgage payment, auto payment, food expenses). Because of that problem, most retailers slightly modify the straight commission plan to allow the salesperson to draw wages against future commissions up to some specified amount per week. For instance, the employee may be able to draw $200 per week, which will be paid back with future commissions.

A major problem with the straight commission plan is that it may provide the retail salesperson with too much incentive to sell. The employee as a result of the income insecurity features of this plan may begin to use pressure tactics to close sales, hurting the retailer's image and long-run sales performance. Similarly, the employee may not be willing to perform other duties such as helping customers with returned merchandise or helping to set up displays. Because, after all, compensation is paid to sell and not to handle customer complaints or displays. Generally, sales personnel for high-priced merchandise or high-ticket items, such as automobiles, real estate, jewelry, and furniture, as well as those industries requiring the sales personnel to prospect or seek out potential customers, such as insurance and door-to door-selling, are paid this way.

An Ernst & Young survey reported that 51 percent of the retailers polled used a salary plus commission plan and 38 percent used straight commission.[22] Exhibit 14.7 summarizes the attributes of each of these plans. During the early 1990s, many retailers began to reduce the commission portion of employee compensation plans and increase the salary portion. This was an attempt to reduce consumer distaste for what was perceived to be high-pressure selling and was highlighted by the problems Sears had with its auto repair centers where service representatives were paid a commission on the amount of service work they wrote up.[23] However, as retailers have faced a tight labor market in recent years, the trend has begun to reverse.

Supplemental Benefits

In addition to regular wages (salary, commission, or both), retail salespeople also can receive four types of supplementary benefits: employee discounts, insurance and retirement benefits, child care, and push money (or spiffs).

Employee Discounts   Almost all retailers offer their employees discounts on merchandise or services they purchase for themselves or their immediate family. About the only line of trade where these discounts are not offered is grocery retailing, because grocery retailers operate on relatively thin gross margins. In other lines of retail trade, the discounts can range from 10 to 40 percent.

Insurance and Retirement Benefits   Historically, retail personnel were not provided any insurance or retirement benefits. However, with recent changes in the federal employment laws this is no longer the case. In addition, many retailers are providing their part-time employees with either free or low-cost group health and life

Exhibit 14.7   Attributes of Compensation Plans

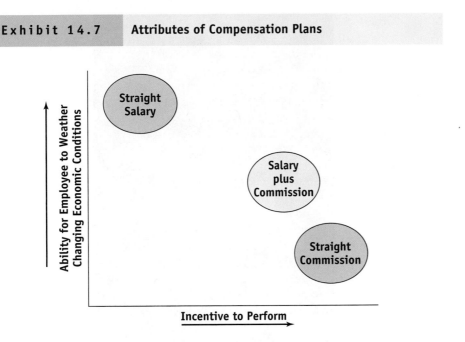

insurance. Still others are making profit sharing, stock ownership, and retirement programs available to salespeople. These benefits are valued between $70 and $260 a month per individual.

Child Care   In an effort to attract employees from two-wage-earner families, some U.S. businesses have begun to provide child care for employees' children during working hours. Retailers have just started providing child care, a program that experts agree will be a necessity in upcoming years. However, with health-care costs rapidly increasing, some retailers have delayed plans to add child care due to the added expenses.

Push Money   A final type of supplementary benefit is "push money," which some may call "prize money," "premium merchandise," or just plain "PM." Retailers commonly called it by another name, "spiffs." The PM, paid to the salesperson in addition to base salary and regular commissions, is said to encourage additional selling effort on particular items or merchandise lines.

PMs can be either retailer or supplier sponsored. A retailer may give a PM in order to get salespeople to sell old or slow-moving merchandise. The salesperson who sells the most may win a free trip to Hawaii or some other prize, or everyone who sells an established quantity of merchandise may get a prize or a premium. Or the retailer may simply offer an extra $10 bonus for the sale of a specific product (e.g., a dining room table). Suppliers, on the other hand, tend to offer PMs to retail salespeople for selling the top-of-the line or most profitable items in the supplier's product mix. These supplier-offered PMs are common in the appliance, furniture, jewelry, and floorcovering industries.

Occasionally there may be a conflict between the supplier and the retailer over the offering of PMs. This conflict arises because the supplier may be offering the retailer's salespeople an incentive to push an item or merchandise line that may not be the most profitable line for the retailer or the best for the customer, although it may be highly

If a retailer does not offer a good compensation plan, it will be constantly losing vauable employees and looking for new employees.

profitable to the supplier. Some retailers prefer to keep all PMs for themselves, because they believe they are already paying a fair wage to their salespeople.

Compensation Plan Requirements

Regardless of what method a retailer ultimately determines to use in compensating its employees, the method should meet the following requirements:

1. *Fairness.* The plan does not favor one group or division over any other group or division or enable such a group to gather disproportionate reward to contribution. It must also keep wage costs under control so that they do not put the store at a competitive disadvantage.

2. *Adequacy.* The level of compensation should enable the employee to maintain a standard of living, commensurate with job position, and to maintain job satisfaction.

3. *Prompt and regular payments.* Payments should be made on time and in accordance with the agreement between employer and employee. In incentive plans, greater stimulation is provided when reward closely follows the accomplishment.

4. *Customer interest.* The plan should not reward any actions by an employee that could result in customer ill-will.

5. *Simplicity.* The plan must be easy to understand so as to prevent any misunderstandings with the resultant ill-will. This should also enable management to minimize the labor hours needed to determine compensation levels.

6. *Balance*. Pay, supplemental benefits, and other rewards must provide a reasonable total reward package.

7. *Security*. The plan must fulfill the employee's security needs.

8. *Cost effective*. The plan must not result in excessive payments, given the retailer's financial condition.

Although none of the three plans we discussed earlier satisfies all of these requirements to the maximum level, awareness of these requirements will aid in the selection of the best plan given the individual circumstances. In fact, it is not uncommon for the same retailer to use more than one plan in the same store as different divisions or departments have different needs.

Job Enrichment

A planned program for enhancing job characteristics is typically called job enrichment. **Job enrichment** is the process of enhancing the core job characteristics for the purpose of increasing worker motivation, productivity, and satisfaction. There are five core job characteristics that should be increased:

1. *Skill variety*. The degree to which an employee can use different skills and talents.

2. *Task identity*. The degree to which a job requires the completion of a whole assignment that has a visible outcome.

3. *Task significance*. The degree to which the job impacts other employees.

4. *Autonomy*. The degree to which the employee has freedom, independence, and discretion in achieving the outcome.

5. *Job feedback*. The degree to which the employee receives information about the effectiveness of his or her performance.[24]

Job enrichment is the process of enhancing the core job characteristics of employees to improve their motivation, productivity, and job satisfaction.

Starbucks Coffee provides an excellent environment for employees, and offers a great variety of benefits to both full- and part-time employees. In fact, Starbucks provides part-time employees full health-care benefits.

Job enrichment programs have their base in motivation theory, which suggest that job factors themselves, such as job challenge, independence, and responsibility, are powerful motivators.

Retail management has long recognized that paying attention to job characteristics and descriptions, work scheduling, job sharing, and employee input programs will have a positive effect on employee productivity and satisfaction. Retailers using the job enrichment program must be careful in presenting it to the employees, otherwise the employees may feel that they are being asked to do too many tasks without being compensated for the extra workload.

Student Study Guide

Summary

LO•1   What steps are involved in planning human resources?

Our discussion of human resource planning and management focused on four major dimensions: planning for human resources, employee hiring, managing existing employees, and human resource compensation.

To properly plan for human resources, retailers should attempt to empower their employees so that both they and the customer are satisfied. However, to gain the benefits of empowerment, the retailer must first identify the myriad of functions that employees need to perform. A useful frame of reference is the marketing functions. Which functions and how much of each does the retailer desire to perform? Each function can then be broken into tasks, which are grouped together into jobs. Finally, the retailer must develop a job description.

In long-range planning, the retailer should carefully examine its projected speed of growth, the predictability of this growth, and geographical and line of trade diversification. In short-run human resource planning, the retail executive should attempt to forecast any weekly, monthly, or seasonal swings in sales activity and then adjust human resource inputs appropriately.

LO•2   What is the process for hiring employees?

Human resources acquisition occurs in a competitive labor market. There are many available sources of applicants; the more common ones include competitors, walk-ins, employment agencies, schools and colleges, former employees, advertising, and recommendations from existing employees. Once the applicants are obtained, they must be properly screened. We suggested a four-step screening process: application blanks, personal interview, testing, and reference check.

LO•3   How do retailers manage existing employees?

Once an employee is hired, the retailer must still be concerned about continuing to train and develop the employee, evaluating the employee, and motivating the employee.

Expenditures on training and development are an attempt by the retailer to increase the productivity of human resources. These programs are ongoing as the employee's responsibilities first become specific then increase in breadth.

The employee's performance should be subjected to an ongoing, formal systematic review process. This process enables the employer to make better decisions concerning wage increases, promotions, transfers or improvement in job skills.

Employee motivation is also a topic of great importance. In our discussion, we looked at two schools of thought: content theories and process theories. Although both theories are extremely important to retailers, more retailers actively use the process models to link together the task, the outcome, and the reward.

LO•4   What methods can retailers use in compensating their employees?

Compensation is crucial to attracting, retaining, and motivating retail employees. A good compensation program includes a fixed component to provide income, a variable component to motivate employees, and a fringe benefit component to provide security and prestige. Special attention was paid to the advantages and disadvantages of the three types of compensation plans: straight salary, straight commission, and a combination of both.

Job enrichment is the process of increasing the skill variety, task identity, task significance, autonomy, and feedback from the job in an effort to improve worker motivation, productivity, and satisfaction and thereby reduce turnover.

Terms to Remember

empowerment
task analysis
bona fide occupational qualification
teamwork
performance appraisal and review
motivation
content theories
process theories
hierarchy of needs model
Herzberg's two-factor theory
Theory X

Theory Y
expectancy theory
goal setting
compensation
fixed component
variable component
fringe benefit package
physiological needs
belongingness and social need
safety and security
job enrichment

Review and Discussion Questions

LO•1   What steps are involved in planning human resources?

1. Are the problems facing a personnel manager in a retail firm any different from the problems confronting a personnel manager in a factory?

2. Why is a job description necessary, if the employee has been told the tasks to be performed?

LO•2   What is the process involved in hiring employees?

3. Why is it so important for a retailer to screen the applicant before hiring the individual?

4. If you were a personnel director for a large department store chain, what traits or characteristics would you look for in a college student under consideration for your management training program? Would those characteristics differ if you were an e-tailer?

5. Should a small retailer have a training program or is this just for large retailers like Kmart and Sears?

6. Develop a list of predictor variables you would use to screen applicants for a sales position in (a) a jewelry department in a high-prestige department store, (b) a used-car dealership, (c) a health club, (d) an antique shop.

LO•3   How do retailers manage existing employees?

7. Why must training be an ongoing operation?

8. Why should a retailer institute an employee performance appraisal plan? What factors make such a plan fair to both employee and employer?

9. Is money the best motivator for every employee?

LO•4 **What methods can retailers use to compensate their employees?**

10. What are the various methods of compensating retail employees?

11. What are the advantages and disadvantages of paying salespeople in a furniture store strictly on a commission basis?

12. If you were the manager of a department store, would you have the entire salesforce under the same compensation plan? Explain your reasoning.

13. If you were to go to work for a retailer today, what would be the most important supplemental benefit the retailer could offer you? Would this benefit change as your lifestyle changed?

14. Why would an increase in task significance enhance a job and increase job productivity?

15. What factors in the retailer's control have a positive effect on employee productivity?

Sample Test Questions

LO•1 **When retailers grant their employees "empowerment," they are**

a. giving them the power to set their own hours
b. giving them the power to kick improperly dressed customers out of the store
c. giving them the power to determine what products should be featured in the retailer's weekly ad
d. giving them the power to make things right with the customer
e. giving them all of the above powers

LO•2 **Which of the following questions can a women's apparel store ask on an employment application?**

a. What is your marital status?
b. What is your age?
c. Have you ever been arrested?
d. Are you handicapped?
e. The retailer is not allowed to ask any of the above questions because each of them can be used to discriminate against particular groups.

LO•3 **Training and development programs should**

a. only be concerned with new employees
b. get rid of the least productive employees within the first two years
c. be an ongoing process
d. rely heavily on senior management's teaching skills
e. only focus on operational skills

LO•4 **For an individual who does not care about security, but only wants to maximize his or her current earnings, which of the following compensation plans would be best?**

a. straight commission
b. straight salary
c. salary plus commission
d. fringe-plus salary
e. teamwork salary

Applications

Writing and Speaking Exercise A vendor has approached your firm, a single-unit furniture store, wanting to know if it can pay push money to your salespeople. At the present time, your store has no set policy on the subject, because no other vendor has ever offered to pay push money or spiffs. The owner has asked that you prepare a memo on the subject for next week's board meeting. Be sure to include the pros and cons of spiffing in your statement.

Retail Project Because retailers often lack legal expertise when making human resource decisions, it is a good idea to review the current laws before doing anything in this area. For your assignment, go to the EEOC's web site (http://www. eeoc.gov). List five circumstances where sexual harassment may occur. Also, explain how an individual may waive his or her rights under the Age Discrimination in Employment Act.

Case

Harold's Fried Chicken[25]

High employee turnover has always plagued the fast-food industry. After being trained, the employee quits for one reason or another. Harold's is taking steps to reduce its turnover rate.

Harold's hires prospective employees at minimum wage for a 28-day period. If the employee remains with the company after the trial period, the employee receives a pay increase of five cents per hour. The training program at the store level includes working for badges that are earned for demonstrated skill in cutting, cooking, and counter service. Employees are given a manual and audiovisual aids to help them learn. A badge and another five-cent-per-hour raise is awarded following the successful completion of both a written and a physical test of skills.

When an employee earns three badges, he or she qualifies as a team leader. Team leaders are eligible to attend one of the five training schools. The training school is a three-week program that combines academic training with the maintenance of management/customer relations.

Because many of Harold's units are located in lower-income areas, many of the students attending the classes have not been exposed to the best education and are unfamiliar with the work world. In order to train and motivate the students, they are paired up with students of comparable ability. They work together and test one another on the concepts and skills they learn. The program uses several steps to teach the trainees how to study. The program is self-paced. A student must master the first step before going on to subsequent steps. Each student is awarded points for every accomplishment, and these points are graphed on a daily basis. Discussion groups are held at the end of the day, and students receive feedback for their work and validation for their accomplishments. Problems are also reviewed at this time.

After the successful completion of the training program, the students return to their respective areas as assistant managers. They hold the position for a minimum of two years before becoming store managers. Harold's also provides store managers an opportunity for store ownership.

1. How would you improve Harold's program?
2. Do you think the employee turnover rate will still be high? Why?

Planning Your Own Retail Business   During the planning process for starting a gift shop in a local resort town you began to question and consider different compensation plans for the retail clerks. It was fairly standard in the area to pay retail clerks $6.25 an hour. However, as you visited gift shops that were paying these rather low wages you noticed that the clerks simply took orders and did not sell or try to answer any questions for customers. In a visit to a gift shop in Ft. Lauderdale last spring you struck up a conversation with the owner. She was more than willing to share her experiences about retail clerks. In fact, after a lot of trial and error she decided to pay upper quartile compensation. This consisted of a base wage of $7.50 an hour and a 3 percent commission on all sales. She mentioned that when she went to this type of system her average transaction size increased by 20 percent and that closure went from 28 to 40 percent. More important, she found that her bottom line profit rose by 32 percent. In short, by paying more for retail clerks she increased employee productivity and the profits of her store.

For the gift shop you are planning you initially estimated that traffic would be 25,000 visitors annually and that closure would be 25 percent. You estimated your average transaction size at $32. Your gross margin percent would be 60 percent and fixed operating expenses would be $60,000 annually. Variable operating expenses would be 20 percent of sales. Under this plan you would pay two full-time clerks $6.25 an hour and you would fill in when things got busy.

Your new plan, which you want to evaluate, calls for paying the clerks $7 per hour plus 4 percent commission on all sales. Thus your fixed operating expenses would go up by $3,000 and variable operating expenses would rise to 24 percent of sales. You believe that closure would rise to 32 percent and average transaction size would rise to $36. Which compensation strategy should you pursue?

Endnotes

1. "Customer Relationship Management," *Stores*, April 2000: 33–36.
2. "Handling Manpower by the Hour," *Chain Store Age*, August 2000: 66–68.
3. "Stores Adopt New Strategies for Seasonal Hiring Challenge," *Stores*, January 2000: 118–120.
4. "Letter from a Productive Lover of Leisure," *U.S. News & World Report*, August 5, 1991: 6.
5. "Dial 800-Prison," *Sales & Marketing Management*, February 1991: 34.
6. "Automated Job Applications Aid in Search for Retail Hourly Workers," *Stores*, May 2000: 38–43; and "Managing HR on the Web," *Chain Store Age*, December 1999: 160.
7. Section 703(e) of Title VII.
8. "Retailers Using Computers to Screen Applications," *Shopping Centers Today*, October 1999: 50.
9. Ibid.
10. "Will My Bad Credit Sink Me?" *Fortune*, October 26, 1998: 302.
11. "Labor of Love," *Progressive Grocer*, May 2000: 59–68.
12. *New Ideas for Retaining Store-Level Employees*, A Study for the Coca-Cola Retailing Research Council by Blake Frank, Ph.D., University of Dallas, 2000: 10.

13. Ibid., 6.

14. Ibid., 5.

15. Ibid., Appendix 4.

16. "Teams, Not Titles," *Chain Store Age*, September 1994: 49–50.

17. "The Talent Search: Attracting and Retaining People with the Skills Your Business Needs," *Retail Insights*, 9 (1) 2000.

18. "Electronics Giants Use Different Battle Plans," *Shopping Centers Today*, May 1997: 64, 70.

19. Sam Walton, *Sam Walton, Made In America: My Story* (New York: Doubleday, 1992): 126–142.

20. "The Talent Search."

21. "The Talent Search."

22. *An Ernst & Young Survey: People in Retail*, September 1990: 11.

23. "How Did Sears Blow This Gasket?" *Business Week*, June 29, 1992: 38; "Sears's Brennan Accepts Blame for Auto Flap," *Wall Street Journal*, June 23, 1992: B1, B12.

24. J. Richard Hackman and Greg R. Oldham, *Work Redesign* (Reading, MA: Addision-Wesley, 1980): 77–80.

25. This case was prepared by Roger Dickinson, University of Texas at Arlington, and used with his permission.

Answers to Sample Test Questions

Chapter 1

1. C is the correct answer. A is wrong because retailing includes credit card purchases. B is wrong because as our Global Retailing box explains, retailing is different in each country. D is wrong because retailing involves selling to the final consumer, not to the wholesaler. E is wrong because retailing is a valued sector of the economy and it does increase economic growth.

2. A is the correct answer as we have pointed out that retailing is changing, challenging, and exciting; the other possible answers certainly don't apply.

3. E is the correct answer as the other four answers where among the five ways of categorizing retailers listed in the chapter. The fifth way, which wasn't listed as a possible answer, was by the Census Bureau's NAICS codes. The manager's gender should have no impact on a store's performance; besides, federal sex-discrimination laws would make this an illegal means for categorizing retailers.

4. B is the correct answer because we would certainly hope that a retailer possesses the other four characteristics as well as being decisive.

5. D is the correct answer as the manager investigated both sources of supply and competition before making her decision. The other possible answers were not covered in the text.

Chapter 2

1. B is the correct answer because market performance objectives seek to establish the retailer's dominance against the competition. A and C are wrong because they are made-up terms. D is wrong because societal performance is concerned with the broader issues of the world, and E is wrong because financial objectives are internally number oriented, dealing with profit or productivity.

2. C is the correct answer. A and B are wrong because price is the poorest way to differentiate yourself. D is wrong because this action would restrict you from selling many of the top brands. E is wrong because the customers really don't see planning, only the results of planning.

Chapter 3

1. B is the correct answer. Americans do move about a dozen times in their lifetimes. A is wrong because some baby boomers are already in their fifties. C is wrong because small markets still represent great opportunities for retailers if they satisfy the consumers' wants and needs. D is wrong because the fertility rate in the United States is near its all-time low. E is wrong because the growth rate has been declining in recent years.

2. C is the correct answer: the boomerang effect is a relatively new phenomenon that describes something many of today's students will face that previous generations did not have to face—returning home to live with their parents. A, B, and D are at least true statements, but they have nothing to do with the boomerang effect. E could be true or not at the time you are reading this, but it also has nothing to do with the question asked.

3. D is correct because discretionary income is disposable income which is all personal income after personal taxes minus the money needed for necessities. E is wrong, because, as we just noted, it is the definition of disposable income. The other three choices are just made up definitions.

4. D is the correct answer. The shopping/purchasing process does not end with the purchase because the consumer will use and evaluate the shopping and purchase experience. This learning experience will in turn influence future shopping and purchasing behavior. Consequently, post-purchase evaluation is the last stage. The buy decision, A, was not identified in the textbook as a unique stage. Active information gathering, B, occurs during the evaluation of alternatives stage and thus is not the last stage. C, the purchase stage, must be followed by post-purchase evaluation. E, the payment stage, was not identified as a unique stage in the model presented in the textbook.

Chapter 4

1. B is the correct answer. E is true in rare cases, but the question asked for what structure *most* retailers are involved in. D, although it is a type of market structure, is wrong because retailers don't operate in environments with horizontal demand curves. A and C, although they sound good, are made-up terms.

2. D is the correct answer because this involves different types of retailers with similar products competing with each other. B is wrong because intratype refers to cases in which the same types of retailers compete with each other and Wal-Mart is a general merchandise store and not a grocer. C (scrambled merchandising) can be used to describe what Wal-Mart is doing, but this term does not refer to a type of competition. E refers to a situation in which a retailer dominates a single line of merchandise, not many lines as Wal-Mart is doing with its supercenters. A is wrong because it is a made-up, nonsense term.

3. D is the correct answer. Some might argue that the retail accordion theory could be used by saying that the small original hamburger stand expanded to the large McDonald's and Burger King restaurants of today and will get smaller as customers rebel. However, this isn't entirely accurate. Nevertheless, we didn't include the accordion theory as a possible answer. B is wrong because it describes stage of growth that institutions pass through and not why they change formats. A is wrong because it is a made-up term.

4. D is the correct answer. A is wrong because retailing is more diverse around the world. B is wrong because success in one country doesn't guarantee success in other countries, witness the hypermarkets in the United States or the fact that Kmart, Sears, and JCPenney have abandoned many of their foreign expansion plans. C is wrong because the size of the average retailer is diverse. E is wrong because other countries have also developed successful new retailing formats, witness IKEA.

Chapter 5

1. C is the correct answer because location analysis is not one of the marketing functions discussed in the text. A, B, D, and E are all marketing functions discussed in this chapter.

2. E is the correct answer because facilitating institutions aid the channel by performing tasks at which they are more capable than the current channel members are. A is wrong because although some facilitating institutions may take possession of the merchandise, none of them take title. B is wrong because facilitating institutions do not take title to the goods. C is wrong because they do not manage the channel and besides the goal of a channel is to minimize sub-optimization as it cannot operate at 100 percent efficiency. D is wrong because they cannot do all eight functions without taking title and beside the text mentions that no one firm would want, or be able, to perform all eight functions.

3. E is the correct answer. A and C are wrong because conventional channels, due to their loose alignment, are by their very nature not efficient. B is wrong because contractual channels are not loosely aligned because the contract directs each member's duties and responsibilities. D is wrong because there is not any feeling of partnership and cooperation in a conventional channel.

4. B is the correct answer. A is wrong, even though it may be true each member wants all the power, a channel member is still dependent on the other members. C is wrong, typically no member can perform all eight functions. D is wrong because a partnership should be committed to the life of the channel. E is wrong because if everybody wanted to work independent of each other, there would not be a channel in the first place.

Chapter 6

1. E is the correct answer because the major price discrimination law, the Robinson-Patman Act, is meant to protect competition by making sure that retailers are treated fairly by suppliers. The other possible answers pertain to laws covering other situations.

2. E is the correct answer because it involved a deceitful action (using another firm's trademark) that caused damage to the other firm. A is wrong because it did not cause damage to the competitor. B is wrong because it was not deceitful, the retailer told the truth. C is wrong because it involves deceptive pricing. D is perfectly legal because you did not do anything wrong.

3. A is the correct answer because an implied warranty of fitness for a particular purpose arises when the customer relies on the retailer to assist or make the selection of goods to serve a particular purpose. B is wrong because an implied warranty of merchantability means that the retailer implies that the merchandise is fit for the ordinary purpose for which the product is usually purchased. C is wrong because it is a made-up answer. D and E are wrong because no verbal or written guarantee was mentioned in the question.

4. B is the correct answer because the purchase of the cat food was tied to the purchase of the unpopular product—litter. The other answers are not related to the question.

5. B is the correct answer. Although there are federal laws governing franchise operations, the most stringent laws are usually state laws because the state government wants to protect its citizens and locally owned franchise businesses, as well as voters, from the unfair practices of out-of-state franchisors.

6. A is the correct answers because it is a merchandising decision regarding the success or failure of merchandise. The other four answers pertain to the ethical decisions discussed in the chapter.

Chapter 7

1. C is the correct answer. It is not essential that a market segment to create high sales; however, it should be profitable. A, B, D, and E are all criteria used to reach a target market successfully and thus are incorrect answers.

2. A is the correct answer. Because free-standing retailers are not part of a shopping center or CBD, they do not have direct competition. B is not correct because it is an advantage of retailers in shopping centers. C is incorrect because free-standing retailers have more difficulty in attracting customers for the initial visit. D is incorrect because free-standing retailers are not able to share advertising costs with other retailers as in a shopping center. E is incorrect because free-standing stores can be either leased or purchased.

3. E is the correct answer. A, B, C, and D are all purposes of geographical information systems and thus any one of these answers is not the single best choice.

4. B is the correct answer. The three steps presented are exactly as discussed in the textbook. A is wrong because the first step is incorrect. C is wrong because the second step is incorrect. D is wrong because all three steps are incorrect. E is wrong because the third step is incorrect.

5. E is the correct answer. A and B by themselves are not the best answer because both are needed to do a site analysis. C and D are incorrect because they are irrelevant to site analysis.

6. C is correct because alternative investments available to the retailer should not be a consideration in the selection of a site. A, B, D, and E are incorrect because they are all important considerations in selecting the best site.

Chapter 8

1. B is the correct answer because current liabilities are listed on the balance sheet but are not included in the merchandise budget. The other answers are all included in the merchandise budget.

2. D is the correct answer because the income statement is a summary of the sales and expenses for a given time period. A is wrong because an expense report, though not mentioned in the chapter, would only cover expenses. B is wrong because although the inventory valuation will affect the retailer's expenses, it also does not include sales. C is wrong because the cash flow statement only deals with the inflow and outflow of cash. E is wrong because gross margin only considers sales and cost of goods sold and does not include operating expenses.

3. C is the correct answer because the cost ($120,000) divided by sales ($200,000) is .6.

Chapter 9

1. A is the correct answer because $425,000 \times 1/2[1 + (\$170,000/\$142,000)] = \$466,901$. E would be the correct answer if the question asked for the basic stock method, not the PVM. D is the average stock for the season, but it is not the correct answer. The other two answers are madeup numbers.

2. Because the key feature of OTB is that it can be determined at anytime during the merchandise period, D is the correct answer. The other answers are wrong because they are time specific.

3. C is the correct answer as the other four are the constraints listed in the text.

4. B is the correct answer because it best describes what is involved in a vendor profitability analysis statement, which was defined in the text as "the record of all purchases you made last year, the discounts granted you by the vendor, transportation charges paid, the original markup, markdowns, and finally the season-ending gross margin on that vendor's merchandise." A is wrong because it is about the vendor's financial statements, which are seldom provided to retailers. C is wrong because it deals with new lines of merchandise. D is wrong because it deals with the retailer's line of credit granted by the vendor. E is wrong because it covers only one factor (discounts) covered by the vendor profitability analysis statement.

5. B is the correct answer. A is wrong because it describes a noncumulative quantity discount. C is wrong because it assumes the discount period starts with the beginning of the year, something that is not always true. D is wrong because it describes a different type of discount. E is wrong because it is based on a specific quantity that may be too high or too low given the circumstances of the sale.

6. B is the correct answer because it is the combination of vendor and retail employees that are most often involved in collusion. A and D are wrong because customers are not involved in vendor collusion. C and E are wrong because although the sales representative or accountant may be involved, the people involved with the delivery person must also be included.

Chapter 10

1. C is the correct answer because the retailer's pricing objectives must be interactive with all the other decision areas of the firm. A is incorrect because pricing cannot be independent of these other decision areas. B is incorrect because pricing cannot be separate from these other areas. D is wrong because the retailer's pricing objectives should not be in competition with these other areas. E is incorrect because multifaced has nothing to do with the question.

2. C is the correct answer because in this case the retailer offered the same merchandise to different customers at different prices. E is incorrect because variable pricing means that the prices for all customers may change as differences in either demand or costs occur. Nevertheless, all customers will pay the same price unless the retailer also uses a flexible policy. A is wrong because there is no such policy as "two-price." B is incorrect because with customary pricing, the retailer seeks to maintain the same price for an item over an extended period of time. D is incorrect because leader pricing involves taking a popular item and offering it for sale to everybody as a means of drawing these consumers into a store.

3. A is the correct answer because markup on selling price is SP − C/SP [($45 − 25)/$45 = 44.4%]. B is incorrect because the question asked for markup on selling price and 80 percent is the markup on cost. The other answers are merely madeup numbers.

4. This question was chosen because many students get confused about reduction percentage. C is the correct answer, because reduction percentage is the amount of the reduction ($29.99 − $19.99 = $10) divided by net sales ($19.99). A is the markdown percentage, which is the amount of the reduction divided by the original selling price ($10/$29.99). The other answers are madeup numbers, although E is the result of dividing the new selling price by the original selling price.

Chapter 11

1. E is the correct answer. Even though the retailer may have a low net worth, this should not be taken into consideration when developing a promotional strategy. After all, the objectives will still be the same. The other four alternatives (credit customers, price level, merchandise, and building and fixtures) are managerial decisions that must be integrated into the retailer's overall plan.

2. A is the correct answer. Institutional, or long-term, advertising tries to create a positive store image and provide public service. B lists the objectives for short-term, or promotional, advertising. C lists the two other types of promotion. D lists how a retailer might seek to obtain short-term results. E lists two other topics covered in this chapter that have nothing to do with the question.

3. E is the correct answer as all four of the alternatives belong as part of an advertising campaign's objectives.

4. E is the correct answer. Premiums are the extra items offered to customers when they purchase the promoted item. When in a limited number of cases premiums could be joint-sponsored sales promotions (alternative A), such promotions would not be beneficial to the retailer because the consumer could purchase the product from another retailer. The other three alternatives (B, C, and D) are other forms of promotion.

Chapter 12

1. C is the correct answer because the text explained that a transient customer is an individual who visits a retailer and finds the service level below expectations or the product out of stock. This transient, or temporary, customer will seek to find a retailer with the level of customer service he or she feels is appropriate. A is wrong because, even though the dictionary defines "transient" as short lived or not long lasting, the term does not refer to length of time spent shopping. The other choices are wrong because they have nothing to do with a transient customer.

2. E is the correct answer because merchandise availability is a transaction service that helps build the relationship with the customer, thus making B and D wrong. A and C are wrong because personal shopping is a service not a cost, despite the fact that there might be some additional costs involved.

3. D is wrong because as shown in Exhibit 12.5 the other alternatives are factors that must be considered when determining the service levels to offer.

4. B is the correct answer because good results are not only dependent on the salesperson's characteristics but also on how satisfied the customer is with the salesperson's performance. Retail selling jobs should be designed to have high levels of variety (C), autonomy (D), task identity (E), and feedback from supervisors (A).

5. E is the correct answer because once the approach has been completed, the salesperson is in a position to present the merchandise and sales message correctly. The key to the presentation, however, is to get the customer to want to buy the product or service. Therefore, the salesperson must have the right price range of products to show the customer. A is wrong because if the price is too high or too low, the sale will be already lost. B is wrong because you cannot select the right product unless you know the right price. C is wrong because the greeting occurs in the approach stage. D is wrong because helping the customer to decide is the last step of the presentation.

Chapter 13

1. B is the correct answer because the two primary objectives around which all activities, functions, and goals in the store revolve are store image and space productivity. Alternatives C and D have two worthwhile activities (merchandise presentation and traffic control, opportunities for impulse buying and shelf management) but by themselves they will not produce high-performance results. A and E are wrong because though its activities are also good traits, sales management (A) and maintaining market share (E) are not objectives of the store environment.

2. C is the correct answer because the store's layout and design must allow the store to be shopable and the merchandise to be effectively presented. A is wrong because even though the retailer would like all the customers to see every high-profit item, this is not always possible and nothing was said about presentation of the merchandise. B is obviously wrong because it would be foolish to give offices, the back room, wall, and aisles as much space as the selling floor as this is not where sales are generated. D is wrong because why would a retailer care to have rapid replacement in a low-turnover area? E is wrong because retailers today want to minimize the space given to back rooms.

3. A is the correct answer because the method of merchandise presentation has an impact on the store's image and space productivity. B is obviously wrong because it would be foolish to hire a psychologist to do the store's displays. C is wrong because by shopping effectively, the customer might not make any impulse purchases. D is wrong because while social factors may influence our behavior, this alternative has nothing to do with the question. E is another obviously wrong choice because it would be foolish for this to be done.

4. B is the correct answer because store design is most responsible for developing a store image, which the other four alternatives are concerned with doing. B, however, would not increase the productivity of the store.

5. E is the correct answer because visual communication is concerned with messages within the store, which are covered by the other four possible answers, and not those external to the store.

Chapter 14

1. D is the correct answer as empowerment gives the employee the power to make decisions so that the customer is taken care of. A is wrong because it is the concept of teamwork, not empowerment, that lets the employees adjust their hours. B is wrong because empowerment is concerned with satisfying customers' problems, not enforcing dress codes. C is wrong because although the employees may make suggestions for featuring products in the weekly ads, this decision is made by the buyer and department manager.

2. E is the correct answer. As noted in the text, none of these would be a valid question to ask an applicant.

3. C is the correct answer because training and development must be viewed as a process of continuing education. A is wrong because existing employees must also undergo training to remind them of how things are done and to teach and inform them of new items. B is wrong because even though employee turnover is expensive, it is better to get rid of unproductive employees as soon as possible. D is wrong because while senior management should be involved in the training process; their time is more efficiently spent doing the things they are an expert in, such as store management, buying, and finance. E is wrong because training should cover all retail activities.

4. A is the correct answer because straight commission offers the greatest potential for instant income. B is wrong because straight salary cannot be influenced in the short run by an individual's performance. C is wrong because the commission in a salary plus commission plan will be lower than the straight commission to compensate for the employer taking some of the risk. D is wrong because it is not a compensation plan. E is wrong because a teamwork salary is based on the entire team's performance, not just an individual.

Photo Credits

p.3	©Tony Roberts/CORBIS
p.9	©A. Ramey/PhotoEdit
p.10	©PhotoDisc
p.12	©Photopia
p.13	©Photopia
p.16	©Photopia
p.19	Amazon.com is a registered trademark or trademark of Amazon.com, Inc. in the U.S. and/or other countries. ©2001 Amazon.com. All rights reserved.
p.21	©Photopia
p.37	Architect: Monighan & Associates, AIA, Inc., Photography: Fred Daly Photographer
p.39	Copyright ©2000 Wal-Mart Stores, Inc.
p.40	Courtesy of Rick Segal, president of Chapter's Online Inc.
p.46	©Michael Newman/PhotoEdit
p.51	©2000 Lane Bryant, www.lanebryant.com
p.58	©Photopia
p.69	©2000 Churchill & Klehr
p.75	©David Katzenstein/CORBIS
p.78	©2000 Dell Computer Corporation. Used with permission. The Dell Precision™ Workstation 220 for Financial Traders.
p.105	www.ebay.com ©2000 eBay.Inc. All Rights Reserved.
p.108	©Andrew Itkoff/Silver Image
p.110	©Reuters NewMedia Inc./CORBIS
p.118	©Photopia
p.121T	©Photopia
p.121B	©2000, Bass Hotels & Resorts, Inc. All Rights Reserved.
p.133	©2000 JCPenney
p.143	©Mike Mazzaschi/Stock, Boston
p.145	www.mp3.com. ©2000 MP3.com, Inc.
p.152	©A. Ramey/PhotoEdit
p.154	©Photopia
p.156	©Owen Franken/Stock, Boston
p.157	©Elena Rooraid/PhotoEdit
p.164	Reprinted by permission from PricewaterhouseCoopers, LLC
p.167	AP Photo/Shizuo Kambayashi
p.170	Reprinted by permission from PricewaterhouseCoopers, LLC
p.171	©Don Couch Photography
p.183	©David Kurtz
p.185	©Owen Franken/Stock, Boston
p.191	©Jon Riley/Stone
p.195	AP Photo/Barry Sweet
p.200	©Photopia
p.204L	Reprinted by permission from PricewaterhouseCoopers, LLC
p.204C	©Don Couch Photography
p.204R	http://niketown.nike.com/catalog. ©2000 NIKE, Inc.
p.206	©Mark Burnett/Stock, Boston
p.213	Reprinted by permission from PricewaterhouseCoopers, LLC
p.225	©Jeff Greenberg/PhotoEdit
p.228	Reprinted by permission from PricewaterhouseCoopers, LLC
p.232	Reprinted by permission from PricewaterhouseCoopers, LLC
p.237	©Don Couch Photography

Company Index

Name Index

Subject Index

TOP 25 RETAILERS

Sales for Year Ending January 2000

1. **Wal-Mart Stores, Inc. (NYSE / WMT)**
   Bentonville, AK
   www.walmart.com
   $165,394,000,000

2. **The Kroger Co. (NYSE / KR)**
   Cincinnati, OH
   www.kroger.com
   $45,352,000,000

3. **Sears Roebuck and Co. (NYSE / S)**
   Hoffman Estates, IL
   www.sears.com
   $41,070,000,000

4. **METRO AG (725750.D)**
   Germany
   www.metro.de
   $40,357,000,000

5. **Carrefour (12017.PA)**
   France
   www.carrefour.com
   $39,780,000,000

6. **Home Depot, Inc. (NYSE / HD)**
   Atlanta, GA
   www.homedepot.com
   $38,434,000,000

7. **Intermarche**
   France
   www.intermarche-le-bugue.com
   $38,390,000,000

8. **Albertson's, Inc. (NYSE / ABS)**
   Boise, Idaho
   www.albertsons.com
   $37,478,079,000

9. **Kmart Corporation (NYSE / KM)**
   Troy, Michigan
   www.bluelight.com
   $35,925,000,000

10. **Ahold (NYSE / AHO)**
    Netherlands
    www.aholdusa.com
    $33,811,000,000

11. **Target Corporation (NYSE / TGT)**
    Minneapolis, MN
    www.target.com
    $33,212,000,000

12. **JCPenney, Inc. (NYSE / JCP)**
    Plano, TX
    www.jcpenney.com
    $32,510,000,000

13. **Tengelmann**
    Germany
    www.tengelmann.de
    $30,881,000,000

14. **Tesco (TSCO.L)**
    Great Britain
    www.tesco.com
    $30,350,000,000